D1561609

THE COMMON CORPS OF
CHRISTENDOM

STUDIES IN THE HISTORY OF CHRISTIAN THOUGHT

EDITED BY

HEIKO A. OBERMAN, Tübingen

IN COOPERATION WITH

HENRY CHADWICK, Cambridge
JAROSLAV PELIKAN, New Haven, Conn.
BRIAN TIERNEY, Ithaca, N.Y.
E. DAVID WILLIS, Princeton, N.J.

VOLUME XXVI

BRIAN GOGAN

THE COMMON CORPS OF
CHRISTENDOM

LEIDEN
E. J. BRILL
1982

THE COMMON CORPS OF CHRISTENDOM

CHRISTENDOM

Ecclesiological Themes in the Writings of
Sir Thomas More

BY

BRIAN GOGAN

LEIDEN
E. J. BRILL
1982

Gogan, Brian — The common corps of christendom:
ecclesiological themes in the writings of Sir Thomas
More / by Brian Gogan. — Leiden: Brill. — (Studies
in the history of christian thought; vol. 26)

UDC 26

ISBN   90 04 06508 3

PRINTED IN THE NETHERLANDS

In memory
of my father and mother

TABLE OF CONTENTS

PREFACE

In the story of the English Reformation the rejection of royal supremacy over the church by Henry VIII's ex-chancellor and court favourite, Sir Thomas More (1477/8-1535), is but one striking incident in a narrative marked by drama, conflict, social upheaval and extraordinary creativity.[1]

Was More an eccentric who delighted in going against the crowd? Or had he some special understanding of the problems involved in declaring Henry Supreme Head of the Church of England which would explain both his own refusal to take the oath of succession as well as his compassion towards those who accepted royal supremacy? These questions marked the beginning of a personal investigation begun in 1955,[2] reopened in 1968, and now reaching a conclusion.

In pursuing this investigation I was led into an area of history lying between two peaks—the Lutheran crisis in Germany and the Henrician schism in England. This shadowy valley is occupied by the early history of Protestantism in England, better described as the Anglo-Lutheran movement.[3] In exploring this, I was obliged to look closely at the attempts of men such as William Tyndale, John Frith and Robert Barnes to initiate a continental style reformation in England, while examining the efforts made by defenders of tradition to ward off this assault.

---

[1] The outstanding biography of Sir Thomas More is still R. W. Chambers, *Thomas More*, London, 1935, repr. Peregrine Books, London, 1963; E. E. Reynolds, *The Field is Won. The Life and Death of Saint Thomas More*, London, 1968 is also indispensable. Further detail is filled out in two works by the same author: idem, *The Trial of St. Thomas More*, London, 1964, and idem, *Thomas More and Erasmus*, London, 1965; Germain Marc'Hadour, *L'Univers de Thomas More, chronologie critique de More, Érasme et leur époque (1477-1536)*, Paris, 1963 is extremely helpful. There is some debate as to whether Sir Thomas More was born in 1477 or 1478. (Hence the celebration of the quincentennial of his birth over a two year period.) Perhaps the best account of this debate can be found in *Marc'Hadour, L'Univers de Thomas More, 34-41*.

[2] This reference is to an M.A. thesis by this writer presented to University College, Dublin: Brian Gogan, *The Idea of the Church on the Eve of the Reformation in England*, 1957.

[3] See among other works H. C. Porter, *Reformation and Reaction in Tudor Cambridge*, Cambridge, 1958; Anthea Hume, *A Study of the Writings of the English Protestant Exiles, 1525-1535*, unpublished dissertation, University of London, 1961 (permission to examine this work was withheld by the author); William A. Clebsch, *England's Earliest Protestants 1520-1535*, New Haven and London, 1964. The following works are also helpful; James P. Lusardi, *The Career of Robert Barnes, Confutation* III, 1367-1415; E. G. Rupp, *Studies in the Making of the English Protestant Tradition*, Cambridge, 1947; Erwin Doernberg, *Henry VIII and Luther. An Account of Their Personal Relations*, London, 1961; H. C. Porter, *Puritanism in Tudor England*, London, 1970.

This was the challenge which converted a talented humanist into an un-
tiring controversialist. Though principally committed to a career in public
life when he joined the King's council in 1518, Sir Thomas More lent his
pen as well as his authority to support the case for traditional orthodoxy
against Luther, Luther's English disciples and in the last period of his life,
against supporters of his erstwhile friend and patron, Henry Tudor.

More's controversial writings are substantial. Having realised this, the
scope of my enquiry expanded from a simple question concerning the
reason for More's adherence to papal primacy to the whole range of his
theology of the church as witness to divine revelation, its inward and outward structure, and its defining characteristics. This in its turn raised further questions concerning the evolution of More's thought, its relation to
tradition as well as to contemporary developments in theology. The
answer to these queries places More at the head waters of a stream of
thought leading up to the *Controversies* of Robert Bellarmine (1586-93), a
dominant current in Catholic thinking on the church till the second
Vatican Council.

This enquiry does not lack contemporary relevance. One might be inclined to think that in the light of present day ecumenical interests, the
study of 16th century religious polemic could be little more than an intellectual cul-de-sac. Such is not the case. In reading the sources for this
work I have become convinced that without a full historical perspective
ecumenical discussion must remain barren and infertile. It is not merely a
question of all parties to the debate admitting to skeletons in the cupboard
but of each church understanding why and how theological division came
about. In studying the controversy which engaged Sir Thomas More's
energies for so many years, one can observe at close quarters the break up
of Christian unity while getting some glimpse of why it happened.

I owe a debt of thanks to many people who have helped me to complete
this work: Professor F. X. Martin of University College, Dublin for his
thoughtful counsel and timely encouragement over the years; Professor
Heiko Oberman of Tübingen University for many helpful references as
well as encouragement to seek publication for this study; the late Mr Denis
Bethell for much useful advice; Professor G. Marc' Hadour of Angers for
many resource materials; Fr Breifne Walker CSSp, Rev. P. Sheldrake S.J.,
Mr Maurice Roche, Mrs Mary Murphy and Mr Michael O'Beirne for
assistance in correcting the text; Dr Joseph Bergin for many valuable
references; the librarians of University College, Dublin, Trinity College,
Dublin, Marsh's Library, Dublin, the National Library of Ireland,
Dublin, the British Museum, London, and the Bodleian Library, Oxford

for their unfailing and courteous service; three good people who spent much time typing out the manuscript: Mrs Marie Jenkins, Mrs Teresa Brennan and Miss Doreen Callan; Mrs Helen Litton who compiled the index, and indeed many others too numerous to name.

A number of individuals and institutions have contributed to the cost of publication of this volume, notably Bank of Ireland, the Catholic Communications Institute of Ireland, C & A Nederland, Lombard and Ulster Banking Ltd., P. J. Carroll Limited, Mr Gregory McCambridge as well as some who wish to remain anonymous. To these benefactors as well as to my own community which so generously gave me time off for this research my sincere thanks are due.

Brian Gogan CSSp
Holy Ghost College,
Dublin

ABBREVIATIONS

ARG = *Archiv für Reformationsgeschichte, Berlin/Leipzig, 1906—.*

BIHR = *Bulletin of the Institute of Historical Research, London, 1923—.*

Confutation = Sir Thomas More, *The confutacyon of Tyndales answere made by syr Thomas More knyght lorde chauncellour of Englonde,* 2 Vols, London, 1532-33; *The Confutation of Tyndale's Answer,* edited by Louis A. Schuster, Richard C. Marius, James P. Lusardi, and Richard J. Schoeck, New Haven and London, 1973, *The Yale Edition of the Complete Works of St. Thomas More, Vol. 8.*

CW = *The Yale Edition of The Complete Works of St. Thomas More,* New Haven and London, 1963—.

Dialogue = Sir Thomas More, *A dyaloge of syr Thomas More knyghte. Newly ouersene by the sayd syr Thomas More chauncellour of England,* London, 1531; *A Dialogue Concerning Heresies,* edited by W. E. Campbell with introduction and notes by A. W. Reed, London, 1927, repr. 1931.

DTC = *Dictionnaire de Théologie Catholique,* edited by A. Vacant, E. Mangenot, E. Amann, 15 Vols with indices (3 Vols), 1899-1972.

DU PIN = Du Pin, M. Lud. Ellies, *Joannes Gersonii...opera omnia...ad manuscriptos codices quamplurimos collata,* & *innumeris in locis emendata...,* 5 Vols, Antwerp, 1706.

EHR = *The English Historical Review,* London, 1886—.

ETL = *Ephemerides theologicae lovanienses,* Louvain, 1924—.

LTK = *Lexikon für Theologie und Kirche,* edited by Josef Hofer and Karl Rahner, 11 Vols, Freiburg, 1957-1967.

MPL = *Patrologia latina,* edited by J. P. Migne, Vols I-CCXXI, Paris, 1844-1864.

NAKG = *Nederlands Archief voor Kerkgeschiedenis, 's-Gravenhage, 1900—.*

Responsio = Sir Thomas More, *Eruditissimi viri Guilielmi Rossei opus elegans,* London, 1523; *Responsio ad Lutherum,* edited by John M. Headley, translated by Sister Scholastica Mandeville, New Haven and London, 1969, *The Yale Edition of The Complete Works of St. Thomas More,* Vol. 5.

RGG = *Die Religion in Geschichte und Gegenwart,* 3. Auflage, edited by K. Galling, 6 Vols and Index, Tübingen, 1956-65.

RHE = *Revue d'histoire ecclésiastique,* Louvain, 1900—.

RSR = *Revue des sciences religieuses,* Paris/Strasbourg, 1921—.

TRHS = *Transactions of the Royal Historical Society,* London, 4th series, 1918—.

WA = *D. Martin Luthers Werke; kritische Gesammtausgabe,* Weimar, 1883—.

INTRODUCTION

Sir Thomas More, Controversialist

Thomas More (1477/8-1535) was the son of Sir John More, a London judge. He became a member of the household of Archbishop J. Morton about the age of thirteen while Morton was chancellor of England. More's early study of the classics held his lifelong interest. It was his father's wish that he study law and this he began in 1494, being called to the Bar about 1501. He lectured in law at Furnival's Inn and in 1504 entered parliament. About this time he had felt the call to religious life and lived for several years with the Carthusians in their London charterhouse. He finally decided that monasticism was not for him and married in 1505 but without giving up his strict manner of life. Because of his interest in the humanities, his house became a meeting place for scholars and humanists. He was on terms of close friendship with men such as John Colet, William Grocyn, and, of course, Erasmus of Rotterdam. More was also a favourite of Henry VIII. With his accession in 1509 to the throne of England, a new period in Thomas More's public career began. He was sent as an envoy to Flanders in 1515, became a privy councillor in 1518, was knighted three years later and elected Speaker of the House of Commons in 1523. He reached the highest point of his career when he was appointed Lord Chancellor of England in 1529, an office he held till 1532 when he was succeeded by Thomas Audley.

More's early intellectual interest in the classics was evidenced by his epigrams, the translations from Lucian, and in a derived sense his most famous work, *Utopia,* published in 1516 at Louvain.[1] However, it is with More the theologian that this study is concerned. More's theological writings fall into two broad categories: spiritual writings which began with his life of the Italian humanist Pico della Mirandola (a translation printed in London about 1510) and ended with the Tower works, notably the treatise on the Passion.[2] In spite of the interest of these compositions, it is

---

[1] Thomas More, *The Latin Epigrams of Thomas More,* (Basle, 1520), edited and translated by L. Bradner and C. A. Lynch, Chicago, 1953; idem, *Utopia,* (Louvain, 1516), edited and translated by Edward Surtz and J. H. Hexter, New Haven and London, 1965, *CW,* 4; idem, *Translations of Lucian,* (Paris, 1506), edited Craig R. Thompson, New Haven and London, 1974, *CW* 3.

[2] Thomas More, *Here is conteyned the lyfe of Johan Picus Erle of Myrandula,* London, (1510?); idem, *A dialoge of comfort against tribulacion,* London, 1553; edited by Leland Miles, Bloomington (Ind.) and London, 1965; edited by Louis L. Martz and Frank Manley, New Haven and London, 1977, *CW* 12; idem, *Treatise on the Passion; Treatise on the Blessed Body; Instructions and Prayers,* edited by Garry Haupt, New Haven and London, 1977, *CW* 13.

in his more formal theological writing that material relating to this enquiry can be found. Most of this was written as a direct response to the threat posed by Wittenberg and its English adherents.

Thomas More's support for Henry was not his first excursion into theology. As a younger man he had lectured on Augustine's *City of God* in the London Jewry and had written a number of essay-letters, some critics say of great originality, on theological method.[3] But the *Responsio ad Lutherum* (1523) was his first major incursion into formal theology. Both as royal official and confidant of King Henry VIII, More had taken an active part in drafting the *Assertio Septem Sacramentorum*.[4] Luther's subsequent replies as well as possible urging from his royal master stirred him to write this, his first major work of religious controversy.

Thomas More's reply to Martin Luther's *Contra Henricum regem angliae* (1522) first appeared under the title *Eruditissimi viri F. Baravelli opus elegans* in 1523 without any indication of the place of printing. A second augmented edition came off the presses under a new title *Eruditissimi viri G. Rossei opus elegans* later the same year (1523) in London.[5] The main difference between these editions, apart from the change of pseudonym, was the expansion of chapter ten (H gathering) to deal with the Roman primacy in some detail. The change of plan was apparently motivated by another work of Martin Luther's of which he had become aware in the meantime, *Responsio ad Catharinum* (1521) in reply to a work composed by

---

[3] See in particular André Prévost, *Thomas More, 1477-1535, et la crise de la pensée européene,* Tours, 1969, 125-141. 'Ce fut la grandeur de More d'avoir pressenti le danger et d'avoir ouvert la route à la théologie moderne, la "Théologie Positive".' Prévost suggests that More was indeed the first to use the term 'positive theology' to describe a theological method based on induction from the sources rather than deduction from *a priori* principles according to the method of scholastic theology. Ibid., 140 and Thomas More to Martin Dorp, Bruges, 21 October (1515), Rogers, *Correspondence,* 45, 608/610: speaking of decadent scholasticism, More says of its exponents '...quaecunque sunt optima, piisima, maxime Christiana, verisque Theologis dignissima, ea, inquam omnia, quod sint (vt ipsi vocant) *positiua*, contemnant...'

[4] See Headley, *Responsio,* 715-731; 775-803. This matter will be dealt with at greater length below. See *Assertio Septem Sacramentorum* in Henry VIII, *Libello huic regio haec insunt,* London, 1521.

[5] The Rosseus edition of the *Opus elegans* was reprinted in the collection of More's Latin works published at Louvain in 1565 by J. Bogard, and in another edition by T. Zangrius. Each of these was reprinted the following year, 1566, as well as in a later edition which appeared in Frankfurt am Main in 1689 under the Gensch imprint. An English translation of part 1 of this work was published some years ago in the U.S.A. by G. J. Donnelly, *A Translation of St. Thomas More's Responsio ad Lutherum,* with an introduction and notes, Washington D.C., 1962. A new edition with notes and translation has since appeared as part of the *Complete Works of St. Thomas More: Responsio ad Lutherum,* 2 Vols, ed. J. M. Headley, tr. Scholastica Mandeville, New Haven and London, 1969, *CW* 5.

Ambrosius Catharinus O. P., an Italian opponent of Luther's, *Apologia pro veritate catholicae et apostolicae fidei ac doctrinae,* printed in Florence in 1520.

In this tract More began to grapple seriously with some of the central problems posed by the Reformation. He identified these principally in terms of the understanding of revelation, the nature and role of the church. More's continued concern with the impact of Luther's innovations reveals itself in his correspondence. He gave it concrete form in his pamphlet against Bugenhagen, taking the Wittenberg publicist to task on a number of classical themes such as justification, ministry and celibacy.[6]

Lutheran influence was felt in Britain within a few years of the Wittenberg eruption. John Dorne records the sale at Oxford of a dozen books by Luther in 1520.[7] At Cambridge interest was more intense. Theology students from a number of colleges 'flocked together in open sight, both in the schools, and at open sermons...' to hear the new doctrines discussed. The White Horse tavern was centre of this ferment. Among early adherents were men later to be reckoned among the founding fathers of English Protestantism such as Tyndale, Coverdale, Joye, Cranmer, Latimer, Barnes.[8] Official opposition could do little to hold back this new growth.

Under pressure from home as well as attraction from abroad many of these men found their way overseas to centres of evangelical reform. The government campaign to forbid entry to Luther's publications was to prove equally ineffectual against the flow of vernacular works which sprang from England's Protestant exiles.[9]

The key work in this publicity campaign was Tyndale's translation of the new testament completed in Worms in 1526. This was followed by a series of other works such as Jeremy Barlowe's *The Burial of the Mass* (Strasbourg, 1528), Tyndale's *Introduction to the Romans* (Worms, 1526),

---

[6] *Epistola, in qua...respondet literis Ioannis Pomerani,* was composed about 1526. It was first published in Louvain, 1568; subsequently in Rogers, *Correspondence,* 323-365. Bugenhagen (1485-1558) was Luther's confessor at Wittenberg, and a supporter of Melancthon. The letter was written in reply to Bugenhagen's *Epistola ad Anglos* (1525) published initially in German and Latin, which reproached the English for their ignorance of the true gospel. See E. F. Rogers, *Sir Thomas More's Letter to Bugenhagen* in *The Modern Churchman* 35 (1946) 350-360.

[7] See F. Madan, *The Day-Book of John Dorne, 1520* in *Collectanea,* I, First Series, ed. C. R. L. Fletcher, Oxford, 1885, 73-117.

[8] See H. Maynard Smith, *Pre-Reformation England,* London, 1938, 497-498.

[9] For an up-to-date list of these works see Anthea Hume, *English Protestant Books Printed Abroad, 1525-1535: An Annotated Bibliography,* in *Confutation* II, 1065-1091; Carl S. Meyer, *Henry VIII Burns Luther's Books 12 May 1521, JEH* 9 (1968) 173-187; for the later fortunes of the subversive book-trade see Louis A. Schuster, *Thomas More's Polemical Career, 1523-1533,* in *Confutation* III, 1155-1252.

Roye's *A Brief Dialogue* (Strasbourg, 1527), Tyndale's *Parable of the Wicked Mammon* and *The Obedience of a Christian Man* both of which appeared in 1528 from an Antwerp press. These works coupled a vigorous criticism of accepted practice in established ecclesiastical circles, often justified, with an appeal to a radical evangelical doctrine on the lines of that advocated by Martin Luther. Publications from abroad were matched by an increasing amount of quiet proselytism at home which touched even More's own household.[10] It is against this background that Cuthbert Tunstal's invitation to Sir Thomas More makes sense. Reasoning, popular appeal, ready wit, and a command of written English, it was hoped, might prove a better counter-balance to subversion than legal threat or even cruel punishment.

In 1528 Sir Thomas More, then Speaker of the House of Commons, was drawn into direct intellectual conflict with the Lutheran movement in England. On 7 March 1527/8 Cuthbert Tunstal, bishop of London, sent him a special commission. In this he asked More to take up the public defence of traditional orthodoxy in the vernacular. He wrote: 'Now you can play the Demosthenes both in English and in Latin, and at every assembly you are the keenest defender of the truth. You can spend your leisure hours in no better way, if any you have, than in writing in English to open the eyes of uneducated people to the crafty deceits of these heretics and so put them on the alert against those who seek to destroy the church. In so doing you will but follow the example of our illustrious king... That you may carry out this mission most effectively I hereby license you to keep and read the works of heresy.'[11] Thus More was commissioned to enter the lists on behalf of orthodoxy.

Why should More, a layman, a non-professional theologian, have been selected for this task? He was marked out for it on several scores—by his political prominence in parliament and friendship with the king, his popularity with the common people achieved in his days as under-sheriff of London, his range of learning established by the widespread acclaim accorded his *Utopia*, his reputation as lecturer in law as well as his theological

[10] Nicholas Harpsfield, *The life and death of Sr Thomas Moore knight.* ed. E. V. Hitchcock, London, 1932, 84-89. Harpsfield was a friend of William Roper, More's son-in-law. Roper went through a prolonged flirtation with Lutheranism about 1526. More stopped arguing and turned to prayer instead. This seemingly proved more succesful in winning his favourite daughter's husband back to orthodoxy.

[11] Cuthbert Tunstal to Thomas More, (London), 7 March 1527/8, Rogers, *Correspondence,* 387/19-388/45. On More's polemical career see Rainer Pineas, *Thomas More and Tudor Polemics,* Bloomington (Ind.), 1968, a collection of articles previously published; idem, *George Joye's Controversy with Thomas More, Moreana* 38 (1973) 27-35; Schuster, *More's Polemical Career,* in *Confutation* III, 1137-1268.

learning and honesty of life. Most decisive of all, perhaps, was his mastery of English as a written language in an age when Latin was the *lingua franca* of cultured society and Europeans generally were only beginning to domesticate the barbarisms of their spoken tongues.[12]

Given this mandate from his bishop, More set to and produced a series of works of controversy in English, the centre-piece of which are his two works directed against William Tyndale. *The Dialogue Concerning Heresies* (1529)[13] brought More directly into conflict with English Lutherans. The *Dialogue* evinced a speedy reply from 'The Masker' as More termed his principal adversary. William Tyndale's response, *An answere vnto Sir Thomas Mores dialoge,* was published probably in Antwerp in 1530. This in turn provoked More's major work of ecclesiological interest, *The Confutation of Tyndale's Answer.*[14] The first part was published in London in the year he resigned as Lord Chancellor, 1532, and the rest the following year, 1533. When we examine these works in detail we discover that while they range over almost all disputed areas, one theme constantly recurs. More repeatedly returned to the authority of the church as bearer and interpreter of revelation. His conviction on this score was something arrived at in the process of argument rather than assumed as an *a priori* position. As already noted, it had arisen first of all in his work against Luther, the *Responsio* (1523). Luther based his case on justification, his rejection of sacraments, the hierarchical church, monastic life and so forth on scrip-

---

[12] See R. W. Chambers, *The Continuity of English Prose from Alfred to More and His School,* in Harpsfield, *Life of Sir Thomas Moore,* ed. E. V. Hitchcock, cxli-clxvii.

[13] *A dyaloge of syr Thomas More knyghte,* was printed in London under the imprint of John Rastell, 1529. It was reprinted in the following year 1530-31 by the same firm. It appeared some thirty years later in *The workes of Sir Thomas More Knyght,* London, 1557, pp. 103-288. This later version was printed in facsimile with a version in modern English spelling in Thomas More, *A Dialogue Concerning Heresies* ed. W. E. Campbell, with introduction and notes by A. W. Reed, London, 1927. A new edition was completed in 1981 as part of the Yale project, with Dr Thomas Lawler of Holy Cross College, Worcester, Massachussetts as chief editor. I am indebted to Dr Lawler for a progress report on this edition and reassurance concerning the almost complete identity of the 1529 and 1531 editions of the *Dialogue.* For some interesting detective work on the text of the *Dialogue* from the clues provided in the printed sheets see E. J. Devereux, *Thomas More's Textual Changes in the 'Dialogue Concerning Heresies',* *Library* (September 1972) 233-235. (I am indebted to Dr Lawler for this reference.) More seems to have treated his printer as a modern newspaper editor treats his printers. Not surprisingly John Rastell passed on the work in mid-stream to a colleague Peter Treveris, better able, presumably, to put up with frequent changes of text.

[14] *The côfutacyon of Tyndales answere made by syr Thomas More knyght,* (pt. I) London, 1532, (pt. 2) 1533 appeared under the imprint of Wyllyam Rastell and was reprinted in his compilation, *The workes of Sir Thomas More knyght,* London, 1557, pp. 339-832. It has appeared in the Yale edition of More's works, *The Confutation of Tyndale's Answer,* edited by Louis A. Schuster, Richard C. Marius, James P. Lusardi and Richard Schoeck, New Haven and London, 3 vols, 1973, *CW* 8.

ture. More found that in order to substantiate his own position he had to turn to traditional interpretations of scripture, the church's theological tradition and established doctrine for support. This in turn led to an examination of church authority together with the nature and origin of the church whose authority he quoted. Finally he came to define the characteristics by which this church can be known. All of this argument is contained in the *Responsio* (1523). It is repeated in whole, in part, or in more developed form in the later works, notably *The Dialogue Concerning Heresies* (1529-31) and *The Confutation of Tyndale's Answer,* (1532-33).

While More directed his attention to other evangelicals besides Tyndale, in 1533 he was obliged to open up a second front, as it were, with critics of the extended powers of the church in English society. In particular Christopher St German (+ 1540), an expert in common law, attracted his attention. St German had published seven treatises attacking ecclesiastical jurisdiction. In 1532 he released an anonymous tract entitled *A Treatise concernynge the diuision betwene the spirytualtie and temporaltie.* In this he blamed the clergy for tensions existing in English society between clergy and laity. In 1533 Sir Thomas More took St German to task in *The Apologye of syr Thomas More knyght* published in London by his nephew William Rastell in 1533. St German's reply, *Salem and Bizance (A dialogue betwexte two Englysshe men)*, came off the presses in the same year. With customary persistence More answered with a further thrust within the year 1533, in *The debellacyon of Salem and Bizance.*[15] It was not without reason that the name of the eastern empire was used in this debate. It was truly Byzantine in its detailed examination of the complications inherent in the interlocking jurisdictions of church and state as well as some outstanding instances in which conflict had arisen.

Sources

This brief review of Sir Thomas More's career as controversialist has already identified the main sources this study will draw on and the order in which they will be discussed.[16] In order of appearance these are the *Respon-*

---

[15] Thomas More, *The Apologye of syr Thomas More knyght,* London, 1533, ed. Arthur Irving Taft, London, 1930; idem, *The debellacyon of Salem and Bizance,* London, 1533, repr. *EW,* 1557. Christopher St German, *A Treatise concernynge the diuision betwene the spirytualtie and temporaltie,* London, 1532; idem, *Salem and Bizance (A dialogue betwexte two Englysshe men),* London, 1533.

[16] More detailed bibliographical information can be found in Frank and Majie Padberg Sullivan, *Moreana. Materials for the Study of Saint Thomas More,* Los Angeles, Ca, 1964-71, a comprehensive bibliography that has appeared in separate fascicules over the years; R. W. Gibson, and J. Max Patrick, *St. Thomas More: A Preliminary Bibliography of his Works and of Moreana to the Year 1750,* New Haven and London, 1961; the review devoted exclusively to Thomas More studies, *Moreana,* Angers, 1964-, and of course the magnificent critical edition

sio ad Lutherum (1523), *The Dialogue Concerning Heresies* (1529-31) and *The Confutation of Tyndale's Answer* (1532-33).[17] For a variety of reasons I have omitted detailed consideration of *The Apology of Sir Thomas More Knight* (1533) and *The Debellation of Salem and Bizance* (1533) even though these shed light on such topics as More's conception of Christendom, church-state relations and his attitudes towards heresy and heretics. I have made this, admittedly regrettable, omission for two reasons. Firstly, the complex nature of the issues discussed: it would be difficult to do them justice within the limits of this already somewhat extended study. Secondly, the editors of the Yale edition of More's works have not yet completed their researches on these treatises.[18] It would seem an unnecessary duplication of effort to get too involved with these tracts while their editors are still at work. However, this should not hide the fact that at a future date the ecclesiological content of the St German controversies will have to be worked into our over-all picture of More's understanding of the church.

One further collection of sources bearing on More's attitudes during the trial proceedings is of importance. These consist mainly of letters, to be found for the most part in Elizabeth Rogers, *The Correspondence of Sir Thomas More,* Princeton, 1947;[19] contemporary accounts of his trial, notably *The Paris Newsletter,* printed as an appendix to Nicholas Harpsfield's, *The life and death of Sr Thomas Moore,* first published in London, 1932;[20] and contemporary biographies, especially those of William Roper and Nicholas Harpsfield.[21]

---

of More's works: *The Yale Edition of the Complete Works of St Thomas More,* Yale University Press, now well advanced. Each volume contains detailed references and bibliographies.

[17] See above notes 5, 13 and 14 for bibliographical details.

[18] The Yale edition of the first of these tracts has appeared since my work was completed: Sir Thomas More, *The Apology,* edited by J. B. Trapp, New Haven and London, 1979, *CW* 9.

[19] The correspondence which developed during More's imprisonment prior to his execution especially with his daughter Margaret and with Thomas Cromwell is important as revealing his thought in regard to the key-issues of royal supremacy and papal primacy. Many of these letters are available in printed sources such as the *The workes of Syr Thomas More knyght* (1557), but are most easily accessible in E. F. Rogers, *The Correspondence of Sir Thomas More,* Princeton, 1947. This resource is complemented by *Erasmi epistolae,* (Oxford, 12 vols, 1906-58) edited by P. S. and H. M. Allen as Rogers does not print letters published by the Allens, as well as Hubertus Schulte-Herbrüggen, *Sir Thomas More. Neue Briefe,* Münster, 1966.

[20] The principal sources for More's trial are the following: *The Paris Newsletter,* reprinted as an appendix to Nicholas Harpsfield, *The life and death of Sr Thomas Moore, knight,* edited by E. V. Hitchcock and R. W. Chambers, London, 1932, 254-266; *Expositio fidelis de morte Di Thomae Mori,* Basle, 1535, ed. Allen, *Erasmi epistolae,* 11, 368-378; H. de Vocht, *Acta Thomae Mori,* Louvain, 1947; J. Gairdner, *The Calendar of Letters and State Papers, Foreign and Domestic of the reign of Henry VIII,* Vol. VIII, No. 974, pp. 384-386. The official documents relating to the trial are extant in the *Baga de Secretis,* pouch 7, bundle 3, M.7 at the Public Record Office,

Any explorer in reformation history owes an enormous debt to those who have provided increasingly brilliant beacons by which to navigate his course. The studies of G. R. Elton in revising many received interpretations of late medieval and early Tudor constitutional history, his perceptive and sympathetic treatment of Secretary Cromwell's *Realpolitik,* as well as his comprehensive treatment of the implementation of royal supremacy—which received the support of many humanists—shed a great deal of light on the issues which confronted Sir Thomas More.[22] While A. G. Dickens has done a great deal to bring the complex history of the English Reformation on to a more human scale,[23] the magisterial treatment of the history of the Council of Trent by Hubert Jedin, together with his other researches, provide us not merely with a multitude of insights into the twisted course of internal Catholic reform, but also manage to illuminate many hidden corners of sixteenth century ecclesiastical history.[24] The history of the Reformation itself continues to be the subject of almost countless studies among which it is difficult to single out star performers.[25] More specifically in relation to the subject matter of this study, the history of ecclesiology, one must point to the brilliant monograph by Yves Con-

---

London. The more important of these have been reprinted as an appendix to Nicholas Harpsfield, *The life of Sir Thomas Moore,* 267-276 in a critical edition which takes account of other extant mss.

[21] William Roper, *The Lyfe of Sir Thomas Moore, knighte,* ed. E. V. Hitchcock, London, 1935, the work of More's son-in-law, Margaret More's husband. Nicholas Harpsfield, *The life and death of Sr Thomas Moore, knight sometymes Lord high Chancellor of England,* ed. E. V. Hitchcock, London, 1932. Harpsfield, like his colleague Roper, a lawyer, was present at More's trial, and later had contact with other members of the More family circle. See also Thomas Stapleton, *Tres Thomae,* Douai, 1588, translated by Phillip Hallett, London, 1928. Stapleton was an exile of Elizabethan vintage, a scholar who spent most of his life at Douai. Cresacre More, *The Life and Death of Sir Thomas More,* (probably Paris) 1631; London 1828. Cresacre was a great grandson of Sir Thomas. Having studied ad Douai, he returned to the family property at Gobions, Hertfordshire. RO: BA, *The Lyfe of Syr Thomas More Sometyme Lord Chancellor of England,* ed. E. V. Hitchcock and P. E. Hallett, London, 1950.

[22] See in particular, on constitutional and related political issues, G. R. Elton, *The Tudor Constitution: Documents and Commentary,* Cambridge, 1960; idem, *The Tudor Revolution in Government: Administrative Changes in the reign of Henry VIII,* Cambridge, 1953. See also the essays collected in idem, *Studies in Tudor and Stuart Politics and Government. Papers and Reviews 1946-1972,* 2 Vols, Cambridge, 1974; on Cromwell and the implementation of royal supremacy, idem, *Policy and Police. The Enforcement of the Reformation in the Age of Thomas Cromwell,* Cambridge, 1972; idem, *Reform and Renewal. Thomas Cromwell and the Commonweal,* Cambridge, 1973; idem, *Reform and Reformation, England 1509-1558,* London, 1977.

[23] See in particular Arthur Godfrey Dickens, *Lollards and Protestants in the Diocese of York, 1509-1558,* London, 1959; idem, *The English Reformation,* London, 1967.

[24] See in particular Hubert Jedin, *Geschichte des Konzils von Trient,* 4 Vols, Freiburg im Br., 1949-75, tr. E. Graf, *A History of the Council of Trent,* 3 vols, London, 1957-.

[25] *Archiv für Reformationsgeschichte* (Gütersloh, 1910-) provides a reliable guide to literature on the Reformation.

gar, a work whose arches span the broad reaches between Augustine and the second Vatican Council without apparent strain.[26] While Congar is particularly effective in providing a vantage point from which to view the many turbulent currents of late medieval ecclesiology, Heiko Oberman has focused attention on the key issues of revelation, scripture, tradition and church.[27] Finally anyone coming to grips with Sir Thomas More must acknowledge his debt to the editors of *The Complete Works of Sir Thomas More,* an edition whose introductions, commentaries and indices provide so many keys to turn, one feels that, given willing hands, the hidden treasure it contains will very rapidly be made available to the public at large.[28]

Historiography

If these are the principal sources on which a study of More's theological ideas can be based, the question naturally arises as to what effort so far has been made to determine the nature and scope of his thought on the church. Not without good reason the French Renaissance scholar Marie Delcourt pointed to two distinct streams of interpretation of Sir Thomas More's thought, the continental European which emphasised the More of *Utopia,* Erasmus's humanist confidant.[29] The English recusant tradition on the other hand turned More into an ikon of God-fearing resistance to unwarranted intervention by secular power in the activity and governance of Christ's church. In this century, however, despite the flurry of hagiographical writing surrounding the canonisation proceedings in the 1930s, the predominant scholarly cult of More in Britain epitomised in the work of R. W. Chambers tended to take up the humanist dimension in his writing. In this case, however, with a renewed stress on the liberal elements in More's thought the tendency was to underline his contribution as *littérateur* and early pioneer of English prose. While *Utopia* still proved a

---

[26] Yves Congar, *L'Église de saint Augustin à l'époque moderne,* Paris, 1970.

[27] Heiko Oberman, *The Harvest of Medieval Theology. Gabriel Biel and Late Medieval Nominalism,* Cambridge (Mass.), 1963. Oberman has carried his researches a stage further in idem, *Werden und Wertung der Reformation, Vom Wegestreit zum Glaubenskampf,* Tübingen, 1977.

[28] *The Yale Edition of the Complete Works of St. Thomas More* published by the St. Thomas More Project, Yale University. Further material less directly related to the subject in hand can be found in other works of More's. These are listed in the bibliography in the end pages of this work.

[29] See Marie Delcourt, *L'Amitié d'Érasme et de Thomas More entre 1520 et 1535,* in *Bulletin de l'Association Guillaume Budé* 50 (1936) 7-29; idem, *Recherches sur Thomas More, la tradition continentale et la tradition anglaise,* in *Humanisme et Renaissance* 3 (1936) 22-42; Delcourt's findings were re-examined and to a large extent confirmed by James K. McConica, *The Recusant Reputation of Thomas More* in *Essential Articles for the Study of Thomas More,* edited by R. S. Sylvester and G. P. Marc'Hadour, Hamden (Conn.), 1977, 136-149.

fertile hunting ground for students in search of a thesis, the content of
More's theological writings remained largely unexplored.

One of the earliest writers in this century to point to the significance of
his theological contribution was the American Charles Kernan in an
article published in *Thought* in 1942.[30] The gist of what Kernan had to say
could be found in some of the early biographies as well as, for example,
Campbell's introduction to his reprint of the 1557 edition of the *Dialogue*.[31]
Nonetheless in subsequent years there has been an increasing focus of attention on More's theological interests and a recognition that theological
and spiritual concerns dominated his writing from 1520 onwards. Martin
Luther killed off the More of *Utopia*. The dream of perfection gave way to
a prolonged struggle for the simple preservation of the structural
framework of western Christendom.

Not surprisingly the doctrine of the church loomed large in this concern.
It has taken some time for historians to identify the centrality of this
theme. Willis J. Egan in his 1952 doctoral thesis pointed the way.[32] In his
analysis of More's concept of the rule of faith, Egan clearly showed the
main elements in More's position. Arguing against Tyndale's simple *scriptura sola* formula, More saw the role of the church both in authenticating
scripture and interpreting it. Divine revelation is broader than scripture.
Unwritten tradition in a variety of forms subsists in the church of Christ
identified by More with the common known Catholic Church. Helpful as
a first exploration of the ground, Egan did not fully perceive the primarily
pneumatic concept of tradition held by More and tended to read back
anachronistically into More a certain degree of ultramontane papalism
unsupported by the evidence.[33]

Paul Huber, a Swiss historian, less concerned with deepening the
analysis of More's theological ideas than with testing out the interpretations of the pre-World War II school of More scholarship in Britain, found
himself focusing on the concept of tradition predominant in More's
thought.[34] He saw More as a man deeply rooted in the socio-cultural and

[30] Charles Kernan, *Thomas More Theologian, Thought* 17 (1942) 281-302.
[31] Thomas More, *Dialogue Concerning Tyndale,* ed. W. E. Campbell, London, 1931,
(63-108).
[32] Willis J. Egan, *The Rule of Faith in St. Thomas More's Controversy with William Tyndale
1528-1533,* published in Los Angeles, 1960. I am indebted to Fr Egan for the use of his
microfilm of *The Workes,* 1557.
[33] See Egan, *Rule of Faith,* 73: 'Thomas More is quite aware, and on more than one occasion he acknowledges, that inerrancy of belief belongs primarily to the *magisterium,* and
especially to the successors of St Peter...'
[34] Paul Huber, *Traditionsfestigkeit und Traditionskritik bei Thomas Morus,* Basel, 1953.

religious tradition of late medieval England, one who wished to advance towards a better world using the mainspring of living tradition rather than promoting its radical destruction, a constitutional reformer in the legal sense of constitution; definitely not a revolutionary.

Huber wrote within the perspective of a historian of culture and society rather than of ideas, still less theological ideas. Nonetheless his analysis as far as it went cast a great deal of light on such themes as More's concept of Christendom as a political entity with a spiritual core and the relation between spiritual and temporal powers, where he adverted to More's stress on the role of laity in the church. Similarly in his interpretation of More's concept of tradition, Huber pointed out that in More's view the bearer of ecclesiastical tradition is not exclusively the clergy. The entire body of believers play a key role. This 'populist' approach to religious faith finds both a political and ecclesiastical counterpart in his theory of consensus. It is characteristic of Huber's method that he presents this stance of More's in terms mainly of popular 'political' consensus rather than one based in spiritual experience and belief. Nonetheless, Huber clearly observed the dominant role of More's doctrine on consensus as a principle of verification: 'nisi rationi consensus accedat...qui consensus aut coalescens usu, aut expressus literis, publica lex est.' Sir Thomas More, Huber recognised, was no counter-reformation papalist but a moderate constitutional thinker in a late medieval mould, one whose political and legal intuitions found a ready parallel in the patristic theology of consensus and communion as well as echoing many voices from the schools of late medieval conciliarism.

The first systematic analysis of More's ecclesiology came in two articles from the Dutch scholar E. Flesseman-Van Leer published consecutively in 1959 and 1960.[35] Concentrating on the More-Tyndale controversy, Flesseman-Van Leer first analysed their respective notions of the transmission of revelation in scripture and tradition. Flesseman-Van Leer's exposition of the controversy revolved around the four classical issues of the Reform. These were:

1. The sufficiency of scripture; 2. the necessity of scripture; 3. the self-authentication of scripture; 4. the transparency of scripture. Exploring these issues Flesseman-Van Leer quickly came up against the doctrine of the church underlying More's antithetical attitudes. Scripture is not suffi-

---

[35] E. Flesseman-Van Leer, *The Controversy about Scripture and Tradition between Thomas More and William Tyndale*, Nederlands Archief voor Kerkgeschiedenis Nieuwe Serie 43 (1959) 143-165; idem, *The Controversy about Ecclesiology between Thomas More and William Tyndale*, Nederlands Archief voor Kerkgeschiedenis Nieuwe Serie 44 (1960) 65-86.

cient. It is complemented by church tradition which is in a certain sense prior to holy writ. While recognising the value of scripture, More admitted the possibility of Christian faith in one who had never read the scriptures through adherence to God's word proclaimed in the preaching of the church. Similarly More affirmed that scripture does not vindicate its own divine origin but is handed on by a church which establishes its credibility through the authority of its own witness and the testimony of miracles.

Not surprisingly More rejected the self-evidence of many scripture passages, insisting that the aid of the church was needed for their interpretation. In disputed readings credence should be given to articles of faith taught by the church rather than to the apparent sense of scripture.

Almost inevitably Flesseman-Van Leer moved on to an examination of the protagonists' opposed views on the nature of the church. For More revelation was not something given once and for all and recorded in writing. It was an ongoing reality—essentially the divine presence in the church, revealing itself to believers of each age, helping them to identify the true scriptures, guiding them in their interpretation as well as leading them into a deeper perception of divine truth either by further revelation or the discovery of new facets to doctrines already made known.

Given the centrality of the church in the appropriation of revelation, More attached a high degree of importance to identifying the true church of Christ. This he saw as the common corps of Christendom, the well known body of believers, not the hidden group of elect whom Tyndale conceived of as the church of Christ. Through its consensus of faith as well as its common voice expressed in council, this church of Christ can determine the meaning of disputed passages in scripture and give authoritative testimony to the broader meaning of any aspect of divine revelation whether made known through scripture or tradition. The church is an organised community with worship and the proclamation of the gospel as its principal activities. Flesseman-Van Leer notes More's nuanced position on papal primacy. While More himself affirmed the divine right of the papacy he did not consider it fully *de fide*. 'He died for the unity of the church, for the upholding of which the primacy was instituted.' Her final word is that the underlying difference between the two writers in their views on the church may be traced back to two different conceptions of what constitutes the substance of Christian faith. More stressed intellectual content, Tyndale the experience of God's loving mercy in trusting to his promise. Whether this analysis is correct remains to be seen. In any event the appearance of these two studies marked a major step forward in a critical examination of More's thought.

In the introduction to the Yale edition of the *Responsio* John M. Headley
presented a picture of its ecclesiology which is a model of both scholarly
expertise and intelligent brevity. Disentangling the two versions of the
Responsio, the earlier Baravellus (late spring 1523) from the later Rosseus
edition, produced probably in autumn of the same year, Headley traces
the evolution of More's thought within the crucial years 1521-1523.[36] He
points out that while the overt question in dispute in the *Responsio* is that of
the seven sacraments, the real underlying question was quickly identified
by More in terms of the authority of ecclesiastical tradition. This led him
subsequently to examine the credentials of the community which claims to
bear and interpret this divine tradition.

More devoted the first book of his treatise to the question of tradition,
going beyond Henry in formulating a theory of unwritten transmission of
revelation. In the *Responsio* this was conceived principally in terms of an
inspirational, pneumatic theory: what the Spirit inscribes on man's heart
through the divine indwelling. This indwelling Spirit of God guides the
church in recognising and interpreting divine revelation whether given in
the form of scripture or unwritten tradition.

Inevitably this led to the question of the church. In the earlier edition's
second book More went on to discuss the question of church authority in
doctrinal matters. He identified this in the main with the consensus of
believing Christians. Headley more accurately than Huber sees the doctrine of consensus principally rooted not in English constitutional practice
nor Roman law theory but in the spiritual conception of a community
uninterruptedly under divine influence, an influence whose aim it is to
bring about communion of mind and heart in common submission to
divine truth.

Only in the H gathering, the addition made to the first edition due
probably to the influence of the German Franciscan Thomas Murner and
More's perusal of Luther's attack on Ambrosius Catharinus Politi, (an
Italian Dominican opponent of Luther's), did More fully perceive the
nature of a further issue of crucial significance, the nature of the church of

---

[36] See Thomas More, *Responsio ad Lutherum,* Part II, ed., John M. Headley, New Haven
and London, 1969, 732-77. Some of Headley's positions were anticipated in earlier publica-
tions and filled out in later ones, mainly the following: idem, *Luther's View of Church History,*
New Haven and London, 1963; idem, *Thomas Murner, Thomas More, and the First Expression of
More's Ecclesiology, Studies in the Renaissance* 14 (1967) 73-92; idem, *More Against Luther: On
Laws and the Magistrate, Moreana* 15 (1967) 211-223; idem, *Thomas More and Luther's Revolt,
ARG* 60 (1969) 145-160; idem, *Thomas More and the Papacy, Moreana* 41 (1974) 5-10. See also
Denis Hay, *A Note on More and the General Council,* in *Moreana* 15 (1967) 249-251. Hay suggests
that More adopted an extreme conciliarist standpoint, a thesis which is not borne out by a
detailed examination of the evidence.

Christ.[37] Both he and Luther had cited Ps 67, 7,—the Spirit of God makes men of one mind to dwell in God's house. Unanimity in faith is the product of the work of the Spirit. But unanimity among whom and in which church? Luther said the hidden church of the elect. What of More?

More identified his church with the common known multitude of believers, what we now call the institutional church, organised hierarchically, which celebrates the sacraments and preaches the gospel of Christ under the presidency of the pope. It is the consensus of this body that More looked on as normative of faith, not that of any 'number of secret and unknown assemblies...who disagree both with the rest of the church and also among themselves about the faith of Christ...'[38]

Headley disagrees with Huber who had argued that More came to recognise the divine origin of papal primacy only about 1528. The former points to the unequivocal nature of his affirmations concerning Christ's wish that Peter and his successors preside over his followers in a ministry springing from an authority not of power but of love. Headley argues convincingly that More's conviction on this matter crystallised in the period between the production of the two editions of his reply to Luther. Thus in terms of the full Rosseus edition Headley is prepared to state that for More the twin focal points of his thought on the church are the institution of papal primacy on the one hand and the authority of ecclesial consensus on the other. Apart from a serious lapse of observation in neglecting the full significance ascribed to conciliar authority in the *Responsio,* this essay of Headley's was the most satisfactory account of More's ecclesiology at its time of publication.

The Abbé André Prévost published in 1969 the first full length survey of More's theological positions extending from his concept of God to practical spirituality. Within this broad ranging synthesis Prévost found time to analyse at length the content of More's ecclesiology.[39] Like his predecessors he began with the rule of faith. The eternal unwritten word of God immanent in tradition as well as scripture is More's yardstick. It is to this divine word mediated through the church that submission is made in the act of faith. The mediation of revelation by the church is an essential

---

[37] On Murner and More, see Headley, *First Expression of More's Ecclesiology,* 73-92; idem, *Responsio,* 786-788. See also Ambrosius Catharinus Politi, *Apologia pro veritate catholicae et fidei ac doctrinae adversus impia ac valde pestifera Martini dogmata,* (1520) ed. J. Schweizer and A. Franzen, *Corpus Catholicorum* 27, Münster Westf., 1956 and Luther's reply: *Ad librum eximii magistri nostri Ambrosii Catharini...responsio,* (1521), *WA* 7, 705-778.

[38] More, *Responsio,* 202/28-33, tr. 203/33-39.

[39] André Prévost, *Thomas More, 1477-1535, et la crise de la pensée européene,* Tours, 1969, 233-287.

part of its function in the world. Prévost like Headley emphasised the inspirational, pneumatic concept of tradition found in More, based on his profound conception of the abiding presence of the divine Spirit within the Christian community.

Because of this divine guidance the church can exercise its ministry in respect of God's word in authenticating, transmitting and interpreting the divine message. This it does through three main organs: the common faith of the visible church; the writings and other commentaries of the fathers; conciliar definition. Prévost recognised More's affirmation of a divinely based papal authority but saw this exercised more in the sphere of discipline and church order than in teaching with special authority. Hence, little is heard of either the 'ordinary' or 'extraordinary magisterium', of the Roman pontiff. In this he was more acute than Headley who failed to see all the nuances possible within a broad affirmation of papal primacy.

According to Prévost the church for More was primarily a social body with ends and means, hierarchically organised with its own discipline and administration. He also adverted to the mystical and communitarian dimensions but these were overlaid by an emphasis on its social characteristics. Nonetheless, he recognised the special significance attached by More to the divine presence which enables the church to outlive the near-fatal effects of the sinful life of so many of its members and officeholders. Prévost's work is invaluable providing as it does a unique synthesis of More's theological outlook. At the same time it lacks a full, historical dimension in that this outlook is presented as a static rather than an evolving picture, one whose lines are drawn in the course of a lifetime, rather than given at birth. Moreover he failed to appreciate fully the profoundly spiritual view of the church underlying More's aggressive polemic.

Richard Marius in his introduction to the Yale edition of the *Confutation* also presents a synthetic view of More's thought, though confined in scope to the work in question.[40] His exposition is systematic rather than genetic in character. Hence one does not have the opportunity to follow the argument as it develops in the course of the book. On the other hand the canvas on which he works is a good deal broader than Headley's though Marius lacks Headley's talent for combining compression with insight.

Marius spells out the context of More's ecclesiology in terms of an awareness of the absoluteness of God, a doctrine of predestination, man's

---

[40] See Richard Marius, *Thomas More's View of the Church* in *Confutation* III, 1271-1363.

sinfulness or God's gracefulness towards man. Marius traverses now familiar territory in describing More's attitudes towards the church, revelation and its transmission. He strikes a nice balance in his presentation of More's view of the church as being at once charismatic and institutionalised, spiritual and terrestrial, sinful and yet inwardly sanctified and sanctifying.

What is a little new in this treatment is the firmer emphasis on conciliar authority in terms of legislation, definition of doctrine, and a certain degree of supervision of the papacy by the council. Marius's treatment of More's attitude to the latter institution is perhaps the most nuanced to date. He notes the dual base of papal authority in divine authority and ecclesial institution. More gave unqualified assent to the second of these affirmations concerning the validity of papal authority. He himself thought the papal office to be of divine institution but did not look on it as a matter beyond the bounds of theological disputation and justifiable dissent.

A number of other shorter studies have appeared on various aspects of More's ecclesiology, some of them an elaboration of positions spelled out in the works referred to above, others derivative from the latter.[41] What then remains to be done? In the first instance only one complete study of More's ecclesiology exists, that of Prévost. This occurs in a larger study covering the whole range of More's theological preoccupations. Moreover valuable as Prévost's study is, it fails to adopt a fully historical perspective in terms of the inner development of More's thought and its relationship to its historical context both as regards medieval background as well as contemporary developments in Britain and the European mainland. The other studies excellent as they are, tend to limit themselves to one or other of the main sources, *Responsio, Confutation,* or in the case of Flesseman-Van Leer, the Tyndale controversy taken as a whole.[42]

Hence there is both room for and need of a study of More's ecclesiology which will examine its development through its various stages of growth as well as in relation to its antecedents in medieval times and parallels in contemporary thought. This makes it possible to identify to some degree the interaction between the various phases of Sir Thomas More's career and thought, to delineate the turning points in the evolution of his positions, to

---

[41] See for example James Hitchcock, *Thomas More and the Sensus Fidelium, Theological Studies* 36 (1975) 145-154, and the later articles by Headley noted above.

[42] Presumably the Yale editors of the *Dialogue Concerning Heresies* will deal with its ecclesiological content.

take stock of his relationships with thinkers of former times as well as his own. In this way it becomes easier to pinpoint his position in the map of an evolving conception of the church and to define in some degree the elements of originality which were his.

Plan of the study

The scope of the subsequent study is worked out within the following framework. The first step is to examine the background of medieval ecclesiology. I then look at some of the principal sources used by More and outline his own approach to theological method. Subsequently I study the development of his thought in four main sources taken in chronological order: the *Responsio ad Lutherum* (1523), *The Dialogue Concerning Heresies* (1530-31), *The Confutation of Tyndale's Answer* (1532-33), and a fourth group of sources, mainly letters, some of which antedate the *Confutation* but most of which were composed during the treason-trial period (1534-35). Finally a synthetic presentation is made from the conclusions of these four chapters showing the development, if any, of More's main positions. These conclusions are reviewed once more in the final chapter, this time against the background of late medieval and reformation ecclesiology.[43]

---

[43] As regards methodology I have followed the American author Clemens J. Fuerst, *Normae scriptis edendis in disciplinis ecclesiasticis,* Rome, 1961, as a basic guide, but modified by T. W. Moody, *Rules for Contributors to 'Irish Historical Studies',* a reprint from *Irish Historical Studies,* Dublin, 1968; *The Victoria History of the Counties of England, Handbook for Editors and Authors,* edited by C. R. Elrington, London, 1970, and R. H. Shevenell, *Recherches et thèses: Research and Theses,* Ottawa, 1963. Normally the full title and author of a work is cited when it first appears in the footnotes; the author with short title is given in subsequent references. A list of abbreviations used is given in the front pages of this work. I have for ready reference inserted biblical references into many of the quotations. These are placed outside the full stop to indicate an interpolation to the text.

CHAPTER ONE

THE COURSE OF MEDIEVAL ECCLESIOLOGY

I. Introduction

'In the Reformation everything was placed in question but most of all the institutional church and ecclesiastical authority. The reformers refused to identify the church of Christ with this institution. Christ's church, understood as the assembly of the truly faithful, was known to God alone and was not, as such, visible. As regards ecclesiastical authority, the reformers wished to admit the authority of God alone and of his word which imposes itself on the Christian conscience within the framework of a religious relationship. Ecclesiastical authority is purely human, social, and utilitarian; all Christians share equally in the priesthood.'[1]

Corresponding to this assertion, Catholic apologists sought to produce a conception of the church which would meet the criticisms of the reformers, retain traditional values, while being at once the mediator of revelation as well as ground for its acceptance. This Catholic reaction reached its culminating point in the work of Robert Cardinal Bellarmine (1542-1621), whose approach to ecclesiology was to predominate in Catholic circles till the emergence of the Tübingen school associated with the name of J. A. Möhler in the first half of the nineteenth century.[2] The debate between Thomas More and the early Lutherans was, unknown to themselves, part

---

[1] Y. Congar, *Kirche*, in *Handbuch Theologischer Grundbegriffe*, ed. Heinrich Fries, I, Munich, 1962, 807-808, French tr. *Église*, *Encyclopédie de la Foi*, I, 427. For a general conspectus of the evolution of the idea of the church in the late middle ages and reformation period, see Congar, *Encyclopédie*, 421-432; idem, *L'Église. De Saint Augustin à l'époque moderne*, Paris, 1970, 11-368; H. Bacht *Ekklesiologie*, I, *Historische Grundlinien*, *LTK* III, 781-784; A. Adam, *Kirche* III, *Dogmengeschichtlich*, *RGG* III, 1304-1312; E. Dublanchy, *Église*, in *DTC* IV (1911), 2108-2224; Friedrich Merzbacher, *Wandlungen des Kirchenbegriffs im Spätmittelalter, Grundzüge der Ekklesiologie des ausgehenden 13., des 14. und 15. Jahrhunderts* in *Zeitschrift der Savigny-Stiftung für Rechtsgeschichte* 70, *Kanonistische Abteilung* 39 (1953) 274-361; another helpful survey can be found in Heiko Oberman, "*Et Tibi Dabo Claves Regni Caelorum*". *Kirche und Konzil von Augustin bis Luther. Tendenzen und Ergebnisse*, *Nederlands Theol. Tijdschrift* 25 (1971) 261-282; 29 (1975) 97-118; E. Mersch, *Le Corps Mystique du Christ*, II, Paris, 3rd ed., 1951, 139-270, tr. J. R. Kelly, S. J., *The Whole Christ*, London, 1938, 441-518. My study does not incorporate the results of significant research into the theological positions adopted in medieval exegesis. See in particular the excellent analysis of medieval psalm commentaries by Scott H. Hendrix, *Ecclesia in Via, Ecclesiological Developments in the Medieval Psalms Exegesis and the 'Dictata Super Psalterium' (1513-1515) of Martin Luther*, Leyden, 1974, 15-140.

[2] Congar, art. cit., 428-429; *Ecclésiologie*, 369-440; Merzbacher, art. cit., 360-361.

of this great movement of thought. Each in his own way was influenced by
a theological tradition extending back more than a thousand years, a tradition which contained embryonically the seeds of later conflict. Hence the
need to fix more precisely the medieval background to More's debates
with Luther and Tyndale.

Among the ecclesiologists of the fifteenth century one can find representatives of the major medieval schools of thought. In this epoch theology
tended to develop around concrete topics, notably that of the role of the
general council, which in its turn raised the whole question of the social
organisation of the church. Thus in order to evaluate the contribution of
the fifteenth century one must go back beyond it to the early middle ages,
in particular to the Gregorian reform to reach the watershed from which
the various streams of thought came to the surface. This is the reason why
so much space is given in what follows to the early and high medieval
period, though what concerns us most is the conciliar epoch, and that
which followed, immediately prior to the Reformation. Our material is
presented under two headings, charismatic and institutional structures,
and the church's role in mediating revelation, as these are the main
themes which will recur at a later date in reformation controversy.

II. The Early Medieval Period

A. *Institutional Structures*

1.*Augustine*

Ultimately the divergences which emerged in the sixteenth century can
be traced back to the manifold description of the church of God contained
in divine revelation. Less remotely they may be seen to stem from contrary elements brought to a living unity by St Augustine in his theological
writings, notably the *De civitate Dei*.[3] St Augustine developed his
ecclesiology in relation to three main concerns: his role as priest and
bishop in expounding the scripture; in debating with the Donatists; in
absorbing into his view of the church the implications of his doctrine on
grace.[4]

In his pastoral presentation of the mystery Augustine emphasised the
theme *ecclesia ab Abel,* the church as the body of the elect. In this sense he

---

[3] Bacht, art. cit., 782-783; Adam, art. cit., 1306-1307. See also Fritz Hofmann, *Der Kirchenbegriff des Hl. Augustinus in seinen Grundlagen und in seiner Entwicklung,* Munich, 1933,
485-516. On Augustine's ecclesiology in general see Joseph Ratzinger, *Volk und Haus Gottes
in Augustins Lehre von der Kirche,* München, 1954.

[4] Congar, *Ecclésiologie,* 11-12.

defined the church as the body of Christ such that Christ and the church form one man, one person, *Christus integer* or *totus*. He illustrated this position by reference to Acts 9, 4: 'Saul, Saul, why persecutest thou me?', and Eph 5, 31 (Gn 2, 24): the bridal image of two in one flesh. Christ prays in us, suffers in us, is our holiness in spite of our own impotence. Significantly for our concern, the gift of grace which pervades this body and binds it together is not the *gratia creata* of scholastic theology but *gratia increata*, the Holy Spirit himself.[5]

The persecution of Diocletian (303-305) had reaped its harvest of conformists. In reaction to their continued presence in the church a group of *illuminati* gathered around Donatus, bishop of Carthage (313-347) to preserve the Christian community in its primitive authenticity.[6] The movement remained confined to small North African enclaves. Augustine rejected their position, arguing that the church was essentially universal by nature. One is only fully Christian when in communion with the great body of believers spread throughout the world. Augustine further developed the notion of the co-existence of good and evil within the church, *ecclesia mixta*. Here Augustine distinguished between the *ecclesia qualis nunc est* and *ecclesia quae futura est*. Only the latter may be described as being without spot or wrinkle in Pauline terms (Eph 5, 28). Sinners, Augustine maintained, form part of the church *numero non merito,* a formula which was to become classic.

The Donatists claimed that only a minister in communion with the Holy Spirit could validly celebrate the sacraments. In response to this threat Augustine affirmed the central role of Christ in Christian worship: 'Peter baptises, it is Christ who baptises...Judas baptises, it is Christ who baptises.' The church does not exercise power, *potestas,* but ministry, *ministerium*, in relation to its own cult. In recognising the validity of sacraments celebrated outside the full communion of the *catholica*, the need arose in order to preserve this unity to emphasise the social elements in the church: communion with legitimate pastors and their authority.

Augustine's neo-platonism led him to postulate two levels of reality within the Christian community: sacramental communion at the empirical level (*communio sanctorum*) and union in the Spirit at the trans-empirical level (*societas sanctorum*). Visible communion in the sacrament is an imperfect realisation of that total immersion in the Spirit which is the goal of Christian life. It is the Spirit which binds the church into one, who

---

[5] Congar, *Ecclésiologie*, 12-13; Fritz Hofmann, *Der Kirchenbegriff des Hl. Augustinus in seinen Grundlagen und in seiner Entwicklung, Munich*, 1933, 485-516.

[6] Congar, *Ecclésiologie,* 13-17.

conferred the gift of the keys to remit sin, who assures the indefectibility in faith of the believing community. Congar points out that later theology materialised Augustine's ecclesiology by applying to the institution texts in which he had described the action of the Spirit through the sacraments.

The *City of God,* composed between 413 and 426, was spread across a canvas coextensive with the creative design of God.[7] The city of God is primarily a heavenly city whose first citizens were the angels. One portion of this city is still in exile on earth, *peregrina,* and its members if predestinate will eventually replace the fallen angels in glory. Augustine, in one sense, takes *church* and *city of God* as synonymous, but in another takes *church* as it applies to those on earth to designate the predestinate. This church even while on earth incorporates to some degree the city of God.

Some have argued to a dual ecclesiology in Augustine. This is true to a certain extent in so far as he used the term *ecclesia* polyvalently: e.g. for the *civitas Dei,* the *ecclesia ab Abel,* the *ecclesia peregrinans.* Similarly it is true to say that for Augustine the *communio sanctorum* and the *societas sanctorum* were not necessarily identical, though he in fact insisted even more than present day theology on the necessity of the sacraments for salvation. Augustine recognised a visible church order in terms of a priesthood which preaches the gospel, celebrates sacraments and promotes peace in brotherhood. He acknowledged the primacy of Rome, not on specifically scriptural grounds but because of its continuity as the apostolic see of Peter. He attributed to it a special role in the confirmation of faith because of its *abundantia gratiae.* Not popes but councils are the normal means of determining doctrinal issues, 'quorum est in ecclesia saluberrima auctoritas'. Conciliar decisions are the expression of the *universalis ecclesiae consensio.*

These Augustinian themes of Christ's mystical body, the *ecclesia mixta,* the objective value of sacraments, the nature of sacramental character, the ministerial role of the church in relation to grace continued to flow powerfully through early medieval ecclesiology.

2. *Carolingian Theocracy*

Subsequently, medieval ecclesiology was to develop not by maintaining the Augustinian synthesis but by taking up particular elements within it and expanding them, often without regard for overall harmony. Global vision was thereby obscured though no doubt to the far-reaching advantage

---

[7] Congar, *Ecclésiologie,* 18-22.

of certain individual elements. The fundamental division arose between a view of the church as a spiritual organism and as an earthly reality. Undoubtedly the medieval emphasis was placed on the latter aspect, though the former was kept alive, in great measure according to some authors, due to Franciscan tradition.[8]

One of the greatest reasons for this emphasis on the temporal reality of the church evinced in medieval times was the extent of her involvement in the socio-political field from the time of Charlemagne onward. This created an urgent need to determine the temporal nature of the church in relation to the structures of feudal society and its political authority. The problem was rendered even more confused by the inherited Carolingian tendency to identify church with society: 'Duo sunt quibus principaliter mundus hic regitur: auctoritas sacrata pontificum et regalis potestas.'[9] In the Carolingian theocratic system church and society are not merely coterminous. They are virtually indistinguishable. It was to take more than a thousand years to disentangle them ideologically as well as politically.

3. *Hildebrandine Reform*

The first major attempt in this field may be associated, curiously perhaps, with Pope Gregory VII. The eleventh century reform was not merely a socio-political movement; it was also ideological. Gregory's practical aim of withdrawing church and churches from lay control was based on theological principle. Arguing from the direct institution by God of the papal power to bind and loose, Gregory proclaimed the subordination of temporal to spiritual power in the service of justice. He did not claim a strictly political power for the papacy but asserted its moral authority of binding and loosing when the justice of God was concerned. Where this infringed on an area of political obedience it could lend itself easily to misuse. Correspondingly he demanded for the church as Spouse of Christ complete liberty in pursuing her tasks and claimed for her the office of *mater et magistra* to all men.[10]

---

[8] Adam, loc. cit.; Ernst Benz, *Ecclesia Spiritualis, Kirchenidee und Geschichtstheologie der Franziskanischen Reformation,* Stuttgart, 1934, 138-174.

[9] This phrase was borrowed from Pope Gelasius I by Gregory VII, except that the word *mundus* replaces *ecclesia*, thereby radically altering the sense. See Congar, *Ecclésiologie,* 52-53; Erich Caspar, *Das Register Gregors VII, Monumenta Germanica Historica, Epistolae Selectae,* Vol. II, fasc. II, *Gregorii VII Registrum,* lib. V—IX, Berlin, 1923, 553, 14-22; Carl Mirbt, *Quellen zur Geschichte des Papsttums und des Römischen Katholizismus,* 4th ed., Tübingen, 1924, no. 187, 85/16-19.

[10] Congar, *Ecclésiologie,* 89-122; Augustin Fliche, *La Réforme Grégorienne,* Vol. II, Louvain, Paris, 1925, 189-204; 309-350; idem, *La Réforme Grégorienne et la reconquête chrétienne*

The papacy succeeded to a large extent in its attempt to achieve the autonomy of the church vis-à-vis the temporal powers but not without cost to itself. Gregory had got his canonists to compile collections of legal texts favouring papal power, many drawn from the False Decretals. In these documents the papacy was presented as *caput, fundamentum, radix, fons et origo* of all authority and power in the church. The church was seen as built upon papal power and depending on it for its right to existence. A further consequence of this trend was that the life of the church tended to be considered and expressed in juridical terms which took little account of her inner life and the realities of charity and grace.[11]

4. *Canonist Ecclesiology*

It is not surprising that those most concerned with systematic reflection on the church in the 12th century tended to be canonists rather than theologians.[12] The *Concordia discordantium canonum* of Gratian was published in Bologna about 1140 A.D. The title itself says a great deal. Within the tradition there are many elements potentially contradictory of each other. To obviate ensuing complications in the daily life of the church Gratian sought to reduce these to unity. Thus from one point of view Gratian was a significant exponent of the Hildebrandine theology of papal authority. In this line he formulated a juridical theory of the church as a perfectly autonomous society. The primacy of the pope is of divine institution. The pope, or *ecclesia romana* which he used as a synonym, is the supreme

---

(1057-1123), (*Histoire de l'Église depuis les origines jusqu'à nos jours.* ed. A. Fliche and V. Martin, Vol. 8), Paris, 1944, 76-83; 110-118; 179-182; Gerd Tellenbach, *Libertas, kirche und weltordnung im zeitalter des investiturstreites, Forschungen zur Kirchen und Geistesgeschichte*, ed. Erich Seeberg, Erich Caspar, Wilhelm Weber, Vol. 7, Stuttgart, 1936, 151-192; tr. R. F. Bennett, *Church, State, and Christian Society at the time of the Investiture Contest*, Oxford, 1940, 126-191.

[11] Congar, *Ecclésiologie*, 107-112; ancient themes of Christian anthropology were used to vindicate papal authority, and the right to depose kings: e.g. Jer 1, 10, 'Ecce constitui te hodie super gentes et super regna,...'; I Cor 2, 15 (6, 3) 'Spiritualis autem judicat omnia,...' The *False Decretals* attributed to Isidorus Mercator saw the light of day in France about the year 850. Their purpose was to establish the independence of the ecclesiastical order by providing texts purporting to come from the earliest centuries in support of this claim. See Congar, *Ecclésiologie*, 62-63.

[12] Congar, *Ecclésiologie*, 145-151; Brian Tierney, *Foundations of the Conciliar Theory, The Contribution of the Medieval Canonists from Gratian to the Great Schism*, Cambridge, 1955, 23-84; idem, *Pope and Council: Some New Decretist Texts*, Medieval Studies 19 (1957) 197-218; J. A. Watt, *The Early Medieval Canonists and the Formation of Conciliar Theory*, in *Irish Theological Quarterly* 24 (1957) 13-31; D. Ed. Heintschel, *The Medieval Concept of an Ecclesiastical Office*, Washington, 1956; L. Hödl, *Die Geschichte der scholastischen Literatur und die Theologie der Schlüsselgewalt*, I Teil, *Beiträge zur Geschichte der Philosophie und Theologie des Mittelalters*, Münster, 1891, 166 ff.; 181-184.

legislator, even the sole legislator. It pertains to the apostolic see to convene councils. The faith of the Roman church is inviolate and indeed normative for the rest of Christendom.

On the other hand Gratian had a conservative strain also running through his thought. He spoke of the pope not as *vicarius Christi* but as *vicarius Petri*. He recognised limits to papal authority and the possibility of the pontiff being deposed in case of heresy; 'a nemine est judicandus nisi deprehendatur a fide devius.'

B. *Mediating Revelation*

One of the most important functions of the church acknowledged by all believers was that of transmitting the word of God. For the medieval mind, however, the opposition or at least clear-cut distinction between the community of believers with its teaching functionaries on the one hand, and the written sources on the other containing this word, whether bible or tradition, did not emerge completely at the reflexive level of consciousness till a relatively late date. The world of creation and the soul of man, it was believed, were only intelligible in any complete sense of the word in the light of sacred scripture. On the other hand it was held with equal conviction that scripture could only yield its fuller meaning in the church where official teaching, the authority of approved doctors, and Christian life itself acted as authentic interpreters of divine mystery.[13] Thus in determining the sources of revelation one is not confronted with a set of atomically-distinct, free standing realities, but a harmonious whole which is the datum of revelation, possessed, understood, and expounded by a living community.

Moreover, when the medieval concept of *scriptura sacra* is examined, it is discovered to have included not merely the book of the bible but also the writings of the fathers, conciliar canons, pontifical decrees, and, less frequently, the works of more outstanding theologians. The bible was considered to be the sacred text *par excellence* but it was also held that the Holy Spirit had been at work in the minds of the fathers, the deliberations of councils, as well as in the decrees of popes, while the idea was also much to the fore that these later writings were but a commentary on and an exposition of the datum of the bible carried on through history by successive

---

[13] Yves M.-J. Congar O. P., *La Tradition et les Traditions*, Vol. I, *Essai Historique*, Paris, 1960, 123-128, tr. Michael Naseby and Thomas Rainborough, *Tradition and Traditions, An historical and a theological essay*, London, 1966, 86-91; J. Beumer, *Die mündliche Überlieferung als Glaubensquelle*, Freiburg, Basle, Vienna, 1962, 45-53.

generations of believers and interpreters.[14] Thus in medieval thought a global view of the church was matched by a global view of its role in mediating revelation. It was for later, more analytical generations to dismantle the globe and expose the inherent tensions it concealed.

III. THE CENTRAL MEDIEVAL PERIOD

A. *Institutional Structures*

1. *Scholastic Theology*

In this period a new strain of thinking emerged concerning the church distinct from that of the canonists namely that of scholastic theologians. By reason of his influence on subsequent generations, Thomas Aquinas is the dominant figure. Aquinas inherited however from Hugh of St Victor (+ 1141) a balanced and essentially spiritual conception of the church. The latter had defined it as the body of Christ animated by one Spirit.[15] Within this 'pneumatic' perspective inherited from Augustine, Hugh of St Victor worked out the plan of the empirical church as a moral body or corporation, hierarchically organised, and presided over by the bishop of Rome.[16] This emphasis on the spiritual aspect of ecclesial reality was maintained by Bonaventure as well as by Bernard of Clairvaux.[17]

From another early scholastic source he received a different perspective on the relation of Christ to his church.[18] The concept of created grace, which may be linked with the *Regulae* of Alain of Lille (after 1194), tended to make of Christ the exclusive source of the life of the body. Two new treatises enter the theological *corpus, de Christo capite* and *de gratia capitis.* On the other hand the formal role of the Spirit in enlivening the body is

---

[14] Congar, *Tradition,* tr. Naseby and Rainborough, 91-93. This usage is attributed initially to the inclusion of the *Decretum Gelasianum* among the canonical collections, and in particular among those chapters which deal with sources and rules.

[15] 'Ecclesia sancta corpus est Christi uno Spiritu vivificata, et unita fide una, et sanctificata. Hujus corporis membra singuli quique fidelium existunt... Hac itaque similitudine Ecclesia sancta, id est universitas fidelium, corpus Christi vocatur propter Spiritum Christi, quem accepit, cujus participatio in homine designatur quando a Christo Christianus appellatur.' in Hugh of St Victor, *De sacramentis christianae fidei,* lib. II, pars 2, *PL,* 176, c. 416.

[16] For Hugh of St Victor see J. de Ghellinck S.J., *Le Mouvement Théologique du XIIᵉ Siècle, sa préparation lointaine avant et autour de Pierre Lombard, ses rapports avec les initiatives des canonistes, études, recherches et documents,* Bruges, Bruxelles, Paris, 2nd ed., 1948, 185-203; Jean Chatillon, *Une ecclésiologie médiévale: L'idée de l'église dans la théologie de l'école de Saint Victor au XIIᵉ siècle, Irénikon* 22 (1949) 115-138; 395-411; Congar, *Ecclésiologie,* 159-162.

[17] Merzbacher, art. cit., 286; Congar, *Ecclésiologie,* 125-129; 224-229.

[18] Congar, *Ecclésiologie,* 161-169.

gradually lost sight of: ecclesiology loses touch with pneumatology. (This is significant for our theme since pneumatology was to be one of the major 'new' insights of Lutheran theology.) It was to be the task of Aquinas to bring the various elements of empirical structure into harmony with one another as well as with the invisible elements, using the Aristotelian concept of *societas perfecta* as a synthesising principle.

Thomas's ecclesiology is not to be found in any one work but is scattered through various treatises.[19] In his work in defence of his fellow-mendicants, Aquinas pointed up the fact that the church of Christ is a *societas perfecta* on the Aristotelian model, 'adunatio hominum ad unum aliquid communiter agendum.' It therefore possesses full autonomy and independence as well as all the means to attain its goal including the right to legislate and to execute laws imposed on its members. This perfect society for Thomas was no mere *moral* unity for, as he explained in the *Summa Theologica,* the church is the body of Christ, a living organism whose energy derives from supernatural sources in a continuous and permanent state of regeneration, according as Christ grows and spreads through the peoples of all epochs and all generations. In its sacramental activity this organism becomes the direct means of communication of divine life by Christ.[20] Thus within one single perspective Thomas brought together the charismatic, sacramental, socio-political and juridical elements of ecclesial reality.

On the question of papal primacy Thomas recognised it as of divine institution, possessing a plenitude of power in the sense that the pope could designate the subjects of orders and episcopal dignity. The 'power of the keys' descends from Peter to the other apostles and so from the pope to the

---

[19] Congar, *Ecclésiologie,* 232-241; E. Mersch, S.J., *Le Corps Mystique du Christ,* II, 171-213, tr. J. Kelly, *The Whole Christ,* 464-485; J. Geiselmann, *Christus und die Kirche nach Thomas von Aquin, Theol. Quartalschr.* 107 (1926) 198-222; 108 (1927) 233-255. A. Darquennes, S.J., *De Juridische Structuur van de Kerk volgens Sint Thomas van Aquino (avec un resumé en français),* Louvain, 1949, 199-216; Yves M.-J. Congar, *Esquisses du Mystère de l'Église,* Paris, 1953 (nouv. éd.), 59-91; idem, *Aspects ecclésiologiques de la querelle entre mendiants et séculiers dans la seconde moitié du XIIIe et le début du XIVe siècle,* in *Archiv. d'Hist. Doctr. et Littér. du Moyen Age* 28 (1961) 35-51; see also F. Merzbacher, art. cit., 287-290; Martin Grabmann, *Die Lehre des Heiligen Thomas von Aquin von der Kirche als Gotteswerk. Ihre Stellung im thomistische System und in der Geschichte der mittelalterlichen Theologie,* Regensburg, 1903; Y. M.-J. Congar, O.P., *Traditio Thomistica in materia ecclesiologica, Angelicum* XLIII (1967) 405-428. For Thomas himself see in particular *Opusculum, contra impugnantes Dei cultum et religionem,* (1256/57) in *S. Thomae Aquinatis doctoris angelici opuscula theologica,* II, ed. R. Spiazzi, O.P., Rome, Turin, 1954, 1-110.

[20] Thomas Aquinas, *In symbolum apostolorum,* a. 9, in ibid., 211-213; *De veritate,* Q. 29, a. 4-5, in *Quaestiones disputatae,* I, 558-562, ed. R. Spiazzi, O.P., Rome, Turin, 1954; also Mersch, loc. cit.

bishops. Similarly, the pope is the supreme judge in matters of doctrine, though Thomas did not ascribe to him the charism of infallibility. Nonetheless, though in no way watering down the role of visible institutional elements in church life, the principal reality of ecclesial life for Thomas remained 'the grace of the Holy Spirit'.[21] At the same time his political theories provided the clearest statement to date of the autonomy of the state vis-à-vis extreme concepts of papal monarchy.

John of Paris (+ 1306) was the most significant of the immediate heirs to Thomas's ecclesiology. His *De potestate regia et papali* was composed during the controversy between Boniface VIII and Philip the Fourth of France.[22] Hence its concentration on church-state relations, which are examined however within the context of a more general theory of the church. Like his master, John of Paris saw the church as the mystical body of Christ, made up of many members, a spiritual unity deriving its life from Christ. Within this vision of the world, Christ alone possesses all power, spiritual as well as temporal. Spiritual power has been conferred on the church, temporal given over to the state, without subordination of one to the other. The role of the pope is to be *dispensator generalis* of the spiritual and material goods of the church, goods which are the possession of the church as a whole, not the pope.

Within the church John of Paris expressed the wish for some sort of body, perhaps along the lines of the college of cardinals to represent the views of the various provinces in Rome. While upholding the divine right of papal primacy he maintained that in matters of faith the final word lies not with the pope but with the assembled council of the church. 'Eo quod orbis maior est Urbe et Papa, concilium maius est Papa solo.' In extreme cases the clergy acting through the college of cardinals may even depose the pope, invoking the cooperation of the temporal power if needs be.

2. *Hierocratic Ideology*

Canonist thought increasingly emphasised the institutional character of ecclesial fellowship in the thirteenth century. Two important consequences followed from this. The first proposed a radical distinction between order

---

[21] Congar, *Ecclésiologie*, 232-241; Aquinas, *Summa Theologica*, I-II, 106, 1 and 2; 107, 1 and 4; 108, 1-3.

[22] Merzbacher, art. cit., 343-346; Jean Leclercq O.S.B., *Jean de Paris et l'ecclésiologie du XIIIᵉ siècle*, Paris, Vrin, 1942, 34: 'Celui... auquel il doit le plus est saint Thomas.' See also 162-165 for a judgement on John of Paris's intellectual lineage. For content of his treatise see ibid., 89-165. See also Congar, *Ecclésiologie*, 282-285; John of Paris, *On Royal and Papal Power*, tr. with intr. by J. A. Watt, Toronto, 1971, esp. 14-63.

and jurisdiction. This opened the way to regarding the pope as source and origin of all ecclesiastical jurisdiction. At a later stage in England this distinction was to cast a cloak of orthodoxy over the affirmation of royal supremacy in regard to ecclesiastical *jurisdiction* as distinct from the relative autonomy of the *sacramental* sphere. A later canonist, Augustinus Trium-phus, was to write, 'papa magis sit nomen jurisdictionis.'

On the other hand the evolution of a theory of the church as a legal cor-poration, a moral body whose authority resides in all its parts taken together, was used to harmonise two ideas, one concerning the headship of a local church, e.g. that of a bishop or abbot, etc.; the other concerning the nature of the church as the *multitudo fidelium*. Huguccio, Innocent IV's master at Bologna, recognised the corporation itself as possessing in the last resort the authority of its head. He even transposed this theory to the relationship between pope or Roman church on the one hand and the church universal on the other. In this concept one can see with Brian Tierney the germ of certain conciliarist positions of the fourteenth and fifteenth centuries.

The reign of Innocent III (1198-1216) witnessed a movement among canonists towards a more hierocratic view of the church.[23] With Innocent IV (1243-1254) and Hostiensis, insistence on the primacy of priesthood was so strong, the position of the pope as supreme judge and the ultimate unitary spiritual goal of both state and church so emphasised, that the dualist theory of two powers was almost emptied of meaning. The *populus christianus* forms one body. To suggest it has two heads, pope and emperor, is to declare it a monstrosity. Not surprisingly, with regard to internal church administration, Innocent IV entered more and more into the allocation of ecclesiastical benefices in the name of his *plenitudo potestatis*. While one school of thought tied this authority not merely to the pope but indirectly to the college of cardinals, thereby laying the foundation for a theory of 'curial primacy', another current extended papal authority over the entire episcopate even when gathered in council. In this latter strain Durandus wrote in the context of the Council of Lyon, 1274: 'Secundum

---

[23] Congar, *Ecclésiologie*, 252-263; W. Ullmann, *Medieval Papalism. The Political Theories of the Medieval Canonists*, London, 1949, 98-104; 152-159. 176-177; Tierney, *Foundations*, 87-147. The latter emphasises the continuity of moderate corporation theory among canonist writers even during this period: ibid., 147-153. J. A. Watt, *The Theory of Papal Monarchy in the Thirteenth Century, The Contribution of the Canonists*, London, 1965, 58-134. Watt also speaks of the continuity of dualist thought in canonist tradition, a current which was to surface later in anti-Bonifatian writers as well as reinforce secularist tendencies inherent in Ockham's thought; see ibid., 142-144.

plenitudinem potestatis potest papa super omne concilium quidquid placet.'[24]

While Thomism exercised its synthesising and moderating influence, a more extreme school of papal canonists was not idle. The very same controversy with Philip the Fourth of France in which John of Paris had been engaged, evoked in the environs of the papal court one of the most extreme statements of hierocratic theory. Foremost among the curial apologists, Aegidius Romanus considered the pope as standing alone at the apex of a body which Aegidius termed: 'Ecclesia sancta et catholica et universalis...mater omnium.'[25] All men, all possessions, all earthly goods, as well as every earthly power are subordinated to the rule of this universal church to which the entire earth belongs.[26] Even worldly power and authority owe their institution to the church alone.[27] Within the church the pope possesses the plenitude of power, a true share in that of God. 'Et sicut Deus hoc agit in regimine omnium creaturarum, ita summus pontifex, Dei vicarius, hoc agit in gubernacione ecclesie et in regimine fidelium.'[28] The writings of Aegidius provided the basis for Boniface VIII's Bull *Unam Sanctam* (1302), it would appear, for although other writers were associated with him, the close parallels which exist strongly suggest the influence of Aegidius on the formulation of this decree.[29]

---

[24] Durandus, *In sacrosanctum Lugdunense concilium sub Gregorio X*, Fani, 1509, fol. 6a cited Congar, *Ecclésiologie*, p. 262, n. 37.

[25] Merzbacher, art. cit., 295-300; Jean Rivière, *Le Problème de l'Église et de l'état au temps de Philippe le Bel*, Louvain, 1926, 191-227. Aegidius Romanus, *De ecclesiastica potestate*, ed. R. Scholz, Weimar, 1929. Merzbacher quotes a phrase without giving the reference, 'papa, qui potest dici ecclesia.' Certainly an extreme statement of the papalist position! I have not been able to trace this reference but statements of a similar character are to be found in *De ecclesiastica potestate*, III, cap. ult., ed. Scholz, 206-209. The apparently extreme form of these statements need not be taken too literally if interpreted in the light of the neo-platonic ideas underlying them, which would see the pope as archetype of the church and therefore possessing in principle all its properties. This of course is not to say that its logic is acceptable.

[26] Aegidius Romanus, op. cit., II, cap. 2, ed. Scholz, 99: 'Omnes ergo homines et omnes possessiones sunt sub dominio ecclesie, ita quod ipsius ecclesie est orbis terrarum et universi qui habitant in eo.' Ibid., II, cap. 12, ed. Scholz, 108: '...omnium temporalium bonorum esset ecclesia domina et magistra...'

[27] ibid., II, cap. 5, ed. Scholz, 59: 'Quomodo potestas terrena est per ecclesiasticam constituta.'

[28] ibid., III, cap. 2, ed. Scholz, 155.

[29] Rivière, op. cit., 394-404; literature on p. 394, notes 1, 2 and 3. For a further account of this controversy, see Merzbacher, art. cit., 298-305; 307-314; Congar, *Ecclésiologie*, 277-281. For the work of James of Viterbo, see H.-X. Arquillière, *Le plus ancien traité de l'Église, Jacques de Viterbe; de regimine christiano (1301-1302), Études des sources et édition critique*, Paris, 1926; Alvarus Pelagius, (+ 1349), *De statu et planctu ecclesiae*, ed. J. T. Rocaberti, *Bibliotheca Maxima Pontifica*, III, 23-266; William Durandus (Junior, + 1330/31), *De modo generalis concilii celebrandi et corruptelis in ecclesiis reformandis*, Lyon, 1531. (This work is a

Conclusion

In so far as the church was discussed by theologians in these centuries, it found its place in Christology.[30] Hence a certain loss in perspective of the mystery of salvation leading to a dualism in thought concerning the church, one stream dealing with the spiritual element, mainly the province of theology, another stream dealing with institutional aspects, very much the concern of canon law. To this transition one may add a change in terminology characteristic of the middle ages though not without its bearing on subsequent developments: *ecclesia peregrinans* becomes *ecclesia militans*. In the same period the term *corpus Christi verum* takes on a new significance. Originally applied to the church, it was now applied to the eucharist. This proved to be a matter of some significance for the understanding of sacramental order. Ecclesiastical office had been hitherto understood in relation to the church and its upbuilding. Increasingly it came to be seen in relation to the eucharist with a consequent reduction of its horizon of concern to liturgy rather than to a broadly pastoral ministry; another issue Luther was to reopen in his treatment of church office and order.

B. *Mediating Revelation*

1. *Scholastic Theology*

As in more general topics concerning the nature of the church, scholastic dialectic set to work analysing the role of the ecclesial community and of its organs in transmitting the Christian message. In particular, Thomas Aquinas was responsible for distinguishing the role of the Holy Spirit in the inspired writing from the general assistance given to men of good will in their reflections on the word of God. He marked off into separate categories the canonical writings, works of the fathers, and magisterial pronouncements on this basis. He attached great weight to the authoritative teaching of bishops and especially to that of the pope as authentic interpreters of a divine revelation contained primarily in the canonical books of the bible.[31] Thomas's views were not universally ac-

---

counter-current to papal absolutism.) Augustinus Triumphus of Ancona (1243-1328), *Summa de potestate ecclesiastica,* (1326), Rome, 1584. On Augustinus Triumphus, see the study by Michael Wilks, *The Problem of Sovereignty in the Later Middle Ages, The Papal Monarchy with Augustinus Triumphus and the Publicists,* Cambridge, 1963, esp. 455-529.

[30] Congar, *Ecclésiologie,* 169-174.

[31] Thomas Aquinas, *Contra errores graecorum,* cap. 36, in *Opuscula theologica,* Vol. I, ed. R. A. Verardo, O.P., Rome, Turin, 1954, 343-344; *Quodlibet* IX, q. VII, a. 16, in *Quaestiones Quodlibetales,* ed. R. Spiazzi, O.P., Rome, Turin, 1949, 194. (Note this work had not been fully authenticated by 1950.) *Summa Theologica,* II-II[ac], q. 1, a. 10, Rome, Turin, (Marietti), 1956.

cepted in his own or subsequent generations. Consequently not a few of his contemporaries continued to consider both revelation and inspiration through an interior suggestion of the Spirit as a continuing feature of the church's existence.[32]

Towards the end of the thirteenth century the more popular attitude towards *scriptura sacra* as designating indifferently biblical and non-biblical expressions of Christian belief began to be modified. A pronounced swing in favour of the decrees of the hierarchy appeared, preference being given to those of the Roman pontiff as the most authentic source of the divine message. This evolution was not uninfluenced by the growth of papal power within the church and the corresponding crisis of authority to which it gave rise. Not surprisingly these attitudes are found more frequently in the writings of papal canonists. The role of the bible as well as that of the believing church was therefore down-graded. The pope's authority took their place and the unquestionable quality of his teaching in certain cases began to be emphasised.[33]

2. *Papal Infallibility—Franciscan Papalism*

A significant development took place in another school of thought about this time, the emergence of a formal theory of papal infallibility. Brian Tierney argues that the emergence of this concept came about '...because an unusual concatenation of historical circumstances arose that made such a doctrine useful to a particular group of controversialists—circumstances involving Joachimite radicalism, Franciscan spirituality and the whole peculiar, ambivalent relationship between the Franciscan Order and the papacy.'[34] In particular Tierney ascribes the formulation of this concept to

[32] Congar, *Tradition*, tr. Naseby and Rainborough, 91-92; J. de Ghellinck, S.J., *Pour l'histoire du mot 'revelare'*, in *RSR* VI (1916) 149-157; idem, *'Pagina' et 'Sacra Pagina'. Histoire d'un mot et transformation de l'objet primitivement désigné*, in *Mélanges A. Pelzer*, Louvain, 1947, 23-59; Beumer, *Mündliche Überlieferung*, 53-62.

[33] P. de Vooght, O. S. B., *Les Sources de la doctrine chrétienne d'après les théologiens du XIVᵉ siècle et du début du XVᵉ*, Desclée de Brouwer, 1954, 148-161; G. H. Tavard, *Holy Writ or Holy Church, The Crisis of the Protestant Reformation*, London, 1959, 22-43; see in particular Aegidius Romanus, op. cit., I, cap. 1, ed. Scholz, 5, et passim; Augustinus Triumphus, *Summa de potestate ecclesiastica*, Rome, 1584, q. X, a. 2, pp. 77-78: '...spectat ad ipsum caprivare, et determinare intellectum uniuscuiusque in obsequium Christi.'

[34] Brian Tierney, *Origins of Papal Infallibility 1150-1350. A Study in the Concepts of Infallibility, Sovereignty and Tradition in the Middle Ages*, Leyden, 1972, 274. See also Paul de Vooght, *Esquisse d'une enquête sur le mot 'infaillibilité' durant la période scolastique*, in *L'Infaillibilité de l'église*, *Journées oecuméniques de Chevetogne*, 1963, 99-146; Congar, *Ecclésiologie*, 244-248. The latter ascribes the earliest use of the term *infallible* in regard to the pope to Guy Terré some time before 1328; see ibid., 247 and n. 17. The subsequent controversy surrounding Tierney's interpretation of the origins of papal infallibility is summarised in Oberman, "*Et tibi dabo*", II, 109-118.

Peter Olivi, a Franciscan theologian of the late thirteenth century.[35] Olivi was, indeed, the first major medieval thinker who posed and answered affirmatively the question, 'Whether the Roman pontiff is...unerring in faith and morals.' Olivi's main argument was based on the assertion that: 'It is impossible for God to give to anyone the full authority to decide about doubts concerning the faith and divine law with this condition, that He would permit him to err...'[36] According to Tierney, however, Olivi's concern in these deductions was largely pragmatic. They were evolved with a view to preserving intact the papal decree approving the Franciscan way of life and in particular their doctrine on poverty as formulated in the decretal *Exiit* of Nicholas III (1279).[37] Subsequently the doctrine of papal infallibility became part of medieval tradition, sustained in the main by Franciscan theologians, only reaching the point of majority opinion in the era of Counter Reformation.

IV. THE LATER MIDDLE AGES

A. *Ockham*

1. *Institutional Structures*

The over-riding practical and ideological problem in the church at the turn of the fifteenth century was undoubtedly concerned with the relative positions of people, episcopate, and papacy in the constitutional scaffolding of the church. Several decades before this had become a burning issue of daily affairs, a revolutionary theologian had set the cat among the pigeons of both accepted orthodoxies, theological as well as canonical, concerning the relative importance of these elements. For although he had affinities with Marsiglio of Padua (1275/80—1342/3),[38] as well as with the Spiritual-Franciscan movement of Michael of Cesena, William of Ockham was a radically original thinker in his own right,[39] who placed the

---

[35] Tierney, *Papal Infallibility*, 93-130.

[36] See ibid., 116.

[37] See *Exiit qui seminat* in *Liber sextus*, ed. E. Friedberg, *Corpus Iuris Canonici*, II, Leipzig, 1879, *Sext.* 5.7.3, col. 1112; Tierney, *Papal Infallibility*, 126-130.

[38] J. Rivière, *Marsile de Padoue*, DTC X (1927), 153-177; P. Mikat, *Marsilius von Padua*, LTK VII, 108-110; Victor Martin, *Les Origines du Gallicanisme*, II, Paris, 1939, 32-41; Merzbacher, art. cit., 321-324; G. de Lagarde, *La Naissance de l'Esprit Laïque au Déclin du Moyen Age*, II, *Marsile de Padoue ou le premier théoricien de l'état laïque*, Saint-Paul-Trois-Châteaux (Drôme), Wien, 1st ed., 1934, 202-243; Congar, Ecclésiologie, 286-290; Jeannine Quillet, *La Philosophie Politique de Marsile de Padoue*, Paris, 1970, 161-274.

[39] Michael of Cesena (+ 1342) was minister-general of the Franciscans. He held the view that the possession of property was incompatible with the church's constitution and on these grounds broke both with his order and the church, finding refuge with Louis of Bavaria then

centre of gravity of the ecclesiastical community solidly in the body of the faithful.

William of Ockham rejected the idea of the church as a visible institution concerned almost exclusively with the communication of grace and salvation, and to whom one's primary obligation is one of obedience. For Ockham the church was primarily the invisible spiritual collectivity of the predestinate, whose main concern is to evoke active sharing in her life through faith on the part of her members. The church as the body of Christ therefore is not the clergy but the body of believers.

The church is ruled and guided by the Holy Spirit but in order to ensure the common welfare, as in political society, there is need for an earthly organisation and system of authority. Ockham accepted the divine institution of the papacy but held its jurisdiction to be of limited scope.[40] The *plenitudo potestatis* is to be found not in the pope nor in the bishops but in the general council which represents the universal body of the faithful.[41] Any single member of the church may fail including the pope; it is only the whole body which is preserved from defection. Indeed the true faith might be preserved in only one individual, an extreme position which effectively undermined the final authority of the council.

Consequently the council, according to Ockham, is superior to the pope and if crises arise, may judge him in the name of the Christian people. Ockham even suggested that the people have the right of election and

---

in opposition to the papacy. Concerning William of Ockham, an English Franciscan, see Merzbacher, art. cit., 324-327; E. Amann, *Occam, DTC* 11 (1931), 864-904; J. R. Reilly, *Wilhelm von Ockham, LTK* X, 1142-1145. Adalbert Hamman, O. F. M., *La Doctrine de l'Église et de l'État chez Occam, Étude sur le 'Breviloquium'*, Paris, 1942, 37-49; Wilhelm Kölmel, *Wilhelm Ockham und seine kirchenpolitischen Schriften*, Essen, 1962, 181-200; H. Köhler, *Der Kirchenbegriff bei Wilhelm von Occam*, Leipzig Dissert., 1937; G. de Lagarde, op. cit., V, *Guillaume d'Ockham. Critique des Structures Ecclésiales*, 3rd ed., Louvain, Paris, 1963, 3-264; Congar, *Ecclésiologie*, 290-295; J. B. Morrall, *Ockham and Ecclesiology* in *Medieval Studies Presented to Aubrey Gwynn, S. J.*, ed. J. A. Watt, J. B. Morrall, F. X Martin, Dublin, 1961, 481-491.

[40] William of Ockham, *Dialogus*, pars I, lib. V, cap. 29-35, in M. Goldast, *Monarchiae S. Romani Imperii, sive Tractatuum de Iurisdictione Imperiali seu Regia, et Pontificia seu Sacerdotali*, III, Frankfurt, 1614, 498-506.

[41] Merzbacher, op. cit., 325, is incorrect in stating that Ockham rejected the divine institution of the papal primacy. See G. de Lagarde, op. cit., 126-127. The text cited by Merzbacher, art. cit., 326, gives in fact the opposite view to that which he attributes to Ockham: '...quia quod in spiritualibus unus praesideat universis fidelibus (etiam si totus mundus esset conversus ad fidem) est immediate ex speciali ordinatione diuina et non humana, ut ex sacris canonibus, qui ponuntur in decretis *dist. 21. c. quamvis* et *dist.* 22. c. omnes et c. sacrosancta, et in aliis locis quam plurimis colligi potest, et ideo nisi Deus aliter ordinaret, et hoc fidelibus revelaret, omnes fideles etiam (si universi mortales suscepissent fidem) deberent uno summo pontifici in spiritualibus obedire: quia non est in potestate hominum divinam ordinationem aliqualiter immutare' in William of Ockham, *Dialogus*, pars III, lib. 1, cap. 8, in Goldast, *Monarchiae*, III, 876-877.

deposition of the pope. This however is not to say that the council as such
is infallible. Sacred scripture and the universal beliefs of the people of God
alone are unerring. Consequently in this scheme of things one finds a certain reversal of both hierocratic and neo-Aristotelian theory. The church is
considered neither as corporation nor as a self-sufficient society of monarchical constitution but as a multitude of individuals united by common
faith in Christ from whom their rulers derive their mandate.

2. *Mediating Revelation*

Ockham carried his anti-authoritarian principles further in his examination of the role of the church in communicating the Christian
message. In characteristic analytical fashion he drew up a list of *veritates
catholicae* in five categories which are normative for all believers including
those in authority. 'Quinque sunt genera veritatum, quibus non licet
Christianis aliter dissentire...Primum est earum, quae in Scriptura sacra
dicuntur, vel ex eis argumento necessario possunt inferri. Secundum est
earum quae ab Apostolis ad nos per succedentium relationem vel Scripturas fidelium pervenerunt, licet in Scripturis sacris non inveniantur
insertae nec ex solis eis possint necessario argumento concludi.' Thirdly
those found in trustworthy chronicles and histories of the faithful; fourth-
ly, truths which may be derived from the foregoing; fifthly, revelations
subsequent to the apostles.[42]

This analysis represents a dramatic change of attitude towards Christian
truth as conveyed through the church's ministry. In place of the older
global approach to mystery, never susceptible of adequate definition, one
is confronted with lists of truths or logical propositions which demand the
assent of the believer. These truths are contained in *literary* sources for the
most part while the role of the church is purely ministerial and in no way
definitive in their regard. Without solving them Ockham had posed questions of vital significance in the reformation crisis. Firstly, what is the rule
of faith? Is it something concretely objective to the body of believers or is
the church her own norm? Ockham subordinated the church to the literary
sources, but did not ignore the obligation implied in official endorsement
by the church of certain truths. But what is the church in this sense? Is it
the pope, the council, the theologians, the faithful? Ockham himself re-

---

[42] Ockham, *Dialogus*, pars I, lib. II, cap. 5: Goldast, *Monarchiae*, III, 415-416. See also G.
de Lagarde, *La Naissance de l'Esprit Laique*, V, 66-74; 128-164; H. Köhler, *Der Kirchenbegriff*,
62-71; H. Oberman, *The Harvest of Medieval Theology*, Cambridge, Mass. 1963, 378-382 emphasises that Ockham adopted an 'orthodox' line with a two-source theory of the transmission of revelation.

jected not merely the infallibility of the pope, but also that of the council, though admitting their magisterial role short of this point.[43] Ockham himself went so far as to suggest that the essential inerrancy of the church as a whole would be preserved even if all but one Christian departed from the truth. This was a minimalistic position adopted by few of his contemporaries, but there was certainly no consensus as to who held the last word in determining doctrinal truth.

The second question which was to prove no small bone of contention in the reformation period was how to account for doctrinal truths commonly held by the church but not attested to by biblical data. Ockham's answer to this was two-fold: extra-biblical, apostolic revelation transmitted through living tradition in the church, *per relationem vel scripturas fidelium*, and secondly, post-apostolic revelation within the church. (This latter notion was possibly a relic of the broader medieval concept of revelation and inspiration.) As in so many other matters, Ockham raised more questions than he answered, and these answers in particular were not to prove satisfying to all. Thus in Ockham's writings one finds not merely a strong tendency to identify the church with the body of the faithful but to give them preponderance of power if not of function within the church vis-à-vis both episcopate and papacy. On the other hand he identified almost exclusively with written sources (he does allow for tradition 'per relationem...fidelium'), the object of the faith of the church, according her a purely ministerial role in their regard. This tendency to enumerate the truths of revelation was carried on by a series of writers from Henry Totting of Oyta (+ 1397) to the great lights of the fifteenth century, Gerson, Torquemada and Biel, and beyond. Ockham's more general ecclesiological ideas were to exert great influence in the course of the conciliarist debate, and beyond that to influence later developments, notably through Biel in Germany, and the Paris school in France.

B. *Conciliarists and their Opponents*

1. *Institutional Structures*

a) Conciliarists

The conciliarist movement developed in relation to a specific historical problem, namely the crisis created in the church by the repudiation by the

---

[43] Ockham, *Dialogus,* Pars III, lib. III, cap. 1: Goldast, *Monarchiae,* III, 819; ibid., pars I, lib. V, cap. 25-26: Goldast III, 494-496; ibid., pars I, lib. V, cap. 3: Goldast III, 470; ibid., pars I, lib. VII, cap. 10: Goldast III, 646-650. ...'omnes veritates, quas determinat vel diffinit ecclesia, sub aliquo quinque generum praefatorum comprehendi noscuntur.' in ibid., 416. Official teaching merely transmits the content of the sources of revelation, which are almost exclusively literary in form.

greater part of the cardinals of Urban VI, whom they had elected as pope in Rome, 8 April 1378. They completed their rejection by electing a rival pope, Clement VII, on 20 September 1378.[44] The whole issue was undoubtedly bedevilled by political considerations and pressures arising from the desire of princes and nations to control to the greatest degree possible the central authority in the church. Nonetheless the practical issue was created by the cardinals' assertion that their original election had been invalid, an emergency measure to placate the Roman mob howling for an Italian pope.

Whatever the truth of their statement, it undoubtedly revealed a constitutional gap in ecclesiastical structures, the absence of an organ of government capable of deciding the issue of a disputed papal election. Indeed, and this aggravated the crisis, the theoretical issues underlying such an institution had not been resolved. Did ecclesial authority reside ultimately in the whole people of God as Ockham asserted? In the pope as Aegidius of Rome had asserted? In the episcopate gathered in council as John of Paris had asserted? Or, as some were later to assert, in the college of cardinals? Or perhaps in some combination of all three? In the light of the answers given to these questions what practical solutions could be offered to the schism? If agreement could not be reached on the theoretical issues, could a practical solution be arrived at acceptable to all parties? These were some of the issues which gave rise to a vast literature relating to the schism.[45]

Broadly speaking, the theologians of the conciliar era could be classified according to their answers to the theoretical question concerning ecclesiastical sovereignty, although some stubbornly clung to a purely pragmatic approach. The overall effect of the debate however was to

---

[44] Louis Salembier, *Le grand schisme d'occident,* Paris, 5th ed., 1922; Walter Ullmann, *The Origins of the Great Schism. A study in XIVth Century Ecclesiastical History,* London, 1948; Fliche et Martin, *Histoire de l'Église,* XIV, E. Delaruelle, E.-R. Labande, Paul Ourliac, *L'Église au temps du Grand Schisme et de la crise conciliaire 1378-1449,* Bloud & Gay, Paris, 1962, 3-44; H. Jedin, *Ecumenical Councils of the Catholic Church. An Historical Outline,* Edinburgh, London, 1960, 105-141.

[45] For a survey of these ideological currents, see H. Jedin, *Konziliarismus,* in *LTK* VI 532-534; *Geschichte des Konzils,* I, 1-48; tr. Graf, I, 5-62; Victor Martin, *Les origines du Gallicanisme,* II, Paris, 1939, 31-84; E. Delaruelle, E.-R. Labande, P. Ourliac, op. cit., 491-528; Ullman, op. cit., 191-231; Brian Tierney, *Foundations of the Conciliar Theory, The Contribution of the Medieval Canonists from Gratian to the Great Schism,* Cambridge, 1955, 157-247; A. Hauck, *Gegensätze im Kirchenbegriff des späteren Mittelalters,* Luthertum (1938) 225-240; Paul de Vooght, *Le Conciliarisme aux Conciles de Constance et de Bâle,* in *Le Concile et les Conciles. Contribution à l'Histoire de la Vie Conciliaire de l'Église,* Chevetogne, Cerf, 1960, 143-181; H. Jedin, *Bischöfliches Konzil oder Kirchenparlament, Ein Beitrag zur Ekklesiologie der Konzilien von Konstanz und Basel,* Basel, Stuttgart, 1962, 5-35; Congar, *Ecclésiologie,* 309-338.

attach undue emphasis to the empirical elements of ecclesial life to the detriment of spiritual or charismatic elements. At the ideological level this must have contributed greatly to the reformation reaction towards inward reality.

Pierre d'Ailly (1350-1425), regarded the church as a community of believers based on scripture.[46] It is an organic whole which in each historical epoch is in a certain sense perfect yet never complete. Hence the need for growth. The faithful in communion with Christ must continue to develop it. Sacramental order confers special authority on the priesthood but not the plenitude of power. The plenitude of ecclesial power resides in the general council which combines the juridical authority of the universal church with the sacramental power of the priesthood. The council can depose the pope if necessary (e.g. in case of heresy or schism) and elect another, for papal office is exercised within the church and in subordination to it. The 'democratic' influence of Ockham is here in evidence though modified by d'Ailly's recognition of the privileged role of those in sacramental orders, one which derives not from the people but from divine intervention.[47]

Conrad of Gelnhausen (1320-1390) was one of the earliest polemicists of the conciliar era.[48] Though sometimes represented as holding extreme views, he was not in fact greatly indebted to either Marsiglio or Ockham, but belonged to the moderate canonist or constitutional tradition while owing something also to the Thomist school. For Conrad the church was essentially a spiritual-sacramental reality whose true nature was best described by the term Christ's mystical body. Therefore the church must

---

[46] Merzbacher, art. cit., 332-335; L. Salembier, *DTC* I, 642-654: Congar, *Ecclésiologie*, 315-316. Also Paul Tschackert, *Peter von Ailli (Petrus de Alliaco). Zur Geschichte des grossen abendländischen Schisma und der Reformconcilien von Pisa und Constanz*, Gotha, 1877, 16-46, and passim. Pierre d'Ailly's work *De potestate ecclesiastica* is printed in Jean Gerson, *Joannis Gersonii Opera Omnia*, ed. E. du Pin, Vol. II, Antwerp, 1706, cc. 925-960, under the title *Tractatus de Ecclesiae, Concilii Generalis, Romani Pontificis, et Cardinalium Autoritate, Liber unicus,* (1417). This represents his final position.

[47] Henry of Langenstein (1325-1397) and Dietrich of Niem (1380-1415) also derived many of their ideas from Ockham. For Henry, see Merzbacher, art. cit., 331-332; Martin, *Les Origines du Gallicanisme* II, 66-70. For Dietrich consult Merzbacher, art. cit., 339-340; E. F. Jacob, *Essays in the Conciliar Epoch*, Manchester, 3rd ed., 1963, 24-43, and the standard dictionaries.

[48] A. Posch, *Konrad von Gelnhausen, LTK* VI, 463-464; Victor Martin, *Comment s'est formée la doctrine de la supériorité du concile sur le pape*, III, *Rev. Sc. Rel.* 17 (1937) 409-417; see in particular Conrad's pamphlet *Tractatus de congregando concilio tempore schismatis* (1380), in E. Martène et U. Durand, *Thesaurus Novus Anecdotorum*, II, Paris, 1717, 1200-1226; also under the title *Epistola concordiae* in F. Bliemetzrieder, *Publikationen des Österreich. Hist. Instituts in Rom*, I, Wien-Leipzig, 1910, 111-140. (Not seen by this writer.)

be considered first and foremost as a community of salvation, 'congregatio fidelium in unitate sacramentorum.' Thus, far from being identified with either the pope or the college of cardinals, it must be seen primarily as the whole body of the faithful.

This community has two heads, Christ and his vicar the Roman pontiff. In the case of defection on the part of the latter, Conrad held that supreme authority in the church devolved on the general body of the faithful, and through it, on the council which represents it: 'ecclesia catholica et universalis, quam concilium repraesentat'. Thus while maintaining the essential authority of the pope in the church, his view of the council tended to be *representative* or 'democratic'. The council in other words was not so much the assembly of bishops each of whom governed his local church by divine right but rather a representative body of all ranks and orders within the church universal.[49] In emergencies regarding papal authority this assembly could exercise supreme rule, drawing its commission directly from Christ.[50]

Jean Gerson (1363-1429) is perhaps the best known of conciliarist theologians.[51] His practical attitudes towards the schism underwent considerable evolution in the course of the crisis. These views, however, were rooted in a solidly based understanding of the church's nature and structure. Gerson upheld the primacy of the spiritual in the inner life of the church, seeing it primarily in terms of biblical images such as body of Christ or spouse of Christ. At the empirical level however he fully recognised the need for authority and order and that Christ himself had provided for this.[52] Gerson, in classical fashion, distinguished two main forms of ecclesiastical authority, one deriving from sacramental order con-

---

[49] 'Concilium generale est multarum vel plurium personarum rite convocatarum, repraesentantium vel gerentium vicem diversorum statuum, ordinum et sexuum et personarum totius christianitatis, venire aut mittere valentium aut potentium, ad tractandum de bono communi universalis ecclesiae in unum locum communem et idoneum conventio seu congregatio' in Conrad of Gelnhausen, *De congregando concilio*, cap. III, Martène et Durand, II, 1217F—1218A.

[50] The famous canonist Cardinal Zabarella (+ 1417) may be placed in the same stream of thought. See K. W. Nörr, *Zabarella, LTK* X, 1295-1296; Merzbacher, art. cit., 336-338; W. Ullmann, *The Origins of the Great Schism*, 191-231; and in particular, Brian Tierney, *Foundations of the Conciliar Theory*, Cambridge, 1955, 220-237.

[51] H. Grundmann, *Johannes Gerson, RGG* II, 1449; R. Bäumer, *Johannes Charlier Gerson, LTK* V, 1036-1037; L. Salembier, *Jean le Charlier de Gerson, DTC* VI, 1313-1330; Merzbacher, art. cit., 335-336; John B. Morrall, *Gerson and the Great Schism*, Manchester, 1960; Congar, *Ecclésiologie*, 316-320; L. B. Pascoe, *Jean Gerson: Principles of Church Reform*, Leyden, 1973, 17-79.

[52] Jean Gerson, *De auferibilitate papae ab ecclesia*, in *Joannis Gersonii Opera Omnia*, II, ed. E. Du Pin, Antwerp, 1706, 213B-C; see also Morrall, op. cit., 89.

cerned mainly with the eucharist, the other connected with jurisdiction relating mainly to the mystical body of Christ.[53]

In his view of the council, Gerson looked on it as the supreme authority in the church, not however on 'democratic' grounds in so far as it represented the whole body of the faithful, but on 'episcopalist' grounds in so far as it was an assembly of the universal episcopate.[54] The council, he held, was superior to the pope, and in certain respects could control and judge him, though not in the ordinary course of law but rather in exceptional circumstances when by his life or actions he was endangering the *res publica ecclesiae*.[55] This authority accorded the council extended even to deposition of the pope.[56]

Nicholas of Cusa (1401-1464) was one of the subtlest thinkers of the conciliarist epoch.[57] In his master work *De concordantia catholica* he drew out an unique view of the church.[58] Beginning with the spiritual dimension, Nicholas declared the church to be a mystical body in so far as it had God for its spirit, the presbyteral order as its soul, and the faithful as its substance. Consequently the church is a living unity, a brotherhood in communion with Christ. The whole church is guided by the Spirit, so that the power of the keys, infallibility, indefectibility, are properties not of any one member but of the whole. The pope is but a member of this church though his office is of divine origin.

The general council is the only adequate representative of the universal church.[59] Because of this it rules over the whole and may even depose the pope as well as binding him by its decrees. At a later stage however, following the emergence of schismatic tendencies at Basle from 1437 onwards, Nicholas retraced his steps and attributed a far greater role to the

---

[53] Gerson, *Propositio facta coram anglicis,* Du Pin II, 128D-129A; *De auferibilitate papae ab ecclesia,* Du Pin II, 211B-212A. See Morrall, op. cit., 81.

[54] Jean Gerson, Le *'De auctoritate concilii' de Gerson,* ed. Z. Rueger, *RHE* 53 (1958) 787; *De potestate ecclesiastica,* Du Pin II, 231D. Note in particular his explanation of papal jurisdiction as deriving its position from the college of apostles, ibid., 238D. See also Morrall, op. cit., 107-108.

[55] Gerson, *Propositio,* Du Pin II, 128B; 129A-129D; *De unitate ecclesiastica,* Du Pin II, 114C-114D. See also Morrall, op. cit., 81-83.

[56] Gerson, *De unitate ecclesiastica,* Du Pin II, 116A-117C; see also Morrall, op. cit., 84.

[57] M. Seidlmayer, *Nikolaus von Kues, RGG* IV, 1490-1492; R. Haubst, *Nikolaus von Kues, LTK* VII, 988-991; E. Vansteenberghe, *DTC* XI (1931), 601-612; Merzbacher, art. cit., 340-343; E. Vansteenberghe, *Le Cardinal Nicolas de Cues, L'action—la pensée,* Paris, 1920; (I have not had access to this work.) Congar, *Ecclésiologie,* 330-334.

[58] Nicholas of Cusa, *De concordantia catholica,* in *Nicolai de Cusa cardinalis utriusque iuris doctoris omnique philosophia incomparabilis viri opera,* Basle, 1565, 683-825; in *Nicolai de Cusa Opera Omnia,* XIV, ed. Gerhardus Kallen, Hamburg, 1963, 1-3.

[59] ibid., II, 18: *Opera Omnia,* Basle, 1565, 738-742; ed. Kallen, XIV, 189-203.

pope, subordinating the council to him and according him the right to administer all benefices.[60]

Another German theologian who was to have an impact on events of the sixteenth century was Gabriel Biel (+ 1495), sometime professor of theology as well as rector at the newly founded university of Tübingen. Biel is commonly regarded as a scholar whose works exercised a profound influence on the young Luther. Present research suggests, however, that in many respects Luther's theological positions represent a negative reaction to his nominalist master rather than a positive development of an earlier trend. For Biel, like Ockham, the church was primarily the *congregatio fidelium,* the body of believers.[61] Faith is the condition for membership in the church as incorporation into Christ. Full incorporation presupposes love as well as faith and brings with it the abiding presence of the Spirit.[62]

Biel recognised the external apparatus of church organisation as flowing from the divine will but, because of the importance of faith in justification, he saw preaching rather than sanctification through sacraments as its primary role.[63] He ascribed a place of importance to priesthood and episcopate and recognised papal primacy as of divine institution. In his interpretation of Mt 16, 18, the rock is Christ. Peter is the first of the apostles who, taken together, form a secondary foundation-stone. Biel recognised in the pope the authoritative centre of the church but also underlined the position of the general council as of key significance, given the special assistance of the Holy Spirit in doctrinal matters.[64] He acknowledged that the pope had the right to convene the council and to confirm its decrees, as had happened at Constance, but he also saw the council as representative of the entire church with authority over every single person including the pope. In this kind of analysis in the event of a conflict of interest the council is superior to the pope.[65] Papal decisions are

---

[60] *Deutsche Reichstagsakten,* XV, ed. Historische Kommission, Munich, 643 ff.; 761 ff., cited Jedin, *Geschichte des Konzils,* I, 16-18; tr. Graf, 22-24. Nicholas's new position was evolved at Mainz in a series of discourses. He tried to reconcile this with his earlier views in a letter to Sanchez de Arevalo, 20 May 1442: see *Nicolai de Cusa opera,* II, Basle, 1565, 825-829; G. Kallen, *Cusanustexte,* II, *Traktate, 3. Brief des Nikolaus von Cues an Rodericus Sancius de Arevalo (1442), Sitzungsberichte der Heidelberger Akademie der Wissenschaften. Philosophisch-historische Klasse, 3. Abhandlung,* Heidelberg, 1935, 106-112.

[61] See the masterly analysis by Heiko Augustinus Oberman, *The Harvest of Medieval Theology, Gabriel Biel and Late Medieval Nominalism,* Cambridge, Mass., 1963, 419-420. This work was curiously overlooked by Congar in his treatment of late medieval ecclesiology.

[62] Oberman, *Gabriel Biel,* 120-121, 355.

[63] Oberman, *Gabriel Biel,* 105; 165.

[64] Oberman, *Gabriel Biel,* 412-415.

[65] Oberman, *Gabriel Biel,* 416-418.

not irreformable apart from the consensus of the church. Thus, as Oberman points out, nominalism in Biel's exposition represented a strongly
orthodox and Catholic movement of thought, though not of course on these
latter issues in identical terms with those of the first Vatican Council.

Conciliar theory in its more extreme forms survived after the Council of
Basle (which finally dissolved in its ultimate location at Lausanne, April
25th, 1449), mainly in Paris where the school of theology remained firmly
conciliarist.[66] Thus as late as March 15th, 1508, the faculty proceeded
against a divine, Maître Jacques Dumoulin, who had advocated Torquemada's opinions regarding the doubtfulness of the Constance decrees,
and obliged him to subscribe to the view that 'the Council is the full and
adequate representation of the Church, and holds its authority from
Christ; it has the power to depose the Pope not only for heresy, but for
other reasons also. Everybody is bound to obey the Council in all that
concerns faith and morals and reform, for the most holy and undoubted
Council of Constance as well as the Council of Basle have defined that this
is Catholic teaching.'[67]

In the course of the controversy which developed following the abortive
Council of Pisa (1511), the leading apologists on the conciliarist side were
Jacques Almain (c. 1480-1515), and John Major (1467/8-1550). Almain
defended a view of the church deriving from Ockham via Gerson.[68] John
Major, a Scot living in Paris, belonged to the more moderate constitu-
tional school of Zabarella.[69] Though accepting the divine institution of the

---

[66] Justus Hashagen, *Papsttum und Laiengewalten im Verhältnis zu Schisma und Konzilien,*
Historische Vierteljahrschrift XXIII (1926) 330-337; idem, *Staat und Kirche vor der Reformation,*
Essen, 1931, 107-110; A Stoecklin, *Das Ende der mittelalterlichen Konzilsbewegung,* in *Zeitschrift*
für schweizerische Kirchengeschichte XXXVII (1943) 8-30; Hubert Jedin, *Geschichte des Konzils*
von Trient, I, *Der Kampf um das Konzil,* Freiburg, 1949, 24-26; tr. Graf, 32-34.

[67] A. Clerval, *Registre des procès-verbaux de la faculté de théologie de Paris,* I, Paris, 1917, 38ff.,
cited by Jedin, *Geschichte,* p. 25, n. 6: tr. Graf, p. 34, n. 1.

[68] V. Oblet, *Almain, DTC* I (1903), 895-897; Jacques Almain, *De auctoritate ecclesiae et con-*
ciliorum generalium adversus Thomam de Vio, Paris, 1512; idem, *Expositio circa decisiones magistri*
Gulielmi Occam super potestate summi pontificis; de potestate ecclesiastica et laica, Paris, 1517. Both of
these treatises are to be found in *Joannis Gersonii Opera Omnia,* II, ed. E. Du Pin, Anvers,
1706, 976-1120.

[69] John Major, *Disputatio de statu et potestate ecclesiae. Excerpta ad verbum, ex eiusdem commen-*
tariis in librum IV. Sententiarum, Paris, 1509; 2nd ed. 1516. ff. ccxiii; *Disputatio de auctoritate con-*
cilii, supra pontificem maximum. Excerpta ex ejusdem commentariis in Matthaeum, cap. XVIII (Paris,
1518) in Du Pin, II, 1121-1145. For Major's life and works, see J. Durkan, *John Major after*
400 Years, in *The Innes Review* I (1950) 131-139; *The School of John Major: Bibliography,* ibid.
140-157; J. H. Burns, *New Light on John Major, The Innes Review* V (1954) 83-100. On Major
and Almain see Remigius Bäumer, *Nachwirkungen des konziliaren Gedankens in der Theologie und*
Kanonistik des frühen 16. Jahrhunderts, Münster Westfalen, 1971, 17-28, 61-82; Olivier De La
Brosse, *Le Pape et le Concile. La comparaison de leurs pouvoirs à la veille de la réforme,* Paris, 1965,
185-310.

papal primacy, he insisted on the pluralist character of ecclesiastical sovereignty. Presbyteral, as well as episcopal power, derives not from the holy see but immediately from Christ.[70] This plurality of powers is represented in the general council. The council, because of this and other reasons, is superior to the pope whom it may correct and, if needs be, depose.[71] It is the last resort in all disputed questions including the tenure of papal office.

Almain's reflection on Mt 18 led him to the conclusion that the church came into existence primarily as a community of believers.[72] Episcopacy and papacy were of divine origin in his eyes but their authority springs from that of the entire community. The source of unity in the community is found in the first instance not in any juridical function but in the gift of the Spirit given to the Christian people as a whole.

In line with this position, the general council, which includes the pope, is immediately and directly representative of the church. Unlike Ockham, Almain insisted on the infallibility of the council in virtue of the divine promises, notably those recorded in Mt 18, 15-18, Mt 28, 20, Lk 22, 32, as well as the precedent of the first council of Jerusalem reported in Acts 15, 28. The pope, it is true, also represents the church but in a distant and remote way. He has authority in doctrinal matters but the ultimate court of appeal is the council even though its convocation normally depends on Rome.

b) Anti-Conciliarists

1. Curialists

Among the opponents of conciliarism one may note the development of what has been termed 'aristocratic theory' concerning the government of the church. This grew up in curial circles in Rome and tended to make of the college of cardinals in conjunction with the pope the supreme governing body in the church, superior to laity and episcopate alike.[73] This

---

[70] John Major, *Disputatio de statu et potestate ecclesiae,* Du Pin II, 1121A—1125A.

[71] John Major, *Disputatio de auctoritate concilii,* Du Pin II, 1132A-1145A.

[72] O. de la Brosse, *Le Pape et le Concile, La comparaison de leurs pouvoirs à la veille de la réforme,* Paris, 1965, 191-194; 200-202; 207-236; 330-335. See Remigius Bäumer, *Nachwirkungen des konziliaren Gedankens in der Theologie und Kanonistik des frühen 16. Jahrhunderts,* Münster, 1971, 62-63, 68-71; 100-101; 147-148; 195-197.

[73] On this group see Merzbacher, art. cit., 346-351; Jedin, *Geschichte des Konzils,* I, 63-74, tr. Graf, 80-93; E. Delaruelle, E.-R. Labande, P. Ourliac, *L'Église au temps du Grand Schisme,* 512-513; B. Tierney, *Foundations of the Conciliar Theory,* 208; 224; and cf. 68-84, 149-153 for the medieval background. O. Prerovsky, *Le idee oligarche nei difensori di Clemente VII,* in *Salesianum* XXII (1960) 383-408.

tendency dates back to the hierocratic ideology of Gregory VII, which was inclined to elevate correspondingly his more immediate collaborators, the cardinals. Pope Boniface VIII gave the college of cardinals a further eleva-tion by placing them next to himself in the hierarchical order; 'sunt mem-bra capitis nostri.'[74] As we have seen, even the moderate John of Paris in his interpretation accorded the cardinalate a position of great importance. In the conciliar crisis however, some of the cardinals themselves went a step forward. They evolved a characteristically 'papalist' view of the church in the tradition of Aegidius of Rome, placing the Roman See ruled over by the pope at the centre of the picture. The position which emerged firmly however, was the suggestion that the cardinals as true successors of the apostolic college are incorporated, juridically speaking, into the papacy. Hence the college of cardinals shares corporately in the over-all authority and dignity of the pope.[75] On them devolves responsibility for the petrine office in case of default on the part of its holder, as the college of cardinals in the only complete personification of the church universal. Thus the extreme papalism of Aegidius of Rome gives place under the stress of schism to the exaltation of the college of cardinals as ruling princi-ple in the people of God to the detriment of people and episcopate alike. St Vincent Ferrer (+ 1419) and a Roman cardinal, Peter Flandrin (+ 1384) were among the leading exponents of this school.

2. *Papal Monarchists*

A more effective opponent of conciliar positions was to be found in the person of Juan de Torquemada O.P. (1388-1468), a Dominican theologian from Salamanca, who expounded his doctrine on the church in a virtually non-polemical way.[76] Torquemada's *Summa de ecclesia* appeared

---

[74] Heinrich Finke, *Aus den Tagen Bonifaz VIII, Funde und Forschungen*, Münster i.W., 1902, 79; *Monumenta Germanica Historica, Scriptorum* XXIV, Hanover, 1879, 479/43 et passim. (This is wrongly cited by Finke as Vol. XXV.)

[75] See the work of St Vincent Ferrer O. P., *De moderno ecclesie schismate* (1384) ed. Père Fages O.P., *Oeuvres de Saint Vincent Ferrier*, I, Paris, 1909, 27-38; on Ferrer, see Merzbacher, art. cit., 351; Michael Seidlmayer, *Die Anfänge des Grossen Abendländischen Schismas, Studien zur kirchenpolitik insbesondere der spanischen Staaten und zu den geistigen Kämpfen der Zeit*, Münster, 1940, 164-171; see also the work of Peter Flandrin (+ 1381), a Roman cardinal, *In facto schismatis*, in F. Bliemetzrieder, *Literarische Polemik zu Beginn des grossen Schismas, (Publikationen des österr. hist. Inst. in Rom, Bd. I)* Wien, Leipzig, 1909, 3-71. On Flandrin, see Merzbacher, art.cit., 348-349; Seidlmayer, op. cit., 137-141.

[76] H. Jedin, *Geschichte des Konzils*, I, 20-22; tr. Graf, I, 27-28; Merzbacher, art. cit., 315-317; Stephan Lederer, *Der spanische Cardinal Johann von Torquemada, sein Leben und seine Schriften*, Freiburg, 1879, 173-260; Karl Binder, *Wesen und Eigenschaften der Kirche bei Kardinal Juan de Torquemada O.P.*, Innsbruck, Wien, Munich, 1955; Congar, *Ecclésiologie*, 340-344.

some time before 1453 (therefore in the wake of conciliarist polemic at Basle) and continued to supply resources to the defenders of papal primacy till the time of the Council of Trent. It was a highly original contribution inasmuch as in one treatise he attempted to synthesize all available ecclesiological data.

In four books Torquemada developed his treatise: the church in general, the primacy, the councils, schism and heresy. He defined the church as the sum total of catholics, *collectio catholicorum*, or the total body of believers, *fidelium universitas,* whether they be predestined or not, living in charity or not, as long as they hold the full catholic faith and are not excommunicate.[77] There is only one church of Christ, the Christian society of those called by God to eternal life, which Torquemada calls at various times *respublica christiana, universitas fidelium,* and *politia christiana.* The distinguishing marks of this church are the traditional four: one, holy, catholic, apostolic.[78]

In spite of his use of political terminology to describe the church, Torquemada saw it as something more than a quasi-political organisation. For him, it was essentially and primarily the mystical body of Christ, united to its head in a communion going beyond the moral order to that of revealed mystery.[79] The head of the body, Jesus Christ, sanctifies those who believe in him through his instruments, the sacraments. Hence the church is also a community of sacramental cult presided over by the bishops under the primacy of the pope. Authority and power therefore within the church do not belong to the strictly temporal or social order but are directed towards the sanctification of those who believe.[80]

Within the church however, Torquemada was a staunch defender of papal prerogative against conciliarism. Neither the church as a whole, nor

For Torquemada's subsequent influence, see Jedin, op. cit., 476, n. 57, tr. Graf, 28, n. 1; idem. *Concilio e riforma nel pensiero del cardinale Bartolomeo Guidiccioni, Rivista di Storia della Chiesa in Italia* II (1948) 39-40; 44; 48; Binder, op. cit., 196-207.

[77] 'Ecclesia in ea significatione impraesentiarum accipimus, secundum quam ecclesia catholicorum collectio, sive fidelium universitas describitur. Fidelium dico, sive sint praedestinati sive non, sive in charitate existant sive non, dum tamen catholicam fidem teneant integram, et pastoris sui censura ab ecclesia, non sint praescisi' in Johannes de Turrecremata, *Summa de ecclesia,* Venice, (no imprint of date), lib. I, cap. 3, pp. 4-5; see Binder, *Wesen und Eigenschaften,* 37-57.

[78] Turrecremata, op. cit., lib. I, cap. 6, p. 7v. These notes of the church are explained in detail in lib. I, cap. 6-19, pp. 7v-23r; Binder, op. cit., 58-106.

[79] Turrecremata, op. cit., lib. I, cap. 43, pp. 50rv; lib. I, cap. 1, p. 2v; Binder, op. cit., 151-195. See also J. F. Stockmann, *Joannis de Turrecremata O. P. vitam eiusque doctrinam de Corpore Christi mystico tractavit,* Bologna-Harlem, 1951, 101-196.

[80] Turrecremata, op. cit., lib. I, cap. 87, pp. 97r-98r; lib. I, cap. 90, pp. 99v-102r; lib. I, cap. 93, pp. 104v-107v.

the council as some advocates of conciliar theory would have it, but the pope is Peter's successor as the depositary of ecclesiastical authority.[81] It is he who imparts authority both to the bishops and to the general council by reason of his act of convocation, appointment of a president, and confirmation of its decrees. The council, Torquemada maintained, is not a representation of all the faithful, nor of the various degrees of the hierarchy; it is essentially a gathering of bishops under the authority of the pope.[82] Hence the council has no power to judge him unless he lapse into heresy. An appeal from the pope to the council is inadmissible.

Torquemada did however see the importance of the council in practical matters, while he continued to look on the council as the church's last refuge in all her greatest needs, the ultimate authority to issue decisions in disputed questions of the faith as well as to reform the pastoral ministry and to check the arbitrariness of certain popes. Though the pope is not bound by the decrees of the councils and may dispense with them or even annul them, honour, *honestas,* binds him to their observance.[83] Hence the importance of the council at the practical level.

In all this it is clear that Torquemada was carrying on the Thomist tradition in ecclesiology, though taking a more rigidly 'papal' line than his predecessor John of Paris. This same tradition was kept alive in conciliar controversy in the early years of the sixteenth century by the noted Dominican theologian Thomas de Vio Cajetan (1469-1534). His principal contribution was made in the course of the controversy which developed following on the failure of the *conciliabulum* of Pisa in 1512 in which Almain had been engaged.[84] Like his predecessors, Cajetan upheld a fundamen-

---

[81] Turrecremata, op. cit., lib. II, cap. 52-56, pp. 166r-173v; lib. III, cap. 28, pp. 304r-306r; lib. III, cap. 32, pp. 309r-311v. See also Pacifico Massi, *Magistero Infallibile del Papa nella Teologia di Giovanni da Torquemada,* Torino, 1957, 36-47.

[82] Turrecremata, op. cit., lib. III, cap. 5, pp. 278rv; lib. III, cap. 11-12, pp. 286v-288v.

[83] Ibid., lib. III, cap. 51-cap. 57, pp. 336r-344r.

[84] Thomas de Vio Cajetan, O.P., *De comparatione auctoritatis papae et concilii,* (Rome, 1511) in *Opuscula Omnia Thomae de Vio Caietani,* I, Lyon, 1562, 5-31: in I. T. de Rocaberti, *Bibliotheca Maxima Pontificia,* XIX, Rome, 1699, 443-492; see also V. M. Pollet, *La Doctrine de Cajétan sur l'Église, Angelicum* XI (1935) 514-532; XII (1935) 223-244; Charles Journet, *L'Âme créée de l'Église selon Cajétan, RT* XVII (nouv. sér.) (1934) 266-274; Jean Rivière, *Cajétan Défenseur de la Papauté contre Luther,* ibid., 246-265; J. D. M. Maes, *Le Pouvoir Pontifical d'après Cajétan, ETL* XII (1935) 705-721; L. Hofmann, *Die Zugehörigkeit zur Kirche nach der Lehre des Kardinals Thomas de Vio Cajetan* in *Ekklesia, Festschrift für Bischof Dr. Matthias Wehr,* Trier, 1962, 221-223; Congar, *Ecclésiologie,* 349-352; A. Bodem, *Das Wesen der Kirche nach Kardinal Kajetan,* Trier, 1971. See also Cajetan, *Apologia tractatus de comparata auctoritate papae et concilii,* (Rome, 1512), in *Opuscula Omnia* I, 31-48: in Rocaberti, XIX, 493-525; *De divina institutione romani pontificis,* (1521), in *Opuscula Omnia,* I, Lyon, 1562, 48-67: in Rocaberti, XIX, 526-561; ed., Friedrich Lauchert, *Corpus Catholicorum,* X, Münster, 1925.

tally spiritual-sacramental view of the church's inner nature as Christ's mystical body, while employing Aristotelian categories to elucidate her social structure. In practice Cajetan's attention was focused by debate on the external apparatus of the church, in particular the relationship between pope and council. He upheld a strictly unitary view of ecclesiastical authority, maintaining on Aristotelian grounds its essentially monarchic institution.[85] Ecclesiastical sovereignty in this perspective resides in the pope as Christ's representative and all other lower forms of juridical authority derive from this and are a participation in it. Even the council is subordinate to the pope since the validity of its decrees depends on papal approbation. The power of the pope is therefore the power of the universal church, as other powers are contained eminently in his. (This is the neo-platonic-Thomistic notion of participation in being applied to socio-political phenomena.)[86] The right of deposition of heretical popes, which the council possesses, is exercised, not as an act of supremacy over the office of papacy but as a subordinate, or ministerial service, linking or severing the link between incumbent and office.

2. *Mediating Revelation*

a) *Conciliarists*

Among the more significant of the conciliarist writers, Jean Gerson was one of those who derived their ideas on the nature of revealed truth largely from William of Ockham. Although retaining the older terminology of *scriptura sacra* to designate the whole body of Christian truth (not merely the bible), in his *Declaratio Veritatum* (published after 1416) he listed six degrees of catholic truth.[87] They all belong, though in various ways, to scripture. The first is the literal sense of the biblical canon. The second consists of 'truths determined by the church, which have been handed on by the apostles through an undoubted and continuous succession,' (what we would term to-day apostolic traditions which have been established as such). The third consists of private revelation, attested to by miracle or by

---

[85] Cajetan, *De comparatione auctoritatis,* cap. VII; I, II, IV, in *Opuscula Omnia,* I, 5-6, 7-8 10-11; in Rocaberti, XIX, 446-448, 450-451, 455-456.

[86] Cajetan, *Apologia,* cap. I; XXII; XXI ad 7um: *Opuscula Omnia,* I, 31-32; 44-46; 44: Rocaberti, XIX, 493-494; 517-518; 518-519; *De comparatione auctoritatis,* cap. XVI, *Opuscula Omnia,* I, 28-30: Rocaberti XIX, 469-471. '...a Petro omnis Ecclesiae potestas derivatur in totam Ecclesiam via ordinaria.' ibid., 449, cap. III, nos. 30-34.

[87] De Vooght, *Les Sources,* 240-249; Tavard, *Holy Writ,* 52-54; Oberman, *Gabriel Biel,* 385-387; Jean Gerson, *De examinatione doctrinarum,* (1423), II, pars principalis, consideratio prima, ed. Du Pin, *Opera Omnia,* I, 12-14.

the church. The fourth and fifth consists of conclusions from the first two types; (some of these are only probable opinions). The sixth category is made up of pious beliefs.[88]

For Gerson these literary expressions of divine truth, even the literal sense of scripture, do not stand alone as self-explanatory. Authentic interpretation is required and this takes place in and through the church. This process of interpretation passes through various stages from that of inspired writing through the privileged expositions of the fathers to the authoritative definitions of councils. Thus although like Ockham, Gerson lists among Catholic truths the word of the bible, he does not see it as standing outside the church, so to speak, but within it and subject to it in so far as its meaning is made manifest through the interpretation of tradition as well as of the magisterial church. On the other hand, neither tradition nor ecclesiastical authority are independent mouthpieces of God. Their role is in a certain sense correlative to and ancillary to the bible as their task is to expound the bible. Thus, in a slightly modified form, Gerson retained the medieval harmony between the various elements constituting the vehicle of divine revelation.[89] Ockham's dichotomies between written word and living church did not work themselves out fully in Gerson's thought. And of course, unlike the *doctor subtilis*, he upheld the authority of the pope though subordinating it to an infallible council.

This was to prove the general trend among conciliarist writers to the eve of the Reformation. Thus Jacques Almain (1480-1515), the Paris theologian, when commenting on Ockham's views on the papacy, recognised the role of scripture as determining the content of faith but subordinated it to the church: 'We are bound to believe first and more in the church than in the gospel... The whole reason why we are bound to believe in the gospel and in the epistles of the apostles and the prophets is that they are proposed by the church.'[90] The authority of scripture depends on the church, and the church may moreover accept points of doctrine not contained in the bible. This does not weaken their credibility since the church received these truths 'orally from the apostles.'[91] Speak-

---

[88] Jean Gerson, *Declaratio Veritatum quae credenda sunt de necessitate salutis*, (c. 1417), Du Pin, I, 22-24.

[89] Jean Gerson, *Tractatus contra heresim de communione laicorum* (1417), propositio I; cap. 2, Du Pin, I, 457; ibid., propositio VI; Du Pin, I, 458-459.

[90] Jacques Almain, *In 3ª Sent.*, d. 24, VIª conclusio, Iª propositio (Paris?), 1527 (no pagination); see also De La Brosse, *Le Pape et le Concile*, 200-202; Bäumer, *Nachwirkungen des konziliaren Gedankens*, 196-197.

[91] Jacques Almain, *Expositio circa decisiones magistri Guillielmi Occam super potestate summi pontificis. De potestate ecclesiastica et laica*, in Du Pin II, 1054. (Almain gives as an example the dispensation given to marry within degrees of kindred forbidden by the scriptures.)

ing in conciliarist fashion, Almain affirms that the pope himself has no other authority than that of the church; his teaching is controlled by the teaching of the church universal, more specifically by that of the council whose definitive magisterial role he recognises.[92]

b) *Biel*

Professor Oberman in his discussion of Gabriel Biel's theology points to two main theories of tradition current in the fifteenth century, one which saw tradition as strictly interpretative of scripture, another which saw it as a complementary channel of divine revelation within the Christian community. Biel, he argues, belonged to the latter group which he traces back, not merely to Gerson, d'Ailly and Ockham but beyond, to Augustine and Bonaventure.[93]

At one point Biel emphasised the authority of scripture for all theological statements. 'All these truths of revelation are contained in Holy Scripture.' He spoke in Hussite terms of a *successio fidei* guaranteed by a *successio doctorum*.[94] On the other hand, following Ockham, he distinguished four categories of truths: (1) direct revelation in scripture; (2) deductions from scripture; (3) conclusions drawn from truths known in these first two ways in the course of apostolic succession, (4) special revelations to individual persons. Hence in Ockhamite fashion revelation becomes identified with its propositional formulation. Category (4) shows clearly that Biel belonged to the second school of thought concerning tradition.

Although there is a certain ambivalence in Biel's positions, as if he would wish at times to make scripture the sole rule of faith, loyalty to the church and its faith will not allow it. The church brought him to believe in scripture. Conversely, he depends on the church for the interpretation of scripture and as guide to belief. This demands faith in propositions not

---

[92] Jacques Almain, *De dominio naturali, civili et ecclesiastico*, conclusio III, in Du Pin II, 972. See V. M. Pollet O.P., *La Doctrine de Cajétan sur l'Église*, II, *Angelicum* XII (1935) 229-236 for a short account of Almain's conciliarism; see also De La Brosse, *Le Pape et le Concile*, loc. cit. For Gabriel Biel's views, see H. Oberman, *The Harvest of Medieval Theology*, Cambridge, Mass., 1963, 361-419.

[93] Oberman, *Gabriel Biel*, 370-371, 393. Oberman takes issue with Tavard, *Holy Writ*, on one point. He argues convincingly that the notion of tradition as a distinct source of revelation is older than Ockham. It can be found in Augustine, Abelard, Bonaventure, and Aquinas. Furthermore, he denies that Ockham held to a theory of the coinherence of church and scripture in the transmission of divine revelation, as De Vooght, *Sources de la doctrine chrétienne* maintained. Ockham, Oberman argues, saw scripture and tradition as separate though complementary channels of divine disclosure. See Oberman, *Gabriel Biel*, 361-373.

[94] Oberman, *Gabriel Biel*, 376, 393-394.

clearly found in nor deduced from the bible, leading to the postulate of
extra-biblical revelation.

Like other theologians, he found difficulty in accounting for beliefs held
in the church not evidently related to clear scriptural affirmation. Hence
he postulated that many truths have been handed down by the apostles
either through oral tradition or through the writings of the fathers. Some
are also of post-apostolic origin, that is, revealed to others than the
apostles. Truths are further defined by councils or popes, truths which are
neither necessarily contained in holy scripture nor conclusions therefrom.
The most forceful argument for the authority of the church thus
understood is that it has the promise of the Holy Spirit and so cannot err.[95]

c) *Papal Monarchists*

It was not merely the conciliarists who fell under Ockham's influence in
determining the criteria of Christian belief in such a way as to ascribe a
leading role to their propositional expression in the written sources. Torquemada also followed Ockham in his distinction of the various types of
doctrinal truth. He even expanded his list of 'truths' from five to eight.[96]
Unlike Gerson, however, Torquemada did not speak of post-apostolic
revelation as assertions demanding a serious assent of the mind within the
context of supernatural faith. On the other hand he agreed with Gerson in
determining the role of ecclesiastical authority as that of interpreting
divine revelation, not of creating new truth. In this ministerial role he attached greater authority to the pope than to the council both of which he
considered infallible.[97] Conciliar decrees of course require papal approbation, so that one may not oppose, strictly speaking, council and pope as
being totally distinct organs of inerrant interpretation.

Hence on the overall view Torquemada's synthesis is relatively balanced between a *scriptura sola* theory and one which ascribes the
preponderant role to the church either as vehicle of divine revelation as a
community of faith, or *magistra* enjoying hierarchical authority to teach the
message of Christ. On the other hand one must recognise him as a definite
ancestor of the two-stream theory of divine revelation, placing church
tradition side by side with the inspired scriptural canon as source of revela-

---

[95] See Oberman, *Gabriel Biel,* 397-401.

[96] Johanes de Turrecremata, *Summa de ecclesia,* lib. IV, pars II, cap. 9,: Venice, 1560,
381v-383r. On Turrecremata, see Tavard, *Holy Writ,* 59-60.

[97] Ibid., Venice 1560, lib. II, cap. 107, 248r-250v; cap., 109-110, in ibid., 252r-256v; lib.
III, cap. 58, in ibid., 344r-346v; lib. III, cap. 28, in ibid., 304r-306r.

tion and measure of the intellectual content of faith. Thomas de Vio Cajetan, upholder of Thomist tradition in the succeeding generation, proposed similar views in the early years of the reformation movement.[98]

C. *The Spirituals*

1. *Institutional Structures*

a) Wyclif

Pre-reformation ecclesiology was not all entirely orthodox by Catholic standards. While extreme conciliarists reacted against the decadence and disruption of the institutional primacy of the Roman pontiff by seeking to replace it with the institutional primacy of a general council, a more radical reaction occurred in England in a movement which had roots in the extreme pauperism of Michael of Cesena (+ 1342) and the Fraticelli, re-echoed in contemporary Bohemia, and was to influence the course of the Reformation. John Wyclif, an English diocesan priest (+ 1384),[99] and to a lesser extent John Hus (1370/71-1415) the Bohemian religious leader, sought to replace the traditional conception of a visible institutional structure, which in their eyes had become corrupt not merely in Rome but throughout Europe, with an almost exclusively spiritual association of those destined to final glory.

Wyclif's starting point was the desire to see a truly worthy church. He was appalled by the decadence of the clergy as well as by the avarice of prelates, especially the rapaciousness of the Avignon papal administration. His own ideal was the church of the poor. He saw the church as spouse of Christ the poor man, and believed this bride should be like her husband in all things. Poverty became for Wyclif an absolute norm to which even sacramental order was subordinated.[100]

As spouse of Christ, he asserted, the true church must be holy and can therefore be identified only with the truly holy, the predestinate: 'Patet

---

[98] For Cajetan's views, see Tavard, *Holy Writ,* 114-116.

[99] See L. Cristiani, *Wyclif, DTC* XV (1946), 3585-3614; E. A. Ryan, *Three Early Treatises on the Church, Theological Studies* V (1944) 113-140; R. Stalder, *Le concept de l'Église selon le 'De Ecclesia' de Wiclif, Bijdragen* XXIII (1962) 38-51, 287-301; Martin Schmidt, *John Wyclif's Kirchenbegriff, Der Christus humilis Augustins bei Wyclif: Zugleich ein beitrag zur Frage: Wyclif und Luther,* in *Gedenkschrift für D. Werner Elert,* ed. F. Hübner, W. Maurer, and E. Kinder, Berlin, 1955, 72-108. Gordon Leff, *Heresy in the Later Middle Ages. The Relation of Heterodoxy to Dissent c. 1250-c. 1450,* II, Manchester & New York, 1967, 494-558; Congar, *Ecclésiologie,* 299-302. See in particular, Iohannis Wyclif, *Tractatus de ecclesia,* ed. Iohann Loserth, London, 1886. (Further bibliography in Cristiani, art. cit., 3613-3614, and Leff, op. cit.)

[100] Wyclif, *De ecclesia,* ed. Loserth, 9-11; 290-292; 169; 307; 308; 289; 177.

ergo ex fide et signacione quid nominis ecclesie catholice, quod ipsa est omnes predestinati praesentes, preteriti et futuri.'[101] This is the vital point in his argument, that the church in its true sense is the eschatological reality, the body of those finally saved by Christ. This body, at the present moment exists in three states, in heaven, purgatory and on earth. In each case it is made up of the predestinate. It is this church, not the Roman communion, which is spouse of Christ and the dwelling place of the Trinity.[102]

The church therefore for Wyclif is identified with those of its members who are predestinate, whether at this given moment they are in grace or not. Those who are not predestinate, the 'foreseen' (*praesciti*) are members of the devil not of Christ, even though in grace at this particular moment.[103] Wyclif's church has for all practical purposes a purely vertical dimension related solely to God since its constitutive principle is the eternal will of God determining the individual to salvation.[104] The individual is constituted member of the church by means of this eternal divine decision, but whether this establishes any relationship of lasting value with his fellow believers or at least fellow-predestinate, is not at all clear. This association is not much more than an aggregate of predestined individuals. Consequently the church of Christ cannot be identified with the church of Rome as it currently exists. Some members of that communion however are members of the church of Christ because predestined to glory.[105]

Logically such a view should have led to the dissolution of the church as a visible temporal society. Wyclif did not quite arrive at this position in his *De ecclesia*. He did, however, approach it, for he made the holding of true authority in the church dependent not merely on present grace, but also on being one of the finally predestined.[106] In his earlier period Wyclif did not draw out the full conclusions of his premises in regard to its sacramental function although he was to do this in his later writings. In the *De ecclesia* he had laid the foundations: 'Hic videtur mihi indubie quod nullus

---

[101] Wyclif, *De ecclesia*, 5; see also 2; 7; 8.

[102] Ibid., 3; 11.

[103] Ibid., 408-409; 410; 416.

[104] Ibid., 110, 111.

[105] Ibid., 414: '...sed illa multitudo est pars illius ecclesie catholice que est in magno tempore et semper post diem iudicii...'

[106] 'Unde videtur nimis blasphemia heresis papam vel collegium suum credere quod in quantum eliguntur in illo officio tenent primatum tocius ecclesie. Oportet enim quod sint filii imitacionis in moribus parentum quorum pretendunt se gerere vicariam potestatem.'; ibid., 89-90.

praescitus est pars vel gerens officium tamquam de sancta matre ecclesiae. Habet tamen intra illam ecclesiam ad sui damnationem et ecclesiae utilitatem certa officia ministrandi.'[107] He was not yet prepared to abandon completely the value of office and sacrament but the seeds of future development were clearly there, for he denied the objective validity of sacraments conferred by those not imbued with the Holy Spirit and therefore greatly reduced their objective value,[108] while casting serious doubts on the value of ordination itself.[109]

The inner logic of his position was therefore to bring Wyclif to the point of denying the visibility of the church at least in its structures. Behaviour is the only clue as to who is or is not a true member and even this is not infallible.[110] The church here below is essentially nothing more than the secret number of those predestined to glory.

Wyclifite ideas lived on in England to some degree in the Lollard movement. This proved a seeding ground for later Lutheran developments which Thomas More was to be called on to deal with. Indeed Wyclif's critique of accepted views on the church and his own particular conception of it were not far removed from those professed at a later stage by Martin Luther and his adherents. It was in Bohemia however and almost within his own life time that Wyclif's influence was greatest. It has been asserted that John Hus took over Wyclif's ideas *en bloc*. Recent research has shown this to be false, in the main. Hus, it is true, borrowed freely from the Englishman, but he selected with care what he wished to use. His theology was basically his own and far closer to Catholic orthodoxy than that of Wyclif.[111]

b) John Hus

This is clearly the case with Hus's ecclesiology. The main lines, the inspiration are apparently Wyclifite, yet the central structure is almost

---

[107] R. Stalder, art. cit.,299, J. Loserth, *Wiclif*, in *Realencyclopedie für protestantische Theologie und Kirche,* XXI, 3rd ed., Leipzig, 1908, 238.

[108] Wyclif, *De ecclesia,* 441-442. See also his comments on the value of Unction, ibid., 399-400; 466; 515.

[109] Leff, *Heresy,* 520-521; 525-526.

[110] John Wyclif, *The English Works of Wyclif hitherto unprinted,* ed. F. D. Matthew, (*Early English Tract Society,* 74), London, 1880, 422.

[111] J. Loserth, *Hus und Wiclif, Zur Genesis der Husitischen Lehre,* Prague, Leipzig, 1st ed., 1884, Munich, 2nd ed., 1925, 156-157; 248-257, and passim, tr. M. J. Evans, *Wiclif and Hus,* London, 1884, 176-177; 280-290; Paul De Vooght, *L'Hérésie de Jean Huss,* Louvain, 1960, 1-6 and passim; M. Spinka, *John Hus' Concept of the Church,* Princeton, New Jersey, 1966, 253-254; S. Harrison Thompson, *Magistri Johannis Hus tractatus de ecclesia,* Colorado, 1956, xxxiii; (Reference to modern Czech scholarship will be found in the above works.) Congar, *Ecclésiologie,* 302-305.

entirely orthodox. Hus's fundamental vision of the church focused on its spiritual nature, its essential relationship to Christ. In other words his vision did not stop at the empirical data of his own time but spanned the phenomena of history to envisage the final assembly of the saved gathered round Christ on the last day. Like Wyclif, John Hus considered the church primarily as the body of the predestined, those whom Christ has called definitively to share glory with him.[112] If this however is taken as the primary concept, it makes of predestination the constitutive and normative element in the church and makes it difficult, to say the least, to apply the same term to the earthly society of Christ's followers, the *corpus permixtum*, made up of good and bad alike. Wyclif was logical in his approach to this, in excluding the *praesciti* from the true church. Hus, who had maintained the orthodox position till 1413,[113] compromised with Wyclif's views by allowing a dual membership of the church, one for the predestinate, *in ecclesia*, the other for those whose loss is foreseen, the *praesciti,* said to be *de ecclesia.* This enlarged body consisting of both groups he termed the *congregatio fidelium,* whose bond here and now consists '*in unitate fidei et virtutum et in unitate charitatis.*'[114]

Upholding therefore an essentially traditional view of the church, he fully recognised the institutional structures of the *congregatio fidelium* in the hierarchical, sacramental and juridical orders,[115] with one exception: the Roman primacy. For while he accepted the divine institution of the office of episcopacy and, unlike Wyclif, the objective validity of the acts of a sinful prelate, he held that the Roman primacy was purely one of honour, its claim to universal jurisdiction deriving from Constantine.[116] Thus except in this respect his view of the church was essentially that of Catholic orthodoxy, though ascribing far more importance to both the spiritual and eschatological dimensions than was current practice in his day.

---

[112] For an account of Hus's ecclesiology, see De Vooght, op. cit., 264-275; idem., *Hussiana,* Louvain, 1960, 9-101; 211-260; M. Spinka, op. cit., 252-289 and passim; Leff, *Heresy* 662-676; 673-675; see in particular John Hus, *Tractatus de ecclesia* (1413), cap. I, A-B; cap. II, A-C; cap. XIV, B, aarv; aaiiirv; lliirv, (referring to foliation), ed. Thompson, 1-2, 8-9, 111-112.

[113] De Vooght, *Hussiana,* 9-15, where he indicates the minor points of similarity between Hus's and Wyclif's position before 1413. Spinka, op. cit., 253 argues that Hus's ideology had been already developed prior to submitting to Wyclif's influence, from 1413 onwards.

[114] Hus, *De ecclesia,* cap. III, H-I; cap. V, A; C; cap. II, D; bbiiirv; cciii rv and passim; ed. Thompson, 17-18; 30; 33; 10.

[115] Ibid., cap. X, A-E, ed. Thompson, 73-77.

[116] Ibid., cap. XV, D-E; F; H; mm passim: ed. Thompson, 122-123; 124; 126-127.

2. *Mediating Revelation*

a) Wyclif

Ockhamite dichotomies in the sources of revelation were carried a step forward by John Wyclif. In his reaction to the abuse and corruption of ecclesiastical power which he saw about him, he rejected for all practical purposes the function of a living *magisterium* in determining with authority the content of faith.[117] The supreme norm of revealed truth he proposed was the inspired word of God[118] which however must be taken not as a series of isolated texts but as a single word (*unum perfectum verbum*) spoken to us by God. Nor is its interpretation something carried on exclusively by the individual believer. The sense of scripture has been rendered more explicit by the *ratio philosophica revelata,* sound theology, but even more so by the great doctors of the past, Augustine, Ambrose, Jerome, Gregory, Bernard.[119] Beyond the views of individual expositors, one finds a sure guide to an understanding of scripture in the common teaching of the fathers,[120] the apostolic creeds, and the common faith of the church.[121] In view of the invisible nature of his church this last proposition had little meaning.

In short, far from proposing a *scriptura sola* theory of the criteria of intellectual faith, Wyclif presented in many respects quite a traditional picture. He insisted however on the primary role of the bible, ascribing to tradition, the faith of the church and the works of theologians a strictly interpretative role in its regard; no hint therefore of a two-font theory of revelation. What separates him most from the normal medieval pattern is his practical rejection of a hierarchical teaching office. Wyclif's notion of the church believing as confined to the predestinate suggests that his idea of the church's faith as vehicle for tradition is to a large extent only in verbal and not real agreement with contemporary opinion. In any given instance the value of any particular testimony is open to question.[122]

---

[117] De Vooght, *Les Sources*, 168-200; Leff, *Heresy*, 511-516; John Wyclif, *De eucharistia*, cap. IX, ed. J. Loserth, London, 1892, 291; *De veritate sacrae scripturae*, cap. X, ed. R. Buddensieg, I, London, 1905, 216-217.

[118] Wyclif, *De veritate,* cap. II, ed. Buddensieg, I, 33-34; ibid., cap. XII, Buddensieg, I, 268-269; ibid., cap. XIX, Buddensieg, II, 112.

[119] Ibid., cap. XIII, ed. Buddensieg, I, 309; Wyclif, *Dialogus, sive speculum ecclesiae militantis,* cap. X, ed. A. W. Pollard, London, 1886, 21; ibid., Epil., Pollard, 93; Wyclif, *De veritate,* cap. II, ed. Buddensieg, I, 39; Wyclif, *De dominio divino,* lib. I, ed. R. L. Poole, London, 1890, 2.

[120] Wyclif, *De veritate,* cap. XV, ed. Buddensieg, I, 385-386.

[121] Ibid., cap. VII, ed. Buddensieg, I, 142; cap. III, Buddensieg, I, 46; cap. X, Buddensieg, I, 217-218.

[122] See Leff's criticism of De Vooght on this issue, Leff, *Heresy*, 516, echoing M. Hurley, 'Scriptura Sola'; *Wyclif and his Critics, Traditio* 16 (1960) 275-352.

b) Anti-Wyclifites

Wyclif's most famous disciple, John Hus, was in fact not over-indebted to him in this regard, for Hus's views on the role of the church in relation to revelation were quite staunchly orthodox.[123] Some of Wyclif's critics however carried the evolution of the theology of tradition a stage further. William of Woodford (+ c. 1397),[124] in particular was one of the earliest to place the church's tradition on a par with the bible as a fully distinct source of divine revelation. William asserted: 'There are a great many truly Catholic doctrines that could not be evidently concluded from the contents of sacred scripture.' These, he believed, derived from 'apostolic institutions confirmed by tradition' and 'institutions reinforced by custom in common use.' In other words where William of Ockham had divided the channels of revelation into three basic categories without stressing their mutual distinction, and Wyclif had reduced these to one for all practical purposes, namely scripture, William of Woodford here places tradition-in-the-church side by side with scripture as a distinct source of divine truth. We are thus faced with two independent categories standing over against one another.[125] The stage is set for conflict between church and scripture as rival masters of the faith.

To Thomas Netter (+ 1430), another English opponent of Wyclifite ideas, has been attributed the doubtful honour of fathering the idea of an independent oral tradition within the church, although in actual fact the term as such does not occur in his writings.[126] Netter's view of the church as well as of revelation was essentially traditional. The church universal is Christ's bride to whom he has left a dowry, namely his own permanent presence which saves her from error. Doubts concerning the faith are resolved by enquiring concerning the teaching of the apostles, that of their successors, and finally what men of sound doctrine have left in their

---

[123] De Vooght, *Les Sources,* 218-233; Tavard, *Holy Writ,* 49-51.

[124] William of Woodford, (alias Waterford, Wodfordus, and Widefordus; he is called William Woodford in F. W. Bateson, *The Cambridge Bibliography of English Literature,* I, Cambridge, 1940, 305), was a Franciscan theologian of the Oxford school. Only one of his works was printed; *Contra XVIII articulos J. Wyclif,* with the work of Aeneas Sylvius Piccolomini noticed below, n. 125.

[125] Paul de Vooght, *Les Sources,* 200-210; Tavard, *Holy Writ,* 42-43; William of Woodford, *Vvilhelmus Vvidefordus adversus Iohannem Vviclefum Anglum,* in *Fasciculus rerum expetendarum ac fugiendarum. In quo primum continentur Concilium Basiliense:...quod Aeneas Sylvius... eleganter conscripsit,* (Cologne?), 1535, art. XVIII, ff. cxxixr—cxxxiiir; see in particular ff. cxxix vDE; reprinted London, Vol. I, 1690, 257-263; see in particular 258-259, '...multa sunt authentice vera...quae non sunt literaliter contenta in sacra scriptura, *nec ex contentis in sacra scriptura possunt clare deduci...*'

[126] Tavard, *Holy Writ,* 58.

writing till the present time. The truth concerning any question can be determined by arriving at a concordance of these data, although generally speaking the teaching of the successors of the apostles is a sure touchstone of belief. The successors of the apostles were, for Netter, not merely bishops and priests, but the laity as well, although bishops deserve more attention, and the bishops of Rome more than any.[127]

To a greater extent perhaps than any of his contemporaries, Netter attached significance to the 'unwritten words of the apostles and their unwritten traditions, preserved and approved by the church, which would all belong to the canon of scripture had they been written.' How exactly these unwritten revelations are transmitted is not clear; partly it would seem in the common teaching of the fathers, partly in popular tradition.[128] (It is the latter which Tavard interprets as oral.) Thus in Netter's view, as in William of Woodford's, the church's constant tradition, whether expressed in patristic tradition or popular belief, is placed side by side with scripture as a vehicle of divine revelation. At the same time he attached great significance to the teaching of the universal episcopate as well as to the authority of the pope in determining doctrinal questions.[129]

D. *Humanists*

1. *Mediating Revelation*

a) Northern Humanists

The humanist movement of Northern Europe constituted a further current of thought in the intellectual waters of pre-reformation Europe.

---

[127] Tavard, *Holy Writ*, 58-59; Thomas Netter, *Thomae Waldensis anglici carmelitae, theologi praestantissimi, doctrinale antiquitatum fidei ecclesiae catholicae,* (composed between 1415-1419), lib. II, art. II, cap. XIX, pr. Venice, 1571, 193/1—197/2.

[128] Netter, *Doctrinale*, lib. II, art. II, cap. XXIII, Venice, 1571, 208/2; 209/2-210/2.

[129] 'Posset forsan alicuius unius sapientis fidelis esse suspitio, posset unius episcopi, et apud pertinacem aliquem est alicujus cleri sive universitatis, sive synodi episcopalis sive etiam decreti communis in Romana ecclesia, immo forsan et generalis concilii patrum orbis, quia nulla harum est Ecclesia catholica symbolica, nec vindicat sibi fidem dari sub poena perfidiae, sed qui sanctionibus sanctorum patrum ecclesiae catholicae et Apostolicae, id est per totum mundum expansae, et a sanctis Apostolis constitutae et per successiones patrum usque ad nostra tempora claruerunt, non statim obedit ipse filius proterviae sine omni scrupulo damnatur a singulis.': Netter, op. cit., lib. II, art. II, cap. XIX, Venice, 1571, 196/2. This notion of continuing and universal belief as being the final determining factor in faith is found later in Thomas More. For Netter's views on papal authority see ibid., lib. II, art. III, cap. XLVII-XLVIII, Venice, 1571, 284/1—289/1. Another Englishman, Reginald Pecock (c. 1393-1461), Bishop of Chichester. led a reaction to Netter, back to a Wyclifian view of the relation between church and scripture. Scripture for him had a uniquely normative place; both church tradition and church teaching are purely expository in its regard. See Tavard, *Holy Writ*, 63-66, and Reginald Pecock, *The Book of Faith*, ed. J. L. Morison, Glasgow, 1909: Pt. II, Ch. 2, Morison, 251-255; Pt. II, Ch. 4, Morison, 279-283; Pt. II, Ch. 5, 302-303.

Christian humanists, having transferred to patristics the Renaissance worship of the classics, took their inspiration in regard to theological questions
from Jerome and Augustine in the first place, and then the other early
Christian writers. This was especially true of those who followed the lead
given in the Brothers of the Common Life, whose intellectual patron was
St Jerome.[130] The humanists were not greatly concerned with the church
as such but their study of the sources of Christian belief raised for them the
question as to the nature of the criteria which determine belief and of the
role of the church in its regard.

Of particular interest for our study is the work of *Johannes Pupper von
Goch* (+ 1475, a Netherlands scholar influenced by the Brothers of the
Common Life), because of the similarities which emerge between his position and that of Thomas More. For Pupper, 'The canonical scripture
alone has determinative value'[131] but he qualified this remark by adding
that, taken by itself, scripture is a dead letter. Only when it is combined
with the 'gospel written by God in the heart through the Holy Spirit' does
it turn into *spiritus vivificans*, the breath of life. This 'law of the gospel' is
the charity poured out by God in our hearts.[132] He thus makes the *church-
believing* of primary importance in the transmission and interpretation of
the bible, a position later adopted by Thomas More. The totality of revelation, in this view, resides existentially as the divine being within the Christian community.

It is for this reason that the interpretations of the fathers are important.
These were men who truly had the Spirit of God within them. Their interpretations taken with the objective content of the bible in its literal sense
are truly normative.[133] Finally, the sense of scripture must be always in
harmony with 'the determination of the church', for it is God-guided
when determining articles of faith.[134] Thus, in practice, Pupper von

---

[130] The Brothers of the Common Life were a religious society founded under the influence
of the Netherlands mystic Gerard de Groote. Their first house was opened in 1380 in
Deventer, whence they spread widely. They were favourable to the humanist movement
especially in its return to the writers of Christian antiquity and communicated this interest
through their works of education to their contemporaries. See R. Haass, *Bruder vom gemein-
samen Leben, LTK* II, 722-723.

[131] Johannes Pupper von Goch, *Epistola Joannis Gocchij de scripturae sacrae dignitate et ir-
refragabili autoritate*, (composed c. 1474) ed. F. Pijper, in *Bibliotheca Reformatoria Neerlandica*
(ed. S. Cramer and F. Pijper), VI, 'S-Gravenhage, 1910, 288.

[132] Von Goch, *Tractatus de libertate christiana* (1473), lib. IV, cap. 5, ed. F. Pijper,
Bibliotheca Reformatoria Neerlandica, VI, 236-237. He quotes Augustine, *De spiritu et littera*, cap.
XVII, 29, *MPL* XLIV, 218.

[133] Ibid., lib. I, cap. 8, ed. Pijper, 56; *De scripturae sacrae dignitate,* loc. cit.

[134] Johannes von Goch, *De libertate christiana*, lib. I, cap. 9, ed. Pijper, 57.

Goch's description of *scriptura sola* implies a four-fold convergence of meaning: the gospel-in-the-heart, the literal sense of the biblical text, the father's interpretations, and the symbols of the church.[135]

b) Pico and Cabalism

Of the southern humanists at least one is deserving of mention, not alone because of his connections with Thomas More but also because of his interpretation of ecclesial tradition, namely *Giovanni Pico della Mirandola* (1463—1494).[136] Pico proposed the somewhat unusual idea that Mosaic revelation was to be found not merely in the Old Testament, but also in the Jewish *Cabala*.[137] The bible, he believed, was the source of written revelation, the *Cabala* the deposit of unwritten revelation passed down over the centuries by word of mouth.[138] As far as this goes it does not affect the

[135] For other writers in this tradition, see Tavard, *Holy Writ,* 69-72. Wessel Gansfort, (c. 1420-1489), a Dutch theologian, stressed the place of the literal text of the bible even more, ascribing a strictly subordinate, interpretative role to the church's tradition as well as to her teaching. On Gansfort, see Oberman, *Gabriel Biel,* 408-412. Johannes Rucherath von Wesel (+ 1481), a Rhinelander, went a stage further, leaving aside ecclesial tradition as a normative interpretation, allowing the bare text of scripture to stand by itself. (See Tavard, op. cit., 71).

[136] Giovanni Pico, Conte della Mirandola e di Concordia (1463-1494), was one of the leading figures of the Christian Renaissance in Italy. Philosopher, literateur, and scholar, he devoted himself to the mystical life, coming in later years under the influence of Savonarola. In his turn Pico exercised a great attraction over More in his earlier years. (See R. W. Chambers, *Thomas More,* London, 1935, 92-94; A. W. Reed, *An Introduction to the Works,* in *The English Works of Sir Thomas More,* I, ed. W. E. Campbell, London, New York, 1931, 18-20; E. E. Reynolds, *Saint Thomas More,* London, 1953, 50-54.) One of More's earliest literary productions was his translation of the life of Giovanni Pico della Mirandola by his nephew Giovanni Franceso: *Here is conteyned the lyfe of Johan Picus Erle of Myrandula,* London, (no date, printed probably in 1510); *EW,* 1-34; modern version ed. W. E. Campbell, *The English Works of Sir Thomas More,* I, London, 1931, 347-396. On Pico, see P. O. Kristeller, *Eight Philosophers of the Italian Renaissance,* London, 1965, 54-71; E. Cassirer, *Giovanni Pico della Mirandola, Journal of the History of Ideas* III (1942) 123-144; 319-346.

[137] *Cabala,* a Hebrew word meaning tradition, was a body of popular commentary on the old testament claiming to be a secret oral tradition of the Jewish people. In fact it originated in Provence (France) in the 12th-13th centuries and thence spread to the rest of Europe. See K. Schubert, *Kabbala, LTK* V, 1233-1236. On Pico's Cabalism and his relations with the English humanists see J. L. Blau, *The Christian Interpretation of the Cabala in the Renaissance,* New York, 1944, 14-16; 19-30; 33-36; F. Secret, *Les Kabbalistes Chrétiens de la Renaissance,* Paris, 1964, 24-43; 228-229.

[138] 'The latter (unwritten revelation) he was forbidden to write down, but was ordered to entrust to seventy wise men, chosen by himself by God's order, who would keep watch over it; and he forbade them to write it down but told them to reveal it to their successors by word of mouth, and these to others, and so on indefinitely.': Giovanni Pico della Mirandola, *Apologia,* q. 5, in *Opera Omnia Ioannis Pici, Mirandulae Concordiaeque comitis, Theologorum et Philosophorum, sine controversia principis,* Basle, 1558, 175-176.

transmission of Christian revelation, but Pico applied the same idea to Christian belief, asserting it too derived in part from an oral tradition passed on from generation to generation independently of the inspired books.[139] It is this point which is of most significance since it may well be that Pico was one of the influences, either direct or indirect, shaping More's attitudes towards unwritten, oral tradition, to which he attached some importance in determining the faith of the church.[140]

V. Conclusion

Towards the end of the conciliar or post-Ockhamist period certain basic positions regarding the principal themes we have considered begin to crystallise. The spiritual-sacramental view of the church had not been abandoned but had been kept very much alive in the writings of Gerson and Torquemada as well as in those of Wyclif and Hus. On the other hand there is no question but that the main concern of the epoch was with the socio-juridical constitution of the empirical church and the location of sovereignty. At the same time, in determining this question, the problem of divine revelation and its sources was raised and the role of hierarchical authority in its regard. It may help to clarify the situation if these various points of view are classified under three main headings and linked with the names of some of their principal exponents in late medieval theology.

A. The Structure of the Church

1. A 'populist' or 'democratic' view of the church was proposed by William of Ockham, and sustained in the sixteenth century by Sorbonne

---

[139] Giovanni Pico della Mirandola, *Oration on the Dignity of Man,* tr. E. L. Forbes, in *The Renaissance Philosophy of Man,* ed. E. Cassirer, P. O. Kristeller, and J. H. Randall Jr., Chicago, 1948, 249-253. See also the more recent study by Henri de Lubac, *Pic de Mirandole. Études et discussions,* Paris, 1974.

[140] We know that Pico's influence was felt in England. Fisher's writings showed Christian Cabalist influence, as in his sermon against Luther, preached in 1521: 'Now almighty god the father taught them by his prophetes. whose prophecyes all be it that they be wrytten in scrypture. yet was there many moo thynges which they spoke unwritten that was of as grete authoryte. as that that was wryten which was the mayster of Jewes calleth cabala. which is derived from man to man. by mouth onely & not by wrytynge.' So also, Fisher argued, unwritten traditions '...that ye have learned of us. other by mouth, or els by wrytyng.' should be respected. See John Fisher, *The English Works,* Part I, (E.E.T.S. Extra Series XXVII), London, 1876, 332-333. Colet though less approving, makes his dependence more explicit by including passages from Pico's *Apologia* in his work on the pseudo-Dionysius; John Colet, *Two Treatises on the Hierarchies of Dionysius,* ed. J. H. Lupton, London, 1869, 236-239: Eng. tr., 109-114. See Blau, op. cit., 34, n. 21, who identified the connection between these passages and Pico's writings.

professors such as Jacques Almain. While admitting the divine institution of episcopate and papacy, Ockhamists placed ecclesiastical sovereignty solidly in the hands of the whole Christian people.

2. The 'constitutional' or 'pluralist' view of the church, expounded by Gelnhausen, Zabarella and John Major, saw it as a plurality of corporations. Within this body pope and bishops possess supreme authority by divine institution but total sovereignty resides in the whole plurality not in any one of its offices. Hence the superiority of a general council representing the whole church over the pope in the last resort.

3. The 'episcopalist' view, as expressed by Gerson and others, recognised the divine institution of both papacy and episcopacy as exclusive organs of authority, but looked on the pope as a member of the episcopate and therefore subordinate to it.

4. The 'curialist' view, as proposed by Ferrer and Flandrin, saw the supreme ruling body as the Roman church, believing this to consist of pope and cardinals considered as one moral personality; hence the key role of the sacred college in all church affairs especially in emergencies. All ecclesiastical power, it was believed, resides in this corporate personality which delegates it to the lower ranks of the hierarchy.

5. A 'monarchical' view of the church was proposed by Thomists such as Torquemada and Cajetan. For them the church was a perfect polity and therefore monarchical in character. Both episcopacy and papacy are of divine institution but the papacy virtually possesses, i.e. *eminenter,* the power spread through the various organs of the church including that of the episcopate.

6. All of these schools upheld the authority of the council though understanding its role and authority in various ways according to their conception of the church.

B: *Ecclesial Tradition as Mediating Revelation.*

1. Medieval theology considered revelation to be transmitted globally by the church in a variety of ways such as scripture, writings of the fathers, church practices and so forth. Each of these expressions of the divine disclosure was carried out, it was held, under the influence of the Holy Spirit. No one medium was thought to exclude another.

2. This somewhat naïve view left itself open to critical analysis especially of a nominalist kind, leading to a descriptive account of revelation in terms of its literary and other sources which tended to leave the transcendental quality of divine disclosure in the background.

3. Three major positions can be discerned in late medieval theology concerning the transmission of revelation:

.1. Scripture and tradition (understood as doctrines of the church, writings of the fathers, common religious practices) are distinct but mutually complementary sources of revealed truth.

.2. Scripture is the primary means of transmitting revelation. Other sources are strictly subordinate to this, being merely explanatory of holy writ.

.3. Revelation is primarily transmitted through the indwelling Spirit of God. Scripture and other expressive media are the objective reflex of this activity of the divine Spirit.

4. Looking at each of these currents of thought in turn, one may briefly note the following:

.1. Ockham made a definite break with his predecessors in identifying revealed truth with the verbal propositions which express it. These propositions he found not merely in the bible but also in complementary sources, mainly the writings of ecclesial tradition and the chronicles and histories of the faithful. Ockham's analytical approach to revealed truth was taken up by many of his successors of various schools, among them Gerson, Torquemada and Gabriel Biel.

.2. A more extreme view than Ockham's was adopted by John Wyclif. Wyclif recognised the primacy of scripture and accorded ecclesial tradition a subordinate, purely interpretative, role in its regard, approaching the later *scriptura sola* position of Luther.

.3. Church tradition, as complementary to scripture, (i.e. containing distinct data) was considered by many to have been passed on not only in literary sources but also *orally* transmitted from one generation to the next. This view may be ascribed to Ockham, Gerson and Biel. It is found more clearly in Netter, and most explicitly of all in the work of Pico della Mirandola and the Christian Cabalists.

.4. An 'existential' dimension was added to the notion of ecclesial tradition by the theory regarding the gospel written in the heart of each believer by the Spirit. One of the most notable exponents of this view was the humanist, Johann Pupper von Goch. In this perspective, ecclesial tradition is purely interpretative, being the conceptual reflex of ongoing interaction between canonical scripture and the Christian consciousness, which, in grace, possesses the totality of revealed truth.

C. *Ecclesial Magisterium as Interpreting Revelation*

1. Wyclif, for all practical purposes, rejected the idea of an authoritative teaching office in the church.

2. Ockham accepted the notion of a teaching office within the church, accepting both episcopacy and papacy as instituted by Christ. He denied, however, finality of infallibility to this teaching, which always is subordinate to the written sources. Divine truth might be preserved in the church if only one person remained faithful. Later nominalist and other writers agreed on this latter point.

3. Netter accepted the divine institution and authoritative interpretations of both papacy and episcopacy, but in his eyes infallibility belonged only to the church universal.

4. Pierre d'Ailly in his early phase, Dietrich of Niem and John Hus accepted the divine institution of episcopacy and the infallibility of the general council, but regarded the papacy as a purely human institution within the church.

5. Gerson upheld the divine institution of both papacy and episcopacy as authoritative interpreters of revelation. Infallibility, however, belongs only to the council as representing the universal episcopate.

6. Thomists and Curialists, (upholders of the 'oligarchical' view of church constitution) held for the divine institution of the episcopal and papal teaching office. Conciliar teaching can be infallible when approved by the pope.

7. Some Franciscan theologians, following Peter Olivi, taught that the papacy was not merely of divine institution but was also infallible when making decisions on matters of faith.

Thus it may be seen that on the eve of the Reformation a wide variety of opinion was current regarding the constitutional structure of the church and the relation between its various organs. Similarly the church's role as vehicle of a divinely inspired message was by no means settled while the relation of her teaching office to this message was also in dispute. Consequently there was ample ground for ideological conflict arising either from an over-emphasis of institutional as against charismatic aspects of ecclesial life, or from clashing interpretations of the mutual relationships between the various elements constituting the empirical congregation of believers, or of the relationship between this body together with its authoritative offices and the initial *corpus* of revelation. The insecurities arising from the ideological indecision of fifteenth century theology were to prove the breeding ground of discord and division in the succeeding century.

CHAPTER TWO

SOURCES AND METHODS

Renaissance humanism brought one benefit to the theological scene. In its stress on the superiority of ancient times, its preference for the classical over the modern it paved the way for a movement in theology which was essentially healthy, a return to the sources. With this background in mind it is easy to appreciate More's impatience with those who by their profession laid claim to a more than passing acquaintance with the mysteries of divinity and who failed rather miserably to vindicate their reputation. In his frequently cited letter to the Louvain theologian Martin Dorp in defence of classical learning More told the story of a discussion with a doctor of divinity as to whether Augustine held that demons were corporeal substances. 'As it was in a shop I took up Augustine's work, *De divinatione demonum* and I showed him the place. He read the section through twice and finally at the third reading with my assistance he began to understand and indeed to express amazement. ''Certainly'', he said, ''I admire what Augustine says in that book but he does not speak in this fashion in the Master's *Sentences,* which is a book of greater authority than this.'''[1] More had no time for a superficial attitude to the study of divinity. Such theologians ignorant both of scripture and the writings of the ancients he compared to students whose knowledge of Latin is limited to a grammar book, and who have no knowledge of literature. For him a knowledge of the sources was fundamental, ignorance a disgrace.[2] Where critical edi-

---

[1] Thomas More to Martin Dorp, Bruges 21 October [1515], in *The Correspondence of Sir Thomas More,* ed. E. F. Rogers, Princeton, 1947, 52/871-53/877 and *passim.*

[2] The principal sources in which More's approach to theology can be found are as follows: Thomas More to Martin Dorp, Rogers, *Correspondence,* 27-74, tr. in *St. Thomas More: Selected Letters,* ed. E. F. Rogers, New Haven and London, 1961, 6-64; Thomas More to the University of Oxford, Abingdon 29 March [1518], Rogers, *Correspondence,* 111-120, tr. Rogers, *Selected Letters,* 94-103; Thomas More to Edward Lee, 1 May, 1519, Rogers, *Correspondence,* 137-154; Thomas More to a Monk [1519-1520], Rogers, *Correspondence,* 165-212, tr. Rogers, *Selected Letters,* 114-144. The translations used below are my own. See also G. Marc'Hadour, *Saint Thomas More,* Namur, 1962, 38-129; idem with H. Gibaud, *Réponse à un moine, présentation du document, traduction française, Moreana* nos. 27-28 (1970) 31-82; A. Prévost, *Thomas More,* 107-141; 363-367. Prévost ascribes to More the original application of the term *theologia positiva* to a scientifically founded study of the data of revelation through their literary sources as opposed to the speculative theories of a philosophically controlled theological method. See ibid., 363-367. On the background to this development in theological method, see among other writers: E. Seebohm, *The Oxford Reformers,* London, 1867; Albert Duhamel, *The Oxford Lectures of Dean Colet, Journal of the History of Ideas* 14 (1953) 493-510; J. K. McConica, *English Humanists and Reformation Politics,* Oxford, 1965, 44-105.

tions of More's writings are available, it is possible to determine with a fair degree of accuracy the works More himself used. This is hardly called for at this juncture. Rather I shall indicate in a general way the main sources he relied on, indicating at the same time how he utilised them. In regard to his literary style, as this varied with each of the works analysed in this study, it will be dealt with in the introductory passages to the chapter in question.

LINGUISTICS

In the light of what has been said above it is easy to understand More's outright condemnation of students who ignore the fonts of revelation in order to concentrate on the 'quaestiunculas... quae vel ad fidei pietatem, vel ad morum cultum minime omnium pertineant.'[3] Knowledge of the sources, on the other hand, postulates a certain competence in the languages of Christian tradition, Hebrew as well as Latin and Greek. Indeed he could not conceive how one might call himself a theologian without a sufficient degree of skill in those languages, '...unless the good man has persuaded himself that enough books have been written in the British tongue, or that all theology is contained in those seven questions concerning which they so assiduously dispute, and to know which, I confess, a small part of the Latin tongue would suffice.'[4] Theology is not limited to those narrow confines, but 'inhabits the scriptures, and passes through all the cells of the most ancient and saintly fathers, such as Augustine, Jerome, Ambrose, Cyprian, Chrysostom, Gregory, Basil and others like them,' men who were studying theology a thousand years before 'argutae istae nascerentur, quae iam prope solae ventilantur, quaestiunculae.'[5] The facility with which More cited the classics as well as his own command of Latin indicate his proficiency in these tongues, lending assurance to his implicit assertion of familiarity with ecclesiastical writers of the Greco-Latin world.[6]

THE SCRIPTURES

The later mellowing of More's attitudes towards scholastic theologians did not imply a reversal of his earlier prejudice in favour of the scriptures over against the *quaestiunculae*. His own writings bear this out fully not

---

[3] To Martin Dorp, Rogers, *Correspondence*, 45/611-614 and *passim;* 32/141-34/202; 49/762-50/799.

[4] To the University of Oxford, Rogers, *Correspondence*, 116/144-148; 115/116-118/202.

[5] Ibid., 116/149-160.

[6] See for example the analysis provided by Headley, *Responsio*, 814-821.

merely in the wide range of his scriptural knowledge but in his fundamentally biblical outlook on all problems of divinity. He could find time to
defend the schools but there is little doubt as to where his own interest lay.[7]

Thomas More's use of scripture in his theological writings inevitably
raises the question of the role of scripture as rule of faith. This in its turn
opens into the somewhat involved relationship of revelation to the bible,
the non-inspired writings of tradition, as well as to the living faith and
teaching office of the church. As these topics are dealt with at length later
in this enquiry, let us concentrate for the moment on his actual approach
to, and use of holy writ as a medium of divine revelation.

In keeping with patristic and medieval tradition More distinguished the
literal and the spiritual senses of the word of God.[8] There is little doubt,
considering both his training as a lawyer and his practice in controversy,
that he preferred the literal sense. Indeed he stated this explicitly in his
debate with Luther. 'Certainly, Luther...I grant that the literal sense, if it
should ever be evident, is almost always the only one effective for proving
anything...'[9] In one forceful passage of his reply to Luther this was
precisely the cutting edge of the argument, that in the vital petrine text,
Mt 16, 16, Luther was electing for a spiritual interpretation of the word
'rock', rather than the literal interpretation which referred it to the apostle
Peter.[10] Thomas's own approach was initially to see the text in its
immediate context and to derive the literal meaning from this.[11]

His training in the classics made it all the easier for More to adopt a
strictly historical method in interpreting the bible. This he used to good effect, though rarely in the same detail as in his criticisms of a number of
Tyndale's translations from the Latin. Here for example, when Tyndale
translated the word *ecclesia* by the English word 'congregation', More was
able to draw up serious arguments based on Greek usage for the inadequacy of this invention.[12] Such painstaking analysis was not the normal

---

[7] On More's use of scripture, see the comprehensive studies of Germain Marc'Hadour,
Thomas More et la Bible. La place des livres saints dans son apologétique et sa spiritualité, Paris, 1969;
idem, *The Bible in the Works of St. Thomas More*, 5 Vols, Nieuwkoop, 1969-71; J.-P. Massaut,
L'Humanisme chrétien et la bible, RHE 67 (1972), 92-112; Thomas More, *Treatise On The
Passion, Treatise On The Blessed Body, Instructions And Prayers*, ed. Garry E. Haupt, New Haven
and London, 1976, *CW* 13, li-lxxxii.

[8] See *Responsio*, 128/29-132/11, tr. 129/36-133/12; G. Marc'Hadour, *Thomas More et la Bible*, Paris, 1969, 458-495.

[9] *Responsio*, 126/5-10, tr. 127/5-11.

[10] Ibid., 128/29-132/11, tr. 129/36-133/12.

[11] See *Confutation*, 349/22-351/14: Dt 12, 32; Dt 12, 29-31.

[12] Ibid., 169/9-172/27, and indeed this entire discussion for further evidence of More's
abilities and tendencies in this field. See in particular his scholarly defence of Erasmus's
translations in To a Monk, Rogers, *Correspondence*, 176/390-184/726.

method he employed. Usually he was content with the immediately evident sense of a particular text but when difficulties arose in interpretation he was prepared to sweep the whole bible in search of illumination. An instance of this was his attempt to show that the metaphorical use of language in scripture permitted the application of the same word to quite distinct and even contradictory realities. This discussion arose as to whether the biblical image 'rock' could apply to one who proved unfaithful, namely Peter. In order to justify this More brought forward analogous usages from the books of Genesis, Kings, Psalms, Apocalypse, and the Gospel of St John.[13] Thus although he insisted on a linguistic approach to the determination of meaning, he did not limit himself to etymology but examined usage in the total context of the bible without of course approaching the precision of present-day philology.

Occasionally More himself lapsed into an allegorical use of scripture as in his application of the story of Sodom and Gomorrah to the problem of contemporary heresy.[14] Somewhat more frequently he made use of typological interpretations as in his application of the images of the paschal lamb and the rock struck by Moses in the desert to Christ as well as that of Noah's ark to the church.[15] This method came more or less spontaneously to him because of his patristic background. From the fathers he learned the fundamental unity of revelation. This freed him from the tendency frequently found among his contemporaries to look to the bible as an armoury of texts from which ammunition could be drawn for verbal warfare against an adversary. Instead, especially in his later works, Thomas More tended to seek the underground stream of meaning, the hidden unity underlying the diversity of scriptural expression. One example of this is the way in which he recognised the organic development of the church of God in the new alliance from that of the old. In doing this he admitted his debt to St Augustine, 'as saint Austin orderly deduceth by a serious goodly process in his book of the city of God.'[16] 'And yet as I say, tyll hym selfe

---

[13] See *Responsio,* 136/2-34, tr. 137/2-39; ibid., 213/32-215/24 for a detailed exegesis of one text: Heb 6, 4-6.

[14] On Gen 19, 4-11 see *Confutation,* 994/16-995/4. For another example of More's exegesis see ibid., 851/24-852/36 on Eph 5, 25-27. (The reference to Eph 2 is incorrect.) More was not totally opposed to allegorical explanations of scripture. He acknowledged that this mode of exegesis had a certain place in the interpretation of the bible provided the literal sense was given pride of place. See G. Marc'Hadour, *The Bible in the Works of St. Thomas More,* Vol. 4, Nieuwkoop, 1971, 163-168.

[15] See *Confutation,* 976/33-977/1; 977/1-10; 976/20-28 on Gen 7, 17-23; Ex 33, 21, 23; Ex 12, 46. See also ibid., 986/1-21 on Ps 21, 7; 988/1-27 on Ps 90, 5-6. (The marginal gloss is incorrect.) For More's use of sacramental typology see ibid., 99/33-105/16.

[16] See *Confutation,* 610/12-17; 103/28-105/17; ibid., 332/1-333/15.

dyd set vp his chyrche/the sinagoge was the very chyrch/and with suche
as were nat wyllyngly blynde, was knowen for the very chyrche of god
diuided from all the world byside, by goddes law, by gouernours of his
assignement, by trewe prophetes/trewe precheours and miracles, for all
the false prophetes and false precheours that were therein byside. And
the right faithe was lerned no where els. And who so had gone out of that
chyrch except onely into Christes/hadde gone wronge.'[17]

What this amounts to is that More had the ability to recognise the fundamental unity of revelation and because of this to recognise the link between various phases of the earthly working out of an eternal plan of salvation. A striking example of this occurs when discussing an assertion of
Tyndale's that 'preachers were ever prophets glorious in doing miracles.'
More takes in the whole span of Judaeo-Christian history: he asks how
many were such from Adam to Noah? from Noah to Abraham? from
Abraham to Moses? and then goes on to compare God's confirmation of
old testament prophecy by miracles with his approbation given in similar
fashion to the 'known catholic church' and to its preachers.[18] The force of
the argument need not trouble us here. What is significant is the writer's
perception of an inner continuity running through the course of God's
dealings with those he has chosen as his people. However it should be
noted that this characteristic is more obvious in the *Confutation*, for example, than in his reply to Luther for, as controversy advanced, More was
obliged to delve deeper into his theological resources.

On the other hand it would not be correct to say that in his use of scripture More's ordinary practice was to trace out the pattern of a biblical
theme. His method was quite varied. Occasionally he used his knowledge
of scripture in an allusive way, as when he compared in rapid strokes the
defection of Tyndale and his associates to the rebellion of Cain (Gen 3) to
that of Chore, Dathan and Abyron against Moses (Num 16), to that of the
ten tribes of Israel under Jeroboam against Roboam (1 Kings 12), as well
as to that of the disciples against the eucharistic teaching of Christ (Jn 6),
and the betrayal by Judas at the Last Supper (Mk 14).[19]

On other occasions he marshalled a whole array of texts directly bearing
on the point in question. Regarding the question of fasting he spread his

---

[17] See *Confutation*, 613/16-24.

[18] Ibid., 274/25-275/29; see also ibid., 308/24-309/35 for a similar argument used
concerning the validity of sacramental symbolism. See also ibid., 327/15-36; 332/1-333/12
for further examples.

[19] See *Confutation*, 670/34-672/30; see also Thomas More to John Bugenhagen, [c. 1526],
Rogers, *Correspondence*, 360/1313-1335.

net wide, drawing support from I Esdras, II Esdras, Judith, Esther, Tobias, Ecclesiasticus, Joel, Jonas, Judges, Daniel, Jeremiah, as well as Matthew and the Acts of the Apostles.[20] This type of argument with its massive organisation of evidence appealed presumably to his lawyer's mind, trained to arrive at certitude by the accumulation of witness rather than the intuitive perception of truth. Such however was his many-sided approach to the word of God that he was willing to abandon this method for those others mentioned earlier as well as for something approaching a simple *lectio cursiva,* or running commentary on the biblical text. This was the method employed in *The answere to the fyrst parte of the poysened booke whych a namelesse heretyke hath named the souper of the lorde,* which is practically a commentary on the sixth chapter of St John's gospel.[21] Here, by means of skilful interpretation, the direct weight of the divine word in all its simplicity is brought to bear on the debate. It may be of interest to note that More's most frequently cited texts were all ecclesiological in content. These have been listed by the Abbé Marc' Hadour as follows: Ps 67, 7; Mt 16, 18; Mt 18, 20; Mt 28, 20; Jn 16, 13; Jn 20, 30; Heb 10, 16.[22]

BIBLE EDITIONS EMPLOYED

The value of Thomas More's exegesis was limited of course by the quality of the scientific instruments at his disposal. As regards the scriptures, apart from the current editions of the Vulgate whose deficiencies he recognised, he was also familiar with the *Quintuplex Psalterium* of Lefèvre

---

[20] See *Confutation,* 64/28-72/22; ibid., 614/18-617/27; ibid., 840/2-841/30; ibid., 997/13-15: More explains his purpose: '...that euerye man myghte by suche collacion of euerye place with other fynde out the trouthe...' An earlier instance of this method can be found in *Responsio,* 196/9-26.

[21] Thomas More, *The answere to the fyrst parte of the poysened booke,* London, 1534; *EW* 1035-1139. See also Egan, *The Rule of Faith,* 9-10.

[22] Marc'Hadour, *The Bible in St Thomas More,* IV, 117-118. The texts in modernised spelling are as follows:

1) Ps 67, 7: 'The Spirit of God makes those who dwell in a house to be of one mind.'
2) Mt 16, 18: 'Thou art Peter and upon this rock I will build my church.'
3) Mt 18, 20: 'God is present in their midst wherever two or three are gathered together in His name.'
4) Mt 28, 20: 'I am with you even unto the end of the world.'
5) Jn 16, 13: 'When He shall have come, who is the spirit of truth, He will lead you into all truth.'
6) Jn 20, 30: 'Many things were done which are not written in this book.'
7) Heb 10, 16: 'I will put my laws upon their hearts and upon their minds I will write them.'

d'Étaples, as well as the latter's translation of the epistles of St Paul.[23] It
goes without saying that More had at his disposal the *Novum Instrumentum*
of his friend Erasmus, a Greek edition of the new testament with a Latin
translation in parallel columns, first published in March 1516. By present
day standards these were of course quite defective but to have an accurate
edition of the new testament in Greek within easy reach in More's day was
a tremendous advantage.

He seems to have had not only the Septuagint at his disposal but
possibly also one of the old Latin versions of the bible. As well as these,
when occasion arose, he was not averse to using a reading adopted by one
of the fathers or the liturgy as a basis for translation. Thus in the case of a
text which constantly recurs in his argument for the essential unity of the
church, Ps 67, 7, More followed neither Septuagint nor Vulgate nor
Erasmus but a reading taken either from Cyprian or possibly the liturgy.[24]
As regards the actual editions he employed it is interesting to note that in
the course of his controversy with Barnes he described an edition
analogous to that published by Froben at Basle in 1498 and 1502 giving
the Vulgate text accompanied by the *Glossa ordinaria,* the *Glossa interlinearis*
and the *Commentary of Nicholas of Lyra.* This may well have been one of his
principal instruments of work, at least in the later stages of his career.[25]

Even with the aid of a relatively reliable text More recognised that the
most diligent student would have difficulty in harmonising the varied data
of scripture. The true student, he held, will carefully collate the parallel
passages of the sacred book with a view to discovering their inner unity;

---

[23] To Martin Dorp, Rogers, *Correspondence*, p. 58, n. 1078; To a Monk, ibid., 176/390-414.
More was also aware of the work of Valla on the Vulgate as well as the much earlier works of
Origen, the *Hexapla* and *Tetrapla;* see ibid., and To Martin Dorp, Rogers, *Correspondence*,
58/1059-1082.

[24] On the background to this topic in general see: B. Smalley, *The Study of the Bible in the
Middle Ages,* Oxford, 1952 passim; G. Marc'Hadour, *Thomas More et la Bible,* Paris, 1969,
497-532; idem, *The Bible in St. Thomas More,* IV, 20-32; Headley, *Responsio,* 821-823;
Marius, *Confutation,* 1349-1363; idem, *Thomas More and the Early Church Fathers, Traditio* 24
(1968) 380-393; J.-P. Massaut, *L'humanisme chrétien et la bible: le cas de Thomas More, Revue
d'histoire ecclésiastique* 67 (1972) 92-112.

[25] See *Confutation,* 1685 for commentary on ibid., 880/35-881/15. John Clement, tutor to
More's children as well as husband to his foster child Margaret Giggs, held in his library a
bible '*in quinque partibus*'. Is it possible these were five of the six volumes of Froben's *Biblia
latina,* Basle, 1498 and 1502 which may have belonged to his father-in-law? See Prévost,
Thomas More, 59-61, and his source: A. W. Reed, *John Clement and his Books, The Library, A
Quarterly Review of Bibliography* 6 (1926) 329-339. Marc'Hadour discredits the suggestion that
More may have had a copy of the *Vetus latina,* quoting a remark of More's: '...hodie non
reperio quenquam, qui praeter hanc Vulgatam sese fateatur unquam vidisse aliam.', To a
Monk, Rogers, *Correspondence,* 176/401; Marc'Hadour, *La Bible,* 497.

'...yet were it not plaine for euery man, nor yet plaine for any man, but for him that coulde so do. And yet not for him neither fullye so playne as a packe staffe, sythe it wyll make some mannes handes rough with tourning the booke so often to and fro, before he trye oute euery suche trouthe on that fashion.'[26] When difficulty or contradiction arises, then the opinions and explanations of 'old holy fathers' are to be preferred to those of newcomers to the theological scene.[27] In *The Dialogue* he expressed his views most succinctly: in interpreting scripture 'the sure way is/with vertue & prayar/fyrst to vse ye iudgement of naturall reason/wherunto seculer litterature helpeth moch. And, secondly, the commentys of holy doctours. And thyrdly aboue all thyng/the artycles of the catholyque fayth receyuyd and byleuyd thorow the chyrche of Cryste.'[28]

There are many examples of this approach to be found among More's writings. One of the most striking perhaps is the case he made for Erasmus's translation of λόγος by the word *sermo* rather than the Vulgate's *verbum*. His adversary in this case was an unknown monk who had criticised Erasmus for departing with insufficient reason from a number of accepted formulae. More, one might have imagined, would have been an upholder of tradition, of the ancient against the recent. And this in fact he proved to be by showing how Erasmus's use of *sermo* received support from early Christian Latin writers as well as more recent commentators.[29] To this end he quoted from Augustine, *Enarratio in Ps 32, 6,* Ambrose, *De fide orthodoxa contra Arianos,* Hilary, *De trinitate,* Lactantius, *Divinarum institutionum libri septem,* Cyprian, *Testimonia adversus judaeos,* the *Glossa ordinaria* once attributed to *Walafrid Strabo* (+ 849), the *Glossa interlinearis* attributed to Anselm of Laon (+ 1117), as well as Nicholas of Lyra (+ 1340).[30] It is

---

[26] See *Confutation,* 997/15-19. Hence, perhaps, his liking for Gerson's gospel harmony, the *Monotessaron.* See More, *Treatise On The Passion,* xliv-xlviii.

[27] On More's use of the fathers see R. C. Marius, *Thomas More and the Early Church Fathers, Traditio* 24 (1968) 379-407. Marius notes that More may have used the *Glossa ordinaria* as an index and even source for patristic comment: ibid., 385; see also idem, *The Pseudonymous Patristic Text in More's Confutation, Moreana* no. 15 (1967) 253-266; R. J. Schoeck, *The Use of St. John Chrysostom in Sixteenth Century Controversy, Harvard Theological Review* 54 (1961) 21-27; Leland Miles, *Patristic Comforters in More's Dialogue of Comfort, Moreana* no. 8 (1965) 9-20.

[28] *Dialogue,* xxxviiir and *passim.* Thomas More to John Frith, Chelsea 7 December [1532], Rogers, *Correspondence,* 446/221-447/256. Regarding the difficulties of scriptural exegesis see *Responsio* 98/22-100/1, tr. 99/28-101/2 where specific mention is made of the problems of Pauline interpretation. See also *Confutation,* 337/17-338/26.

[29] To a Monk, Rogers, *Correspondence,* 179/526-184/691.

[30] On the authorship of the *glossae,* see *Glossa ordinaria* in *The Oxford Dictionary of the Christian Church,* ed. and rev. F. L. Cross and E. A. Livingstone, London, 1974, 572: both the *Glossa ordinaria* and the *Glossa interlinearis* came from the school of Anselm of Laon though the former for long has been attributed to Walafrid of Strabo. More's references to the fathers

possible, as was pointed out above, that these three latter works were available to him in the copy of the bible he worked from. In any event modern scholarship suggests that the *Glossa ordinaria* was never far from his hand,[31] while the commentaries of Nicholas of Lyra formed part of the daily spiritual diet of his home.[32]

Naturally More did not go to such pains in every case to determine the sense of each scriptural phrase. But there is ample evidence available for his belief in searching not merely the inspired books but also their commentators with a view to determining as far as possible their exact meaning.[33] In this his preference was for the more ancient writers, especially of course his beloved Augustine, but he did not neglect the contribution of later scholars, as the names of Walafrid Strabo, Anselm of Laon, and Nicholas of Lyra indicate, not to mention the work of his long standing confidant and correspondent Desiderius Erasmus.

PATRISTIC SOURCES

More did not limit his interest in the writings of the fathers to their commentaries on scripture. He looked on all their works with the greatest respect, not merely because of his Renaissance preference for the classic with its tacit assumption of the superiority of the ancient to the modern,[34] but also, and primarily so, because he looked on these early thinkers as witnesses to the authentic primeval tradition of the church.[35] Whatever the failings of his contemporaries or of the institutions and theological systems they upheld, he felt there was common ground in this inheritance which those who rebelled against the current forms and deformations of Christianity must accept as readily as himself. His expectations in this regard

---

have been identified as follows: Augustine, *Enarratio in Ps 32, 6, MPL* 36, 286; Ambrose, *De fide orthodoxa, alias tractatus de filii divinitate et consubstantialitate, MPL* 17, 554; Hilary of Poitiers, *De trinitate, MPL* 10, 61; Lactantius, *Divinarum institutionum libri septem, MPL* 6, 467, 469; Cyprian, *Testimonia adversus Judaeos, MPL* 4, 726; attributions according to Rogers, *Correspondence,* p. 181, nn. 596, 604, 606, 613.

[31] '...More used the *Glossa ordinaria* frequently as a commentary on the scriptures...': R. C. Marius, *Thomas More and the Fathers,* 385. See also in particular the commentary in *Confutation* III where in many places close analogies have been found between More's views and those advanced in the *Glossa ordinaria.*

[32] Chambers, *Thomas More,* 170.

[33] See *Confutation,* 363/1-18 for More's commentary on Rom 15, 18 and his use of sources. Schuster, *Confutation* III, 1584 points out that More's commentators are identical with those used by Erasmus in his *Novum testamentum, Opera* 6, 647-648, n. 27. See also Egan, *The Rule of Faith,* 9-11 for an examination of More's dependence on commentaries in *The answere to the poysened booke.*

[34] See above p. 64.

[35] This question will be dealt with at greater length later in this work.

were not always fulfilled but this did not deter him nor diminish his trust in 'the old, holy knowen church' of the patristic era.

More's acquaintance with paleo-Christian writings began at an early age, for about the year 1501 we find him writing to his friend John Holt, a schoolmaster in the Chichester Prebendal School, that his tutor William Grocyn had been lecturing on *The Celestial Hierarchies* of Dionysius the Areopagite in the church of St Paul. More apparently did not take this part of his instruction too seriously as he added the comment: 'Nescias an cum maiore sua laude an audientium fruge.'[36] The moderate scepticism More manifested in regard to Dionysius did not extend to other fathers. In another letter written five years later he described Augustine as 'viro gravissimo, hostique mendaciorum acerrimo', an expression of some respect. More had given even stronger indications of his regard for Augustine at an earlier date by choosing his *De civitate Dei* for a series of public lectures given in the church of St Lawrence Jewry about the year 1501, 'to his no small commendation, and to the great admiration of all his audience'.[37] More was also reading Chrysostom with great profit at this early stage in his career.[38] His interest in patristic writing therefore was not something artificially worked up for controversial purposes; rather had it already become part of the fabric of his mind when he became engaged in controversy.

In the *Responsio ad Lutherum* citations from the fathers are not particularly dense. Various indications are given from time to time, but they do not constitute the mainstay in the argument. Its fulcrum comes straight from St Augustine, namely that our faith does not depend exclusively on the

---

[36] Thomas More to John Holt, [London, c. November 1501] in Rogers, *Correspondence*, 4/14-17.

[37] Nicholas Harpsfield, *The life and death of Sr Thomas Moore*, ed. E. V. Hitchcock, with historical notes by R. W. Chambers, London, 1932, 13/15-27; Chambers, *Thomas More*, 77.

[38] See Thomas More to Thomas Ruthall, London, 1506, Rogers, *Correspondence*, 11/18-12/33; R. J. Schoeck, *The Use of St. John Chrysostom in Sixteenth Century Controversy: Christopher St. German and Sir Thomas More in 1533*, *The Harvard Theological Review* 54 (1961) 21-27. Schoeck traces St. German's and More's use of a quotation from the *Opus imperfectum*, at one time attributed to Chrysostom, back through Gerson and the *Catena aurea*, a patristic enchiridion edited by Thomas Aquinas to the original. Although not mentioning it in his debate with St German, More knew of the false ascription of this work to Chrysostom: see *Confutation*, 933/1-12. Sister M. Thecla makes a strong case for the inclusion of the *Catena aurea* among the parcel of books More was allowed to bring to his prison cell in the Tower, implying that the work must have been a favourite reference book of his. See Sister M. Thecla, *S. Thomas More and the 'Catena Aurea'*, *Modern Language Notes* 61 (1946) 523-529. Another enchiridion More availed of was that compiled by Johann Eck: see Pierre Fraenkel, *Johann Eck und Sir Thomas More 1525-1526*, in *Von Konstanz nach Trient. Festgabe für August Franzen*, ed. R. Bäumer, Munich, 1972, 482-495.

gospels since as Augustine says, you could not know which are the gospels except by the tradition of the church.[39] In the *Dialogue* the same type of scattered allusion occurs quite frequently, as well as an appeal to the collective authority of groups of 'old holy fathers' without explicit citation, as for example when defending the traditional attitude to the use of images in worship More remarks: 'And we be very sure that ye thynge is good/& our way good therin/& our byleue therin ryght/not onely by resons & authoryte by whiche I haue proued it you more then ones all redy/but also by that all the olde holy sayntys and doctours of Crystes chyrche as saynt Jerome/saynt Austyn/saynt Basyle/saynt Chrysosteme/saynt Gregory/ wyth all suche other as playnely we rede in theyr bokys/dyd as we do therin/& bylyued therof as we byleue.'[40]

This latter form of recourse to patristic authority occurs not infrequently in the *Confutation*.[41] Moreover one finds there more explicit reference to specific works of the different fathers so that one may trace the origin of some of his leading ideas on the church. We have already adverted to his frequent citation of Augustine's *Contra epistolam Manichaei* in support of the priority he attributes to the church over scripture in determining belief. More used the same work as buttress for his arguments in favour of both the universality of the church as well as its visibility. He found support in Augustine also for the primacy of Rome.[42] The latter's work *Contra Cresconium* was drawn on to establish the fact that the church can be known to men.[43] He drew on this also in his discussion of the coexistence of good and evil within the church.[44] With regard to the value of the church's prayer on behalf of the souls in purgatory he referred to Augustine once more,[45] while he amassed a whole array of witnesses drawn possibly from some compendium in defence of his views on the nature of the church's

---

[39] See *Responsio*, 88/6-10, tr. 89/7-12 where More cites with approval Henry VIII's use of Augustine, *Contra epistolam Manichaei, MPL* 42, 176 in *Assertio* sigs. M3v-M4v. See also *Dialogue,* lix vG.

[40] See *Dialogue,* lxxx rA; vii vE.

[41] *Confutation*, 47/12-26; ibid., 114/23-26; 153/3-8; 478/29-32 as well as numerous other places.

[42] *Confutation*, 735/20-33. More here makes use of Augustine, notably *Contra epistolam Manichaei, MPL* 42, 176 and *Contra Cresconium, MPL* 43, 446-594.

[43] *Confutation*, 733/20-736/3.

[44] *Confutation*, 734/5-735/4; ibid., 963/5-25 for further Augustinian based comment on these issues as well as 963-986 for an extended discussion of a variety of Augustine's works identified by Lusardi, *Confutation*, 1701-1705.

[45] *Confutation*, 967/4-968/38 where More cites Augustine, *De verbis apost., Sermon 32* and *De animabus defunctorum, Sermon 41*. The former sermon is now numbered: 172, *MPL* 38, 936-937. The latter has not been identified. See Lusardi, *Confutation*, 1702.

tradition as vehicle of revelation.[46] Thus on the basis of an initial glance at his explicit citations it would appear that Thomas More's principal source for his ideas on the church was the writings of Saint Augustine even though his direct references on other matters cover a far wider range of patristic scholarship.[47]

MEDIEVAL SCHOLARSHIP

In theology, therefore, More's own preference was for the ancient writers, and in his letter to the University of Oxford the reason is plainly given. It is the Renaissance man who speaks, '...cum in caeteris artibus omnibus, tum in ipsa quoque theologia, qui vel optima quaeque inuenere, vel inuenta tradiderunt accuratissime, fuisse Graecos?'[48] Initially his tendency was to make fun of, even to discredit scholastic theology, referring rather contemptuously to the *quaestiunculae*. Somewhat prophetically he pointed out in his letter to Martin Dorp, which dates probably from the year 1515, that scholasticism is of little value in dealing with heresy: '...non cito hercle opinor, si non vnum magis lignorum fasciculum verentur, quam multos syllogismorum fasces pertimescerent.'[49] At a later stage when faced with Luther's onslaughts on Catholic theological schools he changed his tone and adopted a more positive attitude towards medieval speculation.

---

[46] More claimed the support of the old fathers to show that the view he took of tradition had not been recently invented but belonged to the patrimony of the church. He quoted Ignatius, Polycarp, Dionysius the Areopagite, Cyprian, Chrysostom, Basil, Gregory Nazianzen, Irenaeus, Eusebius, Athanasius, Hilary, Cyril, Sixtus, Leo, Jerome, Ambrose Augustine, Gregory, Bede, Bernard, Thomas, Bonaventure, Anselm, in *Confutation*, 727/16-25. These he referred to without explicit citation. Other lists can be found in parallel passages. What is interesting in this list is the continuity of witness he refers to from patristic to medieval times.

[47] See Egan, *The Rule of Faith*, 10, where he makes a numerical analysis of More's system of patristic quotation in *The answere to the poysened booke*. Egan notes: 'He (More) does not always give exact references to the particular writings of these men, (the fathers) and in the fifteen times he refers to Augustine's opinions he actually quotes him only four times. Cyril he quotes five times; Chrysostom three times; Bede and Theophilactus once each.' Hence it is quite likely that More made use of one or other enchiridion of patristic quotation. See Sister M. Thecla, *S. Thomas More and the 'Catena Aurea'*, Modern Language Notes 61 (1946) 523-529 (The *Catena aurea* was a collection of patristic texts ascribed to Thomas Aquinas); Pierre Fraenkel, *Johann Eck und Sir Thomas More 1525-1526. Zugleich ein Beitrag zur Geschichte des 'Enchiridion locorum communium' und der vortridentinischen Kontroverstheologie*, in Remigius Bäumer, *Von Konstanz nach Trient. Festgabe für August Franzen*, Munich, Paderborn, Vienna, 1972, 481-495.

[48] To the University of Oxford, Rogers, *Correspondence*, 117/182-184 and *passim*.

[49] See To Martin Dorp, Rogers, *Correspondence*, 54/914-916; the date suggested is that proposed by E. F. Rogers, op. cit., 27. See also Edward L. Surtz, *"Oxford Reformers" and Scholasticism*, Studies in Philology 47 (1950) 547-556.

The most remarkable example of this change of attitude on More's part towards scholasticism is to be found in his letter to John Bugenhagen, the Lutheran controversialist, known also as Pomeranus. Bugenhagen had attacked scholasticism for its questioning of truth. More rallied to its support:

'Many debates are held in the schools on such topics as to whether there is any freedom of the will or whether all things are done by chance or are ruled by fate; whether the will of the divine majesty, unchangeable from all eternity, has so determined everything that in the whole nature of creation, the divine will admits nothing at all which can incline itself in either direction; whether the freedom of the human will and the foreknowledge of God conflicts; whether the sin of Adam took away altogether the freedom of our will, or whether the grace of Christ annihilates it. When these questions and others of such a nature are proposed in the schools, if they are discussed with prudence and with a devout purpose, the disputation certainly results in considerable profit...Now when arguments from reason or passages from scripture which they hold to be true and infallible, are produced...they exercise their talents usefully. By the inspiration of God, who makes serious effort prosper, when they arrive at many clear solutions they can give thanks to God. Not only do they themselves receive pleasure therefrom...they bring to others the health-giving fruit of doctrine worth knowing.'[50]

Thus in less than a decade More had come around to recognizing and publicly admitting the real value of scholastic disputation without however condoning its abuse. Similarly, in a later work still, he entered the lists once more to justify the use of pre-Christian philosophy for the elucidation of difficult passages of revelation: '...all that we fynde true therin, is the wysdom gyuen of god, and may well do seruyce to hys other gyftes of hygher wysdome then that is.'[51] However, though More was willing to defend scholastic methods when unfairly attacked, it is clear that his own approach to theology was positive and inductive, seeking always the backing of scripture and tradition for its assertions.

As regards his debt to medieval theologians More's biographer Thomas Stapleton maintained that he was 'thoroughly familiar' with scholastic theology, in particular the works of St Thomas Aquinas.[52] In point of fact,

---

[50] Thomas More to John Bugenhagen, [c. 1526], Rogers, *Correspondence*, 335/341-364.
[51] *Confutation,* 64/32-36.
[52] Thomas Stapleton, *The Life and Illustrious Martyrdom of Sir Thomas More formerly Lord Chancellor of England,* (Part III of *Tres Thomae,* Douai, 1588), tr. Phillip E. Hallett, London, 1928, 38.

however, More did not refer frequently to St Thomas by name and hardly ever cited his works directly. On one occasion he spoke out most forcefully in his favour, describing him as 'that holy doctoure saynt Thomas, a man of that lernyng that the greate excellent wyttes and the moste connynge men that the chyrche of Cryste hath hadde synnes hys dayes, haue estemed and called hym the very floure of theology...'[53] Aquinas was not the only medieval doctor with whom More was acquainted as he mentioned Bernard, Bonaventure, Anselm, as well as Albert.[54] In ascetical matters he was apparently a devotee of Gerson, nor was he ignorant of the *vade mecums* of the contemporary clergy.[55] Nevertheless, although More mellowed in his attitude to the schools in his later years, it could never be asserted that their form of theology ever became his favourite reading.

In the matter of scriptural exegesis we have already noted his acquaintanceship with Anselm of Laon, Walafrid of Strabo, and Nicholas of Lyra. To these one must add the name of Hugh of St Cher, although there can be little doubt that of these latter-day scholars he preferred Nicholas of Lyra to whom he most frequently referred.[56]

---

[53] See *Confutation*, 713/21-28; ibid., 714/7-15; *Dialogue*, lxxiiii verso. W. Egan, *The Rule of Faith*, 13 asserts that St Thomas Aquinas is referred to only four times in More's English writings. This is not quite accurate as the *Confutation* index alone carries six entries for Aquinas.

[54] See *Confutation*, 714/7-15; see also ibid., 984/16-992/13. Note in particular ibid., 727/16-25 where he cites Bede, Bernard, Thomas, Bonaventure and Anselm in the same breath as Cyprian, Augustine and Ambrose.

[55] See also More's handling of *Gersoniana* in *The apologe of syr Thomas More* (1533), ed. A. Irving Taft, London, 1930, 66, 118 and *passim*. See Thomas More, *History of the Passion*, tr. Mary Bassett, ed. P. E. Hallett, London, 1941, 68-71; *Confutation*, 111/5-10 where he refers to the *Rationale diuinorum officiorum*, a book of allegorical explanations of ceremonial insignia. A work under this title was published by the twelfth century scholar Joannes Bolethus (*MPL* 202, 13-166) and a better known work of the same name by Gulielmus Durandus, Bishop of Mende, in the next century. See *Confutation*, 1502 and 1627. Moreover in To Martin Dorp, Rogers, *Correspondence*, 54/918 and note, More speaks humorously of *Dormi secure*, a collection of sermons which enabled parish clergy to sleep soundly on Saturday nights.

[56] The *Glossa ordinaria* was ascribed in medieval times to Walafrid of Strabo, a German scribe who died about 848 A.D. In fact it was the work of the school of Anselm of Laon (+ 1117), a pupil of the Abbey of Bec in Normandy. The *Glossa interlinearis* was also a product of this school. Both of these works exercised a great influence on medieval scripture studies. When the art of printing came in, the first of these glosses was often printed in the margin and the latter between the lines of the biblical text, making for remarkably easy reference. Hugh of St Cher (+ 1264), a French Dominican, was an exegete of some importance in medieval times who sought to restore the study of original biblical texts. Nicholas of Lyra (+ 1349), a French Franciscan, perhaps the most influential biblical scholar of the later medieval period, was referred to frequently by Thomas More. (He merits eleven index entries in *Confutation*, 1805). Lyra sought to have the primacy of the literal sense of scripture universally accepted. On More's views see also: To a Monk, Rogers, *Correspondence*, 172/245-254; *Dialogue*, lxxxv r BC; *Confutation*, 233/15-22; ibid., 811/21-30; ibid., 881/11-15.

More was also familiar with at least some of the writers in the English devotional tradition. One of these figured among the spiritual works he recommended to his readers in the *Confutation* where he referred to Walter Hilton's classic *Scala perfectionis* along with Bonaventure's *Meditationes vitae Christi* and the *De imitatione Christi* which he attributed to Gerson. Walter Hilton (+ 1395) was part of a revival of mysticism in England in the fourteenth century most closely associated, perhaps, with the name of Richard Rolle, author of *The Cloud of Unknowing*. These writers followed the Franciscan idiom in basing their piety firmly on the humanity of Christ while at the same time reflected a similar current in Rhineland spirituality in opening the way to a more sublime vision of the divine being. In Garry Haupt's opinion More's personal spirituality belongs more to the ethical-moral mode of Erasmus than to the transcendental tendency of Hilton and Rolle. Nonetheless it is quite possible that More's predominantly spiritual vision of the Christian community was enhanced by his familiarity with the thought of Walter Hilton.[56a]

Curiously enough perhaps for a lawyer, More showed little interest in canonist writing, an influential body of thought in medieval times. Writing to Nicholas Wilson in the Tower in 1534 regarding the King's divorce, as it had become known that the King's canonists had discovered some faults in the original Bull of Dispensation to marry Catherine, he remarked: 'Now concerning those poyntes I never medled. For I neyther vnderstand the doctors of the law nor well can turne there bookes. And many thynges haue there syns in this greate matter growne in questyon wherin I neyther am suffycyently learned in the law nor full enfurmed of the facte...'[57] When occasion arose he showed himself well able to 'turn their books'. For example in the *Dialogue,* when his imaginary opponent the Messenger used a quotation from St Gregory taken from the *Decretals* of Gratian, More went beyond the secondary source to the original text in St Gregory.[58] There are a number of other instances of More's ability to utilise the canonical sources when called on, notably in 1533 with his work *The apologye of syr Thomas More knyght* and its sequel, *The debellacyon of Salem and Bizance.* The former, among other things, he described as 'a defence of the very good, old and long-approved laws both of this realm and of the

---

[56a] See *Confutation* I, 35/25-33; More, *Treatise On The Passion*, ed. G. E. Haupt, lxxxiii-cxxii, clxvii-clxxx; G. Marc' Hadour, *St. Thomas More*, in *Pre-Reformation English Spirituality*, ed. James Walsh S.J., London, n.d., 224-239.

[57] Thomas More to Dr. Nicholas Wilson, Tower of London 1534, Rogers, *Correspondence,* 536/115-120.

[58] See *Dialogue*, cxxiiii vEF.

whole corpse of Christendom...'[59] And such it was, a learned defence of the position of the *ecclesia anglicana* within the constitutional framework of English laws.

By and large canonical sources did not enter greatly into his discussion on the existence, nature and identity of the church since the reformers were in fact opposed to considering it in juridical terms and were not likely to be moved by arguments based on its laws. On the other hand contemporary scholarship suggests that More was better informed on the principles of ecclesiastical law than he was prepared to admit to his fellow-prisoner. 'We must conclude', writes R. J. Schoeck, 'that Sir Thomas More was more than ordinarily interested and competent in the canon law, in part because of his own extraordinarily wide-ranging interests in legal matters and in ideas of justice, but in part also because of the importance of the canon law in England down to 1535.'[60]

CONTEMPORARY SOURCES

Among More's contemporaries there can be little doubt that Erasmus was his leading inspiration. They were in regular contact with one another almost until More's imprisonment while More remained an ardent supporter of Erasmus's work in biblical and patristic studies.[61] Their relationship is best summed up by the latter's comment on his friend's execution: 'In the death of More I feel as if I had died myself, but such are the tides of human things. We had but one soul between us.'[62] More on the other

---

[59] A citation from *Debellation* in *Apology,* ed. Taft, xli; see also *Apology,* 146; 148; 155-156; 171.

[60] R. J. Schoeck, *Canon Law in England on the Eve of the Reformation, Medieval Studies* 25 (1963) 146 and 125-147; idem, *Common Law and Canon Law in their Relation to Thomas More,* in *St. Thomas More: Action and Contemplation. Proceedings of the Symposium held at St John's University,* October 9-10, 1970, ed. R. S. Sylvester, New Haven and London, 1972, 15-55; idem, *Sir Thomas More: Humanist and Lawyer, University of Toronto Quarterly* 34 (1964) 1-14.

[61] See To a Monk, Rogers, *Correspondence,* 165-206, and the exchange of letters between More and his clerical friend Edward Lee: Thomas More to Edward Lee, Rogers, *Correspondence,* nos. 75, 84, 85.

[62] There can be little profit in rehearsing once more the details of their relationship. It has been adequately treated by numerous writers and relatively recently by E. E. Reynolds, *Erasmus and More,* London, 1964. See also A. Renaudet, *Érasme et l'Italie,* Geneva, 1954, 32-34; 41-45; 99-106; 115-118; 124-127; 179-182; Marc'Hadour, *More et la Bible,* 117-141. Later recusant writers such as Stapleton and Harpsfield, when Erasmus had fallen into some disrepute among Roman Catholics, sought to show that relations between Erasmus and More had cooled in the years following the Lutheran schism. J. K. McConica argues to a continuing relationship in his work: *English Humanists and Reformation Politics,* Oxford, 1965, 36-43; 248-291. See also Marie Delcourt, *L'Amitié d'Érasme et de More entre 1520 et 1535, Bulletin de l'Association Guillaume Budé* 50 (1936) 7-29; idem, *Recherches sur Thomas More: La tradition continentale et la tradition anglaise, Humanisme et Renaissance* 3 (1936) 22-42; A.

hand was a convinced devotee of the Erasmian approach to theological enquiry. As J. Hexter writes: 'From 1515 to 1520 More not only "accepted"
Erasmus' views, he was their most pertinacious and combative
defender...Aside from *Utopia* and an unfortunate and tiresome squabble
with the French humanist Germain de Brie, More directed his literary efforts for five years into a defence of his friend'.[63] Hexter is referring to four
long letters, minor monographs on theological method, to Oxford University, Martin Dorp, Edward Lee, and an anonymous monk.[64] Such involvement implies more than the loyalty of friendship; rather the exposition of a school of thought, indeed the espousal of a cause. That is not to
say that More and Erasmus saw eye-to-eye on every issue. Such a condition would have been entirely out of character on both their parts. In particular More was disappointed with Erasmus's reluctance to take a hostile
stance against Luther in the early stages of religious controversy.[65]
Nonetheless their relationship survived this difference for their agreement
lay at a deeper level of personal empathy and a shared world-view.

Other humanists of a similar cast of thought evidently came within
More's ken. His first published work of substance was *The lyfe of Johan
Picus Erle of Myrandula,* the fifteenth century Italian scholar and lay mystic
whose career had so impressed him as a young man.[66] Besides these connections the pages of his *Correspondence* bear testimony to his constant inter-
course with European humanists of his own day, mainly from the Low
Countries, men such as Peter Giles, Budé, Goclenius and Cranevelt.[67]

Renaudet, *Préreforme et Humanisme à Paris pendant les premières guerres d'Italie (1494-1517),* Paris,
1953, 385-389. Renaudet affirms a profound influence on Erasmus on the part of Colet and
More. The interplay continued throughout their respective lives. On the broader
background to this relationship see Albert Hyma, *Erasmus and the Oxford Reformers,
1493-1503; 1503-1519* in *NAKG* n.s. 25 (1932) 69-93; 97-133; n.s. 38 (1951) 65-85; J.-P.
Massaut, *L'humanisme chrétien et la bible: le cas de Thomas More,* in *RHE* 67 (1972) 92-112;
Heinz Holeczek, *Die humanistische Bildung des Thomas Morus und ihre Beurteilung durch Erasmus
von Rotterdam,* in *Zeitschr. der hist. Forschung* 3 (1976) 165-204.

[63] See Thomas More, *Utopia,* ed. Edward Surtz and J. H. Hexter, New Haven and London, 1965, lxxi and *passim.*

[64] Rogers, *Correspondence,* 111-120; 27-74; 137-154; 165-206.

[65] Rainer Pineas, *Erasmus and More: Some Contrasting Theological Opinions, Renaissance News*
13 (1960) 298-300.

[66] See Thomas More, *Here is conteyned the lyfe of Johan Picus Erle of Myrandula,* London, c.
1510. See also Chambers, *Thomas More,* 86-88; E. E. Reynolds, *The Field is Won,* 42-44; see
in particular Stanford E. Lehmberg, *Sir Thomas More's Life of Pico della Mirandola, Studies in the
Renaissance* 3 (1956) 61-74. Lehmberg notes that More made some notable omissions in his
translation of the life which came originally from the pen of Pico's nephew Gianfrancesco
Pico, notably some references to the papacy and to the value of Cabalist thought.

[67] See Rogers, *Correspondence,* nos. 47; 65; 66; 68; 80; 96; 97; 112; 113; 135; 142; 154; 155;
156; 163; 180.

Northern humanism as a movement was not divorced from theology, and quite soon through its insistence on a return to the sources of theology as well as to classical art and literature had a profound influence on divinity. More's involvement in this movement brought him early on in his career into contact and sometimes conflict with the professional theologians of the schools. Encounters such as these were the occasion of his correspondence with Dorp advocating that theologians return to the sources of revelation, his recommendations on classical studies to the university of Oxford, the controversy with Edward Lee over Erasmus's translation of the new testament, and his even longer letter to an unknown monk on the same subject. All of this tended to bring him within the orbit of professional theology.[68]

When it came to his own task of combating the opponents of orthodoxy he was already, therefore, acquainted to some extent with general trends and the greater names among the theologians. He was not unwilling to draw upon their resources. In his *Responsio* he wrote: Luther's errors '...have been fully disproved by many of the most learned men: by Prierias, Catharinus, Eck, Caspar, Cochlaeus, Emser, Radinus of Piacenza, Faber and many others likewise. Partly through report, partly through my own reading, I perceive that these men have most skilfully exposed the fellow's madness with sound and true reasoning.'[69] Here he was referring to some of Luther's earliest antagonists, and to their controversial efforts. Of the foregoing scholars, Cochlaeus was a personal friend, while he had previously spoken highly of Faber's work both in scripture and in philosophy.

Sir Thomas More also drew inspiration, it seems likely, from Thomas Murner, a German Franciscan of Strasbourg who visited England in the summer of 1523. Murner had published an edition of Henry's *Assertio septem sacramentorum* in August 1522 followed by a German translation as well as a number of polemical works of his own composition. More was instrumental in obtaining a royal subsidy for him from Henry. John Headley believes Murner was mainly responsible for alerting More to the radical nature of Lutheran ecclesiology thus explaining, at least in part, the unusual action of withdrawing a book (the *Responsio*) already in print and making substantial additions to it.[70] In particular Headley argues that

---

[68] Ibid., nos. 15; 60; 75; 83; 143; 162; 165; 166; 180; 184; 194; 196.

[69] See *Responsio*, 138/16-23, tr. 139/20-27.

[70] See G. J. Donnelly, *A Translation of St Thomas More's Responsio ad Lutherum*, Washington, 1962, 13-15; Headley, *Responsio*, 786-803; idem, *Thomas Murner, Thomas More and the First Expression of More's Ecclesiology, Studies in the Renaissance* 14 (1967) 73-92.

More's indebtedness to Murner brought an acute awareness of the extent to which Lutheranism tended to dismantle the social and institutional presence of the church.

As regards immediate sources, it seems likely that Catharinus was the one he drew on most immediately for the *Responsio,* although it is not self-evident that he actually had Catharinus's work and may have known his ideas only through Luther's opposing tract.[71] More cited Catharinus's views with favour on the question of ecclesiastical tradition, and the distinction between church triumphant and militant which explains and justifies the essential imperfection of the latter. Moreover he followed up the Italian's interpretation of the petrine text (Mt 16, 18) with no little interest and vigour.[72]

As might be expected of a work written in support of Henry VIII's *Assertio,* allusions to its contents are far from rare in the *Responsio* though only occasional in More's other writings.[73] The method More adopted in the *Responsio* demanded extensive quotations from the *Assertio Septem Sacramentorum.* It consisted in the main of quoting verbatim both from Luther's works and from relevant passages in Henry's *Assertio* and then supplementing the latter's replies with the author's own comments.[74] The final product makes for heavy reading. It also committed More to adopting Henry's general line on a number of issues, notably the central question of tradition as well as his doctrine on the sacraments.[75] However there is no indication of great reluctance on More's part in doing this nor did it prevent him from developing his own ideas, notably in the H gathering inserted in the second, *Rosseus* edition of his defence of Henry. As this contains much of his thought on the church in this particular treatise, it points to an independent treatment of these issues.

Naturally there is less evidence of his acquaintanceship with the writings of John Fisher, bishop of Rochester, but he too looms large as a fellow pro-

---

[71] Donnelly notes on this question: 'More had no direct quotations from Catharinus, but summarizes his position before directly quoting Luther's answer to Catharinus' argument…it is possible to conclude that More either used Luther's anti-Catharinus work or that he had his own copy of Catharinus' *Apologia,* and preferred to synthesize rather than to quote directly.': see Donnelly, op. cit., 37.

[72] *Responsio,* 122/8-124/4, tr. 123/9-125/4; ibid., 130/19-132/11, tr. 131/24-133/12. See further references to the work of Catharinus, ibid., 120/4-28, tr. 121/3-28.

[73] There are at least two direct references in the *Confutation* to the *Assertio;* sigs. M3-M4, Q4 in *Confutation,* 226/28-30, and sigs. G2v-G3v in *Confutation,* 657/14-32. There are general references in *Confutation,* 27/37-28/1 and 675/29-31. See *Confutation,* 1549 and 1634 for these ascriptions.

[74] See Headley, *Responsio,* 806-807.

[75] See Headley, *Responsio,* 734-737.

tagonist against the Lutheran threat. Although More's personal contacts
with Fisher were of a somewhat limited nature, he had a high opinion of
his ability as a scholar. He described Fisher as 'a man distinguished for his
wealth of learning and above all for the holiness of his life.'[76] He considered Fisher's treatment of Luther's objections masterly. Nonetheless it
was mainly in regard to the primacy of the pope that he drew on the bishop
of Rochester's treatment of the disputed theses, and in fact in this matter
he felt that 'so clearly has the bishop presented the primacy, ... that it
seems vain for me...to attempt to write again on the primacy of the
pope.'[77] More in fact did go on to examine the subject further. This is virtually the only explicit reference to Fisher in the *Responsio* though he may
have come under Rochester's influence in his treatment of some other ecclesiological themes.[78]

In his later writings More showed himself less concerned with what his
fellow apologists were doing than in developing his own thought on the
basis of personal study and reflection. It is evident that he kept in touch
with continental developments[79] but they do not seem to have left obvious
traces of their influence on his theology of the church. Occasional
references to the work of Henry Tudor and John Fisher occur but they remain marginal to the whole.[80] Indeed in More's final climactic experience
of the meaning of his own adherence to the church as he understood it he
was at pains to emphasise the independence of his own judgment. In reply
to his daughter Margaret's reproach that he was too much a disciple of
Fisher in his attitude towards royal supremacy, More replied: 'For where
as you tolde me right now, that such as loue me, wolde not aduise me, that
against all other men, I should lene vnto his mind alone, veryly,
Daughter, no more I doe. For albeit, that of very trouth, I haue hym in
that reuerent estimacion, that I reken in this realme no one man, in
wisdome, learning and long approued vertue together, mete to be matched
and compared with hym, yet that in this matter I was not led by hym, very

---

[76] See *Responsio*, 138/24-25, tr. 139/28-30. See also Rogers, *Correspondence*, nos. 57; 74;
104; 105 which show the superficial nature of their relations. The prison correspondence has
perished. See also Chambers, *Thomas More*, 312-313; 315; 321-322; E. Surtz, *The Works and
Days of John Fisher*, Cambridge, Mass., 1967, 92, 175-178.

[77] See Donnelly, op. cit., 161, tr. of *Responsio*, 140/3-5.

[78] See *Responsio*, 140/5-142/9, tr. 141/7-143/12. See also ibid., 196-198 where use may
have been made of John Fisher, *Assertionis Lutheranae Confutatio*, Antwerp, 1523, 147 v-148r.

[79] See More's correspondence with Cochlaeus, Rogers, *Correspondence*, nos. 162; 164; 165;
166; 184; 189. Cochlaeus was of course a staunch opponent of Luther. See also his references
to Erasmus's dispute with the latter over human liberty in his letter: To John Bugenhagen,
Rogers, *Correspondence*, 357/1214-1225.

[80] See e.g. *Dialogue*, lx verso G; cli verso F; *Confutation*, 187/15-16; 324/23-34; 368/10-18.

well and plainly appereth, both in that I refused the othe before it was offered him, and in that also that his Lordship was content to haue sworne of
that othe (as I perceyued since by you when you moued me to the same)
either somwhat more, or in some other maner than euer I minded to doe.
Verely, Daughter, I neuer entend (God being my good lorde) to pynne my
soule at a nother mans backe, not euen the best man that I know this day
liuing; for I knowe not whither he may happe to cary it.'[81]

Consequently, although More was essentially a scholar taking full account of the source material connected with the matter in question, in this
case scripture and ecclesial tradition, as well as keeping abreast of more recent studies, he was primarily an independent thinker. Not necessarily
that he was outstandingly original but in the sense that what he did bring
forward had been fully assimilated and digested. The evidence presented
was that which had led him to adopt his personal position. Ideas and
arguments he may have borrowed, especially from patristic sources, but
he himself sifted and processed them so that the final product bore upon it
the original stamp of his own judgement.[82] His cast of mind is well
summed up in the phrase just quoted: 'I never entend (God being my
good lorde) to pynne my soul at a nother mans backe, not euen the best
man that I know this day liuing...'[83]

---

[81] See Margaret Roper to Alice Alington, (August 1534), Rogers, *Correspondence,*
520/239-521/253.

[82] On this point see *Confutation,* 602/8-603/16; 346/11-22.

[83] See note 81 above.

CHAPTER THREE

THE RESPONSIO

INTRODUCTION

One of the more remarkable activities of Sir Thomas More in his humanist period had been his concern for sound theology. By this he had meant a theology based on accurate knowledge of the sources read in their original languages.[1] He emphasised as theological resources the literal sense of the scriptures as well as the Spirit guided faith of the church attested to by the corpus of patristic writings. It is unlikely, however, that he realised to what extent the methods he had expounded would be put to the test by an even more radical approach to the nature of revelation and its transmission within the Christian community.

Luther's claim to make scripture the sole rule of faith has often been misunderstood. Catholic controversialists have often taken it to mean a strictly literal and fundamentalist interpretation of the biblical text. Such an interpretation does little justice to the complexity of Luther's opinion on this central issue, which, indeed, he had to develop over a long period of time.[2] The principal elements of his theory as they had developed about the year 1520 were as follows. The central message of divine revelation is concerned with justification by faith in the loving mercy of God made available to us through the saving death of Jesus Christ. It is only when the scriptures are read in the light of this affirmation that they bring life. Moreover, in dealing with the scriptures one must constantly seek to go beyond the letter to the spirit, to the immanent word of God which calls man in the depth of his being to salvation. God's word comes to us in a variety of ways; not only scripture but among others, sacrament and the inner word he speaks through the Spirit in our hearts. In the reading of scripture, nonetheless, careful attention must be given to the literal, historical sense in order to hear God's life-giving word.[3] This latter

---

[1] See above pp. 64-65. In particular, see A. Prévost, *Thomas More*, 109-141; 363-367; More to Martin Dorp, Bruges, 21 October (1515), Rogers, *Correspondence*, 27-74; More to the University of Oxford, Abingdon, 29 March (1518), ibid., 111-120; More to Edward Lee, 1 May 1519, Rogers, *Correspondence*, 137-154; More to a Monk, (1519-20), Rogers, *Correspondence*, 165-206.

[2] G. Ebeling, *Luther. An Introduction to His Thought,* tr. R. A. Wilson, London, 1970, 93-109; H. Bornkamm, *Das Wort Gottes bei Luther*, Munich, 1933; Jaroslav Pelikan, *Luther the Expositor, Luther's Works*, Companion Volume, St Louis, 1959, 48-88.

[3] Ebeling, *Introduction*, loc. cit.

emphasis in Luther's thought, which he further subsequently developed, was summarised in the somewhat misleading phrase, *sola scriptura*.

Luther himself, usually within the framework of the hermeneutical principles outlined above, but not infrequently in a rather fundamentalist sense, made use of this axiom *scriptura sola* as a methodological guideline. This led to damaging attacks on many established positions of medieval theology which naturally disturbed the orthodox. In the heat of battle it came to be regarded by many Catholic controversialists as virtually a complete expression of Luther's criteriology of faith, which in fact it never was.

The work which brought English theologians into direct confrontation with Luther was his *De captivitate babylonica ecclesiae praeludium,* published in 1520. One of the principal themes of this tract was its critical rejection of the Catholic sacramental system.[4] The core of Luther's critique consisted in his declaration that there was virtually no convincing scriptural evidence for any of the accepted seven sacraments except baptism and eucharist. Worried by the increasing interest shown especially by students in this radical challenge to the established order, steps were taken by civil and ecclesiastical authorities to counteract the influence of Luther's writings, among them the public burning of his books at St Paul's Cross in London on 12 May 1521 by John Fisher, Bishop of Rochester.[5]

In Europe an army of controversialists had sprung up to contest the Wittenberg schism.[6] In England none other than Henry VIII, the youthful monarch, felt called on to enter the lists. Though Henry's motives were less than unambiguous, his work, *Assertio septem sacramentorum,* printed by Pynson, and presented to the pope in Rome on 2 October 1521, not only won Henry the title *Defensor Fidei* from the Holy See, it also created quite a stir among the theological dovecotes of the continent. The status of its author won it acclaim far beyond its intrinsic worth. The *Assertio* was reprinted in Rome, Antwerp and Strasbourg as

---

[4] The subsequent account of the theological controversy in which More's *Responsio ad Lutherum* figures is clearly indebted to the detailed analysis provided by J. M. Headley, *Responsio,* 715-822. See also G. J. Donnelly, *A Translation of St. Thomas More's Responsio Ad Lutherum* with an introduction and notes, Washington, 1962, 1-75; A. Prévost, *Thomas More,* 147-151; J. J. Scarisbrick, *Henry VIII,* London, 1968, 110-117, as well as standard histories of the Reformation and biographies of More. Two further studies are worth consulting: N. S. Tjernaegel, *Henry VIII and the Lutherans,* St Louis, Mo., 1965, 5-28; Erwin Doernberg, *Henry VIII and Luther. An Account of their Personal Relations,* London, 1961, 3-35.

[5] Carl Meyer, *Henry VIII Burns Luther's Books 12 May 1521, JEH* 9 (1958) 173-187.

[6] J. Lortz, *The Reformation in Germany,* (1949), tr. Ronald Walls, London, I, 1968, 288-297; E. de Moreau, P. Jourda, P. Janelle, *La Crise religieuse du XVIe siècle,* in A. Fliche et V. Martin, *Histoire de l'Église XVI,* Paris, 1960, 117-123.

well as in two different German translations, one by Jerome Emser, the other by Thomas Murner.

As the title of Henry's treatise indicates, it was mainly concerned with a defence of the seven sacraments, though other matters were dealt with *en route,* including indulgences and the Roman primacy. More fundamentally, however, the whole issue of the criteriology of faith was questioned: *scriptura sola* or scripture and tradition? Henry stood his ground on tradition as a distinct and dependable source of divine revelation whether understood as inner guidance of the church by the omnipresent divine Spirit or as the oral tradition of a living community passing on from hand to hand the divine message.

To what extent Thomas More had a share in the composition of this work has been the subject of much debate. It now seems likely that his own claim to have helped merely with the final editing is close to the mark, though several other scholars including Edward Lee and John Fisher in all likelihood had a significant influence on its content.[7]

Luther's reply was not long in forthcoming. First in German, then in Latin, he made a vigorous and somewhat scurrilous attack on the royal theologian. His *Antwort deutsch* appeared in August 1522 and his *Contra Henricum regem angliae* in September of the same year. A bevy of apologists arose to defend the king including Murner, Eck and Fisher, while Henry himself called on the Saxon dukes to suppress the new heresy.[8] As part of this movement to counteract the spread of Lutheranism and to defend the royal honour, Thomas More took up his pen.

More produced two editions of his work against Luther.[9] In the first version he assumed the mask of a student, one Ferdinandus Baravellus, following courses at a Spanish university. The work was composed purportedly at the request of the uncle of a friend of his at whose house he was staying. It was intended as a direct rebuttal of Luther's *Contra Henricum regem angliae.* The manuscript was completed probably before the summer

---

[7] Scarisbrick, *Henry VIII,* 112-113; Headley, *Responsio,* 720-721; see also Roper, *Lyfe of Moore,* 67/16-19: 'But after it was finished, by his graces apointment and consent of the makers of the same, only a sorter out and placer of the principall matters therin contayned.'

[8] Thomas Murner, *Ob der Künig uss engelland ein lügner sey oder der Luther,* Strasbourg, 1522; Johann Eck, *Asseritur hic invictissimi Angliae regis liber de sacramentis, a calumniis et impietatibus Ludderi,* Rome, 1523; John Fisher, *Assertionis Lutheranae Confutatio,* Antwerp, 1523, and the later *Defensio regie assertionis contra babylonicam captivitatem,* Cologne, 1525; Henry's letter, *Epistola regia ad illustrissimos saxoniae duces pie admonitoria,* Greenwich, 20 January 1523, is bound in with the *Assertio* in some of its earlier editions, e.g. STC 13083. The letter warned the leaders of Saxony of the socio-political dangers implicit in Luther's teaching and called on them to suppress his movement.

[9] See Headley, *Responsio,* 791-803.

of 1523. Subsequently, however. More decided to drastically alter his text.
Only a handful of copies emerged from the printers. In the revised version
More adopted a new *nom de plume*, that of Guilielmus Rosseus, supposedly
an English scholar residing at Rome. This work was completed in the
autumn of 1523 and has reached the contemporary world under the title
Responsio ad Lutherum.[10]

In the first, Baravellus, edition More had dealt with the main areas of
dispute between Henry and Luther. It had become even more evident to
him that the whole question of the criteriology of faith had grown into a
central issue. Book I is largely concerned with this theme. Book II is a
somewhat uninspiring vindication of Henry's defence of the received
sacramental system. What did Rosseus add to Baravellus? The new
material occurs in the H gathering of the first version. Its central theme is
ecclesiology, focusing on such topics as the extent to which freedom from
sin is a condition of church membership and tenure of office. This led
naturally to an attempt to determine the identity of the true church of
Christ. What prompted More into this amplification of a theme to be
echoed throughout the rest of his theological work? The most obvious
answer, as it appears in the body of the text itself, was Luther's reply to a
controversial work published by a distinguished Italian Dominican
scholar, Ambrosius Catharinus Politi.[11] Catharinus, as he is commonly
known, had made a strong case both for the primacy of Rome and the
authority of the church it governed.[12] Luther's counter-attack apparently
made More acutely conscious that he had overlooked matters of extreme
importance in his first draft. Hence the unusual measure of holding up the
publication of a book already in print. A further influence may have been
the presence of the German Franciscan theologian, Thomas Murner, in

---

[10] Headley, *Responsio*, loc. cit., Donnelly, *Responsio*, 2-18; See *Responsio*, 6-25 for More's
own pseudonymous introductions and explanations of the divergence between the two versions. Rosseus claimed that the original manuscript he had sent to the printer had not
reached its destination: '...a compassionate man received it as a child cast off by an
unknown father and brought it out as his own.' This stratagem of More's explained the existence of two editions of the same work under the names of different authors. It did not explain the discrepancies between the texts.

[11] Ambrosius Catharinus Politi (1484-1553) was a Neapolitan humanist who became a
Dominican under Savonarola's influence in 1517. Apart from polemics, his main work was
in mariology and hagiography. See *LTK* I, (1957), cc. 426-427. See Ambrosius Catharinus
Politi, *Apologia pro veritate catholicae et apostolicae fidei ac doctrinae adversus impia ac valde pestifera
Martini Lutheri dogmata*, (1520), ed. J. Schweizer and A. Franzen, *CC* 27, Münster Westf.,
1956; Martin Luther, *Ad librum eximii magistri nostri Ambrosii Catharini defensoris Silvestri
Prieriatis acerrimi responsio Martini Lutheri*, Wittenberg, 1521, *WA* 7, 705-778.

[12] See Catharinus, *Apologia*, lib. II, *De origine potestatis papae*, 87-192.

England at this time. Murner was a firm opponent of Luther and profoundly aware of the ecclesiological implications of his theories.[13] More's
change of mind was fraught with consequence for the future for incorporated into these new considerations were firm affirmations of the divine
origin and transmission of papal primacy.

The literary style adopted by More does not make his work the lightest
of reading.[14] It consisted in the main of citing his opponent's work
paragraph by paragraph and refuting his arguments as they arose. Dr
Headley traces this method back to a variety of sources: the influence of
patristic apologetic, scholastic disputation, humanist dialectic, as well as
legal argument. Whatever its origin, the profit in accuracy was rather
quickly dissipated by the sheer lack of literary appeal. Only the most
dedicated enquirer would wade through this flood as its author sifts his
opponent's case often in vulgar and abusive language. Nor does the literal
presentation of an opponent's work fragment by fragment necessarily
reveal the complete mosaic of his thought. Elementary principles of
hermeneutics point to the necessity of placing any quotation in the larger
context of his whole philosophy. It is questionable whether More ever really penetrated Luther's mind and consequently may have spent a good deal
of his time tilting at windmills. One simple reason for this, of course, was
the limited number of the Wittenberger's books available to him.[15]

---

[13] See Luther, *Ad librum Catharini responsio*, (1521), *WA* 7, 708/26-710/19. See also
Headley, *Responsio*, 786-788, and 802-803: 'Murner undoubtedly introduced More into the
larger world of continental polemic against Luther...By claiming that Luther created a
church like Plato's republic with spiritual walls and doors and burgomasters Murner had in
1520 fastened upon a vital point that defined the issues and which More was now to echo.'
See also an earlier account of this relationship in John M. Headley, *Thomas Murner, Thomas
More and the First Expression of More's Ecclesiology, Studies in the Renaissance* 14 (1967) 73-92; G. J.
Donnelly, *A Translation of St. Thomas More's Responsio ad Lutherum*, Washington, 1962, 13-15.
Donnelly makes the helpful calculation that the twenty-one quotations which supplement the
H gathering come from Luther's reply to Catharinus. This makes for a strong link between
More's revision of the *Baravellus* edition and this new phase of the Lutheran controversy.
Thomas Murner, the friar in question, was a German Franciscan living in Strasbourg who
had published a Latin edition of the king's *Assertio*, a German translation of the same work as
well as a reply to Luther's *Antwort deutsch.* Murner visited the English court in 1523 and was
in contact with More as the latter was instrumental in obtaining a stipend for him from
Wolsey.
[14] See Rainer Pineas, *Thomas More and Tudor Polemics*, Bloomington, Indiana, 1968,
14-28; Headley, *Responsio*, 803-823.
[15] Meyer, *Henry VIII Burns Luther's Books*, 176-178 speaks of the limited circulation
Luther's works had in England at this period. One bookseller, John Dorne of Oxford, sold
only thirteen copies of Luther's writings in 1520. More was not fully informed of all aspects
of Luther's thought. In the *Responsio* he refers to the following works: *De captivitate babylonica
ecclesiae praeludium*, Wittenberg, 1520, *WA* 6, 497-573; *Contra Henricum regem angliae*, Wittenberg, 1522, *WA* 10/2, 180-222; *Ad librum eximii magistri nostri Ambrosii Catharini...responsio,*

Nonetheless, the *Responsio* was crucial for the development of More's own thought while the positive content of his discourse has been looked on as a serious contribution to the theological literature of his age.

CHURCH AND REVELATION

From the very outset of his polemic Thomas More defended Henry's position on the role of the church in relation to divine revelation: '...the church has the power of distinguishing the words of God from the words of men.'[16] This ability to identify and authenticate divine revelation belongs in the first instance not to any individual but to the body of believers as a whole. Henry had paraphrased Augustine in support of his own position: '...as Augustine says, you could not know which are the gospels except by the tradition of the church.'[17] This was a rough translation of Augustine's famous dictum: 'Ego vero Evangelio non crederem, nisi me catholicae Ecclesiae commoveret auctoritas.'[18] These words were frequently cited by More in the course of his controversies. He did not develop his arguments at this point but continued to reiterate a basic position emphasising the role of the church in relation to divinely inspired scripture.[19] When he spoke of the church in this context, it was not so much the hierarchy he had in mind as the authority of living tradition concerning those events 'disclosed to the faithful through the mouths of the apostles' and 'preserved thereafter by the abiding faith of the catholic church.'[20]

Wittenberg 1521, *WA* 7, 705-778; *Acta et res gestae D. Martini Lutheri in comitiis principum Wormaciae,* 1521, *WA* 7, 825-857. He seems to have known of the contents of at least two other works of Luther: *Resolutio lutheriana super propositione sua decima tertia de potestate papae,* 1519, *WA* 2, 183-240 available in Bks II and III of Catharinus, *Apologia; Assertio omnium articulorum M. Lutheri per bullam Leonis X,* 1520, *WA* 7, 94-151, extracts from which were used by Fisher in his *Confutatio.*

[16] See *Responsio,* 70/26, tr. 71/20-30 quoting *Assertio,* sig. S1v-S2.

[17] See *Responsio,* 88/6-10, tr. 89/9-12 quoting *Assertio,* sig. M 3v.

[18] See Augustine, *Contra epistolam Manichaei, MPL* 42, 176. See also: *De baptisme contra Donatistas,* 4, 24, 31, *MPL* 43, 174: 'Quod universa tenet Ecclesia nec conciliis institutum, sed semper retentum est, nonnisi auctoritate apostolica traditum rectissime creditur.'

[19] See *Responsio,* 114/25-116/11, tr. 115/32-117/12; 198/25-29, tr. 199/32-35.

[20] See *Responsio,* 88/5-6, tr. 89/5-7. See also *Responsio,* 396/29-398/4, tr. 397/36-399/5: 'Since, therefore, it is most certain both from the public faith of the catholic church and from the agreement of scripture that the church is ruled by the Spirit of Christ in matters of faith, we do not doubt that what the Spirit says to the church is true and correct even if there is an apparently contrary letter of scripture, knowing either that God has arranged for that text or that it is surely not contradictory but seems so, just as we have no doubt that two texts of scripture which at times seem to conflict are consistent with each other, even though they seem to us to disagree.'; *Responsio,* 102/9-12, tr. 103/9-14: 'Indeed, if any apparently contradictory scriptural text was alleged, the faith written in her heart taught this text was insuf-

Tradition

More could have been more analytical in his exposition of his theory of tradition. Essentially he saw tradition as enduring in the church in two main streams which sometimes merge, sometimes separate, but are always complementary to one another just as both taken together are complementary to scripture. In each case the chemical agent preserving the purity of the waters and indeed the power which keeps them in motion is the Spirit of God. In taking up this stance More was both adopting and defending Henry VIII's approach in the *Assertio*.[21]

Socio-historical tradition

The first of these streams might be termed the socio-historical tradition of the church as a living human community. The basis of this concept of tradition, according to More, lay in the new testament itself. Both Paul and John had made it clear that the word of God was more extensive than its written record '...what does the apostle mean when he says: "Stand firm and hold the traditions that you have learned whether by word or by letters of ours"? (2 Thess 2, 14)... Something, then, was taught, not as though it were a matter of free choice, but as a matter which bound the church beyond scripture...What do you say to the following words of the evangelist: "Many things were done which are not written in this book"? (Jn 20, 30) And to prevent you from saying that such incidents were written down by other evangelists, he says that the whole world could not contain them...Accordingly, it cannot be denied that even necessary articles of faith were among those teachings which were not written down but were transmitted without writing.'[22] Although in Henry's case this was the predominant concept of tradition that he employed, namely the organic processes of a living community, in the *Responsio* More himself emphasised a more transcendental theory of tradition seeing it in terms of the activity of the Spirit of God abiding within each believer.

---

ficiently understood by those to whom it seemed so contradictory, since it was a matter of absolute certainty that Christ does not fail His church on articles of faith, nor does the truthful Spirit of God contradict Himself.' This opinion of More's was based in all likelihood on Augustine, *De doctrina christiana*, III/II/2, *CC* 32 (1962), 78: 'Cum ergo adhibita intentio incertum esse/...peruiderit, quomodo distinguendum aut quomodo pronuntiandum sit, consulat regulam fidei, quam de scripturarum planioribus locis at ecclesiae auctoritate percepit, de qua satis egimus, cum de rebus in libro primo loqueremur.'

[21] See *Responsio*, pp. 86-90; *Assertio*, sig. G4—G4v.

[22] See *Responsio*, 98/3-22, tr. 99/3-27; see also ibid., 98/22-100/1, tr. 99/28-101/2.

The Spirit preserves tradition

The guarantor of the fidelity of tradition to its origins is Christ himself
and the Spirit he has given to the church to guide it into all truth: 'Tell me,
what is the significance of Christ's words: "When the Spirit, the
Paraclete, comes He will lead you into all truth"? (Jn 16, 13) He did not
say, "He will write to you, " or, "He will speak to you audibly," but,
"He will lead you"; that is He will incline you inwardly and by His inspiration direct your hearts into all truth.'[23] These words, according to
More, were addressed not merely to the apostles but to the church of every
age because it was with this church of history that Christ had promised to
remain (Mt 28, 20). The presence of his Spirit would ensure the preservation of his message in its full authenticity.

The gospel in the heart

Very quickly More moved on to one of his favourite themes, namely,
the gospel written by God in men's hearts. The same Spirit who
guarantees the transmission of apostolic tradition within the consciousness
of the community acts in a somewhat different fashion at the preconscious
level in the minds of the faithful: 'Did Christ command the new law to be
recorded on tablets or inscribed on bronze, so that whatever was not read
there would be immediately and totally rejected as worthless? Is not
Luther moved at all by the words of God, mentioned also by the apostles:
"I will put my laws upon their hearts and upon their minds I will write
them."?... He wrote the old law first on stone, later on wood, yet always
externally. He will write the new law inwardly by the finger of God on the
book of the heart...what He has written on the heart will last indelibly.'[24]

---

[23] See *Responsio,* 100/12-28, tr. 101/15-34.

[24] See *Responsio,* 100/12-28, tr. 101/15-34. In this context More had very much in mind
texts such as: Jer 31, 31-34 and Heb 8, 10. In all likelihood he derived this idea directly or indirectly from Augustine, *De spiritu et littera,* XIX/32-XXVI/46, *MPL* 44, cc. 220-229, *CSEL*
60, (1913), 185/20-201/9. This incidentally was not an idea excogitated specifically for the
purposes of this controversy. He had already made it his own some years before. Writing to
Martin Dorp, probably in 1515, he said that in the case of a doubtful reading of a scriptural
text in a manuscript one should have recourse '...aut ad vnius Euangelium fidei, quod per
vniversam Ecclesiam in corda fidelium infusum est, quod etiam, priusquam scriberetur a
quoquam, Apostolis a Christo, ab Apostolis vniuerso mundo predicatum est...' in More to
Martin Dorp, (1515), Rogers, *Correspondence,* 60/1134-1137. A similarly pneumatic concept
of revelation is found in *Assertio,* sig. M3v-M4v, cited by More, *Responsio,* 88/10-13, tr.
89/12-14. More's letter to Dorp shows that he was not dependent on Henry in this respect
though the reverse relationship is possible. On the other hand the concept had gained currency among Christian humanists in the preceding century.

For More this inner gospel was a reality more profound than any writing, even that of scripture. It had enabled the church to resist the onslaught of heresy in the past and would continue to do so in the future. This inner gospel was for More, at least at this time, the primary means by which divine revelation was transmitted from generation to generation within the believing community. 'On the heart, therefore, in the church of Christ, there remains inscribed the true gospel of Christ which was written there before the books of all the evangelists.'[25] As the marginal gloss to the first edition put it: 'The gospel is written with greatest certainty in the hearts of men.'

Inward gospel and faith

This inward gospel is the source of faith. What is communicated by the Spirit at a preconscious level finds its way ultimately into consciousness and the conceptual formulation of faith. This Spirit-inspired faith, not of one individual but of the community as a whole, becomes the ultimate touchstone of Christian truth. How this process takes place, how this transfer occurs from divine presence to credal statement is something More did not elucidate. He simply recorded what he believed to be the case: '...the church of Christ did not doubt that whatever the Holy Spirit inspired in the church was undoubtedly true, whether it was contained in scripture or not. Indeed, if any apparently contradictory scriptural text was alleged, the faith written in her heart taught that this text was insufficiently understood by those to whom it seemed so contradictory, since it was a matter of absolute certainty that Christ does not fail His church on articles of faith, nor does the truthful Spirit of God contradict Himself.'[26] This divinely inspired faith determines the church's acceptance or rejection of any particular formulation of doctrine. In the last resort it may even reject an apparently obvious interpretation of scripture if it is in opposition to a commonly held doctrine of faith. The church of God not merely authenticates the canon of scripture. It also discerns its true meaning. Authentic scripture can never contradict the faith of the church because, in More's scheme of things, the faith of the church is prior even to the apparent content of the inspired word of God as an object of faith.

---

[25] See *Responsio*, 100/25-28, tr. 101/31-34.
[26] See *Responsio*, 100/28-102/12, tr. 101/35-103/14; see also ibid., 224/12-13, tr. 225/14-16.

Material insufficiency of scripture

A further reason for More's preferring the faith of the church even to
the apparent literal sense of scripture was his recognition that the bible did
not comprehend the whole of divine revelation. 'Of these events, some
have been disclosed to the faithful through the mouths of the apostles, and
have been preserved thereafter by the abiding faith of the catholic
church.'[27] More cited as examples of such beliefs not directly attested by
scripture the doctrine of the sacraments, in particular matrimony and holy
orders. In addition he pointed out that certain articles of the creeds such as
'unbegotten' as applied to the Father, 'consubstantial' as applied to the
Son, the procession of the Holy Spirit, as well as the perpetual virginity of
Mary were all formulae not explicitly attested to by the bible. If Luther's
, principle of not accepting any proposition lacking 'the evident testimony
of scripture' is correct, then these articles of faith must be rejected.[28]

The principle, often termed the material insufficiency of scripture, was
as important for More as its converse was for Luther. For all his respect for
holy writ, More's common sense told him that a great many practices of
Renaissance Catholicism as well as some of its beliefs had no clear mandate from scripture. Rather than strain the credulity of his audience by
finding 'places' which might vaguely lend support to a particular proposition, More opted boldly for an alternative source of divine revelation in
the divinely inspired and guided belief of the church. The belief of the
church had to be taken as the criterion of faith, the standard by which any
theological position was to be judged.[29] This applied to tradition as much
as to any other aspect of Christian experience: 'Should you...concede that
the church has been given by God the power of inerrancy in distinguishing
the words of God from the words of men,...then it is necessary for you to
concede also that God will never fail His church...in distinguishing traditions...Christ Himself testifies...: ''I am with you even unto the end of the
world.'' ' (Mt 28, 20)[30]

---

[27] See *Responsio*, 88/5-6, tr. 89/5-7. See also ibid., 88/16-22, tr. 89/19-27 where More cites
the case of the virginity of Mary questioned by Helvidius. In like manner he rejected
Luther's case against the sacraments: '...Nor is there any other proof opposed to him than
the faith of the whole church, which is nowhere greater or stronger than in the sacraments.'
[28] See *Responsio*, 102/13-104/3, tr. 103/15-105/5. See also ibid., 122/8-24, tr. 123/9-27.
[29] See *Responsio*, 100/25-102/12, tr. 101/31-103/14; 108/2-3, tr. 109/3.
[30] See *Responsio*, 114/30-116/14, tr. 115/39-117/15. Cp. *Responsio*, 110/10-112/15, tr.
111/13-113/18. Similarly, ibid., 90/4-8, tr. 91/4-10, having quoted Jn 15, 26-27 and Jn 16,
13, More went on: 'Since the church, then, has had so many and such great teachers, so
many living evangelists, and that Spirit who inspires truth, shall we believe that she has
rashly instituted a sacrament and placed her hope in a meaningless sign? Shall we not rather

The church: criterion of God's word

In the *Babylonian Captivity* Luther had cited Augustine with approval concerning the discernment of true scripture: 'The church undoubtedly has the power to distinguish the word of God from the words of men, as Saint Augustine confesses in saying that he believed in the gospel moved by the authority of the church which proclaimed this gospel.'[31] More naturally agreed with this dictum of Augustine's and tried to turn it against his adversary.[32] He argued that the church not merely authenticates scripture but also interprets it with divine assistance: '...of what use would it be for the church, with God teaching her, to distinguish the true from the false scripture, if in the true scripture she should not distinguish the false from the true meaning?' The church not merely recognises God's word, she understands it and passes it on to her children. More then enlarged the beach-head he believed he had established and extended the principle to cover God's unwritten word as found in tradition: 'It is manifestly clear then...that (as) she has no less the power also to distinguish the words of God from the words of men, that she has no less the power also to distinguish the traditions of God from the traditions of men...since Christ's concern is...that she should not err in any manner.'[33]

---

believe that she has learned from the apostles; shall we not rather believe that she has learned from the Holy Spirit?' In this last section More was quoting verbatim from *Assertio*, sig. G4-G4v. See also *Responsio*, 100/7-12, tr. 101/9-14: 'But tell me, whom will the Holy Spirit lead into all truth? Is it the apostles only, to whom Christ was then speaking personally? Then it was to the apostles only that He also said: "I am with you even unto the consummation of the world." (Mt 28, 20) Who then will doubt that it was of the church that Christ said that the Holy Spirit would lead her into all truth?' Note More's *ducet* reading of Jn 16, 13; other versions have *docebit*. More uses the *ducet* reading to ground his concept of the developing understanding within the church of the content of the self-revelation of God both in the gift of the Spirit and the life and sayings of Jesus.

[31] See e.g. Luther, *De captivitate babylonica*, WA 6, 561/3-5, citing Augustine, *Contra epistolam Manichaei*, MPL 42, 176.

[32] See *Responsio*, 198/25-29, tr. 199/32-35; see also ibid., 248/30-250/14, tr. 249/35-251/15. See especially 110/23-116/11, tr. 111/28-117/15 where More quotes Luther's use of Augustine in his *De captivitate babylonica*, WA 6, 561/3-5 as well as Henry's reply in the *Assertio*, sig. P4-Q1v and gives his own comment on both. See Headley's remarks on this aspect of More's thought. He does not seem to have appreciated how close More was to Luther in his acceptance of the voice of the church understood as the community of faith and therefore as the criterion of revelation. Where he differed with Luther on this particular issue was in determining the limits of the community of faith. More had not fully adverted to this particular difference of viewpoint as yet. In the second *Rosseus* edition he addressed himself to this problem as he had come to recognise its centrality to the controversy. Briefly, while Luther defined this community as a hidden congregation of true believers, More identified it with the multitude of baptised Christians, the common known Catholic Church. See Headley, *Responsio*, 724-743 on this question, and below pp. 96-105; 117-121.

[33] See *Responsio*, 110/24-112/32, tr. 111/28-113/37.

More thus looked to the believing community as the rule of faith.
The church understood in this sense a good deal more than a juridically
structured institution within whose legal provisions one is obliged to act. It
is a living people guided by a living Spirit. This Spirit guides the community in its progressive appreciation and elaboration of divine revelation.[34] The presence of the Spirit ensures the church will never fail in its
essential role of discerning God's word: '...God will never fail His church
in interpreting the scriptures or in distinguishing traditions...To err on
these matters is nothing else than to withdraw one's faith from God and to
place it, not in man, but in empty signs.'[35] What is written in the hearts of
the faithful will remain indestructibly.[36]

Consensus

The question naturally arises as to how in practice the church exercises
her function of discernment in relation to God's word? The post-
Tridentine Catholic turned either to the councils or the Roman *magisterium*
for direction in these matters. More, with his patristic background, looked
elsewhere, to the common faith of the believing community. The unfailing
criterion of orthodoxy for More was not so much the active teaching of the
church as the universal faith of the Christian people spread through space

---

[34] See *Responsio*, 100/4-8, tr. 101/5-10: '''When the Holy Spirit, the Paraclete, comes He
will lead you into all truth...'' But tell me whom will the Holy Spirit lead into all truth?
...Who then will doubt that it was of the church that Christ said that the Holy Spirit would
lead her into all truth?' See also ibid., 90/1-4, tr. 91/1-4: 'And again: ''When He shall have
come, who is the spirit of truth, He will lead you into all truth. For He will not speak of
Himself, but whatever things He shall hear, He shall speak, and the things which are to
come He will reveal to you.''' (Jn 16, 13); ibid., 232/6-10, tr. 233/8-13: Christ promised
'...that the Spirit, the Paraclete, who leads the church into all truth would never fail her;...'
Note that More uses a double Latin reading for 'leads': sometimes *docere* following
Augustine, sometimes *ducere* following Erasmus. See Headley, *Responsio*, 881-882, 907, 911,
943 on this point.
[35] See *Responsio*, 116/6-11, tr. 117/7-12. For More it was unthinkable that the church
could fall from faith as such a collapse would belie Christ's promises. See *Responsio*,
232/6-10, tr. 233/8-13: '...Christ would indeed never abandon His church with whom He
Himself promised that He would remain even until the end of the world; that the Spirit, the
Paraclete, who leads the church into all truth would never fail her...'
[36] See *Responsio*, 192/1-5, tr. 193/1-6: '...the one (church) which Christ long ago established and which has ever remained uncorrupted in the faith of its origins...however great a
part has violently torn itself away from her, it will be a withered branch, lacking the divine
Spirit who will remain only in His own vine, however much it may have been reduced by the
pruning of its branches.' The church remains faithful to Christ and to his message. See
Responsio, 100/25-28, tr. 101/30-34: 'On the heart, therefore, in the church of Christ, there
remains inscribed the true gospel of Christ which was written there before the books of all the
evangelists.'

and time: 'We beg finally that in a disputed interpretation of the sacred writings he believe the consistent judgment of the holy fathers and the faith of the whole catholic church rather than his own opinion.'[37] The consensus of the believing church is the measure of belief. More condemned those who arrogate to themselves the interpretation of the scriptures '...in opposition to so many and such learned and such holy interpreters of so many ages, in opposition to the agreement of the whole Christian world, an agreement which...takes root through the Spirit of Christ...'[38] This agreement induced by the Spirit of God has a dual dimension, one spanning the contemporary church, the other reaching back through time to the apostolic community.

...in space

Consensus at the first level requires that Christians of the existing generation come together in professing certain truths. More could be vehement in his insistence on the value of such a common voice: 'We stubborn blockheads of course demand that we alone be believed; that is, that only the Italians, Spaniards, English, French and finally all men alone should be believed wherever the church of Christ exists today or has ever existed anywhere in the world since the death of Christ.'[39] Such a congruence of opinion does not call for an absolute mathematical degree of unanimity but admits of a certain level of disagreement without its essential force being evacuated.[40]

...in time

Consensus in the church of one historical epoch is a significant index to the presence of God's saving word. Its authority is even greater if it can be

---

[37] See *Responsio*, 300/6-9, tr. 301/7-10. See also ibid., 190/7-11, tr. 191/10-13: '...if there is any true church of Christ on earth, it is this congregation which, begun by Christ, spread by the apostles, taught by the saints, has by God's special care persisted unceasingly through so many ages in the unity of the Christian faith.'

[38] Ibid., 190/20-23, tr. 191/25-29.

[39] See *Responsio* 96/12-16, tr. 97/11-16. See also More's argument for the validity of sacramental order based on Henry's *Assertio*, sig. P3v-P4, in ibid. 116/28-118/9, tr. 117/30-119/9: '...it is quite certain that almost every region of the earth which truly professes the faith of Christ also considers orders as a sacrament. If he could find some obscure corner...in which the sacrament of orders is unknown, nevertheless that corner should not be compared with the rest of the church, which is subject not only to Christ but also for the sake of Christ to the sole vicar of Christ, the Roman pope, and which believes that orders is a sacrament.'

[40] See preceding n. 39. Even though there were 'some obscure corner' in which orders is not recognised as a sacrament, it would not undermine the testimony of other Christian nations. See also the example of Roman primacy where More says that '...*almost all the peoples who sincerely profess the faith of Christ look up to and venerate the successor of Peter as the vicar of Christ*' in *Responsio* 202/26-28, tr. 203/31-33.

shown to extend throughout the generations of believers. It is in this connection that the witness of the fathers of the church is of special value.
More never intended to set up the patristic *corpus* as an alternative literary
source to the bible. The bible is the inspired word of God in writing. The
works of the fathers are not inspired but they do bear a sustained witness to
the faith of the church across the ages. This makes it possible to discover a
moral unanimity of belief not merely in the living generation but extending to the origins of the Christian community. It is important to emphasise
this point. In the *Responsio* More did not look to the fathers in the first instance as literary sources by means of which extra-biblical revelation is
preserved in the church. For him extra-biblical revelation is preserved in
the abiding presence of God with his people, in the gospel engraved on
men's hearts which in its turn finds a voice in the conscious faith of the
church. But as the Spirit is active today, so also in previous times: '...why
do you not also remember the words which Christ Himself says to the
apostles, and through them to other undoubtedly holy men on whom He
deigned to pour out His Spirit: ''He who hears you hears me''? (Lk 10,
16) It is abundantly evident that Christ breathed out His Spirit on the holy
doctors of the church, whose teaching and life He has confirmed by many
miracles. Therefore, even if not a single one being human, has not at some
time been in error, a thing which you also proclaim happened to the
apostles themselves, nevertheless, when they have agreed on a point in
such great numbers through so many ages, it must not be doubted that
they reached this agreement by the inspiration of the divine Spirit who
makes those who dwell in a house to be of one mind...' (Ps 67, 7)[41] The
fathers of the church are to be respected because the Spirit of God was active in their hearts and revealed himself through their teaching.

    More looked to the fathers, therefore, as a means of reaching back
across the years to the faith of previous generations of Christians. 'And yet
I have no doubt that if this same Augustine had read anything in the works
of all the holy fathers preceding him, especially anything harmonizing
with the faith of his own time, he would never have doubted that it was a
true and undoubted article of the Christian faith. For the writings of our
predecessors represent to us the faith of their own times. Nor do we have
any other way of speaking with the dead in order that we can know the
content of their faith. Therefore, out of the books of those who have lived

---

[41] See *Responsio* 128/3-12, tr. 129/3-14. More attached great weight to the testimony of the
fathers. When Luther asserted that he did not care if he were opposed by a thousand
Cyprians, Augustines, Ambroses, More replied: '...you are exposing yourself to the threats
of Christ, who said: ''He who despises you despises me.''' (Lk 10, 16)

before us we find out that knowledge, and thus we discover that this faith which Luther attacks is not, as he falsely asserts, new or proper to any one nation, but that it is the public faith of the whole church through many ages.'[42] When the agreement of living people is supported by the testimony of patristic tradition it becomes an incontrovertible witness to the real substance of divine revelation. 'But if it is certain that on any one point all the ancient fathers long ago agreed, we do not hesitate to oppose such thorough agreement of good men to a single dull-witted scoundrel, when it is clear that they reached agreement through that Spirit who makes those who dwell in a house to be of one mind.' (Ps 67, 7)[43] Even without tangible evidence from scripture, communion in faith is a more reliable guide to the content of divine revelation than the intuitions of any single individual however gifted.

The indices of consent

The question naturally arises as to how such consent is given and how one knows when unanimity is reached? More did not expound at length on these topics, nor does he seem to have regarded them as serious problems. In regard to the first issue of giving consent perhaps the clearest statement of his views is to be found not in his treatment of the word of God but of civil law. Luther had argued that good magistrates were of more importance to the welfare of society than good laws. More replied: '...hardly any judgment is rendered justly which is not rendered according to some established law. For the law of the gospel does not apportion possessions, nor does reason alone prescribe the forms of determining property, unless reason is attended by an agreement...which agreement, either taking root in usage or expressed in writing, is public law.' The Latin text links the thought more expressly to More's theological position: 'nisi rationi consensus accedat...qui consensus aut coalescens usu, aut ex-

---

[42] See *Responsio* 250/13-25, tr. 251/17-29. More was using against Luther his admission that only canonical books are to be believed and that these are known through the church, in *Contra Henricum regem angliae, WA* 10/2, 195. Luther was citing Augustine's dictum in this respect in *Contra epistolam Manichaei, MPL* 42, 176.

[43] See *Responsio* 212/14-18, tr. 213/17-21. See also ibid., 122/8-24, tr. 123/9-27: More approves of Catharinus who, he affirms, presents in support of his case '...the constant agreement of the most holy fathers, of the most ancient interpreters, of the most learned men.'; ibid., 416/7-11, tr. 417/8-17: 'And certainly, of so many holy fathers of the church who have lived from the time of Christ's passion even to the present day, there has never been one who did not believe that the common customs of the universal church concerning the sacraments either were handed down by the order of Christ through the apostles or had developed in the church through the Holy Spirit.'

pressus litteris, publica lex est.'[44] In the background to this dictum is the assumption that customary law is the law of the land and that statutory law is its explicitation carried out with the consent of the people.[45] In this instance the context carries as well overtones of natural law theory: 'nisi rationi consensus accedat...' The two modes in which consent can be given are worth noting: 'aut coalescens usu, aut expressus litteris'. In More's theological approach these appear to be the two principal ways in which the consent of the church to a doctrine, law or practice can be established: the usage of the church and the writings of the fathers.

Regarding the second of these, the testimony of patristic witness, something has already been said above. Concerning usage or custom as a criterion of consent, More's defence of the sacraments in Book II of the *Responsio* depends to a great extent on the practice of the church. He declares repeatedly that God could not have allowed his whole church to err for so long in her acts of piety: 'The whole church, spread throughout the whole world, holds matrimony as a sacrament; it holds orders as a sacrament; it holds penance as a sacrament; and what need is there to recall individual details? These things the church both thinks unanimously now and has thought through so many ages. But if you and your herd believe something different, the church is nonetheless of one mind in its house.' (Ps 67, 7)[46]

The questions raised concerning the manner of giving consent and the measure of its universality are in many ways modern rather than medieval questions. They belong to a world of referenda and opinion polls rather than one governed by immemorial custom. The medieval concept of consent was based much more closely on the assumption of tacit consent expressed through popular usage and accepted tradition. As the influence of various consultative assemblies in the decision making process grew, there

---

[44] See *Responsio* 276/20-25, tr. 277/23-30.

[45] See J. E. A. Jolliffe, *The Constitutional History of England*, London, 1961, 334-341; S. B. Chrimes, *English Constitutional Ideas in the Fifteenth Century*, Cambridge, 1936, 192-214. Note that Chrimes remarks: 'It would be a mistake to assume too readily that *a priori* notions of law had entirely lost their vitality and their practical import in the fifteenth century. The law of God was still a concept to conjure with in practical politics; and Fortescue resorted to the law of nature to prove his views on the succession question. This law of nature, *or of reason*, as the English wisely preferred to call it, which had loomed so large in the speculations of medieval jurists, was still sometimes figuring in the rough-and-tumble of the courts, and could still be a last resort in unprecedented cases.' Hence More was in no way outside his juristic tradition in this manner of speech.

[46] See *Responsio*, 622/16-22, tr. 623/20-26; see also ibid., 672/19-674/15, tr. 673/21-675/17.

was a gradual transition in feudal society from the idea that full numerical agreement was needed for any decision to the principle of majority rule.

In More's day majority rule had been accepted for many decades both in parliamentary elections and parliamentary procedure itself.[47] Within the church it is questionable whether full numerical agreement was ever required either in conciliar procedure or in the determination of extraconciliar consensus.[48] More was reflecting the climate of thought of his own day when he asserted: '...quod in nullo actu multitudinis, requiritur, quod omnes ad unum consentiant...in no action of a multitude is unanimous consent required...'[49] More accepted this axiom in practice so that he was not deterred from adopting a firm position by occasional dissenting voices either in patristic tradition or in the contemporary church.

The source of consensus

While More may have applied general constitutional principles in an analogous fashion to the working of the church, he never allowed himself to think of the church as a purely social organisation. Nowhere is this more marked than in his treatment of the origins of ecclesial consent. We have already seen how he emphasised the role of the Spirit in preserving the truth of Christ's message, in leading the church to a deeper awareness of the meaning of this message, as well as marking it out in some mysterious fashion on the minds and hearts of the faithful. More also recognised the Spirit as the primary source of the unity of the church, a unity of mind and heart: 'Fateris nunc, ubi dei spiritus est, ibi consensus esse.' The same Spirit who writes his law on men's hearts and leads them into all truth, moves them towards agreement on matters of belief.

More expressed this conviction with sustained vehemence when he retorted to Luther's claim that the traditional church had made the pope

---

[47] The principle of majority rule emerged early in English political assembly due in measure to canonist principle. Canon law introduced the idea that *sanioritas* was necessary for corporate decision and the act of a majority raised a presumption of *sanioritas*. The principle of majority rule in parliamentary elections seems to have been established by 1429 and in parliamentary procedure itself by 1476. See Chrimes, *Constitutional Ideas*, 133-137.

[48] See Otto Gierke, *Political Theories of the Middle Ages*, tr. F. W. Maitland, Cambridge, 1900, notes 227-230, pp. 166-167. Gierke remarks on the difference of opinion among theorists as to whether even a majority could always bind an individual to its decisions. For the development of the principle of consent in classical canonist corporation theory see the greatly more nuanced study by Brian Tierney, *Foundations of the Conciliar Theory*, Cambridge, 1955, 108-116, 121-124, 186-188, and in particular his exposé of Zabarella's thought on church and council, 220-237.

[49] See *Responsio*, 608/1-3, tr. 609/2-3.

its source of unity: 'The papistic church places its unity in the unity of its external idol, the pope.'[50] Luther argued that the source of external unity in the Christian fellowship lay in the sacraments of baptism and eucharist; of internal unity in the gift of the Spirit: 'ille inquam internus spiritus solus, unanimes habitare facit in domo.' (Ps 67, 7) More turned Luther's argument against him, insisting that the unity created by the Spirit in fact belied his opponent's case: '...you did not wish to hear, that the Holy Spirit of God interiorly inspires His church with truth, that that interior Spirit renders all taught of God, that He alone makes those who dwell in a house to be of one mind, that He teaches so that they understand the same thing, judge the same, investigate the same, prove the same, confess the same, follow the same, teach the same, that that interior Spirit is the only one who makes men who dwell in a house to be of one mind...Therefore, since you admit that it is the Spirit of God who makes people who dwell in a house to be of one mind and in agreement on necessary matters, you must admit willy-nilly that that church is the catholic church and the house of God in which through so many ages all men have judged unanimously against your irrational opinion...'[51]

This was not the first occasion on which More had stressed the role of the Spirit in bringing about union of mind and heart. He had earlier used the same text Ps 67, 7 to underline the value of consistent patristic tradition, the decision to give communion in one kind only, while in the Rosseus edition he used it once more to underwrite the importance of ongoing tradition in the life and thought of the Christian community.[52] As John Headley points out in his introduction to the *Responsio* and Richard Marius at even greater length in the introduction to the *Confutation,* More was using an Old Latin version of this text rather than the Vulgate. Marius points out the inaccuracy of the Old Latin translation. Headley suggests that More may have picked up this particular version from the Roman missal where it occurs in the mass for the eleventh Sunday after Pentecost.[53]

Wherever More culled this version of a favoured text, its message runs through the whole of More's thinking about the church. Christendom is at heart a spiritual communion created and inspired by the divine Spirit.

---

[50] See Luther, *Contra Henricum regem angliae, WA* 10/2, 219/33-220/4.

[51] See *Responsio,* 622/5-624/9, tr. 623/7-625/11.

[52] See *Responsio,* 212/17-18, tr. 213/17-21. See also ibid., 364/6-7, tr. 365/7-8; 128/11-12, tr. 129/13-14; 300/4-5, tr. 301/5-6.

[53] See Headley, *Responsio,* 823 and 890: note to 128/12; Marius, *Confutation* III, 1352-1353.

The latter guides it through history, watches over and directs all its actions while being the ultimate source of its life and unity. More's eyes continually passed beyond the warped and withered configurations of the earthbound church which surrounded him to a spiritual being and relationship which he looked on as its essential and enduring reality.

Council

It is not surprising that a discussion of consensus would have led to an examination of the place of the general council in the life of the church. More looked on the council as the church in microcosm. His main treatment of conciliar theory followed his examination of Luther's conception of the inner unity of the church based mainly on Jn 6, 45 and Ps 67, 7.[54] It is not elaborate in extent. Taking up a point Luther had made a little earlier, namely his rejection of councils whose decisions go beyond the word of God in scripture,[55] More made a case for the general council somewhat similar to that he had made for the authority of consensus with a parallel undercurrent of constitutionalist assumptions running through it.

Perhaps a little optimistically More presumed the case for consensus to have been made successfully. He then went on to ask whether in order to arrive at consensus it was necessary that '...the whole Christian people from the whole world should be called together at one time, as to an assembly of consuls to the Campus Martius, and their votes sought man by man?' Is it really arrogance if the pastors of the church before all others deal with matters concerning the whole flock? 'To whom should the people rather wish that business delegated than to the bishops, to whom it especially belongs to be anxious about the safety of the people?'[56] Casting

---

[54] For Luther's views on church unity about this time see Luther, *Contra Henricum regem angliae*, *WA* 10/2, 219/33-220/4.

[55] 'Quare videmus hic, omnes Pontifices, omnia Concilia, omnes scholas, qui aliud in Ecclesia sonant quam verbum dei solius, esse lupos, Satanae ministros et falsos prophetas' in ibid., 219/9-11. Note that More did not fully understand Luther's doctrine of the word of God and tended to assume that the latter identified it with a fundamentalist attachment to the literal sense of scripture. For Luther's theory of and appeal to the general council see Peter Meinhold, *Das Konzil im Jahrhundert der Reformation* in *Die ökumenischen Konzile der Christenheit*, ed. H. J. Margull, Stuttgart, 1961, 201-210; Martin Seils, *Das ökumenische Konzil in der lutherischen Theologie*, in ibid., 333-339; A. Ebneter, *Luther und das Konzil*, *Zeitschrift für katholische Theologie* 84 (1962) 1-48, especially 1-29 for the period 1518-1524; C. Tecklenburg Johns, *Luthers Konzilsidee in ihrer historischer bedingtheit und ihrem reformatorischen Neuenansatz*, Berlin, 1966, 179-188 and passim; R. Bäumer, *Luthers Ansichten über die Irrtumsfähigkeit des Konzils und ihre theologiegeschichtlichen Grundlagen*, in *Wahrheit und Verkündigung*, Vol. 2, ed. L. Scheffczyk, W. Dettloff, R. Heinzmann, Munich, 1967, 987-1003.

[56] See *Responsio*, 626/21-27, tr. 627/24-33.

its shadow over this view of council was a populist view of the church. Theoretically, it would appear, all Christians are entitled to attend. But their authority is delegated to the pastors of the church: 'Quibusnam id negocium pocius cupiat delegatum populus, quam episcopis.' More did not speak of an electoral system for the council but did refer to the business of the assembly as 'delegated...to the bishops.' He did not say who was responsible for the act of delegation, God or the people. Nonetheless, underlying his concept of council there appears a concept of representation, related possibly to canonical sources but more likely to parliamentary precedents.

A similar figure was used by Bishop Russell, the fifteenth century constitutional theorist, in a draft sermon for the opening of parliament in the reign of Edward V. He addressed '...ye peple that stonde ferre of...whome for ther gret and confuse nombre and multitude nature can not wele suffre to assemble in oo place apt to the makynge of a lawe...' At a later stage he compared the emergence of parliament to the (mythological) origins of the Roman senate. In Romulus's day the whole people met in one place, and 'the law was made by the assente of alle the peuple togedyr...' But after their number had increased such assemblies became unmanageable and authority to legislate was delegated to the senate 'to the nombre of a.C. noble and wyse men.'[57] We do not know for sure whether More ever read this speech of Russell's. We know he admired the man, must have studied his life to some extent in composing *The History of Richard III*, and may well have met him in his youth at Cardinal Morton's house.[58] Whatever the source there is a strong suggestion of a representative theory of council in

---

[57] The text of this draft sermon for the intended parliament of Edward V (1483) was published by S. B. Chrimes, *English Constitutional Ideas in the Fifteenth Century*, Cambridge, 1936, 168-178. This idea that the whole kingdom was present in parliament through its elected representatives had gained ground through the course of the 15th century. See for example the political verses:

'When all a kingdom gathered is
In God's law, and by one assent,
For to amend what was amiss,
Therefore is ordained a parliament.'

These were published in *Political and other Poems*, ed. J. Kail, *E.E.T.S.*, old series CXXIV, 1904, I, 55, cited B. Wilkinson, *Constitutional History of England in the Fifteenth Century (1399-1485)*, London, 1964, 296; (see p. 280 passim) and in Chrimes, *Constitutional Ideas*, 145.

[58] See Thomas More, *The History of Richard III*, ed. R. S. Sylvester, New Haven and London, 1963, lxii. John Russell was bishop of Lincoln and chancellor to Richard III. He died on 30 December 1494. More spoke of him as '...a wyse manne & a good and of muche experyence, and one of the beste learned menne, vndoubtedlye that Englande hadde in hys time' in ibid., 25/5-8.

More's observations on the subject of the composition of a conciliar assembly. In this context representation could be understood as symbolic as well as electoral. The realities of canonical procedure would suggest that the former notion is in question here while More's own background both as political theorist and practitioner would suggest the second.[59]

This impression of popular participation in the decision making process of council is reinforced by what follows: 'From every part of the church scattered widely throughout the world men gathered for a council, and, as shortly after even you do not deny, very many of the best and most holy men agreed among themselves, each one returned home; the people spread throughout almost the whole world agreed on the same things.'[60] The decision of council is confirmed by the assent of the people. In More's mind there seemed to be an essential complementarity between the consensus of council and the consensus of the people without his working out the full implications of his prejudice. Whatever these might be, the role of council is analogous to that of consensus, in particular concerning the truth or falsehood of doctrine and as maker of law.[61]

More's constitutional experience as well as his explorations in political theory may have influenced his views on the place and structure of general councils. Nonetheless he never failed to place the institutional realities of church life within a theological perspective. Earlier, speaking of the council of Nicaea he had attributed the ultimate authority of that council to the presence of Christ in the assembly, citing Christ's promise in Mt 18, 20 to be present wherever two or three gather in his name. He repeated the same argument when sketching out his *rationale* for general councils, while attributing the universal acceptance of their decrees to the action of the Holy Spirit 'qui habitare facit unanimes in domo'. (Ps 67, 7)[62] Thus, although More appreciated the human dimensions of the church both in terms of personal experience and organisational requirements, he never failed to ascribe its operations to divine influence as their ultimate source.

---

[59] See Gierke, *Political Theories,* 62-67, and the detailed notes to these pages, notes 212-243. For practice at Constance see L. R. Loomis, *The Council of Constance,* New York, 1961, 21-28. 'Symbolic' representation is expressed in such assertions as 'The king represents the nation' without any overtone of electoral process.

[60] See *Responsio,* 626/31-628/3, tr. 627/37-629/3.

[61] This view of the council's powers is found in More's writing more by implication than by direct statement, especially in his criticism of Luther's rejection of the authority first of pope, then of council, and finally of the Christian people. See *Responsio,* 612/21-614/11, tr. 613/26-615/13; 630/12-14, tr. 631/13-18. For the development of Luther's thought on these topics see H. Jedin, *Council of Trent,* I, 172-187.

[62] See *Responsio,* 626/27-30, tr. 627/32-36; 628/3-5, tr. 629/3-6.

Sacramental order

In his younger days Thomas More had not hesitated to speak in criticism of abuses among the clergy. He had denounced abuses concerning wealth, concubinage, as well as simple ignorance. The priests in Utopia were a sober lot indeed. His criticism arose, however, from his concern for the church and the quality of life of those responsible for the cure of souls rather than from doubts concerning the sacrament. In the *Responsio* More took on the task of defending the traditional view of holy orders, in fact adding little to what Henry VIII had said on the subject. At the same time his treatment of the topic is of some significance since it is the foundation of the visible institutional structure of the church.

Luther, during this period, was formulating his own theology of office.[63] Having rediscovered the doctrine of the priesthood of the faithful he had to work out how ecclesiastical office was affected by this new perspective. The Wittenberg reformer evolved a theology of office based on three main foundation stones: charism, the ministry of the word of God, and the role of the local church.

The primary requirements in the minister, Luther argued, are firstly, charismatic gifts necessary for the exercise of the ministry, and secondly, the approval of the local community for his exercising this ministry. Thirdly, the main role of the one appointed to ecclesiastical office is the preaching of the word of God. These ideas were not fully worked out in the reformer's mind in 1520 but they were in process of distillation. There was no doubt concerning his rejection of the Catholic emphasis on the sacramental-sacrificing priesthood set aside irrevocably by a special sacrament for the worship of God and the service of the people. In the traditional conception, this liturgical consecration consisting of prayer and the imposition of hands empowered the recipient from on high for his special mission. Luther rejected all this on the grounds of inadequate scriptural foundation.[64] It was this position More felt called on to attack.

More's basic conviction, like Henry's, was that the seven sacraments could have been established by Christ alone as he alone has the power '...to promise grace with a visible sign.'[65] Holy orders is one of these

---

[63] See Wilhelm Brunotte, *Das geistliche Amt bei Luther*, Berlin, 1959, 34-116, 199-202. For the 1520 period in particular see 34-60. A somewhat different interpretation of Luther's views on office may be found in Hellmut Lieberg, *Amt und Ordination bei Luther und Melanchthon*, Göttingen, 1962, 235-242 and passim. The former emphasises the importance of personal charism; the latter the intervention of the ecclesial community.

[64] See *Luther, De captivitate babylonica, WA* 6, 564/6-14; 569/34-36; *Contra Henricum regem angliae, WA* 10/2, 220/33-221/9.

[65] See *Responsio*, 648/15-650/4, tr. 649/18-651/3.

sacraments conferring grace by the imposition of hands accompanied by prayer. More was content to refer to the scriptural evidence cited by Henry to establish his thesis.[66] He admitted that for a certain time '...when the matter was less well known the bishops permitted the people to name the one whom they judged the best; which practice was more of a kind of commendation of virtue and a testimony of an approved life than the right of election.'[67] More emphatically rejected the idea that the consent of the people was in any way either a precondition or an essential factor in promotion to orders.

Regarding the nature of office More was content to quote verbatim from Henry's *Assertio*, speaking of priests as those who '...labor in the word and in teaching,' in offering sacrifice, and the ministry of the sacraments. Office is conferred by a bishop who consecrates the candidate such that '...both the corporal sign is applied and so much spiritual grace is poured into him that he who is consecrated receives not only the Holy Spirit himself but also the power of conferring Him on others.'[68]

More had nothing to say on the subject of ministry which was new. He reaffirmed medieval tradition already echoed in Henry's tract. In so doing, however, he affirmed his adherence to a view of the church which saw it not merely as a spiritual communion nor as a vast multitude of believers spread in a shapeless mass across the known world, but as an ordered body among whom a special group of men were set aside by God's power and call to minister to the spiritual needs of the others. This fundamental principle provides the basis for the subdivision of the people into distinct groupings and communities. It is evident from other writings of More's that he accepted the medieval church order not merely in its skeletal form but also in its detail.[69] More did not deal with the latter at any length in the *Responsio*. The section on holy orders is the penultimate chapter of the *Baravellus* edition. His second thoughts in the *Rosseus* edition contain a fuller treatment of some aspects of ecclesiastical organisation, notably the Roman primacy and the nature of church jurisdiction.

---

[66] See *Responsio*, 652/14-27, tr. 653/16-30.

[67] See *Responsio*, 654/7-12, tr. 655/10-15.

[68] See *Responsio*, 658/28-660/31, tr. 659/33-661/37. See also *Assertio*, sig. R3v-R4.

[69] See Rainer Pineas, *Sir Thomas More's Controversy with Christopher St German*, Studies in *English Literature* I (1961) 49-62, repr. *Thomas More and Tudor Polemics*, Bloomington, Ind., 1968, 192-213; R. J. Schoeck, *Canon Law in England on the Eve of the Reformation*, Medieval *Studies* 25 (1963) 125-147; *Sir Thomas More: Humanist and Lawyer*, Univ. of Toronto Quart. 34 (1964) 1-14; *Common Law and Canon Law in their Relation to Thomas More* in *St. Thomas More: Action and Contemplation*, ed. R. S. Sylvester, New Haven and London, 1972, 15-55.

The Roman Primacy

In the *Rosseus* edition of the *Responsio*, as we have seen, a large section was added to the H gathering of the original work, seemingly because of More's growing realisation that the identity of the true church of Christ was being increasingly called in question. The heading to chapter X indicates this perception; '...Luther stupidly boggles in trying to make the identity of the church a matter of dispute.' More's main concern was to deal with Luther's objection that the evident corruption of the established ecclesiastical institution inevitably implied its surrender to the power of evil. Consequently, the church of Christ must be sought elsewhere. What prompted More into this prolonged excursus on the identity of the church? Dr Headley suggests two main influences: the presence of Thomas Murner in England and the appearance of a further work from Wittenberg in which Luther attacked Ambrosius Catharinus Politi's *Apologia*. Both these arguments are sustained by the evidence. In any event More's second thoughts led him deeper into ecclesiology, involving him in a consideration of topics such as the Roman primacy, the problem of evil in the church, the origin and meaning of jurisdiction, grace and office, as well as the central issue of the identity of the church of Christ.

More's first serious discussion of the primacy occurs in fact in the *Baravellus* edition. It takes the form of bolstering up Henry's arguments for the primacy based on the continued tradition of the church and its universal acceptance by the Christian world. Henry had argued that the pope could not have seized such universal authority by illegitimate means.[70] Indeed because the origin of his authority antedates human memory it must be presumed to have been legally established. History moreover shows, Henry pleaded, that almost all the churches of the Christian world obeyed the Roman church. Even the Greeks, except when in schism, accepted its primacy. At this point Henry did not take a stand on the question of divine institution but rather on the validity of papal presidency based on the customary law of the church. It was this viewpoint that More initially upheld, arguing against Luther that it could be proved '...from the annals and synods and commentaries and epistles of the Greek fathers...that (the)

---

[70] See *Assertio,* sig. B3-B5. Note that Henry was more emphatic concerning divine institution of the Roman primacy at a later stage of the discussion when defending the validity of public law: '...et indignatur Lutherus, si romanus pontifex successor Petri, vicarius Christi, cui Christus velut apostolorum principi tradidisse creditur claues ecclesiae, ut caeteri per illum *et intrarent,* et pellerentur: ieiunium indicat aut praeculas.' Even still this statement is not without qualification as Henry also says: '...tradidisse *creditur* claues ecclesiae...'

church of both nations (Greek and Indian) acknowledged the pre-
eminence of the Roman see.' Even if it could be shown that 'the Greeks
had continually resisted the Roman church', it would count for little since
Charles is no less 'king of all Spain because several towns have revolted.'
The strength of the papacy '...rests in the agreement of the catholic
church.'[71]

It is interesting to observe that More rests his case for the primacy
precisely on the consent of the church. This suggests that he viewed it at
this time as an organ of government established by the Christian community, possibly something which had grown up over a period of years.
This is consistent with Pole's later assertion that More at one stage in his
life had considered the papacy of purely ecclesiastical institution and that
only serious study had brought him to the point of conviction concerning
its divine origin. The disparity which emerges in More's attitude to the
primacy between the *Baravellus* and *Rosseus* editions of the *Responsio* rein-
forces the argument for dating his change of heart to this period in his life.

In the *Rosseus* edition More claimed that he had wished to avoid discussing the primacy: 'I had not intended, reader, to say anything at all in this
passage on the power of the pope,' but was 'dragged here against my will
by the fellow's confusing discussion in which he has so entangled the question of the church with the question of the pope that I could not answer
him on the one without touching somewhat on both.' More added that he
would gladly have refrained from discussing the primacy and indeed any
other matters except those which concerned Luther's answer to Henry.
Other writers have already dealt with Luther's vagaries, not least John
Fisher, Bishop of Rochester. 'Certainly, as far as the primacy of the pope
is concerned, the same venerable bishop rendered the matter very clear
from the gospels, from the Acts of the Apostles, from the whole body of the
Old Testament, from the agreement of all the holy fathers, not only the
Latin but also the Greek...and finally from the fact that Armenians and
Greeks were defeated, and admitted themselves defeated, by definition of
a general council... Consequently', More asserted, 'I considered that I
would be acting uselessly and opening a closed issue if I were to weave a
fresh web of writing about the primacy of the pope.'[72]

In point of fact, however, though the question of the primacy remained
marginal to More's interest at the time, he did feel obliged to add a few

[71] See *Responsio*, 340/21-348/34, tr. 341/23-349/37. See in particular 348/28-32: '...cuius
robur consistit consensu ecclesiae catholicae: quae plane fuisset in reliquis nationibus: etiam
si perpetuo fecisset Graecia: quod nunc faciunt quaedam rura Boemica.'
[72] See *Responsio*, 138/1-140/5, tr. 139/1-141/6.

skeins to Fisher's web of argumentation. In so doing he revealed a clear
line of development from his brief skirmish with the issue in the *Baravellus*
edition. More's examination of the issue began with the question of the
identity of the church of Christ. He repeated Henry's assertion that the
church of Christ is the one which has the pope as its head. He then went on
to defend Catharinus's case for the same belief. In particular he analysed
Luther's exegesis of the critical petrine text: Mt 16, 18-19.

Luther had argued that 'the keys of the kingdom of heaven' were promised to Peter by Christ, but that there was no evidence that they had ever
been given.[73] More replied, following Catharinus,[74] that whatever Christ
had promised must have been granted. Hence Peter must have received
the power of the keys.[75] The greater part of the discussion revolved around
the earlier part of the text, as to whether Christ had in fact named Peter as
the rock on which his church was to be built? Luther had contended that
the term 'rock' in this text referred not to Peter but to Christ if the text
were understood in a spiritual sense.[76] Catharinus conceded this point but
maintained that this pericope like any other must first be taken in its literal
sense. The literal sense clearly indicated Peter as the 'rock' on which the
church was to be founded.[77] More taunted Luther with inconsistency on
this issue. 'Recently you were saying that not the spiritual and mystical
but only the literal meaning proves anything. But now suddenly, since
Catharinus granted that it is true spiritually that Christ is the rock, but
that in the passage of Matthew Christ was nevertheless not speaking about
His own pre-eminence but about placing a vicar in charge of His flock,
you immediately take a fancy to that spiritual meaning and prefer it to the
literal for proving your point. From his granting that you speak the truth
in some sense, especially in the spiritual sense, you conclude that he speaks
falsely when by means of the decisions of the holy fathers he resists your
distortion of the letter. Even if it is true, as it is, that Christ is most truly
and firmly the rock, most truly the head of the church and most truly the
foundation corner stone of the church who has made both one, nevertheless in that passage Christ was not speaking about His own sovereignty
but about substituting the primacy in His church. Not only do the saints
testify and the Christian world agree to this, but even the sequence of the
line itself seems to demonstrate it clearly; nor does the sense which you

[73] See Luther, *Ad librum Catharini responsio*, (1521) *WA* 7, 711/20-712/7.
[74] See Catharinus, *Apologia*, 93/11-95/16.
[75] See *Responsio*, 122/33-124/16, tr. 123/37-125/17.
[76] See Luther, *Ad librum Catharini responsio*, *WA* 7, 708/15-710/27.
[77] See Catharinus, *Apologia*, 219/19-220/23.

assign seem to fit very exactly. It is as though Christ were saying, "You are Peter, and therefore I shall build my church upon myself."'[78] More concluded, 'Because of the steadfastness of Peter's faith, Christ made him head and primate of His church, as a rock standing in his own place...'[79]

In More's mind there seemed little room for doubt. Christ appointed Peter as head of the church, the foundation stone on which the visible .edifice was to be built but in such a way as not to derogate from Christ's role as spiritual head, foundation and corner-stone.[80] Peter's primacy was to be never more than vicarious. In adopting this interpretation of Mt 16, 18, More was following a tradition of exegesis common though far from invariable among medieval protagonists of the papal cause. Because of his faith in Christ, Peter was named as rock. The term *rock* designated neither Peter's faith nor Christ as other traditional explanations had maintained. It denoted the person of Peter himself.[81] In subordination to Christ himself he was the rock on which the church was to be built.

Transmission of primatial office

More then went on to deal with the question of the passing on of petrine office. To him it seemed abundantly clear that Christ had intended Peter's primacy to be maintained in his successors throughout the history of the church. 'Because of the steadfastness of Peter's faith, Christ made him the head and primate of His church, as a rock standing in His own place, not as though Peter were immortal and so could hold office forever, but many would successively follow him into that office, and these not all of equal merit.'[82] In More's eyes, moral inadequacy did not modify the validity of

---

[78] See *Responsio*, 130/19-132/5, tr. 131/25-133/5.

[79] See *Responsio*, 134/15-17, tr. 135/17-19.

[80] Headley makes a useful observation here concerning More's terminology in regard to the petrine office. He reserves derivatives of *praesidere* for Christ's headship while using derivatives of *praeficere* for Peter's vicariate. The latter usage implies in the context of Roman praxis a clear sense of delegated and subordinate authority. See Headley, *Responsio*, 765-766.

[81] See Franz Gillmann, *Zur scholastischen Auslegung von Mt 16, 18,* in *Archiv fur katholisches Kirchenrecht* 104 (1924) 40-53.

[82] See *Responsio*, 134/15-20, tr. 135/17-22; ibid, 140/21-23, tr. 141/26-28: 'Surely, as regards the pope, God who put him in charge of His church knew what an evil it would have been to have lacked a pope; and I do not think one should desire the Christian world to learn this by experience at its own risk.' More had expressed his respect for the pope as Christ's vicar on previous occasions without commiting himself to any particular view of the origin of his office. Defending Erasmus's translation of the new testament against an anonymous monk he argued from papal approval to its essential authenticity. See Thomas More to a Monk, (1519-1520), Rogers, *Correspondence*, 192/1011-1017: 'Quid quod Summus Pontifex, quod tu vituperas, bis iam accurate probauit? Quod Christi Vicarius velut diuinae vocis oraculo pronunciauit vtile, id tu puer propheta Altissimi vaticinaris esse damnosum. Quod

tenure. In contradistinction to the Wittenberg reformer the English
humanist held to an essential distinction between ecclesiastical office and
personal grace: '...many would successively follow him (Peter) into that
office, and these not all of equal merit. Since this is so, even if the name
"rock" does not fit them, is the power of office for that reason not the
same?'[83] More believed this to be the testimony of scripture. Succession to
Peter's place in the church brought with it the same authority which Peter
enjoyed of binding and loosing, the power of the keys, the commission to
govern the church in the varied aspects of its life on earth.[84]

The nature of petrine authority

More did not expound at length the significance of Peter's role as foundation stone of the church nor develop a conception of his headship of the
church based on this image. He was content to briefly indicate that
supreme authority had been conferred upon him '...to whom as to the
chief of the apostles of Christ is believed to have given the keys of the

---

ex arce religionis summus ille Christiani orbis princeps suo testimonio cohonestat, id tu...
conspurcas.' See also Thomas More to Edward Lee, Greenwich 27 February (1520),
Rogers, *Correspondence,* 210/53-57. More was careful to point out that the petrine office was
not linked irrevocably to the see of Rome: 'And although God seems to have chosen the city
of Rome, as the most renowned place in all the world, nevertheless no one of those who
maintain the primacy of its see has any doubt that wherever the see of Peter may be transferred, there also would be transferred the authority of Peter' in *Responsio,* 166/6-10, tr.
167/5-12.

[83] See *Responsio,* 134/15-23, tr. 135/17-29; ibid., 80/15-82/10, tr. 81/16-83/12, where
More treats with scant respect Luther's rejection of the papacy on the grounds of the immorality of some of its incumbents. He dismisses this argument as absurd, speaking of the
primacy as '*the holy office*'. For Luther's position, see Luther, *Ad librum Catharini responsio, WA*
7, 712, 723; *Contra Henricum regem angliae, WA* 10/2, 190/27-28, 31-32. See also *Responsio,*
140/14-21, tr. 141/16-24 where More dwells on the repercussions on civil society if Luther's
theory of office were applied in the civil sphere: 'I am also much moved by the consideration
that if the faults of men should be imputed to their offices in this manner, not only will the
papacy not endure but also royal power, and supreme magistracy, and the consulate and
every administrative office whatever will fall into ruin and the people will be without a ruler,
without law and order. If this should ever happen, and it seems to threaten in several places
of Germany, then men will finally realize at great loss what a profound difference there is in
human affairs between having bad rulers and having no rulers.' More's fears were partially
realised in the Peasants' War of 1524-25 in Germany. The Lollard experience in England
more than likely lay behind this concern.

[84] See *Responsio,* 148/20-23, tr. 149/23-25: '...the devil will not prevail against the faith of
Peter nor against the power given to Peter of binding and of loosing which has been passed
on in an unbroken succession...' ibid., 150/15-19, tr. 151/17-21: '...Christ was promising
that no wiles of the devil would be powerful enough to extinguish the faith of the church
which He was committing to the care of Peter, or be able to impair his authority and power
of binding and loosing; we see that this promise has been realized up till now.'

church so that by him others might enter and be excluded...'[85] In this phraseology More was viewing petrine authority, still in the context of Mt 16, 18-19, in terms of the right to admit or exclude from the church. In its full signification, however, the promise envisaged a broader sweep of authority to embrace all regulations governing the life and discipline of the church. This interpretation is reinforced by More's use of Jn 21, 17, 'Feed my sheep'. The words were addressed to Peter. They clearly conferred on him authority to govern the church in all aspects of its life.[86]

Against this church 'the gates of hell will not prevail.' (Mt 16, 18) Luther had interpreted the words 'gates of hell' to mean the devil. Whenever men sinned the devil had prevailed. The devil had prevailed in this way over the pope's church. Hence the promise could refer only to the hidden spiritual church of true believers.[87] Luther was here referring to his concept of the true church of Christ as an invisible communion of the just, that hidden body of true believers whose bond with their saving Lord could be broken only by the sin against the Spirit, the explicit rejection of God's saving mercy. More countered by attacking Luther's interpretation, not of the word 'church' but of the term 'gates of hell'. In his view this did not refer to the devil. On the strength of ancient authorities whom he left unnamed, More suggested two possible explanations. Firstly, he suggested that the 'gates of hell' could be a metaphor for '...the rulers and sovereigns of the world who persecuted the infant church but did not prevail against her.' Secondly, he postulated that the phrase could

---

[85] See *Responsio*, 272/25-29, tr. 273/32-36; ibid., 328/25-30, tr. 329/26-32: 'But however much the indulgences of the pontiff may be disputed, the words of Christ necessarily remain unshaken, by which He committed to Peter the keys of the church when He said: "Whatever you shall bind on earth shall be bound also in heaven; and whatever you shall loose on earth, shall be loosed also in heaven." Likewise: "Whose sins you shall forgive they shall be forgiven; and whose sins you shall retain they shall be retained."' (Jn 20, 23) See also ibid., 88/22-28, tr. 89/27-33: 'I certainly think that no one who has the slightest spark of faith can be persuaded that Christ, who prayed for Peter that his faith would not fail, (Lk 22, 32)... would allow her (the church) to be universally bound for so many ages by the empty signs of corporal things...' More also follows Catharinus in arguing that if the keys were promised, they must have been conferred on Peter as Christ could not but fulfil his promise. This was a move against Luther's contention that though the power of the keys was promised there was no scriptural evidence of their having been conferred. See *Responsio*, 122/33-124/2, 123/28-125/2; see Catharinus, *Apologia*, 93-95.

[86] See *Responsio*, 196/14-21, tr. 197/19-25: More asked Luther: '...why do you yourself basely conceal that in the very words of Christ, "Feed my sheep," there is a word which refutes you?...that there is in the repeated word *poimainein* the meaning "to rule"; (Jn 21, 17) but although everyone sees this, it is enough for you to pretend that you do not perceive it.'

[87] See Luther, *Ad librum Catharini responsio*, (1521), WA 7, 708/26-709/33; see also ibid., 712/8-39.

designate 'heretics and antichrists' neither of whom have overcome the church founded on Peter.[88] Even admitting the possibility of Luther's interpretation being correct, i.e. granting that 'gates of hell' is equivalent to evil or the devil, his application of this exegesis does not hold water. The power of evil '...prevails only against the man who is finally so completely overthrown that he cannot rise again to the fight' i.e. when finally damned.[89] The significance of Christ's promises to Peter is precisely this: 'the devil will not prevail against the faith of Peter or against the power given to Peter of binding and of loosing which has been passed on in an unbroken succession...'[90] Although the members of the church and even its visible head may temporarily fail, as a body final defeat can never be theirs. Whichever explanation of the phrase 'gates of hell' is adopted, the church founded on Peter will not succumb completely either to persecution or to infidelity or to sin. So that even if Luther's exegesis is followed, it cannot mean that the church founded on Peter is not Christ's church for in virtue of Christ's own promises the petrine church must survive and triumph over sin. So too will the authority of Peter and his successors.

More concluded his formal treatment of the primacy with a summary of his views: he affirmed he was '...moved to obedient submission to this See' by the arguments which learned and holy men have advanced in support of the primacy; by the fact of history that those who had abandoned Rome in the past ended up by abandoning Christ; by the fear that '...if the faults of men should be imputed to their offices in this manner, not only will the papacy not endure but also royal power, and supreme magistracy, and the consulate and every administrative office whatever will fall into ruin...'[91] What was needed, he felt, was not the undermining of papal authority but prayer that God might bless the church with one or two saintly pontiffs to bring a renewal of spirit to Christian people.

EVIL IN THE CHURCH

Having dealt somewhat summarily with the notion of Roman primacy, Sir Thomas More turned his attention to what he had come to look on as one of the central issues of debate: the problem of moral evil in the church.

---

[88] See *Responsio*, 148/17-150/8, tr. 149/19-151/14. See Headley, *Responsio*, 897 for an examination of some medieval commentaries on this text. Two which fit the reference are the *Glossa ordinaria, MPL* 114, 142 and that of Nicholas of Lyra whose work is not cited.

[89] See *Responsio*, 150/25-28, tr. 151/29-32.

[90] See *Responsio*, 148/17-20, tr. 149/22-26. More probably had in mind Christ's promise to Peter in Lk 22, 31-32.

[91] See *Responsio*, 140/5-18, tr. 141/7-21.

As we briefly saw above, Luther argued from Mt 16, 18 that 'the gates of hell', i.e. sin would not overcome the members of Christ's church. But, he said, *de facto* we know that the pope and his followers have given in to sin.[92] Hence the pope's church cannot be the church of Christ. In many ways, given the scandalous character of a good deal of ecclesiastical administration at the time this was a persuasive argument. More argued on the contrary that Luther was misunderstanding the real nature of Christ's promise. As we have seen according to ancient tradition 'the gates of hell' did not signify personal sin as such but either persecution by the powers of this world or divisive forces such as heresy within the fold. Even granted Luther's interpretation, the powers of evil only overcome the individual irrevocably at death. 'Since this does not happen to anyone in the present life, it is clear that the words of Christ do not prevent even sinners from being able to belong to the Church in this life.'[93] More cited the example of Judas who had still retained his office as apostle after the betrayal of Jesus. Even Peter was seriously rebuked by his master for a misdemeanour shortly after receiving the power of the keys.[94] He went on to list a series of biblical precedents for the presence within God's people of sinners of various kinds: Noah's ark contained clean and unclean; Paul had to censure Corinthians and Galatians for grave immorality; the Spirit rebuked the seven churches in the book of Revelation, while our Lord himself had addressed the Twelve, saying 'and one of you is a devil.'[95]

Sinners always had and always will form part of Christ's church according to More: '...the church of Christ, while she dwells on earth, is not yet so cleansed that some sins do not constantly taint good men; and among the good men everywhere there live the wicked, who for the time being are in the church...For even though these men are not healthy, yet they are somehow still alive and are nourished by a certain warmth of the divine Spirit who animates and preserves the church... But when the day shall come on which, laying aside corruption, she shall be clothed with immortality, then, those rotten and decaying members disappearing, the body of the church will be left utterly pure and gleaming, which in the meantime goes about and will go about diseased, but however diseased, will never go about dead.' Moral evil affects the life of the church in all its aspects and at every level. It makes it no less the church of Christ for one must await the

---

[92] See Luther, *Ad librum Catharini responsio*, (1521), *WA* 7, 710/8-13.
[93] See *Responsio*, 142/19-152/14, tr. 143/23-153/12, especially 152/10-12, tr. 153/9-12.
[94] See *Responsio*, 160/12-30, tr. 161/15-34.
[95] See *Responsio*, 200/15-30, tr. 201/16-32. (See Gen 7, 8; I Cor 5, 1 ff; Gal 3, 1 ff; Rev 2, 5; 3, 16; Jn 13, 10.)

consummation of the kingdom to see the reality of Christ's church in all her glory. Sinners, except the excommunicate, remain part of the church. Even though in a diminished way, they share her spiritual life.[96]

Sin and office

In particular More had to deal with the problem of evil as it affected the holding of ecclesiastical office. It was part of Luther's general theology that church ministry was at heart a charism whose exercise was authorised by the community. He also held, however, that the exercise of office presupposed freedom from sin. In his work against Ambrosius Catharinus, Luther applied this principle to the papacy in particular. He argued that even if Peter had been established as head of the church, an individual could not succeed to Peter's office unless he also followed him in holiness of life.[97] More rejected this opinion: '...the case of a man and his office, of conduct and authority, of virtue and power is so distinct that, even though the heavenly life which God has promised to virtue is taken away from wicked and criminal men, nevertheless the earthly authority which God has joined to their office is not taken away.'[98]

More insisted on this, that appointment to office and the validity of functions exercised in virtue of such appointment were not dependent on the personal sanctity of the subject of office. If some of Peter's successors were not noted for holiness, their authority in the public life of the church was none the less for this. Otherwise, he argued, there would have been no priests in Israel after Moses and Aaron since no one could have matched their devotion. Nor could a man be a bishop unless he was totally the type described in the pastoral letters. Even Paul himself had respect for a bishop of dubious integrity while the evangelist notes that Caiaphas, wicked and ignorant as he was, received the spirit of prophecy on account of his office. The bible offers no support, in More's view, for any total meshing together of worthiness of life and the holding of public function in the church. Holiness is obviously desirable in those who exercise authority. The lack of it does not make their position untenable. They should still

---

[96] See *Responsio*, 202/3-17, tr. 203/3-20.

[97] See for example Luther, *Ad librum Catharini responsio*, (1521), *WA* 7, 709/30-33: 'Cum autem etiam S. Petrus, si praesens esset, non possit sciri, an sanctus esset et permaneret sine peccato, ideo necesse est, nec ipsum esse Petram, sed solum Christum, quem solum sine peccato esse et, permanere certissimum est et cum eo Ecclesiam suam sanctam in spiritu.'

[98] See *Responsio*, 132/33-134/4, tr. 133/38-135/4. See Catharinus, *Apologia*, 137-140.

be respected and obeyed for Christ recommended that the Pharisees be given due honour even though their example was not to be followed.[99]

The English experience of Lollardy probably made More sensitive to this theoretical and practical problem. The troubled decades which preceded Tudor accession to power would have warned him of the dangers of civil strife which could easily be promoted by an application to political life of Luther's theories relating to ecclesiastical office.[100] More looked on the distinction between personal grace and ecclesiastical office as one of the key issues in his dispute with Luther, one of vital importance for the conservation of Christendom, not merely spiritually but politically as well.

Signs of Christ's church

To More's way of thinking, Luther's claim that anyone affected by sin could not be a member of the church dissolved any real church into thin air: '...he reduces the palpable and commonly known church to an invisible one, from an external to an internal one, from an internal one he utterly reduces her to no church at all...'[101] And again: 'Does he not completely abolish every church, external and internal, visible and invisible, spiritual and physical?' Where indeed could the church be found?

Luther replied by pointing to three signs of the presence of a congregation of true believers, '...namely, baptism, the bread, and above all the gospel.' Of these the gospel is the most important. What is involved is not the written gospel but one proclaimed in speech: '...the genuine and authentic word which teaches the true faith of Christ...'[102] More was not

---

[99] More here cited several scripture passages: 1 Tim 3, 1-7, Tit 1, 7-10; Acts 23, 5; Jn 11, 49-52; Mt 23, 1-7. See *Responsio*, 134/23-136/1, tr. 135/27-137/2. More went on to point out that the term 'rock', contrary to Luther's opinion, may apply not merely to those strong in faith and piety as Peter was, but also to the weak and sinful. Similar usage is found in other passages in scripture. The name 'Christ' was applied to David as well as Jesus, (I Kg 24, 7); the name 'giant' given to a sinful man in Deut 3, 11 and, according to Augustine, to Jesus in Ps 18, 6; the term 'serpent' was used of the devil in Gen 3, 1, yet applied to Christ in Jn 3, 14; and so on. Hence the validity of using the metaphor 'rock' for a sinful incumbent of Peter's chair.

[100] See *Responsio*, 140/14-24, tr. 141/16-24 where the implications for civil government of Luther's views are drawn out. See also A. G. Dickens, *Lollards and Protestants in the Diocese of York 1509-1558*, Oxford, 1959, 16-52; M. E. Aston, *Lollardy and Sedition, 1381-1431, Past and Present* 17 (1960) 1-44; J. A. F. Thomson, *The Later Lollards 1414-1520*, Oxford, 1965; G. Leff, *Heresy in the Later Middle Ages*, Manchester, 1967, 494-605. More general accounts will be found in E. F. Jacob, *The Fifteenth Century 1399-1485*, Oxford, 1961, 211-263, 464-645; B. Wilkinson, *The Later Middle Ages in England 1216-1485*, London, 1969, 234-304; M. Keen, *England in the Later Middle Ages*, London, 1973, 226-247; 302-512.

[101] See *Responsio*, 148/5-8, tr. 149/5-9. See also 156/18-19, tr. 157/20-21.

[102] See Luther, *Ad Librum Catharini responsio*, (1521), *WA* 7, 720/32-721/28.

over-impressed with the logic of this argument, claiming that it was inevitably circular in construction: one must know the gospel before one can know the church and vice-versa. His main *riposte*, however, took the shape of a substantial claim that Luther's three signs are in fact embodied in the traditional church of Christendom. Here one finds baptism administered, the eucharist celebrated, the gospel preached in accordance with scripture, and moreover the authentic tradition of the Christian people preserved and respected.[103]

Indeed, More remarked, even the preaching of the gospel in accordance with Luther's criteria cannot constitute an apodictic sign of the presence of Christ's congregation, for although it may be recognised as God's word, this will say more about the preacher's relationship to Christ than it will about his hearers. In fact there is no way of being certain that any one of them is truly justified, truly a member of the church of Christ.[104] Hence this cannot be an unambiguous sign of the church as understood by Luther. Another approach is required. More based his on the assumption that one must first come to a knowledge of Christ's church before committing oneself in faith to his message. This message has been confided to the care of the church. To reach it in its entirety one must first know and accept the church of Christ. If the unbeliever is to discover this church then it cannot be a hidden congregation. It must be palpable, visible, recognisable, located in place.

It was with these ideas in mind that More wrote: '...neither does anyone doubt, even if it is true that there is no place in the whole world where there cannot be a congregation of the faithful, that there must still necessarily be some place in which a definite church may be recognizable and certain. Otherwise no one could be certain which are the true scriptures, nor could anyone know where to turn who, as yet an unbeliever, wishes to be instructed in the faith and to learn thoroughly the Christian teachings.'[105] Where is such a church to be found and how is it to be known? More imagines the case of an unbeliever seeking to know Christ and his church. He wanders through many Christian nations '...and would perceive everywhere the same faith, the same teachings regarding what is necessary for salvation; when he would perceive from the writings of ancient holy men that all the holy doctors from the time of Christ's passion even to the present time have consistently agreed on these same points; then E (the man in question) would have no doubt that, if there is

---

[103] See *Responsio*, 182/5-13, tr. 183/5-14.
[104] See *Responsio*, 186/5-188/22, tr. 187/7-189/26.
[105] See *Responsio*, 166/10-16, tr. 167/13-20.

any true church of Christ on earth, it is this congregation which, begun by Christ, spread by the apostles, taught by the saints, has by God's special care persisted unceasingly through so many ages in the unity of the Christian faith.'[106] The conclusion for him was obvious: '...it follows that this multitude which constitutes the catholic church, this church, I say, from which the faith is learned and the scripture determined, is the common multitude of those who profess the name and faith of Christ, even though their life may not correspond to their profession... this multitude which we all know by the name of the Christian people, almost all of whom acknowledge the primacy of the Roman pontiff...'[107]

The logic of More's exposition is not beyond criticism. He was attempting to do several things at the same time and it is questionable whether the ordering of his argument was the best possible. He had implicitly worked out what he believed to be two essential signs of the church of Christ: its *unity in faith* in the present, its *continuity in faith* with the past. Because these signs are verified in the common multitude of Christians he identified this multitude as the church of Christ. This led him into an initial definition of Christ's church as 'the common multitude of those who profess the name and faith of Christ...' Sinlessness is not an essential quality of the church. Unity and continuity of faith are. We shall leave over a discussion of More's definition of the church till later in order to pass some comment on his apologetic method at this point.

This argument of More's represented a serious attempt to produce sure and convincing signs of the presence of the authentic Christian community. Catholic apologetic was to take a varied course in the centuries to come.[108] There had been little need for apologetic argument in the middle

---

[106] See *Responsio*, 190/2-11, tr. 191/3-13. See also ibid., 190/30-192/5, tr. 191/37-193/6.

[107] See *Responsio*, 172/1-10, tr. 173/1-11. More pointed out in addition that the signs Luther proposed as indicating the presence of his truly spiritual church '...all aply to this very church which he says is not true and which he calls papist.' in ibid., 173/12-15.

[108] See G. Thils, *Les Notes de l'Église dans l'apologétique catholique depuis la réforme*, Gembloux, 1937, x-xiii, 2-8. Thils distinguished four schools of apologetic method: the scriptural, Augustinian, Lerinian, and symbolic. The scriptural group emphasises the indefectibility of the church as well as its universality, visibility, holiness, its unity and the occurrence within it of the phenomenon of miracles. All of this it saw as based on Christ's promise. The Augustinian group emphasised consensus in faith, miracles, apostolic succession, and the name catholic itself. The Lerinian school, following St Vincent of Lérins, took his phrase '*quod ubique, quod semper, quod ab omnibus*' as their programme. The symbolic group based their argument on the ninth article of the creed of Constantinople: '...et unam sanctam, catholicam et apostolicam Ecclesiam.' This latter method came to predominate in the course of the sixteenth century and held the field for many years to come. More might best be grouped with the Augustinian school though the line between this and the scripturally based group, with whom he also had affinities, is rather thin.

ages within the boundaries of Christendom itself. More was probably
drawing on his knowledge of the apologetic writings of the fathers, notably
Saint Augustine, in the method he adopted. As presented, however, it had
serious deficiencies since he failed to show, at least in the immediate context of his argument, that the signs he proposed were necessarily those
which Christ himself had proffered for the identity of his true followers.
More in fact was using for apologetic purposes what constituted his own
personal insight into the inner nature of the church, namely its inner unity
in the Spirit expressing itself in a communion of faith. Unity of faith when
extended in time becomes continuity. So the two signs he proposed as
marking out the presence of the true congregation of Christ were *the common faith of the living community,* in the first instance, and their *communion in
faith with preceding generations* as far back as the fellowship of the apostles, in
the second instance.

Definition of the church

To the present day reader as to Thomas More himself this question of
the signs of the church inevitably raises the question as to what the church
is? More unfortunately tended to treat this question as marginal to his
treatment of other topics rather than sitting down, so to speak, and examining the question systematically and thoroughly. One suspects that he
was so convinced of the rightness of the traditional church that he felt it
needed little careful delineation. Consequently More revealed his views
parenthetically rather than directly. Nonetheless such parentheses recur at
regular intervals so that without too much difficulty it is possible to put
together a composite picture.

The ecclesial dimension to most theological topics inevitably cropped up
in More's mind. Was it an accident that when speaking of the role of the
Spirit in guiding the Christian people into communion he should
characterise the Catholic Church in these terms: 'Therefore, since you admit that it is the Spirit of God who makes people who dwell in a house to be
of one mind (Ps 67, 7) and in agreement on necessary matters, you must
admit willy-nilly that that church is the catholic church and the house of
God...'[109] This was More in his *Baravellus* disguise emphasising the
spiritual power of the world-wide Christian fellowship. When he put on
the mask of *Rosseus* he was more anxious to emphasise the visible and
palpable elements in the church: '...it follows that this multitude which

---

[109] See *Responsio,* 624/5-9, tr. 625/6-9.

constitutes the catholic church, this church, I say, from which the faith is learned and the scripture determined, is the common multitude of those who profess the name and faith of Christ, even though their life may not correspond to their profession.'[110] Or again: '...the common multitude of Christians is the universally known and perceptible catholic church of Christ whose soldiers now conquer, now are conquered, so long as the church still battles on earth...'[111]

In his description of the church More was clearly anxious to ground it in space and time, in contrast to the Platonic concept of the church he ascribed to Luther. Similarly, he wished to make it fully comprehensive in contradistinction to Luther's élitist ideas. The church of Christ on earth is sinful as well as saintly, popular as well as hierarchical, local as well as international, ignorant as well as wise, always imbued with the divine Spirit who guarantees its radical fidelity to its founder.

Papacy and church

More showed some ambivalence in his treatment of the nexus between papacy and church. In some instances he made no bones about making the papacy appear an essential element in this empirical church. Thus he could exclaim: '...this church which you call papist is truly the catholic church of Christ...'[112] At the end of Bk I he exclaimed triumphantly: 'We have proved that the church which he (Luther) calls papistic is the true catholic church of Christ.'[113] At other times, however, he sensed that not all whom he would name Christian accepted the papacy: '...the church is this multitude which we all know now by the name of the Christian people, *almost all of whom* acknowledge the primacy of the pontiff...' And again, postulating that the church might be '...but the number of good men...it is certain that by far the *greatest portion* have for a long time now been among those nations which revere the See of Peter as the mother see.'[114] Thus there can be found a certain tension between a clear-cut affirmation of the papacy as an intrinsic part of the constitution of the church and on the other hand a realisation that this affirmation of the primacy was not as universal as he might have wished it to be.

---

[110] See *Responsio*, 172/8-10, tr. 173/1-6.
[111] See *Responsio*, 192/9-12, tr. 193/12-14. See also ibid., 196/30-33, tr. 197/36-39.
[112] See *Responsio*, 184/28-29, tr. 185/33-34.
[113] See *Responsio*, 318/22-23, tr. 319/27-29.
[114] See *Responsio*, 172/8-10, tr. 173/9-11; ibid., 192/32-194/6, tr. 193/37-195/7. See also ibid., 608/3-5, tr. 609/3-5.

More was undoubtedly aware that the Greeks had rejected the short-lived agreement of Ferrara-Florence reached on 6 July 1439.[115] This may have caused a degree of hesitation in his mind in identifying the church of Christ too unreservedly with the church centred on Rome. He resolved the hesitation by comparing the separation of Greeks and Armenians to a local rebellion against the emperor which in no way disrupted the integrity of the whole circumscription. Yet in a mind for which the principle of consent played such an important role were there no lurking doubts? Certainly it is false to say that he made the papacy one of the distinguishing marks of the church of Christ or that he had arrived in apologetic method at the *via primatus* several centuries before his time.[116] More proved the validity of Roman primacy from the validity of the church rather than the contrary.

It seems to me that Dr Headley overstates the case when he says that '...More's understanding of the church in 1523 had two foci: the papal primacy and the notion of a general consensus—both expressive of unity.'[117] As Dr Headley himself points out, More treated the question of primacy only *en passant* and somewhat unwillingly. When giving his reasons for accepting Roman papacy he said that he had been persuaded by the arguments of learned men, that loyalty to Rome had proven a reliable touchstone of Christian fidelity, as well as by the risk to society if authority and virtue became inextricably interdependent. He did not confess to a thorough personal investigation of the matter, so that as well as recognising the existence of a certain level of dissent in world Christianity on this issue, there may have been at the same time a feeling of dissatisfaction in his mind that he had not seen the evidence himself at first hand. Knowing the kind of man he was, and indeed aware perhaps that he subsequently would make the petrine office a subject of thorough investigation, it is not surprising that he showed some reluctance in discussing it at any length in this work. Consequently, I find it hard to agree with Dr Headley's judgment that at this stage, if ever, More viewed 'the papacy as the touchstone confirming and upholding all.'[118] I am inclined to think it was Luther rather than More who wished to make 'papist' the trade-name for 'this common multitude which constitutes the catholic church.'

---

[115] See J. Gill, *The Council of Florence*, Cambridge, 1959, 227-388.
[116] See Thils, *Les Notes de l'Église*, x, 57, 63, 156, 206-208, 339.
[117] See *Responsio*, 773.
[118] See *Responsio*, 773.

Jurisdiction

More's conception of the church as a social body made up of a vast throng of believers in no way diminished his awareness of the need for, and existence of, an organisational structure for its proper governance. We have already adverted to his acknowledgement of the fundamental principle of church order in his defence of sacramental ministry. In dealing with orders he did not elaborate on its consequences for church life nor on the canonical aspects of ecclesiastical institution. Although emphasising the role of the people in both church and state, More insisted on the need for order and authority in both spheres. Even in his *Utopia* there is no talk of the withering away of the state. Utopia was a highly organised society with a definite system of government designed to promote the welfare of all its citizens.[119] In so far as More opposed authority, it was tyrannical, unjust or inefficient government that he opposed.[120] Hence his concern that the authority of the church to govern its own affairs be upheld.

Martin Luther maintained that within the church there was no divinely-given authority to rule, only the command to love.[121] More on the contrary contended: '...surely, if you were not an utter toper, you would easily perceive that jurisdiction and the function of charity are not altogether the same; even if it is true that there is no Christian jurisdiction which has not been instituted out of charity. But still, the authority of a ruler can and ought to do many things which the charity of any one private individual neither can nor ought to arrogate to itself. Otherwise, if jurisdiction is nothing at all, why did Paul exercise jurisdiction? Why did he deliver a man over to Satan for the destruction of the flesh? Why did he declare most clearly that he who resists authority resists the ordinance of God? Why did he command that what he himself taught should be observed? Why did he command men to obey their rulers?...why do you yourself basely conceal that in the very words of Christ, "Feed my sheep," (Jn 21,

---

[119] See Thomas More, *Utopia*, ed. Edward Surtz and J. H. Hexter, New Haven and London, 1965, 122-125, 397-401.

[120] See Thomas More, *Translation of Lucian* (1506), ed. C. R. Thompson, New Haven and London, 1974, xxxviii-xxxix. See also Erasmus's comment: '...illi semper peculiariter inuisa fuerit tyrannis, quemadmodum aequalitas gratissima.', Allen, *Erasmi Epistolae*, IV, 15/87-89. See also *The Latin Epigrams of Thomas More*, ed. L. Bradner and C. A. Lynch, Chicago, 1953, nos. 91, 92, 93, 94, 96, 97. See also *Utopia*, 123-125, 197, 201.

[121] See Luther, *Ad librum Catharini responsio*, (1521), *WA* 7, 773/33-39. This position had already been adopted by Luther in his *De potestate papae*, (1519), *WA* 2, 194/21-197/39. See Headley's valuable note on this Lutheran concept in *Responsio*, 903-904. Headley also remarks: 'Already Fisher had insisted that *pascere* meant *regere* and that this jurisdiction pertained to the See of Peter, regardless of love' (*Confutatio*, 147 v-148).

17) there is a word which refutes you? You are not unaware, but you basely conceal the fact that Erasmus of Rotterdam, a man extremely learned
beyond all cavil and one who has deserved very highly of the church of
Christ, has noted the fact that there is in the repeated word *poimainein* the
meaning "to rule"...'[122]

It is worth noting here that More accepted Luther's basic contention
that authority in the church is derived fundamentally from the law of love.
Unlike the canonists and scholastic theologians of medieval tradition who
tended to ground the jurisdiction of the church either in the principles of
Roman law or ethics and politics of Aristotle,[123] More stayed strictly
within the biblical orbit, basing the right of those holding office in the
church to exercise juridical authority on the word of Christ as well as
Paul's example. Hence his rejection of Luther's claim that neither pope,
nor bishop, nor any man has any right to impose the slightest obligation
on a Christian man without his consent.[124] Christian authority springs
from love and must be guided by it, but this love expresses itself in positive
decisions binding on those who have submitted to the law of Christ. This
applies to all holding office in the church from the pope downwards.[125]

Holiness of the church

The fact that the church is visible, is involved in the ambiguities of
historical change, that it is subject to the weakness of the flesh, that it
needs to use the ordinary human means of law and administration to
achieve its ends, did not take away in More's eyes from the essential sanctity of this body. He never lost sight of the inner core of divinity hiding
behind the cloak of humanity often tattered and soiled. 'Moreover,
although the body of the church is perceptible to sense, yet the fact that
Christ is her mystical head is likewise shown not by sense but by faith. Indeed, this fact also, that whoever is holy on earth is part of this church,
which is called holy even here on earth not because there is no one in her
who sins but because no one on earth is holy who is not a member of this
church...'[126] A brave claim but one from which he never retreated. Christ

---

[122] See *Responsio*, 196/4-19, tr. 197/5-25. More cites I Cor 5, 5; Rm 13, 2; I Cor 11, 2; 2
Thess 2, 14; Hb 13, 17; Mt 23, 2-3; Jn 2, 13-17; Jn 21, 17 in support of his position. See
Erasmus, *Annotationes,* Basle, 1522, sig. T5v.

[123] See above pp. 23-33.

[124] See Luther, *De captivitate babylonica,* (1520), *WA* 6, 536/7-18. See above for a fuller exposition of Luther's view on this question.

[125] More cited *Assertio,* sig. K lrv and then added his own arguments: *Responsio,*
270/20-272/28, tr. 271/24-273/36 and passim.

[126] See *Responsio,* 200/2-7, tr. 201/2-8.

is always with his church by his presence, his word and his Spirit. More, although never blind to the scandals which afflicted the Christian world of his day, ever lived in the hope of the inner glory of the church being revealed to the whole world. 'But when the day shall come on which, laying aside corruption, she shall be clothed with immortality, then, those rotten and decaying members disappearing, the body of the church will be left utterly pure and gleaming...'[127]

CONCLUSION

In his *Responsio ad Lutherum* Sir Thomas More was drawn into a discussion of certain aspects of the theology of the church partly on practical, partly on theoretical grounds. Faced with the problem of backing up his patron Henry VIII he quickly realised that this task could not be carried out adequately by using scriptural sources alone. The very nature of the controversial ground he was treading obliged him to look beyond scripture to the faith of the church as expressed in past tradition and the living belief of the community. This was not a mere tactical manoeuvre. He recognised on strictly methodological grounds the insufficiency of scripture as a guide to Christian belief. He justified his trust in the faith of the community as criterion of belief by pointing out that scripture itself recognised its own insufficiency.

In discussing the role of the church in relation to faith More's principal emphasis lay on the role of the Spirit. The Spirit of God preserves and guides the church into all truth. The Spirit moreover leaves his mark on men's hearts. Before the written gospel had come into existence this inner gospel had been written on men's hearts. It is this inward gospel and not merely the written word of the bible which is reflected in the faith of the living community. Moreover it is to this gospel as expressed in the faith of past ages that patristic writings bear witness. This gospel and this faith are kept alive in the church by the action of the divine Spirit.

This was the essence of More's theory of tradition. The divine message is more extensive than scripture. The church because of Christ's promises (Mt 18, 20; Mt 28, 20; Jn 16, 13 etc.) retains the message in all its integrity. In order to discover it one must turn not merely to scripture but also to the common and constant faith of the church. Dr Headley is essentially right in associating More with the position adopted by Henry VIII as well as his associate, John Fisher, in proposing a 'two-source' theory of revelation. It might be more accurate, however, to speak of a two-channel theory

[127] See *Responsio*, 202/13-16, tr. 203/16-20.

of the transmission of revelation. More made no bones whatever about claiming tradition as an independent vehicle of the divine oracles. What is of special interest is the manner in which he conceived of tradition. Henry VIII had committed himself to relying in great measure on an independent oral tradition passed on 'from hand to hand'. More, on a different tack, opted for a pneumatic concept of tradition. The gospel for him was a message written by the Holy Spirit in the heart of the believer (Jer 31, 31-34; Heb 8, 10). This gospel expresses itself in consciousness in the faith of the church. What the Spirit writes is essentially complementary to the life and teaching of Jesus. It fills out what the written record has failed to provide and leads to a deeper understanding of holy writ. More did not exclude other media of tradition, neither oral, nor written, nor the living usage of the church. In his mind, however, at this date the over-riding principle was the working of the divine Spirit in the hearts of the faithful.

This latter consideration concerning the role of the church in the transmission of revelation led More into a further set of considerations. If the church transmits Christ's message the unbeliever must needs be in a position to identify this body. Consequently, the church must be visible, perceptible to the senses, located in space and time. The signs of the presence of Christ's followers are their unity in faith in the present and their communion in faith with past generations of Christians. Unity and continuity therefore are the two essential marks of the true church. These signs are verified in no other body than 'the common, known catholic church' presided over by the bishop of Rome. 'The multitude of Christians is the universally known and perceptible catholic church of Christ.' The sinfulness of its members makes this no less the body of Christ. Moral evil is inextricably caught up in the church's existence in the world of time.

More recognised the ordered structure of this community in his defence of sacramental ministry. He did not develop at length a theology of office or ministry. Nonetheless he specifically distinguished office from virtue insisting on the validity of the former independently of the latter. Similarly he advanced a theology of jurisdiction in the church, founding it on the divine command to love, yet recognising that this in turn must lead at the social level to the power of legislation, correction, judgment and punishment. In so far as he discussed office, More concentrated on that of the bishop of Rome, though even here his treatment was not exhaustive.

The arguments he offered for Peter's primacy were based on a straightfoward exegesis of the classical *locus,* Mt 16, 18, with indirect reference to Lk 22, 32, and Jn 21, 16-17. There are indications of a development of More's thought in this area in the interval between the publication of the *Baravellus* and *Rosseus* editions of the *Responsio*. In the former version he spoke of the primacy as a constitutional creation of the church. In the latter he made an unequivocal affirmation both of the conferral of primacy on Peter and of its transmission by divine will to his successors in the see of Rome. More did not expand on the authority of the pope. He spoke of him as *praefectus ecclesiae*, terminology, which as Headley notes, suggests a sense of delegated authority in subordination to Christ, mystical head of the community. This authority is mainly one of governance. There is little mention of a doctrinal magisterium of any great significance on the part of the papacy, though he did appeal to papal authority to vindicate the validity of Erasmus's translation of the new testament.

Nor did Sir Thomas More greatly stress the role of bishops in the conduct of church affairs. He treated briefly of the general council, adopting a 'populist' representative theory of council without necessarily suggesting that representation meant election. In all likelihood his own political and constitutional background underlay his views in this field, which would suggest at least that for him ultimate authority lay with the people. This is confirmed by his theory of consensus.

More relied principally on the consensus of the believing community when it came to the question of authenticating scripture, distinguishing traditions and interpreting the word of God. Because of Christ's promises the common faith of the church can never be in error. Was this a layman's approach, preferring the guidance of the Spirit through the ranks of the ordinary faithful to the decrees of the hierarchy gathered in council? There may have been something of this at work. One must recall as well, however, that More's *Responsio* as a work of polemic was committed to meeting an opponent on his own ground and over-riding his arguments. By 1523 Martin Luther had rejected not merely papal but conciliar authority as well. Hence in appealing to the common faith of the church as guide to belief More was coming as close as possible to Luther's ground, though he had to admit to an essential difference in identifying this community of faith. While Luther spoke of a hidden community of believers, More recognised the common multitude of Christians known as the Catholic Church as the true community of faith.

In the *Responsio* More had not yet become fully aware of the difficulties of identifying the true church of Christ, though his revision of the *Baravellus* shows an increasing awareness of the centrality of this issue. His later work against Tyndale was to bring him 'to the breast of all this matter'. In the meantime he was content to take very much for granted that the visible multitude of Christians was this true church. Their essential sinfulness was not hidden from him but their equally essential holiness was part of the vision to which he clung: '...whoever is holy on earth is part of this church, which is called holy even here on earth not because there is no one in her who sins but because no one on earth is holy who is not a member of this church; this fact, I say, is taught us by faith, not by sense.'[128] Underlying the often shabby clothing of Christ's followers he saw the gleam of divine light. 'For, even if the identity of that church which agrees on matters of faith is evident to sense, yet it is not evident to sense that this agreement does not come about by human conspiring but that it is divinely born and inspired, for this no one grasps except by faith. Moreover, although the body of the church is perceptible to sense, yet the fact that Christ is her mystical head is likewise shown not by sense but by faith.'[129] *Pace* Dr Headley, it is this spiritual dimension I would regard as the central axis of More's thought on the church. It was not he but Martin Luther who wished to make the papacy the most characteristic element in Catholic Christianity. On More's confidence in the abiding presence of the Spirit all else hangs; his respect for scripture, his sense and understanding of tradition, his submission to the consensus of faith, his defence of an often morally dubious hierarchy, his personal assurance of ultimate victory over evil.

---

[128] See *Responsio*, 200/4-8, tr. 201/4-8.
[129] See *Responsio*, 198/30-200/4, tr. 199/37-201/4.

CHAPTER FOUR

THE DIALOGUE

INTRODUCTION

In the years following the publication of his *Responsio* in 1523 More's links with the world of religious controversy remained alive.[1] Circumstances required it. The embargo on the importation of Lutheran publications stemming from Wolsey's commission of May 1521 may have slowed down the drift towards Wittenberg.[2] Nonetheless clandestine groups of reformers continued to flourish and grow.[3] In 1524 More's friend Erasmus was drawn into the battle-lines with his *Diatribe seu collatio de libero arbitrio* which challenged Luther's position on freedom of the will.[4] The following year, 1525, More had the opportunity of meeting Johann Eck, one of the leading German literary opponents of the revolutionary movement and presented him with a copy of his *Responsio ad Lutherum.*[5]

Nor did Wittenberg lose its specific interest in the English scene. That same year John Bugenhagen, a pastor in Wittenberg itself and a close colleague of Luther's, published his *Epistola sanctis qui sunt in anglia.*[6] This was intended to encourage Lutheran sympathisers dismayed by the apparent confusion existing among the reformers on several issues, as well as to get rid of the bad taste left by the savagery of the Peasants' Revolt (1524-25). Bugenhagen attempted to reassure them concerning the central Lutheran

---

[1] See Andre Prévost, *Thomas More,* 167-196; Rainer Pineas, *Thomas More and Tudor Polemics,* 30-119; W. A. Clebsch, *England's Earliest Protestants,* New Haven, 1964, passim; L. A. Schuster, *Thomas More's Polemical Career, 1523-1533,* in *Confutation* III, 1135-1268.

[2] See Clebsch, *England's Earliest Protestants,* 258-270 for an account of the largely unsuccessful attempt to counteract the Lutheran publicity campaign mainly forbidding the circulation and possession of proscribed books, by invoking sanctions against the authors, printers, sellers, buyers and readers of forbidden publications, and finally by developing a counter-propaganda campaign in which Thomas More was to play a leading role.

[3] See Porter, *Reformation and Reaction,* 41-49; Hughes, *Reformation in England,* I, 132-146; Clebsch, *England's Earliest Protestants,* passim.

[4] See Preserved Smith, *Erasmus,* New York, London, 1922, 320-371; Roland H. Bainton, *Erasmus of Rotterdam,* 185 ff.; J. D. Tracy, *Erasmus, the Growth of a Mind,* Geneva, 1972, 167-236; K. H. Oelrich, *Der späte Erasmus und die Reformation,* Münster, 1961.

[5] See H. S. Herbrüggen, *Sir Thoms More, Neue Briefe,* Münster, 1966, 54; Pierre Fraenkel, *Johann Eck und Sir Thomas More 1525-1526,* in *Von Konstanz nach Trient, Festgabe für August Franzen,* ed. R. Bäumer, Münich, Paderborn, Vienna, 1972, 482-495.

[6] See *Joannes Bugenhagen epistola ad anglos,* Wittenberg, February 1525. An English translation (STC 4021) was published in 1536.

thesis of justification by faith in Christ's mercy. More replied in a lengthy letter, refuting Bugenhagen's case paragraph by paragraph on the same lines as his reply to Luther.[7] Martin Luther himself extended an olive branch to Henry on the mistaken assumption that the latter was beginning to evince signs of support for the evangelical cause. Luther's advances were a little premature as a sharp rebuff from Henry soon made clear.[8]

This same year, 1526, witnessed another significant development in the growth of an evangelical faction in England: William Tyndale's first publications.[9] Tyndale, born in Gloucestershire about 1495, received his M.A. in Oxford in 1515 and then transferred to Cambridge. Ordained to the priesthood, he initially took up service as chaplain to a Cotswolds baronet, Sir John Walsh. His first venture into scholarship was probably a translation of Erasmus's *Enchiridion militis christiani,* but in July 1523 he approached Tunstal, Bishop of London, with a view to obtaining support for an English translation of the bible. The times were unpropitious. Following Tunstal's refusal, with the help of a London merchant Henry Monmouth, Tyndale departed for Wittenberg to join the ranks of the evangelical movement. He settled into his project of translating the new testament, and with the help of his amanuensis William Roye, an ex-Franciscan, by March 1526 the first copies were crossing the sea to England.[10]

Tyndale followed up the initial success of his new testament, first printed in Cologne in 1525, with a pamphlet published in 1526 at Worms: *Prologue upon the Epistle of St Paul to the Romans,* largely a borrowing from Luther's *Introduction to Romans* (1522).[11] This was followed some two years later by a further restatement of the doctrine of justification, in *The Parable*

---

[7] See E. F. Rogers, *Correspondence,* 323-365 for the text of this letter. For the general context, see E. F. Rogers, *Sir Thomas More's Letter to Bugenhagen, The Modern Churchman* 35 (1946) 350-360.

[8] Luther's letter arrived in March 1526. An English version may be found in E. Doernberg, *Henry VIII and Luther,* 50-53; see also Henry's reply *Literarium...quibus...Henricus octauus...respondet ad quandam epistolam Lutheri,* pr. Pynson, 2, December 1526.

[9] See J. Mozley, *William Tyndale,* London, 1937; R. Demaus, *William Tyndale,* London, 1886; M. M. Knappen, *Tudor Puritanism,* Chicago, 1939; W. A. Clebsch, *England's Earliest Protestants 1520-1535,* 137-204. Titles of Tyndale's works in the text are taken from the edition by Henry Walter, Parker Society, Cambridge, 3 Vols, 1848-50.

[10] Tyndale's *New Testament* was published in Worms in 1526. A fragment exists of an earlier version printed in Cologne the previous year.

[11] M. Luther, *Vorrede auf die Epistel S. Pauli an die Römer,* (1522), *WA* 10/2; William Tyndale, *A compendious introduccion/prologe or preface vn to/the pistle off Paul to the Romayns,* Worms, 1526.

of the Wicked Mammon,[12] and *The Obedience of a Christian Man* dealing with princely sovereignty.[13] Although Tyndale's new testament was the work which caused most alarm to the authorities, works by other writers also attracted attention. Jerome Barlowe's *The beryeng of the masse,* Strasbourg, 1528, was a vicious satire on the ecclesiastical establishment.[14] The previous year, 1527, had seen the publication of a pamphlet in a different vein, William Roye's *A Brefe Dialoge/bitwene a Christen Father and his stobborne Sonne,* Strasbourg, 1527.[15] The latter publication marked a swing away from Wittenberg and a turning towards Ulrich Zwingli of Geneva for inspiration, (Zwinglian ideas had been brought from Geneva to Strasbourg by Martin Bucer). This current of thought was to have further ramifications in the history of the Reformation but did not enter greatly into Sir Thomas More's sphere of concern.

Propaganda activities of this kind as well as the preaching of evangelists such as Thomas Bilney and Thomas Arthur brought their inevitable reaction. The bishops at Wolsey's instance acted in concert to have as many copies of Tyndale's new testament destroyed as possible, having them publicly burned at St Paul's Cross, 28 October 1526. Agents on the continent were employed to track down pirate printers and get them closed down. In March 1528 a search at Oxford for heretical literature uncovered a collection of one hundred titles in the hands of undergraduates or in circulation among them while the Cambridge circle continued to flourish. Things were clearly getting out of hand.[16] Moreover, at an international level, the problem had been made more pressing by the sack of Rome in 1527, and the defeat of the Hungarian armies by the Turks at Mohacs, bringing the invaders to the very gates of Vienna.

In this situation Cuthbert Tunstal, bishop of London, decided that something more was required. His inclination prompted him to invite his friend Thomas More to take up the case for the defence of traditional

---

[12] See William Tyndale, *The parable of the wicked mammon,* Antwerp, May 1528. This was largely based on a sermon of Luther's *Sermon von dem unrechten Mammon, WA* 10/3, 273-282; 283-292. See L. J. Trinterud, *A Reappraisal of William Tyndale's Debt to Martin Luther, Church History* 31 (1962) 24-25; Clebsch, *England's Earliest Protestants,* 146-149.

[13] William Tyndale, *The obedience of a Christen man and how Christen rulers ought to gouerne,* 2 October 1528 (STC 24446); for a description of the work see *Confutation* II, 1071, No. 7.

[14] See *Confutation,* 1070, for a description of this work.

[15] See Anthea Hume, *William Roye's 'Brefe Dialoge' (1527). An English Version of a Strassburg Catechism,* in *Harvard Theological Review* 60 (1967) 307-321. For a description of the work see *Confutation,* 1069, no. 4. (no. 24223-3 in the revised edition of *STC*).

[16] See Schuster, *Confutation* III, 1173, citing Foxe, 5, ii, Appendix 6. See also H. C. Porter, *Reformation and Reaction in Tudor Cambridge,* Cambridge, 1958, 41-73; E. G. Rupp, *Studies in the Making of the English Protestant Tradition,* Cambridge, 1947, 15-46.

belief and to use his considerable talents as intellectual and *littérateur* to bring home to the general public the absurdity of the new-fangled views. This was the background to the official commission given to More on 7 March 1527/8: 'Because you, dearest brother, can rival Demosthenes in our vernacular as well as in Latin, and are a frequent and brilliant advocate of the Catholic position whenever it is publicly challenged, you will never find a better way of spending any leisure hours you can snatch away from your official duties than in publishing in English for the common man some books that would help him see through the cunning malice of heretics and so keep him alerted and better fortified against these traitorous subverters of the Church.' Tunstal also gave More official permission to read prohibited books as well as a gift of a collection which had been confiscated.[17]

It was against this background and in the light of this commission that More published in 1529 his first major vernacular work of controversy, the *Dialogue Concerning Heresies*.[18]

The original title indicates the main thrust of the work. It was a defence of the peripheral practices of the faithful as well as an attack on what he believed to be the central tenets of the developing theological position of Wittenberg and its outstanding English spokesman, William Tyndale. More's appreciation of Luther's position had not greatly advanced since 1523. His awareness of Tyndale's ideas seems to have been drawn mainly from his translation of the new testament, *The Mammon of Iniquity,* and *The Obedience of a Christian Man*[19] to which explicit reference is made in the course of the work, as well as Barlowe's work on *The beryenge of the masse.*[20]

The general tone of the *Dialogue* is popular. It discusses on the one hand what must have been topics of ale-house or after-dinner conversation, the

---

[17] See Rogers, *Correspondence*, 387/19-26, trans. Schuster, *Confutation* III, 1139.

[18] The full title is as follows: *A dyaloge of syr Thomas More knyghte: one of the counsayll of our souerayne lorde the kyng and chauncelloure of hys duchy of Lancaster. Wheryn he treatyd dyuers maters/as of the veneracyon and worshyp of ymagys and relyques/prayng to sayntis/and goynge on pylgrymage. Wyth many other thyngys touchyng the pestylent secte of Luther and Tyndale/by the tone bygone in Saxony/and by the tother laboryd to be brought in to England.* For a full bibliographical description of the work see R. W. Gibson, *St. Thomas More: A Preliminary Bibliography*, 73-74, nos. 53, 54. The first edition's colophon is dated June 1529; the second, May 1531. This latter edition has been used for the purpose of this study. Cross references are given to W. E. Campbell's edition in *The English Works of Sir Thomas More*, edited by W. E. Campbell, Vol. 2, London, 1931.

[19] Tyndale's *New Testament, Obedience* and *Mammon* are referred to in *Dialogue*, cxlix vE-H, Campbell, 315.

[20] See *Dialogue*, lxxxxix vE-H, Campbell, 212: 'In the preface of his fyrst boke called Mammona he sayth that one frere Hyerom made the other boke that we talke of/whiche frere Hyerom gyuyng vp his order of the frere obseruauntes came to hym where he was/shewyng hym that he wolde cast of his abyte and leue his relygyon/...'

treatment at the hands of the clergy of Richard Hunne, Thomas Bilney, the burning of Tyndale's new testament, the hunting down and general harassment of Lutherans with their sympathisers and supporters. It also deals with the more superficial criticisms of the reformers concerning the use of relics, images, the promotion of pilgrimages and the poor quality of life of the clergy. As well as these relatively trivial matters it discusses at length some of the central issues of the Reformation: faith, justification, good works, while a large section is given over to examining the relationship between church and revelation in an even more explicit manner than in the *Responsio.*

Allowing for the multiplicity of topics discussed it is possible to observe a certain logical order which may have been intentional. In the first book More gave a great deal of attention to the question of miracles. He then went on to discuss the relation of church to revelation as well as the nature and authority of the church, using miraculous intervention as a key index to the true community of Christ. With the authority of the church established, More in the latter parts of Bks II and III dealt with individual matters which had been raised regarding, for example, the use of vernacular bibles, clerical morals and so forth. Finally in Bk IV he investigated a variety of theological issues raised by Luther and Tyndale, depending in most instances on the authority of the church to ground his argument. Hence the centrality of his treatment of the church to the whole debate.

So much for the essential contents of the work. The literary framework adopted was the dialogue form, in one shape or another More's preferred literary device. In this instance the fiction More assumed took the following form. 'For where as a ryght worshypfull frende of myne sent ones vnto me a secrete sure frende of his...' with a set of queries touching several matters '...of late by lewde people put in questyon.' More spoke at length with the Messenger and sent him on his way. He then felt that for the sake of security the dialogue should be put in writing. Having done this he realised that his manuscript might be put to ill use by his enemies and decided to have it printed. Thus it is set in the form of a conversation interspersed with refreshment of various kinds. The whole text is spiced with proverb, witticism and anecdote. Nor is the personality of the Messenger without significance. He is a university student specialising in classics with a special interest in scripture, possibly based on the character of his son-in-law, William Roper, an early dabbler in Lutheranism.

The human scene then of the late 1520's constitutes both the historical and literary context of the work.[21] More's lightness of touch does not take away from its high seriousness. He was determined to lay bare what he believed to be the real meaning of the Reform: '...wherby they take away all dylygence and good endeuour to vertue/all withstandyng and stryuyng agaynst vyce/all care of heuyn/all fere of hell/all cause of prayer...layng theyr syn to goddes ordenaunce/and theyr punysshment to goddes crueltye/and fynally turnyng the nature of man in to worse than a beste/and the goodnes of god into worse than the deuyll...'[22] Whatever the inaccuracy of his analysis, the vehemence of More's tone indicates the passion with which he wrote.

The book was written probably between the summer of 1527 and the spring of 1529. The title page dates the first edition to 1528 but, as Dr Schuster points out, according to our calendar this could have extended till March 1529.[23] A revised edition was published in 1531, 'newly ouersene by the sayd syr Thomas More chauncellour of England.' More had reached the summit of his career at this stage. The reissuing of the *Dialogue* without substantial alteration made it more clear than ever where the Chancellor stood on many of the debated issues of his day.

I. The church inerrant

Fundamental postulate: the church cannot err

The *Dialogue Concerning Heresies* was primarily concerned with practical and political issues such as the execution of Bilney, the burning of Tyndale's translation of the new testament, opposition to Luther, the rights and wrongs of the persecution of heretics and so on.[24] Characteristically, these practical considerations led the author back to the problem of the church. More turned to the church as bearer, custodian and criterion of divine

---

[21] The work abounds with topical references to the Hunne and Bilney cases, the king's exchange with Luther, the peasant revolt and other political disturbances in Germany and Switzerland, as well as the Turkish threat to Vienna and the rest of Western Europe.

[22] See *Dialogue*, cli rAB, Campbell, 318.

[23] See Schuster, *Confutation III*, 1187, and n. 1 'Made in the yere of oure Lord, M. D. xxviii' is the date given on the title page. The colophon reads, however, June 1529. This extension allowed More time to assimilate Tyndale's later works, *The Parable of the Wicked Mammon*, and *The Obedience of a Christian Man* both published in 1528. The later of these appeared only on 2 October 1528, according to Anthea Hume: *English Protestant Books Printed Abroad, 1525-1535, An Annotated Bibliography, Confutation II*, 1071, no. 7.

[24] See *Dialogue*, vii r B, Campbell, 13; More terms three doctrines for which Bilney was noted as heresy: '...that we sholde do no worshyp to any ymages/nor pray to any sayntes or go on pylgrymagys/whiche thyngys I suppose euery good crysten man wyll agre for heresyes.'

truth, the standard by which not merely theory but Christian custom and behaviour must be judged: 'And therfore can it not in no wyse be/that the chyrche can be deceyued in that they take for sayntes these holy doctours of the chyrch. Nor they so beynge/can it in any wyse be that the doctryne wherin they consent and agree can be false or vntrue. Amonge whiche doctryne syth the thyngs wherof we speke/I mene the praynge to sayntes/the worshyp of ymages/reuerencynge of relyques/and goynge in pylgrymages is a parte as by theyr bokes playnly doth appere/we may well and surely conclude that none of these thynges be dampnable or dyspleasaunt to god/but thynges hyghly to his contentacyon and pleasure.'[25] Once more it is to the faith of Christ's church, as in the case of the sacraments against Luther, that More turned to vindicate devotional practices.

This illustrates a change of method in More's argument. In his work against Luther he had, as it were in the course of discussion, to clarify his own mind in relation to the vital question of criteriology and the relation of church to revelation as its bearer in tradition as well as its interpreter. With Luther, More based himself on scripture but went on to postulate extra-biblical tradition carried on within the church, while he more or less took for granted that the common consent of the church is the ultimate guide to faith.[26] This last was the vital point. Having affirmed this principle of judgment, he could apply it to whatever matter was brought forward, theoretical or practical, making it possible for him to distinguish clearly between basically good practices and their abuse.[27]

The criterion of judgment adopted by More was the common consent of the church. In order to establish its validity he examined once more the divine presence within the church, her indefectibility in life and faith, the presence of divine revelation within her members as unwritten gospel, inspired writings, and living tradition. He sketched out in passing the structure this church takes as an organised society as well as an object of faith.

---

[25] See *Dialogue*, lxxxii v G, ed. Campbell, 175; ibid. xvii r D—xvii v E, ed. Campbell, 32: '...the force of my tale (in favour of pilgrimages) was not the myracles/but the thynge that I holde stronger than any myracles/...the fayth of Crystes chyrche/by the comon consent wherof. These matters be decyded and well knowen that the worshyp of sayntes and ymages ben alowed/approbate/and accustomed for good crysten and merytoryous vertues/and the contrary oppynyon not onely reproued by many holy doctours/but also condempned for heresyes by sundry generall counsayles.'

[26] See above, pp. 96-103.

[27] See *Dialogue*, Book I, for example, where the discussion passes from an examination of practical questions such as praying to saints, the honouring of images, going on pilgrimage, to the question of miracles, and thence to the inerrancy of the church which approves such practices. At a later stage, (Book II, Chapter 10) he brings out the value of miracles as confirming the testimony of the church's preaching.

Finally however he had to deal with the question: which is this church that
can verify divine revelation? How can it be recognised? The line of argument is somewhat different from the *Responsio,* the emphasis slightly
changed, certain points receive greater development. The picture is
basically the same; its expression more popular in tone.

Inerrancy based on divine presence in the church

Beginning therefore with this assumption regarding the agreement in
faith of the church as a measuring rod of Christian truth and behaviour,
More also practically assumed the fact of the founding of a community of
faith by Christ and of its continuity till the present day: 'ye do quod I
agre/that suche thynges as are mencyoned in the gospell/spoken by Cryst
vnto saynt Peter and other his apostles and dysciples/were not only sayd to
them selfe/nor onely for them selfe/but to them for theyr successours in
Crystes floke/and by them to us all/that is to wyt euery man as shall apper-
teyne to his parte.'[28]

More's principal concern was to emphasise the supernatural reality of
the Christian community. Christ is present in this community by reason of
his godhead: 'Cryst also sayd/I am with you tyll the ende of the worlde/not
I shall be/but I am/whiche is the worde appropryed to his godhed. And
therfore that worde am/is the name by whiche our lorde wolde as he tolde
Moyses/be named vnto Pharao/as a name whiche from all creatures, (syth
they be all subiecte to tyme) clerely dyscerneth his godhed/whiche is euer
beynge and present with out dyfference of tyme past or to come.' Christ,
he continued, also promised to be present to his church with his Father
and to send the Holy Spirit and 'is also present amonge us bodyly in the
holy sacrament/...'[29] Christ therefore is present to his church in various
ways, not merely in scripture but also in the sacrament of the eucharist,

---

[28] See *Dialogue*, xxxi v E, ed. Campbell, 65; see also *Dialogue* xxxiii rv CD, Campbell, 69,
where More notes other statements of Christ addressed not merely to Peter or the Twelve
but to the wider church. 'And thou beyng one of these dayes conuertyd/conferme and
strength thy bretherne.' (Lk 22, 32): '...fede my shepe...' (Jn 21, 16); the promise of the
Spirit's guidance (Jn 14, 26); '...where so euer be .ii. or .iii. gathered togyther in my name
there am I my self among them.' (Mt 18, 20); 'Lo I am with you all the dayes to the worldes
ende...' (Mt 28, 20). The church therefore was not merely to consist of apostles and die with
them, but continue through time empowered by Christ's promises.
[29] See *Dialogue*, xxxv v E-G, Campbell, 74. See ibid., xxxv v H—xxxvi r A, ed. Campbell,
74-75, where the assistance of the Spirit to those appearing before hostile judges is promised
to inspire them not merely with the memory of scripture but 'wordys new gyuen theym by
god inspyred in theyr hartys...' See also *Dialogue* xxxiii r D, Campbell, 69, where the author
insists that the special mode of Christ's presence in the assembled congregation did not cease
with apostolic times (Mt 18, 20).

and the special presence of the Trinity ever assisting the community whether assembled or dispersed.

In particular More made use of Johannine images to bring out this closeness of communion between the body of faithful and their Lord. 'Doth he not in the. xiiii. xv. and xvi. chapyter of saynt Johan agayne and agayne repete/that after his goynge he wyll come agayne to them/...[30] And again, 'I am sayth he a very vyne/and my father is a gardyner. I am the vyne and ye be the braunches. And euery braunche that bereth in me no frute/my father taketh it away. And euery braunche that bereth frute/he purgeth it to make it brynge the more frute. And as the braunche can do no good beynge taken from the tree/ryght so can ye do no good nor serue for nought but for the fyre/excepte ye abyde in me.'[31] (Jn 15, 5-6) The thought is familiar but the rendering has a certain savour of its own as of words long mulled over, the picture of his own Chelsea garden with its autumn bonfires before his mind on the one hand, of fires burning the bodies of unfortunate apostates on the other, something for which as chancellor he would have to accept responsibility. On the other hand there is no escaping the impression that deep in More's mind was sealed a conviction concerning the presence of Christ in and through his church, a presence never to be ignored by its members ever so unworthy.

This divine concurrence guarantees the continued existence of the church through history. Both More and his companion agreed on this point that Christ intended 'to gather a flocke and congregacyon of people that shold serue god and be his specyall peple.' Citing Ps 2, 8: *Postula a me et dabo tibi gentes hereditatem tuam,* he argued that this inheritance should last 'tyll domys day/and after in heuen eternally.'[32] This was not a question which More felt needed much delving into. Rather was it something he

---

[30] See *Dialogue,* lviii v E, Campbell, 121; the quotation continues: 'Let us adde now therunto the wordes before reherced/that he wyll be with them tyll the worldes ende/and it appereth playne that he ment all this by his hole chyrch that sholde be to the worldes ende.' (Mt 28, 20) More cited in this context, as well as the foregoing text, Jn 14, 18; Jn 15, 15; Jn 13, 34; Jn 14, 26; Jn 16, 13; Jn 14, 16-18.

[31] See *Dialogue,* lxiiii r CD, Campbell, 134; see also *Dialogue* xlvii r BC, Campbell, 97-98, speaking of '...heretykys that rebell and refuse to be obedyent to god and his chyrche. Who be therby cut of from the lyuely tre of that vyne/and waxynge wythered braunches/be kepte but for the fyre fyrste here and after in hell/excepte they repent and call for grace/that may graft them into the stocke agayne.' More also made use of the Pauline imagery of body and spouse: see *Dialogue* lxviii rv C-E, Campbell, 143: 'But our lorde in this his mystycall body of his chyrche/caryed his membres/some seke/some hole/and all sekely...god shall with his spouse this chyrch of cryst entre in to the pleasaunt weddyng chambre to the bed of eternall rest/...' See ibid., lxviii v GH, Campbell, 144.

[32] See *Dialogue,* lvii rB, Campbell, 118.

took entirely for granted as a postulate of argument: '...his chyrche be and euer shall be contynuall without any tymes bytwene (in which there shall be none)...' He went on to argue from this to the preservation of true faith within this community. For More 'the chyrche of cryste also is a thynge that alway hathe stande and contynued.' It was not so much this as the preservation of faith he envisaged as problematic.[33]

This same divine concurrence, he argued, ensures the lasting fidelity of God's people to the message they have received: '...haue we so sone forgotten the perpetuall assystence of the trynyte in his chyrche/and the prayour of Cryst to kepe the fayth of his chyrche fro faylynge/and the holy gost sente of purpose to kepe in the chyrche the remembraunce of Crystys wordys and to lede them into all trouthe. what wolde it haue profyted to haue put you in the remembraunce of the assystence of god with the chyldren of Israell/walkyng wyth them in the cloude by day/and in the pyler of fyre by nyght in theyr erthly vyage/and therby to haue prouyd you the moche more specyall assystence of god with hys crysten chyrche in theyr spyrytuall vyage/wherein hys especyall goodnes well declaryth his tender dylygence/by that he doth vouchesafe to assyste and comforte vs with the contynuall presence of his precyouse body in the holy sacramente. All thys wolde not helpe/yf manyfeste reason that I made you/and euydent scrypture that I rehersed you/can not yet prynte in your harte a perceyuynge that the assystence of god in his chyrche must nedys preserue his chyrche frome all damnable errours in the fayth/and gyue hys chyrche so ferforth the vnderstandynge of scrypture/that they may well percyue that no parte therof well vnderstande/standyth agaynst any artycle that the chyrche byleuyth/as parcell of theyr crysten fayth.'[34] God guided his chosen people across the desert; now he guides the new chosen people in such wise that they may never fail in their understanding of the divine message. '...god kepeth and euer shall kepe in his chyrche the ryght fayth and ryght byleue by the helpe of his owne hande that hath planted it/...'[35]

II. REVELATION IN THE CHURCH

This of course immediately brings us to the dividing line between More and the innovators whose mouthpiece is the composite figure, the

---

[33] See *Dialogue*, xxxvi vG, Campbell, 76; ibid. lxiii r D, Campbell, 132; ibid. xxxiiii r B, Campbell, 70: '...god made not his chyrche for a whyle/but to endure tyll the worldes ende.' The words are the Messenger's but his partner in dialogue is in complete agreement with him on this issue.

[34] See *Dialogue*, lx r BC, Campbell, 125; see also *Dialogue*, lvii r BCD, Campbell, 118.

[35] See *Dialogue*, xxxiiii v F, Campbell, 72.

Messenger, namely the manner in which the seed of divine revelation is planted and preserved in the church. For while the Messenger reiterated a simplified version of the *scriptura sola* doctrine of the Wittenberg school, More repeated his basic affirmation concerning the form of divine revelation in the Christian dispensation as a compound of words and inward guidance preserved in the church not merely by inspired scripture but also by the gospel written in the heart of man by the Holy Spirit.

The role of scripture

More never undervalued the role of scripture in the formation of faith. The bible for him was the written source *par excellence* of divine revelation. 'There was neuer thynge wrytten in this worlde that canne in any wyse be comparable with any parte of holy scrypture...And of dyuynyte reken I the best parte to be conteyned in holy scrypture. And this I saye for hym that shall haue tyme thereto/and from youth entendeth to the chyrch warde/and to make hym selfe with goddes helpe mete for the offyce of a precher.'[36] From More's own writings, apologetic as well as devotional, there can be little question of his attachment to the scriptures.[37]

This clearly emerges in his dialogue with the Messenger. One of the questions he placed in his mouth concerned the vernacular use of scripture. The distribution of unauthorised versions of the bible had been long ago forbidden by the Council of Oxford (1408), while Tyndale's translation of the new testament had been publicly burned. More defended the destruction of Tyndale's testament on the grounds of its distortion of Christ's teaching. He listed a number of key instances where Tyndale had departed from accepted usage with, he alleged, deliberate intent to mislead. Among these More noted: *love* for *charity*, *congregation* for *church*, *senior* for *priest*, *fervour* for *grace* and so forth. It was this kind of tendentious translation which justified restrictive legislation in More's opinion. He was at pains to point out that the laws had been aimed initially at Wyclif and the Lollards. All translations had not come under the ban, only those deemed liable to lead the innocent astray.[38]

Under questioning from the Messenger, More himself made a strong case for vernacular translation of the scriptures: 'There is no tretyce of scrypture so harde but that a good vertuous man or woman eyther/shall

---

[36] See *Dialogue*, xxxix v FG, Campbell, 82.
[37] See *Dialogue*, lxxxiiii vG—lxxxvi rB, Campbell, 180-182.
[38] See *Dialogue*, lxxxxvii r—lxxxxix r, Campbell, 206-211; ibid., c rD—vG, Campbell, 213-214; ibid., cix B; cxiiii vE—cxv vG, Campbell, 232, 242-245. (Note misnumbering of 1530 edition at this point. The number cxi when it first appears should read cix.)

somwhat fynde therin that shall delyte and encreace theyr deuocyon...for
no doubte is there/but that god and his holy spyryte hath so prudently
tempered theyr speche thorowe the hole corps of scrypture/that euery man
may take good therby and no man harme/but he that wyll in the study
therof lene prowdely to the foly of his own wytte.'[39] This was essentially a
positive view of holy writ, in harmony with opinions of his expressed
before the storms of Reformation had blown up. In fact More went even
further, giving guidelines for the use of scripture by the laity as well as
making suggestions for a translation project that would have made a
suitable text available for circulation to one and all.[40]

    The problem posed by the Reformation, however, was the relation be-
tween scripture and the church. Did holy writ stand over and above the
church as something radically distinct from it or did it somehow fall within
its compass? The reformers' position affirming the transcendence of scripture arose from an inherent tendency to emphasise the written word of
God as the acid test of revelation. On this More was clear. He drew a clear
line between revelation and the inspired writing of scripture.

    This tendency becomes apparent in his treatment of faith and its rela-
tion to church and scripture. Thus he asked how it happened that in the
days 'of Noe hym selfe/though ther were few saued a lyue/yet proueth not
that the people to be all myscreantes/and without fayth.' Did not Abraham
and Moses and those that followed in their footsteps have true faith in
God's promises before any bible was published?[41] The gospel of Christ
was preached before the gospels were written. This revelation conveyed in
the preaching of the church informs her members as to which scriptures
are inspired. The outer word of the preacher is confirmed by the secret
working of the Spirit guiding the community to agreement.[42] The fact that
More was prepared to prove the authenticity of the church out of scripture

---

    [39] See *Dialogue*, cxvii v FG, Campbell, 249. See also ibid., cxviF—cxviiG, Campbell,
247-248.
    [40] See *Dialogue*, cxvi rD—vE, Campbell, 246-247; ibid., cxviii rC—vE, Campbell,
249-250.
    [41] See *Dialogue*, lxxxiiii vG—lxxxv rC, Campbell, 180-181.
    [42] See *Dialogue*, lxxxv v E, Campbell, 181: 'I praye you tell my what scrypture hath taught
the chyrch to knowe whyche bookys be the very scrypture/and to reiecte many other that
were writen of the same maters/and that in suche wyse wryten/and in the namys of suche
men as (sauynge for the spyryte of god geuen to hys chyrch) a naturall wyse man had bene
lykely ynough/eyther to haue taken both for holy scrypture/or to haue reiected both as none
holy scripture. And surely in the receyte of the tone/and reieccyon of the tother/there wolde
haue ben at the lest way suche dyuerse opynyons that the hole chyrch had neuer taken all the
tone sorte and reiected all the tother/had not that holy spyryte inspyred that consent/qui facit
unanimes in domo/whyche makyth the chyrche all of one mynde and accorde.' (Ps 67, 7).

need not hide the fact that, while recognising the prior importance of divine revelation, he considered this revelation to have been committed to the care of the community as such.[43] Inspired writings are one means by which this revelation is preserved but they do not supplant the work of the Spirit still living in the hearts of the faithful, nor replace the gospel written in the mind of all true believers, nor the living tradition of that community as evidenced in the legacy of the past as well as the actual practice of the present.[44]

Gospel in the heart

This inward gospel unfolds itself both in the traditions of the church and in the development of certain theological themes beyond the semantic limits of their biblical premises. The Christian law, he wrote, '...is called the lawe of Crystes faythe/the lawe of hys holy gospell. I mene not onely the wordes wrytten in the bookes of hys euangelystes/*But moche more specyally the substaunce of our fayth it selfe/whiche oure lorde sayd he wolde wryte in mennes hartes*/not onely bycause of the secrete operacyon of god and his holy spyryte/in iustyfyenge the good crysten/eyther by the workynge with mannes good wyll/to the perfeccyon of faythe in his soule/or with the good intente of the offerers/to the secret infusyon of that vertue in to the soule of an innocent infant. But also for that he fyrste without wrytynge reuelèd those heuenly mysteryes by hys blessyd mouth/thorowe the eres of his appostles and dyscyples in to theyr holy hartes/or rather as it semeth it was inwardely infused in to saynt Peter his harte/by the secrete inspyracyon of god/without eyther wrytynge or any outwarde worde. For whiche cause when he hadde vppon Crystes questyon demaundynge/of whome saye you that I am/answered and sayd. Thou arte Cryst the sonne of the lyuynge god/whiche arte commen in to this worlde. Our sauyoure sayd agayne vnto hym. Thou arte blessyd Symon the sonne of Johan/for neyther flesshe nor blode hathe reueled and shewed this to the/but my father that is in heuen. (Mt 16, 15-17) And thus it appereth that the fayth came into saynt Peter his harte as to the prynce of the appostles without herynge by

---

[43] Here I am using a later language to express More's thought. He himself was not as yet able to define his position as closely as this.

[44] See *Dialogue*, lxxxv v G, Campbell, 182. See also ibid., lix v G, Campbell, 124: 'But the gospels and holy scrypture/god prouydeth that thoughe percase some of it may perysshe and be lost/(i.e. divine revelation) whereby they myght haue harme/but not fall in erroure (for the faythe sholde stande thoughe the scryptures were all gone) yet shall he neuer suffre his chyrch to be deceyued in that poynte/that they shall take for holy scrypture any booke that is not.'

secrete inspyracyon/and in to the remenaunt by his confessyon and Crystes holy mouthe. And by theym in lyke maner/fyrste without wrytynge by onely wordes and prechynge/so was it spredde abrode in the worlde/that his fayth was by the mouthes of his holy messengers put into mennes eres/and by his holy hande wrytten in mennes hartes or euer any worde therof almost was wrytten in the boke. *And so was it conuenyent for the lawe of lyfe/rather to be wrytten in the lyuely myndes of men/than in the dede skynnes of bestes.* And I nothynge doubte/but all had it so ben/that neuer gospell hadde ben wrytten/yet sholde the substaunce of this fayth neuer haue fallen out of crysten folkes hartes/but the same spyryte that planted it/the same sholde haue watered it/the same shold haue kepte it/the same shold haue encreased it. But so hathe it lyked our lorde after his hye wysdome to prouyde/that some of his dyscyples haue wrytten many thynges of his holy lyfe/doctryne and faythe/and yet farre frome all/whiche (as saynt Johan sayth) (Jn 21, 25) the worlde coulde not haue comprehended.'[45]

In this lengthy quotation we are given in summary form More's concept of Christian revelation and its transmission. Peter's is the archetypal case. By inward revelation he came to confess Christ to be the Son of God. This outward proclamation in conjunction with an inward movement of the Spirit was taken in by the apostles. Two actions work concurrently therefore on those living subsequently to Peter, the preaching of the word and the inward movement of the Spirit marking out this revelation on the inward mind of faithful believers. At a later stage this same revelation was written down in inspired books. But that is not to say that the written word is the exclusive extrinsic vehicle for the transmission of revelation. Not everything was written. Hence the life and preaching of the church are an ongoing medium for the transmission of divine revelation, a revelation kept fresh in the minds of its bearers by the inward action of the Spirit.

Socio-cultural tradition

More developed a second concept of tradition which he looked on as working in tandem, so to speak, with the gospel in the heart. This might be termed the socio-cultural tradition of a living society, serving a purpose analogous to that of customary law in the juridical theory of feudal society. Living custom is the law of the land. Statutory law is merely a clarification and refinement of this to meet the needs of the times. Thomas More, significantly enough and in contrast to Henry, maintained his emphasis on the pneumatic concept of tradition. Nonetheless he also acknowledged

---

[45] See *Dialogue*, xlv v H—xlvi r B, Campbell, 95-96.

the presence of a living tradition within the community distinct from this, though depending on it for its authenticity: '...all the deuout rytys and ceremonyes of the chyrch/bothe in the deuine seruyce as encensynge/ halowyng of the fyre/of the funt/of the pascall lambe/and ouer that the exorcysmys/benedyccyons/and holy straunge gesturys vsyd in consecra-cyon or mynystracyon of the blessyd sacramentys/all whiche holy thyngys *greate parte wherof was frome hande to hande left in the chyrche*/from the tyme of crystys apostels/and by them left vnto vs...'[46]

Here More clearly had in mind as the bearer of tradition not another set of writings to be placed on a par with scripture, but the living tradition of a human society which will find expression in the totality of its life, theological, liturgical and pastoral.

The fathers of the church

This socio-cultural concept of tradition does not incorporate his dependence on patristic testimony: 'And we be very sure that the thynge (honouring of images) is good/and our way good therin/and our byleue therin ryght/not onely by resons and authoryte by whiche I haue proved it you more then ones allredy/but also by that all the olde holy sayntys and doctours of Crystes chyrche as saynt Jerome/saynt Austyn/saynt Basyle/saynt Chrysosteme/saynt Gregory/wyth all suche other as playnely we rede in theyr bokys/dyd as we do therin/and bylyued therof as we byleue. And syth we se what they byleued/we nede not to doubte what is best that we byleue.'[47] In other words, More was not looking to the fathers as an independent literary *source* of apostolic tradition but as *witnesses* to the *faith* of the church, which in its turn comes from the Spirit. In short he was looking to the fathers as further evidence of the faith of the church concerning the value of a particular type of devotional practice, using their writings to discover a concordance extending not merely in space but through time to its origins. This is another version of the internalistic view of tradition, the vehicle of divine revelation in this case being primarily the presence of God within his community, inspiring each one as he did Peter with a true vision of faith.

---

[46] See *Dialogue*, xiiii r A, Campbell, 27.

[47] See *Dialogue,* lxxx r AB, Campbell, 169. See also *Dialogue*, lxxxii v G, Campbell, 175: 'Amonge whiche doctryne (concerning which the church cannot be deceived) syth the thynges wherof we speke/I mene the praynge to sayntes/...is a parte *as by theyr bokes playnly doth appere*/we may well and surely conclude that none of these thynges be dampnable or dyspleasaunt to god/but thynges hyghly to his contentacyon and pleasure.'

Continuing revelation

Thus although More, in the *Dialogue,* oscillated to some extent between externalist and internalist views of tradition, his emphasis remained on the internal guidance of the Spirit. Hence he could speak in terms of a continuing revelation in the church supplementary to the content of holy writ: 'But as it may be that many thyngys be there not all at onys reuelyd and vnderstanden in the scrypture/but by sondry tymys and agys mo thyngys and mo by god vnto his chyrche dysclosyd/ and that as it shall lyke his hygh goodnes and wysdome to dyspence and dyspose/so in thyngys to be done maye fall in his chyrche varyete mutacyon and chaunge/...'[48] Here More was grappling with the perennial problem of the development of doctrine.

In the same place he cited the example of the definition of the equality of Father, Son and Holy Spirit, a credal statement not found explicitly in scripture, yet the first relationship was defined in the council of Nicea, (consubstantiality of Son with Father) and the second included in the creed of Athanasius.[49] Although his interpretation of this dogmatic fact used the language of revelation: '...many thyngys be there not all at onys *reuelyd and vnderstanden* in the scrypture/but by sondry tymys and agys mo thyngys and mo by god vnto his chyrche *dysclosyd/*...', it seems more reasonable to consider it in terms of the Spirit given to the Christian community recalling all things to their minds, and guiding them into all truth, a process normally taking the shape of theological reflection.

In short More did not differentiate with full logical rigour between the various modes in which divine revelation is preserved, transmitted and interpreted. His vision was not so much analytical as global and ultimately rested on the promises of Christ concerning the abiding presence of God within the community. For More the precise mode of transmission of any particular definable element of divine revelation was secondary. The primary element for him was the divinely imbued character of 'the common knowen christian people'. It was their agreement in belief which was the inescapable sign of the presence of a divine voice inviting the believer's assent.

---

[48] See *Dialogue*, xlvii r CD, Campbell, 98. See also ibid., xlvii v E: 'And therfore ouer this as it may be that as I sayd before/some thynges in holy scrypture be not yet fully perceyued and vnderstanden/so am I very sure/that the chyrch neyther doth nor can do dampnably conster it wronge/...As if they sholde by mysse construccyon of the scrypture brynge vp and byleue that Cryst were one god and egall with his father and with the holy goost/yf the trouth were otherwyse in dede.'

[49] See Denzinger-Schönmetzer, *Enchiridion symbolorum definitionum et declarationum de rebus fidei et morum,* (23rd ed.), par. 150 and par. 75.

Church's faith prior to scripture

One important consequence follows from this position. In the logic of faith the church is prior to scripture since it is from the church we learn which be the true scriptures, while in their interpretation account must be taken of traditional belief and practice as well as, above all, the articles of faith.[50] Indeed in the last resort, these must be adhered to in preference to any particular text of scripture. This assertion perhaps best illustrates More's priorities in faith. Faith is posited in relation to God revealing himself in and through his people. God's word is known primarily through their active teaching. The word of scripture forms part of this doctrine but in any particular instance a definition of the church is preferable to a problematic interpretation of a scriptural text. This constituted no contradiction for More. It is the same God who speaks through the mouth of Christ as through his church as well as through the written gospel. In the event of a clash between these mouthpieces More's preference was for the unwritten gospel in men's heart, whose conceptual reflex is found in the common faith and teaching of Christ's church.

III. CHURCH AND REVELATION

Church authenticates scripture

This position of More's concerning the priority of church to scripture comes through quite clearly in his dialogue with the Messenger. He asked the Messenger how he knew the scriptures to be true? The Messenger admitted that books may be falsely ascribed to their authors. This in no way diminishes the value of their contents. More pressed him further as to how he knew the contents to be true? The Messenger answered that God

---

[50] See *Dialogue*, xl r AB, Campbell, 83: '...For the sure auoydybge wherof/(of deception by the devil) my pore aduyse were in the study therof/to haue a specyall regarde to the wrytyngys and commentys of olde holy fathers. And yet or he fall in hande with the one or the other/nexte grace and helpe of god to begotten with abystynence and prayour and clennes of lyuynge/afore all thynge were it necessary/to come well and surely enstructyd/in all suche poyntes and artycles as/the chyrche byleuyth.' In the case of apparent contradiction between the truth of scripture as expressed in different texts, the student will seek to reconcile them by collation with other places, as well as by examining the comments of the fathers. Failing this, let him assume, as Augustine suggests, a scribal error: 'And so let hym reuerently knowlege his ignoraunce/lene and cleue to the fayth of the chyrche as to an vndoutyd trouthe/leuynge that texte to be better perceyuyd whan it shall please our lorde wyth hys lyght to reuele and dysclose it.' See ibid., lxxxiiii v F, Campbell, 179: 'And so byleue you the chyrche/not bycause it is trouth that the chyrche telleth you/but ye byleue the trouth of the thynge bycause the chyrche telleth it.'

had shown him so. In what way? asked More. Through a revelation made
to one man in the beginning who was known and believed because of his
miracles and the goodness of his life. 'And the knowledge went forth from
man to man.' This gave More his opening for the note he had so often
trumpeted in defiance of Luther: it is only through the church that true
scripture can be known: '...yet shall he neuer suffre his chyrch to be
deceyued in that poynte/that they shall take for holy scrypture any booke
that is not. And therefore sayth holy saynt Austyne/I sholde not byleue the
gospell/but yf it were for the chyrche. And he sayth good reason. For were
it not for the spyryte of god kepynge the trouthe therof in his chyrche/who
coulde be sure whiche were the very gospels?'[51]

This was a familiar reference of More's, one which Henry had used in
his *Assertio* and which More himself had employed on several occasions in
the *Responsio*. The fictional structure of the dialogue in no way diminishes
either the strength of the writer's conviction or the value of the evidence. It
was a matter of fundamental importance to his whole case that the church
had been given the gift of distinguishing God's word from the words of
men. Hence her ability to reject apocryphal gospels, authenticate others
and so guarantee the preservation of true faith.

Church interprets scripture

While emphasising the value of scripture in Christian life, Thomas
More was also keenly aware of the difficulties its interpretation could pose
to the naïve or unlearned. The understanding of scripture is enlightened
by faith but guided by right reason. In order to do its task properly, reason
must be 'by study, labour and exercise of logic, philosophy and other
liberal arts corroborate and quickened, and that judgement both in them,
and also in orators, laws, and stories much riped.'[52] To make the point
clearer he asked the Messenger at what age he thought people should
begin to study the scriptures. His friend answered that he would have a
man begin when very young and continue all his life. More then gave a
number of examples to show how the untrained mind might easily be led
astray by a superficial reading of the text. For example, one who read and
accepted at their face value those pericopes which speak of the subordination of Jesus to his Father might well end up in Arianism. What is always
required is the comparison of text with text, the apparent sense of scripture

---

[51] *Dialogue*, lix v GH, Campbell, 124. The quotation is from Augustine, *Contra epistolam
Manichaei*, 'Ego vero Evangelio non crederem, nisi me catholicae Ecclesiae commoveret auctoritas', *MPL* 42, 176.

[52] *Dialogue*, xli vG, Campbell, 87.

with traditional exegesis, and the compound of both with the common
faith of the church, if balance is to be maintained.[53]

Earlier More had in fact given guidelines for the interpretation of scripture borrowed from St Augustine.[54] Among the points he listed were: pure
and prayerful living, careful examination of the interpretations of the
fathers, and a sound knowledge of the articles of faith. If the sense of any
portion of holy writ '...seem to stand against any of them, (the articles of
faith) either shall the light of natural reason, with the collation of other
texts, help to find out the truth, or else (which is the surest way) he shall
perceive the truth in the comments of the good holy doctors of old to whom
God hath given the grace of understanding.'[55] If however none of these
measures prevail, then, as Augustine indicated, let him assume there is
some fault either in the translator, or in the writer, or now-a-days in the
printer, or that for some other reason he has failed to get the point. 'And
so let hym reuerently knowlege his ignoraunce/lene and cleue to the fayth
of the chyrche as to vndoutyd trouthe/leuynge that texte to be better
perceyuyd whan it shall please our lorde wyth hys lyght to reuele and
dysclose it.'[56]

Teaching of church preferable to scripture

More returned to this theme at later stages of his discussion. 'What', the
Messenger asked, 'if the clear text of scripture is in direct opposition to the
glosses of the fathers?' More reiterated his fundamental principle of the
priority of the common faith of the church over any apparent difficulty
arising from the biblical text. 'With this myght I also laye and very well
conclude/that syth those holy doctours and the chyrche/be...all of one
fayth in this poynte...I wyll rather proue you the truth of them by the truth
of the chyrch/than the truth of the chyrche by the truth of them...For surely syth they were but membres of his chyrch god had his specyall cure vpon
them moost especyall for the profyte of his chyrch/by whose hole corps he
more setteth than by any membre therof/saynt/appostle/euangelyst/or
other.' In the final analysis it is the common faith of the church which
must be upheld against any particular passage of scripture for to the

[53] See *Dialogue*, xxxix v F—xl r C, passim, Campbell, 82-83.
    [54] See Augustine, *De doctrina christiana*, III, II, 2,*CC* 32 (1962), 78: 'Cum ergo adhibita in-
tentio incertum esse peruiderit, quomodo distinguendum aut quomodo pronuntiandum sit,
consulat regulam fidei, quam de scripturarum planioribus locis et ecclesiae auctoritate
percepit, de qua satis egimus, cum de rebus in libro primo loqueremur.'
    [55] See Campbell, 83, (see *Dialogue* xl rBC).
    [56] See *Dialogue*, xl r B—xliii v F; xlvi r D, Campbell, 84—91, 96.

church has been given the office not merely of authenticating holy writ but also of correctly interpreting it.[57]

IV. WHICH IS THE CHURCH OF CHRIST?

Thomas More was emphatic that the counter-testimony of heretics in the past in no way diminished the value of consensus in determining the content of faith. Such groups had continually arisen and then perished in the history of Christendom. Their very transience precluded their being reckoned worthy of consideration in terms of a frame of reference extending across the whole span of the church's life.[58] This thesis, however, enabled him to raise another issue: what or which is the church? This had been a problem for him in the *Responsio,* one he had not faced up to in a fully systematic way, and yet which he had dealt with several times *en passant.* Now it is clear he wanted to deal with it *ex professo.* The years between 1523 and 1528 had seen the continued spread of Lutheranism in Germany, its gradual infiltration into established church institutions in some instances, the establishment of its own in other situations, as well as posing a growing threat to the established order in Britain.

The church of the predestinate

This presumably was the background to the objection the Messenger put to his summary dismissal of heretics as being unworthy of consideration in any assessment of the common mind of the church: 'Well quod he peraduenture they wyll not stycke moche to assygne you a place and shewe you a company and congregacyon/whiche they wyll saye is the very chyrche. For what yf they wyll shewe you Boheme and nowe in Saxony where Luther is/ and peraduenture in a good parte of Germany.'[59] This allowed More to tackle directly and formally for the first time the question of the nature of the church. He began with a general definition of the *ecclesia ab Adamo* to bring out the point that the church of Christ had been always in existence prior to any heresy: 'E nobis profecti sunt, sed non

---

[57] See *Dialogue,* lvi vFG; liiii v G—lviii r A passim; lx G, Campbell, 117, 113-120 passim and 126: '...since God will not suffer his church to mistake a book of scripture for peril of damnable errors that might ensue thereon—and like peril may there ensue by the misconstruing of the sentence as by the mistaking of the book—it must needs follow that God will in things of our faith no more suffer them to take a false sentence for true than to take a false book for scripture' (Campbell's text).

[58] See *Dialogue,* lxiii rv C-G, Campbell, 132-133.

[59] *Dialogue,* lxiii vF, Campbell, 132.

erant ex nobis' (1 Jn 2, 19): '...we myght fetche the chyrche of Cryst far aboue/and begynne it at Adam. For frome the fyrste good man to the last/ all shall in conclusyon be his chyrche tryumphant in heuyn.'

But, he went on to say, he was more concerned to define the church in terms of those who profess explicit faith in Christ: '...that congregacyon that berynge his name/and hauynge his ryght fayth/and beynge begon to be gathered by hym selfe and sprede abrode by his apostles hath and doth and shall tyll his comyng to the dredefull dome/contynue styll in this worlde...'[60] Was this church in existence prior to Luther? 'Yes', answered the Messenger. More had sketched out a description of Christ's church acceptable to both orthodox and dissidents alike. The question still remained, however, which among the Christian communities answering this description was Christ's church? Could it be more clearly defined?

Negative limits of Christ's church: not infidels

More began negatively by showing that heretics could not be members of the church since living faith was an essential condition for a real relationship with the body of Christ. Even grave personal guilt is compatible with a certain level of inner communion but not formal heresy. Faith of some description is an essential condition for membership in the church of Christ. 'And out of the stocke of the vyne be all/that be not graffed in by fayth/or fallen of by open professyon of heresye/or cut of and caste out for infydelyte. For faythe is the gate into goddys chyrche/as mysbyleue is the gate in to the deuyls chyrche. For as the apostle saythe, Accedentem ad deum oportet credere/(Heb 11, 6) a man can not come to god without fayth.'[61]

Such faith may achieve full integrity through a lively hope and an active charity. But even the man who while retaining faith has lost the friendship of God through sin still remains a member of the church. He is still somehow attached to the body of Christ and may receive from it the vital impulse to become once more a fully organic part of the body, a true branch of the vine (Jn 15, 5). Thomas More did not explore the nature of this *fides informa*. It was and still is a common datum of Catholic theology that only the sin against the Holy Spirit cuts one off completely from the life of the body.[62]

---

[60] *Dialogue*, lxiiii rA, Campbell, 133.
[61] See *Dialogue*, lxiiii vE, Campbell, 134.
[62] See *Dialogue*, lxiiii A-E, Campbell, 134.

Concerning those who have sinned against faith, More made several distinctions. A secret unbeliever is still in the church but not of it 'as a ded hande is rather a burden in the body/than verely any membre organe or instrument therof.' In other words he still belongs to the visible communion although any internal link has been broken off. On the other hand one who professes his disbelief openly before any ban of excommunication has been issued has already left both community and communion. He is no longer a branch of the living vine but rather ready for burning: 'And as the braunche can do no good beynge taken from the tree/ryght so can ye do no good nor serue for nought, but for the fyre/excepte ye abyde in me.'[63] It follows from this that open heretics can never be members of or still less constitute the church of Christ.

...not merely the predestinate

More then went on to exclude another possible concept of the church in terms of the predestinate. He had already himself opened the way for such a definition in speaking of the *ecclesia ab Adamo*. The Messenger was allowed to take the hint and propose that the church of Christ be made up only of those sure to be saved. More did not delay long in dealing with the issue nor indeed treat of it thoroughly in terms of scripture or tradition. He had already acknowledged the body of the predestinate as one valid analogous concept of the church. But for him it was evidently not the principal analogue which he saw in terms of a concrete historical community. The body of the predestinate cannot be identified with such an earthly church since there could be no question of anyone joining it as one is predestinate from conception or birth not from baptism; nor of leaving it through sin since one remains predestined in spite of temporary lapses.

This hypothesis concerning the church of the predestinate is wide of the mark for '...we speak of the church of Christ militant here in earth, and therefore goeth their frame as far wide from the place they should set it on, as heaven and earth stand asunder.'[64]

...not merely the just

The Messenger then brought up the notion of the church proposed by Luther. 'Well quod he yet may it be/that the very chyrche of Cryst/ is all suche as byleue a ryght and lyue well where so euer they be/though the

---

[63] See *Dialogue*, lxiiii rv C-H, Campbell, 134-135.
[64] Campbell, 135-137; see *Dialogue*, lxv rB.

worlde knowe them not/and thoughe fewe of them knewe eche other. For god as saynt Poule saythe/knowe who be his.'[65] (2 Tim 2, 19) He went on to cite Luther's interpretation of Mt 16, 18: 'agaynst his chyrche the gates of hell shall not preuayle...' namely that the gates of hell symbolised personal sin. No one conquered by sin could be a member of the church. More rejected this view.

Luther by sin, however, had meant the sin against faith and had rather gratuitously ascribed such sin to a large proportion of the empirical ecclesiastical community. More, as in the *Responsio*, took Luther to mean sin in the more general sense of grave moral evil. He consequently rejected first of all the Wittenberger's interpretation of Mt 16, 18 as he had done in the *Responsio* and further insisted that the church of Christ on earth must always be afflicted with moral evil. This, our Lord had foreseen.[66] Instead of crossing lances, therefore, the two cavaliers somewhat ungracefully lurched past one another. One significant point More made in this connection concerned the visibility of the church. If the church be unknown even to its own members how could any honest enquirer come to find Christ, be he Turk or Saracen?[67] If the church is to lead men to Christ and to his message it must be known. 'But the chyrche of Cryste is a chyrche well knowen. And his pleasure was to haue it knowen and not hyd. And it is bylded vpon so hygh an hyll of the holy stone/I meane upon cryste hym selfe/that it can not be hyd.' (Mt 5, 14)[68]

Positive limits: visibility

If the church is a road to faith, there must be some means of discovering it. Against the Messenger More argued that the church of Christ always existed in visible form, never as a purely hidden communion in faith. Even in the period of persecution it was always a known visible body coming together for preaching and prayer, the celebration of the sacraments, with fastings and vigils kept in private houses.[69] Such manifestations of

[65] *Dialogue,* lxv vG, Campbell, 137.

[66] *Dialogue,* lxvii vF—lxviii vF, Campbell, 141-143.

[67] *Dialogue,* lxvi vEFG, Campbell, 139.

[68] *Dialogue,* lxvii rD, Campbell, 140.

[69] See *Dialogue,* lxiii rA, Campbell, 131: 'The chyrche of Cryste where so euer it was in all the persecucyon/vsed to come togyther to the prechynge and prayer/thoughe it were preuely in wodys or secrete housys. They vsed also the sacramentes among them selfe/as baptysme/confyrmacyon/matrymony/holy order/prestes and byshoppes amonge them/ fastyngs/vygyls kepte/the sondayes halowed/the masse sayd...And partely well apppereth by a pystle of Plinie wryten to the Emperour Traiane. And suche thyngys must there be therin/yf it be any chyrche or congregacyon of Cryste.' This is a reference to the famous letter of the

community activity, he maintained, belong to the very substance of the church. They are also, in so far as they make it visibly manifest, a necessary condition for enabling someone seeking faith to discover its whereabouts. More, aware of the difficulty facing such a person, posed the case of a Turk or Saracen who, having heard of Christ's name, 'did long to know his scripture and his faith.' How could such a one distinguish between faithful and heretic Christians unless the church be visible?

And indeed visible it is. The apostolic church in Jerusalem and Judea was well known. When Christ said that a man who would not amend his fault should be complained to the church, he clearly envisaged a body which was well known (Mt 18, 17), as did Paul writing to the Corinthians advising them to settle their lawsuits among themselves (1 Cor 6, 4). This indeed is the mind of Christ: 'The cyte can not be hyd that is set on an hyll. (Mt 5, 14) And he wolde haue his fayth dyuulged and spredde abrode openly/not alway whyspered in hukermoker. And therfore he bounde his prechers to stande thereby and not to reuoke his worde for no payne. For he sayd that he dyd not lyght the candell to put it and hyde it under a bushell/for so wolde no man do/but he had kyndeled a fyre which he wolde not sholde lye and smolder as coles dothe in quenche/but he wold it shold burne and gyue lyght.' (Mt 5, 15; Lk 12, 49)[70] Without any doubt, More concluded, Christ intended his church to be clearly visible to all who sought him.

...an empirical, organised community of faith

More had cleared the ground for a clearcut statement as to what he understood the church to be. He had recognised the validity of using the term church to designate the body of the predestinate from all time, *ecclesia ab Adamo*. He had gone on to delineate its elements, relating it specifically to Christ but located in time and space: the congregation bearing Christ's name, having his right faith, spread abroad by his apostles, and awaiting his coming till the end of time. Such a formula however would have been acceptable to both Tyndale and Luther so More set himself to define more closely the reality he intended. He began by explicitly excluding certain notions: that it could include heretics, since true faith was required; that it

---

younger Pliny (c. 112 AD). The governor of Bithynia in this letter asked the Emperor Trajan whether Christians should be punished for bearing the name of Christian or only for specific crimes. It includes a reference to the liturgical practices of the Christian community. See Pliny, *Letters*, X; Eng. tr. in *A New Eusebius, Documents Illustrative of the History of the Church to AD 337*, ed. J. Stevenson, London, 1957, 13-16.

[70] *Dialogue*, lxvii rvD-E, Campbell, 140-141.

consisted only of the predestinate, since visible membership was assumed; that it was not an invisible congregation of the just, since it must be visible to unbelievers and possess tangible elements such as priests and bishops, word and sacrament. Finally he asked the question: what is the church? Unlike the *Responsio* he devoted one single chapter to anwering the question. The chapter as such is short, less than one page of the 1531 edition. Nonetheless the approach adopted and the emphasis given it clearly shows that he had come to regard this as a matter of crucial importance in dealing with his opponents, as indeed it was. The experience of the *Responsio* had now crystallised into formal conviction.

And so to answer the question: 'Is it not this company and congregayon of all these nacyons/that without faccyons taken and precysyon from the remenaunt/professe the name and fayth of Cryst...this is the very chyrch/and this hath begon at cryst/and hath had hym for theyr hed and saynt Peter his vycar after hym the hed vnder hym/and alway synce the successours of hym contynually/and haue had his holy fayth and his blessyd sacramentes and his holy scryptures delyuered/kept and conserued therin by god and his holy spyryte.'[71] More was quite explicit. The church of Christ is the visible body of Christian nations. This body is in historical continuity with its founder Jesus Christ. It is headed by the pope, successor of Peter, Christ's vicar. It preserves the faith of Christ, his sacraments and the scriptures. Primarily, for More, the church is the people, 'all the crysten people whom we call the chyrche' as he had put it a little earlier; 'the comen knowen multytude of crysten men good and bad togyther.'[72] Hence he adopted an essentially popular view of the church recognising the multiplicity of nations which made it up. This people can trace its beginnings back to Christ: thus historical continuity with its origins is important. Unambiguously he placed subordination of the church to the Roman pontiff as head under Christ in succession to Peter as one of its distinguishing characteristics. But the papacy is not the sole symbol of its historical presence for it conserves the faith, sacraments and scriptures of Christ by the power and grace of God.

All of this tends to emphasise empirical elements in the church, the social and institutional in a manner almost the converse of the reformers' emphasis. More never allowed the empirical and tangible aspects of ecclesial life to predominate in his thought, but the church needs to be clearly identifiable so that we may receive the authentic word of God from her

---

[71] See *Dialogue*, lxviii vG, Campbell, 143-144.
[72] *Dialogue*, lxviii rAB, Campbell, 142.

hands: 'By this chyrch knowe we the scrypture.' The spiritual elements of faith, scripture and sacrament are conserved, not by ecclesiastical officialdom but 'by god and his holy spyryte'. Very quickly in the same passage More went on to underline the inner spiritual reality of this historically tangible body of believers: only this '...chyrch of cryst is the vyne that cryst spake of in the gospell/which he taketh for his body mystycall...'[73] This social body is the true vine of John's gospel, the body of Christ of Paul's epistles imbued with divine life flowing from its inner source in Christ its root and head.

For More there is no radical distinction, in contrast with the Lutheran position, between the spiritual communion of believers and the empirical body of the faithful. The spatio-temporal dimension of the people of God constitutes the physical presence of what is at its core a spiritual reality. One may share in varying degrees the inner life of this body, the minimum being that of the man in grave sin just as one may share in varying degrees its external manifestation, in this case the minimum degree being that of a secret heretic. Essentially the two are twin aspects of a single unity, inextricably bound together as body and soul.

Church order: presbyterate

For all its unity in spirit and in faith, this body is differentiated at the empirical level according to the gift each one receives.[74] More assumed the basic distinction of cleric and lay, of 'spiritualty and temporalty' without presenting a detailed exposé of church order. This was something given in the accepted nature of things.[75] In keeping with his populist views he recognised that the mission to preach was given to all believers, that is to the church as a whole. Nevertheless he saw this function as the special province of the clergy[76] as the celebration of the sacraments is primarily their

---

[73] *Dialogue*, lxviii H, Campbell, 144.

[74] See *Dialogue*, cxv vFG, Campbell, 245: 'And surely syth as the holy appostle saynt Poule in dyuers of his epystles sayth/god hath by his holy spyryte so instytute and ordeyned his chyrch/that he wyl haue some reders and some herers/some techers and som lerners/we do playnly peruerte and tourne up so downe the ryght order of Crystes chyrch/whan the one parte medleth with the others offyce.' (Eph. 4, 11)

[75] See *Dialogue*, vi vG, Campbell, 13.

[76] See *Dialogue*, liiii r A-D, Campbell, 111-112: 'For as his (Christ's) father sayd of hymselfe here hym/so sayd he of his chyrche whan he sent it abrode to be spred forthe. For whan he had gathered his chyrch of his apostles and his dyscyples/and therupon sent them forth to preche/sayd he not vnto them/he that hereth you hereth me. Dyd he not also commaunde that who so wolde not here the chyrche sholde be reputed and taken as paynyms and publycans...the chyrche is the person whom ye be by Cryst commaunded to here and byleue and obay.' See ibid. xxxiii r CD, Campbell, 69, regarding Jn 21, 16: 'fede my shepe...' and Jn 14, 26: '...the holy goste shold enstructe them of all thynges.'

role, not to be usurped by unqualified laity.[77] In the *Responsio* More had upheld the jurisdiction of the church though basing it on the law of love rather than on any theories of power or juridical right. So too in the *Dialogue* he recognised the right of the clergy to legislate for the good of the church.[78]

In dealing with Tyndale's translation of the Greek *presbyteros* as *senior*, More expanded somewhat his ideas on ministry. He gave a garbled version of Luther's theology of office, ascribing to the latter the view that the office of preacher came solely by popular election and was essentially impermanent, while any man, woman or child could celebrate the other sacraments. This concept, he felt, underlay Tyndale's use of *senior* for *presbyteros* as well as appearing in *The Obedience of a Christian Man*.[79] More upheld the traditional view of orders as a consecration to God making of the recipient an anointed person. Putting his rejection of Tyndale positively, one can assume on More's side the special role of the priesthood in the sacramental ministry.[80] More emphasised that neither the value of this, nor indeed the validity of office itself depended on the quality of life of its holder.[81] Indeed he made a special point of defending the virtue of the clergy in England affirming that man for man they were better than their counterparts elsewhere. This, however, did not blind him to the need for practical reform.[82]

...Episcopate and papal primacy

More did not dwell at length on the episcopal office as such but he did have more to say concerning the primacy of Rome. He included the

---

[77] See *Dialogue*, lxiii vG, Campbell, 133: 'And yet all they (heretics and schismatics) knowledge that they can not haue the sacramentes mynystred/but by suche prestys as be made by authoryte deryued and conuayed frome the pope whiche is vnder Cryste vycary and the hedde of our chyrche.'

[78] See *Dialogue*, xxxii r A, Campbell, 66: More quotes Mt 23, 4 in support of his position where Christ speaks of burdens imposed by Scribes and Pharisees: 'And yet for all that he bad the peple do what theyr prelatys wolde byd them/though the burden were heuy/And let not to do it though they sholde se the bydders do clene the contrary. For whiche he addyd/but as they do/do not you.' See also ibid. xxxii rv B-F, Campbell, 66-67 where More attempts to persuade his readers that ecclesiastical legislation is less oppressive than might at first appear.

[79] *Dialogue*, lxxxxviii vG, lxxxxix rA, Campbell, 210. More referred to William Tyndale, *The Obedience of a Christen man and how Christen rulers ought to gouerne*, Antwerp, 2 October 1528.

[80] ibid.

[81] See *Dialogue*, cii vEFG, Campbell, 218: ibid., vi vH—vii rA, Campbell, 12-13. More argued that the authority of judges in an ecclesiastical court was independent of their own private moral conduct.

[82] See below pp. 158-159.

petrine office in his definition of the church: '...this is the very chyrch/and this hath begon at cryst/and hath had hym for theyr hed and saynt Peter his vycar after hym the hed under hym/and alway synce the successours of hym contynually/and haue had his holy fayth and his blessyd sacramentes and his holy scryptures delyuered/kept and conserued therin by god and his holy spyryte.'[83] St Peter and his successors, according to More, were appointed heads of the church by Christ: 'But syth that vpon his fyrst con-fessyon of the ryght fayth that Cryste was goddys sonne/our lorde made hym his vniuersall vicare/and vnder hym hed of his chyrche. And that for his successour he sholde be the fyrst vpon whom and whose ferme con-fessed fayth he wolde bylde his chyrch/and of any that was onely man make hym the fyrst and chefe hed and ruler therof/...'[84] It is interesting to note that More here conflated two distinct interpretations of the petrine text, one which considers the rock on which the church is founded to be the faith which Peter professed, namely that Christ is the Son of God; the sec-ond that Peter in his successors is the rock on which the church is founded: Peter's 'successour he sholde be the fyrst *upon whom and whose ferme confessed fayth he wolde bylde his chyrch...*' In his *Responsio ad Lutherum* More had insisted that the literal interpretation of this text referred the term rock to Peter;[85] the first view like Catharinus he regarded as an alternative, spiritual sense of the text. Now however, arising out of a discussion of Lk 22, 31-32: 'sathanas hath desyred to syfte thee as men syfte corne/but I have prayed for thee that thy fayth shall not fayle/...' he admitted the significance of the first interpretation. He was willing to agree that Peter's personal faith did fail him in the passion of Christ but that this belief was kept alive in the church in the heart of Mary who never ceased to believe in her Son. Perhaps somewhat illogically, he inferred from this that Peter had a decisive role in communicating faith to the rest of this brethren: 'And therfore our lorde added therto. And thou beyng one of these dayes con-uertyd/conferme and strength thy bretherne. (Lk 22, 32) In whiche by these wordes our sauyour ment and promysed that the fayth sholde stande for euer. So that the gates of hell shold not preuayle there agaynst.'[86] This opinion of More's appears a little clearer in another text concerned with Mt 16, 18-20: 'And thus it appereth that the fayth came in to saynt Peter his harte as to the prynce of the appostles without herynge by secrete inspyra-

---

[83] See *Dialogue*, lxviii vG, Campbell, 144.
[84] See *Dialogue*, xxxiii r AB, Campbell, 68.
[85] See above pp. 108-111.
[86] See *Dialogue*, xxxiii r C, Campbell, 69.

cyon/and in to the remenaunt by his confessyon and Crystes holy mouthe.'[87]

Thus while More had some difficulty in giving a full, mutually harmonious rendering of the various petrine references, he did not waver in his assertion regarding the appointment of Peter and his successors as heads of the church, the rock on which the church is founded and endures. Faith is communicated to the rest of the apostles by Peter's 'confessyon and Crystes holy mouthe.' Peter's faith does not fail, at least in the sense that once it has been passed on to the church it will always be kept alive. The paradigm for this, offered by More, was Mary. During the passion of Christ Mary never lost faith in her son.

More even made of the pope the ultimate authority in sacramental matters, saying: 'And yet all they (heretics of Bohemia) knowledge that they can not haue the sacramentes mynystred/but by suche prestys as be made by authoryte deryued and conuayed frome the pope whiche is vnder Cryste vycary and the hedde of our chyrche.'[88] Papal primacy therefore is not merely one of honour but one of authority as well. Christ's command to Peter to feed his sheep (Jn 21, 16) was also addressed to his successors.[89]

The church for More was primarily a spiritual, divinely constituted and animated body of people, not left however as a shapeless mass but organised, taught and guided by duly appointed leaders under the supreme direction of the Roman pontiff.

Sinfulness of the church

As it exists in this world, Christ's church is very much a mixed body, comprising not merely '...all suche as byleue a ryght and lyue well where so euer they be/though the worlde knowe them not/and thoughe fewe of them knewe eche other...' as the Messenger, More's interlocutor would have it in Lutheran fashion.[90] No, 'The chyrche therfore must nedys be

---

[87] See *Dialogue*, xlvi r A, Campbell, 95.

[88] See *Dialogue*, lxiii v G, Campbell, 133.

[89] See *Dialogue*, xxxi v E, Campbell, 65: '...ye do quod I agre/that suche thynges as are mencyoned in the gospell/spoken by Cryst vnto saynt Peter and other his apostles and dysciples/were not only sayd to them selfe/nor onely for them selfe/but to them for theyr successours in Crystes floke/...'

[90] See *Dialogue*, lxv v G, Campbell, 137; ibid. lxvi r A, Campbell, 138: '...And so may it be peraduenture nowe/that the very chyrche of Cryste is not nor many dayes hath not bene the people that semeth to be the chyrche/but some good men scatered here and there unknowen/tyll god gather theym togyther and make theym knowen/and happely those that byleue agaynste ymagys and whome we nowe call heretyques.' More totally rejected this view as he could not conceive of any man being free from sin. If sinlessness be a condition for membership in the church, then it makes nonsense of any realistic conception of the church.

the comen knowen multytude of crysten men good and bad togyther/whyle the chyrche is here in erth. For this nette of Cryste hath for the whyle good fysshes and bad. And this felde of Cryste bereth for the whyle good corne and cocle/tyll it shall at the day of dome be puryfyed/and all the bad caste out/and the onely good remayne.'[91] Sinfulness is a characteristic of the church from earliest times. Judas the apostle was to betray our Lord. The latter was sure of this for early on in his public life he said: 'and one of you is a devil.' (Jn 6, 71) St Peter because of his betrayal could not be accounted a faultless member of the church over which Christ appointed him as head. In the earliest communities the apostles had to deal with the greatest sins such as incest at Corinth (I Cor 5, 1-5). Evil belongs almost to the very being of the church in this world. Sin as such, consequently, does not cut one off *ipso facto* from membership of the body: 'But our lorde in his mystycall body of his chyrche/ caryed his membres/some seke/some hole/and all sekely. Nor they be not for euery syn clene caste of from the body/But yf they be for fere of infeccyon cut of/or els wyllyngly do departe and seperate them selfe as do these heretykes/that eyther refuse the chyrch wylfully them selfe/or els for theyr obstynacy be put out.'[92] Freedom from sin is not a condition for membership in the church on earth. Far from it, its members are 'all sickly.'

Need for reform

On the other hand, More's recognition that the church is essentially imperfect did not imply any kind of compromise. This came out clearly when he dealt with the Messenger's objections to established orthodoxy based on the clergy's low level of morality. More's initial response was to defend the clergy: '...so dare I boldely say that the spyrytualty of Englonde/ and specyally that parte in whiche ye fynde most faute/that is to wyt that parte whiche we comenly call the secular clergye/is in lernyynge and honeste lyuyng well able to matche and...farre able to ouer matche number for nomber the spyrytualtye of any nacyon crysten.'[93] More went on to add that criticism of the clergy was often unbalanced and that while many might be indifferent the whole church was indebted to those of outstanding goodness.

Having thrown a few bouquets, he outlined a programme for clerical reform. The laws as they existed, he maintained, were adequate. What

---

[91] See *Dialogue*, lxviii r B, Campbell, 142.
[92] See *Dialogue,* lxviii r D, Campbell, 142.
[93] See *Dialogue*, ci rA, Campbell, 215.

was needed was their strict implementation. The main problem was the large number offering themselves for holy orders. Time was when men thought twice of asking for this holy office. 'Nowe ronneth euery rascall and boldely offreth hym selfe for able. And where the dygnyte passeth all pryncys/and they that lewde be/desyreth it for worldely wynnynge...' More had few illusions about the quality of life of many of the clergy. His anger against time-servers and position-seekers breaks out: 'But for the number/I wold surely se suche a way therin/that we sholde not haue suche a rabell/that euery meane man must haue a preste in his house to wayte vppon his wyfe/whiche no man almost lacketh nowe/to the contempte of presthed in as vyle offyce as his horsekeper.' The sight of a clergy becoming religious grooms to the wealthy houses of England turned his stomach.[94] The same problem arose concerning clerical celibacy. More admitted the existence of abuses and called for the full enforcement of existing law.[95] 'But nowe yf the bysshops wolde ones take vnto presthed better ley men and fewer...all the matter were more than halfe amended.'[96]

Destined to be perfect

On the other hand, the church is not destined to remain always in this mixed condition of holiness and sin. She is caught up in a movement of history extending from Adam to the end of time. The day will come when in fact the church will coincide with the body of the predestinate and evil will disappear from the midst. 'But whan the tyme shall come that this chyrche shall hole chaunge her place and haue heuyn for her dwellynge in stede of erth/after the fynall iudgement pronounced and gyuen whan god shall with his spouse this chyrch of cryst entre in to the plesaunt weddyng chambre to the bed of eternall rest/than shall all these scalde and scabbed peces scale clene of/and the hole body of Crystes holy chyrch remayne pure/clene and gloryous/without wem/wrincle or spot/which is (and for the whyle I wene wyl be/as long as she is here) as scabed as euer was Job/...'[97] It is precisely because of this paradoxical character of the church on earth, and the hidden nature of the church in glory that faith is needed to believe in her. The Christian community itself must be an object of

---

[94] *Dialogue,* cii vE—ciii vH, Campbell, 218-221.
[95] *Dialogue,* ciiii rA—cviii r A, Campbell, 221-229.
[96] *Dialogue,* ci r B, Campbell, 215.
[97] See *Dialogue,* lxviii v E, Campbell, 143. See also ibid., lxiiii r A, Campbell, 133: 'Yf we sholde go quod I to that rekenynge/we myght fetche the chyrche of Cryst far aboue/and begynne it at Adam. For frome the fyrste good man to the last/all shall in conclusyon be his chyrche tryumphant in heuyn.'

faith: 'For we besyde the scrypture do byleue the chyrch/bycause that god hym selfe by secrete inspyracyon of hys holy spyryte/doth (yf we be wyllynge to lerne) teche us to byleue hys chyrche/...'[98]

V. CHURCH AND REVELATION: FURTHER PRECISION

Consensus

The presence of the divine Spirit preserving life in this mixed bag of saints, sinners and indifferent Christians alike ensures that this multitude remains a community, not only in discipline and practice but also in faith. The Spirit of God accomplishes this by an inner movement of the mind. He 'enclyneth theyr credulyte to consent in the byleuyng all in one poynt whiche is the secrete instyncte of god/thys is the sure meane that neuer can in any necessary poynte fayle here in Crystys chyrche.'[99] Because of the divine guarantee underlying its consensus the common faith of the church becomes the sure guide to orthodox doctrine: 'And therby do I playnly know it for an heresye/yf an heresy be a secte and a syde way (taken by any parte of suche as ben baptysed/and bere the name of crysten men) from the comen fayth and byleue of the hole chyrche besyde.'[100] This consensus is spread over space and time, the agreement being not merely that of contemporary Christians but those of previous ages as well. Hence writing of the cult of saints recorded in antiquity, More said: 'And syth we further perceyue that theyr bokes be wryten in dyuers regyons and sondry ages/we therby well perceyue that these thynges be parcell of the rytes vsages and byleue of Crystes chyrch/not onely nowe and of late/but continually from the begynnynge hytherto. And syth it is playnly proued you that the chyrche can in no wyse be suffred of god to fall in to any damnable errour therby/it is yet most surely concluded/that these thynges be none suche.'[101] Surety in judgment is given where communion in faith is found not only in the local, contemporary body of believers but most certainly when spread through space and time.

Development of doctrine and consensus

On the other hand it can happen that agreement in regard to any particular proposition is not immediately arrived at. In regard to certain

---

[98] See *Dialogue*, lxxxv v H, Campbell, 182.

[99] See Dialogue, lxxiiii v G, Campbell, 157-158: 'For goddes holy spyryte that anymateth his chyrche and gyueth it lyfe/wyll neuer suffer it all (to) consent and agre togyther vpon any dampnable errour', ibid., lxxv r A, Campbell, 158.

[100] See *Dialogue*, vii r D, Campbell, 14.

[101] See *Dialogue*, lxxxii v GH, Campbell, 175; see also *Dialogue*, lxxx r AB, Campbell 169.

beliefs past generations had already arrived at consensus, More pointed out. In that case we must remain true to their positions no matter how many abandon them. Nonetheless, '...yf there were any thyng that was peraduenture such/that in the chyrche somtyme was doubted and reputed for vnreueled and vnknowen/yf after that the holy chyrche fall in one consent vpon the one syde/eyther by common determynacyon at a generall counsayle/or by a perfyte perswasyon and byleue so receyued thrughe crystendome/that the crysten people thynke it a dampnable erroure to byleue the contrary/than yf any wolde after that take the contrary waye/ were it one or mo/were it fewe or many/were they lerned or vnlerned/ were they ley people or of the clergye/yet can I nothynge doubte whiche parte to byleue yf I wyll byleue the chyrche.'[102] This view concerning the gradual growth of agreement among Christian people regarding points at one time deeply disputed creates some difficulties concerning the doctrine of consensus. What is in question here is clearly not agreement in the fuller sense, extending across the centuries, but agreement arrived at from varying positions at a particular point of history subsequent to apostolic times. Looking at More's position critically, strictly from the stand-point of consensus, this agreement would seem to carry less weight than one of a more extended character. On the other hand, the viewpoint expressed here is quite in keeping with his position in regard to possible growth in understanding of the teaching of Christ brought about by the action of the Holy Spirit within God's people. Even though a consensus did not always exist, present consensus is binding.

The position he adopted at a later stage himself, regarding the oath of supremacy, is already contained embryonically in this statement of the binding force of the consensus of the contemporary church, even in matters not immediately evident in scripture. Given such agreement, '...were it one or mo/were it fewe or many/were they lerned or vnlerned/were they ley people or of the clergye/(who held the contrary opinion) yet can I nothynge doubte...' The lonely position of the man imprisoned in the Tower is already foreshadowed. On the other hand, it must always be added that More never felt himself completely alone when in tune with the 'common corps of Christendom' even against the councils of his own realm.

The faith of the Christian people was for More the final and lasting touchstone of belief. '...the force of my tale was not the myracles/but the thynge that I holde stronger than any myracles/whiche as I sayd in the

---

[102] See *Dialogue,* liii v G, Campbell, 111.

begynnyng I reken so sure and fast/and therwith so playne and euydent
vnto euery crysten man/that it nedeth none other profe/and that thynge is
as I sayd afore the fayth of Crystes chyrche/by the common consent
wherof. (sic) These matters be decyded and well knowen that the worshyp
of sayntes and ymages ben alowed/approbate/and accustomed for good
crysten and merytoryous vertues/...'[103]

There is little of originality in More's treatment of consensus in terms of
an evolution of his position since the *Responsio* of 1523. The main difference is one of language as he was now writing in English. The terms he
used to designate *consensus* were commonplace enough: 'consent', 'agreement and consent'; 'consent and agree', 'perfect persuasion and belief';
all of these were synonymous with the recurrent formula 'common faith
and belief'. The idea is straightforward, the position if anything less
nuanced than in the *Responsio*, as More did not delve for example into the
question of what might constitute an acceptable level of dissent compatible
with an authoritative and binding consensus. This he had dealt with in the
Responsio with the trenchant phrase: 'in no action of a multitude is
unanimous consent required.'[104] One area in which a certain degree of
innovation did occur was in dealing with the development of doctrine.
This had been touched on implicitly in the *Responsio* in his recognition that
certain credal statements, such as that of the consubstantiality of Son with
Father from the Nicene Creed,[105] were not to be found explicitly in scripture. In the *Dialogue* there was a more explicit recognition that while at one
time opposing views may coexist in the church on particular issues, over a
period of time, possibly centuries, these may merge into a single voice
which must be heard as that of Christ. Consensus may not always be
spread over the history of the church but may be of more recent occurrence. Such an agreement is no less binding than one of ancient origin.
More was to speak further on this subject later in his career.

The theological basis for his doctrine on consensus was again in no way
novel. It sprang first of all from the abiding presence of God with his
church promised by Christ. The texts used were familiar: Mt 18, 20; Mt
28, 20; Jn 14, 16-18. The second foundation of the doctrine lay in his conviction that the church would never fail in faith. This too was based on the
promise of divine presence and assistance, but more specifically on Mt 16,
18, 'the gates of hell will not prevail', and Lk 22, 32, Christ's prayer for

---

[103] See *Dialogue*, xvii rv DE, Campbell, 32.
[104] *Responsio*, 608/1-3, tr. 609/2-3: 'quod in nullo actu multitudinis, requiritur, quod
omnes ad unum consentiant.'
[105] *Responsio*, 102/13-27, tr. 103/15-32.

Peter that his faith fail not.[106] The third support for More's platform of
consensus lay in the scriptural texts emphasising unity and promising the
gift of the Spirit to bring it about. Here his treatment was a little more explicit. For example in one place he began with Christ's promise to return
to his disciples (Jn 14, 18) and went on to his exhortation to them to
become a brotherhood of love (Jn 15, 15 and Jn 13, 34). He then spoke of
Christ's promise to send them a comforter to bring to mind all things
which he had spoken to them (Jn 14, 26). The role of the Spirit however, is
not only to remind the apostles and his church of Christ's teaching but to
lead them into all truth (Jn 16, 13). This is the purpose of his abiding with
them (Jn 14, 16-18), to bring them as a body to a right understanding of
his revelation to them.

More also used 1 Cor 1, 10, Paul's exhortation to the Corinthians to be
of one mind, to buttress his claim that unity of belief was essential to the
church. Similarly he used Acts 4, 32 'Erat multitudo credentium, anima
una et cor' to underline the quality of such agreement among the early
Christians. He also deployed what had been virtually his favourite citation
in the *Responsio*: Ps 67, 7: 'qui facit unanimes in domo' translated:
'whyche maketh all of one mynde in the house of god/that is in the
chyrche.'[107] More used this text more sparingly than in the *Responsio*. His
case for consensus did not rest on one mistranslated pericope from the
old testament but on three columns, three themes central to the new
testament, of which one was illustrated by the earlier, over used Ps 67, 7
quotation.

Councils

More did not greatly stress the role of the general council in the *Dialogue*.
The decisions of such gatherings are one way in which the voice of the

---

[106] More here draws up the problem raised in late medieval theology as to whether the
faith of the church did fail during Christ's passion. The answer offered was that true faith
was kept alive in the heart of at least one person, namely the Virgin Mary. Ockham had
used this objection to argue that no consensus could be absolutely binding since the same
case might be repeated at a later stage in history. Through Panormitanus this position
reached Martin Luther and was used by him to justify his rejection of the general council.
So paradoxically, the same example used by More to vindicate the indefectibility of the
church's faith and so ground consensus was used by Luther to reject consensus, at least as
evidenced in the general council. For Luther, see *WA* 2, 404/26-31: '...plus credenduum uni
privato fideli quam toti concilio aut Papae, si meliorem habeat autoritatem vel rationem.'
Cf. also *WA* 568 ff.; *WA* 1, 279. For Panormitanus, see idem, *Commentaria in decretales*, Lyon,
1512, 1, 6, 4, no. 2. fol. 85.

[107] See Headley, *Responsio* 823 and 890 (comment on 128/12); Marius, *Confutation* III,
1352-1353.

whole church can be heard. As we have seen when discussing the development of consensus, in regard to questions at one time disputed he
remarked: 'yf after that the holy chyrche fall in one consent upon the one
syde/eyther by common determynacyon at a generall counsayle/or by a
perfyte perswasyon and byleue so receyued thrughe crystendome/...'[108]
Here More seemed to equiparate the agreement of a general council with
the common consent of the church. Does this make of the council the voice
of the whole people, and not merely their teacher? Is there a 'democratic'
view of the council underlying this position, or is it a mere turn of phrase?

The other important conciliar reference in the *Dialogue* suggests the
'democratic' view as does the whole context of More's thought concerning
the presence of the Spirit within the general body of the church. Quoting
presumably the Second Council of Nicea (787)[109] in its approval of the cult
of images and condemnation of iconoclasticism he said: 'Nor besydes this
haue I nothyng spoken of the generall counsayls condempnyng your parte
by good and substancyall authoryte *comprobate and corroborate* by the hole
body of crystendom/led therunto bothe long before and euer synce/thorow
the secret operacyon of the holy gost/...'[110] The conciliar statements are
taken by More, not as standing on their own but within the general context
of the common faith of the Christian community. This common faith
preceded the conciliar decree, followed upon it and added weight to it. This
may have been a debating technique for use against a Lutheran position
which by this time had abandoned the traditional notion of conciliar
authority. It may also have been a symptom of the post-conciliar epoch
when the authority of councils had been weakened by mutual contradiction
as well as conflict with the papacy. Or it may more likely have represented
an implicit belief in the primacy of the Spirit within the whole people of
God, recognising the council as the mouthpiece not of the hierarchy alone
but of the entire church. We shall have to await a study of his later writings
for further clarification on this issue.

The subject of the general council received little further formal treatment in the *Dialogue*, less even than in the *Responsio*. More referred occasionally to the authority of the council but preferred to lean on ecclesial
consensus as the main support for his positions. Perhaps this arose from

---

[108] *Dialogue*, liii v G, Campbell, 111.

[109] See C. Emereau, *Iconoclasme*, *DTC* 7/1, (1922), 584-587; P. Bayerschmidt,
Bilderverhehrung, *LTK* II, (1958), 464-467; for the teaching of the Second Council of Nicea see
H. Denzinger and H. Schönmetzer, *Enchiridion Symbolorum*, 32nd ed., Herder, Barcelona,
1963, 200-202, nos. 600-603.

[110] See *Dialogue*, lxix v G, Campbell, 146.

his realisation that already in the *Contra Henricum* Luther had placed severe limits on the authority of councils.[111] More claimed that he had thrown them over completely, though this was hardly true. Nonetheless, though he himself recognised the general council's role in voicing the consensus of the church he did not underline it. He was careful moreover to see the council in the context of such consensus both as expressing a pre-existing agreement and in having its decisions 'comprobate and corroborate' by their acceptance in the believing community. Perhaps the conciliar history of the previous century lay behind this, perhaps his awareness that the Greeks and Armenians had subsequently rejected the hard-won agreement on papal primacy drawn up at Florence.[112] Perhaps he sensed that he was somewhat closer than traditional conciliarists to the Lutheran position on church authority in matters of doctrine in stressing the agreement of the believing community. Whatever the cause at this stage in the debate, conciliar thought played little part in More's ecclesiology.

VI. SIGNS OF CHRIST'S CHURCH

Having established, at least to his own satisfaction, the nature and authority of the Christian community in relation to revelation in particular, the question naturally arose as to how this community might be identified with any degree of certainty.

More was now moving into what was for him new ground, the area of apologetics. What are the distinguishing features by which the church of Christ can be known from any other congregation claiming the same name? Western Christendom had had few doubts concerning its identity since Charlemagne. By argument from scripture and by common sense More had established the necessity of the essential visibility of the Christian people. But this left open other possibilities which he did not as yet fully envisage but may have been lurking at the back of his mind. What of the case where two or more visible communities claimed to be those instituted by Christ?

---

[111] See *Dialogue*, cxxv vF-cxxvi rD, Campbell, 267; Luther, *Contra Henricum*, (1522), *WA* 10/2, 219/9-11. 'Quare videmus hic, omnes Pontifices, omnia Concilia, omnes scholas, qui aliud in Ecclesia sonant quam verbum dei solius, esse lupos, Satanae ministros et falsos prophetas.' For Luther's theology of and appeal to the general council see A. Ebneter, *Luther und das Konzil, Zeitschrift für katholische Theologie* 84 (1962) 1-48; especially 1-29 for the period 1518-1524; Peter Meinhold, *Das Konzil im Jahrhundert der Reformation* in *Die ökumenischen Konzile der Christenheit*, ed. H. J. Margull, Stuttgart, 1961, 201-210; Martin Seils, *Das ökumenische Konzil in der Lutherischen Theologie*, ibid., 333-339.

[112] See J. Gill SJ, *The Council of Florence*, Cambridge, 1959, 227-388.

One indication of the identity of Christ's church, he suggested, is its
unity in faith: '...besydes all thys/ye can not say that these be the chyrche
whom we call heretyques/but ye must tell whiche kynde of them is the
chyrche. For all can not be/sythe the chyrche is and must be all of one
byleue/and haue all one faythe. And as it was wryten in the actys of the
apostles. Erat multitudo credencium anima una et cor unum. (Acts 4, 32)
The multytude of faythfull byleuynge men were all of one mynde and of
one harte. And in the chyrche is the holy goste/qui facit unanimes in
domo/(Ps 67, 7) whyche maketh all of one mynde in the house of god/that
is in the chyrche/But as for amonge heretyques/there be as many dyuers
myndys almoste as there be men.'[113] Unity of faith is a mark which
characterises the church of Christ, a characteristic of that common known
multitude whose consensus concerning things to be believed had been
accepted by More as one of the principal criteria of faith.

Miracles

More also developed an argument for the identity of Christ's church
based on the phenomenon of miracles. Miracles he argued, were they not
performed by God 'to the entente to make his messengers knowen and the
trouthe of his message? As when he sent Moyses to Pharao/were not the
myracles done by god to make Pharao perceyue therby the trouth of his
worde?' This was the pattern in both old and new testaments. More's conclusion was that miracles have been worked in the Christian church 'for
the knowlege of his doctours and declaracyon of hys doctryne/...' In other
words just as miracles testified to the mission of Moses and the twelve
apostles, so also they witness to the validity of the traditional doctrine
handed down by the 'old holy doctors' of the 'catholic knowen church' and
consequently to the points More had been trying to establish in the course
of his controversy.[114] The performance of miracles testifies to the substantially accurate transmission of authentic doctrine within Catholic tradition.

More carried the argument a stage further for he noted that miracles do
not appear to be performed among heretical sects, notwithstanding the
Messenger's claims. Some wonders, it is reported, are claimed for pagan,
Turk, and Saracen peoples but curiously the source of miracles seems to
have dried up within the Jewish people as if to underline their error. It is

---

[113] See *Dialogue*, lxiii r C, Campbell, 132-133: '...the chyrch of Cryst is a people of one
faythe/...'; ibid. lxiiii r B, Campbell, 134.

[114] See *Dialogue*, lxxx v G—lxxxi r A, Campbell, 170-171, and passim.

within the Catholic community that such wonders happen: '...and the doynge therof in his onely chyrche/may be among many other thynges one good marke and sure token/wherby all these false sectys of them may be dyscernyd and knowen frome hys very true chyrche/that is to say from the hole congragacyon of true crysten people in this worlde/...'[115] The working of miracles by God only within this Christian people is an unmistakable sign that they are the true church of Christ.

Thus without making it one of his major concerns Sir Thomas More had worked out for himself a simple form of apologetic by means of which the true Christian people could be distinguished from the various sects claiming to be the church of Christ. The first characteristic he had earlier established: its visibility. Only a visible church can be known. The second was its essential unity in faith since this seems demanded by the example of the Christian community and the promise of scripture. The third is the working of miracles within the community of Christian people spread throughout Christendom. These miracles testify to the validity of traditional doctrine, and point to this community as being the elect of God. This latter argument for him had special force as such wonders did not seem to have occurred among other religious groups.

By the discernment of these signs the unbeliever can discover for himself the true congregation of Christian believers and so prepare himself for the gift of faith, since 'god hym selfe by secrete inspyracyon of hys holy spyryte/doth (yf we be wyllynge to lerne) teche vs to byleue hys chyrche.'[116] It is of interest to note a certain change of direction here from the *Responsio ad Lutherum* where, in so far as any apologetic was provided, it depended mainly on the argument from continuity, the essential organic connection between the living church and that of patristic, and through that, of apostolic times.[117] This shift, perhaps, corresponds to a certain change of status on the part of the Lutheran community in Germany where by 1527, having survived the turmoil of the peasant revolt, it was beginning to take on the appearance of a rival establishment to that of traditional orthodoxy. Since in many areas Evangelicals represented practically the entire community, the argument from organic continuity was no longer as pressing as in 1523 when urged against what then could

---

[115] See *Dialogue*, lxxxii r C, Campbell, 174 and passim.

[116] See *Dialogue*, lxxxv v H, Campbell, 182 and passim.

[117] In the *Responsio*, I have found only one reference to miracles, and that in a purely negative sense. More points out sarcastically that Luther is not proving the divine origin of his mission by miracle, *Responsio*, 236/5-9, tr. 237/8-12.

have been dismissed as a handful of agitators within the larger body of believers.

The apologetic issue was growing in importance as polemic was failing to achieve its objective. More's approach, though undergoing a certain development in terms of a new emphasis on the testimony of miraculous intervention, still remained within the category of scripturally based apologetic. Though similar initiatives were being taken by writers elsewhere in Europe, this developing dimension of his thought indicates that he remained close to the heart of the debate. Through his experience in *Responsio* and *Dialogue* he had succeeded in clarifying for himself the answer to the question: what is the church of Christ? The further question was now growing more pressing: among rival communities claiming the name, which is the true church of Christ? This was to constitute, nominally at least, his central preoccupation in the major controversial work to follow, the *Confutation of Tyndale's Answer*.

VII. CONCLUSION

More's treatment of ecclesiology is a good deal more lucid and relaxed in the *Dialogue* than in the *Responsio*. The *Responsio* reads like the work of a man intervening in a two-sided argument to back up a friend, except perhaps in the additional H gathering. The strategy and field of battle were not of his choosing. It also reads like the work of a man who is not entirely sure as to what the quarrel is about and has to resolve the issues as he writes, *solvitur ambulando*. The first book was concerned mainly with tradition, the second with the sacraments. The question of the church remained always in the background, entering obliquely into many aspects of the discussions, principally as bearer of the divine message and guarantor of authenticity in sacramental practice. Then in the H gathering it became the central theme, not so much in terms of a clearcut attempt at definition as in negative terms. More had to overcome Luther's arguments concerning the irreconcilability of sin with membership of the church. Inevitably this led to a definition of the church in tangible, visible terms in opposition to Luther's ghostly communion of the justified. The main thrust, however, was negative.

In the *Dialogue* More seems to take up where he had left off in the *Responsio*. Basic issues had been settled in his mind and had had several years to mature. The faith of the church is an unfailing and sure guide to belief. Divine revelation has been given to the Christian people not only in the eminent form of inspired scripture but also in the socio-cultural tradi-

tion of a living community. Most important of all, the divine word is inscribed in the hearts of the faithful by the Holy Spirit. This operation of
the Spirit has found historical expression in the faith of a community
extending in time back to its origin in Christ. A common faith does not
preclude development, a passage from divergent opinions to consistent
belief, a new accent in the *Dialogue*. But the ultimate guide for the believer
is the church of Christ for it is the church which points to the scripture and
provides a reliable interpretation of its message.

   This leads naturally into the direct question of the definition of the
church. More devoted a separate chapter to the topic. Here perhaps we
may notice a new emphasis being forced on him through the controversial
nature of his work, an emphasis which was to become more pronounced in
Catholic theology in the course of the reformation debate. In the *Responsio*
the stress throughout was on the spiritual dimension of the community,
the divine presence within each believer, guiding their fellowship both in
preserving and expounding the divine message. In the *Dialogue* the same
note is repeatedly sounded, but when More comes to a formal definition of
the church the social, visible and institutional elements are placed in the
foreground: 'this company and congregation of all these nations...that
profess the name and faith of Christ', presided over by Christ's vicar, the
Roman pontiff, and endowed in faith with the twin tangible sources of
sanctification: sacrament and scripture. Only obliquely is reference made
to the spiritual dimension of this corporation as 'true vine' and 'mystical
body'. In context, from More's point of view, this constituted a logical
progression from a presumed virtually common ground in the spiritual
concept of the church. But *post factum* it amounted to an increasing stress
on the visible, institutional elements in the church, a current of thought
which was to reach its peak in Catholicism in the writings of Robert Bellarmine and was only transcended within the Roman Catholic communion at
doctrinal level in the *Constitution on the Church (Lumen Gentium)* of the
Second Vatican Council.

   Concurrent with this, several institutional elements received appropriate treatment from More in the *Dialogue*. He recognised the division
of the ecclesial community between cleric and lay and briefly defended its
divine origin in the sacrament of order. He had little to say on the
episcopate, but although he did not deal *ex professo* with the Roman
primacy he made no bones concerning its divine institution nor in making
it along with sacrament and scripture one of the distinctively visible institutional elements of corporate Christianity. He said little of its powers
and nothing on its teaching authority. The empirical expression of the
common faith of the church he identified, as in the *Responsio*, with the *con-*

sensus fidelium, principally of the existing church though receiving reliable reinforcement from the agreement of consistent patristic tradition. More also recognised the authority of councils but perhaps because of the experience of the previous century tended to refer their authority back to that of the believing community for corroboration.

As in the *Responsio,* More acknowledged both the sinfulness of the church and its need for reform especially in its clergy. This in no way weakened his faith as he believed its imperfections to have been envisaged by Christ in its founding just as he had also promised its transformation in its final consummation. Thus the weakness of the church in no way diminished its authority in More's eyes. Perhaps a little alarmingly he used that authority of common belief to validate not merely credal statements not found *ipsissimis verbis* in the bible as well as the traditional forms of the seven sacraments, but also to underwrite peripheral practices such as devotion to saints, pilgrimages and the use of relics. In short what a later Catholicism was to make of papal authority in all fields of Christian life, More's 'populist' Catholicism made of the common faith and practice of the believing community, a corporate mind which can never err. Presumably this undiscriminating anxiety to provide a sound basis to the entire fabric of medieval tradition greatly diminished any possibility of a common ground emerging between orthodoxy and its radical critics.

Inevitably of course this raised the increasingly important question as to which community one must look to for sure guidance? An apologetic rather than polemic response was called for. More grappled fully with this question in neither *Responsio* nor *Dialogue,* though the latter marked a step forward towards an answer. Challenged on the issue of miracles he composed as a peroration to the main part of his work a short treatise on the subject and then used its conclusions for his own controversial purposes. For him the two distinguishing characteristics of the true church of Christ which mark it off for enquiring unbelievers were its unity in faith and the gift of miracle. In the *Responsio* unity in space and time had been the principal indices to Christ's community. In an atmosphere of growing confusion as to the possibility of establishing true continuity and identity, the ongoing actuality of divine intervention in human life which he believed unique to the visible community to which he adhered became its dominant symbol. These symbols establish for the sincere enquirer the identity of the real Christian community and enable him to discover the meaning of divine revelation. On receiving faith he is accepted into full mystical communion with Christ and into fellowship with the other members of the common corps of Christendom, the 'common knowen catholic church' More defended so strenuously.

CHAPTER FIVE

THE CONFUTATION

INTRODUCTION

In the years between the first printing of More's *Dialogue* and his *Confutation,* (i.e. from the spring of 1529 to the spring of 1533) significant changes appeared on the European scene.[1] Several years' negotiation of a settlement of religious strife ended in failure at Augsburg in 1530. With no sign of agreement emerging, Lutheran, Zwinglian and Catholic positions consolidated on a regional basis under the political and military aegis of local princes. This provided a firmer foundation than ever for infiltration of reformist ideas from Europe into Britain. In spite of continued acts of repression the illegal book trade flourished as one pamphlet after another rolled off the presses and was sent on its way.

Henry, meanwhile, was changing political course. Wolsey's efforts to obtain a divorce for him were about to end in failure. On 23 July 1529 Campeggio dissolved the legatine court for the summer recess. It was not to meet again. In October a writ of *praemunire* was issued against Wolsey and on 18 October he surrendered the Great Seal. Sir Thomas More was Henry's surprising choice as Wolsey's successor. The King's motives were not altogether transparent, for although he hesitated for some time about his course of action, it was soon clear that a marriage to Anne Boleyn was very much on his mind. The direction he was to take gradually crystallised with the progress of the 'Reformation Parliament' convened in November 1529. Ecclesiastical jurisdiction was undermined by one enactment after another until by 15 April 1536 Henry's divorce had been granted by Cranmer and the church in England was completely under royal control.

In the midst of this turmoil More soon discovered that he had little influence over the main stream of events. He had taken office with hopes

---

[1] See in particular L. A. Schuster, *Thomas More's Polemical Career, 1523-1533,* in *Confutation* III, 1190-1268. See also Grimm, *The Reformation Era,* 178-233; Elton, *England under the Tudors,* 122-150; Scarisbrick, *Henry VIII,* 198-354; Clebsch, *England's Earliest Protestants,* 42-204; Chambers, *Thomas More,* 226-277; Reynolds, *The Field is Won,* 193-277; E. Flesseman Van Leer, *The Controversy about Scripture and Tradition between Thomas More and William Tyndale,* NAKG new ser. 43 (1959) 143-165; idem, *The Controversy about Ecclesiology between Thomas More and William Tyndale,* NAKG new ser. 44 (1960) 65-86; R. C. Marius, *Thomas More's View of the Church,* in *Confutation* III, 1269-1364; E. Birchenough, *More's Appointment as Chancellor and his Resignation,* Moreana no. 12 (1966) 71-80.

of defending the church and promoting the unity of Christendom. He soon found that his effective sphere of public action lay in the proscription of heretical books, the pursuit of heretics, and in a less public way, the advocacy of the Aragon cause.[2]

Nor did he cease to work in private in the field of religious controversy. In spite of the burden of office he still found time for serious writing of which the principal fruit was to be his monumental *Confutation of Tyndale's Answer*. Following the submission of clergy on 15 May 1532 More resigned from office as chancellor and devoted himself to the completion of this massive work as well as other publications.

A novel aspect of Henry's approach, probably masterminded by the rising star Thomas Cromwell, was the use of propagandist publications to win popular approval for his policies. Books such as *A Glass of Truth* (1532) argued for royal supremacy over the English church, the justness of the divorce proceedings and, sounding strangely in the English air, trumpeted the case for conciliar supremacy in the universal church. Henry's argument was upheld by support from many writers, some unsolicited such as that of Christopher St German who called for the limitation of ecclesiastical jurisdiction within the realm.[3]

Nor were the reformation publicists idle. Joye, Frith and Barnes among others contributed their share to the flood of literature which sought to wean the English away from established religious loyalties. William Tyndale was perhaps the busiest of all. To this period belong, among other works, *The Practice of Prelates* (1530), his translation of the *Pentateuch* with prologue and controversial glosses (1530), his translation of Jonas, (May 1531), *A Pathway into the Holy Scripture* (1530-31) and *Exposition of I John* (September 1531). With even greater relevance to our theme, it was a period which saw Tyndale's *An Answer unto Sir Thomas More's Dialogue* (1531) come to light.[4]

---

[2] See G. R. Elton, *Sir Thomas More and the Opposition to Henry VIII, Moreana* no. 15 (1967) 285-303, repr. *BIHR* 41 (1968) 19-34, repr. *Studies in Tudor and Stuart Politics*, I, 155-172; idem, *Thomas More, Councillor*, in *Thomas More: Action and Contemplation*, ed. R. S. Sylvester, New Haven, 1972, 86-122, repr. *Studies*, I, 129-155.

[3] Christopher Saint German, *The Division Between the Spirituality and the Laity* (1532); *Salem and Byzance* (1533) among others. See P. Janelle, *L'Angleterre Catholique à la veille du schisme*, Paris, 1935, passim; P. Hughes, *The Reformation in England*, I, London, 1950, 249-269, 330-341; F. Le Van Baumer, *The Early Tudor Theory of Kingship*, (1940), repr. New York, 1966, 211-224; W. G. Zeeveld, *Foundations of Tudor Policy*, Cambridge, Mass., 1948, 111-156; J. J. Scarisbrick, *Henry VIII*, London, 1968, 241-304; G. R. Elton, *Policy and Police, The Enforcement of the Reformation in the Age of Thomas Cromwell*, Cambridge, 1972, 171-216.

[4] See Anthea Hume, *English Protestant Books Printed Abroad, 1525-1535: An Annotated Bibliography*, in *Confutation* II, 1065-1091 for details of Tyndale's book production.

In this latter work Tyndale attacked the institutional church, claiming it had departed from authentic Christianity during the previous eight hundred years. He then examined the relation of church to gospel, the validity of tradition, and the inerrancy of the church. Tyndale defended his translation of certain key words of the new testament as well as systematically and at length refuting More's *Dialogue.*

Another work which was to engage More's attention was that of Friar Robert Barnes.[5] Barnes, an Augustinian priest, was a graduate of Cambridge, Louvain and a member of the Cambridge White Horse circle. Accused of heresy in 1528, he fled to Wittenberg. There he produced two works, the second of which, *A supplicatyon vnto kinge henrye the eyght,* printed in Antwerp in 1531, brought him into direct conflict with More. In this pamphlet Barnes gave his own version of Luther's ecclesiology. The true church of Christ is not the visible organised community but an invisible communion of those '...that beleue yt Chryst hath wasshed them from their synnes/and styke fast vn to his meryttis and to the promysse made too them in him only.'[6] This church is invisible to carnal eyes though inwardly sanctified in the Spirit. She cannot err because she is taught by Christ. Only this hidden church spread throughout the world is inerrant in its appropriation of God's word. Visible signs of the presence of this congregation are: '...the word of god is trewly and perfytly preached...' and '...good workes that doo openly agre wyth the doctrine off the gospell...'[7] More devoted Book VIII of *The Confutation of Tyndale's Answer* to a refutation of these basic Lutheran tenets.

Barnes got into trouble with the authorities following a fiery sermon preached in St Edward's church on Christmas Eve 1525. After an episcopal enquiry he publicly retracted and was placed in a house of observance. In 1528 it was discovered that he was still involved with the evangelical movement and was put under further restrictions. Barnes escaped, however, to Europe where he betook himself to Wittenberg. Here he wrote two books: *Sentenciae ex doctoribus collectae,* published in Wittenberg in autumn 1530, and the one already referred to, *A supplicatyon unto kinge henrye the eyght* (Antwerp, 1531). A revised edition was published in London in November 1534 which took some account of More's strictures in Book VIII of his *Confutation of Tyndale's Answer.* The previous summer

---

[5] On Barnes see J. P. Lusardi, *The Career of Robert Barnes,* in *Confutation* III, 1367-1415. See also G. Rupp, *Studies in the Making of the English Protestant Tradition,* Cambridge, 1947, 31-46; Clebsch, *England's Earliest Protestants,* 42-77.

[6] See Barnes, *Supplication,* in *Confutation* II, 1041/20-23.

[7] Ibid., 1048/33-38.

Barnes had returned to London and continued to live in England. Never fully in favour with the king, though employed on several diplomatic missions by Cromwell, Barnes led a somewhat chequered career. Not satisfied with the Henrician settlement, his continued preaching of evangelical doctrine finally led to his execution at Smithfield on 30 July 1540.

The first volume of the *Confutation* appeared in 1532. It had been composed during More's term of office as chancellor. The 383 pages it fills in the Yale edition comprise the preface and three books. The preface deals in general with the spread of heresy in England and the dangers this entails for church and state. The first three books deal successively with the preface to *Tyndale's Answer*, mainly concerned with a description of the lifestyle and faith of 'the spiritual man', Tyndale's defence of his translation of the new testament, and the reception and transmission of revelation. The second volume, composed after More's retirement, was published in 1533. It fills 647 pages of the Yale edition. It deals in five books with the inerrancy of the Christian community, the authenticity of the Catholic Church, its anteriority to heretical groupings and its role in relation to scripture. Book VIII is concerned with an attack on Barnes's theses concerning the church, while Book IX is an incomplete summary of the whole argument.

More's method, as in the *Responsio*, consists in taking sections of his opponents' work and exhaustively refuting those he finds unacceptable. Refutation of any particular detail in Tyndale's case tends to draw down a recapitulation of the whole of More's overall position—hence a vast amount of repetition. In the expression of his ideas More approaches the popular style of the *Dialogue*. Together with strictly theological evidence and reasoning there is a rough sauce of earthy wit, homely anecdote and personal interpretation which not infrequently overflows the main dish by its sheer quantity. Hence the density of a work which, in spite of its sauce, remains largely indigestible. Nonetheless it is of key importance in the exposition of More's thought on the church and related topics.

To avoid falling into the trap of endless repetition that More himself fell into, his ideas will be expounded in the following way. The main order of topics followed by More will be used, namely the definition of the church, as it arose in Bk II; divine revelation and the church as discussed in Bk III/1 and Bk VI; the transmission of revelation as examined in Bk III/2 and Bk VII; the inerrancy of the church as developed in Bk IV; and the authenticity of the Catholic Church as discussed in Bk V taken in conjunction with Bk VIII. Matter relating to these topics drawn from other parts of the *Confutation* will be incorporated in accordance with this general line of thought at the appropriate moment.

I. THE NATURE OF THE CHURCH

Meaning of the word 'church'

In his reply to Tyndale More examined a number of interpretations of the word 'church' proposed by the former.[8]

1. '...a howse where crysten men were wont to resorte in olde tyme to here the word of god/...

2. 'Then he sayth it hath a seconde sygnyfycacyon, but that is he sayth but mysse taken and abused by whyche it sygnyfyeth the clergye/...

3. 'A thyrde sygnyfycacyon he sayth it hath/by whych it betokeneth a congregacyon, a multytude, or a company gathered to gyther in one, as a man may call the chyrche of London/meanyng not the spyrytualtye onely but the hole body of the cytye of all kyndes, condycyons, and degrees. And in thys thyrde sygnyfycacyon he sayth that though it be lytell knowen amonge the comon people now a dayes: yet in this sygnyfycacyon is he sayth the chyrch of god or Cryst taken in the scrypture for the hole multytude that receyue ye name of Cryste to byleue in hym...

4. 'Not wythstandynge yet yt is some tyme taken generally, for all that embrace the name of Criste, though theyr faythes be nought, or though they haue no fayth at all.

5. 'And sometymes yt is taken specyally for the electe onely/in whose hartes god hath wryten his law wyth his holy spyryte, and geuen them a felynge fayth of the mercy that is in Cryste Iesu our lorde.'[9]

Writing in this same context More himself found a number of other meanings for the term:

6. 'One is that this worde chyrch besyde all the sygnyfycacyons that Tyndale hath here shewed vs: doth sygnifye that parte of the chyrch that in synodis and counsayles do represent the whole chyrch...lyke wise as a parliament representeth the hole reame...

7. 'The chyrch also sygnifyeth sometyme a mych lesse nomber that is to wyt/the onely rulers or hedes of the chyrche. as where we be commaunded to complayne to the chyrch/yt is not ment to all ye whole towne nor to all the clergy therof, but to rulers and gouernours.'[10]

8. At a later stage in the discussion More discussed another hypothesis proposed by Tyndale, the church understood as 'the pope and hys

---

[8] See Tyndale, *Answer,* 11-13.

[9] See *Confutation* I, 145/15—146/9.

[10] See *Confutation* I, 146/12-25.

generacyon...' More commented: 'For here wolde I wytte what thynge
Tyndale meaneth by the pope and popys generacyon. If he meane hys
carnall kynredde, or the pope and his cardynallys eyther: he then
wynketh of wylynesse, and wyll not se the marke. For he knoweth very
well yt neyther of these is the thyng that we call the chyrche, when we
speke of the catholyke chyrche of Cryste that can not erre. If he meane
by the pope and hys generacyon, all the crysten nacyons not beynge cut
of nor caste out for theyr obstynate malyce, nor of wylfulnesse depar-
tyng out by sedycyouse scysmes: then seeth he ye marke at the leste
wyse.'[11]

More himself preferred to have the word 'church' taken 'of such onely
people as be crysten people, and them not in one cytye onely, but that hole
nomber of euery cytye, towne, and village thorow out all the hole
world...there is of the chyrch no synifycacyon neyther more great nor
more comen...'[12] More had already given expression to this concept at the
beginning of this discussion: '...but yt he knoweth and so hereth the clergy
preche also them selfe, that of the chyrche of Cryste is euery crysten
man/and that the hole chyrch is the hole crysten people/and therfore they
call it the catholyke chyrche that is vnyuersall/...'[13]

Amidst the many usages of the word which More admitted it is clear
that he opted for one normative usage denoting the key concept of the
church as existing in history, namely, 'that hole nomber of every cytye,
towne, and village thorow out all the hole world...' the common known
church of Christian people, saint and sinner, cleric and lay, this is the
church which received Christ's promises and gifts, sent by him to preach
his word, and guaranteed the active assistance of his presence and that of
the Holy Spirit throughout its existence. More followed his mentors

---

[11] See *Confutation* I, 387/5-30. More had earlier dismissed the same view proposed by
Tyndale: *Confutation* I, 131/20-30: 'When Tyndale speketh of the pope with hys/here vseth
he a lytell sophystrye. For he leueth vs in dowte what he meaneth by these wordes, the pope
wyth hys. If he meane the pope wyth hys cardynals/then speketh he lytell to the purpose. For
I neuer called nor no man ellys, the pope and the cardynals the hole catholyke chyrche. But
yf he meane by the pope and hys, the pope and all the crysten reames and countrees that
haue not by scysmes and heresyes departed and seuered them selfe from ye corps of crystendome: he that then iudgeth the pope and hys to be the chyrche of cryste, iudgeth as it is in
dede.' It is worth noting that while More never conceived of the church as 'the pope and
hys', this was in fact Tyndale's approximation to an interpretation, reputable at the time
and finding support in Rome for the term *ecclesia romana*. Its most noted proponent was, of
course, the notorius Giles of Rome. In the fifteenth century, it survived in the 'oligarchical'
school of ecclesiology which sought to attribute to the pope with his college of cardinals the
prerogatives Giles had reserved to the pope alone. See above pp. 30,43-44.
[12] See *Confutation* I, 147/3-17.
[13] *Confutation* I, 164/25-29.

Cyprian and Augustine in this: '...men may well perceyue, that both saynt Cypryane and saynt Austayn to, dyd take the chyrch for none other then the knowen catholyke chirch...'[14] In contrast with Tyndale's élitist concept of the church as the congregation of the elect, of the truly just, More opted for the general body of believers in all of their social and moral states as most fully realising Christ's idea of his church on earth.

More continued the discussion in Book III with an analysis of other disputed translations of new testament terminology by Tyndale. For our purposes rather than follow him on this excursion, it may be more helpful to enlarge here on More's concept of the church so as to see it in its broader aspects. He had already defined its main characteristics in *Responsio* and *Dialogue*. These views were established in his mind when tackling the specific issues raised by Tyndale and Barnes. Let us briefly see how he gave expression to these in the *Confutation*.

Presence of Christ in his church

To this common known Christian people the pledge of divine presence, support and enlightenment was given. More refers to this presence in two ways, in terms of Christ and in terms of the Spirit. He repeatedly made use of Mt 28, 20 with its promise of Christ's continuing assistance to his church in preaching the gospel till the end of time.[15] In certain contexts he interpreted this text in terms of the abiding presence of Christ in the reserved sacrament: '...Chryst when he turned the brede into his own precyouse body, and the wyne into his blessed blode, and commaunded the same to be done for euer in his chyrch after in remembraunce of his passyon, and dyd in so commaundyng make a faythfull promyse, that hym selfe wolde be for euer with hys chyrch in that holy sacrament/...'[16]

Whatever nuances More attached to this text, it was one aspect of his thought that Tyndale had failed to come to grips with in the *Answer*, to the point of virtually ignoring More's repeated claims for the continuing assistance of Christ to his people.[17]

---

[14] *Confutation* II, 734/29-31.

[15] See *Confutation* I, 467/13-14: 'I am with you all dayes vnto the ende of the worlde ...'; ibid., 155/7-8; see also pp. 107, 133, 259, 286, 345, 379, 388, etc.

[16] See *Confutation* I, 467/8-14. The text continues: '...& for a perpetuall memory of hys bytter passyon that he suffered for vs, wolde gyue hys owne flesshe that suffered passyon, & hys owne blode that was shedde in hys passyon, to abyde perpetually with vs, accordynge to hys owne wordes spoken vnto hys chyrche when he sayed, I am with you all dayes vnto the ende of the worlde...'

[17] See L. A. Schuster, *Thomas More's Polemical Career, 1523-1533*, in *Confutation* III, 1257-1258.

Using another biblical image, that of the loving husband, More spoke of
Christ's continuing care for his church. He has given himself up for his
church, More said in commentary on Eph 5, 26-27, 'to thentent that the
sacrament of baptysme myght weshe them all and clense them from all
theyr synnes. For wythout his deth the sacrament shold not haue hadde
any effycacye to clense them.' Why has he cleansed them by the sacrament
'...and by the infusion of his grace in fayth, hope, and charyte, sanctyfyed
them in spyryte? surely (as saynte Poule sayth) to thentent that he myghte
make her to hym selfe a gloryouse chyrche wythout spot or wryncle/that is
to wyt, that they myght and sholde perseuer in vertue, and ...so lyue here
wyth his grace, that he myghte after this worlde brynge them to his glory,
and there haue them a gloryouse chyrch fyrst in soule and after in body
to/where they shall neyther haue spot nor wryncle...'[18] Here More was
speaking of Christ's presence to his church under the image of a
bridegroom caring for his wife in the spousal theme common to old and
new testaments. He stressed in contradistinction to Barnes that full
glorification of the bride takes place only in the final eschatalogical state
which is prepared for in the course of temporal history.[19]

More also used the familiar image of the mystical body in a similar way
to bring out the closeness of Christ's presence to his church, his continuing
action upon it and care for it.[20] This body is conformed though not yet
perfectly to its head in all things even to the extent of suffering oppres-
sions, persecution and all other things that may be laid unto it.[21] In other
contexts More makes use of the Spirit theme drawn largely from Jn 16 to
emphasise the continuing inflow of guidance and direction to God's

---

[18] See *Confutation* II, 852/6-20.

[19] See Robert Barnes, *Supplication,* in *Confutation* II, 1040/26-40.

[20] See *Confutation* II, 855/2-17: '...And specyally is yt (the church) holy bycause of the holy
hed therof our holy sauyour hym selfe, whose mystycall body is the whole knowen catholyke
chyrche/in whych for all the cure done vppon yt in the baptysme, yet are there many sykke
members by many great new synnes...of those sortes ordynaryly doth and shall our sauyour
(the sore cancred members that wyll not in conclusyon be cured, left vnto the rotte and
shaken into the fyre) brynge forthe and make perfyte his gloryouse chyrche, and present yt to
his father bryghte and smothe, wythoute any spot or wryncle to lyue and endure in
heuen/but neuer shall his chyrche be clerely wythout spot or wryncle, whyle yt wandereth in
this wreched worlde.' See also ibid. II, 669/27-32; ibid. II, 944/16-29, where More relates
Mt 18, 15-19 concerning fraternal correction with I Cor 12, 26 where 'as saynt Poule sayth,
if one member taketh hurte all the members be greued therwyth.' From the freedom with
which More moved from one image to the other of the church, it is clear that what was principally in his mind was the underlying relationship between its members with each other and
their Lord.

[21] See *Confutation* II, 953/12-32.

chosen people. The Spirit abides with them, guides them, and leads them into all truth.[22]

Church Order

Faith is the gateway to the church

If the church is a definite company of believers guaranteed the abiding presence and assistance of Christ, one may ask how does one become a member of this definite company of 'the catholic church'? The first requisite is faith or what would appear to be its equivalent, a strong desire to belong to it: '...euery person in euery other parte of the worlde that is chrystened or longeth to be chrystened & consenteth with that chyrche in fayth is a member of the same/...'[23] Note that More did not insist on an explicit act of faith but recognised desire to belong to the church as implicitly the same thing.   `

Curiously enough, More's position on implicit faith was not too far removed from Tyndale's concept of justifying faith. For Tyndale the central element in faith was surrender to the caring mercy of God, the total inner acceptance of Christ as personal saviour bringing with it unfailing trust in the mercy of God towards the repentant sinner. Such faith he regarded as a gift of God, not the result or conclusion of a rational process. He also linked it closely with religious experience, describing it as 'a feeling faith'—the result of something akin to direct sensory experience. He did not look on the conceptual content of faith as of extreme importance, assuming that the man who had made his submission to God's loving mercy would also accept his word so far as it became known to him.[24] Hence for Tyndale the key element was the intuitive apprehension of God's mercy in Christ, a position not as remote as either contestant might have thought from More's views, traditional Catholic views at that, on implicit faith. The difference was more one of emphasis for whereas for Tyndale this implicit, virtually aconceptual surrender to the person of Christ was central, for More it tended to be matched by the full appropriation of divine revelation as mediated through the church.

---

[22] *Confutation* I, 107-109; 133-134; 158-160; 225-226; 285-286; 376-377.

[23] See *Confutation* II, 942/17-20. See also ibid. II, 962/19-22: 'But we deny not but yf there be dwellynge amonge Turkes or Sarasyns any chrysten, or men that longe to be chrysten, whych agre with the knowen chyrche of these chrysten contynued nacyons in fayth/all those folke are of thys knowen chyrche also.' See also ibid II, 924/17-34, where More discusses the case of those entitled to attend a full assembly of the church.

[24] Tyndale, *Answer,* 30-39; 50-52.

It is regrettable that More did not discuss at greater length the question
of implicit faith, which he attributed to those sincerely desiring to be
members of the church. Had he done so, it might have brought him closer
to an appreciation of Tyndale's understanding of feeling faith in Christ as
being sufficient to constitute one a member of the elect church, with the
corollary that assent to any given proposition of revelation was purely
relative to this. Looking at the matter with hindsight, one can see that
these positions are not too far apart. If according to More the implicit faith
of one who has not been instructed is sufficient for salvation, even to be
accounted a member of the church, the conceptualised data of revelation
are in fact of secondary importance. In short it could be argued that on the
question of faith, in spite of verbal disagreement and a definite difference
in emphasis, one can point to a certain convergence of position.

It is on the secondary issue of how the data of revelation are made
known to the believer and the constitution of the body of believers that
fundamental disparity occurs: '...who was euer so madde to thynke that
the trouth of goddes worde, depended vppon the mouthes of any mortall
men or any creature eyther in erthe or heuen? but wythoute any outwarde
dependens, hath his solydyte substaunce and fastenes of and in yt
self...But syth you se well as I say that oure questyon is not what thyng
maketh goddes worde to be trew...but by what meane men know whyche
is the trew word of god, and whether we know not whyche is the trew
gospell by the meane and teachynge of the knowen catholyke chyrch or not
by yt, but by some other chyrch or congregacyon vnknowen...'[25]

The genesis of faith

In the case of *infants*, faith is infused with grace in the moment of their
baptism,[26] though later they will have to make an adult form of assent
grounded in extrinsic reasons. This is so from the start in the case of the
adult approaching the Christian mystery: '...we haue in geuynge credence
vnto the catholyke chyrche two maner of mocions/one kynde of outwarde

---

[25] See *Confutation* II, 800/2—801/6. Cf. n. 32 below for remarks on E. Flesseman-Van
Leer's analysis of the root of division between More and Tyndale.
[26] See *Confutation* II, 768/19-30: 'And in such as are baptised yong, ye inwarde mocyon is
the same goodnes of god preuentynge theym, with the habytuall fayth infounded in the
sacrament of baptysme. Vppon the seed wherof wyth the good helpe of goddes grace, there
spryngeth after in the good and well appliable wyll of man, the frute of credence and bylyefe
whyche they geue vnto crystes catholyke chyrche, accordyng to his owne commaundement
vppon the preachyng of the same chyrch/in the reasons whyche the same chyrche by goddes
good ordynaunces geueth as outwarde meanes of credence and enducynge to the bylyefe,
both of yt selfe and of the scrypture...'

causes such as myght yf the mater were worldely, moue mannys reason to
the full agrement and consent therof. And that the tother mocyon is in
them that byfore theyr baptysme haue vse of reason, the goodnesse of god
fyrste preuentynge them, wyth the occasyons of some outwarde
mocyon/and then walkynge and workynge wyth theyr conformable wyllys
into the consent of that godly treuth, and therwyth geuynge theym by baptysme that grace to is rewardable wyth glorye, but yf some other synne be
the let vpon theyr part.'[27]

This outward motion is related to the visible appearance and tangible
structure of the church: '...as Criste was both by fayth byleued, and yet
was also by syght and felyng knowen, as well as was in such wyse knowen
any draper or mercer eyther/for the false Iewes knew hym by the tone
meane onely & his trew discyples knew hym by both/and saynt Thomas of
Inde after he hadde both sene hym and felt hym, dyd by syght and felynge
know his manhed, and therewyth by fayth byleued his godhed: euen so we
know the chyrche by syghte, herynge and felynge as we know drapers &
mercers. And we byleue the spyryt of god abydynge therwyth and ledynge
yt into all trouthe, and Cryste the chyefe hedde therof assystyng yt, and
preseruyng yt from faylynge agaynste all the gates of hell.'[28] Thus in the
genesis of the adult's act of faith there is a dual motion: the perception of
the church as a socio-historical reality, an act of common sense similar to
that involved in recognising any individual's trade or profession; the second is a commitment in trust to the Spirit dwelling in the church.

This latter decision deserves a word of elaboration. The church in
More's conception is not the main object of faith. It is God dwelling within
the church whom I believe. 'And we byleue the spyryt of god abydynge
therwyth and ledynge yt into all trouthe, and Cryste the chyefe hedde
therof assystyng yt...'[29] It is in the godhead dwelling within the church as
in the historical body of Jesus that we believe, not the human institution:
'And therfore in byleuynge the chyrche, we put not I saye our trust in the
men whom we byleue/but we put our truste in god, for whome and by
whome we byleue the men.'[30] Though the church may draw me to the
point where I wish to believe, my faith is in God: '...but vnderstand you
that we byd you and dyd bydde you, that beynge conuersaunt in the holy

---

[27] See *Confutation* II, 768/11-18.

[28] See *Confutation* II, 974/33—975/10.

[29] See *Confutation* II, 975/6-9.

[30] See *Confutation* II, 764/8-10. See also ibid., 763/34-764/3: 'But now good chrysten
readers I haue declared you before, that saynt Austayne in byleuynge the scrypture bycause
of the authoryte of the chyrche, *and all we that do the lyke/do not therby put our truste in man but in
god, that by hys inwarde spyryte and outwarde myracles, enclyneth vs to byleue hys chyrche therin...*'

catholyque chyrche, you sholde byleue in god, and that you sholde byleue also the resurreccyon of the fleshe that ys to come.'[31] God is the object of belief, but God dwelling in the church as in the body of Christ.

To sum up then, the role of the church in relation to faith is to prepare the ground for faith in God's word by providing tangible evidence for his presence; once faith is given to God abiding in the church to determine and guide the believer in his assent to its propositional formulation.[32] At the same time implicit faith in certain circumstances is sufficient for membership in the church.

Sin and Church Membership

Once membership in the church has been attained, it cannot be lost by sin alone. 'For it is the comon knowen chyrche of all crysten people, not gone out nor caste oute. Thys hole body bothe of good and badde is the catholyke chyrche of Cryste, whyche is in thys worlde very sikely, & hath many sore membres/as hath somtyme the naturall body of a man, and some sore astonyed, and for a tyme colde and dede/whyche yet catcheth

---

[31] See *Confutation* II, 982/7-9. More is here paraphrasing St Augustine. He insists: '...we asked you not after that maner, that you sholde euen in the same maner as you byleue in god, byleue in the catholyque holy chyrche/...'; loc. cit.,/1-3.

[32] A later theology will express these distinctions by saying that (a) the church forms part of the *motivum credibilitatis revelationis,* part of the ground which makes the act of faith a reasonable human option; (b) it also forms part of the material object of faith, in the sense that an important part of revelation is the supernatural mission of the Catholic Church (We have not touched at length on this here but cf. the many places where More speaks of scripture authenticating the church, once the scriptures are received from the church); (c) the church is a permanent witness and guide to the believer in his assent to the content of revelation. God, however, is the one who is believed, or as scholastic theology expressed it, is the *objectum formale fidei.* More did not examine the motive or grounds of the act of faith itself, although recognising that in so far as it is a supernatural action, it comes from God. In this, I must differ from E. Flesseman-Van Leer, *The Controversy about Ecclesiology between Thomas More and William Tyndale, NAKG* (1960) 85: 'For More faith is the acceptance of truths to which God binds man through his church. It might be either a matter of ceremonies—the way in which the mass should be celebrated or fastdays to be kept—or it might be a matter of doctrines, such as Jesus Christ was God and man, or Mary remained a Virgin.' As an account of More's understanding of faith this provides the correct emphasis. More was concerned with defending particular doctrines. On the other hand, I think it misses an important point which More himself recognised, that he, like Tyndale, believed primarily in God not the church. The division between them was not fundamentally therefore as to *whom* one should believe, but as to *what* one should believe and *how one knew what one should believe.* It is here the difference lay, Tyndale believing that God speaks exclusively through the literal sense of scripture; More that God speaks through the consensus of the living community whether in her teaching, her preaching, her traditions of practice and belief, her interpretations of scripture, as well as through the literal sense of holy writ itself, something which receives the tacit assent of the community in its affirmation of canonicity.

hete and lyfe agayne, yf it be not precyded and cut of from the body.'[33] Here More parted company with Tyndale for the latter wished to restrict membership of the church to 'repentyng synners': 'I saye that Crystes electe chyrch is the hole multytude of all repentyng synners that byleue in Cryste...'

For More in this life even unrepentant sinners remain part of the church: 'Chryste hath chosen hys catholyke chyrche out of the Iewys and Gentyls, to be hys chyrche here in erth: in thys kynde are there penytentes and impenytentes bothe.' Christ had foreseen this from the beginning as can be seen in the image of Noah's ark containing clean and unclean animals (Gen 7, 1-5), the parables of the net collecting good and bad fish indifferently (Mt 13, 47-50), and the field of corn and cockle (Mt 13, 24-30) as well as the apostolic college itself one of whom was 'a deyll' (Jn 6, 70-71).[34]

More also took issue with Barnes on this point. The latter cited Eph 5, 25-28 and I Cor 6, 11 to prove that the true church on earth is all pure and bright. More pointed out that these words really contain a promise for the future, of the glory in store for those who persevere. In the meantime, he pointed out, Paul himself had no illusions concerning the impeccability of his neophytes. He had had repeated occasion to admonish and correct them, even for the greatest offences.[35]

More saw membership of the church as the prerogative of all baptised persons, and indeed all that 'longeth to be chrystened...' He did not go into the possibility of loss of membership in any depth apart from recognising that some leave the visible communion and are known 'yf from the socyete therof for scismatikes, yf from the fayth therof, for heretykes.'[36] At the same time he seems to have accepted that radical membership of the church could not be lost, membership conferred according to Christian tradition by the sacramental bond or character of baptism. This view is suggested, for example, in his concession to Friar Barnes when discussing

---

[33] See *Confutation* I, 398/27-35; see ibid. II, 392/29-393/2: 'For penitentes are accompted amonge the good/and in thys chyrche be there bothe good and badde, as our sauyour sheweth hym selfe in the parables bothe of the felde wyth good corne & cocle, and also the nette with fysshes good and badde/and the scrypture sheweth by the arch of Noe with bestes clene and vnclene/and Cryste wyth hys aforesayde wordes to his apostles: Haue I not chosen you twelue and one of you ys a deuyll...' see also ibid., II, 834/4-11, where the parable of the net is once more cited; ibid. II, 854/5-24.

[34] *Confutation* I, 392/26—393/2.

[35] See Barnes, *Supplication*, in *Confutation* II, 1040/26—1041/5; More, *Confutation* II, 851/24—855/2.

[36] *Confutation* II, 669/11-14.

a hypothetical council at which literally all Christians would be physically present, that all manner of 'open heretykes, and scismatykes' might be present, a privilege he would not have accorded even in jest to one who belonged in no way to the church of Christ.[37]

In this More of course differed fundamentally from Tyndale who identified the church of Christ with those possessing 'feeling faith' in him. Membership in this body could be lost by radical rebellion against God, the rejection of his grace, the sin against the Spirit. Tyndale used this as a sort of 'Catch 22' to show that the church of Christ could not err and could not sin in this central sense. *Ipso facto* one who did sin in this way ceased to be a member of the church of the predestinate. Hence the church was made up of members without sin, i.e. against the Spirit.

The Church of the Elect

When More came to discuss the church in the narrower sense, namely those who are now *de facto* on the road to salvation, he insisted that a good deal more is required than implicit faith or the sacramental tie. This discussion arose out of his attempt to take Tyndale on his own grounds and to discuss the church in terms of the predestinate, or more accurately in More's frame of reference, in terms of the conditions required for salvation. He deliberately avoided talking of the church of the predestinate as being present here and now in history in order to make it easier for him to insist on the necessity of man's co-operation with God's saving will in the performance of good works. Here of course he differed from Tyndale who looked on the church as the body of elect, justified once and for all by faith in Christ's salvation.[38] More accepted this terminology but gave it his own meaning. 'And I call here the elect chyrche in thys world, neyther all that are chosen in to crystendome and the professyon of the catholyke fayth, nor onely those that shall be fynally saued/but all suche as for the present tyme so stande in the state of grace, that yf they dye before they fall therefro they shalbe saued. Of whiche folke many fall after from it, and so be dampned in dede/whyche folke before theyr fall be the chyldren of god saye I. And when they be fallen into dedely synne, then ceace they to be

---

[37] See *Confutation* II, 942/12-22; see also ibid. II, 924/6-34, where More to please Friar Barnes included in an imaginary assembly of the universal church 'not onely all false secrete heretykes openly professynge the chrysten fayth and secretely muterynge the contrary,' but 'all false open heretykes, and scismatykes, whych by playne professyon of theyr scismes and heresyes, are gone out or cast out of the knowen catholyke chyrche, & are knowen for her mortall enemyes.'

[38] See Tyndale, *Answer,* 30-33; 35-39; 50-52; 54-56.

the chyldren of god, and be become the chyldren of the deuyll tyll they be
borne of god agayne by grace thorowe penaunce, and become the chyldren
of god agayne. And in whyche so euer of these two states a man fynally
dyeth in/in that he perpetually dwelleth, and is therby for euer eyther the
chylde of god in hys chyrche of the fynall electes in heuen, or ellys the
chyld of the deuyll in the chyrche of the fynall reprobatys in hell/accordyng
to the word of holy wryte...'[39]

To belong to the church in this more limited sense of those that 'stande
in the state of grace' more is required than faith in Christ and his salvation, '...whych besyde that fayth hath instytuted ye fayth in his blessed
sacramentes & dyuers other artycles besyde/and which hath playnely
declared yt all be it ye knowlege of hym & hys pleasure by fayth, be such a
way toward heuen, yt without it we can not come thyther: yet if we ioyne
not to yt knowlege good dedes or purpose of good workes neyther can that
knowlege nor repentaunce neyther serue vs for a suffycyent waye to
heuen.'[40] Faith, where possible, must extend to the full range of revealed
truth. It must be accompanied by a sincere effort to live well. Only those
who meet these standards qualify for membership 'in the church of the
elect', i.e. the body of those moving positively towards final salvation.
Membership in this group is not permanent. It can be lost through grave
sin. Only those who persevere to the end will join the church in glory.

More patently misunderstood Tyndale's position on the question of
moral responsibility.[41] There is no question but that for Tyndale, as for his
mentor Martin Luther, saving faith brought with it the gift of divine love.
This love, he believed, must express itself in acts of kindness towards his
neighbour as well as praise of God.[42]

More was quite incorrect in assuming that in Tyndale's view saving
faith alone guaranteed one a place in the church of glory. What Tyndale

---

[39] See *Confutation* I, 429/4-19; see ibid. II, 852/13-18: commenting on Eph 5, More insists
that final purification comes only as the conclusion of a life well spent. God has cleansed his
church in the water of baptism, '...that they myght and sholde perseuer in vertue, and yf
they fall then ryse agayne by penaunce/and thus in good workes of charyte and worthy frutes
of penaunce so lyue here wyth his grace, that he myghte after this worlde brynge them to his
glory, and there haue them a gloryouse chyrch fyrst in soule and after in body to/...'

[40] See *Confutation* I, 417/27-33; see ibid. II, 867/10-18: 'But god hath not so ordered
yet/that euery man which hath age & dyscrecyon shold so trust vnto that satysfaccyon by
whyche Cryste wyth his passyon satysfyed for all mennes synnes at onys/that he sholde for
hys owne synnes by the frutefull wurkes of penaunce make no satysfaccyon hym selfe, no
more than he wold though Cryst be our aduocate & pray for vs, that we shold therfore, be the
more slacke and remysse in prayenge also dylygently for our selfe.'

[41] *Confutation* I, 416/29-34.

[42] Tyndale, *Answer*, 21; 95; 173-174; 182; 195-199; 204-205.

was saying was this. Firstly, the reward of glory comes not in repayment for work done but as a further gratuitous gesture of divine love. Secondly, the only deed which excludes one who has come to true faith from the circle of divine mercy is the sin against the Holy Spirit.[43] Here a significant difference lay between More and Tyndale. More accepted the moral teaching of medieval tradition. He tended to see the path of glory as one fraught with far greater perils due to a concept of sin which envisaged the possible loss of grace and glory for lesser moral delinquencies than the formal sin against the Spirit. Consequently, while More had an extremely broad concept of church-membership in this life, he was more rigorous than Tyndale in his criteria for acceptance into the church of glory.

Summary

Membership in the common known church, according to More, comes about principally through faith in God revealing through the church. This faith however must be accompanied by hope and charity, gifts conferred not by man but by divine means, normally through sacramental baptism, though he was prepared to admit without exploring the nature of their membership, that catechumens and others sincerely desirous of belonging to the faith of the church, without being christened in fact, belong to the body of the church. So indeed do sinners but as dead branches to a vine. Excluded from visible communion are non-believers and all open heretics and schismatics. On the other hand to belong to the church of the elect, that is to those unquestionably on the way to final election, one must be in the state of grace and prove one's sincerity by the performance of acts of virtue. Only the virtuous man will be confirmed by the grace of final happiness. In the meantime, pursuing its pilgrim way, the church remains afflicted with sin.

Hierarchical Structure

Regarding the hierarchical structure of the church, More had not a great deal to say in the *Confutation*. He recognised the office of priesthood, its sacramental character and ministry: 'For graunted that presthed was an offyce/yet myghte that offycer be consecrated wyth a sacrament, and so was in dede. And a parte of hys offyce was also to mynyster the sacramentes to the people.'[44] The priesthood's role of preaching the gospel

---

[43] Ibid., 30-34; 35-39; 142-143; 204-206.
[44] See *Confutation* I, 305/31-34.

was exemplified in the missions which accompanied the new discoveries overseas.[45] The episcopate as such receives even less attention, except for passing references such as More's insistence that the validity of the principle of authority in the church is not voided by the reprehensible behaviour of certain of its holders, as authority is necessary for the good order of any society,[46] a theme he had elaborated on in the *Responsio*. This acceptance of the established order is implied in his proposal of two distinct meanings, valid in themselves, of the word 'church' as applied to 'that part of the church that in synods and councils do represent the whole church', as well as to those we are commanded to complain to (Mt 18, 15-17) which is 'not ment to all ye whole towne nor to all the clergy therof, but to rulers and gouernours.'[47]

More's reticence on this particular issue need not be cause for comment. He had already defended the sacramentality of holy order in his reply to Luther.[48] His present work was a work of polemic concerned with a specific problem, not with setting out in full the nature of the church. When the occasion arose he was not slow to expose his convictions regarding the role of the clergy in the church.

In answer to Tyndale's charge that the clergy were usurping the place of Christ and the apostles More replied: '...then hath euer the clergye of euery age bene that parte of Chrystes very chyrche, to whome Chryste specyally spake, speketh, and euer shall speke these wordes, Go ye and preche the gospell to all creatures. (Mk 16, 15) And also these wordes: who so hereth you hereth me/and who so dyspyseth you dyspyseth me. (Lk 10, 16) And these wordes also, who so receyue you receyueth me/and what so euer cytye receyue you not, Sodome and Gomorre shall be more easely delt wyth then that cytye in the daye of iugement. (Mt 10, 15; Lk 10, 12) And also sithe they must be the techers/it foloweth that they be & must be that parte of his chyrche, to which parte these wordes were also specyally spoken: I shal sende you the holy goost whiche shall teche you all trewthe and lede you into euery trouthe/and I am with you my selfe vnto the worldes ende.' (Jn 16, 13; Mt 28, 20)[49]

---

[45] See *Confutation* I, 190/29—191/21.

[46] See *Confutation* II, 911/3-32.

[47] See *Confutation* I, 146/24-25.

[48] See *Responsio*, 648-663.

[49] See *Confutation* II, 614/20-35. See also *The Apologye of Syr Thomas More, Knyght*, ed. A. I. Taft, (*Early English Text Society, No. 180*) London, 1930, 112, where More declares his certainty that '...in such thynges as the whole clergy of chrystendome techeth and ordereth in spyrytuall thynges...' there is no room for error, '...syth I no thynge dowte in my mynde but in that congregacion to goddys honour gracyously gathered together the good assystence of

There can be no questioning the significance More attached to the place of the ordained clergy in the church, nor of his belief in the special assistance granted them by the Lord in the exercise of their function.[50]

The Roman primacy

It is More's treatment of the papacy in the *Confutation* that needs to be developed.[51] From his statements in the *Confutation* alone it is difficult to form a correct assessment of his attitude towards the role and office of the papacy in the church. Shortly before his death in a letter to Cromwell he declared that he had deliberately avoided raising the issue because at the time the lines of conflict between king and pope were already drawn.[52] However certain facts do emerge from a consideration of the *Confutation* which are not devoid of significance. It is noteworthy that More in this work, in contrast with the *Responsio*, interpreted two key petrine texts in a general rather than petrine sense. The first of these, Mt 16, 18, 'vppon thys rocke I wyll byelde my congregacyon', Tyndale had interpreted as referring to faith: the rock on which the church is founded is faith in Christ; '...agaynst the rocke of this fayth, can no synne, no hell, no deuyll, no lyes, none errour preuayle.'[53] More in replying to Tyndale gave three possible interpretations of the latter's words, but did not, significantly, re-interpret the text in relation to the person and office of Peter. Rather he

---

the spyryte of god is accordynge to Crystes promyse as veryly present or assystante as it was with his blessed apostles.' More, of course, recognised the fallibility of particular councils: ibid., 113.

[50] For all this discussion regarding the role of the clergy in bearing witness to Christ's message, see *Confutation* II, 615/5-33; *Confutation* I, 361/35-362/2. Note More's terminology here. The church, not the clergy only, is Christ's apostle. See ibid. I, 252/3-8.

[51] Regarding apostolic succession, More has this to say, *Confutation* I, 614/12-20: Since Christ '...entended that hys chyrche here in erthe sholde alwaye haue amonge them techers and prechers/syth he entended that hys chyrche sholde as Tyndale agreeth as longe laste in erthe as the worlde sholde endure/& none other hath there ben had synnys Chrystes dayes and hys apostles in chrystendome, but the clergye by contynuall successyon...' See also *Confutation* II, 1011/4-11 (not in first edition) for a passing reference to the episcopate as succeeding to the apostolic college. Granting for the sake of argument that Peter was not appointed by Christ head of the known church, More goes on: '...yet at the least he appointed saint Peter with other, and that they were all knowen heades. And they dyd also substytute other whyche were knowen heades also. And euer after by succession knowen heades to succede, of suche as bi the blessed sacrament of holye orders were by special consecracion, as by a certain spirituall generacion borne enherytable to those roumes.'

[52] See More to Cromwell, Chelsea, 5 March 1534, Rogers, *Correspondence*, 500/273-283: 'But where as I had written therof at length in my confutation byfore, and for the profe therof had compyled together all that I could fynde therfore...whan I after that sawe the thing lykely to drawe toward such displeasure bytwene theym I suppressed it vtterly and never put word therof in to my booke but put owt the remenaunt with owt it...'

[53] See *Confutation* I, 410/35-411/3; Tyndale, *Answer*, 31.

admitted the general contention that the church is founded on faith in
Christ. His question to Tyndale concerned the notion of faith and the
meaning of its invincibility.[54] Similarly, Lk 22, 31-32 'Symon Symon...I
haue prayed for the that thy faythe shall not fayle' was taken by More as
referring mainly to the personal faith of Peter. His role in confirming the
faith of his brethren was not enlarged on.[55] Thus there is a notable
reticence in regard to Peter's place in the apostolic church.

Writing against Barnes, More was a little more papal in outlook;
'...Christ was himselfe a knowen head vpon his church of his twelue
apostles, and vppon all his disciples that he tooke into him both the good
and ye bad, and than he appointed sainte Peter for his successour, and
head and chiefe shepherde to feede and gouerne hys whole flocke after his
death, and so foorthe the successors of him euer after...' On the other
hand if his opponents rejected the place of Peter as supreme head More
was willing to admit that '...if Christ dyd not appoint saynt Peter for the
chiefe shepherd ouer al his flocke, yet can they not say nay, but that yet at
the least he appointed saint Peter with other, and that they were all
knowen heades.'[56] Thus while More's personal inclination seemed to find
expression in his first option, i.e. the appointment by Christ of Peter and
his successors as heads of the church, he admitted the legitimacy of
discussing the possibility of an episcopally governed church. In a similar
vein he explained that although for many generations Christians have
recognised the pope, 'not as the byshop of rome but as the successoure of
saynt Peter, to be theyr chyefe spyrytuall gouernour vnder god, and
Chrystes vycar in erth/...yet dyde I neuer put the pope for parte of the dyffynycyon of the chyrche, dyffynyng the chyrche to be the comon knowen
congregacyon of all chrysten nacyons under one hed the pope.' More
deliberately refrained from such a definition as it would but complicate the
issue. His basic argument for the authenticity of the 'common knowen
church' sprang from its unity in faith. To add the issue of primacy to this
would only weaken its force by raising without need many secondary problems. Moreover, he continued, to leave the pope out of the formal definition of the church is no harm, 'syth yf he be the necessary hed, he is included in the name of the hole body.'[57] He therefore rejected out of hand

---

[54] See *Confutation* I, 411/10-414/20.
[55] See *Confutation* I, 554/23-560/36; Tyndale, *Answer,* 38-39.
[56] See *Confutation* II, 1010/16-21; 1011/4-8; (not in first edition).
[57] See *Confutation* II, 576/23-577/23; see also ibid. I, 398/36-399/3: 'Thys catholyke
knowen chyrch is that mystycall body be it neuer so syke, wherof the pryncypall hed is
Cryste. Of whyche body whyther the successour of saynt Peter be his vycar generall and hed
vnder hym, as all crysten nacyons haue now longe taken hym/is no parte of this questyon.'

any attempt to define the distinguishing characteristic of the church exclusively in terms of the papacy. Moreover, he vehemently rejected any suggestion that the pope with the college of cardinals were of such significance that the universal church could be identified with them.[58]

More took cognisance of other views concerning the headship of the universal church. Explaining his omission of the papacy from the definition of the church he said: '...there myghte be peraduenture made a secunde questyon after yt, whyther ouer all that catholyke chyrche the pope muste nedes be hed and chyefe gouernour or chyefe spyrytuall shepherde/or ellys that ye vnyon of fayth standyng among them all, euery prouynce myghte haue theyr owne chyefe spyrytuall gouernour ouer it selfe, wythout any recourse vnto the pope, or any superyoryte recognysed to any other outwarde person. And then yf the pope were or no pope/but as I say prouyncyall patryarches, archbysshoppes, or metropolytanes, or by what name so euer the thynge were called: what authoryte & what power eyther he or they sholde haue among the people, these thynges well I wyste wolde rayse among many men many mo questyons then one.'[59] In saying this he recognised the openness of theological debate on this issue, conceding the *a priori* respectability even of some of the more extreme views on the position of the pope within the Christian body.

On the other hand he stressed his own conviction that the Christian nations '...now do and longe haue done, recognysed and knowleged the pope, not as the byshop of rome but as the successoure of saynt Peter, to be theyr chyefe spyrytuall gouernour vnder god, and Chrystes vycar in erth/...'[60] This body of opinion was stretched by More to include even the Greeks.[61] He quoted, moreover, St Austin's affirmation that St Peter's

---

[58] See *Confutation* I, 131/21-25: '...when Tyndale speketh of the pope wyth hys/here vseth he a lyttel sophystrye. For he leueth vs in dowte what he meaneth by these wordes, the pope wyth hys. If he meane the pope wyth hys cardynals/then speketh he lytell to the purpose. For I neuer called nor no man ellys, the pope and the cardynals the hole catholyke chyrche.' See ibid. I, 387/22-26, for a similar statement.

[59] See *Confutation* II, 577/3-23.

[60] See *Confutation* II, 576/28-32.

[61] See *Confutation* I, 131/33-132/9: 'For yf there eyther yet be, or any tyme hath ben, that eyther the Grekes or any other parte of trewe crystendome dyd not recognyse the pope for theyr chyefe spyrytuall gouernour vnder god: yet alwaye those that were lernyd or good men amonge them, and the hole people wyth them, in the necessarye artycles were of the same fayth, and confyrmed them selfe to the see of Rome, in such thynges as amonge them bygan to be disputable/as well appereth not onely by saynte Chrysostome and other olde holy doctours of the Grekes, but also by the generall counsayles, in which the Grekes in matters of dowte and questyon, fynally confermed them selfe to the Latyns and to the see apostolyke.' On the temporary reunion of Latins and Greeks reached at Ferrara—Florence, 6 July 1439, see Jedin, *Ecumenical Councils*, 132-134.

successor is 'the chief head in earth of the whole catholic church.'[62] In short, while More quite correctly recognised that papal primacy was still a subject of theological debate, his own inclinations were apparent. These latter statements of his come close to saying that there exists within the church a consensus, (though not unanimous) on the primacy of Peter and his successors. When the behaviour of individual popes was called in question, More did not dispute Barnes's assertion that individual popes have erred. He did not distinguish between their role as teachers and private theologians.[63] He also accepted the principle commonly held by medieval canonists and theologians alike that popes may be corrected for their failings and even deposed.[64]

To summarize therefore his attitudes to the papacy, one may say that More on political, polemical and theological grounds did not insist on the divine right of the papacy as of a matter beyond dispute. He even admitted the legitimacy of views which would deny the Roman primacy to be of divine origin or even of practical desirability. In contrast with this, however, he sketched out, not always with complete accuracy, the outline of an embryonic ecclesial consensus concerning the primacy of the pope within the church, hinting therefore at his own personal conviction. This did not prevent him from admitting the possibility of error on the part of a pope (not distinguishing clearly personal and functional impropriety) as well as the legal possibility of correcting and deposing an unworthy holder of office. In this last position of course he was in no way unorthodox as the provision could be found in the law books at least since Gratian (c. 1140) and found support even among more extreme papalists such as Torquemada and Cajetan.[65]

CONCLUSION

The Christian people form a definite and distinguishable body, composed both of temporalty and spiritualty alike. This body is an organised

---

[62] See *Confutation* II, 962/35-963/1: 'For saynt Austayn called the successoure of saynt Peter the chyefe hed in erth of the hole catholyke chyrche, as well as any man doth now.' More was referring here to e.g. Augustine, *Contra epistolam Manichaei, MPL* 42, 175.

[63] See *Confutation* II, 910/4-911/2. See also ibid., 579/35—580/8.

[64] See *Confutation* II, 590/13-15: 'There are orders in Christes churche, by which a pope may be bothe admonisshed and amended/and hathe be for incorrigible mynde and lacke of amendement, finally deposed and chaunged.' On the other hand, he insisted that this may not be done by 'euery lewde lorell vppon euery false tale that he hereth.'

[65] Gratian's crucial phrase was 'Papa a nemine est iudicandus, *nisi deprehendatur a fide devius*'—this qualification opened the door to much legal speculation. See Tierney, *Foundations of Conciliar Theory*, 56-67; 82-83 and passim.

body in so far as the spiritualty have the duty of preaching the gospel, administering the sacraments and making suitable laws for the whole body. Sir Thomas More did not stress institutional elements in his description of the church. His emphasis was always on the church as the whole Christian people, distinguished above all by their community in faith with one another as with the church of previous centuries: '...all crysten nacyons professyng the trew fayth of Cryst, that is to say the comen catholyke fayth wherin the knowen catholyque chyrch agreeth, be the very holy chyrche of Cryste here in erth, and make amonge them the comen knowen catholique chyrch/of whyche the very good men are parte, and are all called the faythfull people of Cryste, bycause of the vnyte of the trew fayth of Cryste.'[66] This community in faith however is no mere ideological agreement but grows out of a deeper community in Spirit, for '...thys body mystycall of Cryste this catholyk chirch, is yt body yt is animated, hath lyfe spyrytuall, & is enspyred with ye holy spyryt of god yt maketh them of one fayth in the howse of god, by ledyng them in to the consent of euery necessary trouth of reueled fayth, be they in condycyons & maners neuer so syke, as longe as they be conformable & content in vnyte of fayth to cleue vnto ye body.'[67]

II. REVELATION AND CHURCH

Curiously enough, it was only at the end of the *Confutation* that More succeeded in providing himself with a relatively clear-cut conceptualisation of the basic phenomenon underlying the controversy between orthodox and reformers, namely that of divine revelation. In his earlier writings he had used various descriptive phrases, the preaching of Christ, the preaching of the apostles, the gospel, the word to denote a divine message. These latter in particular tended to be ambiguous. Which in fact is the divine word? The Word pre-existing in God, the word infused into the minds of prophets or the apostles, the word preached by Christ, the word written in the bible? The whole problem of communication between each side in the controversy was inextricably confused by the ambiguity of the language employed. Often each side was arguing at cross-purposes to the other.

In the final book of the *Confutation*, however, More reached a definite realisation that the common ground to their debate lay in the belief shared by both camps in a divine revelation: 'Now they and we be bothe I sup-

---

[66] See *Confutation* II, 912/10-17.
[67] See *Confutation* I, 339/3-10.

pose agreed, that reuelacion is in generall, the shewing of a thing by God
vnto hys creature, eyther immediatelye or by a meane, in some such wyse
that the same creature by his onely naturall powers, should either not at
all, or not so fullye wythout that shewyng haue attayned the perceiuing
therof. 'But now begynne they and we to varye vpon the meanes of
reuelacion. For we saye that God hath made his reuelacions to hys churche, partelye by wryting, partely wythout, and that in those twoo maners
the reuelacions of God styl abyde and continue in his churche, in scrypture
and tradicions delyuered by theuangelistes and apostles of Christ vnto the
churche, and that ouer that, Christe hymselfe and hys holye spyryte, do
stil by secrete inspiracion, reuele & open vnto his churche, euery
necessarye truth, that he wyl haue his churche farther know and bounden
to belieue.

'But of thys saye they the contrarye. For they saye that God albeit that
vnto the church of Christ he dyd geue all hys reuelacions without
wrytinge, and not one by writing (for the true exposicions of the olde scripture by him taughte and before not perceiued, he gaue his church in the
beginning without writinge) yet they sai that the euangelistes and apostles
did wryte all those thinges, as farforthe as shoulde be necessary for saluacion, so that the corps of scripture being fynished in the apostles daies, our
Lord neuer gaue anye necessarye reuelacyon synce, nor neuer wyl agayne
whyle the world shall stand...But God they wyll in no wise that any man
shall belieue wythout wrytinge.'[68]

In this summing up More had arrived at a clear picture of the common
basis for agreement as well as the dividing lines between the two parties.
Both agreed on the fact of a divinely communicated message. The difference lay in the manner in which each perceived how this message is
preserved and transmitted to successive generations of believers. This immediately raised the issue of the church, as has been noted in the earlier
works, both in respect of its inner constitution, its relation to the gift of
revelation and the manner of God's acting within it. One task More set
himself in the *Confutation* was to establish on a monumental basis the fact of
the primacy of the living community of the church both as recipient and as
means of communication of divine revelation.

The principal way in which God revealed his mysteries to his church
was of course in the life and teaching of Christ. This was More's often
unspoken assumption, that the most important means which God adopted

---

[68] See *Confutation*, II, 996/9-35. (As this citation belongs to Book IX, it is not found in the
first edition).

to reveal himself to men was in the historical figure of Jesus, his deeds and
words. It also goes without saying that he accepted the old testament as a
preliminary and complementary form of revelation. These views he
shared with Tyndale. What was in dispute was more the question of how
this revelation is received, recorded, and finally re-transmitted to successive generations within the church.

Presence of the Holy Spirit

When More spoke of the presence of the Spirit within the church it was
usually in terms of his role as counsellor, guiding the church in her pursuit
of truth, that is primarily in relation to the intellectual aspect of the
church's life.[69] Thus in commenting on Jn 16, 8: 'the holy ghost shall
come and rebuke the world of judgement', More insisted against Tyndale,
who thought the judgment applied to the leaders of the orthodox church,
that it referred to Jews and pagans who rejected true faith. Indeed the role
of the Spirit is to illumine not condemn the church of Christ: 'For the holy
goost hathe not fayled to teache his chyrch all such kinde of truthe from the
begynnynge hytherto, nor neuer shall ceace so to do, as well by his owne
holy secrete worde vnwrytten in the scrypture, and yet by hym selfe wrytten in chrysten mennys hartys/as by his holy scripture eyther wryten in
tables of stone or in bestes skynnes/accordynge to his owne wordes spoken
as well by ye mouth of ye prophete Ezechiel, (Ezech 11, 18-20) as of the
blessyd apostle saynt Paule.' (2 Cor 3, 1-3).[70] Here More makes of the
Holy Spirit the source of divine revelation as well as the recorder of the
message, whether on tablets of stone, parchment, or the inward heart of
men. Notice the equiparation between these modes of preserving the divine
message while on the other hand there is no mention of any other extrinsic
form of recording it other than the scripture.

---

[69] It is worth noting that More considered this Spirit to be given to each one in baptism:
'...suche as are baptysed and recyue the spyryte of god, may yf they wyll farre more easyly
folowe the spyryte and resyste the flesshely mocyons...' Through baptism we have the Spirit
of God dwelling in us and therefore we are sons of God. It is our duty to follow the Spirit and
mortify the flesh. See *Confutation* II, 755/30-34.

[70] See *Confutation* I, 45/6-15. More emphasised this inward writing of the gospel on men's
hearts. See ibid. I, 332/10-15, quoting Jer 31, 33-34: 'I shall geue my law in theyr bowels/& I
shall wryte yt in theyr hartes.' That is, God made no promise of written books but promised
that the Holy Spirit would come to teach his church and lead them into every truth. 'For the
prophete (Is 54, 13) and the euangelyste (Jn 6, 45) sayth, that they shalbe all goddes owne
scolers/whych sygnyfyeth that the congregacyon and companye shall be taught by god and
his spyryte, that shall wryte the new law the ryght fayth in the hartes of hys chyrche. And our
sauyour sayd, I shall sende ye holy goost that shall teache you all thynge, and lede you into
euery trouth' (Jn 14, 26) in ibid. I, 332/30-37. See ibid. II, 752/30-753/28 for similar texts.

Continuing Revelation

Nor is revelation of divine truth necessarily closed with the ending of the apostolic era: 'For what so euer Tyndale saye: neuer shall he proue the contrarye, but that god is at hys lyberte styll and euer styll shalbe, to teache hys trouthes more and more, as his pleasure shall be to haue them known, and to gouerne his chyrche to hys pleasure in dyuerse ages after dyuerse maners, such as hym self lyste for to dyuyse/wherof his church is by theyr hole consent sure.'[71] More was not over-specific in explaining how this continuing revelation takes place. God, he suggested 'hath dayly stered vp & dayly doth sterre vp new prophetes in sundry partes of hys catholyke chyrche, holy doctours, and preachers, and faythfull men, and good lyuers/...'[72] Are these the recipients of the divine oracles? He did not answer directly but insisted that the power of miracles the Spirit actuates in the church testifies to the value of their teaching.[73]

Rather than the prophetic spirit given to individuals, for which he did of course allow, More stressed the role of the Spirit in deepening the understanding of the church in general of the basic datum of divine revelation. Commenting on I Cor 2, 15, 'the spyrytuall iudgeth all thynges, and his spyryte sercheth the depe secretis of god,' More remarked that to no one more than the old holy fathers could the appellation 'spiritual' be given in this sense.[74] The fact that they disagreed at times should not be cause for rejecting their doctrines, as God's Spirit works in varied ways: 'For god doth reuele hys trouthes not always in one manner/but sometyme he sheweth yt out at onys, as he wyll haue yt knowen and men bounden forthwyth to byleue yt/as he shewed Moyses what he wolde haue Pharao do. Sometyme he sheweth yt leysourly, suffryng his flokke to comen and dyspute theruppon/and in theyr treatynge of the mater, suffreth them wyth good mynde and scrypture and naturall wisedome, with inuocacyon of his spirituall helpe, to serche and seke for the treuth, and to vary for the whyle in theyr opynyons, tyll that he rewarde theyr vertuouse dylygence wyth ledyng them secretely in to the consent and concorde and bylyef of the trouth by his holy spirite *qui facit unanimes in domo* (Ps 67, 7),

---

[71] See *Confutation* I, 249/9-16.

[72] See *Confutation* I, 339/25-27.

[73] See *Confutation* I, 339/28-32; ibid. II, 690/25-35.

[74] See *Confutation* I, 47/32-48/3: '...I wote well that all those holy fathers were reputed for good crysten/and I wene they were all baptized and borne agayne of water and ye spyryte as our sauyour sayd vnto Nychodemus/...these thynges seme well to shewe that they were borne agayne of god and new created wyth his spyrite/and so by Tyndalys owne tale shold seme able to vnderstande the thynges of the spyryte of god.'

whyche maketh his flokke of one mynde in hys house, that is to wyt his chyrche.'[75] Whether it be the working of prophetic vision or the less dramatic insight of progressive reflection, underlying each advance in the understanding of the mystery of God lies a movement of his Spirit. Similarly changing observance and ordinance within the church should not be regarded as mere human decision. The Spirit is at work in these affairs of the church as in any other.[76] Where disagreement exists within the church one should be slow to give complete assent to one side or the other: 'For god byddeth vs that we shold not be lyght of bylyefe, nor by and by byleue euery spyryte/but proue the spyrytes whether they be of god.'[77]

So it is the Spirit, the principle of revelation within the church, who guides her to an understanding of what she has received whether recorded in men's hearts, inspired scripture, or popular traditions. 'And I saye that god by hys worde vnwryten dyd teache his chyrche to know his wordes wryten, and his tradycions also, whyche he taught the chyrche by his apostles/and made the chyrche agre therin by his spyryte, whiche maketh men of one mynde and one custome in the chyrche, and whyche spiryte kepeth both the wordes wryten and the wordes vnwritten in perpetuall knowledge and obseruaunce in his chyrche/accordynge as the very worde of god vnwryten, that is hys naturall worde of hym selfe bygoten seeth necessarye abydynge wyth his chirche for euer accordynge to his owne promyse.'[78] Here More combined within one perspective the presence of the divine personal Word of God within the church with the presence of the Spirit. His aim was to emphasise the priority of God's unwritten word in the sphere of revelation. God's own Word, an unwritten word, lives on in the church. It is both the principal form of revelation and norm of its interpretation. It performs this latter function of interpreting revelation in

---

[75] See *Confutation* I,248/11-24. See also ibid. II, 769/8-18.

[76] See *Confutation* I, 322/33-36: speaking of the Sunday observance, More says: 'I say that the chyrch as yt made yt so yt may breke yt. That is to wyt that as yt made yt by the spiryte of god, so yt may breke yt by the same spiryte. That is to say that as god made yt, so hym self may breke yt, yf yt so shall please hym.' See ibid. I, 377/10-24, where More sees the guidance of the Spirit underlying such adaptations as baptism in the name of Jesus, rather than in that of Father, Son and Holy Spirit as Christ commanded in Mt 28, 20; the abolition of circumcision by St Paul: '...how knew he when he shold do the tone and when the tother? by bare ymagynacyons of hys owne mynde? naye by that spiryte they knew yt/whyche as yt ruled them, so ruleth yt the chyrch in the necessary poyntes of fayth and euer shall vnto the worldes ende.'

[77] See *Confutation* II, 889/32-890/2: 'For god inwardly worketh with the will of man walkyng with god, in well vsynge and applyenge conuenyent occasyons towarde yt outwardely geuen by god...'

[78] See *Confutation* I, 381/26-35.

conjunction with the illuminating and uniting Spirit who brings all men
together in common belief.

Record of Revelation

The transcendent Word of God becomes immanent in the inspired
writings of prophets, evangelists and apostles. More important still, in
More's eyes, it becomes immanent in the gospel written in men's hearts
by the Holy Spirit. Thus he had no hesitation in affirming the insufficiency of scripture by itself as a guide to divine revelation: 'But now syth god
entended not to gyue his new lawe by bokes, but specyally by the necessary
poyntes therof wryten in mennys hartes/wherof hym selfe wolde be the
specyall inwarde mayster: he hath prouyded ye scrypture to serue for
parte, but not to serue alone for all.'[79] The written word of God is complemented by the gospel in the heart.

It is interesting to note in this case how More made of the latter the principal record of divine revelation in the new alliance. God gives his new law
*'specyally by the necessary poyntes therof wryten in mennys hartes; dede stony hartes
sholde waxe tender, softe & quycke, and wyth wyllyng and applyable myndes shold by
the spyryte of god haue the lawe, that is the trewe bylyefe, good hope, and well
wurkynge cheryte, gracyously wryten in them.'*[80] It is of this inward law that the
divine presence is the 'speciall inwarde mayster', guiding the Christian
consciousness in its own self-awareness and in its interpretation of what
the Spirit says within it.

On the other hand there is a certain ambiguity in More's mode of
speech. At times by 'the gospel in the heart', as in the foregoing quotation,
is meant apparently an effect, distinct from the Spirit, produced in the
mind and heart of man. At other times it appears identical with the
abiding Spirit, as in the following quotation: '...in the same maner remayneth wryten in the same chyrche by the same spyryte, a ryghte rule

---

[79] See *Confutation* I, 257/33-37. See ibid. I, 270/18-23: 'For I say that the trewth of that artycle taught and byleued as the chyrche wythout any doute or questyon byleueth/may be so
surely grauen in mannys harte, that though he neuer haue redde nor herde neyther any
scrypture in that poynte: yet presupposynge yt for an vndouted trouth, he shall set at nought
all the false wrested scrypture of the false prophete...' See also ibid. I, 332/1-333/12;
380/25-381/35.

[80] See *Confutation* II, 753/14-17. See also *Confutation* I, 312/36-313/2: 'If a man seke
amonge the other euangelystes: he shall fynd mo necessary thynges then one lefte out in
saynt Iohan/and in eche of them somwhat that some other hath. And yf a man loke ferther in
the boke of fayth, wryten in the hartes of Cristes hole catholyke chyrche: he shall fynde some
thynges yt none of them all hath wryten, and yet necessary poyntes of fayth/as I haue shewed
you samples and shall.'

lefte by god, techynge the chyrche to enterprete and vnderstand the
wrytynge that hys holy apostles haue wryten after, & hys holy prophetes
haue also wryten before. And thys wrytynge from tyme to tyme in the
hartes of hys chyrch is the writyng that Cryst so often promised vnto his
chyrch/that is to wyt that he wolde sende the holy gooste to teche it all
thynge, and to lede it into all trouth, & be wyth it hym selfe all dayes also
euyn vnto the worldes ende.'[81] Here More seems to identify the unwritten
gospel with the Spirit of God, or better the presence of God. This is where
the ambiguity lies, as he emphasises at one time the presence of God, at
another the word written in men's hearts. In any event his basic purpose is
clear: to affirm that the over-riding criterion in the interpretation of
revelation is the indwelling presence of God and his continued influence in
the mind and heart of the believer. The God who gives revelation in the
first instance to those who believe guides believers in their explanations of
that same message no matter in what form it is recorded.

Priority of Gospel or Church?

On the basis of this divine guidance More sought to answer the question
posed by Tyndale 'whether the chyrche were byfore the gospell, or the
gospell before the chyrche'? The question as posed in one particular instance by Tyndale illustrates the basic confusion arising from the use of the
term 'word' in this context. Arguing from Rom 10, 14 that unless the
gospel be preached no faith can be given, Tyndale claimed the priority of
word to church.[82] More, without the slightest hesitation, conceded this
point as the issue at stake was not the priority of revelation or even of the
preaching of the gospel to the church. This seems evident enough from a
consideration of how Christ called his apostles. Not merely is the Word-
made-flesh but so also his spoken word is prior to the church. The point at
stake is whether the *written word* of God is prior to the church? And here
More was adamant, turning the very text of Romans against his
antagonist. In the normal course of events after Christ's coming it is the
church which preaches the gospel. When faith has been aroused by
preaching a man turns to the church and accepts from her the written
word of God.

Once more in this debate More relied on a familiar place in the writings
of Augustine for support: 'And thus I saye good reders, ye may perceyue
by that place in saynt Austayne whyche I haue rehersed you, and by hys

---

[81] See *Confutation* II, 753/19-28.
[82] Tyndale, *Answer*, 24-26.

other foure chapyters immedyate before, that the mynde and entent of saynt Austayne is playne, that god of his goodnesse offereth men occasyon, and by good and substancyall causes helpeth them that are wyllynge fyrste of all to knowe the trewe chyrche, of whyche euery trewe precher is a member. And then lyke as god vseth myracles & dyuers other meanes, by whyche meanes his helpe and grace maketh the well wyllyng person to perceyue & know whyche is his very chyrch: so doth he after vse the same chyrch for a meane, by whych he maketh a man know whych is the very scrypture/ye and ouer that in thynges necessarye for saluacyon, whych is the very sense and the trew vnderstandynge of the very scrypture.'[83] As in his previous works the spokesman for orthodoxy insisted that it is through the church we recognise the written word of God and discover its authentic meaning.

Moreover it is in the Christian community that the scriptures are correctly interpreted. Not merely do we receive the text but its faithful rendering within the context of the living church. 'And of these thynges I saye yt yt foloweth necessaryly, that though the chyrch be not aboue the scripture and holy wryt: yet yt is so taught by the spyryte of god and his holy secrete inwarde worde vnwrytten, that yt can not be dampnably deceyued in the vnderstandynge of his holy scrypture wryten. And theruppon yet farther foloweth, that all such as so conster the scrypture, that they wolde make the scrypture seme to be contrarye to the fayth of Cristes chyrch: do damnably conster yt contrary to the teachynge of god and his holy spiryte.'[84] In all matters concerning the interpretation of scripture, let a man '...lene therin vnto the iudgement of the olde holy enterpretours passed, and specyall to the sense receyued of the hole catholyke chyrche...'[85] The exegesis of scripture is never a matter of purely private intuition. It takes place within a living community and a living tradition. Only a recognition of this fact can save one from serious error.

As we have seen earlier, More did not clearly distinguish between the presence of the Spirit within the human person and the effect such

---

[83] See *Confutation* II, 739/9-21. More is referring here of course to *Contra epistolam Manichaei, MPL* 42, 175. See also *Confutation* II, 792/27-35.

[84] See *Confutation* I, 133/31-134/2.

[85] See *Confutation* I, 62/7-12. See ibid. I, 337/26-338/2: '...there may lye yet therein for all ye vnderstandyng yt men haue therof, many a great mystery hyd that neuer shalbe clerely vnderstanden/tyll such tyme as god vppon the thynge done and shewed, shall by his spyryte promysed, sente, and assystent vnto his chyrche in the tymes conuenyente, and by god appoynted therunto, reuele yt/whyche thynges shall then be necessary poyntes, to be byleued, and nowe neyther necessarye to byleue, nor possyble to be thought vppon. But when yt shall please god any suche thynges to do, shew, & reuele...he shall send suche holy messengers as he hath ben euer wonte about such besynesse to send...'

presence might produce.[86] On this point his mind was not quite decided but the fundamental issue was evident enough. He did not place the church above revelation but related revelation to the living presence of God within the community and each member of that community which he established. Revelation is received not merely in words, deeds, and images, but also and more significantly in the mysteriously transcendental manner of divine presence. This presence produces its reflex in the mind of its recipient as well as continuing to guide and inspire chosen individuals as its mouthpiece. Revelation cannot be restricted to the written word of inspired scripture which occurs subsequently to the initial revelation made to the early Christian community. The God who spoke to that community is still present to that which has succeeded it. He still speaks to the community as he did to that of earlier generations enabling it to piece together the message he makes available to it through a variety of channels.

III. TRANSMISSION OF REVELATION

Tyndale's central position in opposition to More was concerned with the transmission of revelation. He acknowledged that '...Christ and his apostles preached an hundred thousand sermons, and did as many miracles,' but these he claimed, '...had been superfluous to have been all written.'[87] Instead the core, the pith, the substance of everything necessary for salvation, '...both of what we ought to believe, and what we ought to do, was written...or drawn out of that which is written.'[88] Consequently anything which cannot be supported by the written words of scripture is not binding in faith or conscience.[89]

The sign that the word of God is being preached is the conformity of the preacher's doctrine to scripture. The only other sign Tyndale would admit was that of miraculous intervention to confirm the word of the preacher or prophet. He used this latter position to evade the difficulty of the late appearance of writing in the old testament '...the preachers were ever prophets, glorious in doing of miracles, wherewith they confirmed their

---

[86] This is one of the more ancient debating points in Christian theology. As St Thomas expressed it: 'utrum gratia ponat aliquid in anima?', i.e. whether grace is identical with the Spirit or whether the Spirit's presence produces secondary, created effects within the person he inhabits? See *Summa Theologica* I-II, cx, 1.

[87] Tyndale, *Answer*, 26.

[88] Tyndale, *Answer*, 26. See also ibid., 99; 133-137.

[89] Tyndale, *Answer*, 26; 96-99.

preaching...'[90] The rule of scripture applies even to general councils, for by holy writ have they '...concluded such things as were in them determin-ed...And by the same scripture we know which councils were true, and which false.'[91]

Tyndale took his stand on a strictly biblical rule of faith rejecting any position that could not be clearly validated from its writ. Moreover the on-ly sense of scripture that Tyndale was prepared to take seriously was the literal sense: 'Thou shalt understand, therefore, that the scripture hath but one sense, which is the literal sense. And that literal sense is the root and ground of all, and the anchor that never faileth, whereunto if thou cleave, thou canst never err or go out of the way. And if thou leave the literal sense, thou canst not but go out of the way.'[92]

More, of course, had the highest regard for the inspired word of God. He himself was deeply immersed in scripture and recognised it as the cen-tral medium for the transmission of revelation within the Christian com-munity, second only to the personal action of the Holy Spirit in the hearts of the faithful. He could not accept Tyndale's position that all significant revealed truth was contained in the bible. He subscribed rather to the position advanced by Henry VIII and Fisher that the word of God was passed on 'partly by wrytynge partly by worde wythout wrytyng.'[93]

One of More's main concerns was to establish that the divine message is communicated not merely by written word but also by the preaching of the church. Beginning with Christ, he asserted, God has taught the world by word of mouth accompanied by the inner action of the Spirit. '...our sauyour fyrste by hym selfe & after by his holy spyryt taught his blessed apostles, & by them the world that wold lerne/...'[94] '...by hys worde he sheweth hys trewth/and by his worde we byleue that he doeth it/and by hys apostles and euangelystes we byleue that he sayed it/and by the chyrche of euery age folowynge, we be taughte and byleue that the euangelystes and the apostles preched and taught partly by wrytynge partly by worde wythout wrytynge, suche thynges as the catholyke chyrche of Cryste

---

[90] Tyndale, *Answer*, 27; ibid., 100: 'Christ's disciples taught Christ's doctrine; confirming it with miracles, that it might be known for God's, and not theirs. And even so must the church, that I will believe, shew a miracle, or bring authentic scripture that is come from the apostles, which confirmed it with miracles.'

[91] Tyndale, *Answer*, 99-100.

[92] Tyndale, *The Obedience of a Christian Man*, 304. See also ibid., 305-306 and passim.

[93] See the excellent summary history of the concept of tradition in Headley, *Responsio*, 734-736; 738-739.

[94] See *Confutation* II, 885/3-5.

telleth vs to haue bene taughte by them.'⁹⁵ Tyndale had argued from Jn 5,
34: 'I receyue no recorde of men' that the truth of Christ's preaching did
not depend on the teaching of the church. More agreed that the gospel is
not true because it is taught by the church. It is true because it is God's
word.

On the other hand he affirmed that it was very definitely Christ's intention that witness to his doctrine would be borne by men throughout the
ages. In support of his position he cited Lk 24, 44-49 where Christ provided that '...penaunce and remyssyon of synnys sholde be preached in his
name amonge all nacyons begynnynge at Hierusalem: he sayed vnto them
forther, and ye are wytnesses of these thynges...' The same command was
given in Acts 1, 8: 'ye shalbe wytnesses vnto me in Hierusalem, & in all
Iewry, and in Samary, and euen vnto the worldes ende.' This text of St
John cited by Tyndale therefore does not deny the need for human witness
to divine truth. It does affirm that this truth does not depend principally
on such witness for its verification, but on the inward testimony of the
Spirit and the outward attestation of miracle.

There is no clash between divine and human witness to the same truth,
as can be seen in Jn 15, 26-27: '...the spyryte of trouth that procedeth of
the father, he shall bere wytnesse of me/and ye shall bere wytnesse also,
bycause ye haue ben wyth me from the begynnynge.' All this 'clerely proueth that Crystes catholyke chyrche is a very specyall wytnesse. For onely
in that chyrch is the number of trewe byleuynge menne/...'⁹⁶

This emphasis on the preaching of the church brought More to
underline an aspect of tradition to which he had paid less attention in the
Responsio. Speaking of the new testament, More observed that the apostles
and evangelists had not recorded all Christ's deeds and words: '...but that
of goddes wordes they wrote not all/but dyuers thynges were by god to
them and by them to other taughte by mouth, and by tradycyon from
hande to hande delyuered, and from age to age hytherto contynued in
Crystes chyrch.'⁹⁷

This short passage makes three important points. Firstly, scripture is an
incomplete record of revelation. Secondly, what is lacking from scripture
is supplied, in part at least, by the tradition of the church, 'from hande to
hande delyuered', a phrase which occurs in Henry's *Assertio*.⁹⁸ Moreover
the most specific means mentioned for this handing on is when God's

---

⁹⁵ See *Confutation* I, 246/10-16.
⁹⁶ See *Confutation* I, 239/14-240/39.
⁹⁷ See *Confutation* I, 152/37-153/3.
⁹⁸ See Headley, *Responsio*, 734-736 citing Henry VIII, *Assertio*, sigs. G4; M3 v.

revelation is 'to other taughte by mouth', that is in oral tradition. This is a
new element in More's thought.

Initially one might think it brings him into line with the Christian
Cabalists who spoke of a secret oral tradition supplementing scripture.
From the context it is clear that this is not so. More had in mind the ordinary teaching procedures of Christian people: parents to their children,
clergy to their parishioners and so forth[99] Nonetheless, this contribution
brings a new dimension to the fore in his treatment of tradition, namely
the living tradition of an age-long community which now assumes a complementary significance to the inner activity of the Spirit in the preservation and ongoing communication of the divine message.

In More's scheme of things in the *Confutation*, the testimony of the
church's preaching plays an essential part in the transmission of revelation. This realisation may have led him to broaden the concept of tradition
expounded in the *Responsio*. In the latter work he emphasised the direct
role of the Spirit in the transmission of revelation. The Spirit inscribes the
gospel on the hearts of the faithful. The constant faith of the church
traceable in her beliefs and practices is the outward reflex of the inward
movement of the Spirit. As we have seen in discussing More's concept of
divine revelation and its modes, this idea was frequently adverted to in the
Confutation.

In the *Dialogue*, faced with the problem of vindicating such clearly un-
biblical usages as worship of images, relics, and pilgrimages More had
given new stress to the idea of unwritten traditions existing within the
church, mainly in the form of customary practices dating back to apostolic
times, their value authenticated by the divinely guided consent of the
church. In the *Confutation* More also made ample use of this second concept of tradition which is prominent in Henry's *Assertio* as well as Fisher's
Confutatio, namely tradition understood as the handing on by a community
of its socio-cultural behaviour patterns and values from one generation to
the next: '…the comen fayth of the catholyke chyrch…whych from hande
to hande hath ben taken & kepte from Crystes dayes and hys apostles
hytherto…'[100]

When one comes to examine examples of such unwritten tradition in the
church, one finds the range rather large. Thus More will argue from tradi-

---

[99] See above pp. 59-60 for a note on the Christian Cabalists. It is worth observing that the
concept of tradition in the *Responsio* is not exclusively pneumatic. There are traces of the
socio-cultural concept of tradition with less specific reference to oral tradition. See *Responsio*
240/29-32, tr. 241/33-38.

[100] See *Confutation* I, 389/30-35.

tion for the seven sacraments,[101] the virginity of Mary as well as her assumption.[102] This latter doctrine, he urged, is as worthy of belief as 'to byleue that Enoch or Hely, is bodye and soule in paradyse, syth he maye do the tone that doth the tother. And he sayth the tone that sayth the tother/though he saye them not bothe in one maner, but the tone by wrytynge the tother by mouth.' This is another explicit reference to a strictly 'oral' tradition within the church.[103] Other examples he cites of unwritten tradition are the change in the sabbath day, purgatory, and some a little more banal such as the fact of women baptizing when Christ's command to baptize was given only to men (Mt 28, 20). Even more so, the custom of putting water into wine used in the celebration of mass.[104] This tendency on the part of More and other controversialists to defend indiscriminately the total medieval heritage by the same argument from anonymous ecclesial tradition weakened its force when applied to key questions in sacramental or Marian theology.

Thus in the *Confutation* one finds side by side with a pneumatic concept of revelation and its transmission, a concept of tradition which depends greatly on the social continuity of the church body. This body of belief is passed on 'partly by wrytynge partly by worde wythout wrytynge.' This involved a modification of his position as expressed in the *Responsio* where he had viewed the written monuments of Christian tradition as the visible result of the inner working of the Spirit, the primary, almost exclusive, channel of the word of God besides scripture.

----

[101] See *Confutation* I, 157/3-22.

[102] See *Confutation* I, 366/15-367/35; ibid. I, 477/31-37 for the virginity of Mary. See ibid. I, 285/4-30, for the assumption: 'If thys be a new byleued artycle/lette Tyndale tell when thys bylyef beganne/& he shall fynde that yt hath ben thus byleued euen from the tyme of her deceace. And now ye thyng that almoste .xv. C. yere hath ben byleued/he calleth a new artycle.' This tradition, he continues, is as worthy of belief as the word of scripture. 'For the inwarde inspiracyon of hys spyryte/is his mouth vnto his resonable creatures.'

[103] See *Confutation* I, 389/31-35 for a further example of a similar manner of speaking regarding the manner of tradition: '...the catholyke knowen chyrche can not erre in that fayth, whych from hande to hande hath ben taken & kepte from Crystes dayes and hys apostles hytherto.' See ibid. I, 79/22-26 for the same phraseology employed in connection with the sacraments: 'And yf that of any suche sacramentes or ceremonyes gyuen of olde by god vnto his blessyd apostles, and by them delyuered vnto hys chyrche, and therin euer synnys fro hand to hand contynued/it hath pleased the spyryte to let his people haue and enioye the profyte...'

[104] See *Confutation* I, 261/19-21. The only reason he sees for the custom of women baptizing is that: 'I see ye tone euer vsed euery where in Cristes hole chyrche, and the consent of holy sayntes approuynge and allowyng the same.' As regards the custom of adding water to wine, cf. ibid. II, 657/14-35.

Fathers of the church

It is true at the same time that the pneumatic theory of tradition lived on in the *Confutation*. His respect for the fathers of the church was not diminished. The fathers of the church, More claimed, have a special role to play in the transmission of extra-bibilical tradition. Because they were spiritual men, born anew of water and the Spirit, they seem well fitted 'to understande the thynges of the spyryte of god.'[105] Because of the special influence of the Spirit upon them, their interpretations of scripture are to be treated with great respect and not departed from except for serious cause.[106] The fathers have maintained the spirit of prophecy in the church as their miracles attest.[107] But as well as their function in prophecy, the continuity of their teaching is a guide to the constant faith of the church: '...syth that they maye well wytte, by the authoryte of saynt Austayn, saynt Hierom, saynt Gregory, saynt Ambrose, saynte Cypriane, saynt Basyle, saynt Chrysostome, & all the olde holy sayntes vnto theyr owne dayes, and all the whole catholyke chyrche of Cryste, and by hys holy spyryte gyuen to those holy doctours of his chyrche and euer abydynge therin/..'[108]

Development of doctrine as continuing revelation

The understanding of revelation within the church is not a static thing fixed forever in the deposit of revelation in one particular formulation. Rather is the Spirit active in the church continually leading her on to a further understanding of divine truth. More would even say revealing this understanding to the church or to some of its specially endowed adherents: '...yet is it (scripture) not so open but yt there is many a place in euery

---

[105] See *Confutation* I, 47/31-48/5: '...but I wote well, that all those holy fathers were reputed for good crysten/and I wene they were all baptized and borne agayne of water and ye spyryte as our sauyour sayd vnto Nychodemus/& after yt they lyued well and spyrytually, and dyed well and spyrytually, as apperyeth by theyr bookes and hystoryes wryten of theyr lyues, and myracles shewed for them of god after theyr dethys. And vnto suche symple groce carnall peopell as we be/these thynges seme well to shewe that they were borne agayne of god & new created wyth his spyrite/and so by Tyndalys owne tale shold seme able to vnderstande the thynges of the spyryte of god.'

[106] See *Confutation* I, 62/7-10: '...but let vs lene therin vnto the iudgement of the olde holy enterpretours passed, and specyall to the sense receyued of the hole catholyke chyrche...'

[107] See *Confutation* II, 623/3-6; see also ibid., 695/34-695/3: 'How be it of treuth, holy prophetes hath there bene sent vnto the worlde by god and into the chyrche of Chryst, mo then an hundred syth the deth of Chryste, to kepe in the ryghte fayth and calle home the people fro synne, by the trewe doctryne of the spyryte, inspyrynge theym the ryghte sense of scrypture & what so euer god wolde haue knowen besyde...'

[108] See *Confutation* II, 589/25-30.

parte therof, so darke & of such diffyculty/yt there neyther is nor I wene neuer was synnys ye apostles dayes, nor peraduenture euery man amonge them neyther, yt durst haue ben so bold to say yt all thyng was so open to him/but yt there may lye yet therein for all ye vnderstandyng yt men haue therof many a great mystery hyd that neuer shalbe clerely vnder-standen/tyll such tyme as god vppon the thynge done and shewed, shall by his spyryte promysed, sente, and assystent vnto his chyrche in the tymes conuenyente, and by god appoynted therunto, reuele yt/whyche thynges shall then be necessary poyntes, to be byleued, and nowe neyther necessarye to byleue, nor possyble to be thought vppon.'[109]

Notice in what sense More speaks of a continual revelation in the church: a revelation by the Spirit of an intuitive understanding of the basic content of revelation, in this case that which is contained in scripture. Once again More did not work out a coherent theology distinguishing the assistance of the Spirit in understanding the elements of the primitive message from the manner in which such secrets are made known to men. His language suggests, in fact, a continuing revelation within the church: 'Christe hymselfe and hys holye spyryte, do stil by secrete inspiracion, reuele & open vnto his churche, euerye necessarye truth, that he wyl haue his churche farther know and bounden to belieue.'[110]

Hence although More had moved closer to Henry VIII and Fisher in emphasising the place of natural process in extra-biblical tradition, he maintained at the centre of the picture the abiding presence of the Spirit of God leading the church further into truth. His continued regard for the authority of patristic testimony as well as his openness to theological and doctrinal development must be understood in this light.

In his work on Gabriel Biel, Professor Heiko Oberman has illuminated the issue of tradition by speaking of two broad concepts prevalent in later medieval theology, one which viewed tradition as the explicitation of scrip-ture; a second which saw it as supplementary to and independent of scrip-ture. Seen in these terms More clearly falls into the second category, em-phasising tradition as an independent source of information concerning the divine message. While Oberman's categories enable one to organise and arrange a good deal of the evidence, one wonders whether they fully comprehend all aspects of the problem. Surely what is at stake is not mere-ly the relation of scripture and tradition but the much larger question of

---

[109] See *Confutation* I, 337/21-31.
[110] See *Confutation* II, 996/20-23. (This section belongs to Bk IX; not found in the first edi-tion.)

divine revelation; how it was originally given and received as well as how it survives in its man-made vehicle?

Are there not also key supplementary questions concerning the nature of tradition considered in itself? Perhaps More's contribution is of significance precisely because he continually pushed the discussion beyond an immediate confrontation of scripture and tradition to an awareness of the presence of a transcendent God present to his people and revealing himself to them. This emphasis was at its strongest in the *Responsio*. A pneumatic concept of tradition makes it consist mainly in the ongoing self-revelation of God in the Christian consciousness. In the *Confutation* as well as this pneumatic concept of tradition he admitted a socio-cultural transmission of belief and practice of some significance. Nonetheless he continued to accord over-riding importance to the indwelling Spirit and the gospel in the heart as the primary mode of divine communication. 'For the inwarde inspiracyon of hys spyryte/is his mouth vnto his resonable creatures.'

One wonders whether, if Luther and More had been able to pursue a friendly dialogue on this subject, they might not have been able to reach some common ground, since Luther in the early 1520's did not identify divine revelation with the literal sense of scripture nor see it as coterminous with it. If it had been possible, a common search into the concept of divine revelation might have led to a narrowing of the gap between the two men. With Tyndale, however, the evangelical movement in England had come to see God's word as irrevocably formulated in the written word of the bible. There was little space for an irenic exchange between Tyndale and More on that issue. For More in his *Confutation* had come to rely even more than hitherto on a socio-cultural tradition, even an oral tradition, though he never dabbled in Christian Cabalism as did Fisher, as a vehicle of divine revelation.

In his use of the *partim...partim* formula, (partely by wrytynge partely by worde wythout wrytynge) More echoed a phrase found in Henry VIII, John Fisher, and which was to be a major source of controversy at Trent, indeed to the present time. Trent rejected the *partim...partim* formula, replacing it with *et...et*, without determining whether 'both...and' implied the preservation of the essential source of revelation in scripture alone or not. In the *Dialogue* and *Confutation* More took a further step towards recognising in tradition a separate record of revelation containing elements of the divine message both formally and materially distinct from that contained in scripture. In this he contributed towards a hardening of division between the reformers and the established churches.

At the same time he retained his central focus on what might have
proved a point of reconciliation. He consistently insisted that God in his
self-revelation transcends any of his immanent images whether in scripture or the traditions of the church. It is the voice of God one must hear.
This must be sought beyond and behind any particular utterance whatever
form it may take and wherever it may be found.

IV. CHURCH AND REVELATION

The church of Christ on earth for Tyndale was essentially identified
with those who had been justified by faith in Christ. In the first chapter of
his *Answer to Sir Thomas More's Dialogue* he had discussed a variety of meanings of the word church.[111] Finally he had opted for one in particular
where '...it is taken specially for the elect only; in whose hearts God hath
written his law with his Holy Spirit, and given them a feeling faith of the
mercy that is in Christ Jesus our Lord.'[112] Membership in this church is
brought about through loving surrender to the Lord Jesus whom one
encounters in the living word of God mediated through preaching and
scripture.[113]

The members of this church can neither sin nor err. This sounds a
rather sweeping statement. It is less so when understood in the context of
Tyndale's thought. What he meant by error and sin was primarily the
total rejection of God's grace or word. Men might commit sin through the
weakness of the flesh, or might have an erroneous opinion concerning the
interpretation of certain passages in scripture. Still, as long as the believer
maintains loving trust in the mercy of God he remains within the circle of
God's grace. Such believers '...never sin of purpose, nor hold any error
maliciously, sinning against the Holy Ghost; but of weakness and infirmi-
ty.'[114]

Tyndale was able to maintain this position on the intrinsic inerrancy of
the church of the elect for this reason. He did not look on the sacramental
character of baptism as constituting any real title to membership in this
hidden body. Membership belongs to those who have living faith.
Membership could be lost only by the sin against faith, by the rejection of
the Spirit: 'But they which maliciously maintain opinions against the

---

[111] See Tyndale, *Answer*, 11-13.
[112] See ibid., 13.
[113] See ibid., 30-31; 50-51; 139; 195-196.
[114] See ibid., 30-35; in particular p. 32.

scripture are fallen from Christ, and make an idol of their opinions.'[115] Thus not merely does loss of grace follow on this sin, but also loss of membership in the true church of Christ whose permanent purity is thereby assured.

It is evident that fidelity to the gospel, especially as found in scripture was, for Tyndale, a key element in retaining membership in the church. The scripture contains all truth necessary for salvation. 'By which scripture the councils general have concluded such things as were in them determined...And by the same scripture we know which councils were true, and which false. And by the same scripture shall we, if any new question arise, determine it also.'[116] Thus the teaching of the church as a whole as well as that of the individual preacher must be measured against the rule of written scripture. The church is strictly subordinate to the holy writ.

More's starting point was, of course, different. For him the church was mainly the common multitude of the baptised, be they sick or well. Membership could not be finally lost in this world. It was to this body that God revealed himself and within it he promised to dwell. Through its mediation his word reaches the world. Hence the key role of the church both in handing on and interpreting the divine message.

More constantly reiterated in opposition to Tyndale that revelation had been given to the care of the church for transmission to the people of the world and so to succeeding generations of believers. The principle means of this act of communication is the preaching of the word. The validity of such preaching springs from its concordance with the general faith of the community. Preachers have credence '...bycause they be membres of her that is trew, and theyr doctryne agreeth with hers, whom god wyll not suffer to saye dampnably false...'[117]

The gift of inspired scripture is a unique treasury of the divine word, a privileged way of coming to know God and his message. Nonetheless it can pose problems. More had dealt many times in the past with the preliminary question: how does one know whether scripture is authentic or not? The answer he repeatedly gave, paraphrasing St Augustine's *Contra epistolam Manichaei* and the *Contra Donatistas* did not change: the authority of the church. Scripture is received from the church and not vice-versa.[118]

---

[115] ibid., 33. See also Tyndale, *A Prologue upon the Epistle of St Paul to the Hebrews* in *Doctrinal Treatises and Introductions to Different Parts of the Holy Scriptures,* ed. Henry Walter, London, 1848, 521-524.

[116] ibid, 99; 135-137; 139.

[117] *Confutation* II, 891/24-27.

[118] *Confutation* II, 735/5-739/38, citing Augustine, *Contra epistolam Manichaei, MPL* 42, 175; *MPL* 33, 403-404, as well as the *Confessions, MPL* 32, 733-780.

The church's ministry in this area is not limited to the vindication of scripture but extends to its interpretation. More insisted that the bible was no transparent document. On the contrary, '...is it not so open but yt there is many a place in euery parte therof, so darke, & of such diffyculty/yt there neyther is nor I wene neuer was synnys ye apostles dayes..' any man '...yt durst haue ben so bold to say yt all thyng was so open to him...' that no further mystery remained.[119] On the contrary, scripture needs careful elucidation and he who will grasp the divine message must exercise the greatest care. In all disputed passages the patristic tradition of exegesis and the teaching of the church is an unfailing guide.[120] Ultimately, however, the interpretation of revelation belongs not to exegetes or scholars but to the church at large: '...though the church be not aboue the scripture and holy wryt: yet yt is so taught by the spyryte of god and his holy secrete inwarde worde vnwrytten, that yt can not be dampnably deceyued in the vnderstandynge of his holy scrypture wryten.'[121]

At the same time the church does not necessarily appropriate in consciousness the full content of revelation at any given moment in history. Rather is there a gradual unfolding in time of the mystery made known by God, a mystery '...that neuer shalbe clerely vnderstanden/tyll such tyme as god vppon the thynge done and shewed, shall by his spyryte promysed, sente, and assystent vnto his chyrche in the tymes conuenyente, and by god appoynted therunto, reuele yt/...'[122]

Process of interpretation

The process by which a deepening awareness of the meaning of divine mystery takes place in the Christian community was not fully analysed by More. At first sight he seems to appeal mainly to a continuing revelation to vindicate in part beliefs and practices not incontrovertibly found in scripture. It would be fairer to More's matter-of-fact approach to look at these references to post-apostolic revelation in the light of another statement: 'For god doth reuele hys trouthes not alwayes in one manner/but sometyme he sheweth yt out at onys, as he wyll haue yt knowen and men bounden forthwyth to byleue yt/as he shewed Moyses what he wolde haue

---

[119] *Confutation* I, 337/18-28.

[120] *Confutation* I, 61/36-62/14.

[121] *Confutation* I, 133/31-35.

[122] *Confutation* I, 337/27-33. See also *Confutation* II, 996/20-23. 'Christe hymselfe and hys holye spyryte, do stil by secrete inspiracion, reuele & open vnto his churche, euerye necessarye truth, that he wyl haue his churche farther know and bounden to belieue.'

Pharao do. (Ex 3 ff.) Sometyme he sheweth yt leysourly, suffryng his flokke to comen & dyspute theruppon/and in theyr treatynge of the mater, suffreth them wyth good mynde & scrypture and naturall wisedome, with inuocacyon of his spirituall helpe, to serche and seke for the treuth, and to vary for the whyle in theyr opynyons, tyll that he rewarde theyr vertuouse dylygence wyth ledyng them secretely in to the consent and concorde and bylyef of the trouth by his holy spirite, *qui facit unanimes in domo* (Ps 67, 7), whyche maketh his flokke of one mynde in hys house, that is to wyt his chyrche.'[123]

Thus More used the word 'revelation' in a rather broad sense to cover not only a direct divine intervention in consciousness but also the gradual process by which the community using natural resources as well as the grace of God slowly pieces together the fragments of divine truth to make of them a coherent pattern. It is in this sense, therefore, as well as in terms of infused knowledge that one must understand More's references to continuing revelation. At the same time he does not seem to have had any acute awareness of a closure put to direct divine intervention in the mind of believers with the closing of the apostolic age.[124]

Church consensus—guide to truth

In the last analysis the agreement of the church concerning any points of doctrine, morals, devotional or other practices provides a sound guide to the believer: '...the comen consent of Crystes catholyke chyrche can not in crystes very trew fayth erre and be dampnably deceyued, whyther the thynges byleued be wryten in scrypture or not/...'[125] Tyndale is wrong, More asserted, when he declares that a thing is not of necessity to be believed, '...though all the catholyque chyrche of Cryste both do byleue, and many hundred yeres haue byleued yt the thyng is of necessyte to be

---

[123] See *Confutation* I, 248/11-24. See also ibid. I, 249/9-14: '...god is at hys lyberte styll and euer styll shalbe, to teache hys trouthes more and more, as his pleasure shall be to haue them known, and to gouerne his chyrche to hys pleasure in dyuerse ages after dyuerse maners, such as hym self lyste for to dyuyse/wherof his chyrche is by theyr hole consent sure.' Speaking of private scriptural interpretation he says: '...yet it is peryllous for any man *except certeyn reuelacyon of god*, to take hymselfe for so far forth renewed wyth ye spyryte of god, that he boldely lene in such thynges to hys owne wyt...' in ibid. I, 62/3-6.

[124] *Confutation* II, 996/15-38.

[125] See *Confutation* I, 362/22-24; see ibid. II, 714/33-715/4: '...we neuer bynde hym (Tyndale) to any thynge of necessyte vppon the saynge of any one doctoure be he olde or yonge/but eyther by the comen faste fayth of the whole catholyke chyrche, growen as yt euer doth by the spyryte of god, that maketh men of one mynde in his chyrche, or by the determynacyon of the chyrche assembled for such causes in the generall counsayles.'

done or byleued.'[126] For More the test of faith is the assent of the whole church to a particular doctrine, when '...the comon knowen catholyke people, clergy, lay folke, and all/whych what so euer theyr lyuynge be...do stande to gether and agre in the confessyon of one trew catholyke fayth, wyth all olde holy doctours and sayntes.'[127] This consensus is strongest when it extends not merely to the living church but across space and time to the apostolic age, to '...the interpretacyon of all holy doctours and sayntes, and the comen fayth of all trewe crysten people. xv. hundred yere before them...'[128] While the church's common faith was the basis for rejecting Arianism, on the other hand it justifies the continuing acceptance of a doctrine such as that of the assumption of the virgin Mary into heaven.[129]

Source of consensus

Indeed the doctrine of the assumption is a characteristic example of how such consensus comes about. There is no question here of a purely democratic process but of guidance by the Spirit of God of the minds of believers through history to arrive at agreement on a matter of faith: '...it is trew and taught vnto the chyrche by the spyryte of god, whyche ledeth the chyrche into euery trouth/and the chyrche growen into the consent and agrement therof by the same spiryte of concorde and agrement, whych maketh all the house of one mynde/and though the bylefe therof were very new...'[130]

Councils and consensus

One of the ways in which consensus on any particular issue becomes evident is in the decision of a general council. Conciliar decisions, for More, form part of the extrinsic determinants of the content of faith and

---

[126] See *Confutation* I, 310/25-27.

[127] See *Confutation* II, 480/36-481/2.

[128] See *Confutation* I, 157/12-14. See ibid II, 660/1-4: '...we proue well and suffycyently, that there is not an olde chyrche of Cryste and hys apostles, & an other newe chyrche now/but one whole chyrche from that tyme to thys tyme in one trewe fayth contynued.' See also ibid. II, 715/4-6: 'And then the comen fayth of olde tymes byfore our dayes, we presume to be suche of lykelyhed, as we perceyue by the olde holy sayntes bokes that they were of them selfe.'

[129] See *Confutation* I, 341/5-19. More asserts that the doctrine of the assumption has been believed for 1500 years; see *Confutation* I, 285/1-29. See also ibid. I, 78/11-20, where More points out that the common faith of the people is one major ground upon which sacramental belief rests.

[130] See *Confutation* I, 285/10-16.

are in fact equiparated to a general consensus. More, for example, called
for Tyndale's assent to propositions held '...eyther by the comen faste
fayth of the whole catholyke chyrch, growen as yt euer doth by the spyryte
of god, that maketh men of one mynde in his chyrche, or by the determynacyon of the chyrche assembled for such causes in the generall counsayles.'[131] More even recognised a certain equivalence between church
and council, seeing in the council a valid sense of the word church, inasmuch as '...counsayles do represent the whole chyrch...lyke wise as a
parliament representeth ye hole reame...'[132] A council therefore has the
right to determine matters concerning faith. Its authority in this area was
represented as equivalent to that of 'the catholic consent of all christian
people'.

Whence does it derive this authority? More rejected out of hand Tyndale's thesis that the authority of any particular conciliar decree is no
stronger than the scriptural evidence on which it is based:[133] '...what
scrypture alledged the apostles for theyr determynacyon in the .xv.
chapyter of the actes, where they in theyr counsayle sayde, & by theyr pystle wrote, ye holy goost & we haue sene yt good, to put no more burden vppon you, then these necessary thynges/that is to wyt that you abstayne
from thynges offred to idolys, and from blood...Was not the authoryte
thereof by the reason of Crystes worde: He that hereth you hereth me/(Lk
10, 16) whych worde hadde as great strength byfore yt was wryten, as euer
yt hadde synnes. Now this same authoryte hath Crystes chyrche assembled
in the generall counsayles/and the same spiryte enspyreth them, and the
same wordes of Crist byndeth his flokke to obay them that bounde them to
obay his apostles.'[134] These words More insisted are '...mych more properly ment of the whole vnyuersale chirche yt self/and of the counsayles
generall representynge that hole chyrche, wherof euery pertyculer chyrche

---

[131] See *Confutation* II, 714/34-715/4; ibid I, 355/30-35; see also ibid. II, 872/23-29, where
More, referring to Barnes's theory of church teaching, remarks: '...the poyntes of the fayth
that they and we varye for, be for oure parte not onely determyned by counsayles, but also
receyued and approued as parte of the comen catholyke fayth, by the faythfull consent and
bylyef of all crysten nacyons/and the contrary parte not onely condemned and abhorred by
holy generall counsayles, but also by ye sentence of all old holy sayntes wrytynges and by the
catholyque consent of all crysten people...'

[132] See *Confutation* I, 146/15-20.

[133] See Tyndale, *Answer*, 99-100.

[134] See *Confutation* I, 344/21-345/3. See also ibid. II, 941/21-27: 'I say that the counsayle
in the makynge so muste do, and so do in dede, and that the spyryte of god guydeth them
therin & ledeth them into all necessary trouth of fayth. And that when they haue done: theyr
determinacyon is not than to be examined by frere Barns, or such other as lyste to mysse
constre the scrypture to the contrary to defend theyr false heresyes.'

is but a member.'[135] In short the authority of the council, although not independent of holy writ as its basic charter comes from a command of
Christ recorded therein, is not tied immediately to the letter of scripture
but rather to the divine guidance which underlies both scripture and the
life of the church.

The bases of conciliar authority

This raises the question of the precise form of conciliar authority. As we
have seen there were various schools of thought on this matter in existence
in the fifteenth and early sixteenth centuries. More did not delve very
deeply into these problems. On the other hand a certain trend of thought
can be discerned which may well indicate on which side he would have
come down had he been obliged to face up squarely to the issues involved.
Even in the statement quoted above this orientation is hinted at, for while
he derived conciliar authority to teach authoritatively from Lk 10, 16: 'He
that heareth you, heareth me,' he interpreted this text in terms of the
whole church and not merely the episcopate or clergy for he went on to
say: 'Now this same authoryte hath Crystes chyrche assembled in the
generall counsayles...' In short, as he put it himself, the whole church is
assembled in council by means of its representatives. It is this which
justifies the use of the term 'church' when applied to conciliar decisions,
'...as a parliament representeth ye hole reame, & is by the comen speche so
called to/as when we say yt the realme hath made a law that heretikes
shalbe burned.'[136] In short, More's tendency was towards a represen-
tational-populist theory of council. As the general council represents the
whole church, the whole church is one of the institutional pillars on which
conciliar supremacy is built. It draws its authority from the entire people,
not merely from the episcopate.

This impression is reinforced by another passage from More's debate
with Barnes. In order to establish the force of conciliar decisions as in fact
representing the full ecclesial consensus, he asked him to imagine a
hypothetical council meeting in Salisbury plain at which all those entitled
to come might attend. All believing Christians from all parts of the world

---

[135] See *Confutation* I, 346/2-5.

[136] See *Confutation* I, 146/18-20; ibid. I, 345/29-346/5, where More comments on the
words of Christ, 'if any man here not ye chirch, take hym for an hethen; (Mt 18, 17)
euery man well woteth that thys is manifestly spoken not of the apostles onely for theyr tyme,
but of the chirch as longe as ye world shall laste...*so is it mych more properly ment of the whole
vnyuersale chirche yt selfl and of the counsayles generall representynge that hole chyrche, wherof euery pertyculer chyrche is but a member.'*

would be present: '...who so euer crysten man or woman were in any nacyon yet vncrystened' (catechumens presumably); 'who so euer in suche
place had a chrysten purpose, & fauored the name and fayth of Cryste
wyth entent to be chyrstened.' Having assembled in his mind's eye this
vast concourse of people, More went on: 'I doute nothynge but that yf this
had be thus proponed, yt wolde haue ben there in that full counsayle
agreed and ordered and decreed, that the generall counsayles shold be
after, not of the whole nomber of all crysten people, but of some suche
conuenyent nomber as conuenyently myghte assemble/and the same
though yt were not the whole catholyke chyrch in dede, but as frere Barns
saith only representatyue, sholde yet haue the same authoryte and the
same full credence geuen vnto yt, as though there were at yt all the whole
crysten people.'[137]

In short, More fully recognised that the church is made up of all believing Christians, extending its ranks to catechumens, and even to those explicitly desirous of membership in the church. It is the whole church which
is possessed of the Spirit; it is the whole church which the Spirit guides to
agreement.[138] On the other hand such vast assemblies are in practice impossible. Hence the convention of a convenient number of people, who,
More said explicitly, though 'only representatyve, sholde yet have the
same authoryte...as though there were at yt all the whole crysten people.'
The authority of the council within this perspective derives from its role as
representing the whole Christian people.

This view is strengthened by consideration of a further statement made
within the same context: 'And also that the dew assemble of certayne
partes representynge the whole body, sholde haue the full authoryte of the
whole body/is a thynge by the comen assent and experyence of the whole
worlde crysten and hethen so fully seen and perceyued, that no man can
doute but that it wold haue be so there determyned, for the power and
authoryte of euery generall counsayle of crystendome lawfully called and
assembled to gether, that though they were not...the congregacyon of all
the whole crysten people, yet sholde theyr determinacyon and decre be of
lyke strength and power as yf they hadde ben all assembled there to gether
on a grene.'[139]

In other words More here appears to be appealing to a general principle
of representation valid in civil life among Christian and pagans alike to
vindicate the authority of the general council. Ultimately of course, the

---

[137] See *Confutation* II, 938/14-23, 924/9-34.
[138] See above pp. 211-212 re consensus.
[139] See *Confutation* II, 940/33-941/8; see also ibid., II, 937/13-938/14.

implication of such a view (whose implications he may not have fully realised) is that sovereignty within the church resides in the whole body and not in the hierarchy alone. It is because of this that conciliar decrees have authority for in virtue of a general principle of representation, the authority pertaining to the whole body is brought to bear on any given issue.

As in parliament unanimity is not a requirement for conciliar decisions to be binding. Within the council, the 'spyryt of god inclyneth euery good man to declare hys mynde, and inclyneth the congregacion to consente and agree vppon that that shall be the beste, eyther precysely the beste, or the beste at the leste wyse for the season...But when the counsayle and the congregacion agreeth and consenteth vppon a poynt/yf a few wylfull folke, farre the lest both in nomber, wyt, lernynge, and honest lyuynge, wolde reclayme and say that them selfe wolde not agre, yet were theyr frowardnes no let vnto the determynacyon or to the makyng of the law/but that it must stand tyll yt be by a nother lyke authoryte chaunged.'[140] This was of course a rebuttal of the Lutheran view that *maior pars* is not necessarily *sanior pars,* that strength does not rest in mere numbers, that the truth of God might be preserved within the church and even within the council by one individual.[141]

More did not agree with this principle. According to his doctrine of consensus, the role of the Spirit is to bring about agreement among the members of the church, to make of them a harmonious household. The quality of individual prophecy must be measured against the opinion of the whole body. The agreement of the church in general or assembled in council is a surer sign of the action of the Spirit than any individual charism can be. Hence the dissidence of a small number may be ignored, not merely on the grounds of common parliamentary procedure, but because of a deeper under-pinning in the theology of consensus for such a course of action.

The council, for More, speaks as representative of the whole church, not merely the hierarchy. Its authority derives from the divine command to speak the truth issued not only to the apostles but to all who would follow in their footsteps. The strength of any particular decree is not immediately proportioned to the scriptural evidence that may be advanced in its support but rather to the over-riding authority of God residing in his church, capable of speaking through its conciliar representation as

---

[140] See *Confutation* II, 922/33-923/11.
[141] See *WA* I, 568 ff; *WA* I, 279; *WA* 2; 404; *WA* 40, 334/30.

through the letter of holy writ. This does not place the council above the scriptures as its basic charter is recorded in scripture but relates it more directly to the revealing God who animates the church as well as the written word of scripture. It would be premature to class More with a populist or democratic theory of council and church as he did not examine these alternatives in comprehensive fashion. Nonetheless from what we have seen it can certainly be said that his sympathies leaned in that direction and that such an interpretation of council was consistent with his view of the church.

Common faith cannot be in error

The consensus of the Christian community whether expressed in its common faith, ordinary teaching, or in council has been guaranteed divine protection against failure, especially in its fidelity to original revelation: '...we be sure that the comen fayth of the catholyke chyrch is trewe/ and that the catholyke knowen chyrche can not erre in that fayth, whych from hande to hande hath ben taken & kepte from Crystes dayes and hys apostles hytherto? Whyche fayth muste nedes be trewe by Crystes promyse made vnto hys apostles, as teachers of hys chyrche, (Mt 16, 17-19; 28, 20) and not for them selfe but for hys chyrche/that is to wytte the fayth that saynte Peter professed shulde not fayle, and that god wolde be wyth them all dayes vnto the ende of the worlde. And that the fayth of the knowen catholyke chyrche...is the same fayth whyche the holy doctours of Cryste chyrche in euery age haue beleued and taught...'[142] This divine concurrence extends to the exegesis of scripture, such '...that yt can not be dampnably deceyued in the vnderstandynge of his holy scrypture wryten.'[143] The Spirit of God ever rules the church 'in the necessary poyntes of fayth, and euer shall vnto the worldes ende.'

---

[142] See *Confutation* I, 389/30-390/8; ibid., I, 223/28-31: '...and I proued also that the chyrch of Cryste can not fall in dampnable errour, but hath ben, is, & euer shall be, taught by the spyryte of god euery necessary trouth to the bylefe wherof god wyll haue them bounden/...'

[143] See *Confutation* I, 133/34-35: '...though the chyrch be not aboue the scripture and holy wryt: yet yt is so taught by the spyryte of god and his holy secrete inwarde worde vnwrytten, that yt can not be dampnably deceyued in the vnderstandynge of his holy scrypture wryten. And theruppon yet farther foloweth, that all such as so conster the scrypture that they wolde make the scripture seme to be contrarye to the fayth of Cristes chyrch: do damnably conster yt contrary to the teachynge of god and his holy spiryte.' See also ibid. I, 62/1-14; ibid. I, 377/5-9.

Infallible in moral teaching

Inerrancy extends to other matters including its moral teaching: '…all
be it our lord doeth suffer his chyrche to erre in the knowledge of a facte or
dede done among men: yet wyll he neuer suffer yt to erre and be deceyued
in the knowlege of hys lawe, to whych he wyll haue it bounden, and in the
tyme in whyche he wyll haue it bounden therto. And therfore wyll he
neuer suffer hys chyrche to take, repute & iudge a thynge for synfull and
damnable, that is of trouthe good & pleasynge to god.'[144] God's assistance
is forthcoming even in the determination of sanctity, for God '…shall not
suffre it as that holy doctour saynt Thomas sayth, to erre and be deceyued,
in takynge for a saynt any dampned person, & ther by geue to goddes
enemye the honour dew to hys frende.'[145] This unfailing teaching may
emanate from the common faith of the church or from a general council.[146]
Its certainty is due to the indwelling Spirit of God guiding the church into
all truth.[147] Because of this the church is the pillar and ground of truth,
'vppon whose doctryne euery man may reste and stande sure.'[148]

Which church?

To make such radical claims for any given body immediately raises the
question as to which congregation possesses this transcendental power?

---

[144] See *Confutation* I, 133/12-20. See ibid. II, 689/37-690/2: God '…wyll haue the
catholyke chyrch to be to suche as wyll lerne, the pyller and sure stablyshement of trouth, as
well in doctryne of fayth as of maners.'

[145] See *Confutation* II, 711/13-25. Note, however, More's caution in regard to the popular
beliefs regarding the saints: 'The legendes of sayntes lyues were wryten in dyuers tymes, as
the sayntes in dyuerse tymes lyued, and in dyuers dyed/of whose lyues the chyrch none other
knoweth, but as they fynde wryten or herde by good folke that knew them/…'

[146] See *Confutation* II, 923/22-28 and passim: 'But in artycles of fayth, as necessary artycles
to be byleued/frere Barons shall neuer fynde whyle he lyueth, that any one generall counsayle orderly called to gether, impugned and reproued a nother/that grace our lord be
thanked hath he geuen his knowen catholyque chyrche euer hytherto…' See ibid. II,
941/28-32: 'Now shall I ferther saye, that what so euer all chrysten people wolde determyne
yf they came to one assembly togyther/loke what strength it sholde haue yf they so dyd, the
same strength hath it yf they be all of ye same mynde, though they make no decre therof, nor
come not togyther therfore.'

[147] See *Confutation* I, 377/5-9: 'If the spyryte of god gouernynge the chyrche, and ledynge
it in to all trouth, put vs not in surety and certaynte of the trouth: how coud he be to vs as he
is named *paracletus*, that is a comforter, yf we were lefte so comfortelesse that we were vncer-
tayne whyther the hole chyrche were in damnable errour in stede of the ryght fayth.' See
Confutation II, 720/18-20: 'For it is inough to me that the chyrch of Crist hath that gyfte of
god by his great promyses, that it shall euer be by him & his spyrit led into euery necessary
treuth…'

[148] See *Confutation* II, 617/17-19: '…the chyrch is as saint Paule saith, the pylar & the fote
or grounde/that is to say the sure strengthe or fastenynge of the trouthe.'

'And now if Tyndale aske with which chyrche? I saye wyth hys catholyque chyrche/wyth hys chirche in whyche onely chirche he wurketh miracles wyth his chirche, whyche he commaundeth men to here and obay/and fynally wyth the same chirche, by whyche chirche Tyndale lerned to know whych is the scripture.'[149] This church is the congregation of 'all cristen people, all the crysten nacyons/all the whole corps and body of the catholyque chyrche, that agaynste paynyms, Iewes, heretyques, and scysmatykes, agree in the professyon of the comen crysten fayth, both in the poyntes of bylyef/and in the rules of lyuynge/though theyr lyuyng haue in dede many spottes, and many blottes, and many wrythen wryncles...'[150] This church is not the body of the elect, a coterie of chosen souls, but a definite company of saints and sinners with its own order, discipline, and authority, as well as the promise of the unfailing presence and guidance of its lord and master.

V. THE SIGNS OF THE CHURCH

The question of the signs of the church was not a matter to which Tyndale applied himself with any degree of depth. For him the central issues were Christ and his revelation in scripture. Christ is known directly through his scripture. Scripture is known not through the testimony of a community but immediately by an inner instinct: 'Who taught the eagles to spy out their prey? Even so the children of God spy out their Father, and Christ's elect spy out their Lord...'[151] Hence there is no need to know the church prior to this central act of justifying faith. Following on this commitment Tyndale did not seem to have envisaged any need for further testimony. His underlying assumption was that anyone who had submitted himself to the mercy of God in Christ and accepted the scriptures as his rule of faith was assuredly a member of the church. In any event he does not seem to have considered the identification of the true church a matter of major significance. Once one had scripture one was secure.

One qualification must be made in this respect. Tyndale recognised the power of miracle in authenticating the divine origin of a preacher and his

---

[149] See *Confutation* I, 381/35-382/1.

[150] See *Confutation* II, 914/10-15. See also ibid. II, 846/33-847/26, where More insists on the perceptibility of the church on which men may lean 'as vnto a sure pyller...' This is the known Catholic Church according to the definition he elected as the primary meaning of the word 'church': 'a multitude gathered to gether in one...but of such onely people as be crysten people, and them not in one cytye onely but that hole nomber of euery cytye, towne, and village thorow out all the hole world.' See *Confutation* I, 147/3-6. See also ibid. I, 119/17-36; II, 855/20-856/33 for similar descriptions.

[151] Tyndale, *Answer*, 45-49.

mission. He acknowledged this in the case of preachers and prophets of the old testament as well as in the ministry of Jesus and his apostles. The purpose of miracles, he maintained, was to draw attention and credence to the one who preached.[152] Hence, in support of any doctrine he looked to the testimony either of miracles or authentic scripture: '...wherwith should the true preacher confound the false, except he brought true miracles to confound the false, or else authentic scripture of full authority all ready among the people.'[153] However, even in this respect Tyndale's ultimate confidence was in scripture, '...in so much that Christ and his apostles might not have been believed without scripture for all their miracles.'[154] The miracles More claims for his church are false miracles, the work of Antichrist. These wonders are overcome by scripture for '...when the scripture is fully received, there is no need of miracles.'[155]

Barnes, sharing Luther's and Tyndale's views of the essentially hidden character of Christ's church, seems to have been somewhat more aware of the need for a minimal physical evidence of the presence of a congregation of true believers. He offered two principal signs of the presence of this church: 'So lykewysse/where the word of god is trewly and perfytly preached with out the damnable dreames of men/and where yt is welle of ye herars reseued/and also where we se good workes that doo openly agre wyth the doctrine off the gospell these be good and suer tokens where by that we may iudge/that there be some men of holy church.'[156] Following Luther he proposed the true preaching of the word of God as one, and godly living in accordance with the gospel as a second sign of the presence of the true church of Christ.

The church can be known

The apologetic argument which More evolved in his *Confutation of Tyndale* was based on the premise that the church of Christ is a known and therefore knowable church. This adjective recurs repeatedly in his description of Christ's church: 'the catholyke knowen chyrche of all crysten nacyons'; 'thys comon knowen chyrche, that hath from Crystes dayes

---

[152] Tyndale, *Answer*, 130-132; idem, *Obedience*, 286-290.

[153] See Tyndale, *Answer*, 26.

[154] Ibid., 27.

[155] Tyndale, *Answer*, 132.

[156] Robert Barnes, *Supplication*, in *Confutation* II, 1048/33-38. See James P. Lusardi, *The Career of Robert Barnes, Confutation* III, 1365-1470 for a thorough study of Barnes's life and views.

hytherto contynued';[157] thys vnyversall knowen people of all crysten nacyons'; 'the comon knowen chyrche of all crysten people, not gone out nor caste oute'[158] and so on.

This was a vital point to establish, '...yt this chyrch is knowen well inough/& therfore maye be well vsed as a sure iudge, for to decerne bytwene ye trew doctrine & the false, and the trew precher and false, concernyng the ryght fayth and the decernyng of the trew word of god wryten or vnwryten, from ye counterfete word of man...'[159] This was the source of all his argumentation: that we have in the church's faith and teaching a sound criterion by which we may judge the authenticity of any practice or belief. In order that she be such a criterion the church must of necessity be known.

He supported this argument from scripture, citing St Paul's epistles as well as Mt 5, 14 to show that the church as a city built on a mountain cannot be hid.[160] On the the other hand, he did not accept Barnes's suggestion that the preaching of the gospel is an infallible sign of the presence of the church as it may well be that a man preach the gospel and it be not accepted.[161] Clear evidence is available to indicate the true known church of Christ.

Augustine's influence

In his apologetic for the church More depended to a large extent on Augustine. He developed some arguments at length according to his own inspiration. Others he allowed to stand on Augustine's authority alone. Thus for example he cited Augustine's work against the epistle of Manichaeus in which the former recited the reasons for his own conversion: '...that is to wytte the consent of the catholyke chrysten nacyons/and that he had the catholyke chyrche in authoryte, fyrst for the myracles that

---

[157] See *Confutation* I, 119/19-29.

[158] See *Confutation* I, 224/4; 398/26-28; II, 576/26-28.

[159] See *Confutation* II, 399/23-27. See also ibid. II, 891/20-34.

[160] See *Confutation* II, 915/8-16; ibid. II, 855/26-30: '...those chyrches to whome saynt Poule wrote were very trew partes, and of the nature and maner of the whole chyrche. For as those partyculare chyrches were knowen chyrches: euen so is the whole chyrche a knowen chyrche.'

[161] See *Confutation* II, 882/17-27: 'And that it shold not in euery place take hold/appereth by the wordes of our sauyour, where he sayth to hys dyscyples whom he sent to preche, In to what house so euer ye entre, fyrste saye ye peace be to thys house. And then yf the sonne of peace be there/your peace shall reste vppon hym, or ellys your peace shall retourne agayne vnto your selfe. (Lk 10, 5-6) In whyche oure sauyour sheweth vs, that yf a good man preche well, though there were not one in all hys audyence that wold be ye better for it/yet shold it not be voyde/...but not of necessyte take holde in euery audyence...'

were shewed therin/and that therupon his fayth and credence geuen
therunto, was nurysshed and fostered wyth hope encreaced wyth cheryte,
and confermed with antiquite. There helde hym he sayd in the gyuynge of
fayth and credence to the catholyke chyrche thys thynge also, that is to wyt
that he sawe the successyon contynued in the see of saynt Peter, to whom
our lorde had after his resurreccyon commytted the fedynge of his shepe
sayth saynt Austayne, from saynt Peters dayes vnto hys owne tyme. And
fynally euyn the very name he sayth of catholyke, that is to say vniuersall,
gaue toward the gettyng of his credence the catholyke chyrche great
authoryte/whych name of vniuersall the same chyrche alone amonge so
many heresyes hadde so obtayned...'[162]

More went on to refer to the proofs which Augustine gave from scripture
that the Catholic Church is Christ's church. Once one receives the scriptures from the church, and one believes their message, then their message
in turn confirms one's belief in the church. Augustine had argued this in
the account of his conversion in the *Confessions*[163] and in his epistle against
the Donatists.[164] The African doctor, moreover, claimed in other works
that the Catholic Church is the only Christian community universally
known throughout the world.[165] In short, on the basis of his reading in
Augustine More had mustered up a body of evidence in favour of identifying the known Catholic Church with the church of Christ. This was based
on scripture, miracles, continuity in faith, the petrine succession, and
universality. More himself did not develop all of these arguments at equal
length. His principal line of reasoning in the *Confutation* rested on the principle of continuity in faith among the contemporary, patristic, and
apostolic churches and the testimony of miracle. He merely touched on
other elements.

Continuity

In his discussion of the church's continuity through history, More
started with the Jewish synagogue. He saw an essential, organic link between the history of Israel and the evolution of the people called together
by Christ: 'For I thynke that no man wyll desyre to haue it proued that the
chyrche or Synagoge of the Iewys was not ordayned to laste for euer/but to

---

[162] See *Confutation* II, 735/16-29.
[163] Augustine, *The Confessions*, Books 7-9, *MPL* 32, 733-780.
[164] Augustine, *Epistolae*, 105, *MPL* 33, 403-404.
[165] See Augustine, *Against Parmenian*, Book III, *MPL* 43, 104; idem, *Epistle to Vincentius*, *Epistolae*, 93, *MPL* 33, 333.

ceace and gyue place vnto Chryste at hys commynge/and that he sholde
then in stede of the synagoge of the Iewys, begynne and contynue hys
chyrche bothe of Iewys and Gentyls/and that then sholde be of the Iewys
peculyar chyrche & peculyar lawes and sacramentes and ceremonyes an
ende/and that the chyrche of Chryst as longe as the world sholde laste,
sholde neuer haue ende. Nor no man wyll I suppose desyre to haue it
proued, that the chyrche of Chryste can be but one.'[166]

The church takes over the revelation of the old testament, making it her
own and incorporating it with that of the new alliance, being duly
enlightened in the understanding of both.[167] On the other hand one cannot
ignore the breach which exists between church and synagogue for '...there
is yet in maner as great dyfference, as is bytwene the fygure and the
thynge, the shadow and the body/...' Of these differences, one of the
greatest is the pledge made by Christ to send the Holy Spirit to his
followers 'to lede it into al trouth, (Jn 16, 13) and that it sholde dwell
therin for euer, and hym selfe be permanent also therin for euer.' (Mt 28,
20)[168]

Within the strictly Christian tradition More argued that the church had
maintained unspoiled the faith of ancient times: 'For the knowen catholyque chyrch haue styll the byliefe of the same necessary artycles, that the
olde holy sayntes of euery age agreed and consented in, agaynste the sectes
of these heretykes.'[169] Indeed this continuity in faith goes back beyond the
patristic era to the very origins of Christianity, 'in that that from the
begynnynge it hath euer styll bene by ordynary course of successyon kepte
and contynued one/and the olde fayth from the begynnynge (as by the
bokes of holy sayntes of euery age well appereth) all waye contynued

---

[166] See *Confutation* II, 606/19-28. See also ibid. II, 607/16-19: 'Fynally Chryste went wyth
hys apostles out of the old chyrche to begynne a newe, that was prophecyed to be a
perpetuall chyrche wythout ende, agaynste whych the gates of hell sholde neuer preuayle.'
Ibid. II, 682/6-11: 'But our sauyour Cryste hath begonne and contynued his chyrche, this
knowen catholyque chyrche gathered of Iewes & gentyles both to gyther. And he toke not the
olde scryptures of you, nor of you neyther lerned to know them, nor of you to vnderstande
theym/but he made theym all, and by the writers therof hym self endyghted them.'

[167] See *Confutation* II, 682/14-17: 'And then he taught and euer teacheth and euer shall
teache, hys catholyque chyrche to knowe as well those holye wrytynges as those other holy
thynges vnwryten, wyth all necessary vnderstandynge of those holy wrytyngs to.'

[168] See *Confutation* II, 719/35-720/10. See also ibid II, 753/4-17 where More contrasts the
old law of Moses 'wryten in bokes eyther of stone or in dede skynnes' with the new, where,
'dede stony hartes sholde waxe tender, softe, & quycke, and wyth wyllyng and applyable
myndes, shold by the spyryte of god haue the lawe, that is the trewe bylyefe, good hope and
well wurkynge cheryte, gracyously wryten in them.'

[169] See *Confutation* II, 650/11-14. See also ibid. I, 136/10-137/5, where a similar assertion
is made with special reference to the sacraments.

therin/and the olde ryghte maner of interpretacyon of the scrypture, concernynge the fayth (as by the same sayntes holy bokes appereth) all waye
contynued therin/...and that it was promysed that it sholde euer contynue
tyll the worldes ende...'[170] This continuity in faith is witnessed to by a long
line of saints stretching from 'saynt Ignatius, saynt Polycarpus, saynt
Deonise, saint Ciprian,' to 'saynt Bernard, saynt Thomas, saynt
Bonauenture, saynt Anselme, and many an holy man mo of euery age
synnys the apostles dayes/which were all lefte by god for seed in the
knowen catholyke chyrch/whyche knowen catholyke chyrch they euer
knowleged for the very chyrch of Cryste...'[171]

This argument from identity in faith among the generations, More felt,
had been sufficiently established in his treatment of the sacraments,
mariology, as well as other beliefs and practices. It was also grounded in
scripture in one of his favourite themes, the guaranteed indefectibility and
inerrancy of the church.

Indefectibility

The Christian community, More believed, is indestructible, ever-
lasting: 'For I say playnly that ye chyrch muste nedes be. For all the
deuylles in hell, nor all theyr instrumentes vpon erth, shall neuer be able to
destroy yt, but pull they neuer so many from yt, & leue they the remanaunt
neuer so few: yet shall the remanaunt alway be the chyrch, and a well
knowen chyrche, so byelded vppon that hygh mountayne, that is to wyt
vppon Cryst, that yt shall alway be syghtely & can not be hydde.'[172]
However it is principally with its permanence in faith that he was concerned. He affirmed this repeatedly basing himself on the promise of the
Spirit in Jn 16, 13 who is to lead men into all truth;[173] the promise of his
abiding presence in Mt 28, 20;[174] the pledge that the church is to be the

---

[170] See *Confutation* II, 669/36-670/23. 'Fynally good chrysten reders vppon these thynges it
foloweth, that we proue well and suffycyently, that there is not an olde chyrche of Cryste and
hys apostles, & an other newe chyrche now/but one whole chyrche from that tyme to thys
tyme in one trewe fayth contynued...' in ibid. II, 659/36-660/4.

[171] See *Confutation* II, 727/18-27; ibid. II, 739/1-8.

[172] See *Confutation* II, 915/1-8; see also ibid. II, 942/14-16: '...and as it styll contynueth
and alwaye contynue shall in the olde approued trouth, so is it alwaye styll, and alway styll
shall be the very trewe chyrche of Cryste/...' See also ibid. II, 606/19-607/28 where similar
assertions are made.

[173] See *Confutation* I, 45, 107, 130, 133, 151, 155 etc.

[174] See *Confutation* I, 107, 133, 155, 259, 286, 345 etc. where it is said that Christ promised
'...that he wold be wyth hys chyrch of crysten people all dayes vnto the ende of the worlde...'

pillar and ground of truth to all generations (I Tim 3, 15);[175] the promise
that the gates of hell shall not prevail against it (Mt 16, 18); and Christ's
prayer that Peter's faith should not fail (Lk 22, 32).[176] The community to
which these promises have been made can be none other than '...that
knowen catholique chyrche/of whiche from age to age the scripture hath
ben receiued, and the people taught...'[177] Within this basic continuity
there may be found variations in practice but these in no way affect the
substance of ongoing tradition, being no more than variations on a
theme.[178] Thus in matters of belief, in the event of a general council proposing certain things 'as necessary artycles to be byleued', it will never be
found 'that any one generall consayle orderly called to gether, impugned
and reproued a nother/...'[179] Continuity in this respect is absolute. Even
though other matters may be added to the content of belief, mutual contradiction is excluded. The faith of the body of believers does not repudiate
that of a previous generation. Rather it constitutes an essential link with
the founder members of the Christian fellowship as well as providing a
pledge of future glory.

Apostolic Succession

In short, Sir Thomas More thought of apostolic succession more
in credal terms than of hands imposed upon a series of spiritual leaders.
In one passage, however, he did appeal to apostolic succession in
ecclesiastical leadership in this latter sense. This instance, however, was
intended to vindicate the visibility of the Christian body rather than the
identity of the contemporary known church with that of the apostolic age
although this latter idea was implied: '...passing ouer al the tyme from
Adam to Christ, Christ was himselfe a knowen head vpon his church of his
twelue apostles, and vppon all his disciples that he tooke into him both the
good and ye bad, and than he appointed sainte Peter for his successour,

[175] See *Confutation* II, 617/16-19: '...it shal euer be trew to say that the chyrch is as saint
Paule saith, the pylar & the fote or grounde/that is to say the sure strengthe or fastenynge of
the trouthe.' See also ibid. I, 383, 397; II, 645-646; 668 etc.
[176] See *Confutation* II, 693/22-24.
[177] See *Confutation* II, 617/19-21.
[178] See *Confutation* II, 922/32-923/5: 'And in a counsayle of crysten men the spyryt of god
inclyneth euery good man to declare hys mynde, and inclyneth the congregacion to consente
and agree vppon that that shall be the beste, eyther precysely the beste, or the beste at the
leste wyse for the season: whyche when so euer yt shall be better at any other tyme to
chaunge, the same spyryte of god inclyneth his chyrche eyther at a new counsayle, or by as
full and whole consent as any counsayle can haue, to abrogate the fyrste &turne yt into the
better.'
[179] See ibid. II, 923/22-26.

and head and chiefe shepherde to feede and gouerne hys whole flocke after his death, and so foorthe the successors of him euer after...' If it were denied that Peter was the known head of the church by Christ's appointment, '...we shal not neede to dispute thys poynt with them for thus farre forth as yet. For if Christ dyd not appoint saynt Peter for the chiefe shepherd ouer al his flocke, yet can they not say nay, but that yet at the least he appointed saint Peter with other, and that they were all knowen heades. And they dyd also substytute other whyche were knowen heades also. And euer after by succession knowen heades to succede, of suche as bi the blessed sacrament of holye orders were by special consecracion, as by a certain spirituall generacion borne enherytable to those roumes.'[180] In other words if the succession to the Roman see could not establish More's point at least the succession in the presbyteral-episcopal line could. Implicit in the argument of course is the assertion that only the 'common known church' can lay claim to apostolic succession in terms of its sacramentally ordained human leadership and through it to a visibly ordered succession in apostolic authority.

The Sign of Miracle

Philosophically speaking More had no difficulty in accepting the possibility of miraculous intervention by God in the existing world order. He did not evolve a theory of miracle but assumed its possibility. He accepted biblical evidence for the occurrence of such prodigies in old and new testament times as well as conventional human testimony for their continued appearance in the course of church history. He even used the analogy of miraculous intervention to explain the causality of the sacraments. Just as prophets, saints, and the Lord himself used material things such as water (4 Kg 5, 9-14; Jn 5, 4), the touch of a garment (Lk 8, 43-48) clay and spittle (Jn 9, 6-7) to bring bodily healing, so God can use corporeal things to bring spiritual healing.[181]

More attempted to establish the authority of his church by appeal to miraculous occurrences. Divine intervention authenticates the preaching of the word of God. God's institution of the church of Israel as well as the mission of its prophets was attested by miracle.[182] The phenomenon continued among the followers of Christ to vindicate its founder as well as the

---

[180] See *Confutation* II, 1010/15-1011/11. (This text is not in the first edition of the *Confutation*.)

[181] See *Confutation* I, 103/28-105/17.

[182] See *Confutation* II, 620/1-10.

company he left after him.[183] Those who accept scripture on the authority of the church do so because they put their trust not in men but in God '...that by hys inwarde spyryte and outwarde myracles, enclyneth vs to byleue hys chyrche therin/and yet by the same scrypture also confermeth the same bylyefe by hys great promyses therin conteyned...'[184] This power of miracle points to the presence of the Spirit in the church[185] as well as confirming the gospel which the Spirit writes in men's hearts.[186]

Each individual preacher is not necessarily endowed with the gift of miracles. The wonders which some work give evidence of divine approval to all who spread the same message. They '...shewe and make profe that hys catholyke chyrche is hys perpetuall apostle...'[187] In like manner in the case of those ranked as 'holy doctors' God 'hath with moo than a thousande myracles declared (them) to be his messangers.'[188] Using the lesson he had learnt from his master Augustine, More employed the argument from miracle to vindicate the divine mission of Christ's disciples as well as the supernatural origin of their message and its bearers throughout the history of the church.

More's use of the argument from the miraculous ties in closely with his concept of faith. Prior to one's actual commitment in faith to God in Christ or in his church there is a process of reasoning which must be gone through in order to establish the credibility of those who claim to purvey a

---

[183] See *Confutation* I, 252/40-253/5: 'And we se that in the catholyke chyrche god hath done and dayly doeth for hys sayntes, bothe whyle they were here and after theyr departynge hense/and hath also done and dayly doeth at dyuerse ymages and pylgrymages, as greate myracles in confyrmacyon of our fayth in that behalfe, as euer he dyd in the tyme of the apostles.' See also ibid. I, 275/7-276/33; ibid. I, 347/7-24.

[184] See *Confutation* II, 764/2-5. See also ibid. I, 347/7-21, where More points out that not every point of doctrine nor every authoritative statement needs confirmation from miracles.

[185] See *Confutation* II, 760/36-761/7: 'For well he woteth that Cryste promysed and sent the same spyryte to hys chyrche, to teche it & lede it into all trewth, and hym selfe also to dwell therin for euer. (Jn 16, 13; Mt 28, 20) And that the knowen catholyke chyrche is it that onely hath the same spyryte, appereth clerely by thys that onely the knowen catholike chyrch hath in it declared and contynued the power. For none other chyrche of Chryste is there in whyche the myracles contynue.'

[186] See *Confutation* I, 270/29-36: 'And by this fayth in the worde of god vnwryten in theyr bokes/and yet wryten in theyre soules: dyd there many martyrs stand and shede theyr blood in wytnesse of the trouth therof, that neuer red nor herde the scrypture in theyr dayes/and wold in the same word vnwryten, wyth goddes grace haue wythstanden false myracles to, whych had yet bene vndoutedly the sorest pynche, sauying for the mo and more meruelouse myracles that them selfe saw or byleued done on the tother syde for the trouth.' For the connection between miracle and prophetic gift see ibid. I, 339/25-32: '...and therby approueth the fayth and workes that they lyued and dyed in...'

[187] *Confutation* I, 252/2-253/11; ibid., 247/28-35 and passim.

[188] See *Confutation* II, 623/3-24.

divine message. Miracles are an incontrovertible testimony of divine
favour. With their assistance true messengers can be distinguished from
false, and final assent given to divine truth.[189] More attached a good deal
of importance to the *prolegomena* of faith. Tyndale, on the other hand,
dismissed this antecedent relative certitude as historical faith which he opposed to 'feeling' or justifying faith. This latter type of faith in his view
was engendered by a gift of God which takes the form of connatural
knowledge or spiritual intuition. By means of this Christ and his word are
recognised and accepted unreservedly. Hence the secondary importance
for Tyndale of a rationally constituted threshold to faith. More agreed that
the central act of faith arose from divine gift. He also insisted on the need
to establish the prior credibility of its object at a rational level. Hence the
significance for him of miraculous and other signs of the church's divine
origin and mission.

If Tyndale looked on scripture as self authenticating, Friar Barnes offered 'tokens' which if they did not prove any individual to be a member of
the church, at least indicated the presence of a congregation of true
believers. The tokens named were the true preaching of the word of God
and the performance of good works in accordance with the gospel. With
shrewd common-sense, More picked the obvious hole in the first argument. He posed the case of two illiterate women, the wife of a London
merchant, (had he his own Dame Alice in mind?) and the good wife of
Botolph's wharf. Neither could read, consequently they were in no position
to know whether any given sermon was in accordance with scripture or
not. Nor for that matter could they judge with any assurance the
evangelical quality of anyone's behaviour.[190] More did not delay long in
dismissing the second of the signs proposed by Barnes—good works. He
pointed out that Barnes himself saw the weakness of this position
'...bycause they (good works) may be fayned by hypocryse.'[191] Hence the
essential inadequacy of the tokens Barnes proposed as signs of the true
church.

---

[189] See *Confutation* I, 476/24-477/20 and passim.
[190] See in particular *Confutation* II, 893/29-895/4 and in general ibid., 873-908. 'And thus
are we now good reders wyth these onely women vsynge no reason but suche as a woman
myght fynd, ...comen to a poynte of frere Barnes vnperfayt tokens, by whych we may so
knowe his chyrche, as we be neuer the nerer for the knowledge of yt...' in *Confutation* II,
905/19-27.
[191] See *Confutation* II, 880/10-13; 893/36-894/3; cf. Barnes, *Supplication* in *Confutation* II,
1049/9-20.

Universality

Other aspects of Augustine's apologetic were not developed at length by More. We have already seen earlier, as in other works of his, the importance he attached to the role of the church in authenticating scripture. There is hardly need to discuss this again. Augustine had also inferred from the universality of the traditional church its identity with that of Christ. More did not stress this reasoning. Finding it used against him by Friar Barnes he quietly agreed that the church of Christ is universal and that anything Barnes had to say about the universality of the Christian communion applied equally well to the common known church.[192] Similarly he did not feel himself bound to go to great lengths to establish the uniqueness of the congregation called together by Christ. He took for granted that Christ left only one church. There is only one true vine, and 'this one comen well knowen catholyke chyrche of all crysten nacyons, as I byfore haue specyfyed, left to gether in the stocke of vnite of the knowen catholyque fayth, dystyncte and dyuyded from all the manyfolde wythered braunches of so many soundry scysmys and sectes, as from the begynnyng vnto these wreched dayes haue wyth obstynate malyce wylfully fallen therfro.'[193]

Holy and Sinful

Realist that he was, More did not fail to face the fact of evil in the church about him. How could he when Wolsey had been his master? In his younger days he had castigated the church for her imperfections. In maturity he faced the reality of evil in the lives of many Christians as well as their leaders, recognizing that this was part of the Christian's condition in his pilgrim state: 'And that company yt shalbe gloryouse, shall yet not be gloryouse here in this world/but shall be here in this world gracyouse, that they may in a nother worlde be gloryouse. And yet not at euery tyme gracyouse in this world neyther/but some tyme fall frowardely or neglygently from grace, and so stande longe in suche vngracyouse state/...[194] A man may well indeed pass all his days in sin and still remain a

---

[192] See *Confutation* II, 858/15-26.

[193] See *Confutation* II, 992/7-13; see also ibid. II, 670/24-28: 'These thynges I saye beyng thus, that the very chirch can be but one, and muste endure as longe as the worlde lasteth, and can in this worlde haue no new chyrche to succede yt as the synagoge hadde/and then that all these chyrches of these sectis be rysen and gone oute of the catholyke chyrch, and yt contynueth styll...'

[194] See *Confutation* II, 957/16-20; ibid. II, 964/8-31 where More quotes Augustine to the same effect: *MPL* 38, 980; *MPL* 42, 47-50. See also ibid. II, 865/16-36, where he cites the example of the people of Israel, not all of whom reached the promised land.

member of Christ's body the church. He may adhere to the body as the
dead branch remains on a tree. But as long as he retains faith he is to that
extent subject to the influence of the Spirit and retains the possibility of
repentance.[195]

Nor did the presence of abuses within the ecclesiastical institution in-
hibit More from recognising the essential holiness of God's people. '...for
that cause is yt called holy chyrche/not for that euery man is holy that is in
yt, but for that many suche be in yt, and none can be holy that wyll not be
in yt.'[196] Later he explained why the church may be called holy, '...for
that it hath holy professyon, wherby it is dedycated vnto Chryst. The
secunde, that there is in thys world none holy that goth to any other
chyrche out of it, or that wyll not be of it. The thyrde cause is, for that the
holynesse that is in it be there neuer so few holy therin, is farre fayrer and
holyer, and more plesaunt in the syght of god, than the fowlenesse and
vnholynesse of all that are fowle & vnholy therin/specyally for the bewtye
and holynesse of the very cheyfe & pryncypall hed therof our sauyour Cryst
hym self.'[197]

More's view is mainly optimistic, for while recognising the presence of
evil within the community of faith he trusted in the surpassing goodness of
the body's head, Christ himself and in the profession of faith by the church
itself. He assumed in consequence that the good to be found among its
members must outweigh the bad. His ultimate cause for hope lay in his
assurance that the words of Paul would finally be realised and that Christ
one day would '...brynge forthe and make perfyte his gloryouse chyrche,
and present yt to his father bryghte and smothe, wythoute any spot or
wryncle to lyue and endure in heuen/...'[198]

Thomas More, therefore, in contrast with Tyndale emphasised the need
for visible signs to authenticate the mission of Christ's church, its
preachers, and their message. Scripture for More was not self-
authenticating; nor indeed was revelation. He accepted divine revelation
through whatever channel it reached him because of the testimony of
Christ's church. He accepted Christ's church as witness to revelation
because of divinely given indices of its origin. These are effective,
however, only in so far as the church of Christ is a known church, perceptible to sense as well as faith. In drawing up his list of indices More drew

[195] See *Confutation* II, 957/10-34.
[196] See *Confutation* II, 735/1-4, More based this view on Augustine, *Contra Cresconium,*
MPL 43, 476.
[197] See *Confutation* II, 907/37-908/7.
[198] See *Confutation* II, 855/14-16; ibid. II, 970/23-34; ibid. II, 865/16-36.

heavily on Augustine. Yet he himself stressed the importance of two elements: firstly the communion in faith of the living church as well as its continuity with that of preceding generations back to the apostles themselves; secondly, the gift of miracles. These qualities mark off the true church of Christ from any other body and prepare the neophyte for that commitment in faith to the Lord who comes and speaks through this community. Its evident sinfulness may obscure but in no way call in question its divine origin. Its failings were envisaged by Christ just as its future glory is promised with a word as unshakeable as God himself.

Conclusion

Thomas More's laborious refutation of Tyndale's *Answer* contains a rich and in many ways, for his time, original understanding of the nature and role of Christ's church. Having examined many definitions of the church, he preferred to see it as a visible body composed of laity and clergy alike. He emphasised repeatedly that every baptised Christian is a full member of this 'common corps of Christendom.' Although one may be excluded from the visible community for schismatic action or heretical conviction, radical membership once gained cannot be lost. The church in time, indeed, remains always crippled by sin. But one day it will appear 'without spot or wrinkle'.

Without resolving all the difficulties this view creates, More also recognised that implicit faith could make one a member of the church. Consistent with this, More insisted that the proper object of faith is not the church but God. God speaks through the church. It is God we believe, not his messengers. On the other hand by its activity the church prepares us for faith. Its nature and structure moreover form part of the divine teaching. But the primary object of faith is God alone.

Sir Thomas fully recognised the role of the clergy in transmitting divine revelation as well as acting as leaders of the Christian people in life and worship. He showed a marked reticence in the *Confutation* on the Roman primacy, a reticence he later explained to have been deliberately adopted on account of Henry VIII's marital problems. He showed a marked openness on the question of its divine institution, admitting the legitimacy of contrary opinion in the theological context of his day. Nonetheless he sketched out an embryonic argument from ecclesial consensus for the divine right of petrine office. At the same time he saw definite limits to the *plenitudo potestatis,* acknowledging with other contemporary theologians that the pope might personally err in faith or morals. In such cases he might be legitimately deposed.

More did not develop a full theory of the general council. In justifying
its existence and authority he appealed to the abiding presence of God with
all his people as well as to general theories of representation. Taken
together, this implied that sovereignty, spiritual as well as social, resides in
the people as a whole and not exclusively with the clergy. While avoiding
the tangled issues of pope and council, More hints here at quite a 'liberal'
concept of conciliar function, drawn in part at least from parliamentary
analogies, including the principle of majority rule and a clear recognition
of the principle of popular representation.

In the *Confutation* More reached a new clarity on the question of revelation. He saw it as a truth made known by God to man which he 'by his
onely naturall powers, should either not at all, or not so fullye wythout that
shewying haue attayned the perceuing therof.' In this he found himself in
agreement with Tyndale. Similarly he did not find great cause for dispute
as to how God reveals himself; through his Spirit in the inward heart of
man, the words of his prophets, interventions in history, and most
specifically in the life and teaching of Christ. More, however, also held for
an ongoing revelation in the post-apostolic church, not always clearly
distinguished from the influence of the Spirit in aiding the community
penetrate more deeply the revelations of old and new testament times.

Tyndale did not accept this position. For him revelation was closed with
the apostolic church. Its main substance is adequately recorded in the inspired word of scripture. The bible, for Tyndale, was the indispensable
source and unique means for the transmission of revelation to subsequent
generations.

Sir Thomas More, on the other hand, ascribed first place to this living
community in the transmission of revelation. He held to this because he
believed that God still speaks his message in the heart of each believer and
at the same time leads the community to a deeper knowledge of the
original revelation made under both old and new dispensations.

In this view, revelation is transmitted through the community in the
written word of scripture. In addition, however, the community's written
records reflect what the Spirit has been saying in the minds and hearts of
any particular generation. Both *Dialogue* and *Confutation* stressed the importance of socio-cultural tradition by means of which many of the sayings
and doings of Jesus are transmitted from hand to hand in the church from
apostolic times onwards. Inspired scripture is not an adequate record of
revelation. It needs to be completed by ecclesial tradition taken in this dual
way of pneumatic inspiration and community tradition.

The interpretation of the divine message is a further step. It takes place within the community and moves along three tracks: the infusion of new ideas by the Spirit; the acquisition of a new understanding of revelation under the guidance of the Spirit; and coupled with this, the articulation of revelation in conceptual form through the rational discourse of theological investigation. This forward movement leads to the development of doctrines such as the hypostatic union of Christ, the assumption of Mary, and indeed the nature of papal office. As a general rule, More did not look on the formulation of doctrine as new revelation, but rather as the appropriation in consciousness by the community of the significance of primitive revelation.

Hence though the word of God is prior in time to the Christian community, indeed calls it into being, the community once in existence is both means of transmission and authoritative interpreter of the word. This does not place it 'over' the revealing word of God. More recognised that God who reveals himself in various ways and calls the church into being, also ensures the transmission of this revelation through various channels in the believing community's life and action. He also provides for an authoritative and meaningful interpretation of this revelation within the community.

The whole church of God is called to take part in the transmission of revelation and in a certain sense in its interpretation. In disputed issues, however, More consistently returned to ecclesial consensus as the ultimate arbiter. This consensus may exist in the dual dimension of time and space where a continuing tradition exists within the community from apostolic times. On the other hand, it may exist only in the here and now, a consensus which has been arrived at, not from unity but from diversity as happened, for example, in the case of the doctrine of Mary's assumption into glory.

More recognised in the general council one means of identifying the existence of consensus in the church. General agreement at a council is a sure sign of the meaning of divine truth. Its authority is in no way weakened by the dissent of a small minority. More's grounds for this position were two-fold. Firstly Christ's promise to be with his church always. If the whole church were to err in faith, then the promise of divine assistance would have been emptied of meaning. The other was his conviction concerning the Spirit's role as a uniting force within the church, *qui facit unanimes in domo*. The fact that the church reaches agreement on any point is a sure sign of the guidance of the Spirit in fulfilling Christ's promise to lead the church into all truth.

If the true church of Christ plays such an important role in the transmission and interpretation of revelation, how can it be recognised from other communities making the same claim? By 1533 this was a real problem, in particular with the growth in visible influence of evangelical churches in Germany and Zwinglian communities in Switzerland. Tyndale had not given much thought to this. For him the scriptures are the key to divine revelation. These are recognised by the true believer not because of any external signs as such, but by a secret instinct of God. Tyndale's fellow protagonist Barnes felt the need for more visible evidence of divine authority. He proposed the practice of good works and the true preaching of the gospel as sure tokens of the presence of Christ's church.

More rejected these. The first, on Barnes's own admission was inadequate, due to the impossibility of real assessment of other people's behaviour. The second was inadequate, being of no value to those unable to read the scripture. Only the literate could know whether a preacher's doctrine was in accordance with scripture or not. This brought More back to his earlier contention that revelation is mediated through a living community, fully visible to the world, equally accessible to literate and illiterate alike. How can it be shown to be trustworthy? More assembled a body of apologetic argument drawn from Augustine: the testimony of scripture, miracles, continuity in faith, petrine succession, and its universality in space and time.

He did not dwell at equal length on each of these arguments preferring for his own purposes to underline the continuity in faith of the 'common knowen church' and the evidence of miraculous intervention to confirm its divine origin. God does not abandon his church. He is ever present, corroborating its claim to teach with divine authority. His Spirit draws all its adherents into one living communion of faith and love. An idealised picture perhaps but one to which Sir Thomas More himself gave full credence, a credence shortly to be put to the test.

CHAPTER SIX

THE TRIAL PROCEEDINGS

INTRODUCTION

This study so far has concerned itself with three major works of religious controversy belonging to the public arena. If however one wishes to get to the heart of More's thought on certain vital issues there is a further body of sources to be consulted: the largely informal literary production of the years intervening between his resignation as chancellor 16 May 1532 and his execution 6 July 1535. These sources consist in the main of a body of letters addressed to a variety of friends and enemies explaining his reasons for refusing the oath to the royal succession of the new queen Anne Boleyn. More's final address to the court which tried and condemned him for refusing to acknowledge royal supremacy over the church in England, was recorded for posterity albeit with some ambiguity by contemporary biographers. It concludes the series of sources on which this chapter is based.

Though some of this literature antedates the *Confutation*, I have elected to treat this material separately as it possesses a certain unity of its own in thought and expression. This is not a set of theological treatises but the literary self-revelation of a man under the dual stress of political pressure on the one hand and of life-long affection for his loved ones on the other. Such a procedure involves a slight departure from the chronological order followed hitherto. This loss of tempo may well be compensated by the filling of *lacunae* from an earlier stage of More's development as well as to some extent explaining their occurrence by describing the context in which they took place.[1]

On 16 May 1532 Sir Thomas More surrendered his seal of office as Lord Chancellor. The pretext he offered for his action according to his son-in-law Roper was increasing ill-health.[2] Ostensibly at least king and

---

[1] See *Sir Thomas More's Indictment* in Harpsfield, *Thomas Moore*, 269-76; G. de C. Parmiter, *Saint Thomas More and the Oath*, in *The Downside Review* 78 (1960) 1-13; idem, *The Indictment of Saint Thomas More*, ibid., 75 (1957) 149-166; J. Duncan M. Derrett, *The Trial of Sir Thomas More*, in *The English Historical Review* 79 (1964) 449-477; E. E. Reynolds, *The Trial of St. Thomas More*, London, 1964, 33-56.

[2] See Roper, *Lyfe of Sir Thomas Moore*, 51/7-12; '...for certaine infirmities of his bodye, he pretended himselfe vnable any longer to serve.' This assertion is confirmed to some extent by More's letter to Erasmus complaining that '...a disorder of I know not what nature has

minister parted on good terms. Henry thanked More for his years of dutiful service and pledged his support '...in anye sute which he should after haue vnto him, that either should concerne his honor...or that should appertaine vnto his profitt...'[3]

It was fortunate for More that he had a credible excuse for asking to be relieved of office since voluntary withdrawal from service could easily have been construed as opposition to royal policy. Nonetheless, in spite of the polite pleasantries exchanged, it is unlikely that either party had any illusion concerning the deeper motives underlying More's decision.

From the beginning of his brief term of office as Lord Chancellor, More had made it plain to the king probably as early as 1527 that he could not support his case for an annulment of his marriage to Catherine. This was not something decided upon without prolonged heart-searching. The conclusion he reached following a detailed examination of the issue was in favour of the validity of the original dispensation permitting Henry's marriage to his sister-in-law.[4] Henry treated this disagreement with apparent tolerance. It did not prevent him from appointing More to an elevated position of state nor did it stop him from pursuing his divorce with dogged persistence.[5] When normal channels ended at a brick wall, he turned in another direction. During this shift of course Henry was guided in all likelihood by the one who was to replace Wolsey as his principal political navigator, Thomas Cromwell.

Cromwell's solution to the king's difficulties was simple and direct. 'He offered to make a reality out of Henry's vague claims to supremacy by evicting the pope from England.'[6] The implementation of this policy meant a divorce for the king, acquisition of immense power and wealth, and on the way to these goals, a gradual invasion of ecclesiastical rights

---

attacked my chest...For when it had plagued me without abatement for some months the physicians whom I had consulted gave their opinion that the long continuance of it was dangerous' in More to Erasmus, 14 June 1532, *Erasmi epistolae* 10, 31/1-32/38, tr. E. F. Rogers, *St Thomas More: Selected Letters*, New Haven and London, 1967, 44.

[3] Roper. op. cit., 52/5-12.

[4] See More to Cromwell, Chelsea, 5 March (1534), Rogers, *Correspondence*, 493/48-497/199. More made it clear that the matter had already been raised before his appointment as chancellor, probably following his return from Calais in 1527. See Rogers, *Correspondence*, p. 493, n. 54. See also More to Dr. Nicholas Wilson, Tower of London, 1534, Rogers, *Correspondence*, 534/33-536/125.

[5] See G. R. Elton, *England under the Tudors*, London, 1963, 98-126.

[6] Elton, op. cit., 129. See also Elton, *King or Minister? The Man behind the Henrician Reformation*, in *History* NS 39 (1954) 216-232; *Studies in Tudor and Stuart Politics and Government*, Cambridge, I, 1974, 173-188. See also *The Political Creed of Thomas Cromwell*, *TRHS* 5th series 6 (1956) 69-92, repr. *Studies* II, 215-235.

and liberties reaching its turning point in the enactment of effective royal
supremacy over the ecclesiastical institution in England.

The precise moment at which Henry's mind was made up remains hidden in the mists of the past. Once the decisive option was made the
political machinery moved rapidly and swiftly under Cromwell's careful
pilotage. Henry's marriage with Catherine was declared void in May 1533
by Archbishop Cranmer who had taken over responsibility for the hear-
ings. On 1 June 1533 Anne Boleyn was crowned queen.[7] The legal take-
over of ecclesiastical jurisdiction was completed in a series of statutes
passed in the two parliamentary sessions of 1534. The addition of the title
'Supreme Head of the Church of England' to Henry's style late in
1534 merely marked the end of a phase in the king's proceedings as well as
constituting an ominous portent of further developments to come.[8]

The campaign against papal authority and ecclesiastical autonomy
had begun in desultory fashion with the meeting of parliament on 3
November 1529. It gathered momentum as the clergy submitted to a
variety of demands and threats emanating from parliament as well as war-
nings of possible action against them in virtue of *praemunire*. The pace
quickened with the admission of Thomas Cromwell to the inner ring of
royal advisers in 1531. A major breakthrough had come with 'the submission of the clergy' on 15 May 1532. A 'rump' group of the upper house of
Southern Convocation agreed to submit all new legislation to royal approval. Not insignificantly it was the day following this surrender that Sir
Thomas More resigned. His previous three years as Henry's chief
minister must have been a little trying. Not merely could he not approve
of the divorce proceedings but the whole campaign against the independence of the church must have been entirely repugnant to him. The
depth of this repugnance may be measured in the effort involved in
devoting the greater part of his leisure time in the preceding six years to
the defence of the church and its beliefs. Indeed two of the last works of

---

[7] See G. de C. Parmiter, *The King's Great Matter*, London, 1967, 227-243.

[8] See Elton, *England under the Tudors*, 127-159; G. Constant, *The Reformation in England*, tr.
E. I. Watson, London, II, 1942, 91-199; H. Maynard Smith, *Henry VIII and the Reformation*,
London, 1948, 42-74; P. Hughes, *The Reformation in England*, I, *The King's Proceedings*, rev.
ed., 1963, 247-279; J. J. Scarisbrick, *Henry VIII*, London, 1968, 198-354; G. R. Elton, *The
Reformation in England*, in *The New Cambridge Modern History*, II, (1958), 234-235. For a critique
of Elton's interpretation of Cromwell's role in these affairs, see G. L. Harriss and P.
Williams, *A Revolution in Tudor History?*, Past and Present 25 (1963) 3-58. See also A. G.
Dickens, *The English Reformation*, London, 1967, 162-175. Elton's latest work provides a
helpful review of his researches: G. R. Elton, *Reform and Reformation: England 1509-1558*,
London, 1977. See also Stanford E. Lehmberg, *The Reformation Parliament 1529-1536*, Cambridge, 1970, 64-248.

controversy which he published deal specifically with the rights and privileges of the church in English society. These were written not in flagrant opposition to royal policy but rather as a counter-blast to the anti-ecclesiastical propaganda of Christopher Saint-German.[9] Nonetheless the undercurrent of feeling for the inner core of the Christian community as well as care for its institutional expression was undoubtedly revealing not merely to subsequent generations of devotees but also to the subtle politicians who had taken both Wolsey's and More's places at the king's side. *The Apologye of Syr Thomas More Knyghte* (April, 1533) and *The Debellation of Salem and Byzance* (October, 1533) clearly demonstrated More's regard for the traditional liberties of the church in England.

The essential content of the policy which Thomas Cromwell helped crystallise in the mind of his royal master has already been outlined: take over the supreme governance of the church in England; obtain a divorce through the good offices of a government appointee; enrich the monarchy and expand its political influence through the spoliation of church property. The early objectives in this campaign were gained through the subjugation of the hierarchy and the compliance of a cooperative parliament in passing the necessary statutory authorisation. Both Cromwell and his royal master knew that this was not enough. It is one thing to pass laws even in a fully democratic assembly, something the Tudor parliament never was. It is another thing to have them obeyed, and still another to have them respected.[10] It was this sensitivity to the feelings of the masses which perhaps most distinguished Cromwell's contribution to the political and constitutional developments of these years. He clearly recognised that it was not enough to crush overt resistance to the royal will. People at large must be persuaded that Henry's course of action was really in their better interest. The movement forward had to be double-pronged. Each prong had its bearing on the ultimate fate of Sir Thomas More as well as accelerating the final distillation of his convictions concerning the nature and ordering of the common corps of Christendom.

'The tasks of enforcement, (of the reformation statutes) from clarifying the new truths to dealing with the irreconcilables, not only existed; they

---

[9] See More, *Apology*, ed. Taft, xxxvii-xlvii; Rainer Pineas, *Sir Thomas More's Controversy with Christopher St. German, Studies in English Literature* 1 (1961) 49-62, repr. *Thomas More and Tudor Polemics*, Bloomington, Indiana, 1968, 192-213; A. Prévost, *Thomas More*, 213-227.

[10] See G. R. Elton, *Policy and Police, The Enforcement of the Reformation in the Age of Thomas Cromwell*, Cambridge, 1972, 171-425. Indeed the entire book may be read as a somewhat discursive treatment of the whole subject. Its special merit lies in focusing attention on this topic. See also A. G. Dickens, *The English Reformation*, London, rev. ed., 1967, 175-182. See also Scarisbrick, *Henry VIII*, 302-354.

were pressing, constant and pervasive.'[11] Both tasks were carried out concurrently. The policy of persuasion took various forms, mainly the preaching of sermons, publication of pamphlets and the administration of oaths to the succession and, implicitly, to royal supremacy. The propaganda campaign is of particular interest.[12] It brought into the foreground an issue of some importance which may well have provoked in More a clarification of his own thought concerning the place and function of the general council in the life of the church. It is not remarkable that this topic received little attention in both *Responsio* and *Dialogue*. Conciliarism had barely stirred the surface of English ecclesiastical life in the 14th and 15th centuries; still less in the early decades of Tudor rule.[13] What is noteworthy is that conciliar issues received attention from More not only in the *Confutation* (1532-33) but also in the transactions leading to his arrest and execution. This interest on More's part is not unconnected with the Henrician strategy of mass persuasion.

Cromwell's programme to eliminate opposition to his royal master led to an early move against More.[14] In February 1534 he had his name included in the Act of Attainder for misprision of treason in keeping silence on the subject of treacherous talk attributed to Elizabeth Barton, the 'Nun of Kent'. Because More had acted with the greatest discretion in all of this affair he escaped temporarily.[15] A second line of attack was to follow in connection with Henry's propaganda campaign. This latter tactic involved the sponsored publication of a collection of tracts justifying Henry's actions in the divorce case in subordinating the ecclesiastical order to royal

---

[11] See Elton, *Policy and Police*, 170.

[12] See F. Le Van Baumer, *The Early Tudor Theory of Kingship*, New Haven, 1940, 211-224; W. G. Zeeveld, *Foundations of Tudor Policy*, Cambridge, Mass., 111-156; P. Hughes, *The Reformation in England*, I, rev. ed., 1963, 248-269, 330-342; J. K. McConica, *English Humanists and Reformation Politics under Henry VIII and Edward VI*, Oxford, 1965, 106-149; Scarisbrick, *Henry VIII*, 265-266; Elton, *Policy and Police*, 171-216.

[13] See S. B. Chrimes, *English Constitutional Ideas in the Fifteenth Century*, Cambridge, 1936, 301-303; E. F. Jacob, *Essays in the Conciliar Epoch*, Manchester, 3rd ed., 1963, 44-84, esp. 54-56; B. Wilkinson, *Constitutional History of England in the Fifteenth Century (1399-1485)*, London, 1964, 382-384.

[14] There are indications that More had been associated for some time, at least indirectly, with a small opposition group to Henry's policy especially as it concerned the Divorce. Most of its members were favourable to Catherine. It still remains to be established that this was the principal reason for his becoming the object of royal ill will. See G. R. Elton, *Sir Thomas More and the Opposition to Henry VIII*, Bull. Inst. Hist. Research 61 (1968) 19-34, repr. *Studies in Tudor and Stuart Politics* I, 155-172; Elton, *England under the Tudors*, 137-140.

[15] See Elton, *England under the Tudors*, 137-138; Chambers, *Thomas More*, 218-284; Reynolds, *The Field is Won*, 278-293; Elton, *Policy and Police*, 401; J. D. M. Derrett, *Sir Thomas More and the Nun of Kent* in *Moreana* no. 15 (1967) 267-284.

authority as well as other policies he was to pursue in later years. The propaganda campaign was not limited to the transitional years of royal
supremacy while its influence spread through the public support of those
who for one reason or another backed Henry's line.[16] Characteristic of this
literature in its early stages was one work which led to official accusations
against More: *Articles devised by the holle consent of the kynges most honourable
counsaylles,* published in 1533.[17] This work contained two important
arguments, one in favour of the king's divorce, the other claiming that the
final court of appeal in cases such as Henry's marriage problem lay not
with the pope but with the general council. This last marked a significant
rediscovery by Henrician apologists of conciliar theory. The publication in
England of Marsiglio of Padua's *Defensor Pacis* in 1535, a project for which
Thomas Cromwell himself personally advanced the money, was symptomatic of this trend.[18] Marsiglio's treatise was of an entirely different
quality to the productions of Cromwell's pamphleteers. Nonetheless a
course had been set, new coordinates taken. The general council was to be
looked on as a highly respected ecclesiastical institution presumably
replacing the Roman primate as supreme governing authority and final
court of appeal in Christendom.[19]

   In a letter to Thomas Cromwell, More rejected the charge laid against
him of having openly criticised the *Articles of the kynges counsaylles.*[20] Was it
not typical of More's legal mind that he should reach out and use an argu-

----

   [16] This literature, official and unofficial, is by now quite well catalogued. See n. 12 above.
For subsequent developments, see J. K. McConica, *English Humanists and Reformation Politics,*
150-281; G. R. Elton, *Reform and Renewal. Thomas Cromwell and the Commonweal,* Cambridge,
1973, 38-65, 158-166.
   [17] See *Articles devised by the holle consent of the kynges most honourable counsaylles,* pr. Berthelet,
London, 1533, repr. Pocock, *Records of the Reformation, The Divorce 1527-1533,* Oxford, II,
1870, 523-531. For an account of this literature, see P. Janelle, *L'Angleterre Catholique à la
veille du schisme,* Paris, 1935, 232-319; F. Le van Baumer, *The Early Tudor Theory of Kingship,*
49-56; W. G. Zeeveld, *Foundations of Tudor Policy,* 87-89; 130-131; 135-137; P. Hughes, *The
Reformation in England,* I, 248-269. For a summary of the *Articles,* see ibid., 253-255.
   [18] See Elton, *Policy and Police,* 186, and 186, n. 2; H. S. Stout, *Marsilius of Padua and the
Henrician Reformation, Church History* 43 (1974) 308-318.
   [19] On these developments, see n. 12 above. On some of its later ramifications see P. E.
Sawada, *Two Anonymous Tudor Treatises on the General Council, JEH* 12 (1961) 197-214; *Das Imperium Heinrichs VIII und die erste Phase seiner Konzilspolitik,* in *Reformata Reformanda, Festgabe für
Hubert Jedin,* ed. E. Iserloh and K. Repgen, Münster, I, 1965, 476-507; R. W. Albright,
Conciliarism in Anglicanism, CH 33 (1964) 3-22. On Gardiner's contribution the most significant of the early period, see P. Janelle, *Obedience in Church and State,* Cambridge, 1930,
67-171.
   [20] See More to Cromwell, Chelsea, 1 February (1533-34), Rogers, *Correspondence,*
467/1-469/61. See also Chambers, *Thomas More,* 280-281; Reynolds, *The Field is Won,*
283-284.

ment of opposing counsel and utilise it to further his own case? While the growing emphasis on royal supremacy undoubtedly underlay his remarkable silence on the issue of papal primacy in the *Confutation*,[21] increasing interest in the general council evinced among Henry's publicists may well explain the more extensive treatment it received in More's later work as well as the extent to which it figured in the exchanges prior to his execution, as he used the argument from conciliar anthority to justify his stand on royal supremacy.

The nub of all these discussions was of course the dual issue of royal succession and supremacy. The historical and biographical details of these affairs need not detain us here as they have been well and often told before.[22] Suffice it to recall that More was initially imprisoned in the Tower on 17 April 1534 for refusal to take the oath of succession. The following November an act of attainder guaranteed his imprisonment for life as well as the reduction of his family to penury.[23] The Act of Supremacy was passed in parliament the same month. Subsequently several attempts were made to induce More to accept the oath of succession. His consistent refusal led to his trial for treason and final conviction based, many of his friends believed, on perjured evidence. It was the manoeuvres leading to this outcome which provoked from More some significant statements on church, council and primacy.

THE CHURCH OF THE SPIRIT

At the centre of More's preoccupations at this time lay his own personal relationship with Christ. André Prévost has shown how this concern lay

---

[21] See More to Cromwell, Chelsea, 5 March (1534), *Correspondence*, 500/273-281: 'But where as I had written therof at length in my confutation byfore, and for the profe therof had compyled together all that I could fynde therfore, at such tyme as I litle loked that there shold fall bytwene the Kyngis Highnes and the Pope such a breche as is fallen synnys, whan I after that sawe the thing lykely to drawe toward such displeasure bytwene theym I suppressed it vtterly and never put word therof in to my booke but put owt the remenaunt with owt it...'

[22] The whole question of More's indictment, the oaths he was asked to take, as well as the conduct of his trial have been the subject of much recent investigation. For a masterly summary of these findings, see Elton, *Policy and Police*, 400-425. See also G. de C. Parmiter, *The Indictment of St Thomas More*, *The Downside Review* 75 (1957) 149-166; G. de C. Parmiter, *St Thomas More and the Oath*, *The Downside Review* 78 (1959-60) 1-13; E. E. Reynolds, *An Unnoticed Document*, *Moreana* no. 1 (1963) 12-17, and reply to criticisms: ibid., no. 3 (1964) 20-22; R. W. Chambers, *Thomas More*, 278-334; E. E. Reynolds, *The Field is Won*, 294-382; *The Trial of St. Thomas More*, London, 1964, 33-159; J. D. M. Derrett, *The Trial of Sir Thomas More*, EHR 79 (1964) 450-477; J. D. M. Derrett, *The 'new' Document on Thomas More's Trial*, *Moreana* no. 3 (1964) 20-22; B. Byron, *The Fourth Count of More's Indictment*, *Moreana* no. 10 (1966) 33-46.

[23] 26 Henry VIII, c. 23 (SR iii, 528), cited Elton, *Policy and Police*, p. 402, n. 3.

close to the centre of More's consciousness for the greater part of his life.[24]
His devotion to Christ brought the life of the church and his own personal
life within the same perspective through the mediating concept of Christ's
mystical body: 'Each time we see the moment approach when Christ, the
Son of Man, is handed over to sinners, each time we perceive the danger
that threatens the mystical body of Christ of being handed over into the
power of men and the Christian people destroyed.'[25] This faith in Christ
and in his abiding presence with his true disciples lay at the core of More's
own personal life of prayer and liturgical worship. Writing on the
eucharist to John Frith in December 1532, he spoke of the presence of the
risen Christ in this sacrament: '...and all hys trewe faythfull byleuyng and
louyng peple with hym, whom as the mystycall membres of hys gloryous
body he shall than, and from thens forth for euer pleasauntly nurysh and
fede and sacyate theyr insacyable hunger...' As Prévost remarks: 'It is this
idea of a people united to Christ as his mystical body in which the
mysteries of Incarnation and Redemption extend themselves in time that
gives to More's thought its most solid foundation and to his Christian
humanism its *raison d'être.*'[26] Prévost might have added that it provided
More as well with the inspiration to accept death so readily.

CHRISTENDOM

Although More never lost sight of the spiritual dimensions of the
church, another co-ordinate of his thought was never distant from his
mind: his understanding of the church as the common corps of Christendom. In these later years the unity of Christendom was a matter of burning concern. As ever, he conceived of it in a unitary way though existing at
several levels. Christendom is a name for that geographical region where
Christians for the most part live; a habitation and a place.[27] More than

---

[24] André Prévost, *Thomas More 1477-1535 et la crise de la pensée européene,* (Mame), 1969,
291-315. See also G. Marc'Hadour, *Thomas More's Spirituality,* in *St. Thomas More: Action and
Contemplation,* ed. R. S. Sylvester, 125-159, and L. Martz, *The Tower Works,* in ibid., 59-83.

[25] 'Nihil potest esse validius ad salutem et Christiano pectori quodque virtutum genus in-
ferendum, quam si quis pio cum affectu seriem passionis Christi meditatur...toties
timeamus tempus appropinquare quo filius hominis Christus tradetur in manus pec-
catorum: quoties conspicamur imminere periculum ne in manus hominum corpus Christi
mysticum Ecclesia Christi, Christianus videlicet populus pessundatur.' in *Expositio Passionis,*
(1534-35), *Opera Latina,* Louvain, 1565, 126C-D. See also More to John Frith, Chelsea, 7
December (1532), Rogers, *Correspondence,* 463/859-870.

[26] Prévost, *Thomas More,* 314.

[27] See for example More to Cromwell, Chelsea, 5 March (1534), Rogers, *Correspondence,*
498/232-499/247: More was arguing to the importance of general councils in settling
disputes among Christian people: '...or ellys were there in no thing no certayntie, but

this, Christendom is a political reality which needs to be conserved, extended and protected. This latter aspect occupied a good deal of More's attention during his years of royal service.[28] However, Christendom meant a great deal more to him than a convenient conceptual tool with which to organise the experience of daily life; it was a cause to which he was passionately attached. Witness his conversation with his son-in-law Roper as they walked the bank of the Thames, probably early in 1529: 'Now would to our Lorde, sonne Roper, vpon condition that three thinges were well stablished in Christendome, I were put in a sacke, and here presently cast into the temmes.' More's three wishes were for universal peace in Europe, unity of faith, and the happy settlement of Henry's marriage problem.[29]

The source of More's passion lay in all likelihood outside the arena of politics in a vision of Christendom as a spiritual unity bound together by common faith, life and law. The solidarity of Christendom is a frequent theme in his writings: 'And therfore sith all Christendom is one corps, I can not perceive how eny membre therof may withowt the comen assent of the body depart from the comen hede.'[30] Here More was thinking of Christendom in social terms, a body of people bound together by a com-

---

thorow Christendom vppon every mannys affectionate reason, all thing myght be browght fro day to day to contynuall ruffle and confusion, from which... every such counsaile well assembled kepeth and euer shall kepe the corps of his Catholique Chirch.' Here there is a clear interaction in view between the social and ecclesiastical dimensions of Christendom.

[28] See for example, More to Wolsey, Windsor, 16 March (1528), Rogers, *Correspondence*, 390-391. Negotiations were on foot between the monarchies of France and England to unite in common cause against the Emperor Charles V; 'And that it were to great pitie...if the thre gretteste princis of Christendom cummyng to so nere pointis of peace and concord shold in so nere hope and expectatione of peace sodaynly fall at warre...' More reported Henry's reply in these terms, that the latter would do anything to promote peace '...if with th'Emperor either resonable respecte of his awne honor, profite and suertie or eny regard of the comen weale of Christendome myght haue taken place.' Henry cautioned, however, that he and his friends must '...defende his and theire good cause and the comen state of Christendome...' Whatever the force of the argumentation, the political quality of the concepts employed is evident.

[29] See Harpsfield, *The life and death of Sr Thomas Moore, knight*, ed., E. V. Hitchcock, London, 1932, 67/22-68/24. See also ibid., 196/5-10. Harpsfield's account is dependent on Roper, 24/5-25/8. This conversation is not dated in the above sources. It would seem to have taken place some time before the peace of Cambrai, August 1529. On this, see Chambers, *Thomas More*, 220-221; Reynolds, *The Field is Won*, 276. A great deal of More's anger against heretics originated in his fears for the political security and integrity of Christendom. See More to Erasmus, Chelsea, (1533), in *Erasmi epistolae*, pp. 258-261. See also More, *Dialogue*, 1st ed., cxxviii-cxxix v, *EW* 257D-259E, ed., Campbell, 272-275.

[30] More to Cromwell, Chelsea, 5 March (1534), Rogers, *Correspondence*, 498/232-234; see also ibid., 226-231: '...that primatie is at the leist wise instituted by the corps of Christendom...'

mon way of life and a common discipline. He used this concept to underline the subordination even of English civil law to the common law of Christendom in relation to the papacy: '...thorowe the corps of Christendome the Popes power was recognished for an vndoubted thinge...' He went on '...a man is not by a lawe of one realme so bounde in his conscience, where there is a lawe of the hole corps of Christendome to the contrarie in mater towchinge belief, as he is by a lawe of the hole corpes though there happe to be made in some place a lawe locall to the contrarye...'[31] More here confused to some extent law and faith, but what was evidently on his mind was the right of Christendom to establish its own socio-legal as well as credal structures for the regulation and ordering of its religious life. He had been always ready to resist unwarranted intrusions by the spiritual power into the temporal sphere.[32] The reverse was also true.

More did not limit his concept of Christendom to its social dimension but clearly affirmed it to be a commonwealth of faith. This aspect of his thought was very much in evidence in the account by Margaret Roper of a conversation with her father and reported on in a letter dated to August 1534. The letter purports to quote More's words verbatim as he speaks of the authority of 'the general counsell of the whole body of Christendome' being guided by 'the spirit of God' so that it may never make any decision 'to Goddes displeasure'. The individual Christian is bound by such decisions as he is 'by a generall faith growen by the workynge of God vniuersally thorow all Christian nacions.'[33] It is, perhaps, in his last speech before his judges that More's sense of Christendom as a community of faith comes through most powerfully. He argued that if the weight of learned opinion were to count for so much in determining what one should believe, then he saw no reason to modify his conscience on the issue of royal supremacy. For in Christendom the majority '...of these well

<hr/>

[31] More to Margaret Roper, Tower of London, 2 or 3 May 1535, Rogers, *Correspondence*, 558/84-100. See also More's address to his judges immediately before judgement was passed upon him, in Harpsfield, *Thomas Moore*, 193/1-194/24.

[32] See for example More's warning to Henry regarding the latter's exaggerated concessions to the political authority of the papacy in the *Assertio Septem Sacramentorum*. Before the book was published More helped Henry rearrange the materials as well as reminding him of the purely political character of certain papal pretensions. He also recalled to his monarch's mind the existence of the statute of *praemunire* and advised him to do nothing that might undermine its authority. See Harpsfield, op. cit. 159/13-160/17. See also Roper, op. cit. 67/8-68/23. These represent expanded, possibly embroidered accounts of that given by More to Cromwell, Chelsea, 5 March (1534), Rogers, *Correspondence*, 498/200-214.

[33] See also Margaret Roper to Alice Alington, (August 1534), Rogers, *Correspondence*, 524/386-525/417.

learned Bishopps and vertuous men that are yet alive...are of my minde therein. But if I should speake of those that are already deade, of whom many be nowe holy Saintes in heauen, I am very sure it is the farre greater part of them that...thought in this case the way that I thinke nowe; and therefore am I not bounden...to conforme my conscience to the Councell of one Realme against the generall Councell of Christendome.'[34]

Thus within the boundaries of a single landscape Thomas More saw Christendom as a place inhabited by Christians, as a loose political confederation of principalities, as a socio-moral body with its own constitutional procedures bearing on religious life, and a body of believers bound together by their common faith and life in Christ. For him these elements were inextricably intertwined such that each aspect made up, as it were, one wall of a quadrangle. Take one element away and the quadrangle no longer existed. Consequently each element in the building must be defended for the sake of the whole.

Consensus

The latter notion of Christendom as a community of faith underlay the familiar theme of consensus which More used so frequently as his ultimate court of appeal in disputed questions of Christian thought and practice. There is little in these letters to add to what has been already said on this subject, though one or two points are made with greater precision than hitherto. This arose in particular in his discussion on the relationship between consensus and the formation of conscience, obviously a matter of central significance during these final days. More insisted that in the absence of consensus each one is free to form his conscience according to his own lights. No one is bound to disobey a law promulgated for a particular region unless there be a definite contrary indication from a general council or a universally established belief or practice of the Christian community.[35] It is significant that he deliberately placed this popular consen-

---

[34] Harpsfield, *The life and death of Sr Thomas Moore, knight,* 195/15-196/4, and passim. See also Roper, op.cit. 94/23-95/9.

[35] Margaret Roper to Alice Alington, (August 1534), Rogers, *Correspondence,* 525/405: 'Now if it so hap, that in any particular parte of Christendome, there be a law made, that be such as for some parte therof some men thinke that the law of God can not beare it... (one is not) bounden to chaunge his owne conscience therin, for any particular law made any where, other than by the generall counsaile or by a generall faith growen by the workynge of God vniuersally thorow all Christian nacions: nor other authorite than one of these twayne (except special reuelacion and expresse commaundment of God)...' Note the degree of authority More attached to 'special reuelacion', putting it on a par with that of the general council in the formation of individual conscience. This would seem to be the measure of his faith in the presence of the Holy Spirit in the heart of each believer. See also ibid., 526/455-470.

sus on a par with the authority of a general council. Indeed in some instances it is not altogether clear whether he is referring to a general consensus or a conciliar decision since he spoke of the whole church virtually as if
it were a council. At first glance one might ascribe this ambiguity to confused ideas. Reflection suggests that his own representative theory of
council may well have been the source of this manner of speech.[36]

The relative insecurity of his own stance on the issue of primacy must
have been weighing heavily on More's mind. One of the topics to which he
drew his daughter Margaret's attention was that of the development of
doctrine. He used the doctrine of the Immaculate Conception of the
Virgin Mary to illustrate his point. This had been hotly disputed at one
stage in the course of the middle ages. In prison More could not recall
whether it had as yet been defined by a general council but he assumed it
to be a generally received belief of his own day. In any event he could see
in this as in other issues that the consensus of the common corps of
Christendom was not necessarily given throughout history to all doctrines
currently received in the church. Some positions the people of God now
looked on as of faith had been reached through a centuries-long process of
growth: '...a generall faith growen by the workynge of God vniuersally
thorow all Christian nacions'.[37] More, because of his personal study of the
matter, felt the doctrine of papal primacy had this kind of backing from
age-long Christian tradition.[38] He also realised that his own depth of
knowledge was entirely exceptional. Hence his reluctance to judge others
in a negative way on the one hand and the firmness of his own stand on the
other.

---

[36] We find this usage in such phrases as: 'the generall counsell of the whole body of
Christendome'; 'his whole catholike church lawfully gathered together in a generall
counsell'. See Roper to Alington, Rogers, *Correspondence,* 524/393-525/404. Another example
of this usage occurs in Harpsfield's account of More's 'speech from the dock'. Having referred to all those who throughout the course of history had held the same opinion as himself
concerning the primacy, More went on '...and therefore am I not bounden, my Lorde, to
conforme my conscience to the Councell of one Realme against the generall Councell of
Christendome.' See Harpsfield, *Thomas Moore,* 195/22-196/4. See above pp. 212-217 for
More's theory of council, and below pp. 264-265 for the constitutional background to these
views which to a large extent justify this interpretation of More's terminology. His phrase
'the generall Councell of Christendome' may well be the ecclesiastical counterpart of a view
of parliament which looked on it as the whole realm gathered to advise and consent.
[37] See Roper to Alington, Rogers, *Correspondence,* 525/416-418.
[38] '...thorowe the corps of Christendome the Popes power was recognised for an
vndoubted thinge which semeth not like a thinge agreed in this realme and the contrary
taken for truthe in other realmes...' in More to Margaret Roper, (Tower of London, 3 June
1535), Rogers, *Correspondence,* 558/87-90; see also More's final speech to the Commissioners
in Harpsfield, *Thomas Moore,* 195/15-196/9, cited above.

THE GENERAL COUNCIL

In the letters and interviews of his period of retirement, as in the *Confutation*, Thomas More placed a new emphasis on the function of the general council within the body of the church. He did not elaborate on its nature and powers yet he appealed on several occasions to its authority. He saw it as standing on a par with the unanimous opinion of believers as a guide to faith, the supreme legislative body in Christendom on religious matters, as well as the voice of Solomon in deciding disputes among theologians. There are echoes in these writings of a representative view of conciliar constitution hinted at in the *Responsio*, and elaborated in the *Confutation*. He used such phrases as '...the general counsell of the whole body of Christendome...'; '...his whole catholike church lawfully gathered together in a generall counsell...'[39] Similarly in his final appeal to the king's commissioners, having cited the authority of Christian tradition for his stand, he declared: '...and therefore am I not bounden, my Lorde, to conforme my conscience to the Councell of one Realme against the general Councell of Christendome.'[40] What seems to hide behind these phrases is a concept of council which sees it as the whole church gathered together for deliberation. Because all cannot meet in one place, they do so through the social convention of representative assembly. Consequently, however, the deliberations of the representative body are not those of an élitist group but of the whole corporation of believers. In other words, the 'populist' idea of council which appeared in the *Confutation* seems to be echoed here in the trial period.

Seen in these terms, it is easy to understand the equiparation of conciliar and ecclesial consensus in More's thought, as when he argues that no one '...is bounden vpon paine of Goddes displeasure to chaunge his owne conscience...other than by the generall counsaile or by a generall faith growen by the workynge of God vniuersally thorow all Christian nacions...'[41] At the same time More appears to have granted a certain practical superiority to the council in deciding disputed questions. While consensus may have to grow gradually over the centuries till dissident voices have been quieted, councils may decide issues which are still in dispute till the time for determination arrives within the assembly. Once the decision is given, then all are conscience-bound to assent. 'But lyke as after the determinacion of a well assembled generall counsaile, euery man

---

[39] Roper to Alington, Rogers, *Correspondence*, 524/399-525/404.
[40] Harpsfield, *Thomas Moore*. 196/1-4.
[41] Roper to Alington, Rogers, *Correspondence*, 525/414-417.

had been bounden to geue credans that way, and confirme their owne conscience to the determinacion of the counsayle generall, and than all they
that helde the contrary before, were for that holding oute of blame...'[42]

In matters of constitutional law More allows the council authority to
revise what has been determined by the common consent of the church.
This implication occurs when he urges the illegitimacy of departing
'...from the comen hede' without 'the comen assent of the body'. 'And
than if we may not lawfully leve it by our selfe I can not perceive (but if the
thing were a treating in a generall counsaile) what the question could
avayle whither the prymacie were instituted immediately by God or ordeyned by the Chirch.'[43] Perhaps with one eye on the *Articles devised by the
kynges counsaylles* (pr. Berthelet 1533), he left a theoretical door open to a
revision of the common consent regarding the primacy by a future general
council. However, as will appear later, this common assent in regard to
the primacy, in More's eyes, could be fully verified only in relation to the
legal, constitutional position of the Roman pontiff. Its theological standing
was less secure. Hence what More envisages here is either a change in the
constitutional law of the church to be carried out by a general council, or
possibly a doctrinal decision of even greater authority still. Given his personal opinions concerning the primacy, it is likely that this was written
with his tongue in his cheek. Nonetheless it is an interesting comment on
the relationship between the authority of universal consensus and general
council. Consensus, though binding, is subject to revision by the council
at least in legal matters.

Regarding the ordinary powers of an ecumenical council, More seemed
to be in line with the ordinary thought of his time. Understandably in a lay
theologian, he was not over precise in drawing a line between the
legislative and magisterial authority of these assemblies. Indeed the
vocabulary he employed is often suggestive of his forensic and parliamentary background. He regarded the council as the supreme legislative body
in the church capable of making ordinances binding on all Christians.
Such ordinances are in themselves reformable but because of the divine
promises one has a guarantee of their not contradicting the law of God:
'...to institute any thinge in such wise to Goddes displeasure, as at the
makinge might not lawfully be perfourmed, the spirit of God that
gouerneth his churche, neuer hath it suffered, nor neuer here after
shall...'[44]

---

[42] Ibid., 526/448-452.
[43] More to Thomas Cromwell, Chelsea, 5 March (1534), Rogers, *Correspondence*,
498/232-499/278.
[44] Roper to Alington, Rogers, *Correspondence*, 524/393-525/404.

Concerning the teaching authority of the general council, Sir Thomas More was quite emphatic: 'As for the generall counsailis assembled lawfully, I never could perceive, but that in the declaration of the trewthis it is to be byleved and to be standen to, the authorite therof owght to be taken for vndowtable, or ellys were there in no thing no certayntie, but thorow Christendom vppon every mannys affectionate reason, all thing myght be browght fro day to day to contynuall ruffle and confusion, from which by the generall counsailis, the spirite of God assisting, every such counsaile well assembled kepeth and euer shall kepe the corps of his Catholique Chirch.'[45] The same Spirit of God who guides the whole church into union of mind and heart guides the council in its function of providing clear headlines for the individual believer in his interpretation of divine revelation. Spurred on by the recovery of conciliar thought by Henry's propaganda machine as well as by the deepening divisions in European Christendom, More depended to an increasing degree on conciliar decisions to resolve disputed questions.

For his day, More seemed to have a remarkably clear perception of how the troubled gestation period of theological dispute can eventually lead to a calm and universal acceptance of a new theological position. In conversation with his daughter Margaret he had given as one example of such development the tenet of the immaculate conception of the Virgin Mary. This had been hotly disputed in the course of the Middle Ages. Aquinas himself had held serious reservations on the issue.[46] 'Nor neither parte was ther bounden to chaunge ther opinion for thother, nor for any prouinciall counsell either. But lyke as after the determinacion of a well assembled generall counsaile, euery man had been bounden to geue credans that way, and confirme their owne conscience to the determinacion of the counsayle generall...'[47] Thus while allowing liberty to the speculative mind, More also assumed that faith demands decision as to what it affirms at particular moments in time. When that time arrives and the common corps of Christendom gathered in council decides an issue, then for More speculation should cease and religious assent take over. In this view, the ecumenical council has two main functions, one legislative, the other doc-

---

[45] See More to Cromwell, Rogers, *Correspondence,* 499/238-247.

[46] See X. Le Bachelet, *Immaculée Conception, DTC* 7 (1921), cc. 995-1129.

[47] See Roper to Alington, Rogers, *Correspondence,* 526/445-451. See also Thomas More to Dr. Nicholas Wilson, Tower of London, 1534, Rogers, *Correspondence,* 537/136-140: 'Many thynges every man learned woteth well there are, in which every man ys at lyberty withowte peryll of dampnation to thyncke whiche waye hym lyste tyll the one parte be determyned for necessary to be beleved by a generall counsayle...'

trinal. In disciplinary matters More admitted the reformability of conciliar decrees. In doctrinal matters his silence suggests the reverse.

One further point remains to be made concerning More's conciliar theory. He was careful to insist that councils must be lawfully assembled. Not any council claiming ecumenicity deserves the title or the obedience of Christians. The general council '...in the declaration of trewthis...is to be byleved and to be standen to...' provided that it be 'lawfully assembled'. Later on in the same letter, he spoke of the value of validly convened councils in preserving the unity of 'the corps of his (Christ's) Catholique Chirch'.[48] The condition for validity is that they be 'well assembled'. The same qualification occurs in his conversation with his daughter Margaret already referred to above: '...after the determinacion of a well assembled generall counsaile, euery man had been bounden to geue credans that way...'[49] This requirement of legitimate assembly is as much needed for legislative as for doctrinal decision.[50]

All of this shows that More was not unacquainted with some of the canonical and theological problems of the conciliar movement. His parliamentary experience as well as his knowledge of the past would have convinced him of the need for due convocation and correct procedure. The unhappy outcome of conciliar manoeuvres at Basle (1431—c. 1449) and Pisa (1511) may well have been on his mind when making these provisos regarding conciliar procedure.[51] His caution may have had another inspiration as well. He may have been covering his flanks against any *force majeure* on Henry's part in promoting a council of the universal church in despite of Rome. In this way, while espousing an orthodox conciliar theory without spelling it out in detail, he made it clear that he could not go along with unlawfully convened or conducted assemblies such as those mentioned above. Still less could he adopt the position of a Marsiglio of Padua whose views were being touted at court and whose work Thomas Cromwell himself was making vigorous efforts to promote.[52] More did not

---

[48] More to Cromwell, *Correspondence*, 499/238-247.

[49] Roper to Alington, Rogers, *Correspondence*, 526/448-450.

[50] See ibid., 524/399-525/404.

[51] See H. Jedin, *Ecumenical Councils of the Catholic Church*, Edinburgh, 1960, 105-141; P. Hughes, *The Church in Crisis. A History of the Twenty Great Councils*, London, 1960, 241-252, 256-257. See also Tierney, *Conciliar Theory*, 179-237; H. Jedin, *Council of Trent*, I, (1957), 5-61; 101-138.

[52] The translation of Marsiglio's *Defensor Pacis*, did not appear till 1535. Marsilius Menandrinus, *The defence of peace*, tr. from laten (by W. Marshall) fol. R. Wyer, f. W. Marshall, 1535. The translation had been finished before 1st April 1534 in all probability. Apart from this it is reasonable to suppose that the whole issue was the subject of some discussion among politicians, ecclesiastics, and humanists alike. See Elton, *Policy and Police*, 186, and 186 n. 2; H. S. Stout, *Marsilius of Padua and the Henrician Reformation*, CH 43 (1974) 308-318.

spell out what he meant by the terms: 'lawfully assembled' or 'well assembled'. One may speculate concerning their meaning within the context of his thought. Such guesswork is perhaps best left over to a discussion of pope-council relations. First we must examine More's views on the primacy as they emerge at this period.

THE ROMAN PRIMACY

As pressure built up on More concerning the succession and, later, royal supremacy, he expressed regret that Henry VIII should feel that he was in opposition to him '...concernyng his great mater of his mariage or concernyng the prymatie of the Pope.' He seemed quite willing to expound his views on these issues and to explain his position to the king: 'Never wold I wishe other thinge in this worlde more liefe, than that his Highnes in these thingis...as perfetely knewe my dealyng, and as thorowly saw my mynde as I do my selfe.'[53] Curiously enough these statements were made in a letter to Thomas Cromwell which has not been exactly dated but was composed in Chelsea, probably in March 1534, about the time both the Act of Succession and the Heresy Act which declared it no longer a felony to deny Roman primacy were either before parliament or in the pipe-line. (Both of these statutes were passed in the spring session of 1534.)[54] A man with his ear as close to the ground as More must have had a fairly clear idea of what was afoot. In addition there had been the matter of more specific charges against him in the 'Nun of Kent' affair, the Divorce issue, and the matter of a general council to which appeal had been made by the *Articles of the kynges counsaylles*.[55] Consequently this letter to Cromwell bears the quality of both confession and apologia made not in a naïvely self-revelatory fashion but in a diplomatic style which adopts a shrewd compromise between basic truth and conciliatory presentation. His hope was perhaps to gain a temporary respite or even permanent peace for himself and his family. Much of what follows is either drawn or deduced from this missive.

It is in this letter that More makes his often-quoted statement that it was through reading Henry's *Assertio Septem Sacramentorum* that he came to ac-

---

[53] See More to Cromwell, Rogers, *Correspondence*, 492/30-35.
[54] See Elton, *England under the Tudors,* 135; Hughes, *The Reformation in England,* I, 256-261; A. G. Dickens, *The English Reformation,* 162-175; Elton, *The Reformation in England* in *The New Cambridge Modern History,* II, (1958), 234-235; Scarisbrick, *Henry VIII,* 324.
[55] See above pp. 236-240.

cept the divine institution of the Roman primacy.[56] More's claim, though surprising and undoubtedly slanted in his own favour, is credible. Reputable theologians of the conciliar epoch had not been convinced of the divine foundation of the papacy. Neither was Desiderius Erasmus, More's friend and intellectual intimate especially during his humanist period, which in fact the Lutheran schism succeeded in bringing to an end. Erasmus looked on the papacy as an ecclesiastical institution entirely valid within the context of a world-wide religious body but nonetheless of human origin, at least until 1526.[57]

Sir Thomas More, as we shall see, adopted at a later date two distinct though complementary positions on the Roman primacy, one 'maximalistic', affirming its divine institution, the other 'minimalistic', where like Erasmus he argued that there can be no doubt that the position of the Roman pontiff within the Christian community had evolved out of the exigencies of the latter's existence and with its full consent. The account he gives of this development is similar to that given by Bishop Russell, the fifteenth century constitutional theorist, of the origin of political power, sovereignty, and their subsequent institutionalisation.[58] Hence it is not impossible that some such position had been adopted by More with regard to the papacy before he was obliged to examine it more thoroughly when called to play a role in the preparation of Henry's onslaught on Luther.

John Headley has effectively demolished the hypothesis put forward first by R. W. Chambers, and later by Paul Huber that doubt may have remained in More's mind concerning the divine origins of Roman

---

[56] See More to Cromwell, Rogers *Correspondence*, 498/200-214: 'As towching the thyrde point, the prymatie of the Pope, I no thing medle in the mater. Trowth it is, that as I told yow, whan yow desyred me to shew yow what I thowght therin, I was myselfe some tyme not of the mynd that the prymatie of that see shold be bygone by thinstitution of God, vntill that I redd in that mater those thingis that the Kyngis Highnes had written in his moost famouse booke agaynst the heresyes of Marten Luther, at the fyrst reding wherof I moved the Kyngis Highnes either to leve owt that point, or ellys to towche it more slenderly for dowt of such thingis as after myght happe to fall in question bytwene his Highnes and some pope as bytwene pryncis and popis dyverse tymis have done. Whervnto his Highnes answered me, that he wold in no wise eny thing minishe of that mater, of which thing his Highnes shewed me a secrete cause wherof I neuer had eny thing herd byfore.'

[57] See Harry McSorley, *Erasmus and the Primacy of the Roman Pontiff: Between Conciliarism and Papalism, ARG* 65 (1974) 37-54, who argues that by that date Erasmus had become aware of the decrees of the Council of Florence and accepted them.

[58] See Bishop Russell, *Parliamentary Sermon: Draft prepared for the intended Parliament of Edward V (1483)*, in Chrimes, *English Constitutional Ideas*, 173-174. More was an admirer of Russell's: '...he was a wyse manne and a good, of muche experyence, and one of the beste learned menne, vndoubtedly that Englande hadde in hys time' in More, *Richard III*, 25/5-8.

primacy until the late 1520's.[59] The evidence of the *Responsio* points to the adoption of a clear-cut position in the course of its composition, probably even in the interval between the printing of the *Baravellus* and *Rosseus* editions. On the other hand, whatever about More's flattery of Henry on what had become a delicate issue between them in 1534, it is on the cards that he was even more indebted to his fellow controversialist John Fisher than to his temperamental monarch for clarifying his views on the papacy.[60] Nonetheless, this does not preclude a strong possibility that prior to his work on the *Assertio* More regarded the papacy as of human origin rather than divine.

If 1523 marked a turning point in More's views on the petrine see, it did not mean an end to his study of the matter, rather a beginning. The more deeply he read the deeper grew his conviction: 'But surely after that I had redd his Gracis boke therin, and so many other thingis as I have sene in that point by this continuaunce of these x yere synnys and more...' Denial of the primacy to have been 'provided by God' had become personally unacceptable to More.[61] His claim to serious and prolonged study of the matter was repeated on other occasions and indeed offered as a reason for

---

[59] See Chambers, *Thomas More,* 182-187; P. Huber, *Traditionsfestigkeit und Traditionskritik bei Thomas Morus,* Basel, 1953, 132-136, and p. 133, n. 61 in particular. Chambers did not attempt to date the crystallisation of More's convictions. Huber placed it in 1527 at the earliest. The basis of this hypothesis is the report of a conversation between More and his Italian friend Antonio Bonvisi, referred to by Reginald Pole, and recorded in J. Strype, *Historical Memorials, Ecclesiastical and Civil,* London, III, 1721, 244-245. In this conversation More, it is alleged, said that he looked on the primacy of Rome as a human ordinance. After a short period of study he returned to Bonvisi to announce a complete change of heart on the matter. In More's letter to Cromwell, he said he had studied the question of the primacy 'these x yere synnys and more.' This was a correction in his own hand of 'vii yere'. Huber argued that the original 'vii yere' was the correct figure. He related this to the Bonvisi conversation, and suggested it had taken place seven years earlier than the letter to Cromwell, namely in 1527. The correction, however, was in More's own hand; the time designated imprecise: 'x yere synnys and more.' This brings one back to 1524, near enough to the revision of the *Responsio* a year previously, in the autumn of 1523. On this matter, see More, *Responsio,* ed. Headley, II, 770, 792-793. See in particular ibid., 768: 'By the autumn of 1523 he had assumed a stance that was to be revealed at his trial twelve years later.' See also Reynolds, *Saint Thomas More,* 161-163, and idem, *The Field is Won,* 310-312 for a similar interpretation. [Note: Bonvisi was of Italian parentage but had lived most of his life in London. He had been a friend of More's for forty years. See More to Bonvisi, Tower of London, 1535, Rogers, *Correspondence,* 560/5-13, and *DNB* II (1917-), 827-828.]

[60] See *Responsio,* 138/29-140/5. Following Fisher's treatment of the issue in his *Assertionis Lutheranae Confutatio,* Antwerp, 1523, More could say: 'Consequently, I considered that I would be acting uselessly and *opening a closed issue* if I were to weave a fresh web of writing about the primacy of the pope.'

[61] More to Cromwell, Rogers, *Correspondence,* 498/214-231.

his own almost unique stand as well as his equally unique tolerance of those who followed a different line.[62]

While he had dealt at some length with the promises made to Peter as well as the petrine office itself in the *Responsio,* More pointed out to Cromwell that in his 'boke agaynst the Maskar (*The Dialogue*), I wrote not I wote well fyve lynys.' In the *Confutation* he had intended to treat the question at some length. The original draft had contained a substantial treatment of papal office, presumably the fruit of his ten years of study. At a later stage he had decided to drop this passage: '...whan I after that sawe the thing lykely to drawe toward such displeasure bytwene theym I suppressed it vtterly and never put word therof in to my booke but put owt the remenaunt with owt it...' More never intended, he insisted, to intervene positively on this issue against 'the Kyngis graciouse pleasure, what so ever myn awne opinion were therin.'[63] His public stance was to remain strictly negative and passive. He would not speak out against royal policy but he would refuse to take any oath involving a denial of the pope's primatial function. More thus trod a delicate tightrope between his open affirmation of papal primacy and a careful silence concerning royal supremacy. The latter tactic was a simple application in the legal forum of the ancient maxim: *qui tacet consentire videtur.* In this way he achieved a subtle balance between his moral duty to affirm his faith on the one hand and to preserve his life on the other. Under interrogation he steadfastly refused to give his reasons for not accepting royal supremacy but did not hesitate to explain his attitude to papal primacy.[64] Within the law his position was

---

[62] See Thomas More to Margaret Roper, (Tower of London, c. 17 April 1534), Rogers, *Correspondence,* 505/110-506/112 and passim. More had been called to appear before the King's commissioners at Lambeth, 13 April 1534. The archbishop of Canterbury urged More to swear the oath of succession which included an abjuration of loyalty to any foreign potentate. While willing to accept the succession, More saw in the latter clause a rejection of papal sovereignty over the English church. He consequently refused the oath. 'Wherin I had not enformed my conscience neither sodeinly nor sleightley, *but by longe laysure and diligent serche for the matter.*' See also Pole's remarks reported in Strype, loc.cit. See also More's remarks to Dr. Nicholas Wilson in his letter of 1534: '...of all those that I talked with of the matter...the moste, as I trow you wote well, was yourself.' Here More was referring to the Divorce rather than the primacy. Concerning the link between the latter and the oath of succession, he said: '...I am not he that take vpon me to diffyne or determyne of what kynd or nature euery thyng is that the othe conteynethe, nor am so bolde or presumptious to blame or disprayse the consyence of other men, theyr treuthe nor theyr learning neither, nor I medle with no man but of my selffe, nor of no mannes consyens ellis wyll I medle but of myne owne.' See Thomas More to Dr. Nicholas Wilson, Tower of London, 1534, Rogers, *Correspondence,* 534/33-41 and 537/140-145.

[63] See More to Cromwell, Rogers, *Correspondence,* 499/268-500/283.

[64] See note 22 above for reference to recent publications on this matter. Elton, *Policy and Police,* 400-420 follows Derrett, *The Trial of Sir Thomas More, EHR* 79 (1964) 450-477, who

secure. The reason his tactic failed to save his life is disputed: was it a fatal slip on his own part or the perjury of an erstwhile beneficiary of his? Opinions differ. In any event it is possible to reconstruct the gist of the missing passages of the *Confutation* from More's 'confessions' during this period.

It may be helpful in elucidating the complex theological, moral and legal situation in which More found himself to make the following observations concerning the nature of revealed truth as understood within Catholic tradition. Catholic theology assumes that divine revelation can be interpreted in logical propositions: e.g., 'God is the creator of heaven and earth.' Because of the essentially objective character of the content of revelation contained in a message addressed by God to the believing community, and on the other hand the different ways in which this message may be received, theologians distinguish between the objective and subjective weight to be ascribed to individual propositions. To use More's own example of the immaculate conception of the Virgin Mary: a twelfth century theologian might have been personally convinced of the truth of this belief. It still remained, however, objectively speaking a debatable opinion, one the ordinary believer might accept or reject with impunity. As agreement grew on the matter, its objective weight increased till finally the point of unanimous consent or conciliar definition would have been reached. At that juncture, within More's frame of reference, debate was over.[65]

When one looks at his views on the primacy in the light of these distinctions, it would appear that he looked on this doctrine, objectively speaking, as an open question on which dissent was acceptable. Subjectively speaking, he himself had reached the point of personal conviction concern-

---

assumes the truth of the testimony contained in the fourth count of the official indictment based on Rich's report of his conversation with More. Elton takes stock of Reynolds, *An Unnoticed Document, Moreana* no. 1 (1963) 12-17, but not of the critique of Derrett's article by Brian Byron, *The Fourth Count of More's Indictment, Moreana* no. 10 (1966) 33-46. The basis of Derrett's view lies in his doubts concerning Roper's credibility as a reporter of the meeting between More and Rich. Byron argues convincingly to the value of Roper's account of the trial based in all probability on information drawn from eye-witnesses who were trained lawyers. The more common opinion in recent years until the appearance of Derrett's article had been that Rich perjured himself in his evidence given at More's trial, and that this perjured testimony was the basis of the judges' verdict. See Chambers, *Thomas More,* 322-323; Reynolds, *The Trial of St Thomas More,* 106-117. The nub of the question is whom should one believe, Roper/More or Rich and the Crown? Elton and Derrett have opted for Rich and the Crown.

[65] See above pp. 247-251 for More's treatment of this topic in a general way. For a contemporary treatment largely inspired by Aquinas, see Edward Schillebeeckx, *Revelation and Theology,* tr. N. D. Smith, London, 1967, 81-92.

ing its divine institution in 1523. Further study, far from changing his mind, had merely reinforced his opinion.

This still leaves open a further dimension to the question. Apart altogether from the *doctrinal status* of the papacy, there remained also the issue of its standing within the *canon law* of the church. As far as More was concerned there was no question on this score. The common corps of Christendom had the right to develop constitutional forms necessary for the ordering of its affairs. Given his background in medieval law More would readily have seen this in terms of the evolution of customary law as well as the enactment of statutory provisions.

Hence the somewhat complex nature of his stance on the primacy. It could be taken at two levels: one of *law,* the other of *dogma.* The question of law was simply a matter of fact. Was the Roman primacy part of the accepted legal structure of the Christian community? The question of dogma in its turn had to be viewed at two levels, the subjective and the objective.

Taking the legal standing of the papacy first, More's position was clear and unambiguous: the primacy of the Roman pontiff has the force of law throughout Christendom. This law had been implicitly and explicitly accepted throughout the Christian world from time immemorial: '...ffor that primatie is at the leist wise instituted by the corps of Christendom and for a great vrgent cause in avoiding of scysmes and corroborate by continuall succession more than the space of a thowsand yere at the leist ffor there are passed almoost a thowsand yere sith the tyme of holy Saynt Gregory.'[66] Not merely did previous generations give their consent to papal prerogative and continue to do so through the ages, but across the length and breadth of Christendom in More's own day papal authority was *de facto* established and acknowledged. This is how More put it in Harpsfield's account of his last defiant challenge to the conscience of the court which condemned him: 'And forasmuch as this Inditement is grounded vpon an Acte of Parliament directly repugnant to the lawes of God and his holye Church...it is therfore in lawe amongest christen men, insufficient to charge any christian man...this Realme, being but one member and small part of the Churche, might not make a particuler lawe disagreable with the generall lawe of Christes vniuersall Catholike Churche...and therefore am I not bounden, my Lorde, to conforme my conscience to the Councell of

---

[66] See More to Cromwell, Rogers, *Correspondence*, 498/227-231. See also More to Margaret Roper, (Tower of London, 3 June 1535), Rogers, *Correspondence*, 558/95-110. More was reporting on a conversation he had held with Cromwell in the course of which he had pointed out that a Christian is exempt from local law '...where there is a lawe of the hole corpes of Christendome to the contrarie in mater towchinge belief...'

one Realme against the generall Councell of Christendome. For of the foresaide holy Bisshopps I haue for euery Bisshopp of yours, aboue one hundred; and for one Councell or Parliament of yours (God knoweth what maner of one), I haue all the Councels made these thousande yeres. And for this one kingdome, I haue all other christian Realmes.'[67]

The argument is rhetorical rather than scientific. Nonetheless its burden is clear. The primacy of the bishop of Rome has been accepted in Christendom from time immemorial. The Act of Supremacy is out of kilter with the general law of Christendom which every Christian is bound to uphold. What Henry and his parliament have proposed is a radical and unwarranted departure from mainline Christianity. Since Maitland's work: *Roman Canon Law in the Church of England* (1898)[68] there has been little question of the continued submission of the medieval English church to Roman authority whatever the extent of its practical compromise with royal intervention. The place of the pope in the Christian scheme of things was so emphasised both in church and state that until the repeal of the Heresy Act in 1534 rejection of papal primacy was a civil offence. Moreover, possibly the strongest statement of papal prerogative in early Tudor times had come from the hand of Henry VIII himself. Consequently, in making this case, although today one might find the argument from canon law in a civil court a little weak, More was speaking from the heart of English ecclesiastical tradition as well as from an awareness of the broader European scene. From his point of view, the position of the Roman pontiff in law was both subjectively and objectively beyond dispute.

DOCTRINAL STATUS OF ROMAN PRIMACY

An analysis of More's views of the doctrinal standing of the Roman primacy calls for a certain amount of theological sophistication. In the first instance, there is little doubt that he looked on the divine institution of

---

[67] See Harpsfield, *Thomas Moore,* 193/13-196/9. See also More to Margaret Roper, loc. cit., where he explained how he had justified to Thomas Cromwell his own methods of interrogation as Lord Chancellor. These interrogations of suspect heretics usually included some questions concerning the papal primacy, '...because that at that time as well here as ellys where thorowe the corps of Christendome the Popes power was recognised for an vndoubted thinge which semeth not like a thinge agreed in this realme and the contrary taken for truthe in other realmes...'

[68] See F. W. Maitland, *Roman Canon Law in the Church of England,* London, 1898, 1-50 and passim; Pickthorn, *Early Tudor Government,* 101-108; Hughes, *The Reformation in England,* I, 196-206; R. J. Schoeck, *Canon Law in England on the Eve of the Reformation, Medieval Studies* 25 (1963) 125-147.

papal primacy as a matter of debate among theologians rather than an
unambiguous proposition of faith. On this score, he seems to have been a
little more aware of the complexities of the situation than a recent
historian, Philip Hughes, who could write concerning the 'King's Proceedings': 'It is the repudiation of the doctrine, and the fact, that the pope
is primate over the Church of Christ wherever this be found, (by divine
institution) that is the really substantial change, by the side of which all
other changes are mere detail. For here is the act by which the mass of
Englishmen cease to be what all Englishmen have been for a thousand
years nearly...'[69]

It must be said, however, that More himself alternated in mood
somewhat, emphasising at one time the weight of tradition for the Roman
primacy, and at another, recognising the existence of dissent both in past
and present. The former attitude comes through in explaining his own
personal option; the latter in his remarkable comprehension of the attitude
of those who followed another road. This theological openness on More's
part underlay his reluctance to condemn those willing to take the oath. Indeed, in one of the interviews prior to his trial, the Archbishop of Canterbury, Thomas Cranmer, almost slipped under his guard. Cranmer argued
that if More would not condemn the conscience '...of those that sware,
...it apered well, that I did not take it for a very sure thinge and a certaine
...but rather as a thinge vncertain and doubtfull.' That being the case,
Cranmer argued that More should allow his conscience to be formed by
the royal demand for submission which was beyond doubt. More was initially unsettled by this argument but recovered his balance by sticking to
his basic thesis that in his view the weight of evidence lay in favour of papal
primacy. Nonetheless he freely admitted the possibility of differing opinion, speaking of it as one of those '...matters (on which) the doctours
stande in great doubt...'[70] In a letter to his fellow prisoner Dr Nicholas

[69] See Hughes, *The Reformation in England,* I, 196. The parenthesis 'by divine institution'
has been inserted to bring out the full sense of Hughes's argument as expressed, ibid.,
199-206. 'The question at issue is...whether Catholics then believed that he is its (the
church's) head by divine appointment...'

[70] See More to Margaret Roper, (Tower of London, c. 17 April 1534), Rogers,
Correspondence, 505/92-506/116. The oath in question was the oath of succession. The in-
terview mentioned took place on the 13 April 1534. More's refusal to accept was based on its
implicit rejection of papal prerogative. Presumably this was the matter on which some
degree of doubt existed. See G. de C. Parmiter, *Saint Thomas More and the Oath, Downside
Review* 78 (1959-60) 1-13; E. E. Reynolds, *The Trial of St Thomas More,* London, 1964, 33-51;
Marc' Hadour, *L'Univers de Thomas More,* 493, who agrees with the above interpretation of
More's attitude to the oath of succession. See also More's letter to Cromwell where he
recognised that there were some who admitted the personal primacy of Peter while denying

Wilson, More described his position in such a way as to suggest that it had further matured since his interview with Cranmer in April 1534. More wrote as follows: 'Many thynges every man learned woteth well there are, in which every man ys at lyberty withowte peryll of dampnation to thyncke whiche waye hym lyste tyll the one parte be determyned for necessary to be beleved by a generall counsayle...' Apparently, he rated the primacy as one of these. Hence his conclusion: '... of no mannes consyens ellis wyll I medle but of myne owne.'[71] On account of his knowledge of Christian tradition and in spite of a certain amount of dispute on the matter, More could take no oath which implicitly or explicitly violated the principle of Roman primacy over the whole church of God including that of England.

While More then recognised that divine institution of papal prerogative could not be upheld as *objectively* outside the realm of dispute, subjectively he had little doubt on that score. He had expressed himself at some length on the subject eleven years earlier in the *Responsio* (1523). In his letter to Cromwell of 5 March 1534 he reiterated this position: 'But surely after that I had redd his Gracis boke therin, and so many other thingis as I have sene in that point by this continuaunce of these x yere synnys and more have founden in effecte the substaunce of all the holy doctors from Saynt

---

he had any authentic successors. See More to Thomas Cromwell, Rogers, *Correspondence*, 499/268-500/273; Roper to Alington, Rogers, *Correspondence*, 528/531-537: 'I am also, Margaret, of this thinge sure ynough, that of those holy doctours and saintes, which to be with God in heauen long ago no Christen man douteth, whose bookes yet at this day remayne here in mens handes, there thought some such thinges, as I thinke now. I say not that they thought all so, but surely such and so manye as will well appeare by their wryting, that I pray God geue me the grace that my soule may folow theirs.' See also G. Glez, *Primauté*, *DTC* 13, (1936), cc. 266-318. A study of the fathers must have shown More that while there was a long tradition of respect and honour for the see of Peter, not every patristic writer was explicit in his attribution of divine institution to the primacy of that see. Even Cyprian, one of More's favourites among the ancients, was not a little ambiguous on this matter. Similarly, among the moderns, he may have known that theologians of repute such as Pierre d'Ailly and Nicholas of Cusa had reservations about the divine origin of papal primacy. Not least, his close friend Erasmus considered it a creation of the Christian community, at least till 1526, if McSorley's interpretation is correct. See H. McSorley, *Erasmus and the Primacy*.

[71] See More to Dr. Nicholas Wilson, Tower of London, 1534, Rogers, *Correspondence*, 537/136-537/147. See also Roper to Alington, ibid., 528/520-526: Margaret quotes her father, '...in some of my causes I nothing doubte at all, but that though not in this realme, yet in Christendome about, of those well learned men and verteouse that are yet alyue, they be not the fewer parte that are of my minde. Besides that, that it were ye wot well possible, that some menne in this realme too, thinke not so clere the contrary, as by the othe receyued they haue sworne to saye.' This letter, composed probably in 1534, antedates that to Wilson which is more compassionate in tone to those who accept the oath. At the same time this comment of More's clearly shows his awareness of the strength of the evidence from tradition for the primacy and yet that it was not sufficient by itself to create an inescapable certitude of faith.

Ignatius, disciple to Saynt John th'Evangelist, vnto our awne dayes both
Latynis and Grekis so consonaunt and agreing in that point, and the thing
by such generall counsailis so confirmed also, that in good faith I neuer
neither redd nor herd eny thing of such effect on the tother syde, that euer
could lede me to...deny the primatie to be provided by God...'[72]

More made the same assertion on several other occasions. Writing to his
daughter Margaret from the Tower c. 17 April 1534, in explanation of his
refusal to take the oath of succession, he claimed to have in support of his
position: 'as great a counsail and a greater (than parliament)...the generall
counsail of Christendome.'[73] At a later stage, probably August 1534,
Margaret Roper repeated to her step-sister Alice Alington an account of
her conversation with her father concerning his refusal to submit. He
claimed, according to Margaret, the overwhelming support of Christian
tradition for his stand. To change course would have been unforgiveable
treachery on his part.[74]

It has been suggested by some of More's biographers that in his final
speech to the royal commissioners he lifted the veil on his inner thoughts
and exposed his private reasons for refusing the oath.[75] In fact the veil had
been lifted long before and in a way easily accessible to government. His
letter to Cromwell was as frank a statement of his position as his speech
from the dock. Hence Derrett's interpretation of this speech as a serious
attempt to escape condemnation at the hands of the court is undoubtedly
correct.[76] More put together, if his early biographers can be trusted, a
series of arguments to which he had already given vent in a variety of
places: '...And forasmuch as this Inditement is grounded vpon an Acte of
Parliament directly repugnant to the lawes of God and his holye Churche,
the supreme Gouernment of which, or (of) any part whereof, may no tem-
porall Prince presume by any lawe to take vpon him, as rightfully belonging to the Sea of Rome, a spirituall preheminence by the mouth of our
Sauiour himselfe, personally present vpon earth, onely to St Peter and his
Successours, bisshopps of the same Sea, by speciall prerogatiue
graunted...' He went on to give his reasons: the uninterrupted flow of

---

[72] See More to Cromwell, Rogers, *Correspondence,* 498/214-225.
[73] See More to Margaret Roper, (Tower of London, c. 17 April 1534), Rogers, *Correspondence,* 506/120-129.
[74] See Roper to Alington, Rogers, *Correspondence,* 528/531-537.
[75] See Bridgett, *Sir Thomas More,* who makes this implication by the manner of ordering
his narrative; Chambers, *Thomas More,* 324-327; Reynolds, *Saint Thomas More,* 346-350;
idem, *The Trial of St Thomas More,* 120-133; idem, *The Field is Won,* 367-371.
[76] See Derrett, *The Trial of Sir Thomas Moore, EHR* 79 (1964) 468. This view is supported
by Elton, *Policy and Police,* 409-410.

Christian tradition, the weight of contemporary opinion and '...all the Councels made these thousande yeres.'[77] The moment was unique, the argument familiar both to his bitterest enemies and dearest friends. Unfortunately for More, it proved unconvincing to his judges.

On the issue of the temporal power of the pope as distinct from his strictly ecclesiastical authority within the Christian community, More had serious reservations, more even it would seem than his royal master had held in 1521, if the former Lord Chancellor's testimony is to be believed. In the forementioned letter to Cromwell More claimed that he had tried to persuade Henry to tone down his presentation of papal prerogative but the latter had refused.[78] More may have been deliberately ambiguous in this assertion, allowing Cromwell to assume that the point at stake was papal primacy itself. If Roper's and Harpsfield's accounts are correct, it was mainly on the question of the political pretensions of the Roman see that More hesitated. In his discussion with the king, More reminded Henry of the content of the statute of *praemunire* as well as possible political implications of being over enthusiastic about the temporal authority of Rome. Henry's reply was to declare that he owed his imperial crown to the pope. Presumably what Henry had in mind was the fictitious *Donation of Constantine* which granted the pope temporal jurisdiction over the western isles.[79] This topic is referred to indirectly in the *Assertio* and may well have been the occasion for More's intervention.[80]

In any event, while More never openly questioned the pope's position as an Italian prince (except perhaps in *Utopia*), he showed no inclination to

---

[77] Harpsfield, *Thomas Moore*, 193/13-196/9; Roper, op. cit., 92/15-94/10.

[78] See More to Cromwell, Rogers, *Correspondence*, 498/200-214.

[79] See Harpsfield, *Thomas Moore*, 159/7-160/17; Roper, 67/20-68/23. See also H. Leclercq, *Constantin: XIII Donation de Constantin, DACL* III/2, (1914), cc. 2676-2685.

[80] See Henry VIII, *Assertio Septem Sacramentorum*, pr. Pynson, London, 1521, sig. B 4 rv, where he says that by divine right and special title all peoples, cities, kingdoms, and provinces acknowledged the authority of a foreign prelate. For Henry's imperial pretensions, see R. Koebner, *The Imperial Crown of this Realm: Henry VIII, Constantine the Great and Polydore Vergil, Bulletin of the Institute of Historical Research* 26 (1953) 29-52. Koebner argues that Henry's imperial aspirations had a basis in popular legend, namely, that the Emperor Constantine's mother Helena was the daughter of an English prince. 'So it happened that Constantine, their son, had united British Kingship with Roman emperorship.' The British link with the imperial crown was celebrated in another legend that King Arthur was descended from Constantine. This was in turn embellished by claiming that the Tudor dynasty embodied the Arthurian lineage. In this way, convenient genealogical arguments for imperial pretensions were constructed. On the score of dependence on Rome for his imperial pretensions, Henry presumably had in mind the equally mythological *Donation of Constantine* according to which Constantine had renounced his imperial claims in the west and had surrendered them to Pope Sylvester and his successors. If Henry could now claim an imperial title, it could only be with papal permission.

see his temporal power extended and even upheld the limits imposed on his pastoral jurisdiction by the statute of *praemunire*. Thus while fully committed to upholding the divine origin of the petrine office as well as its spiritual and pastoral role in the church, More was no fanatical supporter of papal intervention in strictly secular affairs.

POPE AND COUNCIL

The final point to be examined is Thomas More's position concerning the relationship between pope and general council. To recall briefly his views on the council, More held it to be the supreme law-making authority in the church. He also looked on its doctrinal decisions as binding on all the faithful and equivalent to a general consensus of believers. On occasion it could anticipate the arrival of consensus in the church at large and by its own decisions settle issues previously disputed. Such determinations by councils lawfully assembled were, according to More, binding on all parties in the debate. On the other hand only councils which were duly assembled were entitled to this kind of influence over the life and faith of the Christian community.[81] This latter phrase is worth bearing in mind in the present context. What constituted lawful assembly in terms of sixteenth century ecclesiology and constitutional theory?

Another key statement of More's calls for examination along with this. It occurs in the course of his letter to Cromwell. Having expressed the hope that Henry would do nothing '...to derogate and deny not onely the primatie of the se apostolique, but also the authorite of the generall counsailys...' he went on: '...yit neuer thowght I the Pope above the generall counsaile nor neuer have in eny boke of myn put forth among the Kyngis subgietis in our vulgare tunge, avaunced greatly the Popis authorite.'[82] This phrase concerning the relation of pope to council could be interpreted in any one of three principal ways:

1. The council is independent of the pope and superior to him.
2. The council works in harmony with the pope but is superior to him.
3. The council is coordinate with the pope and equal to him.

We shall examine each of these possibilities in turn bearing in mind the imprecise nature of More's statement of position.

The first of these possibilities is in all likelihood ruled out by More's proviso concerning the due assembly of councils. The fifteenth century

---

[81] See above pp. 247-251.

[82] See More to Cromwell, Rogers, *Correspondence*, 499/252-264.

had witnessed a running battle between papalists and conciliarists concerning the respective roles and rights of pope and council. The popes consistently upheld their privilege of convening a general council on the one hand and approving its acts on the other. The other side of the story was put by a number of conciliar theologians from Constance onwards, seeking virtual autonomy for the general assembly. This current of thought expressed itself among other ways in the breakaway councils of Basle and Pisa.[83] These precedents may well have been in the background to More's careful insistence on lawful assembly. Another current of thought militating against this hypothesis of the autonomy of councils is found in contemporary English constitutional practice. The English parliament met in the sixteenth century only when convened by the king. Its acts attained the force of law only under his seal and signature. It is not unlikely that More would have viewed conciliar procedure in a similar light, putting the pope in the place of the king.[84]

The further questions remain as to whether More considered the pope subordinate to or coordinate with the council. He was unambiguous on one point: the council may depose the pope. Indeed this was one of the hopes he held out to Henry, possibly a trifle speciously, that if a general council were convened it would depose the current pope Clement VII. (Clement died in fact in September 1534).[85] This assertion cannot be taken as implying the supremacy of council over pope in all affairs. Even unequivocal papal monarchists such as Thomas de Vio Cajetan acknowledged the right of council to depose a pope for heresy or equivalent moral dismeanour. A long canonical and theological tradition lay behind this.[86] More was merely echoing a commonplace of Christian thought in the knowledge that Clement VII was not the most saintly occupant of Peter's throne.[87]

---

[83] See above p. 250.

[84] See Chrimes, *Constitutional Ideas*, 344-349; Elton, *'The body of the whole realm'. Studies in Tudor Government* II, 28-29; 35-37; Wilkinson, *Constitutional History*, 278-294.

[85] See More to Cromwell, Rogers, *Correspondence*, 499/252-259: '...it could be no furtheraunce there vnto his Gracys cause, if his Highnes shold in hys awne realme byfore, either by lawys making, or bokys putting forth, seme to derogate and deny...the authorite of the generall counsailys to, which I veryly trust his Highnes intendeth not, ffor in the next generall counsaile it may well happen, that this pope may be deposed and a nother substituted in his rome, with whom the Kyngis Highnes may be very well content...'

[86] See Brian Tierney, *Foundations of the Conciliar Theory. The Contribution of the Medieval Canonists from Gratian to the Great Schism,* Cambridge, 1955, 56-67; 82-83; 170-176; 212-218; 227-230.

[87] See L. von Pastor, *The History of the Popes from the Close of the Middle Ages,* IX, London, 1910, 242-254, and 272-466 passim; X, 1910, 1-387 passim.

Consequently we must look elsewhere for some indication as to More's thinking on this matter. In truth it must be stated that he probably had given the question little study. As we have earlier suggested, More's interest in the council was probably less the fruit of prolonged reflection than a skilful debater's reaction to a new twist in Henry's political programme. What More has to say concerning the role and origin of conciliar authority bears more the stamp of English constitutional thought than that of strict conciliar theory. If this be true, then the relationship between pope and council may well have been envisaged by him on the analogy of that existing between king and parliament.

Unfortunately for our purposes, little is yet known of More's views on constitutional law. Two strands of his thought, however, may help to draw our understanding a little closer to the target. More was both a theorist and a practitioner of politics. Given his long standing bias towards an elective system of government it is reasonable to assume that he would have welcomed the widening of parliamentary powers brought about by the reformation parliaments even though he might have objected to the content of many of the statutes passed.[88] In practice, however, his thinking on constitutional matters as such may well have been that current in the late fifteenth and early sixteenth centuries. This position on the relationship between king and parliament has been summarised by the eminent constitutional historian, G. R. Elton, as follows: 'To the fifteenth century, influenced by the doctrine of the three estates, it was in fact obvious that Parliament consisted of the lords spiritual, the lords temporal, and the commons. The king formed no part of Parliament, which was his court; they stood to each other as the king stood to the court of Common Pleas or the King's Bench. A parliamentary sermon of 1467 stated this plainly enough when it spoke of the three estates and one further above them, the king. In 1483, Bishop Russell, drafting his address to Richard III's only

---

[88] See Huber, *Traditionsfestigkeit und Traditionskritik bei Thomas Morus*, 171-227. Huber cites an early epigram of More's on the selection of princes:
   'Alter ut eligitur populo, sic nascitur alter:
   Sors hic caeca regit, certum ibi consilium.'
See *The Latin Epigrams of Thomas More,* ed. L. Bradner and C. A. Lynch, Chicago, 1953, no. 182, p. 83. The whole of this epigram is an argument for a senatorial-elective system of government as against monarchy. In his younger days More did not think too highly of the monarchical system of government; see ibid., nos. 190, 227, and especially no. 103, p. 175: 'Any man who has command of many men owes his subjects this: he ought to have command not one instant longer than his subjects wish. Since kings, not their own masters, rule on sufferance, why are they proud?' The Utopian form of government may not have been too remote from More's real ideal.

Parliament, spoke of "three estates as principal members under one head"...and when he actually delivered himself he was more precise still in describing "this high and great court" as composed of three estates of lords spiritual and temporal and the commons. The same definition appeared in the same year in the statute affirming Richard III's title to the crown, which declared him to be king "at the request and by assent of the three estates of this realm, that is to say the Lords Spiritual and Temporal, and Commons of this land, assembled in this present Parliament.""[89]

Thus the late medieval concept of the relationship between king and parliament tended to see it as one between coordinate but distinct organs of government mutually dependent on each other. The king rules but only with the assent of the lords and commons of the land assembled in parliament. On the other hand parliament only meets when convened by the king while the legitimacy of its decisions requires his approval.

The other element in More's thought which may shed some light on his view of the general council is the emphasis he repeatedly placed on the consensus of the believing community as ultimate guide and norm to the content of faith. This conviction of his was based on his profound awareness of the action of the Holy Spirit in the mind and heart of each believer rather than on any reflected political prejudice. If the general council in More's view is the people of God gathered to decide on matters of discipline or faith, it is reasonable to assume that for him the balance of power would lie with the people over against the pope.

Without going too far into a purely hypothetical reconstruction of More's theology of council, it is not unrealistic to postulate that assumptions such as these underlay what he wrote concerning the links between pope and council. It is more than likely that in his view the balance of authority between pope and council lay with the representatives of the Christian people. It is quite clear that More was no ultramontane born out of due time. In saying that he never thought the pope above the council he clearly ruled out the papal monarchist view of council held by some theologians of his own day. He believed in the divine institution of papal primacy. But to him the church as a whole was immensely more important. The church gathered in council must of necessity be the principal mouthpiece of the unifying Spirit of God even though it might not act independently of the Roman pontiff and without his consent.

---

[89] See G. R. Elton, "*The Body of the Whole Realm*". *Parliament and Representation in Medieval and Tudor England*, Charlottesville, Va., 1969, 19-20 and passim; in *Studies in Tudor Politics* II, 1974, 32-33; Chrimes, *English Constitutional Ideas*, 81-126.

CONCLUSION

These considerations in a sense gather together many of the threads of More's thinking as revealed in the informal writings of the pre-trial period. The spiritual dimension of the church as mystically related to Christ was an ever present reality to More in these last days. This perspective provided a spiritual horizon to his passionate concern for the unity of Christendom as a religious as well as a socio-political reality. The fundamental source of this unity, in his view, was to be ascribed to the action of the Holy Spirit in promoting a communion in faith whose authentic expression is guaranteed by the consensus of believers. More saw the general council as a constitutional mechanism to enable the common corps of Christendom to resolve with ease those questions touching its common destiny. It seems likely that his late accession to conciliar theory was in part at least a pragmatic reaction to its exploitation by Henrician publicists in their effort to bolster up their master's policies.

On the primacy of the bishop of Rome, More held a dual position. He saw it in the first instance as an ecclesiastical institution established and approved by the Christian community and therefore as part of the common law of Christendom. He was a good deal less assertive concerning its doctrinal standing. He acknowledged the divine institution of the primacy to be a matter of open debate among theologians; hence a subject on which consensus had not yet been fully reached nor an indisputable conciliar decision taken. On the other hand his own reading of the evidence left him no personal option than to believe that Christ himself had given supreme authority in the church to Peter and to his successors. Hence the contrast between the firmness of his own stand on the oath of supremacy and his tolerance of those who acted differently.

Finally on the relationship between pope and council, More never thought the pope above the council. Given his predispositions in political theory, constitutional practice as well as in theology, it seems likely that he looked on pope and council as a pair in tandem, so to speak, drawing the Christian community along its path through history, but with the council as lead horse. 'As for the generall counsailis assembled lawfully....the authorite therof owght to be taken for vndowtable or ellys were there in no thing certayntie, but thorow Christendom vppon every mannys affectionate reason, all thing myght be browght fro day to day to contynuall ruffle and confusion, from which by the generall counsailis, the spirite of God assisting, every such counsaile well assembled kepeth and euer shall kepe the corps of his Catholique Chirch.'[90]

---

[90] See More to Cromwell, Rogers, *Correspondence*, 499/238-246.

CHAPTER SEVEN

SYNTHESIS

INTRODUCTION

In his approach to the question of belief raised by the reformers Sir Thomas More progressed from a casual incidental approach to the problem of the nature and order of the church to a striking awareness of its centrality in the issues raised by the Reformation—'the breast of all this battle' as he termed it. In the *Responsio ad Lutherum* his main concern had been to vindicate Henry's embattled positions on the seven sacraments. As John M. Headley so convincingly argues, it was only as an afterthought, though an afterthought which led to a rapid re-publication of his *opus,* that he began to analyse in detail his understanding of the church. On its implications so many of his other arguments rested.

Similarly in the *Dialogue Concerning Heresies* it was practical issues such as the treatment of heretics, the burning of Tyndale's new testament, the maintenance of Catholic practices such as the honouring of images and relics, pilgrimages and sacramental devotions that occupied his attention. It was when he had dealt with these questions that he realised, so to speak, that he had committed himself to an ecclesiology and felt constrained to develop it as grounding the rest of his argument. It was only with the *Confutation of Tyndale's Answer* that More acknowledged the full importance of the role of the church in relation to faith. He now saw it as the kernel of debate. If this problem could be settled, so it seemed to him, the other pieces of the jig-saw would fit relatively easily into place.

Ironically it was the development of a fully articulated view on the nature and authority of the church, of its role in relation to divine revelation, and specifically its function in the formation of conscience of the individual believer which provided More with a solid intellectual basis for the final critical decision of his life. Arguments carefully drawn up while in a position of privilege to counter the intrusions of continental reformers eventually brought him to a position where he could himself be condemned for sedition by the courts of his own land. Surely one of the cruellest tricks history has played on one who had aspired to guide its course.

In the ensuing presentation of More's principal persuasions concerning the church of Christ his views are presented in a synthetic fashion, creating a unity not fully evident to the cursory reader of his works. At the same

time a genetic perspective will be maintained, seeking to point out how the
main planks of his platform were shaped in the course of his major excur-
sions into the theology of the church. As it was mainly in relation to revelation and faith that More dealt with ecclesiological issues, it is from this
standpoint that his thought will be summarised in the following sequence:

1.   The nature of revelation, its reception and elaboration by the
     Christian community.
2.   The inner life of the church of Christ and its visible structures.
3.   The role of the church in mediating divine revelation.
4.   The signs of Christ's church.

I. REVELATION

The nature of revelation

Sir Thomas More never fully tackled the problem of the nature of divine
revelation but rather assumed it as a fact which needed no analysis. In the
Responsio and in the *Dialogue Concerning Heresies* he showed himself aware
that the concept of revelation is a good deal broader than that of inspired
scripture. Yet it was only in passing that he referred to the plurality of
ways in which this divine truth is transmitted. In the *Confutation* he arrived
at a formal statement about the nature of revelacion and the manner of its
communication: '...revelacion is in generall, the shewing of a thing by
God vnto hys creature, eyther immediatelye or by a meane, in some such
wyse that the same creature by his onely naturall powers, should either not
at all, or not so fullye wythout that shewyng haue attayned the perceiuing
therof.'[1] Revelation then is the making known to man of some information
or understanding of reality which he might not possess by reason of his
own powers. This divine truth, God's word, is prior to the church and is
the norm which regulates and guides its activities.

This word has been communicated to the members of the church, initially the apostolic community, in two ways: 'immediatelye or by a
meane'. It is crucial to grasp the significance of the first of these ways for
an appreciation of Sir Thomas More's approach to Christian truth. He
continually stressed the immediacy of divine revelation to the church, not
merely the church of the apostles but the church of all time. Ultimately it
was on this principle that he based his advocacy in respect of many
elements of traditional belief and practice not explicitly founded on
scripture.[2]

---

[1] *Confutation* II, 996/10-14.
[2] *Confutation* I, 249/9-16; 339/25-32; II, 889/24-890/11.

The modes of revelation

In the *Dialogue Concerning Heresies* More had already pointed to a real duality in the means of divine communication.[3] These mysteries are revealed in two ways: firstly, by the Lord's '...blessyd mouth/thorowe the eres of his appostles and dyscyples'; secondly, 'as it semeth it was inwardely infused in to saynt Peter his harte/by the secrete inspyracyon of god/without eyther wrytynge or any outwarde worde' (that Christ was the Son of the living God). This inner revelation was confirmed by Christ saying: 'Thou arte blessyd Symon the sonne of Johan/for neyther flesshe nor blode hathe reueled and shewed this to the/but my father that is in heuen' (Mt 16, 15-17).[4] More took the first form of revelation and its transmission for granted and did not expand largely upon it.

The latter form calls for more explanation. More made of it the paradigm of one of the principal modes of divine revelation in the subsequent history of the church. For though the apostles shared the secrets made known to them by God with other men both in spoken and in written words, God himself continues to address the individual believer in his consciousness and to make his secrets known without book or teacher. So Thomas More believed.

The Transmission of Revelation

1. *The record of revelation: scripture*

In respect of the written record of revelation, More ascribed the first place to scripture.[5] The study of scripture had been one of his earliest loves. Part of his contribution as a humanist to the scholarship of his day had been to recall his fellow-scholars to a study of the scriptures in their original languages as the basis of theological scholarship. In the course of his controversies, however, he was obliged to define the limitations of an exclusively biblical approach to revelation. The first of these boundaries has been marked out above in speaking of the on-going possibility of a direct address by God to the mind of the believer. The second boundary lay within the bible itself. The gospels themselves testify, More repeatedly noted, that not everything that Christ said or did was recorded in the new testament (Jn 21, 25).[6] Hence the intrinsic possibility of transmitting

---

[3] *Dialogue* xlv vH-xlvi rB, Campbell, 95-96.

[4] Loc. cit.

[5] *Dialogue,* xxxix vF, Campbell, 82: '...of dyunyte reken I the best parte to be conteyned in holy scrypture.'

[6] See *Responsio,* 98/3-22, tr. 99/3-27. See also ibid., 98/22-100/1, tr. 99/28-101/2; 88/5-6, tr. 89/5-7; 88/16-22, tr. 89/19-27; *Dialogue,* xlv vH-xlv rB, Campbell, 95-96; *Confutation* II, 996/15-35.

revelation by some other method and consequently of apprehending some element of the divine message not recorded in scripture. It was on this postulate of the 'material insufficiency of scripture' that More built his defence of the sacraments and other traditional practices.

2. *The record of revelation: the living faith of the church.*

In proposing a second manner of coming to the knowledge of divine mysteries More's first recourse was to what he termed 'the gospel in the heart.' Greatly influenced by Augustine, he continually stressed the abiding presence of God in the church.[7] This was a constant refrain from the *Responsio* onwards. He cited repeatedly certain groups of texts, notably Jn 16, 13 and Mt 28, 20, to which he often added Ps 67, 7 in an Old Latin reading. With these he associated Jer 31, 33 and Heb 8, 10. Revelation did not cease with the apostolic church. God is present to the individual believer and writes his law in his heart, i.e. reveals the law directly to each individual member of the community. This inner revelation manifests itself in consciousness in the faith of the Christian people. The church of Christ makes and formulates its act of faith under the impulsion of the abiding Spirit. It thereby gives expression to what the Spirit has spoken in the inner heart of each believer.

While the individual believer may err in not giving full or adequate expression to the message written by the Spirit on his heart, the collective consciousness of the church is protected from error. The role of the Spirit is not only to reveal God to the disciple of Christ. He leads the whole church into truth. Most particularly he leads the church to a consensus about divine truth. The Spirit of God is not a Spirit of contradiction but one of unity who makes men of one mind to dwell in one house. (Remember More's translation of Ps 67, 7.) Thus where unanimity or better, consensus is found, this is a sure sign that the Spirit has spoken to the members of the church. This testimony may well bear a content over and above that of the scriptures.[8]

The response of the believer to divine revelation in whatever form it reaches him is faith. The living faith of the community is symbolised in the

---

[7] *Responsio*, 100/3-28, tr. 101/2-34; 100/25-28, tr. 101/31-34; '...the substaunce of our fayth itselfe/whiche oure lorde sayd he wolde wryte in mennes hartes/...', *Dialogue*, xlv vH ff., Campbell, 95 ff; *Confutation* I, 45/6-15; 332/10-22; II, 752/30-753/28.

[8] *Responsio*, 100/4-8, tr. 101/5-10; 90/1-4, tr. 91/1-4; 232/6-10, tr. 233/8-13; 116/6-11, tr. 117/7-12; 190/7-11, tr. 191/10-13. ibid., 128/3-12, tr. 129/3-14; *Dialogue* lxxiiii vG, Campbell, 157-158; ibid., lxxv rA, Campbell, 158; ibid., liiii vE, Campbell, 111; *Confutation* I, 248/11-24; 381/26-35.

concrete life of the Christian community, in its worship, institutions and activities. Both the living practice of the church and the monuments which record its past testify to what the Spirit has written on the hearts of the faithful. Hence long-standing practices of devotion are to be treated with greatest respect as possible bearers of such a divine communication. The writings of the fathers are a particularly valuable index to this mode of revelation. The authenticity of their lives is a guarantee of the fidelity of their record of the Spirit's intimations. Not that any one father on his own account is to have his writings put on a par with holy writ. But when a constant current of thought is found among the fathers of all ages and all churches, this is a reliable indication of the Spirit's influence. It points to the fact that he has been infusing his wisdom into human hearts and guiding their efforts to formulate these insights in a consciously rational fashion.[9]

3. The record of revelation: oral tradition

The dominant concept of tradition in More's thought is that expressed in the preceding paragraph, as in his view the primary mode for the transmission of revelation and its preservation in the church is the gift of the Spirit to each one of the faithful. This is notably the case in the *Responsio* where, although he uses the *partim-partim* formula eventually rejected by Trent, he opposed to scripture not so much a hidden oral tradition as the ongoing revelation of God to his people in the gospel written on their hearts.[10]

In the *Dialogue Concerning Heresies* he was more closely pressed on matters of religious practice. Here we see a new emphasis on another mode of the transmission of revelation, namely the informal way in which any society transmits by a type of cultural osmosis its folk ways, values and customs to its most recent candidates. At the back of this hypothesis is the assumption drawn from Jn 21, 25 that Christ had done many things which went unrecorded by the evangelists. Thus More postulated that many teachings of the Lord became part of the folk tradition of the Christian community. This is not the Cabalistic view, traces of which can be found in both Fisher and Colet, of a secret tradition handed down among initiates, but rather a view of tradition similar to that underlying, for example, the acceptance of

---

[9] *Confutation,* I, 47/31-48/5; 62/7-10; II, 589/25-30; *Dialogue,* lxxx rA, Campbell, 169; ibid., xlvii rCD, Campbell, 98.

[10] See Headley, *Responsio,* 733-739 for an excellent account of More's thought on this point.

customary law as part of the law of the land. Tradition is handed on not by a chosen few as the Cabalists held but by the whole community.

More did not speak of an 'oral tradition' as such, but of 'tradicions delyuered by theuangelistes and apostles of Christ vnto the churche...', '...whych from hande to hande hath ben taken and kepte from Crystes dayes and hys apostles hytherto.'[11] Examples of such traditions to which he referred are the assumption of the virgin Mary, accepted positions relating to the sacraments as well as several of the devotional practices of his day. More himself did not enlarge on the manner in which these traditions are transmitted. Given his legal background in common law as well as his pronounced sense of history, it can be inferred that he had in mind the passing on of values and conventions in the socialisation procedures which characterise most living communities. The two principal testimonies to these traditions are the writings of the fathers on the one hand and the living practice of the church on the other. This social concept of tradition appears in the *Confutation* side by side with the pneumatically based one described above.

Although the predominant influences on More in respect of this position were probably his own innate and cultivated sense of history as well as his feeling for the cumulative weight of common law provision and jurisprudence, he may also have been influenced both by Colet and Fisher. The first of these in particular was a disciple of Reuchlin. He admitted the existence within the Christian community of a neo-cabalistic tradition, that is a secret oral tradition going back to apostolic times which would justify many contemporary practices having little evident foundation in scripture. Pico della Mirandola, one of the preceptors of More's youth, had been a fervent disciple of the *Cabala*.[12] More probably had too much common-sense to adopt such a recondite theory. Nonetheless, the trend of his thinking may well have been influenced by his friends. Henry VIII, moreover, in his *Assertio* had also attached great importance to extra-biblical tradition, an indication that this view was current in the intellectual circle in which More moved. Hence over and above the practical needs of controversy there were many influences close to his experience to explain his insistence on the importance of this particular folio in the many-sided register of divine revelation.

---

[11] See *Confutation* II, 996/19-20; I, 389/31-35; see also *Dialogue*, xiii rA, Campbell, 27.

[12] See K. Schubert, *Kabbala, LTK* V, 1233-1236; Blau, *The Christian Interpretation of the Cabala in the Renaissance,* 14-16; 19-30; 33-36; Secret, *Les Kabbalistes Chrétiens,* 24-43; 228-229; Colet, *In ecclesiasticam hierarchiam,* 56; 110; 112; 135; Fisher, *The sermon agayn Martin luuther, English Works,* 336.

4. Development of doctrine

The notion of the development of doctrine has become a familiar theme in theological writing of the last hundred years. It is perhaps a little surprising to find it so clearly marked out in the controversial theology of the sixteenth century, if only in an embryonic way. Sir Thomas More tended to combine two distinct elements in his treatment of these issues, linking together and perhaps not adequately distinguishing what may best be described as on-going revelation through the inspiration of the Holy Spirit and the development of doctrine through the discursive activity of Christian thinkers. In the first instance development takes place through a direct infusion of insights, in the second it occurs as a result of prolonged thought and reflection. This is essentially a rational process though carried out facing the horizon of faith and under the guidance of the Holy Spirit. Thus in general it appears that the message conveyed by the Spirit to the Christian community is not something static, permanent, unchanging, but rather dynamic, growing, evolving with the course of history.

In the *Responsio*[13] More speaks of the abiding presence of the Spirit leading the church towards a deeper appreciation and understanding of the revelation given in Christ. Here the message is figured as static but the church's understanding as progressing under the guidance of the Spirit. In the *Dialogue Concerning Heresies* on the other hand he speaks of many things 'not all at once reuelyd and understanden in the scrypture/but by sondry tymys and agys mo thyngys... by god vnto his chyrche dysclosyd.'[14] He offers as an example of this new disclosure the development of the Christological dogmas in the Nicene and Athanasian creeds. At least *vi verborum* this suggests an ongoing revelation in the church, not completed with the adoption of the canon of scripture but going on through the ages. This theme is not elaborated at this juncture while the examples offered at least in the light of present knowledge point more to the development of theology and of doctrine than of further revelation.

In the *Confutation* More brings out both aspects clearly. He underlines the role of the Spirit guiding the church into further truth. He speaks of the Spirit imparting his truth in a way which is tantamount to further revelation. This activity of the Spirit is complemented on the one hand by the activity of the prophets and on the other by the continuing intellectual activity of the church's thinkers, slowly spinning out the full implications

---

[13] See *Responsio*, 100/3-7, tr. 101/5-9.
[14] *Dialogue*, xlvii rCD, Campbell, 97-98.

of what is already contained in the twin storehouses of scripture and the gospel written in men's hearts.[15]

More did not specifically discuss the scriptural canon. Reading between the lines it may be said that, although the canon was only fully formulated in the Catholic Church by the Council of Trent, More accepted that the canon of scripture was closed in the apostolic era.[16] However, revelation for him was a much broader concept than inspired writing, broader even than the idea of private revelation made to charismatic individuals. Every Christian of every age is the recipient of direct divine revelation. Even though the canon of inspired scripture is closed, revelation is not. This is of course a rather problematic doctrine leaving the Christian community open to fraudulent claims from self-styled divine oracles. The solution on More's terms lay in the doctrine of consensus which he regarded as a sure touchstone of religious authenticity.

Conclusion

Revelation, then, although it was a concept More fully formulated only towards the end of the *Confutation,* includes a broader range of reality than that of inspired scripture. Revelation is God's word given to his church both through the speech and actions of Jesus Christ and the inward communication of his Spirit to individual believers. The record of revelation is firstly the scriptures and secondly the tradition of the church. In the latter case there is also duality. More spoke on the one hand of a living tradition of truths 'handed down' from one generation to the next. But on the other hand he spoke of God's word given directly to the church of each generation. This concept itself is broader than tradition and might be better treated as revelation itself. This revelation may be given to specially chosen individuals as was the case with the prophets. In a fuller sense it is given to each believer. Each one is taught directly by the Spirit of God. The gospel the Spirit writes in the heart of each believer is a testimony to the whole of divine revelation. It is, moreover, the basis for an ongoing development of the church's awareness of divine truth, both in the rational and systematic unfolding of what has been already revealed as well as the Spirit-inspired communication of further enlightenment.

The consensus of the community is the authentic sign of the action of the revealing Spirit behind any particular formulation of doctrine or institution. Hence the importance of the writings of the fathers testifying

---

[15] See *Confutation* I, 248/11-24; 337/21-31; II, 996/20-23.
[16] At least there is no evidence to the contrary.

to the expression of the community's faith throughout time as well as documenting traditions handed on through the socio-historical institutions of the Christian people.

Within More's approach to the sources of revelation a certain shift took place in the course of his career as controversialist. In his humanist period he attached the greatest importance to the inspired scriptures, albeit as interpreted by the fathers. In his *Responsio ad Lutherum,* while in no way denying the importance of scripture, he evolved the notion of the 'gospel in the heart' as the primary locus of divine truth. In the *Dialogue Concerning Heresies* and even more decisively in the *Confutation* he came to the conclusion that this was the primary mode of divine revelation,[17] while recognising at the same time the key significance of social tradition as a means of transmitting earlier revelation. Scripture, he asserted, must always be read in the context of the Christian community, more particularly in the light of what the Spirit has said to the church of this and of all generations. The primary and controlling mode of divine revelation is not, therefore, the written word of scripture but the transcendental word imprinted on the inner consciousness of each believer and attested to with certainty by the common faith of the community: '...in the same maner remayneth wryten in the same chyrche by the same spyryte, a ryghte rule lefte by god, techynge the chyrche to enterprete and vnderstand the wrytynge that hys holy apostles haue wryten after, & hys holy prophetes haue also wryten before.'[18]

II. CHRIST'S CHURCH

The structure of the church

The analysis of Sir Thomas More's concept of revelation and of its transmission in the Christian community has inevitably involved a consideration of the Christian people as primarily passive recipients of divine

---

[17] See *Confutation* I, 45/6-15; 332/10-15; II, 752/30-753/28; I, 381/26-35.

[18] *Confutation* II, 753/20-23. Flesseman-Van Leer, *The Controversy about Ecclesiology,* 86 places the main divide between More and Tyndale in the doctrine of faith. On this subject there was a strong verbal disagreement between the two men. The case could be argued with hindsight that the disagreement was one more of words than facts, of emphasis rather than essential faith since, if analysed, the traditional doctrine of salvation by implicit faith upheld by More is not too far removed from the Lutheran doctrine of justification by faith. On the other hand, I believe, much more could be made of a radical division in their respective concepts of revelation, More favouring a fluid, pneumatic, ongoing intervention by the divine in the minds of believers; Tyndale identifying revelation with holy writ, a static message fixed for all time.

confidences. Now we move on to an examination of the more active role of the community in relation to the message entrusted to it. Before doing this, however, we must look in some detail at the character of this people so favoured by God and entrusted by him with an onerous mission. This will include a study of the origins of this community, its future, its inner life as well as its visible constitution.

Definition

In the *Baravellus* edition of the *Responsio* More was hesitant in speaking explicitly of the church. By the time he came to produce his revised *Rosseus* version he had inserted into the H gathering a substantial treatment of ecclesiological issues in large measure concerned with the question of authority in the church including the papacy. He incorporated into this a number of assertions identifying what he believed to be the church of Christ. This he described as '...the common multitude of those who profess the name and faith of Christ, even though their life may not correspond to their profession...the church is this multitude which we all know now by the name of the Christian people, almost all of whom acknowledge the primacy of the pontiff...[19] At this stage More did not press the distinctive qualities of what he considered to be the true church. He was content to point out that the signs Luther spoke of as identifying the church of Christ were equally applicable to the common multitude of Christian people.[20] He included the papacy in his description of the church but was not unambiguous in making of it an essential element and distinguishing characteristic. The phrase: 'almost all of whom acknowledge the primacy of the pontiff' suggests some lurking doubt about its real position rather than a clear-cut affirmation of its necessity. In the *Responsio*, at a time when Luther's followers were still a dissident body within the orbit of the 'common corps of Christendom', this description was given from the vantage point of a universally recognised institution with a history extending back for hundreds of years. The church of Christ was so self-evident to More at this time that it needed little definition.

When he came to compose the *Dialogue Concerning Heresies* (1529), he was confronted with a recognisable body of dissidents gradually assuming the position and organisational structure of a distinct ecclesiastical organism

---

[19] See *Responsio*, 172/1-10, tr. 173/1-11.

[20] *Responsio*, 172/12-14, tr. 173/14-16: '...all these signs...apply to this very church which he says is not true and which he calls papist...'

in several German principalities as well as in parts of Switzerland.[21] More could envisage a similar situation arising in Britain. Hence the need for more precise definition of the church. This occurs several times throughout the *Dialogue Concerning Heresies*. Perhaps the best statement is as follows: '...this company and congregayon of all these nacyons/that without faccyons taken/and precysyon from the remanaunt/professe the name and fayth of Cryst...and this hath begon at cryst/and hath had hym for theyr hed, and saynt Peter his vycar after hym the hed under hym/and alway synce the successours of hym contynually...'[22] Elsewhere More identified this visible body with the true vine and its branches of which Christ speaks in Jn 15, 1-8, as well as the mystical body described in Paul's epistles (1 Cor 12, 12-27; Rm 12, 4-5 etc.). Thus in More's conception of the church there was no disjunction between the charismatic and institutional aspects.

There is a slight shift in emphasis from the *Responsio*. Instead of speaking of 'this multitude' of individuals, as it were, he now speaks of 'this company and congregacyon of all these nacyons...' Although this type of language with its national undertones has a background in the new testament,[23] in the historical context as well as the context of More's own perspective it seems to refer concretely to the historical peoples of Europe. In this respect it places his view of the church within that stream of thought which reached its first institutional expression in the Council of Constance, where the gathering of the universal church was organised explicitly on the basis of national representation rather than on dioceses or provinces.[24] The same movement of thought underlay the Gallican movement in France. It had a good deal to do with the nationalistic aspects of the con-

---

[21] By June 1525 the Peasants' Rising had been crushed. The Diet of Speier held in June 1526 saw the beginnings of the implementation of the principle *cujus regio illius religio*. Saxony, Hesse, Prussia, Schleswig-Holstein, Silesia, and a number of smaller provinces as well as cities supported the evangelical movement and allowed either a take-over of established church institutions by evangelicals or the setting up of distinct evangelical congregations within their borders. This movement was reinforced by the Diet of Speier held three years later in February 1529. In Switzerland the cantons of Zurich, Bern and Basel had opted for the reformation movement under Zwingli's inspiration. See Atkinson, *Luther*, 278-282; Grimm, *Reformation Era*, 188-189; Lortz, *The Reformation in Germany*, II, 31-91.

[22] *Dialogue*, lxviii vG, Campbell, 143-144.

[23] See Apoc 5, 9: '...for thou wast slain and by thy blood didst ransom men for God from every tribe and tongue and people and nation, and hast made them a kingdom and priests to our God...' See also Apoc 10, 11; 11,9; 13, 7 etc.

[24] See Fliche et Martin, *Histoire de l'Église* 14, 173-174; J. Gill, *The Representation of the 'Universitas Fidelium' in the Councils of the Conciliar Period* in G. J. Cuming and Derek Barker, *Councils and Assemblies, Papers Read at the Eighth Summer Meeting and the Ninth Winter Meeting of the Ecclesiastical History Society*, Cambridge, 1971, 182-188.

tinental reforming movement and was to exercise a pronounced influence on the development of the *ecclesia anglicana* as a national entity.

It is interesting to notice More's ability to retain this particular datum within an orthodox view of the universal church. It is significant also to notice his concession to the defections from this unity, especially one assumes, among the German nation: '...without faccyons taken/and precysyon from the remanaunt.'[25] With all this, his attitude towards the papacy had grown firmer. Instead of speaking of the Roman pontiff as acknowledged by almost all Christian people, he spoke unambiguously of Peter as vicar of Christ, and under Christ, as head of the Church: 'and alway synce the successours of hym contynually...' He does not speak here of divine institution of the primacy but there is a clear implication of belief that the primacy belongs to the apostolic and therefore abiding constitution of the church.

The general direction of More's thought was maintained in the *Confutation*. Here, in response to a thesis of Tyndale's identifying the church of Christ with the church of the elect, More examined systematically a variety of possible meanings to the word *church*: a building; the clergy; the local church of a particular place; all those that call themselves Christian; the elect; synods and councils; the rulers and governors of Christian peoples; the pope and his generation; the pope and all Christian nations. More did not reject the validity of any one of these usages except when the phrase 'the pope and his generacyon' was used to signify either the pope and his kindred, or the pope and his cardinals. Neither of these instances warrant the use of the term *church*. On the other hand if it were used to designate the pope and the Christian nations 'not being cut off nor cast out for their obstinate malice', it was quite acceptable.[26]

Indeed this last was the preferred sense of the word in More's own vocabulary as it pointed to '...such onely people as be crysten people, and them not in one cytye onely, but that hole nomber of euery cytye, towne, and village thorow out all the hole world...there is of the chyrch no sygnifycacyon neyther more great nor more comen...'[27] In this affirmation he combined two views of the church, one based on a sense of Christendom made up of nations and indeed national churches with another which focused on a multitude of individuals who taken together make up the universal church.

---

[25] *Dialogue*, loc. cit.
[26] *Confutation* I, 146/12-25; 387/5-30; 147/2-17; 131/20-30; 164/25-29; II, 734/29-31.
[27] *Confutation* I, 147/2-17; 361/34-362/2; 398/27-399/10.

Inner constitution

With regard to the foundation of the church by Christ, More had no doubt whatsoever. This was something he affirmed as an almost self evident truth in each one of his writings.[28] In the *Responsio* he singled out as the moment of institution Christ's promise to Peter in Mt 16, 18. In his later works he did not feel compelled to indicate any particular point of time at which Christ set up his community of disciples.

Of greater concern to More was his conviction of the abiding presence of God with his church.[29] This is one of the poles which defines his position on a great number of other issues. It was axiomatic in each one of his treatises as he based on it his concept of revelation, the fidelity of the church to its founder and mission, its indefectibility and intrinsic holiness. He presented this proposition through the medium of a number of biblical images. He repeatedly cited Christ's promise in Mt 28, 20: 'I am with you always, to the close of the age.' He turned often to the Johannine promises of the gift of the Spirit: Jn 15, 26 and Jn 16, 13, while referring in general on many occasions to chapters 14, 15 and 16 of John's gospel. In this connection, especially in terms of the unifying effect of the Spirit he frequently made use of Ps 67, 7, though in an Old Latin version,[30] as well as Jer 31, 31-34 as cited in Heb 8, 12. Moreover, he applied to the church biblical images of the divine presence, such as the pillar of cloud and the pillar of fire (Ex 33, 10; 14, 24) from the old testament; the vine and its branches from John, (Jn 15, 1-8) and the mystical body theme from St Paul (1 Cor 12, 12 etc). In spite of much evidence to the contrary in the everyday life of the church around him, not least the dubious witness of his predecessor as chancellor, Cardinal Wolsey, Sir Thomas More saw the inner reality of the church in terms of an abiding divine presence binding its members into a trans-empirical and trans-historical communion. His view of the social reality of the church he lived in was invariably caught up in this perspective. Hence the depth of compassion he showed for those guilty of the most reprehensible behaviour. Only deliberate heresy, which for him meant a conscious repulsion of the divine offer of grace, fell beyond the range of his merciful eye.

---

[28] *Responsio*, 88/22-28, tr. 89/27-33; 190/2-11, tr. 191/4-13; 190/30-192/5, tr. 191/37-193/6; 238/24-27, tr. 239/26-29; *Dialogue*, xxxi vE, Campbell, 65; ibid., xxxiii rvCD, Campbell, 69. *Confutation* I, 345/15-346/22.

[29] *Responsio*, 100/3-7, tr. 101/5-9; *Dialogue*, xxxv vE-G, Campbell, 74; *Confutation* II, 755/30-34; I, 332/16-37.

[30] See the discussion of this by Headley, *Responsio*, 823, and at greater length, Marius *Confutation* III, 1352-1353.

For More, then, this divine presence was a continuing guarantee of the
holiness of the church. Christ cleanses it in baptism, sanctifies it by the gift
of the Spirit, and thereby pledges it final perfection in glory. In the *Responsio* More affirmed little concerning the essential holiness of the church.
Ironically, he was more concerned to establish its sinfulness, i.e. the com-
patibility of its foundation and continuing guidance by Christ with the
weakness of its members. In the *Dialogue Concerning Heresies* and likewise in
the *Confutation* he added a further line of argument to his case. He pointed
on the one hand to the essential holiness of the church because of the
presence of Christ with it, citing Eph 5, 26-27, a favourite text of both
Tyndale and Barnes, to argue that one day the church of Christ would be
indeed without spot or wrinkle when it enters upon its reward in glory.[31]

It was this basic assumption concerning the divine presence working
through the human organism of the Christian community that enabled
him to integrate within his synthesis the presence of moral evil among its
members. Luther, and following him Tyndale and Barnes, had stressed
the holiness of the church of Christ. Their manner of speaking was
somewhat misleading, creating the impression, at least in so unsym-
pathetic a listener as More that the true believer was without sin. In fact
the reformers recognised the possibility of sin in the members of Christ's
predestinate church, though not the sin against the Spirit. Men commit
sin not in so far as they are subject to Christ but subject to the flesh. Hence
their sin can neither be ascribed to Christ nor to his body, the church. In
this sense the church on earth is without sin.[32]

It is questionable whether More ever understood this particular viewpoint due to a different focus in his thought. The reformers tended to
locate the centre of gravity of Christian life within the individual. More on
the other hand had a more communitarian vision of the church. Whatever
affected each member affected the body as a whole. Corresponding to this,
a man was a member of the church with the whole of his being, mind and
heart, body and soul. If a Christian sinned he did not lose church-
membership. On the other hand, the evil he committed was in a certain
sense attributable to the church. Hence his willingness in the *Responsio* to
admit the possibility of sin within the church.[33] Indeed in his eyes it was

[31] *Dialogue*, lxviii vE, Campbell, 143; ibid., lxiiii rA, Campbell, 133; *Confutation* II,
852/6-22; 855/2-17.

[32] Tyndale, *Answer,* 30-33.

[33] *Responsio*, 142/19-152/14, tr. 143/23-153/12; 200/15-30, tr. 201/16-32; 202/3-17, tr.
203/3-20.

too real an occurrence to be glossed over. He clearly recognised this in the *Dialogue Concerning Heresies* and the *Confutation.*[34]

At the same time he was careful to insist that although evil affects the church here and now, such sinfulness does not invalidate the official actions of those holding and exercising authority in the community.[35] This was a recognised position which had received a great deal of attention in medieval theology due specifically to widespread abuses on the one hand and the radicals' reaction against them on the other. This latter movement had reached its most extreme expression, perhaps, in Wyclif's doctrine carried on within Lollardy, denying even elementary human rights to those who had fallen from grace.[36] More's realistic view comprehended both sanctity and sin among both office-holders and rank and file members. He was not as concerned as Luther was with the coexistence of evil and grace. Paradoxically, More adopted a biblical approach to the whole matter, accepting as a temporary phenomenon the existence of evil which in the course of the history of salvation of each individual and the community as a whole will eventually be abolished by the saving intervention of the Lord.[37]

Closely linked with these ideas was his approach to predestination and divine election. The only practical meaning of the word *elect* in his eyes was in reference to those enjoying the gift of divine grace at the present moment. Their persistence in grace is always at risk and must be earned by godly living. Election is not definitive till death. Any attempt to limit the concept of the church in time to the number of those who will finally reach eternal beatitude must be resisted. The church in history is always made up of good and bad alike. Because of the divine promises it will endure for all time whatever the vagaries of its members.[38]

Membership in the church

This was not a matter More discussed at any length in the *Responsio*. In the *Dialogue* he insisted on the necessity of faith for membership in the

---

[34] *Dialogue*, lxviii rB, Campbell, 142; ibid., lxviii rD, Campbell, 142; *Confutation*, 1007/1-1021/33 and numerous other places.

[35] See *Responsio*, 132/33-134/4, tr. 133/38-135/4; 134/23-136/1, tr. 135/27-137/2; 140/14-21, tr. 141/16-21.

[36] See for example Wyclif, *De ecclesia*, ed. Loserth, 89-90; 399-400; 441-442; 515. On Wyclif's views see Leff, *Heresy in the Later Middle Ages*, II, 520-526. On the 'spiritualist' current of thought, see Congar, *Ecclésiologie*, 198-214.

[37] *Dialogue*, lxviii vE, Campbell, 143; *Confutation* I, 392/26-393/2; II, 851/24-855/17.

[38] 'tyll domysday/and after in heuen eternally', *Dialogue*, lvii rB, Campbell, 118.

church.[39] In the *Confutation* he examined in some detail the conditions for acceptance into the Christian community.[40] He extended these to include not only faith but also the desire at least for baptism, though regarding the actual reception of the sacrament as the normal mode of entry. Faith in the case of infants is conferred in the ritual of initiation by God himself. In the case of adults faith is given by the Spirit prior to the sacramental celebration. Membership is not confined to those in grace. Sinners may and do belong to the Christian community. So also do catechumens who have not yet received the sacrament. Unbelievers, open heretics, and schismatics are excluded. More did not explicitly discuss the fate of those who through no fault of their own do not realise the significance of the Incarnation. He did restrict his definition of the church to those who have some knowledge of Christ to the point of desiring to be baptised. Whether he restricted the possibility of salvation to this number is not clear from his writings,[41] though his friend Erasmus unequivocally opened the gates of heaven to good pagans.

The believing Christian must approach the church with faith. Faith, as understood by Sir Thomas More, is a gift of God. It is given in baptism to infants; through the Spirit to adults aspiring to be Christian.[42] Such faith goes through two distinct stages in its process of crystallisation. In the initial stage of conversion a 'worldly assent' is given, one posited on tangible reasons in the life and witness of Christian people. Ultimately, however, this must be superseded by an unconditional assent to revealed truth. Such a commitment is not based on the laws of evidence or on deductive reasoning but on a movement of the mind which arises from a divine impulse and can have no other source.

This faith is at heart faith in God. It has God as its object. But in concrete existence it becomes faith in God-dwelling-in-his-church, and ultimately faith in God-acting-through-his-church. God enlightens the believer by revealing his truth to him and enlivens him by conferring his grace upon him. It is this faith in God-dwelling-in-his-church that underlies the acceptance by the believer of further guidance from the church in relation to the content of faith. Behind the empirical guidance of the church More perceived the hand of the Spirit leading the disciples of

---

[39] *Dialogue,* lxiiii vE, Campbell, 134.

[40] *Confutation,* II, 942/17-20; 669/11-14; I, 417/27-33. I, 429/4-21; II, 852/9-22.

[41] *Dialogue,* lxiiii rA, Campbell, 133; *Confutation* II, 942/17-20: '...euery person in euery other parte of the worlde that is chrystened or longeth to be chrystened & consenteth with that chyrche in fayth is a member of the same...'

[42] *Confutation* II, 768/11-30.

Christ towards the fulness of truth. The individual believer is called on to participate in this movement through the concrete expression of his faith in life and word. This living expression of faith manifests the gospel which has been written in his heart. In the last analysis, however, implicit unformulated divinely aroused faith is sufficient for membership in the Christian community.[43]

Visible organisation

The community thus created by the divine call to faith is not an amorphous mass of people. It has visible organisation and shape. A large part of the *Responsio* was given over to a defence of one of the corner stones of the institution of Christian life and worship, namely the sacrament of order. In recognising the origin of this sacrament with Christ Sir Thomas More implicitly accepted the division of Christian people into two orders, the 'temporalty and spiritualty'.[44] Coupled with this division went the establishment of local congregations around individual bishops, their sub-division in parishes and other structures of ecclesiastical life. More did not develop a detailed rationale for this aspect of Christian corporate existence. It was rather something that he assumed as part of a given reality received from earlier ages and canonised by the guarantee of the Holy Spirit's guidance. There is little trace in his vision of the church of the influence of either Roman canon law or Hellenistic political philosophy such as can be found in the work of contemporary scholastic theologians and canon lawyers alike. This was typified in More's view of the recipient of holy orders. The dominant image is the biblical one of pastor, who must care for his flock and tend it with love.[45]

In the *Dialogue* the same positions were upheld. The need for authority in the church was maintained and while, significantly, More saw the mission of preaching as conferred on the entire community of faith, he attributed special responsibility to the clergy in this respect.[46] Most of this was reiterated in various places in the *Confutation*. He expanded somewhat

---

[43] *Confutation* II, 942/17-20; 962/19-22; 924/17-34.

[44] See for example Luigi Prosdocimi, *Chierici e laici nella società occidentale del secolo xii: A proposito di Decr. Grat. c. 12. q. 1. c. 7: 'Duo sunt genera christianorum'* in *Proceedings of the Second International Congress of Medieval Canon Law*, ed. S. Kuttner, and J. J. Ryan, Rome, 1965, 105-122: C. Duggan, *The Reception of Canon Law in England in the Later Twelfth Century*, ibid., 359-390; Schoeck, *Canon Law in England on the Eve of the Reformation*, 125-147.

[45] *Responsio*, 658/28-660/31, tr. 659/33-661/37. On the pastoral image in particular see his treatment of *poimainein* ('Feed my sheep...') in ibid., 196/4-20, tr. 197/5-25.

[46] *Dialogue*, vi vG, Campbell, 13; ibid., liiii rA-D, Campbell, 111-112; ibid., lxiii vG, Campbell, 133. *Confutation* I, 305/31-34; II, 614/12-615/9.

the scriptural basis for his position, citing such places in particular as Mt 28, 19-20, Lk 10, 1-15, Lk 10, 16, while returning frequently to Jn 16, 13 to retain the spiritual perspective within which, he felt, the empirical church must be viewed. It is interesting to note that More was careful not to attribute the teaching mission exclusively to the clergy with his own personal task possibly in mind. He did recognise their special role, 'to which parte these wordes were also specyally spoken...' Given his own treatment at the hands of the English bishops it is not unremarkable that he had so little to say about the specific role of the episcopate.[47]

The Roman primacy

Sir Thomas More was a good deal more explicit on the Roman primacy than on the function of bishops. The *Baravellus* edition of the *Responsio* had largely avoided the issue. Provoked apparently by Luther's reply to Catharinus and perhaps prompted by Thomas Murner, he withheld his manuscript from publication and inserted a lengthy if somewhat unsystematic rebuttal of the Lutheran theses in the revised *Rosseus* edition.[48] In this latter work More argued strenuously for Peter's primacy on the grounds mainly of a literal interpretation of Mt 16, 18-19. Christ is the true foundation and cornerstone of the church. Peter is head of the church but in a subordinate capacity, appointed rock because of the steadfastness of his faith. Peter the 'rock' is subordinate, in More's view, to Christ who '...is most truly and firmly the rock, most truly the head of the church...' But this did not preclude the conferring on Peter of a special, vicarious function in the church. By reason of the gift of the keys, More argued, Peter was given authority to admit and exclude from the church. In the context of the promises made to Peter such authority has broader significance encompassing the regulation of ecclesiastical life and discipline. This view was reinforced by Christ's commission recorded in Jn 21, 17 to feed his sheep. Christ's word clearly signifies authority to govern in all phases of church activity. This assertion is based largely on his explanation of the word *poimainein* in Jn 21, 16, 'feed my lambs', which he saw as ascribing to Peter in the church a function analogous to that of a shepherd with his flock, i.e., one of full responsibility and direction.[49]

Thomas More did not expose in detail a case for the enduring character of the petrine office. He seems to have assumed it to have been included in

---

[47] The title *bishop* is not used as an index heading in the Yale editions of either *Responsio* or *Confutation*.

[48] See Headley, *Responsio*, 775-803.

[49] See *Responsio*, 196/4-20, tr. 197/5-25.

the promises made to Peter. He may have had in mind in this respect his interpretation of Mt 16, 18, 'the gates of hell will not prevail against it.' He understood this to mean 'that the devil will not prevail against the faith of Peter, nor against the power of binding and loosing given to Peter and perpetually to his successors.' More already had assumed that the church and the petrine office as well as Christ's promise of assistance were indefinitely valid. In confirmation of his views he pointed to the universal consent of the Christian people, comparing the dissidence of oriental Christians to 'local rebellions', in no way weakening the force of more general opinion concerning the primacy. While his treatment of the issue was by no means complete, in referring his readers to Fisher's treatment of the same question he indicated that the matter had been dealt with adequately elsewhere.[50]

In the *Dialogue* More briefly repeated the doctrine outlined in the *Responsio*. Christ had conferred the primatial office on Peter (Mt 16, 18-19). Peter and his faith constitute the rock on which the church has been founded. In this connection he now added a reference to Lk 22, 31-32: 'I have prayed for thee that thy faith shall not fayle.' He admitted that Peter's faith had failed at the time of the Passion but asserted that it was subsequently confirmed by Christ so as to enable the first apostle to become the cornerstone of the church. Peter's decisive role in the Christian congregation is intimately connected with communicating this faith. The *transmission* of the petrine office did not seem to merit special treatment in the *Dialogue*. More did however attribute supreme authority to the pope, arguing for example, that only 'such priests as be made by authority and conveyed from the pope' may administer the sacraments. More did not make the scholastic or canonical distinction between valid and licit celebration. Presumably what he had in mind was lawful administration.

Nonetheless, his insistence on the point, triggered perhaps by recent events in Germany where Lutheran pastors were being installed in a number of parishes, not all of whom had been ordained according to the traditional rite, did point to a high conception of papal authority within the church. Specifically it points to a close nexus in his mind between juridical communion with the papacy and sacramental communion in the church's liturgical worship.[51]

As More explained in a letter to Cromwell shortly before his execution, he had avoided the issue of papal primacy in the *Confutation*, being aware

---

[50] *Responsio*, 138/1-140/5, tr. 139/1-141/6.
[51] *Dialogue*, lxiii vG, Campbell, 133.

of the ongoing confrontation between London and Rome on the issue of the royal divorce. Nevertheless, an examination of the text does reveal him committing himself to certain positions. In his study of Mt 16, 18-19 he interpreted Christ's words concerning the rock on which the church is founded as referring to faith in Christ, not Peter's primacy. Similarly Christ's promise to Peter in Lk 22, 31-32 was interpreted in respect of Peter's personal commitment rather than his role in the church. Moreover he rejected out of hand any 'aristocratic' view of church organisation which would identify the essence of the church with the pope and his cardinals, such that participation in church life would involve close identification with the Roman authorities.

   All of this represents a minimalising of the primatial position both in terms of its grounding in scripture and of the pretensions of some of its more extreme advocates. More than this, he recognised the *theoretical admissibility* of alternative views of church government including the following:

1.   Christ did not appoint Peter and his successors as heads of the whole church though *de facto* and *de iure humano* the Roman pontiff is such a head.
2.   Each province in the church is an independent unity presided over by its own spiritual governor be he patriarch, archbishop or metropolitan.

Hence the care he took not to include the papacy in his definition of the church in the *Confutation*.

   On the other hand, if only briefly and in passing, More's own *personal* position emerged. As a private individual he looked on the primatial office as of divine institution, conferred on Peter and intended to endure in his successors. He found this view confirmed by the virtually unbroken consensus of Christian people throughout the centuries. For More, such a consensus was an infallible sign of the authenticity of any given doctrinal position. Consequently, though he acknowledged the legitimacy of contradictory views on the matter, his own mind was clear at this moment in time. The primacy of Rome was instituted by God for the welfare of the church. This did not make him an ultramontane born *hors série*. He did not hesitate to admit the fallibility of the pope, without distinguishing public or private matters. Nor was he reluctant to admit the right of the church to correct or even depose the pope for heresy or serious misconduct. But on the divine origin of primatial office More's *personal* stance was unambiguous.[52]

In the course of the correspondence and other proceedings surrounding his trial further elements were added to this picture. In a letter to Cromwell written from his home in Chelsea early in 1534, Sir Thomas More indicated that he had not been convinced of the divine origin of the Roman primacy at the time Henry was composing his *Assertio Septem Sacramentorum* probably early in 1521. On the occasion he had advised Henry against including certain assertions concerning the Roman primacy or alternatively to moderate his opinions. Subsequent study of the fathers, together with the testimony of both Greek and Latin Christians as well as the teaching of the councils had made it impossible for him to deny that Christ had conferred supreme authority in the church on Peter and his successors. More's conviction on the issue seems to have come to fruition in the period he was revising his first *Baravellus* edition of the *Responsio* and to have been reinforced in subsequent years as to reach its final critical affirmation in his closing speech before the court that condemned him.

On the other hand More's own personal theological position did not prevent him from recognising that the doctrinal standing of the Roman primacy was not beyond question. This is apparent not merely in the *Confutation* where he was under some pressure to moderate his views. It is also evident in the correspondence of the trial period where he spoke of it as one of those '...matters (on which) the doctours stande in great doubte...'.[53] In other words More acknowledged that the doctrine of Roman primacy was still a matter of debate among theologians even though his own *private* conviction following lengthy study was extremely firm.

Over and above this personal conviction concerning the divine origin of Roman primacy lay another position which he felt to be much more solidly grounded in evidence and beyond objective doubt. This was his view concerning the *legal status* of the petrine office. Here one must bear in mind More's conception of the unity of Christendom. Made up of many kingdoms and principalities, it was nonetheless both a religious and a political entity. The supreme laws of Christendom were established either by the consent of Christian people or the determination of the councils of

---

[52] *Confutation* II, 1010/16-21; 1011/4-11; 576/23-577/23; especially 576/28-32 coupled with I, 131/33-132/9 and II, 962/35-963/1 for the more 'pro-papal' viewpoints found in the *Confutation*. Limits on papal immunity from error touched on briefly in ibid. II, 910/4-911/2 and ff; II, 579/35-580/8; II, 590/13-15.

[53] More to Margaret Roper, Rogers, *Correspondence*, 505/9-506/118.

Christendom, presumably the general councils. On this score there could be no question of the authority of the Roman pontiff: '...ffor that primatie is at the *leist wise* instituted by the corps of Christendom and for a great vrgent cause in avoiding of scysmes and corroborate by continuall succession more than the space of a thowsand yere at the leist...' This being so his attitude to royal supremacy voiced in his final address to the commissioners at his trial follows on logically: '...this Realme, being but one member and small part of the Churche, might not make a particuler lawe disagreable with the generall lawe of Christes vniuersall Catholike Churche, no more then the Citie of London, being but one poore member in respect of the whole Realme, might make a lawe against an Acte of Parliament to binde the whole Realme...'[54]

Thus while More was privately convinced of the divine institution of the papacy, he was even more emphatic concerning the constitutional position of the papal office within the legal framework of Christendom as he understood it at that time. He acknowledged in the pope the supreme authority in the daily administration of ecclesiastical affairs, entitled to rule and guide the whole church. There was no mention of an infallible teaching office and little reference to the teaching function of the pope as of significance in the life of the church. Sir Thomas More forcefully affirmed the obligation to show respect to the Roman pontiff. On the other hand he made no bones about admitting his human frailty. In particular he denied out of hand the validity of one provision in Gratian—the classic text cited by medieval canonists in defence of papal sovereignty *Si papa* with its key phrase *a nemine est iudicandus*. More simply pointed out this to be a quotation from St Boniface and of no more authority than the saint's voice.[55] This is indicative of a balanced approach to the papacy, recognising its legitimacy but adverting to its potential weaknesses and refusing to deify it or exaggerate its role beyond that of an ecclesiastical organ of government.

Nor did he show any interest in extending papal authority in temporal affairs. He had no qualms of conscience over the implications of *praemunire* and indeed, according to himself, had sought to prevent Henry VIII from ascribing too much authority to the pope in secular affairs.[56] The latter's role was seen more in terms of governing the church, preserving its unity, and of preventing and healing schisms. Nor was he seen as superior to

---

[54] See More to Cromwell, Rogers, *Correspondence*, 498/227-231; Harpsfield, *Life of Sr Thomas Moore*, 193/25-194/5.

[55] See E. A. Friedberg, *Corpus Iuris Canonici*, Vol. 1, Leipzig, 1879, 146: D. 40, c. 6, and *Confutation*, 590/8-593/35. See Marius, *Confutation*, 1306 for more detailed discussion.

[56] Roper, 67/20-68/23; Harpsfield, 159/7-160/17.

the general council: '...yet never thought I the Pope above the General Council.'[57]

The general council

More did not develop a theory of the relationship between pope and council. The burden of his thought on the general teaching office in the church was to view it in terms of consensus expressed either outside or inside a general council. Councils as such did not figure largely in his view of the church. He did however see them as a means of manifesting the universal consensus of the church and therefore as one expression of the supreme teaching authority of the church in general. He attributed to councils the power to correct and even depose holders of the papal office who had been guilty of heresy or conduct gravely harmful to the church. Hence, while defending the papacy in its essential position, it can be argued that More was of a conciliarist bent, verging on a neo-democratic view of the church's constitution.[58]

Sir Thomas More discussed the general council within the context of a theory of consensus. The sure test as to whether any particular doctrine or practice forms part of or is in accord with divine revelation is its acceptance by the general body of believers. He referred only in passing to the council in the course of the *Responsio*, though the ground of his later thought was already laid in that work.[59] There he spoke in defence of a council made up almost exclusively of bishops. Such a council is truly representative of the church since 'To whom should the people rather wish that business (concerning doctrine or practice) delegated than to the bishops, to whom it specially belongs to be anxious about the safety of the people.'[60] The bishops in council are thus looked on as delegates or representatives of the entire people of God. The agreement they reach is

---

[57] In this presentation of More's views on the papacy I clearly disagree with Egan, *Rule of Faith*, 73 who makes a papal monarchist out of More, as well as with Headley, *Responsio*, 773. Headley suggests that the papacy was one of the two main foci of More's ecclesiology. While More clearly recognised the need for authority in the church, the whole trend of his thought was away from identifying authority with any one individual. More saw the papal office canonised by the Spirit-guided consensus as well as founded in scripture rather than the reverse. The papacy was for More in all probability part of the divinely constituted governing body of the community. The mainspring of the community is its inner life not its outward cloak nor its system of government. On the other hand I find myself in close agreement with the interpretation of Marius, *Confutation*, 1299-1315.

[58] *Confutation* II, 938/14-23; II, 940/33-941/12; II, 937/13-938/14; II, 922/33-923/11; I, 146/15-20; II, 714/34-715/4.

[59] See Marius, *Confutation*, 1310 who corrects Headley, *Responsio*, 765 on this point.

[60] See *Responsio*, 626/16-628/8, tr. 627/21-629/10.

no merely human compromise but the result of the guidance of the divine
Spirit. Their agreement is ratified in the ensuing assent of the people to
what has been decided. This already sketched out a representative theory
of council with a theological basis in the guarantee of divine assistance
such that decisions reached in council can be looked on both as decisions of
the whole church and as sure intimations of the divine will.

More referred only briefly to conciliar theory in the *Dialogue* where he
viewed it as a means to an explicit formulation of ecclesiastical
consensus.[61] In the *Confutation*, however, probably under the influence of
Henry's pragmatically inspired conciliarism, he began to make more use
of conciliar authority. Quoting Lk 10, 16 'He that hereth you hereth me',
he went on to say: 'Now this same authoryte hath Crystes chyrche
assembled in the generall counsayles...'[62]

More's theory of council is strongly representative in character. Writing
against Barnes he took up an image already found in the *Responsio* of a
gathering of the whole church which would embrace all its living
members. In the *Responsio* he pictured it as taking place in the *Campus Martius*; in the *Confutation* on Salisbury Plain. Such a gathering would certainly
be entitled to give authoritative guidance to the Christian people. While
not admitting that such a cumbersome gathering was out of the question,
More argued that a general council representing the whole church '...haue
the same authoryte and the same full credence geuen vnto yt, as though
there were at yt all the whole crysten people.' The authority of the council
within this perspective appears to derive from the people whom it
represents though ultimately grounded on Christ's promises to his
disciples. This view is reinforced by another statement: '...that the dew
assemble of certayne partes representynge the whole body, sholde haue the
full authoryte of the whole body/is a thynge by the comen assent and experyence of the whole worlde crysten and hethen so fully seen and
perceyued...'[63] Here More appealed not to any particular conciliar theory
but to a general principle of representation to vindicate the authority of the
general council.

Without becoming over-involved in the niceties of conciliar theory
More upheld what may be termed a 'neo-democratic' view of the church
and its government with particular reference to the role of the council.
This becomes more evident in the comparison he drew between council

---

[61] *Dialogue*, liii vG, Campbell, 111; ibid., lxix vG, Campbell, 146.
[62] *Confutation* I, 344/34-345/5.
[63] *Confutation* II, 940/33-941/8.

and parliament. Councils represent the church '...as a parliament representeth ye hole reame, & is by the comen speche so called to/as when we say yt the realme hath made a law that heretikes shalbe burned.'[64] Conciliar decrees are binding as decrees issued by the whole church. Conciliar doctrine bears the authority of the whole church. Conciliar consensus represents and expresses the consensus of the whole church.

Nor did More identify consensus with numerical unanimity either in the church or in council. Even though a minority of unspecified size 'a few wylfull folke' dissent from the general consensus, the decision making power of the council is in no way imperilled. More justified this stance by reference to parliamentary procedure as well as by a common sense approach to unanimity in the Spirit. In this way he disarmed, at least to his own satisfaction, the theoretical position of Luther derived from William of Ockham and which had found echoes in More's own work, that the true faith might be preserved in the church and in the council by one protesting individual. This position also safeguarded to some degree his reliance on consensus in the face of the defection of increasing numbers especially on the continent from the prevailing Catholic consensus.[65]

It follows logically from Sir Thomas More's view on the origins of conciliar authority that the council may speak on any matter that the church can. Hence matters of discipline, the ordering of church life and activity as well as moral and doctrinal issues fall within its purview. He clearly looked on the council as the supreme teaching organ and legislative body within the ecclesiastical structure. This was the burden of several references made to the conciliar role during the trial proceedings. It comes through clearly in Margaret Roper's letter to Alice Alington, More's letter to Cromwell, as well as in his concluding speech from the dock: '...and therefore am I not bounden, my Lorde, to conforme my conscience to the Councell of one Realme against the generall Councell of Christendome. For of the foresaide holy Bisshopps (who had accepted royal supremacy) I haue for euery Bisshopp of yours, aboue one hundred; And for one Councell or Parliament of yours (God knoweth what maner of one), I haue all the Councels made these thousande yeres.'[66] Conciliar jurisdiction extends beyond institution and discipline to morals and doctrine. In the last analysis conciliar teaching on doctrine is unfailing. More did not develop a theory of inerrancy for the council as he did for the church but it was

---

[64] *Confutation* I, 146/18-20.

[65] For greater detail on all this see above pp. 212-216.

[66] See Harpsfield, *Life of Sr Thomas Moore*, 196/1-8. See also: Reynolds, *Trial*, 126; idem, *The Field is Won*, 369.

implicit in his view that councils do not contradict each other as well as grounded in the inerrancy of ecclesial consensus of which the council is one important mouthpiece.

Pope and council

On the relationship between pope and council Sir Thomas More did not have a great deal to contribute. Through the first sixty years of the fifteenth century this had been a much debated question. The so-called Gallican articles reaffirmed by the Pragmatic Sanction of Bourges (1438) had reiterated as far as the French monarchy was concerned the administrative autonomy of the French church as well as the doctrine of conciliar supremacy. This view continued to influence ecclesiastical life in France in succeeding centuries. England, on the other hand, had remained to a large extent on the fringe of the western schism and attendant controversies. The general trend of English thought was in support of the papacy. Henry's treatment of the papal prerogatives in his *Assertio Septem Sacramentorum* (1521) is fairly indicative of the main thrust of late medieval ecclesiology in this area.[67]

In Thomas More's key letter to Cromwell written in 1534 from his Chelsea home, he touched on the matter specifically. Speaking of the Roman primacy he said: '...yit neuer thowght I the Pope above the generall counsaile nor neuer have in eny boke of myn put forth among the Kyngis subgietis in our vulgare tunge, avaunced greatly the Popis authorite...'[68] This does not give us a great deal to go on. Yet it contains some vital information. Firstly, it is concerned with More's *personal* position, not his assessment of current thought on the subject of pope-council relationships. Secondly, he asserts that he never looked on the pope as above the council. Hence, in line with general conciliar theory he must have thought of him as either coordinate with or subordinate to the council. Given his theology of consensus underlying his theology of council, it seems probable that More would have ascribed a subordinate role to the pope in conciliar affairs.

On the other hand, More was careful to insist on the principle of due assembly. Councils are to be believed provided that they be 'lawfully assembled.' They are of value in preserving the unity of the Catholic Church on condition that they be well assembled. Presumably several considerations underlay these careful provisos. One must have been English

---

[67] Henry VIII, *Assertio,* sigs. B5-C1; K1-K2; P3v-P4.
[68] More to Cromwell, Rogers, *Correspondence,* 499/261-264.

constitutional practice where parliament convened at the king's request while its decisions only obtained the force of law from his approval. Another factor probably in his mind was the running battle between conciliarists and the papacy which had taken place in the course of the fifteenth century concerning the autonomy of councils. The papal position maintaining the right of popes to convene councils and approve their *acta* won out as far as the greater part of Christendom was concerned and presumably also with Sir Thomas More.

Because of his imprecision on a number of these issues it is impossible to place More with certainty in any particular school of conciliar thought. Nonetheless, the burden of his expressed attitudes would tend to place him closer to contemporary conciliarists such as Jacques Almain and John Major rather than with papalists such as Catharinus or Cajetan.[69]

The sources of More's conciliar theory are not immediately evident. Was it Erasmus, or Dionysius Carthusianus, or Gerson? There is no evidence in More's works for any direct dependence on any of these. Indeed the main influence suggested by his statements on the council lies with a more general theory of representation evolved during his career as lawyer, parliamentarian and statesman as well as in connection with his theoretical writing on political matters.[70] Medieval theories of representation, developed initially by canonists in relation to the church's constitution, played an important role in the growth of constitutional thought and law and so ultimately in the emergence of fully representative government.[71] Representation does not necessarily imply election; a hereditary monarch may, symbolically, represent his whole people as a feudal baron may represent his subjects in the King's council. Similarly bishops in council may represent the people of the dioceses from which they come. The fact that they are *ex officio* members of the assembly to which they belong in no way derogates from the fact that they stand in council not as isolated individuals but representing the corporation of which they are head. Correspondingly, however, their headship of their local community depends on the consent of the people even though this consent may not be given through the medium of popular election but by tacit assent and practical cooperation. Because of this the council is a gathering of the whole

---

[69] See above pp. 42-7.

[70] This question is discussed at some length in the following chapter pp. 347-348.

[71] See the classic examination of these issues in Gierke, *Political Theories,* tr. Maitland, 37-67; Tierney, *Conciliar Theory,* passim. Among more recent works on English constitutional history see Donald W. Hanson, *From Kingdom to Commonwealth,* Cambridge, (Mass.), 1970, 97-216.

church. Its agreement is equivalent in authority to the general consensus of believers.

More spoke at length of the council only in his later writings from the *Confutation* onwards. Had his doctrine on consensus proven too volatile to deal with the subtle vigour and persistence of his opponents? Had he come to realise a need for more explicit authority and formal definition in dealing with his opponents? Was the force of popular consensus losing its clear thrust through the growing and marked separation of Christendom into separate camps? Or was he simply appealing somewhat opportunistically to a form of authority which was finding new adherents among Henry's followers in the period leading up to the royal assumption of control of the English church? Whatever the inner reasons for More's discovery of the importance of conciliar thought, in his last years the general council had come to play a significant role in his conception of ecclesiastical authority.

III. The Church and Revelation

The teaching office of the church

This church, made up of saints and sinners, governed and taught by a duly appointed clergy and strengthened by the abiding presence of the Spirit, is the means God has chosen to transmit his message to mankind. In More's mind there was no shadow of doubt on this issue. God's word as divine revelation is prior to the church. Indeed it brings it into existence. As infused by the abiding Spirit it continues to guide the Christian people in their journey through time. The church moreover, once constituted, has the mission to witness to this message, to share it with believers and unbelievers alike. In this respect, then, the church is responsible for the word, for its recognition, transmission, and interpretation. The truth of the message does not depend on the church but men depend on the church to discover the truth of God's message. The church testifies to the existence of divine revelation and has the gift of discerning its real meaning when this is not self-evident. Hence the church not only receives revelation. She interprets this message before transmitting it to those willing to hear it. All of this is done under the guidance of God's indwelling Spirit, so that he who hears the church hears Christ.

The church identifies divine revelation

In the *Responsio* More made it patently obvious that he looked on the church as playing a key role in identifying for believers and enquirers alike both the literary sources and the content of divine revelation. In unambiguous terms he affirmed his conviction that God has given 'the church the power to distinguish the word of God from the words of man.'[72] He did not work out all the implications of this thesis in a systematic way. He had little of significance to say, for example, as to how the recipient of a direct illumination from the Spirit might protect himself from self-delusion. Yet he himself based a good deal of his case against the reformers on the unspoken assumption that this gift of discernment is available to the believer or at least to the church in general. Perhaps he may be excused a certain lack of rigour in his argument regarding this point since his opponents made equally bland assumptions regarding the infallibility of spiritual intuition on the part of the true believer.[73] More was not completely inconsistent in this position since his theory of consensus protected the community at least from the pretensions of mountebanks and pseudo prophets.

Sir Thomas More's blanket assertion concerning the role of the church in discerning God's word covers all forms of revelation whether that given to the believer in his heart, prophetic inspiration of individuals, or the socio-historical revelation in the deeds and words of Jesus Christ. More himself did not spell this out in detail but it is implied in many of his assertions concerning the nature of revelation itself. It was in connection with the records and interpretation of revelation that he discussed the function of the Christian community in some depth.

The most important aspect of this task is that of identifying authentic scripture. It is through the church we come to know which scriptures be true and which false. Unless the church pointed out certain writings as the inspired expression of revelation we would remain in ignorance of their existence or at least have no sure guarantee of their divine origin. In *Responsio, Dialogue* and *Confutation* More consistently used this argument to counter the reformers' claim that scripture is self-authenticating and prior to the church in every respect. Because of his broader view of the scope of divine disclosure he was able to by-pass their position. Resting his argument on the authority of St Augustine in his reiterated citation of the latter's *Contra epistolam Manichaei*,[74] More subordinated the bible to the church in the sense of claiming that, in the logic of faith, assent to the

---

[72] *Responsio*, 70/26, tr. 71/29-30 citing *Assertio*, sig. S 1v-S2.

[73] See for example Tyndale, *Exposition of the First Epistle of St John* in *Expositions and Notes on Sundry Portions of the Holy Scriptures*, Cambridge, 1849, ed. H. Walter, 138-139: '...whosoever hath the profession of baptism written in his heart, cannot but understand the scripture...'

[74] *MPL* 42, 176.

church is prior to assent to God's word in scripture. That is not to say that
the church is above scripture. The church is indeed subject to God's word
in so far as its charter is contained in scripture. Rather is there a mutual
relationship whereby once the church has established *the fact of revelation* she
herself becomes subject to this message correctly understood while at the
same time by her witness making it available to others.[75]

More attached great importance to tradition as a vehicle of divine
revelation, whether understood as the objective reflex of the inner
guidance given by the Spirit to the multitude of believers or as the human
means of transferring from one generation to the next those elements of
Christ's sayings and doings not recorded in the new testament. Just as
there can be false scriptures so also false traditions can take hold in the
church. Through the guidance of the Spirit the Christian people have the
gift of discerning true from false tradition. In exercising this gift the
church must carry out a critical function carefully sifting what is of purely
human origin from what can be traced to divine influence. It may be
recalled that More himself was rather generous in his ascription of divine
influence allowing great latitude to the activity of the Spirit within 'the
common corps of Christendom' in post-apostolic generations. However
the power is exercised, there still remains a need for careful assessment of
religious practice and belief.[76]

The church interprets revelation

The role of the church is not confined to identifying divine revelation
and authenticating the sources which contain it or express it. Because of its
obscurity or apparent contradictory assertions, the Christian people have
the responsibility of interpreting the gospel message. More affirmed this in
the *Responsio* as well as in *Dialogue* and *Confutation*. In the *Responsio* he emphasised the task of harmonising the data of revelation in so far as these
reach the believing community through tradition in its various forms.

He did not reflect at length on the nature of this process except to stress
two points. One is something he had already worked out in his humanist
days, namely that in the interpretation of scripture great respect must be
shown to the constant tradition of the fathers in their exegesis of particular

---

[75] *Responsio*, 110/24-112/32, tr. 111/28-113/37; *Confutation* II, 739/9-27; II, 792/27-35;
Dialogue, lix vGH, Campbell, 124; ibid., xxxix vF-xl rC passim, Campbell, 82-83; ibid., xlvi
rD; ibid., xl rB-xliii vF, Campbell, 84-91; 96.

[76] *Responsio* 190/20-23, tr. 191/25-29; ibid., 128/3-12, tr. 129/3-14; *Confutation* I,
379/16-28.

passages. Though More's preference was for the literal sense, the over-
riding sense of scripture for him was not its immediate historical sense as
seen from the vantage point of the present moment, but its sense as seen
by the age-long reflection of the Christian community especially as
mediated through patristic tradition.[77]

The *Dialogue* did not add substantially to More's thought in this area
though he spelled out in some detail how the Holy Spirit can work on the
minds of the faithful to lead them from apparently opposed positions to
unity on basic issues. He worked this out at greater length in the *Confutation*. Here he demonstrated how God sometimes reveals truth directly to
the church such that it is immediately understood. At other times he allows
his flock to draw out the hidden meaning through the exercise of reason
using scripture and natural wisdom to discover his intent. Ultimately, of
course, divine guidance is required so that men may arrive at 'consent and
concorde and bylyef of the trouth...'

Hence it is both the action of the Holy Spirit as well as the critical power
of the human intellect which lead to the deeper penetration of the mystery
of faith. In all of this More was careful to insist that God cannot contradict
himself. One revelation cannot contradict another nor can the apparent
sense of scripture be in real contradiction with the articles of faith. When
in doubt the latter should be adhered to pending a deeper illumination of
the sense of scripture.[78]

Thus in her task of interpreting divine revelation in whatever form it
comes, 'the Gospel in the heart,' holy scripture, or the church's ongoing
tradition of faith and practice, a lengthy process of elucidation may be
called for. This can take the form of a living, unsystematic interaction between the revelation of God given in grace and in consciousness to the
believer on the one hand and the written word of scripture on the other.
Or a dialectical process may take place, where reason and common sense
using the resources of natural wisdom, presumably philosophy, history
and other natural sciences with a bearing on the subject, are used to draw
out conclusions from the given data of revelation. Even this logical procedure demands divine assistance, for this is the essential factor leading to
the solution of difficulties and eventual agreement among the faithful.

---

[77] *Responsio*, 126/26-128/15, tr. 127/29-129/18; 300/6-9, tr. 301/7-10; *Confutation* I,
62/7-12; I, 133/31-134/5.
[78] *Responsio*, 100/1-102/12, tr. 101/2-103/14. See also More to Martin Dorp, (1515),
Rogers, *Correspondence*, 60/1134-1137; *Confutation* I, 337/18-33; I, 61/36-62/14; I, 133/31-35;
Dialogue, xl rB-xliii vF; xlvi rD, Campbell, 84-91; 96.

The rule of faith

In all of this discussion there is no question that in More's mind, to use a later terminology, the proximate rule of faith is the church. In other words the final practical guide as to what is to be believed or not is the belief of the church. Here he differed radically from the stand taken by the reformers in that their guidance was *scriptura sola*, though even this was understood by some in a special sense not understood by their English opponent. This is not to say that More was an ultramontane before his time or even a papalist theologian in the mould of Thomas de Vio Cajetan or Ambrosius Catharinus. While their school of thought insisted both on the role of the episcopate and the papacy in determining the content of faith, for More the line to be followed was set not so much by hierarchical authority but by the consensus of the believing community.

Consensus

Sir Thomas More's doctrine on consensus was worked out initially in the *Responsio* and maintained throughout his controversial career. Consensus for him, technically a legal or political term, implied the agreement of virtually all believing Christians concerning a doctrine of faith. In the first instance More spoke of a consensus throughout time. Where all believers in the course of history have held to a particular doctrine this is an unfailing sign of its being a truth revealed by God. This in practice amounts to a *consensus patrum*. Since it is hardly feasible to question the dead, the normal way of sounding the opinion of earlier generations is through the writings of the fathers. These were men of sanctity and probity and therefore of profound faith. Their writings can be looked on as a reliable index to the faith of the Christian community in their generation. When a line of agreement in patristic opinion can be found extending throughout time, this may be taken as a sure indicator of the common faith of the historic church of Christ. Consequently it points to what the present generation must hold fast if it is to remain faithful to apostolic tradition.[79]

The other dimension of consensus is the contemporary one, namely that of the faith of the common corps of Christendom at the present day. Using this as a background More could argue against Luther: 'We stubborn blockheads of course demand that we alone be believed; that is, that only

---

[79] *Responsio*, 128/3-12, tr. 129/3-14; 250/13-25, tr. 251/17-29; 212/14-18, tr. 213/17-21; *Dialogue*, lxxxii vGH, Campbell, 175; ibid., lxxx rAB, Campbell, 169; *Confutation* I, 47/31-48/5; I, 62/7-10; II, 623/3-8; II, 589/25-30.

the Italians, Spaniards, English, French, and finally all men alone should be believed, wherever the church of Christ exists today or has ever existed anywhere in the world since the death of Christ.'[80] The church More believed in was 'the common corps of Christendom' made up of the believing nations of the world. It is their agreement in faith which is binding on the individual Christian as a sure guide through the intricate and often badly-signposted maze of divine revelation.

The *Dialogue* did not bring any noteworthy development of More's thought in this respect, except perhaps a remarkably firm preference for doctrine clearly held in the church over against any apparently learned explanation of biblical passages. He also expressed graphically his sense of the universality which often characterised such testimony from the fathers' books '...wryten in dyuers regyons and sondry ages/(we) therby well perceyue that these thynges be parcell of the rytes vsages and byleue of Crystes chyrch...'[81]

In the *Dialogue* and even more explicitly in the *Confutation* More discovered a new significance in the consensus of the living body of believers. In the course of time, as we have seen, he observed that doctrine develops through the inter-action of the indwelling Spirit and the imprint he leaves on consciousness on the one hand and the letter of scripture on the other. In the *Confutation* he also envisaged development taking place both through continuing revelation from God, and through the divinely guided conclusions of the human mind. In each of these instances divine guidance is required. The acid test as to whether development has been authentic or not is the consensus of the present-day church. The Spirit so assists the faithful in their search that '...he rewarde theyr vertuouse dylygence wyth ledyng them secretely in to the consent and concorde and bylyef of the trouth...'[82] Or as he put it in another passage '...god is at hys lybertye styll...to teache hys trouthes more and more, as his pleasure shall be to haue them known...wherof his chyrch is by theyr hole consent sure.'[83] This consensus is not an agreement of scholars only, or the clergy only, or the bishops only, but of '...the comon knowen catholyke people, clergy, lay folke, and all/whych what so euer theyr lyuynge be...do stande to gether and agre in the confessyon of one trew catholyke fayth...'[84]

[80] *Responsio*, 96/12-16, tr. 97/11-16.
[81] *Dialogue* lxxxii vG, Campbell, 175.
[82] See *Confutation* I, 248/20-23.
[83] *Confutation* I, 249/9-14.
[84] *Confutation* I, 480/36-481/1. On development of doctrine, see for example ibid., II, 923/12-28; '...in dyuerse times there may be mo thinges farther and farther reueled, and other then were desclosed at the fyrst...'

300

SYNTHESIS

Councils and consensus

This last point brings into the foreground More's trust in the common man in religious matters, the man of simple faith and belief. It also sheds light on his approach to councils and conciliar decisions. He tended to see these as an expression of the common faith of the church. His passing references to the role of councils in the *Responsio* already hinted at this viewpoint. There he spoke of a hypothetical council of the whole church in the Campus Martius in Rome. This being hardly feasible the representatives of the Christian people, the bishops, meet in council. Their consensus is shortly after matched by the consensus of the Christian people in accepting the decisions. More did not explore the subtleties of this relationship. It sufficed in his estimate to say that the consensus of the council is either based on or confirmed by the consensus of the whole church.[85]

In the *Dialogue* More equiparated the consensus of the council with that of the church. In disputed matters. '...yf after that the holy chyrche fall in one consent vpon the one syde/eyther by common determynacyon at a generall counsayle/or by a perfyte perswasyon and byleue so receyued throughe crystendome...'[86] Here council and the common faith are treated as virtually independent functions of the church. In the *Confutation*, however, where he spelled out in some detail a representative theory of council, More suggested that as the authority of the council springs from its role as representing the church so its consensus is a reflection of the consensus of the church in general.[87]

In dealing with the question of consensus More was careful to insist especially in the *Confutation* that what is required is not a mathematically complete degree of unanimity but a moral unanimity. In the event of agreement being reached by 'the counsayle and the congregacion' (presumably the world-church) 'yf a few wylfull folke, farre the lest both in number, wyt, lernynge and honest lyuynge, wolde reclayme and say that them selfe wolde not agre,' their dissidence would in no way weaken the decisions arrived at. What is in question is a virtual unanimity similar to a parliamentary majority. Such a majority in ecclesiastical affairs, however, did not draw its credentials from a theory of majority rule but rather from a theology of consensus which saw in the moral unanimity of the church an infallible sign of the guidance of the Spirit.[88]

---

[85] *Responsio*, 626/21-628/5, tr. 627/24-629/6.
[86] *Dialogue* liii vG. Campbell, 111.
[87] *Confutation* I, 146/15-20; I, 345/29-346/5; II, 938/14-23; II, 940/33-941/8.
[88] *Confutation* II, 922/30-923/11.

Consensus grounded in the Spirit's presence

This is perhaps the most important factor in Sir Thomas More's view of the theory of consensus. For while he emphasised the value of the testimony of each individual's act of faith on the one hand and on the other spoke of the constitutional position of the council within the ecclesiastical institution in the language of representational-political theory, the ultimate ground for his doctrine of consensus lies in his pneumatic view of the Christian community. This spiritual perception of the church is found throughout his writings from the *Responsio* to the trial proceedings. Christ is with his church directing and guiding it. He is the vine, the Christian people its branches. He is the head, the Christian community his body. Through this body flows his life-giving Spirit.

The Spirit has the special function of inscribing in the heart of each believer the true sense of divine revelation, of recalling to the mind of the Christian community the full range of Christ's teaching, of leading the community to an ever more complete appropriation of his truth. Most important of all, the Spirit exercises a unitive role within the Christian people as he draws them together in a communion of life and faith. Repeatedly More cites Ps 67, 8, *qui facit unanimes in domo*: 'whych maketh all the house of one mynde' in reference to the Spirit's activity.

Dr Richard Marius has shown in some detail the textual origins of this citation in an old Latin version that More received in all likelihood through the mediation of Cyprian and Augustine. This version, according to modern scholarship, is a mistranslation of both Septuagint and Massoretic texts.[89] Whatever the origin of one of his favoured biblical quotations, this assumption underlay More's challenge to the Reformation: *Fateris nunc, ubi dei spiritus est, ibi consensum esse.* The unifying action of the Spirit draws men together in a common confession of faith: 'enclyneth theyr credulyte to consent in the believying all in one poynt whiche is the secrete instyncte of god...'

However, it would be erroneous to conclude that More based his whole position on this one text of scripture. Rather should one see his use of this text in a symbolic light as an expression in abbreviated form of his profound conviction of the abiding presence of God with his church. This presence of God guarantees the fidelity of his people to divine revelation and ensures their ultimate indefectibility in faith. If God allowed his

---

[89] See Marius, *Confutation*, 1352-1353; also Headley, *Responsio*, 823, who suggests that More may have found this reading in the Latin liturgy, viz., the *Introit* text for the 11th Sunday after Pentecost.

church to err, the gates of hell would have triumphed, his help would have proved ineffectual, he would have been shown as something less than omnipotent. This is a constant theme of More's writing and of his faith from *Responsio* to his final sacrifice. His view can be best summarised perhaps in his own words: '...god hath & euer shall according to his manyfold promises, so prouyde that the doctryne therof shall neuer be any dampnable errour/but as Cryste came hym selfe to begynne yt, and sent his apostles dyuerse in dyuerse partes to instructe yt, and they set other vnder them, as saynt Poule set Timothe: so god hath from age to age sent into euery good crysten countrey good & holy vertuouse men, as hath appered by theyr godly lyuynge and holy wrytynge and manyfolde myracles, whyche god hath wrought and wurketh by them/and wyth whiche wonderfull myracles god bereth wytnesse for them/and wyth hys owne grace and assystence whyche he promysed sholde euer abyde, wurketh wyth the towarde wylles of the people of hys knowen catholyke chyrche, to the consentyng and agrement of the same doctryne/so that the catholyke chyrche is the house of god, and the pyller & sure grounde of trouth, that euery syngulare person in the clerynge of all dowtes concernyng the sure auoydynge of all dampnable errours, maye stande and lene vnto.'[90]

The church communicates divine revelation

Sir Thomas More did not dwell at length on the ordinary teaching mission of the church in spreading Christ's message to the world. He took it very much for granted. There are few direct references in *Responsio* or *Dialogue*. In the *Confutation* he expounded in some detail on the topic in an effort to relate the witness of the church to the inner witness of the Spirit in the communication of the word. In keeping with his general principles, it is the whole church which receives this commission from Christ as 'hys perpetuall apostle.'[91] When Christ said: 'He who heareth you heareth me' (Lk 10, 16), he intended this to refer to the church as a whole and not exclusively to clergy or episcopate.

At the same time More recognised the special function of the clergy in the task of spreading the gospel.[92] The mission given the church as a whole is given to them in particular. This mission is not something carried out by purely human power. The preaching of the word is guided by the Spirit

---

[90] *Confutation* II, 855/33-856/15. *Responsio*, 88/5-90/8, tr. 89/5-91/10; 108/9-116/14, tr. 109/9-117/15; Dialogue, lx rBC, Campbell, 125.

[91] *Confutation* I, 252/5-8; ibid., 467/3-19.

[92] *Confutation* I, 305/31-34; I, 190/29-191/21; II, 911/3-32.

who also exercises a complementary function in the inner hearts of those who hear the word. Nevertheless the activity of the 'perpetuall apostle' is required to bring them to faith. The outer word of preaching counter-points the interior witness of the Spirit: '...yet was yt ordeyned yt he (Christ) shold haue also ye witnesse of saynt Iohan, & so afterwarde of hys euangelistes & apostles, ye & after yt of his other holy doctours & sayntes of euery age, & specyally, ye wytnesse of his hole catholike chyrch...by whych man shold come to fayth for his saluacyon.'[93]

IV. Signs of the true Church

Given the central role of the church in the identification, transmission and interpretation of revelation it evidently becomes a matter of key importance to determine which is in fact the church founded by Christ. The question of the credentials of Christ's church had been the subject of much discussion in the patristic period. In the course of the middle ages it had fallen from view to some extent due to the limited awareness within western Christianity of the existence of Christian churches other than those of western Europe. Medieval apologetic was more concerned with Islam than with dissident Christians. Hence it is not surprising that it took some time for sixteenth century controversialists to focus their attention on this as a living issue. It is to Sir Thomas More's credit that in the *Responsio* itself, his first venture in to apologetics, he isolated this question as being one of central concern. He complained of Luther: '...while pursuing and manifesting a kind of concealed and hidden wisdom, he reduces the palpable and commonly known church to an invisible one, from external to an internal one, from an internal one he utterly reduces her to no church at all.'[94] His conclusion from this was that '...there must still necessarily be some place in which a definite church may be recognizable and certain. Otherwise no one could be certain which are the true scriptures, nor could anyone know where to turn who, as yet an unbeliever, wishes to be instructed in the faith and to learn thoroughly the Christian teachings.'[95]

---

[93] *Confutation* I, 240/17-22. In this presentation of More's doctrine on consensus I am in agreement with the final phase of Huber's presentation where he sees the centrality of the inspirational, Spirit based view of consensus in More's theological views as distinct from a juridico-political concept which he espoused in other matters. See Huber, *Traditionsfestigkeit*, 148-152. Other commentators have reached the same conclusion. See Headley, *Responsio*, 741-745, 762-773; Prévost, *Thomas More*, 259-264; Marius *Confutation*, 1294-1297.

[94] *Responsio*, 148/2-8, tr. 149/2-9.

[95] *Responsio*, 166/10-16, tr. 167/13-20.

In the *Dialogue,* More put the question even more succinctly: how could a Turk or Saracen in search of Christ identify the true scriptures or the true church? The church must be visible and embody recognisable indices to its true identity.[96] In the *Confutation* he came to realise that this is 'the very brest of all this batayle/that is to wyt the questyon whych is the chyrche.'

Visibility

The visibility of the church was a basic element in More's ecclesiology. The church he followed and loved was the common church, the common corps of Christendom. In the *Responsio* he met the problem directly in dealing with Luther's spiritualised concept of the *ecclesia.* John Headley suggests that it may well have been Thomas Murner who drew More's attention to this aspect of the Wittenberger's thought.[97] Be that as it may, More did not delay in denouncing the Lutheran conception as '...imperceptible and mathematical—like Platonic ideas—which is both in some place and in no place, is in the flesh and is out of the flesh, which is wholly involved in sins and yet does not sin at all.'[98] In opposition to this view he emphasised the empirical character of the Christian community without providing a massive justification for his position.

In the *Dialogue* he took the discussion a stage further, listing a number of scriptural passages which point to the perceptibility of the Christian community. He spoke of it as a city set on a hill (Mt 5, 14); a candle set on a bushel (Mt 5, 15); a blazing fire (Lk 12, 49); a church whose authority can be clearly invoked in time of dispute (Mt 18, 17 and I Cor 6, 4).[99] Virtually the same citations recur in the *Confutation.*[100] Hence in More's eyes the question of the accessibility of the church to an outside enquirer as well as to its own members was something grounded in scripture as well as tradition and evident common sense. What then are the most striking qualities of this visible community?

Unity

In the *Responsio* Sir Thomas More pointed to a number of indices of the true Christian community. Unity in mind and heart is something he

---

[96] Campbell, 137; 139; 140-141.

[97] See Headley, *Responsio,* 900, comment on 166/20-21.

[98] *Responsio,* 166/17-23, tr. 167/21-28.

[99] *Dialogue* lxvii rC, Campbell, 142 and passim.

[100] See e.g., *Confutation* II, 915/8-11 for Mt 5, 14; ibid., I, 146, 243, 345, 388 etc. for Mt 18, 17.

looked on as an essential quality of this congregation. Throughout space
and time the same Christian faith is shared by all believers. Such unity in
essentials does not preclude diversity in areas of debate. These latter
however remain subordinate to the central themes of tradition. In the
Dialogue More repeated these affirmations. He gave reasons from scripture
as to why unity of belief must be a distinguishing characteristic of the
church of Christ, citing texts familiar from a slightly different context in
the *Responsio*, notably Ps 67, 7 and Acts 4, 32.[101] In the *Dialogue* unity in
faith at the present time received a certain emphasis. In contrast with the
inner divisions found among the reformers More found in the uniform
doctrine of the established church a sure sign of the presence of the Holy
Spirit and therefore of its obedience to and communion with Christ. In the
Confutation the same line of argument was taken up.[102] Underlying this
profound affirmation of the church of Christ was More's spiritual view of
the church centred on the abiding presence of Christ and his Spirit. The
same insight which controlled his theory of consensus is operative here in
terms of visible evidence of divine action among the followers of Christ
which can be interpreted by unbelievers as an indication of their fidelity to
their Lord and master.

Continuity

The argument from unity is organically linked with another theme, that
of continuity. The church of Christ is universal. Throughout Christian
lands but one authentic Christian church is to be found sharing the same
faith. This has been so throughout the course of history. This same body of
believing Christians is in communion with those of preceding generations
in a spiritual lineage which goes back as far as the apostolic community. A
verifiable historical continuity of faith with the original body of believers is
a further guarantee of the legitimacy of 'the common knowen church'.
More developed this point at greatest length in the *Confutation*. Influenced
by Augustine, notably in *De civitate Dei*,[103] he traced the origin of the
Christian church back to the synagogue, as he termed it, the Jewish *Qahal
Yahweh*. The church of Christ takes over old testament revelation as its
own. In the years since its foundation the church has maintained unspoiled the faith of ancient times. This consistency in faith is witnessed to
by a long line of saints from Ignatius of Antioch to Thomas Aquinas,

---

[101] *Dialogue*, lxiii rC, Campbell, 132-133; ibid., lxiiii rB, Campbell, 134.
[102] See *Confutation* II, 604/6-12; II, 606/19-607/28; 668/19-669/35 and ff.
[103] See Augustine, *De civitate dei*, *MPL* 41, 475-619.

Bonaventure and Anselm. While allowing for development in belief he was careful to insist that such growth is organic in the sense that it will never be found 'that any one generall counsayle orderly called to gether, impugned and reproued a nother'; similarly the general consensus of the faithful.[104]

In short More looked at apostolic succession primarily in terms of belief rather than of church order. In the light of his theology of consensus this is not surprising. It is the fidelity of the church to the original teaching of Christ as handed down through the apostolic community which makes it truly authentic. This position was partly forced on him; or perhaps better, he was obliged to work out this conclusion in response to the constant claims of the reformers that established orthodoxy had departed from the original inspiration of the founder. It is very much in terms of a counterclaim that this assertion is made. On the other hand apostolic succession in terms of church order was not clearly worked out in More's treatises. There are allusions to it, as for example his statement in the *Confutation:* '...they (the Twelve) were all known heades. And they dyd also substytute other whyche were knowen heades also. And euer after by succession knowen heades to succede, of suche as bi the blessed sacrament of holye orders were by special consecracion, as by a certain spirituall generacion borne enherytable to those roumes.'[105] However, he did not develop this into a full blown apologetic argument. Similarly John Headley argues that in the *Responsio* 'More increasingly looked to agreement with the Roman See as the identifying mark of the church.'[106] This puts the case a little too strongly. More included the pontiff in his description of the 'common knowen church' and in his case too recognised the reality of a continuous line of succession.[107] But neither in *Responsio* nor later writings did he make of succession in church order a mainspring of his apologetic argument. Rather did his case rest on the principles of unity and continuity in faith. To these twin characteristics of the church of Christ, he added a third, the gift of miracles.

Miracles

Sir Thomas More made little use of the appeal to miraculous intervention in human affairs to vindicate 'the palpable church' of the *Responsio*. In

[104] *Confutation* II, 923/14-26.
[105] *Confutation* II, 1011/6-11.
[106] Headley, *Responsio*, 763.
[107] See *Confutation* II, 1010/18-21; II, 1011/4-7, '...yet dyde I neuer put the pope for parte of the dyffynycyon of the chyrche, dyffynyng the chyrche to be the comon knowen congregacyon of all chrysten nacyons vnder one hed the pope.' in *Confutation* II, 576/33-37; see also ibid., 577/1-23.

the *Dialogue*, partly because the reality of miracles was cast in doubt by his imaginary opponent, he treated of miracles at some length. In the *Confutation*, however, he made of miraculous intervention one of the principal signs of divine revelation and the authenticity of the church of Christ. In the *Dialogue* More pointed out that miracles were performed by God as credentials for his messengers and the truth of their message. This has been the tradition of old and new testaments, he asserted, as well as the experience of the Catholic Church where the testimony of its fathers and doctors has been validated by supernatural intrusion in the order of nature. Indeed, More claimed that such occurrences are exclusively a privilege of the Catholic community. Some wonders are reported from pagan, Turk and Saracen peoples. They certainly do not occur among heretical sects. Hence the Catholic Church, which is the only religious body visited by these acts of divine benevolence, he argued, must be the bearer of true doctrine.[108]

In the *Confutation* More came to value the testimony of such intervention even more highly. He arrived at this position for a number of reasons. Tyndale himself admitted to the value of miracle as validating revealed truth. Miracles were stressed by St Augustine, More's principal mentor in theology. In dealing with the ultimate core of Lutheran argumentation regarding the authority of scripture More found it necessary to appeal to the testimony of miracles.

This arose in the following way. When it came to a question as to how one knows whether any particular person has divine guidance or not, either as bearer of a divine message or author of an inspired book, Tyndale's solution was to appeal to connatural knowledge: 'As the eagle spieth out her young etc...' More felt this unsatisfactory in the extreme, feeling the need for some objective, empirically based ground for commitment in faith especially in the case of enquiring unbelievers. His solution was to appeal to miracles as confirmation of divine mission or inspiration.

More had little difficulty in accepting the reality of divine incursions into the fabric of terrestrial life. God the all powerful, he felt, can intervene dramatically in human affairs, using created things to achieve results beyond the limits of their natural powers. This occurs daily, he believed, in the celebration of the sacraments where the material symbols become the means of producing interior grace. Indeed such was his acceptance of the miraculous that he justified his view of the sacraments by reference to

---

[108] *Dialogue*, lxxx vG-lxxxi rA, Campbell, 170-171 and passim; ibid., lxxxii rC, Campbell, 174, and passim.

miraculous phenomena recorded in the bible. These miracles he saw as a
vindication of the mission of the prophets of the old testament as much as
that of Jesus in the new. The same gift accompanies the teaching of
Christ's church throughout the ages: 'And by the myracles done in the
same catholyke chyrche, we know that the same chyrche is the very
chyrche of god/and that the doctrine of the same chyrch is reueled and
tought vnto yt by the spyryte of god/and that all other congregacyons
teachynge the contrary be false chyrches...'[109] Such miracles God works
daily 'in his catholyque chyrche' to cause it to be recognised as 'his very
chyrche' and firm credence given thereunto. While keeping an open mind
regarding wonders reported in other religions, he vigorously denied the
possibility of miracles being worked in support of his opponents' teaching.
God could not intervene in support of falsehood but '...wolde leue all those
congregacyons voyd of all myracles...'[110]

[109] *Confutation* I, 246/15-19.
[110] *Confutation* I, 246/27; 271/6-9.

CHAPTER EIGHT

SIR THOMAS MORE'S ECCLESIOLOGY IN ITS CONTEXT

I. THE MODES OF DIVINE REVELATION

The nature of revelation was not a major issue between More and the reformers. It was of course one of the axes of Luther's world of thought. Luther's personal rediscovery of the central role of the revealing word of God and its response in justifying faith was the starting point of the new theological synthesis he created. His concept of the word of God itself was a good deal broader in scope than More's. The term word of God for Luther referred either to the God who speaks, or the speech of God. It is the latter usage that concerns us here. God speaks in various ways, through the act of creation, the saving deeds which marked his interventions in history from Abraham to Jesus as well as the message of the prophets culminating in the revelation of Jesus Christ.[1]

Tyndale had little to add to his master's thought on this subject. For both Tyndale and Luther the word of God was more than event and message. It was also the recital or memorial of both within the church so that its redemptive effect might continue among those prepared to listen. It was on this last point, what has been termed the transmission of revelation, that division occurred.

Seen against the medieval backdrop More's concept of revelation as the unveiling of divine mystery belongs to a movement of thought which Luther himself, perhaps unconsciously, sought to transcend, the late medieval tendency to identify revelation with lists of revealed 'truths' rather than the divine mystery from which they spring. This development had been fathered, among others, by another Englishman, William of Ockham, and found an echo in figures as diverse as Jean Gerson, Juan Torquemada and Gabriel Biel.[2] The counter current flowed strongest in

---

[1] See H. Bornkamm, *Das Wort Gottes bei Luther,* Munich, 1933; Jaroslav Pelikan, *Luther the Expositor, Luther's Works, Companion Volume,* Saint Louis, Mo., 1959, 48-88; H. Beintker, *Luthers Offenbarungsverständnis und die gegenwärtige Theologie, Zeitschrift für systematische Theologie* 24 (1955) 241-265; see in Luther's works: *WA* 40/II, 329; *WA* 40/II, 52; *WA* 46, 543-545; *WA* 42, 13; *WA* 47, 65; *WA* 40/II, 231; *WA* 14, 675; *WA* 40/III, 605-606; *WA* 10/I-I, 626; *WA* 10/II, 48.

[2] See Ockham, *Dialogus,* pars I, lib. II, cap. 5, Goldast, *Monarchiae,* III, 415-416; Jean Gerson, *De examinatione doctrinarum,* secunda pars principalis, consideratio prima, Dupin, *Opera Omnia,* I, 12-14. See also Du Pin, I, 22-24; Turrecremata, *Summa de ecclesia,* lib. IV, pars II, cap. 9, Venice, 1560, 381v-383r.

the Low Countries where the mystical movement associated with the Brothers of the Common Life as well as figures such as Johann Pupper von Goch and Wessel Gansfort instinctively perceived the immensity of divine being and in consequence the relativity of human statements concerning it, even those embodied in divinely-inspired scripture.[3] While Fisher seems to have belonged to the Ockhamist strain,[4] More's colleague Desiderius Erasmus, though in a slightly different key, stressed the transcendence of divine mystery and the limits on human endeavour in coming to grips with it. Speaking critically of the methods of certain theologians, mainly scholastics, he said 'qui animis rudibus, repente ad divinitatis arcana non ingredimur, sed irrumpimus, non adscendimus, sed involamus, et tanquam gigantes, exstruetis in coelum molibus, invito Jove arcem illius occupare conamur?'[5] The mystery of God lies hidden in the mist; best approached by a *via negativa,* hence beyond the power of any formula to encapsulate.

II. TRANSMISSION OF REVELATION

In this over-all approach to the transmission of revelation, recognising the complementarity of scripture and tradition, Sir Thomas More was in the main stream of late medieval thought. He had moved away, it is true, from the global concept of *scriptura sacra* of the patristic and early medieval church which tended to view the facts of revelation as a global, synthetic system, rather than as separate circuits each channelling its own peculiar set of message impulses.[6] Not surprisingly More had many companions in the late medieval period in presenting the transmission of revelation as flowing in two distinct streams, scripture and tradition, as well as in the significance he attached to primitive apostolic revelation. This concept can be found in William of Ockham, implicit in his listing of *veritates catholicae* in five categories including those: '...quae in Scriptura sacra dicuntur'; those '...quae ab Apostolis ad nos per succedentium relationem vel Scripturas fidelium pervenerunt, licet in Scripturis sacris non inveniantur insertae nec ex solis eis possint necessario argumento concludi,' and, he

---

[3] See von Goch, *De scripturae sacrae dignitate,* ed. Pijper, 288; idem, *De libertate christiana,* lib. IV, cap. 5, ed. Pijper, 236-237; ibid., lib. I, cap. 8, ed. Pijper, 56; ibid., lib. I, cap. 9, ed. Pijper, 57; Tavard, *Holy Writ,* 69-72; Oberman, *Harvest of Medieval Theology,* 408-412.

[4] See Surtz, *Fisher,* 232-233.

[5] See Erasmus, *Antibarbari, LB* X, 1738F. See Kohls, *Die Theologie des Erasmus,* I, 58-59; 71.

[6] See Congar, *Tradition,* 86-93; Beumer, *Die mündliche Überlieferung,* 45-53.

added, the content of revelations subsequent to apostolic times.[7] Ockham
the philosophical sceptic was almost a fideist in the nineteenth century
sense when it came to divine revelation. This pluralistic concept of tradition continued through the fifteenth century to the Council of Trent and
indeed subsequently. Even to the present time it has acted as a watershed
marking off Catholic and Protestant approaches to Christian revelation.

Scholars have noted two important trends within this school of thought,
one which emphasised the co-inherence of scripture and tradition, namely
that all essential truths are contained in scripture and other traditions are
merely the explicitation of scripture's hidden truth. The second school of
thought saw both scripture and tradition as distinct tributaries each one
carrying its own separate outflow of divine truth from the original reser-
voir in the divine act of self-communication.[8] William of Ockham was undoubtedly a key figure in the explicit emergence of this second school of
thought. It was echoed in the writings of men as diverse as Thomas Netter
of Walden, the English Carmelite opponent of John Wyclif, Jean Gerson,
Turrecremata, and Gabriel Biel the Tübingen theologian whom Luther
studied in depth while at Erfurt.[9]

Within Catholic theology a further school of thought emphasised the
role of the Holy Spirit in the church as bearer of tradition. This school, as
we saw above, was linked with the *devotio moderna* and other movements in
spirituality and theology in the Low Countries, a significant *motif* in the
harmonious development of the Northern Renaissance. The rediscovery
of Augustine, and in particular his work *De spiritu et littera* led thinkers
such as Johannes Pupper von Goch (+ 1475) to relate tradition to the
ongoing inspiration of the Holy Spirit in the hearts of the faithful, citing in
particular Heb 10, 16. Within this perspective they viewed the interpretation of God's word in Christian tradition as a verbalised expression of the
inward guidance of the Spirit. Another writer of this school, Wessel
Gansfort, who entered into Luther's ambit, having taught at Erfurt from
1455-1460, carried this view of tradition to a clear conclusion in seeing
tradition understood in this way as explanatory of scripture rather than as
a complementary body of revealed truth.[10]

---

[7] See Ockham, *Dialogus,* pars I, lib. II, cap. 5, in Goldast, *Monarchiae* III, 415-416.

[8] See Oberman, *Harvest of Medieval Theology,* 365-393.

[9] See e.g. Gerson, *De examinatione doctrinarum*, (1423), secunda pars principalis, consideratio prima, ed. Du Pin, *Opera Omnia*, 12-14; Turrecremata, *Summa de ecclesia*, lib. IV,
pars II, cap. 9, Venice, 1560, 381v-383r; Netter, *Doctrinale antiquitatum*, lib. II, art. II, cap.
XIX, Venice, 1571, 193/1-197/2. See also Tavard, *Holy Writ,* 22-66; Congar, *Tradition,*
94-101; Oberman, *Harvest of Medieval Theology,* 365-408.

[10] See Tavard, *Holy Writ,* 67-72; Oberman, *Harvest of Medieval Theology,* 408-412; von

Sir Thomas More himself, in company with many Catholic theologians subsequently, understood Luther to stand for a simplistic *scriptura sola* approach to the manner in which divine revelation is relayed to successive generations of believers. This does little justice to the depth and complexity of the Wittenberger's views. Luther emphasised first and foremost the transcendence of the divine Word which becomes immanent in a variety of ways, the created world, historical event, prophetic utterance, as well as the gospel written on the inner heart of the believer by the Holy Spirit. Its central message is God's loving mercy towards those who submit in faith to Jesus as saviour.

The church's preaching and written word of scripture is the memorial of the revelation of God. It actually becomes God's word when listened to or read with faith.[11] In this regard the bible has a key role to play. The believer comes in contact with the transcendent word of God when, inspired by the Spirit, he reflects on the literal sense of scripture in faith and in the light of its own central theme, sinful man's redemption in Christ. It is in this sense that scripture is the rule of faith, an indispensable and unique *means* to encountering the living Word of the transcendent God. The letter can never contain the divine Spirit but for sub-apostolic generations the letter read in the Spirit is the norm of proclamation and of faith. It is an exclusive and unique means, *scriptura sola,* of coming to know the God revealed to us in Christ.[12]

In the early years of his breach with the established church this was the theme Luther stressed. In the period following the emergence of Anabaptist and other sects he found a new value in patristic tradition but only as an aid to the interpretation of scripture. He could not accept the notion that grains of divine wisdom were unattainable in scripture but could be gleaned from other sources.[13] Still less would he abide the concept of further communication of salvific significance after that made to the apostolic community in an ongoing revelation.

Goch, *De libertate christiana,* lib. IV, cap. 5, ed. Pijper, 236-237, where he quotes Augustine, *De spiritu et littera,* cap. XVII, 29, *MPL* 44, 218; von Goch, ibid., lib. I, cap. 8, ed. Pijper, 56.

[11] '...verbum est verbum Dei originaliter et autoritative, non ecclesiae nisi passive et ministerialiter. Ergo ecclesia est sub verbo et mandato Dei et non supra.' See *WA* 30/II, 682. See also: Pelikan, *Luther the Expositor,* 48-88; G. Ebeling, *Luther, An Introduction to his Thought,* tr. R. A. Wilson, London, 1970, 93-109.

[12] 'Nolo omnium doctor iactari, sed solam Scripturam regnare, nec eam meo spiritu aut ullorum hominum interpretari, sed per se ipsam et suo spiritu intelligi volo.' See *WA* 7, 98 ff; 7, 721; *WA* 39/I, 184-197. See also *WA* 51, 515; *WA* 30/III, 342-343.

[13] See *WA* 13, 242; *WA* 8, 98-99; *WA* 43, 94. See Pelikan, *Luther the Expositor,* 81-85.

Luther's disciple, Tyndale, failed also to grasp the complexity of his master's thought. He opted for a somewhat fundamentalist identification of revelation with the written word of God in scripture. The historical sense of scripture was the principal key to this revelation, though he also recognised the need for collation with 'a like text of another place', the need to '...make Christ the foundation and the ground, and build all on him...' and to ensure '...that the exposition agreeth unto the common articles of the faith and open scriptures.' Tyndale did not expand on his concept of 'the common articles of faith'. Flesseman-Van Leer is probably right in suggesting that little else besides the doctrine of justification by faith meant a great deal to Tyndale in this respect. He constantly reiterated his thesis concerning the essential openness of scripture, its own inner harmony, and its intelligibility to the ordinary reader.[14]

More to a larger extent failed to grasp Luther's position regarding the memorial of revelation and its relation to the transcendent Word. He understood him to hold a position close to that of Tyndale, whereas, although their positions were far from identical, More's view of tradition in the *Responsio*, where he almost identified it completely with the indwelling Spirit of God and his interior action on the mind and heart of the believer, could bear comparison with Luther's concept of the transcendent Word immanent in scripture but attainable only by interior illumination by the Spirit of God. Both controversialists cited the same texts: among others Jer 31, 33 and Heb 10, 16, in support of their respective positions. The nuance of difference lay perhaps, firstly, in More's emphasis on the immanence of the revealing God in the believing community whereas his opponent laid greater stress on the presence of God in scripture; secondly, in More's insistence that tradition even in this pneumatic sense contained revelations both materially and formally distinct from those of holy writ. In his later development in *Dialogue* and *Confutation* of a doctrine on tradition which leaned substantively on a socio-cultural transmission mechanism More moved even further away from both Luther and Tyndale to a position where the literary monuments and religious customs of the church are placed almost on a par with scripture as media of divine disclosure.

Henry VIII had no hesitation in fastening on church tradition as an alternative source of transmitted revelation to the inspired word of scripture. Henry decried Luther's confidence in the sufficiency of scripture,

[14] See Tyndale, *The Wicked Mammon*, ed. Walter, 46-54; *Obedience of a Christian Man*, ed. Walter, 156; 304-305; 167; 329-330.

citing Jn 20, 30 in defence of his position that Jesus had done and said many things not recorded in the bible. These have been presented and transmitted to successive generations in the church under the guidance of the Holy Spirit. Henry also spoke of another gospel written in the hearts of the faithful by the Spirit (Heb 10, 16). In practice, however, he opted for a socio-cultural concept of tradition which contrasts with that used predominantly by More in the *Responsio*. On the other hand texts which More called on frequently were also part of Henry's staple: Lk 22, 32, Jn 16, 13, Jn 20, 30.[15] More summarised the king's argument thus: '...uerbum dei probauit aliud scriptum esse, aliud non scriptum: sed uel ab apostolis tradita quaedam, uel a Christo ecclesiae suae dicta diuinitus...Sacramenta septem; et reliquos articulos fidei: *partim scripto, partim non scripto,* sed tamen dei uerbo fulciri; utrumque uerbum ex aequo certum, ex aequo uenerabile.'[16] More here used the *partim...partim* formula to express the king's thought, a formula which has been traced variously to St Basil and the pseudo-Dionysius's *Ecclesiastical Hierarchies.* More may have in all likelihood borrowed the phrase from Fisher's *Confutatio,* reputedly the first theologian to use the formula to explain the relationship between revelation and its conveyance within the Christian community.[17]

Fisher, More's fellow controversialist had a deep devotion to scripture all his life. This did not prevent him acknowledging its limits and the worth of other sources of divine revelation. Indeed he went further than either Henry VIII or Thomas More in promoting the concept of a distinct oral tradition. In his sermon against Luther he spoke of tradition as one of the three foundations for the church: '...Fyrst the prophetes that were instructed by the father almyghty god. And also theyr Cabala...Secondly the apostles. whiche were instructed by oure sauyoure chryst Jesu. and also

---

[15] See Henry VIII, *Assertio,* sig. M4 rv; *Responsio,* 88/1-90/8; ibid., 240/31-242/6; Headley, *Responsio,* 734-739.

[16] See *Responsio,* 240/31-242/6.

[17] See J. R. Geiselmann, *Das Konzil von Trient über das Verhältnis der Heiligen Schrift und der nicht geschriebenen Traditionen,* in *Die mündliche Überlieferung,* ed. Michael Schmaus, Munich, 1957, 123-206; 140 in particular. The *partim...partim* formula may have originated in St Basil's treatise *De spiritu sancto* where his adverbial form *ta men...ta de* could have been rendered *partim...partim.* Or possibly more likely, pseudo-Dionysius's, *Ecclesiastical Hierarchies* which in the translation of Ambrosius Traversari Camaldulensis, printed in Strasbourg in 1498, contained this *partim...partim* formula. Given John Colet's predilection for the pseudo-Dionysius, it is conceivable that Fisher could have derived the formula from Traversari. See John Fisher, *Assertionis Lutheranae Confutatio,* (Antwerp, 1523), 12v and *Opera Omnia,* Vvirceburgi, 1597, 295, where he cites Traversari: 'hi multa, partim scriptis, partim non scriptis institutionibus suis...nobis tradiderunt.'

theyr tradycyons not wryten in the byble. Thyrdely the holy fathers and doctours of the chyrche. that were enformed by the holy spyryte of trouthe. as well in theyr exposycyons of scrypture. as also by theyr general assembles and counceyles had here to fore.'[18] Thus side by side with the scripture, Fisher envisaged the word of God handed on from generation to generation in a tradition oral, written, and indeed non-verbal as well, in the life and custom of the Christian community.

It is interesting to note Fisher's explicit use of Cabalistic ideas though referring them strictly to the old testament. In making this reference he was probably under Colet's patronage who had brought these ideas into currency in England partly under Pico della Mirandola's influence, partly under that of the pseudo-Dionysius. Colet's interest in Cabalism waned in later years due perhaps to the discrediting of Dionysius. Fisher, however, in the heart of reformation controversy retained this somewhat dubious approach to tradition, a decision which underlines the importance he attached to extra-biblical ecclesiastical tradition in all its forms. In this, like Henry, he was more than likely affected by the guidance of Colet, pioneer of Christian humanism in England as well as a sturdy advocate of church reform several years before Luther or Tyndale appeared on stage.[19]

Fisher, indeed, well after Colet's interest in Cabalism had cooled, continued to be impressed by it.[20] In June or July 1517 he had written to Erasmus complaining that a copy of *De arte cabalistica,* with which Reuchlin had presented him, had been held up by Thomas More to whom it had been transmitted by Erasmus, '...as he did before with the *Oculare speculum.*' In fact More had passed the work on with Erasmus's permission to Colet, and it was the latter who had delayed delivery.[21] This happening

---

[18] See John Fisher, *The sermon...made agayn the pernicyous doctryn of Martin luuther...,* (1521), *The English Works of John Fisher,* Part I, ed. J. E. B. Mayor, London, Early English Text Society, 1876, 331-336. On this see Edward Surtz S. J., *The Works and Days of John Fisher,* Cambridge, Mass., 1967, 100-113. See also Fisher, *Confutatio, Opera Omnia,* cc. 278-290; 290-296: 'The apostolic traditions, although they have been set forth in no way in holy scripture, are nevertheless to be observed by persons truly Christian.'

[19] See John Colet, *In ecclesiasticam divi Dionisii hierarchiam* in *Ioannes Coletus super opera Dionysii, Two Treatises on the Hierarchies of Dionysius, by John Colet, D. D.,* ed. J. H. Lupton, London, 1869, 56; 110-112.

[20] See John Colet to Erasmus in *The Epistles of Erasmus,* tr. F. M. Nichols, Vol. II, London, 1904, 596-597: Colet commenting on Reuchlin's *De arte cabalistica:* 'Ah, Erasmus, of books and of knowledge there is no end; but there is nothing better for this short term of ours, than that we should live a pure and holy life...Wherefore it is my most earnest wish, that leaving all indirect courses, we may proceed by a short method to the Truth.'

[21] See Erasmus to More, Allen, *Erasmi epistolae,* II, pp. 494, 496; Fisher to Erasmus, ibid., II, p. 598; Fisher to Erasmus, Allen, *Erasmi epistolae,* III, p. 75. Fisher had, apparently, a very high regard for Reuchlin; see Erasmus to Johann Reuchlin, Antwerp, 29 Sept. 1516, Allen, *Erasmi epistolae,* II, 350: 'Adorat te propemodum Episcopus Rossensis...'

itself is of little significance except as a human incident illustrating the genesis and lineage of certain currents of thought at work in the reformation controversy.

More, who was aware of the Cabalist movement, steered clear of it, while at the same time adopting a 'two-source theory' of the transmission of revelation. Moreover, his earliest emphasis on a pneumatic theology of tradition gave ground to a socio-cultural theory in his later writings. Erasmus too looked on Cabalism with a sceptical eye without losing touch with it.[22] Erasmus indeed clove even closer to the bible than his English colleagues, opting for a view of tradition as explanatory of scripture rather than as in any way independent of it.

Prior to Luther's critical breach with Rome in spring 1520, Erasmus's main concern had been scripture and what it had to say about the Christian life. Living in the church, he implicitly accepted the canon of scripture approved by tradition.[23] In his approach to the content of faith, Erasmus ascribed the primary role to the literal sense of scripture. His greatest theological work at this time was his *Novum Instrumentum* (1516), a controversial edition and translation of the Greek new testament. Here he affirmed his belief in the primacy of scripture: '...scribit Chrysostomus, ad confirmandum Evangelium non esse opus humana philosophia, sed sufficere sibi Scripturam;...'[24] His opinion in this respect did not change, as appears from a letter to Jean Carondolet seven years later: 'This indeed is true theology, to define that only which is clearly contained in sacred scripture.'[25]

Erasmus was not one sided in his approach to revelation. He also recognised the role of ecclesiastical tradition not separate or distinct from

---

[22] See Erasmus to John Caesarius, 3 Nov. 1517, Allen, *Erasmi epistolae*, III, 127/13-38.

[23] Thus Erasmus in his younger years. See Kohls, *Die Theologie des Erasmus*, 127-243. In his later writings one finds him referring to the function of the church in authenticating scripture; see Erasmus to Willibald Pirckheimer, 19 October 1527, Allen, *Erasmi epistolae*, VII, 216/55-217/70: '...sequor interpretem Ecclesiam, cuius autoritate persuasus credo Scripturis canonicis.'; idem, *In Psalmum* XXII, (1530), *LB* 5, 323.

[24] See Erasmus, *Novum instrumentum*, marginal note to 1 Cor 2, 13, *LB* 6, 668F. See also Franz Otto Stichart, *Erasmus von Rotterdam, seine Stellung zu der Kirche und zu den kirchlichen Bewegungen seiner Zeit*, Leipzig, 1870, 234-253; Georg Gebhardt, *Die Stellung des Erasmus von Rotterdam zur Römischen Kirche*, Marburg, 1966, 44-51; Kohls, *Die Theologie des Erasmus*, 77-78; 84-87; A. Renaudet, *Érasme et l'Italie*, Geneva, 1954, 118-121; *Études Érasmiennes (1521-1529)*, Paris, 1939, 139-144; 322-328; 338-340; 347; F. de Maesener, *De Methode van de Theologie volgens Erasmus*, Rome, 1963, 84-99.

[25] 'Imo hoc demum est eruditionis theologicae, nihil ultra quam sacris literis proditum est, definire...' in Erasmus to Jean Carondolet, 5 January 1522/23, Allen, *Erasmi epistolae*, V, 178/229-230; Erasmus, *Modus orandi deum* (1524), *LB* 5, 1115E-1116B. See also his preface to *Novum instrumentum* (1516), *LB* 6, ii r.

the bible as regards content but explanatory of it.[26] In his own thought he
showed the highest regard for the fathers: his monumental editions of
patristic writing are sufficient evidence of this. On the other hand he did
not allow himself be led into making of theological tradition a rival literary
source of revelation to scripture. He fully recognised the discrepancies to
be found within the individual writers of the patristic era as well as in
tradition as a whole.[27] His attitude towards ecclesial tradition was
threefold. Firstly he recognised the value of the individual witness and interpretation of the individual writer while fully alive to the possibility of individual error. Secondly he recognised the possibility of apostolic tradition
preserved within the church in the writings of the fathers. Thirdly he
acknowledged the possibility of an ecclesial consensus demonstrable by a
constant agreement across the centuries evidenced in the records of tradition. Within this framework, however, Erasmus consistently upheld the
primacy of scripture as a means of entering into living contact with the
mystery of God.

III. Definition of Church

In the course of history the definition of the church has been the subject
of several dialectical tensions, among them those between inward communion and outward association, between people and priesthood, between
local congregation and universal fellowship, and on the temporal axis, between the church of this world and that of other worldly glory. The
patristic age notably in Augustine had created a tentatively balanced
understanding of these various elements. Thus Augustine measured his
conception of the *societas sanctorum* united in the Spirit against the visible
communio sanctorum, united in the sacraments. He qualified his concern
with the *ecclesia ab Abel,* the church of the predestinate, with the *ecclesia
qualis nunc est* which includes those who are members *universo non merito.*
While recognising the full franchise of every baptised Christian in the
body of Christ, he also acknowledged the need for order and the ministry

---

[26] See Erasmus, *Ratio verae theologiae* (1518), *LB* 5, 82AB. See Allen, *Erasmi epistolae,* XII,
30-34 for the list of patristic editions which Erasmus edited. See also *Ratio verae theologiae, LB*
5, 92D: 'Proximum his (scripturis sacris) locum tenet quaedam nobis ceu per manus tradita,
vel ab ipsis Apostolis ad nos usque profecta, vel ab iis certa, qui vicini fuerunt temporibus
Apostolorum.' See also A. Renaudet, *Études Érasmiennes,* 141-144; 340-341; F. Stichart,
Erasmus von Rotterdam, loc. cit.; Denys Gorce, *La Patristique dans la réforme d'Érasme,* in *Festgabe
Joseph Lortz,* II, *Glaube und Geschichte,* ed. Erwin Iserloh and Peter Manns, Baden-Baden,
1958, 233-276; de Maesener, *De Methode van de Theologie,* 107-113.

[27] See Erasmus to Henry Bullock, 22 August 1516, Allen, *Erasmi epistolae,* II, 323/65-67;
idem, *Lingua* (1523), *LB* 4, 703D; D. Gorce, *La Patristique,* 248-249.

of those 'quorum est in ecclesia saluberrima auctoritas'. He gave due place to the local congregation, but Augustine continually emphasised the essentially universal character of the *ecclesia catholica*.[28]

These same dialectical tensions ran through the development of ecclesiology in the whole medieval period. The greater theologians, whether of the school of St Victor, Aquinas, William of Ockham, or the conciliarist thinkers among whom Jean Gerson stands out, managed each in his own way to create a certain harmony between the various elements of this mystical and social polygon.[29] This is not to say that all was light and harmony in the evolution of medieval conceptions of the church. The canonist tradition on the one hand tended to emphasise the institutional at the expense of the charismatic, the international at the expense of the local, the temporal as opposed to the eschatological, and while carrying within its tradition strong currents of populist, 'neo-democratic' thinking, generally tended to emphasise authority at the expense of the place of the people.[30] This latter trend reached an extreme height in the thought of papalist apologists such as Aegidius Romanus and later 'aristocratic' theorists who sought to make either the Roman see or the cardinalatial college a social archetype of the church, containing potentially within itself the spiritual and temporal powers of the whole *ecclesia*.[31] In polar opposition to this current of thought stood that of the 'Spirituals' from Michael of Cesena to Wyclif and the English Lollards. This body of opinion sought to emphasise the spiritual character of Christian fellowship, often emphasising the eschatological nature of such communion to the neglect of the *cor-*

---

[28] See Congar, *Ecclésiologie*, 11-24, and above pp. 21-22.

[29] See for example: Hugh of St Victor, *De sacramentis christianae fidei*, lib. II, pars 2, *MPL* 176, c. 416; Thomas Aquinas, *In symbolum apostolorum*, a. 9, ed. Spiazzi, 211-213; idem, *De veritate*, Q. 29, a. 4-5, ed. Spiazzi, *Quaestiones disputatae*, I, 558-562; Ockham, *Dialogus*, pars I, lib. 5, cap. 29-35, ed. Goldast, *Monarchiae* III, 498-506; Gerson, *De auferibilitate papae ab ecclesia*, ed. Du Pin, *Opera Omnia*, II, 212D-213C.

[30] See Congar, *Ecclésiologie*, 145-151; Tierney, *Foundations of the Conciliar Theory*, 23-84; J. Watt, *The Early Medieval Canonists and the Formation of Conciliar Theory*, Irish Theological Quarterly 24 (1957) 13-31; W. Ullman, *Medieval Papalism, The Political Theories of the Medieval Canonists*, London, 1949, 76-114 and passim; idem, *The Growth of Papal Government in the Middle Ages*, 3rd ed., London, 1970, 262-309; idem, *Principles of Government and Politics in the Middle Ages*, 2nd ed., London, 1966, 32-56.

[31] See for example Aegidius Romanus, *De ecclesiastica potestate*, lib. III, cap ult., ed. Scholz, 206-209; ibid., II, cap. 2, ed., Scholz, 99; ibid., II, cap. 12, ed. Scholz, 108; ibid., II cap. 5, 59; ibid., III, cap. 2. ed. Scholz, 155; see Rivière, *Le Problème de l'Église*, 191-227. On 'oligarchical' ecclesiology, see Merzbacher, *Wandlungen des Kirchenbegriffs*, 346-351; O. Prerovsky, *Le idee oligarche nei difensori di Clemente VII*, Salesianum XXII (1960) 383-408; see for example Ferrer, *De moderno ecclesie schismate*, ed. Fages, 27-38; Flandrin, *In facto schismatis*, ed. Bliemetzrieder, 3-71.

pus permixtum of the here and now. Not infrequently this led to an identification of the church with a small body of *electi* as opposed to the universality of believers, ambiguous in their witness to their profession of faith.[32]

Luther and Tyndale to a large degree fall within this latter current of
thought. Reacting against the emphasis on institution in canonical and a
good deal of scholastic thinking, Luther opted for a predominantly
spiritual conception of the church at some point between 1515 and 1520.[33]
The only church which is worth considering is that of the justified, those
here and now in vital contact with the Spirit of Christ, those who both
numero et merito belong to Christian fellowship. This fellowship is essentially
a hidden group bound by spiritual ties to Christ the Saviour.[34] A similar
conception underlay Tyndale's ideas of the church. The church of Christ
for him was essentially the church of the elect, 'the whole multitude of all
repenting sinners that believe in Christ, and put all their trust and confidence in the mercy of God.'[35] As real faith is difficult to discern, the
fellowship of which it is the foundation must of necessity be somewhat
nebulous in character.

As John Headley so acutely observes, More himself was living in a
world of implicit assumptions concerning the nature of the church. It was
Luther's vigorous assault on Catharinus together with some prompting
from Thomas Murner which in all probability led More to recognise the
other worldly, transcendental quality of the congregation his opponent
designated as the church of Christ. Caught in this dialectical tension, and

---

[32] See for example Wyclif, *De ecclesia,* ed. Loserth, 5: 'Patet ergo ex fide et signacione *quid nominis ecclesie catholice,* quod ipsa est omnes predestinati presentes, preteriti et futuri.' See also ibid., 2, 7,8, 11; 408-416. See also Leff, *Heresy in the Later Middle Ages,* 494-558 and passim; Congar, *Ecclésiologie,* 299-303.

[33] A more detailed account of Luther's ecclesiology and literature relating to it will be found in the works listed in n. 34.

[34] Whatever the outcome of the debate concerning the precise time at which Luther broke with the traditional view of the relation between outer community and inward communion, there is little question that at the time of the More-Luther disputation Luther had already advanced to a 'spiritual' conception of the church. The hidden congregation of true believers is composed of those who have been justified by faith in the saving work of Jesus Christ. This inward communion is the mystical body of Christ. It makes its presence perceptible mainly in the preaching of God's word. See Karl Holl, *Die Entstehung von Luthers Kirchenbegriff,* (1915), in *Gesammelte Aufsätze zur Kirchengeschichte,* Tübingen, 1927, 288-325; Holsten Fagerberg, *Die Kirche in Luthers Psalmenvorlesungen 1513-1515, Gedenkschrift für D. Werner Elert,* ed. F. Hübner, Berlin, 1955, 109-118; W. Maurer, *Kirche und Geschichte nach Luthers Dictata super Psalterium,* in V. Vajta, *Lutherforschung Heute,* Berlin, 1958, 85-101; H. J. Iwand, *Zur Enstehung von Luthers Kirchenbegriff,* in *Festschrift für Günther Dehn,* ed. W. Schneemelcher, Neukirchen, 1957, 145-166; S. H. Hendrix, *Ecclesia in Via,* Leyden, 1974, 284-287 and passim.

[35] See Tyndale, *Answer,* 30; see also ibid., 13, 113, 108-110.

even though he himself was possessed by a deeply spiritual insight into the nature of Christian communion, More opted in practice for an 'empirically' based, temporal, and institutional description of the church of Christ. Within this definition he maintained a real balance between popular and authoritarian elements, but on the spiritual-empirical axis, nominally at least, he fell into the dialectical trap of opting for a definition of Christian community in socio-political terms.

This dialectical tendency is all the clearer in the *Dialogue*, where the process of the argument from common ground to specifying difference culminates in the definition of the church of Christ once more in socio-political terms: 'Is it not this company and congregayon of all these nacyons/that without faccyons taken...professe the name and fayth of Cryst...'[36]

More's emphasis on the empirical church is in contrast with that of his spiritual guide John Colet. Through his study of the fathers, notably the neo-platonic work of the pseudo-Dionysius and his meditation on scripture, Colet had recovered a deeply spiritual vision of Christian fellowship: 'This composite Body also, formed of God and men, is sometimes called God's temple by the sacred writers, sometimes his Church, sometimes his House, sometimes his City, sometimes his Kingdom...'[37]

While Colet, if with some ambiguity, included in this perspective the role of office and institution, he insisted that the essential bond keeping this body together lay at the level of spirit not law or organisation. Speaking of the function of bishops he said: 'In this mutual love consists all order, duty and office in the Church; and the whole Ecclesiastical Hierarchy in it rests on the love of God and of our neighbour.'[38] The greater the bishop is, the more he should serve in the office of love and ministration. Clearly, then, this was no juridical institution endowed with temporal power but a charismatically inspired communion of believing persons.

Fisher, like Colet, adopted a predominantly spiritual view of the church. 'Just as Eve was formed from the side of Adam so the life of the church comes from the side of Christ himself...'[39] And again: 'Just as Eve

---

[36] *Dialogue*, lxviii vG, Campbell, 143-144.

[37] John Colet, *Enarratio in primam epistolam S. Pauli ad Corinthios. An Exposition of St Paul's First Epistle to the Corinthians*, ed. J. H. Lupton, London, 1874, 7; see also ibid., 248-249, tr. 123-124; 254-255, tr. 140-142; 260-261, tr. 143-144.

[38] See Colet, *In ecclesiasticam hierarchiam*, 50-51; See also: idem, *Enarratio I Cor, 87*: 'For there never lived the man, who loved even the most indulgent father or mother so exceedingly, and with such dutiful affection, as every true son of God loves one who is truly his brother in God.'

[39] See John Fisher, *De veritate corporis et sanguinis Christi in eucharistia, Opera Omnia*, 1068.

came forth from Adam so we who are the church and spouse of Christ through sharing in his body and blood are formed into one body. We are members of the body of Christ as two are made one body (in matrimony).'[40] This theme was reiterated on numerous occasions by Fisher under the familiar biblical images of the temple, the spiritual house, the spouse of Christ. At the same time Fisher made it clear that he identified this body with the organised, visible community of Christians with its visible hierarchy and due system of authority.[41] Fisher seems to have been influenced by Colet in his vision of the church[42] as spiritual reality, yet in the heat of controversy and in dependence perhaps on a more formal scholastic tradition, also emphasised the institutional and hierarchical elements in its make up.

Erasmus, in his earlier writings, did not attempt a formal definition of the church. The focus of his concern was the quality of individual Christian life. The church was part of the context within which the drama of personal existence was staged.[43] At the same time, as Ernst-Wilhelm Kohls points out, in the *Enchiridion militis christiani* certain significant assumptions were made which constituted the ground plan of later, more formal, theological developments. Recent studies suggest that Kohls's thesis is to a great extent verified in Erasmus's later writings on the church.[44] Erasmus presents his view of the church in the *Enchiridion* within the *exitus-reditus* schema of patristic theology. Love emanates from God and eventually returns to him. The church is a historical, social and institutional manifestation of divine love.[45] For Erasmus in the strictest sense, there is only one office within the church, that of love. Hence the in-

---

[40] See Fisher, *De veritate corporis, Opera Omnia,* 1134.

[41] See Fisher, *Assertionis Lutheranae confutatio,* art. XXV, *Opera Omnia,* 565-569, where Rochester argues to the multiple headship of this mystical body; Christ in the spiritual order, the pope in the temporal order. See also G. Duggan, *The Church in the Writings of St. John Fisher, Dissertation presented for the Doctorate in Theology,* Angelicum, Rome, 1937 (mss), 78-80.

[42] 'Have we not seen that Christians are born of priests, priests of bishops, and bishops also are generated (propagari) by the sovereign pontiff. The latter, who is the greatest, is descended in direct line from Peter...' in Fisher, *Confutatio, Opera Omnia,* 567. Cp. Colet, *De sacramentis ecclesiae,* ed. J. H. Lupton, London, 1867, 35-45. Idem, *In ecclesiasticam hierarchiam,* 53; 128-130.

[43] See Ernst-Wilhelm Kohls, *Die Theologie des Erasmus,* 159-160.

[44] Kohls, *Die Theologie des Erasmus,* 192-194. See Gebhardt, *Die Stellung des Erasmus zur römischen Kirche,* 404-417 and *passim*; W. Hentze, *Kirche und kirchliche Einheit bei Desiderius Erasmus von Rotterdam,* Paderborn, 1974, 213-217 and passim; among several important contributions see especially C. Augustijn, *The Ecclesiology of Erasmus,* in *Scrinium Erasmianum,* ed. J. Coppens, Vol. II, Leyden, 1969, 135-156.

[45] See Erasmus, *Enchiridion,* ed. Holborn, 67/32-35; Kohls, *Die Theologie des Erasmus,* 162-164.

stitutional aspect of church life has value and meaning for him as an expression of the inner dynamism of the Spirit and as leading towards a
deepening participation in the life of charity on the part of each of its
members.[46] This naturally leads to a spiritual conception of the church as
the body of Christ (Rm 12, 5; 1 Cor 12, 12-26) whose many-faceted activities are preserved in harmony through the action of the Spirit. The
Christian fellowship then is essentially one of love. Its visible, perceptible
social life and structures must be seen as a function of this central reality.
This did not lead to a rejection of sacrament, office, or law but rather to
placing them in a particular perspective and relationship to the primary
reality.[47] The final evolution of this view may be seen in one of Erasmus's
later works, the *Explanatio symboli* (1533). 'Laudatur Christiana concordia,
sine qua nulla est Religio, nulla felicitas. Huius absolutum exemplum
habes in Patre, Filio et Spiritu sancto, habes proximum in nomine Ecclesiae, quae tot vinculis connectitur, habens unum Deum, unam fidem,
unas leges, unum baptisma, eadem sacramenta, eumdem Spiritum,
eamdem expectans haereditatem.'[48]

IV. THE INWARD CHURCH

More's theology of the interior life of the church belongs to the main
line of Christian ecclesiology from the new testament onwards. His
awareness of God abiding with his church, whether attributed to Father,
Son or Spirit, was nothing new to Christian tradition. For while it is true
that on the one hand canonists in ecclesiastical administration, as well as
theorists of the hierocratic school tended to stress and to some extent virtually idolise the institutional aspects of church life, and on the other, those
involved in the conciliarist debate were deeply concerned with organisational structures, throughout the medieval period there was a constant
flow of reflection and comment on inward aspects of Christian community.

Here too a certain shift in value systems took place. The role of the
Spirit as enlivening the church was taken over by the humanity of Christ.
The broadly sacramental view of the visible structure of the church
became obscured. Nonetheless, apart even from the activity of the
'spirituals' on the frontiers of orthodoxy, the great medieval doctors,

---

[46] See Erasmus, *Enchiridion*, ed. Holborn, 107; ibid., 76/27-77/7; Kohls, *Die Theologie des Erasmus*, 164-165.

[47] See Erasmus, *Enchiridion*, ed. Holborn, 82-83.

[48] See Erasmus, *Explanatio symboli*, (1533), *LB V*, 1185BC.

Hugh of St Victor, Bernard, Aquinas, Gerson, down to Turrecremata and Nicholas of Cusa gave due prominence to the spiritual dimension of Christian community, each within his own conceptual and linguistic frame of reference and with his own personal degree of emphasis.[49]

More did not make of God's word and man's response a major parameter of his thought on the church as did Luther and his followers.[50] Yet the centrality of faith in divine revelation as a condition of membership and indeed the basis on which the church of Christ was founded was a significant element in his thinking.[51] Within the act of justifying faith itself there was a different focus of interest, Luther and Tyndale downgrading the need for any rational preamble to faith and underlining as key element the surrender to God's loving mercy in Christ made possible by divine gift.[52] It is true that More affirmed the need for reasonable grounds for positing an act of faith, which he also recognised as a divine gift. He also laid stress on unreserved acceptance of the articles of faith, that is on the doctrinal content of revelation.[53] At the same time one can at least identify in his recognition of the possibility of justification by implicit faith the point at which a real dialogue as distinct from a disputation might have developed on the nature of faith leading to justification. The direction this might have taken can be seen most clearly, perhaps, in his interpretation of the 'petrine' text (Mt 16, 18) in the *Confutation,* not in a 'petrine' sense but in a sense which saw in the confession of Jesus as saviour the foundation on which the church of Christ is built.[54] However, this observation is more in the nature of being wise after the event than strictly historical comment, since as far as More was concerned polemic not dialogue was the way to deal with dissidents.

---

[49] See Hugh of St Victor, *De sacramentis christianae fidei,* lib. II, pars 2, *MPL* 176, c. 416; Bernard of Clairvaux, *Epist.* 126, 6, *MPL* 182, c. 275; idem, Serm. 2, 6, *In nativ., MPL* 183, c. 122; idem, *In Ps 90,* 14, 3, *MPL* 183, 240B; Aquinas, *In symbolum apostolorum,* a. 9, ed. Spiazzi, *Opuscula theologica* II, 211-213; idem, *De veritate,* Q. 9, a. 4-5, in *Quaestiones disputatae* I, ed. Spiazzi, 558-562; Gerson, *Propositio facta coram anglicis,* Du Pin II, 124 AB and 127CD; Nicholas of Cusa, *De concordantia catholica,* ed. Kallen, 1-3; Turrecremata, *Summa de ecclesia,* lib. I, cap. 43, Venice ed. 50 rv; ibid., lib. I, cap. 1, Venice ed. 2 v. See also Congar, *Ecclésiologie,* 159-161; 125-129; 232-241; 316-320; 330-334; 340-344.

[50] For Luther's views see—*WA* 3, 179/9; *WA* 3, 259/18 ff; *WA* 3, 371/24 ff.; *WA* 4, 379/26 ff., 38 ff.; Tyndale, *Answer,* 24-25.

[51] See *Dialogue,* lxiiii r B, ed. Campbell, 134; ibid., lxiiii v E, ed. Campbell, 134; *Confutation,* 942/17-20; ibid., 962/19-22.

[52] See Tyndale, *Answer,* 50-54; 108-109.

[53] *Confutation,* 507/33-511/12; ibid., 744/35-745/15; ibid., 389/15-390/16; ibid., 477/21-478/6.

[54] See *Confutation,* 410/35-413/25; see also *Dialogue,* xxxiii r AB, ed. Campbell, 68; ibid., xxxiii r C, ed. Campbell, 68-69.

Given the different coordinates within which their respective ecclesiological patterns were worked out, one finds an area of agreement between Catholic and Lutheran disputants in a common recognition of inward communion between those belonging to Christian fellowship. The
inner gift of the Spirit flowing from the risen Christ brings men together in
an invisible relationship to the risen Lord binding them into one body,
making of them the spouse of Christ, the new temple in which true worship is offered to the Father. For More this inner fellowship could be
broken more easily than in Luther's or Tyndale's eyes, for while he held to
the medieval doctrine on grave sin,[55] the latter argued that only the sin
against the Spirit could disrupt this bond.[56] At the same time it may be
necessary to repeat that while Luther and Tyndale adopted this concept of
inner fellowship as the defining factor of the church of Christ on earth,
More never accepted this view, insisting that the normative concept must
be the tangible, historically perceptible community implicitly including in
this the body of elect. Indeed More went further on occasion, explicitly
identifying the 'mystical body' and the 'true vine' with the empirical
Christian community without, however, either describing or analysing the
problems this created in regard to the nature of church adherence.[57] At
the same time More consistently maintained an emphasis on the spiritual
dimension of the church. He spoke uninterruptedly of the abiding
presence of Christ, the inner working of the Spirit, the outpouring of
charity that binds the Christian people into a communion of life, mind and
heart, expressed in the biblical images of body, ark, vine, spouse, temple,
living house, city, kingdom.[58] This direction of his thought was to some
extent at variance with his formal definition of the church. Unconsciously
he had allowed himself to be placed in the dialectical position of defining
the church in socio-empirical terms as a corrective to what the Abbé
Prévost has termed the *désincarnation* of the church in Luther's and Tyndale's ecclesiologies. In point of fact, however, when More's theology of
the church is examined in full, it can be seen to have a great deal in
common with that of his opponents.

More clearly belongs to the main line of spiritual ecclesiology. His first
concern is not with organisation and structure but with the presence of

---

[55] See *Confutation*, 429/4-19.
[56] See for example Tyndale, *Answer*, 30-34.
[57] See *Dialogue*, lxviii v GH, ed. Campbell, 144.
[58] See *Responsio*, 100/3-7, tr. 101/5-9; ibid., 202/3-17, tr. 203/3-20; ibid., 200/13-16, tr.
201/16-17; *Dialogue*, lxiiii r CD, ed. Campbell, 134; ibid., xlvii r BC, ed. Campbell, 97-98;
ibid., lxviii rv CDE, ed. Campbell, 143.

Christ and the activity of the Spirit within the hearts of the faithful. In his emphasis on the Spirit he represents a return to the more pneumatic and dynamic view of the church current in the patristic period. In developing this intuition it is quite likely that one of the major influences was John Colet, who acted as counsellor as well as spiritual director to More for many years. Colet had been greatly taken, not merely with the biblical revival of the Italian Renaissance but in particular with neo-platonic theology which he encountered mainly in the writings of the pseudo-Areopagite. Largely through the latter's influence Colet produced an image of the church predominantly spiritualistic in perspective and tone, coloured by a profound belief in the presence and activity of the Holy Spirit. 'God however, like a soul, is wholly in the whole, and wholly in every single part. Not that He makes godlike all parts alike; for this is what to animate means, in the case of God. But He does this in various measures, as is meet for the fashioning of that one in him, which consists of many.'[59]

Colet ascribed this life primarily to the Spirit. By the Spirit the church is governed, moved, and sustained in a wonderful order. The harmony and mutual agreement of the parts is caused by that one and same Spirit who cements them all into one. If the Spirit departs, the fabric falls to pieces by its natural tendency.'[60] Colet's reformist ideas were largely based on his awareness of the need for a release of the Spirit within the church of his own time. At the same time his neo-platonic perspective enabled him to incorporate the imperfect participation of the degenerate Christians of his own day within a scale of participation extending from the one who lay at the centre to the many at the periphery of the divine scheme.

More himself had a healthy scepticism with regard to the pseudo-Dionysius, justified by the uncovering of his false identity by William Grocyn among others.[61] At the same time, in view of his close relationship to Colet, the latter's essential vision must have rubbed off to some extent on his disciple and may well have been, together with Grocyn, one of the influences which directed More towards the study of Augustine. More lec-

---

[59] See Colet, *Enarratio I Cor,* ed. Lupton, 7; ibid., 246, tr. 120.

[60] See John Colet, *De corpore Christi mystico,* in *Joannis Coleti opuscula quaedam theologica,* ed. J. H. Lupton, London, 1876, 36; see also ibid., 31, 34, 37.

[61] See Chambers, Thomas More, 77; More was somewhat sceptical of Grocyn's involvement with the pseudo-Dionysius. Writing to John Holt, a schoolmaster at Chichester prebendal school concerning Grocyn's lectures in St Paul's on the *Celestial Hierarchies* he remarked somewhat superciliously: 'Nescias an cum maiore sua laude an audientium fruge.' See Thomas More to John Holt (London, c. November 1501), Rogers, *Correspondence,* 4/14-22. For an expression of More's deep attachment to Colet, see Thomas More to John Colet, London, 23 October (1504), Rogers, *Correspondence,* 8/60-68.

tured on the *City of God* in the church of St Lawrence Jewry as a young
man in 1501. The Augustinian vision of the church, also neo-platonic and
predominantly spiritual in character,[62] continually comes through in
More's writing and is probably largely responsible for the predominantly
spiritual view of the church that he adopted.

Henry VIII's vision of the church, though less steeped in the spiritual
than More's, also brings within its compass several of the key texts used by
the latter to bring home the abiding presence and guidance of the Spirit,
Jn 16, 13, Jn 20, 30, Heb 10, 16, as well as Lk 22, 32.[63] Fisher dealt a
good deal more explicitly than Henry with the spiritual dimension of
Christian community. Like More, he too saw the charismatic aspect in the
foreground of the picture underpinning and enhancing everything else.
Familiar images recur in Fisher; the church is a spiritual house built with
living stones;[64] 'as Eve came forth from Adam, so we who are the church
and the spouse of Christ, by eating his flesh and drinking his blood, are
made one body and members of the body of Christ, and from two is made
one flesh.'[65] Indeed so intense was Fisher's idea of communion that he saw
bodily union merging into union of Spirit. 'So great indeed is the unity of
this mystical body (which is the church) that all we Christians are called,
and actually are, not only one body but also one Spirit on account of the
Holy Spirit dwelling in us.'[66] At the same time, Fisher never allowed a
total dichotomy to develop between mystical communion and ecclesiastical
institution. He identified the mystical body, like More, with the social
body of the Catholic Church, and even spoke of the pope as head of the
mystical body.[67]

Erasmus's view of the church, like More's, was predominantly
pneumatic, from the *Enchiridion* (1503) onwards. Christ is 'head of the
church', the church is his body. Individual Christians are members of the
body. Making use of the Pauline imagery of Rom 12, 5 and 1 Cor 12,
12-26, Erasmus evolved an ecclesiology which hardly justifies the accusa-
tion of extreme individualism sometimes levelled against him,
'...whatever happens one member affects the whole body. What happens
you and the other members of the body, happens to Christ, affects even

---

[62] See Congar, *Ecclésiologie*, 16-20.

[63] See Headley, *Responsio*, 736, who makes this observation in relation to *Assertio*, sigs
M3 v-M4 v, in particular.

[64] See John Fisher, *This treatyse concernynge the fruytful saynges of Dauyd the kynge & prophete in
the seuen penytencyall psalmes, English Works*, ed. Mayor, 175-180.

[65] See John Fisher, *De veritate corporis et sanguinis Christi in eucharistia, Opera Omnia*, 1134.

[66] See Fisher, *Confutatio*, proem., veritas 7, *Opera Omnia*, 289.

[67] Fisher, *The sermon agayn luuther, English Works*, ed. Mayor, 322.

God himself' (1 Cor 12, 26). Together God, Christ, the body and its members make up one single communion.'[68]

That is not to say that Erasmus reduced the church to a body made up of identical parts. Rather did he underline the distinct character and function of the individual member. This diversity is bound together into harmonious unity by the action of Christ the head.[69] Thus by reason of one's baptism, the Christian is born anew by the action of the Holy Spirit and grafted in this body whose life is summed up in brotherly love.[70] Similarly, the eucharist is a means of deepening this life of Christian love. Through it one becomes one spirit with the spirit of Christ, one body with the body of Christ: 'If you feel as if you are being formed in a very clear way into the likeness of Christ, and live ever less for yourself, then be grateful to the Spirit, who alone awakens such love.....'[71] This motif of the church as Christ's body persisted through Erasmus's theological career, resounding even more loudly in his later writings.[72]

The Holy Spirit receives even more formal attention, his dynamic influence is perceived at work at every level of church life from the very beginnings to the working of the sacramental mysteries. 'Est hominis vita quaedam peculiaris, quam bruta nesciunt. Hac (sic) vivunt qui Spiritu Dei aguntur, hac vivunt, qui pie vivunt.'[73] Concerning the action of the Spirit in and through the celebration of baptism: '(a) The material in which the power of the sacrament acts is the soul of man. (b) The shape produced is the work of the Holy Spirit. (c) The ultimate cause is the Blessed Trinity. Thus the priest or any other who baptises is no more than a living instrument or servant.'[74] Without losing sight of the sacramental and institutional aspects of ecclesiastical existence, Erasmus kept the strictly divinising activity of the Spirit of God in the foreground of his vision of the church of Christ. In this he was very much on the same wave length as his old master John Colet and his intellectual Jonathan, Thomas More.

The breadth of vision this opened up for Erasmus was as extensive as humanity in its span from creation to final judgment. The church of Christ for him was not confined to those who formally believed in Christ. It began with creation, *ecclesia ab Abel,* and ended only with the last

---

[68] See Erasmus, *Enchiridion,* ed. Holborn, 100/21-25.
[69] See ibid., ed. Holborn, 100/25-28.
[70] See ibid., ed. Holborn, 82/16-83; ibid., 83/13-17.
[71] See Erasmus, *Enchiridion,* ed. Holborn, 73/25-35.
[72] See Gebhardt, *Die Stellung des Erasmus zur römischen Kirche,* 105-138; Hentze, *Kirchliche Einheit,* 47-49.
[73] See Erasmus, *Enarratio in Ps 33* (34), (1531), *LB* V, 403C.
[74] See Erasmus, *Ecclesiastes II,* (1535), *LB* V, 933E.

trumpet. The essential condition for membership in his view was a sincere desire to live well. This church is composed of those '...Christ draws together , whether among inhabitants of east, west, north or south. It may well be that in the world there are certain regions, islands or continents not yet known to sailors or geographers where nonetheless Christian faith is to be found.'[75] Indeed holiness can flower outside the Judaeo-Christian tradition as in the lives of philosophers and sages such as Zeno, Xenocrates and Socrates. Erasmus was inspired in this view by a theology of Christ, Logos of the world, in whose being all may participate even unconsciously.[76] Although Colet might have approved such a standpoint, Erasmus went beyond More who did not extend the boundaries even of the inward church beyond the limit of those with formal if implicit faith in Judaeo-Christian revelation. And of course it brought Erasmus directly under Luther's ban, as the latter made conscious surrender to God in Christ the condition of election to eternal life.[77]

V. INSTITUTIONAL STRUCTURES

In basing his view of the institutional structure of the church on the sacrament of order More was fully in accord with the main tide of Christian tradition. It is true that in certain influential currents of medieval theology a distinction had been drawn between the 'power' of order, relating specifically to the eucharist, and the 'power' of jurisdiction relating to Christ's mystical body the church.[78] This left the door open to the exponents of hierocratic theory to locate the source of jurisdiction in

---

[75] See Erasmus, *Explanatio symboli*, (1533), *LB* V, 1175 A.

[76] Erasmus saw in Christ 'immortalis ille rerumenum moderator' who created the world: '...ratione summa constituit universa': in Erasmus, *Antibarbari*, (1495?), *LB* X, 1712C. See also his later work: Erasmus, *Hyperaspistes* II, (1527), *LB* X, 1529F: '...mihi probabilius videtur...nulli aetati, nulli hominum generi divinam providentiam defuisse. Siquidem ante proditam Mosi Legem constat in lege naturae multos fuisse sanctos.' See also Gebhardt, *Die Stellung des Erasmus zur römischen Kirche*, 144-232; Hentze, *Kirchliche Einheit*, 76-79.

[77] In Colet's view, the members of Christ's body apart from the head '...are the rest of mankind, as many as are brought under the quickening influences of the Divine Spirit...' Colet, *Enarratio I Cor*, ed. Lupton, 6-7; see also idem, *In ecclesiasticam hierarchiam*, ed. Lupton, 29.

[78] See Congar, *Ecclésiologie*, 169-174. The disjunction made between sacramental ministry and juridical authority left the door open to those working in the legal field to elaborate a theory of authority which saw all juridical power embodied in the papacy which delegated it as it saw fit to subordinate offices. This led on the one hand to the exaggerations of *Unam Sanctam* and the fantasies of an Augustinus Triumphus (*papa magis sit nomen jurisdictionis*), and an impoverished theology of episcopate and presbyterate on the other. It also opened the door to Henry VIII who could claim juridical authority in the church without sacramental power.

the pope with a consequent depreciation of elements in the Christian community; not only the people but also the bishops. More was not fully aware of this disjunction nor of its significance, tending to see the whole church in a state of mission while recognising that within the community certain members were permanently designated by means of sacramental ordination to act as leaders both in preaching and worship. In this he reverted to a patristic vision of church order.

He was quite at variance with the 'spiritual' tradition still alive in Lollardy and indeed with the Lutheran movement in affirming that office was distinct from grace and could exist without it.[79] This provided the basis for a definition of the church which included as one of its principal parameters a permanent institutional structure based on sacramental order.

Luther's position on church office was in part evolved in antithesis to one medieval conception of ecclesiastical authority. This predominantly canonical view of authority saw it as a legal function, delegated from a higher level. Hence preaching, teaching, worship were ultimately reduced to legal categories, while authority was seen as exercised 'from above, over subjects' in a manner similar to that of civil authority.'[80] Luther rejected on grounds of lack of scriptural basis the traditional ceremony of ordination by imposition of hands and prayer.[81] In so doing he rejected the idea of a permanent designation to ministry in the church.

Tyndale followed him in this. He asked concerning the grades of office from subdeacon to pope: 'Are these all sacraments, or which one of them? Or what thing in them is that holy sign or sacrament? The shaving or the anointing? What also is the promise that is signified thereby? But what word printeth in them that character, that spiritual seal? O dreamers and natural beasts, without the seal of the Spirit of God; but sealed with the mark of the beast and with cankered consciences!'[82]

Office in Luther's concept comes about, first through an inner gift both charism and vocation, to a member of the Christian community of priests. This charism is primarily concerned with the ministry of the word, though

---

[79] See John Wyclif, *De ecclesia*, ed. Loserth, 89-90, 441-442; Leff, *Heresy*, 520-521, 525-526.

[80] See *WA* 6, 536/7-12; *WA* 10/II, 215/20-27; *WA* 2, 22; *WA* 6, 24.

[81] See *WA* 10/II, 220/33-221/9; '...I denied that orders is a sacrament, that is, a promise and sign of grace added, such as are baptism and the bread... I stated emphatically that it is a calling and instituting of a minister and preacher, whether this is done by the authority of one apostle or by that of the pope alone, or by that of the people agreeing together makes no difference...'

[82] See Tyndale, *Obedience of a Christian Man*, in *Doctrinal Treatises*, ed. Walter, 254-255.

it also involves presiding over the life of a local Christian community including its worship. No individual is allowed to exercise this office without
authorisation of the community.[83] The only authority the pastor has is one
of love; feeding the sheep meant, for Luther, loving them.[84] Installation in
office is a simple ceremony. Tyndale, who followed Luther on these issues,
put it thus: 'Neither is there any other manner or ceremony at all required
in making of our spiritual officers than to choose an able person, and then
to rehearse him his duty, and give him his charge, and so to put him in his
room.'[85]

Henry VIII in his work against Luther had taken as one of his tasks the
defence of the sacramentality of order within the church, affirming both
that the sacramental ceremony had been instituted by Christ and that the
office conferred and the institutional structures which ensued were in
keeping with the mind of Christ.[86] Significantly, perhaps, for Henry's
subsequent assumption of administrative authority over the church, he
maintained the medieval tradition of distinguishing order and jurisdiction.
He condemned Luther for '...being so blinded by malice as not to discern
jurisdiction from order at all... If the bishop then who has care of the
whole diocese, commits any part of his care to a priest, does not reason
teach us that this man can bind or loose no more than what the other has
committed to him...'[87] Supreme jurisdiction of course lies with the pope.
Henry, therefore, accepted the late medieval conception of church structure, seeing authority in the church in a dualistic way, but with sacramental and pastoral authority subordinated to that of jurisdiction.

Needless to remark Fisher defended the visible structures of the church
with great conviction and vigour. 'His conception of the church as hierarchical, that is, as a society in which the rulers receive authority immediately from God and not mediately through the people, is so evident and insis-

---

[83] On this see Wilhelm Brunotte, *Das geistliche Amt bei Luther,* Berlin, 1959, 34-60 in particular, but also 61-116, 199-202. Brunotte underscores the charismatic element. Hellmut
Lieberg, *Amt und Ordination bei Luther und Melancthon,* Göttingen, 1962, 235-242 affirms that
Luther attached proportionate significance to the intervention of the community. This latter
element is still to the fore in Luther's *De captivitate babylonica, WA* 6, 564/6-9: 'If priests were
forced to admit that as many of us as are baptized are all equally priests, as in fact we are,
and that the ministry alone is given to them, *yet by our consent,* and that no right of command
over us is granted them except insofar as we allowed it by our free choice...'

[84] See for example Luther, *De potestate papae,* (1519), *WA* 2, 194-197; idem, *Assertio omnium
articulorum,* (1520), *WA* 7, 130/15-21 where he denied that Christ's command to Peter to feed
his sheep in Jn 21, 17 implied authority other than that of love.

[85] See Tyndale, *Obedience,* ed. Walter, 259; see also ibid., 254-256; idem, *Answer,* 18-20,
170-180.

[86] See Henry VIII, *Assertio,* sigs Pv2—Rr4; L rv2.

[87] Henry VIII, *Assertio,* L rv2.

tent as hardly to need statement.'[88] Fisher treated of these aspects of the church on several occasions. A summary of his views occurs in his *Defence of the Royal Assertion* (1525) where he lists ten axioms on the Christian priesthood. 'The first shows that for six undeniable reasons there must be placed over the multitude men to care for its interests. The second, that in fact Christ appointed such men to feed, govern and teach his, i.e., the Christian flock. The third, that such men need a more abundant grace that they may the better discharge their office. The fourth, that in fact Christ did bestow such grace upon the pastors he appointed. The fifth, that these offices must necessarily be continued in the Church until the Last Day. The sixth, that no one lawfully discharges such an office, unless he be duly called, ordained, and sent. The seventh, that those who are legitimately appointed to such offices are undoubtedly to be believed to be called by the Holy Ghost. The eighth, that at the moment when they are thus appointed they receive always the grace of the same Spirit unless they place a hindrance in the way. The ninth, that the Holy Spirit infallibly gives this grace at the performance of some external rite, i.e., the imposition of hands. The tenth, that the pastors and priests so ordained by the imposition of hands, are truly priests of God and offer sacrifice both for themselves and for their flock.'[89]

Fisher recognised the threefold function of the priesthood without attempting to describe the relation between the power of jurisdiction and that relating to ministry of word and sacrament.[90] It is not without significance that unlike More, he completely divorced the authority of jurisdiction from Christ's precept of love in discussing Jn 21, 17. 'And for the last time it is false that without love this power (of ruling) is unable to exist. For just as the power of absolving and baptizing and even of consecrating the eucharist remains, with love having been removed by sin, still this power remains although love shall have been lost occasionally.' Peter's authority and his love for Christ are quite distinct. So also, presumably, the authority of others holding office in the church.[91]

---

[88] See Surtz, *Fisher*, 51.

[89] See Fisher, *Sacri sacerdotii defensio contra Lutherum*, (Cologne, 1525), *Opera Omnia*, cc. 1242-1269, tr. P. Hallett, *The Defence of the Sacred Priesthood*, London, 1935, 22-76, esp. 74-75.

[90] See Duggan, *The Church in the Writings of St John Fisher*, 143-148.

[91] Fisher, *Confutatio*, Art. XXV, fol. 147 v, Antwerp, 1523, cited Headley, *Responsio*, 766-767. Headley may exaggerate the significance of this passage since Fisher was evidently seeking to show that office in the church was independent of the holiness of life of the incumbent, a position he shared with More and long-standing Catholic tradition. Fisher viewed church-office precisely as a service of charity, its aim the growth of Christ's body in spirit and truth. See Duggan, *The Church*, 143-148; Fisher, *Confutatio, Opera Omnia*, 556.

As far as Erasmus was concerned, only one office existed in the church, that of love of God and neighbour. This office is conferred on each Christian in baptism. Every other function which church worship and administration call for is subordinated to this. Erasmus underlined that various titles such as 'apostle', 'pastor', 'bishop' are names given to forms of service not of overlordship. 'Pope' and 'abbot' are symbols of love not power.[92] In this service of love the Christian community can carry with it the weak as well as the strong, while at the same time it spreads the message of Christ and wins new members through the love it shows for the world.[93]

This did not involve Erasmus in a denial of the institutional forms of the church. Rather it provided a context and perspective within which formal office must be viewed—as growing from love, being the occasion of exercising love and serving the growth of a community of love. Even ceremonial law takes on a meaning in this context.[94]

In his later writings Erasmus expounded more explicitly the nature of office. He recognised a threefold office, pastoral, magisterial, and priestly, conferred in the sacrament of order. Thus while recognising the common priesthood of the faithful, Erasmus affirmed the special role of the clergy as set aside in ordination and strengthened by the Spirit for these tasks.[95] He considered the division of function between bishop and presbyters as a matter of historical evolution, whereas the apostles had combined both roles in themselves.[96] The archetype of office is the bishop whom he viewed not primarily as a ruler but as a steward of Christ, Christ's vicar; 'Episcopus es, Christi vicem geris.' The bishop exercises the three-fold ministry of priest, teacher, pastor. This is the model of institutional authority in the church; from it flows a variety of provisions which in their turn are intended to enable the community to live as a brotherhood of love. Thus Erasmus went behind medieval tradition to revive an image of bishop and church united in brotherhood, where authority in the com-

---

[92] See Erasmus, *Enchiridion*, ed. Holborn, 107/14-16; Kohls, *Die Theologie des Erasmus*, 163-165.

[93] See Erasmus, *Enchiridion*, ed. Holborn, 5/2-7, 20; ibid., 106/11-107/13.

[94] Erasmus, *Enchiridion*, ed. Holborn, 76/27-77/7.

[95] See Erasmus, *Explanatio symboli*, (1533), *LB* V, 1176 E: 'Qui vero deliguntur ad mysticas functiones, iis per sacramentum Ordinis augetur donum Spiritus ad digne administrandum munus delegatum.'; idem, *Christiani hominis institutum*, (1514), *LB* V, 1358 D. See also idem, *Ratio verae theologiae*, (1518), ed. Holborn, 253/16-19 where he upheld the validity of priestly office in spite of the unworthiness of its holders. See also Gebhardt, *Die Stellung des Erasmus zur römischen Kirche*, 240-267; Hentze, *Kirchliche Einheit*, 62-64 and passim.

[96] See Erasmus, *Ecclesiastes*, (1535), *LB* V, 1056 E.

munity springs from divine love and serves it, and where a threefold pastoral office is conferred by the Spirit in the sacramental ordination.[97] He thus restored the medieval concept of jurisdiction to its pastoral function, grafting it once more to its parent plant of sacramental order, a perspective fundamentally the same as that of Sir Thomas More, though even more explicitly pneumatic in concept and intention.

It may well be that the original inspiration for both Erasmus and More was John Colet. The Dionysian perspective of the *Ecclesiastical Hierarchies,* while not without its ambiguities, provided a breadth of canvas which allowed for the incorporation of spirit and institution, charism and order, sanctity and evil within the same frame.[98]

VI. ROMAN PRIMACY

The supreme form of office in the church for More was the Roman primacy. His own position in course of time became quite definite. He regarded its legal standing as beyond question, its divine origin he looked on as still a subject for debate, while privately convinced of its institution by Christ. At the same time he was no exponent of hierocratic ideology. His 'populist' view of the church as well as his stance on the sacrament of order precluded any totalitarian concept of papal power within the church. In church-state affairs he had no scruple in upholding *praemunire*, an indication of a pluralistic rather than a monolithic approach to the organisation of Christendom.

More was clearly at odds with Luther on the issue of the primacy, though it is quite probable that his own convictions were crystallised during his debate with the reformer. By the time of writing of his *Contra Henricum regem angliae* (1522) Luther's position had already passed through various stages of acknowledging the papacy as of divine law, to human law, to a rejection of papal office as an act of usurpation of authority leading to the degradation of Christianity. The pope is Antichrist.[99]

---

[97] See Erasmus, *Expositio concionalis in Ps 85 (86),* (1528), *LB* V, 554A; idem, *Ecclesiastes,* (1535), *LB* V, 801C, 830E, 777E, 826D, 831D, 791 E.

[98] See John Colet, *Epistolae B. Pauli ad Romanos expositio,* in *Joannis Coleti opuscula quaedam theologica,* ed. J. H. Lupton, London, 1876, 88; idem, *In ecclesiasticam hierarchiam,* 114, 128-130, 53, 62-63, 83-84. The ambiguity arises in such statements as the following: 'He is not a priest, which is one outwardly, with the tonsure in the flesh; but he which is one inwardly, in the spirit' in Colet, *Epistolae B Pauli ad Romanos expositio,* 88. While at first glance this sounds like a Wyclifite position, given a neo-platonic frame of reference it can be understood in a sense compatible with the traditional doctrine on the permanent character of priestly ordination.

[99] See Ernst Bizer, *Luther und der Papst,* Munich, 1958, 5-56.

In this Luther was closely followed by Tyndale. The latter consistently rejected all arguments of papal apologists in favour of the primacy. In the 'petrine' text Mt 16, 18, the rock on which the church is founded is 'Christ, the faith, and God's word,' not the person of Peter. The keys of the kingdom (Mt 16, 19) were given to all the apostles indifferently (Jn 20, 22-23), when all received power to forgive sins. The power of binding and loosing (Mt 16, 19) similarly was given to all the apostles (Mt 18, 18). Indeed the latter pericope shows that this promise must be understood in terms of fraternal correction not of juridical power.[100] The pope can claim no special authority for his mission, 'Seeing now that we have Christ's doctrine, and Christ's holy promises, and seeing that Christ is ever present with us his own self; how cometh it that Christ may not reign immediately over us, as well as the pope which cometh never at us.'[101] Still less then has the pope power in the temporal sphere.[102]

Luther and Tyndale on the issue of papal primacy were in reaction against a theological and institutional development which had its roots in the effective emergence of Roman authority in the post-Constantinian period, but which received its greatest impulse in the years following the Hildebrandine reform.[103] The attention of historians in the nineteenth and early twentieth centuries tended to focus on the papal-imperial conflict. More recent studies have shown that the affirmation of papal autonomy in relation to the temporal power and in some instances the claim to papal hegemony over the temporal sphere were based on an increasing emphasis on the role of papal authority within the church, to the detriment of provincial, diocesan and local self-determination.[104] This movement culminated in fourteenth century juridical and theological theories of papal *plenitudo potestatis* as expounded by apologists such as Giles of Rome, Augustinus Triumphus, and most markedly among the popes, Innocent IV and Boniface VIII.[105] This school of thought which initially had fo-

---

[100] See Tyndale, *Obedience*, ed. Walter, 318-321; idem, *Answer*, 102-110, 99-100, 52-54. See also idem, *The Practice of Prelates*, 255-288.

[101] See Tyndale, *Obedience*, 211.

[102] See Tyndale, *Obedience*, 188-198; idem, *The Practice of Prelates*, 259-280.

[103] See Congar, *Ecclésiologie*, 25-38, 102-155; Walter Ullman, *The Growth of Papal Government in the Middle Ages*, 44-86, 167-228, 262-343, 413-446.

[104] See Innocent III: '...in capite viget sensuum plenitudo, ad membra vero pars eorum aliqua derivatur...' Reg. VII, 1: 215, 279, cited Congar, *Ecclésiologie*, 255.

[105] See Innocent IV, *In decretal. Cum super his*, in *Apparatus*, Venice, 1570, f. 255 v, cited Congar, *Ecclésiologie*, 258: 'Cum enim Christus habuerit super omnes potestatem, unde in psalmo *Deus iudicium tuum regi da*, non videtur diligens paterfamilias nisi vicario suo quae (quem) in terra dimittebat, plenam potestatem super omnes dimisisset.'; Boniface VIII, *Unam Sanctam*, in Denzinger, *Enchiridion Symbolorum*, no. 875: 'Porro subesse Romano Pon-

cused on the administrative sphere extended its concern to the sphere of doctrine. In the development of a theory of papal infallibility whose paternity is ascribed to the French Franciscan Peter Olivi and its subsequent patronage by theologians of his order, papal authority reached a culminating point.[106] Counter currents were not absent in the medieval period. Canonist theory itself recognised definite boundaries to papal authority.[107] In the dispute between mendicants and seculars in the 13th century on the right of religious to preach and hear confessions, a pluralist conception of the church was kept alive by the latter.[108] The conflict with Philip the Fair evoked a large literature tending to minimise the temporal pretensions of the papacy.[109] The crisis of western schism gave rise to a broad range of ecclesiological speculation concerning the nature of the church and the role of the papacy. The prolonged debate produced a variety of views ranging from theorists of popular sovereignty, Ockhamist in inspiration,[110] through exposés of episcopal collegiality of the school of Gerson[111] to the exponents of papal monarchy in accordance with canonist or Thomist principles, notably Vincent Ferrer and John Turrecremata.[112]

---

tifici omni humanae creaturae declaramus, dicimus, definimus et pronuntiamus omnino esse de necessitate salutis.' See also Aegidius Romanus, *De ecclesiastica potestate,* III, cap. ult., ed. Scholz, 206-209; cf. ibid., 99; 155. Augustinus Triumphus, *Summa de potestate papae,* (1324) q. 4, a. 2, pub. Rome, 1584, 42: 'papa magis sit nomen jurisdictionis quam ordinis'.

[106] See Brian Tierney, *Origins of Papal Infallibility 1150-1350,* 93-130; P. de Vooght, *Esquisse d'une enquête sur le mot 'infaillibilité' durant la période scolastique,* in *L'Infaillibilité de l'Église. Journées oecuméniques de Chevetogne,* Chevetogne, 1963, 99-146; Congar, *Ecclésiologie,* 244-248. The controversy surrounding Tierney's study of papal infallibility is summarised in Oberman, *"Et tibi dabo",* II, 109-118.

[107] 'The pope cannot dispense from natural law, nor divine law; he cannot change the sacraments nor create new ones; he cannot act against the *generalis status ecclesiae,* i.e., in practice its divine constitution and (with certain reserves) against the decrees of ecumenical councils, especially the first four' in Congar, *Ecclésiologie,* 260. It was generally accepted that the pope lost his jurisdiction in the event of death, resignation, mental illness, heresy, and schism. Hence the principle that the pope 'a nemine iudicatur' had definite limits which came to be more clearly recognised when openly discussed in the conciliar epoch.

[108] See Yves Congar, *Aspects ecclésiologiques de la querelle entre mendiants et séculiers dans la seconde moitié du XIIIe siècle et le début du XIVe,* in *Archives d'Histoire Doctrinale et Littéraire du Moyen Âge* 28 (1961) 35-151; idem, *Ecclésiologie,* 248-252.

[109] See V. Martin, *Les Origines du Gallicanisme,* I, 149-242; F. J. Pegues, *The Lawyers of the Last Capetians,* Princeton, 1962, 36-60 and *passim;* J. Leclercq, *Jean de Paris et l' ecclésiologie du XIIIe siècle,* Paris, 1942, 89-165; Jean Rivière, *Le Problème de l'église et de l'état au temps de Philippe le Bel,* 191-227.

[110] Among these we may count Pierre D'Ailly, (1350-1425), Henry of Langenstein (1325-1397) and Dietrich of Niem (1380-1415). On these see Merzbacher, *Wandlungen des Kirchenbegriffs,* 332-335, 331-332, 339-340.

[111] On Gerson himself, see Morrall, *Gerson and the Great Schism,* passim; Pascoe, *Jean Gerson, Principles of Church Reform,* 17-79; Congar, *Ecclésiologie,* 316-320.

[112] On Ferrer, see Merzbacher, *Wandlungen des Kirchenbegriffs,* 351; on Turrecremata, see Binder, *Wesen der Kirche bei Torquemada,* passim; Congar, *Ecclésiologie,* 340-344.

The early part of the fifteenth century witnessed a struggle for supremacy between conciliarists and papacy culminating in victory for the latter in the persons of Eugenius IV and Nicholas V.[113] Subsequently, though conciliarism survived as a theory, it did so in general in a more moderate form based mainly on a pluralist concept of the church. This tended to see the *plenitudo potestatis* in the confluence of popular, episcopal and papal authority in duly convened and approved assemblies of the univeral church.[114]

As a general rule medieval canonists and theologians accepted the establishment by Christ of the petrine office, whatever their persuasion concerning its nature and of its relationship to other sovereign bodies in church and state. Even William of Ockham, who advocated a strongly 'populist' view of the church, upheld the divine institution of Roman primacy.[115] It was mainly thinkers who went into schism, such as Michael of Cesena, Marsiglio of Padua, John Wyclif and John Hus who tended to deny divine origin to the petrine office. In England the principal opponents of Wyclif, Richard Fitzralph, William of Woodford, Thomas Netter, and even the slightly equivocal Reginald Pecock upheld the divine right of the papacy.[116] Indeed it was so much part of established ecclesiastical thought in England, that not merely was papal jurisdiction over the church fully recognised both in canonical theory and practice, but recognition of the papacy was regarded as a test of doctrinal orthodoxy

---

[113] This 'victory' consisted in the transfer of the council of Basle to Ferrara by Pope Eugenius IV on 18 September 1437. The majority attending Basle remained in that city. They progressively lost credibility and support for the anti-pope Felix V they had elected on 5 November 1439. By 1449 the rest of Christendom had renewed allegiance to the Roman Pope Nicholas V as sovereign pontiff. The papacy had scored both a strategic and theological advantage over the more extreme conciliarist factions. The prevailing right of the pope to convene a council and approve its acts was established even against the decrees of Constance, *Sacrosancta* and *Frequens*. For a brief account of this see Jedin, *Ecumenical Councils,* 112-136. Note in particular the change of attitude on the relationship of pope and council evinced by Nicholas of Cusa; on this see Jedin, *Council of Trent,* I, 22-24.

[114] See for example the work of the Scottish exile in Paris, John Major (1467/8-1550): John Major, *Excerpta ex eiusdem commentariis in librum quartum sententiarum dist. xxiv* and *Excerpta ex eiusdem commentariis in Matthaeum* in *Opera Omnia Joannis Gersonii,* II, ed. Du Pin, cc. 1121-1130; cc. 1131-1145. On Major and his contemporary, Jacques Almain, see Remigius Bäumer, *Nachwirkungen des konziliaren Gedankens in der Theologie und Kanonistik des frühen 16. Jahrhunderts,* Münster Westfalen, 1971, 17-28, 61-82 and *passim*; Olivier de la Brosse, *Le Pape et le Concile,* 185-310.

[115] See Ockham, *Dialogus,* pars I, lib. V, cap. 29-35, in Goldast, *Monarchiae* III, 498-506 ibid., 876-877.

[116] See for example Netter, *Doctrinale,* lib. 2, art. 3, cap. 47-48, (Venice, 1571), pp. 284-289; Reginald Pecock, *The Repressor of Over Much Blaming of the Clergy,* (1447), ed. Churchill Babington, Vol. 2, (Rolls Series, vol. 19), London, 1860, 433-443, esp. 438.

by the state.[117] However, some noted conciliarists such as Pierre d' Ailly while respecting the importance of the papal institution in the structure of the church, questioned its foundation by Christ.[118]

More's position on the papacy, seen against this background, emerges as one of great moderation. It seems in his earlier years he himself doubted its divine institution and that his views only crystallised in the course of the Lutheran controversy. He of course upheld the constitutional position of the pope in keeping with medieval custom with great vigour in terms of positive ecclesiastical law. As regards the authority he ascribed the pope, while recognising in him the supreme governor, the *praefectus ecclesiae*, his views on the church suggest that he be placed in the pluralist tradition of those who saw authority in the church spread proportionately throughout the whole body. The evidence suggests he ascribed to the pope the right of convening and approving the acts of the general council in the spirit of moderate fifteenth century conciliarism.[119]

On the other hand the indications are that, unlike papal monarchists of the school of Turrecremata and Cajetan, he upheld the proper autonomy of the council in its own sphere.[120] In matters of church and state, while defending the privilege of clergy, he saw no need to allow any invasion of temporal authority by the papacy. In this we may see him in the moderate constitutional line which descends from John of Paris, through Dante, carried on even more radically by William of Ockham, and upheld in More's own day by the Spanish philosopher Francisco de Vitoria.[121]

More's early scepticism regarding the Roman primacy is not easy to grasp precisely because it was out of harmony with English medieval tradi-

---

[117] See F. W. Maitland, *Roman Canon Law in the Church of England,* London, 1898, 1-50 and *passim*; Pickthorn, *Early Tudor Government,* 101-108; R. J. Schoeck, *Canon Law in England on the Eve of the Reformation, Medieval Studies* 25 (1963) 125-147.

[118] See Pierre D'Ailly, '*Quis enim in Petri infirmitate Ecclesiae firmitatem stabiliat?*' *Recommendatio sacrae scripturae,* (c. 1380) in *Gersonii Opera Omnia,* ed. Du Pin, I, 604. In his later works D'Ailly returned to an affirmation of divine institution of the papacy. Other conciliarists influenced by Marsiglio of Padua continued to reject it. See Dietrich of Niem, *De modis uniendi ac reformandi ecclesiam in concilio universali,* (c. 1410) in Du Pin, II, cc. 163-166. See on this V. Martin, *Les Origines du Gallicanisme,* II, 127 ff.

[119] See for example Nicholas of Cusa to Sanchez de Arevalo, 20 May 1442, in G. Kallen, *Cusanustexte, II, Sitzungsberichte der Heidelberger Akademie der Wissenschaften, Philosophisch-historische Klasse,* 3. Abhandlung, Heidelberg, 1935, 106-112; Dionysius Carthusianus, *De auctoritate summi pontificis et generalis concilii libri tres* (Cologne, 1532), *Opera minora* IV, Tournai, 1908, 567-568, 570, 573-577, 583-584.

[120] See Turrecremata, *Summa de ecclesia,* lib. III, cap. 5, Venice ed. 278 rv; ibid., lib. III, cap. 51-57, Venice ed. 336 r—344 r; Cajetan: '...a Petro omnis Ecclesiae potestas derivatur in totam Ecclesiam via ordinaria' in idem, *De comparatione auctoritatis papae et concilii,* (1511), cap. III, nos. 30-34, ed. Pollet, Rome, 1936, cited Congar, *Ecclésiologie,* 351.

[121] See Congar, *Ecclésiologie,* 281-296.

tion. His attitude at the time of writing of Henry VIII's *Assertio* contrasts with the fervour of his master, even though the latter's ardour for the papal cause may not have been completely disinterested. Henry had no reservations concerning the divine right of the papacy, its primacy of jurisdiction expressed in a way Boniface VIII would have found agreeable[122] and, if Roper and Harpsfield are correct, attributed his 'imperial crown' to papal gift.[123]

One reservation must be made, however, and that is concerning the arguments Henry offers for the divine authority of the petrine office based as they are not so much on scriptural evidence but on the prescriptive right of established custom. 'Any (institution) whose origin cannot be known is assumed to be legitimate. It is forbidden to alter such institutions which have remained so long unchanged in accordance with the unanimous consent of all peoples (*omnium consensu gentium*)... Indeed if anyone will examine ancient monuments or read the histories of former times he will easily find that since the conversion of the world all Christian churches have been obedient to the see of Rome...'[124]

This approach of Henry's curiously resembles that adopted by More in the *Baravellus* edition of the *Responsio*. Was there a certain reticence among humanists concerning papal credentials? Colet did not treat *ex professo* of the Roman primacy. He contented himself with an expression which, while acknowledging the due preeminence of the Roman pontiff, could be read in terms of either ecclesiastical or divine institution: among bishops, '...he especially who is the highest, whom we call the Pope; that what by his authority he diffuses over the Church, quickening it to life eternal, he may draw wholly from God...'[125] What Colet had in mind here of course within his pneumatic perspective was not juridical authority but the gift of divine light and life of which the pope should be an eminent source by reason of his absorption in God. Is it coincidental that another English humanist of a younger generation, Reginald Pole, for many years in all

---

[122] Henry VIII, *Assertio*, sigs. B v3—v4 '...all the faithful honour and acknowledge the authority of the sacred Roman see as their mother and supreme head. Distance of place nor danger of travel hinder no one from having access to its embrace. Even the Indians separated from us by such vast distances of both land and sea submit to the Roman pontiff...How can anyone believe...that all nations, cities, even kingdoms and provinces should be so indifferent to their rights and liberties as to acknowledge the authority of a foreign priest who had no claim over them...'

[123] See Roper, 66/15-68/23; Harpsfield 158/17-160/17; on this see Koebner, *The Imperial Crown of this Realm*, 29-52.

[124] Henry VIII, *Assertio*, loc. cit.

[125] See Colet, *In ecclesiasticam hierarchiam*, 150.

likelihood regarded the papacy as a creation of the Christian community?[126]

When one looks at Erasmus's views on the issue of primacy one finds that his positions must have reinforced the doubts of his correspondents and disciples. In his earlier writings Erasmus took the papacy with other church-offices for granted while emphasising their role as instruments of divine love.[127] At a later stage he had to explain his attitude at greater length. He understood the 'petrine' text, Mt 16, 18, in terms of the faith on which the church was founded rather than as reference to a personal foundational role for Peter.[128] The papal office he looked on as a legitimate development within the church analogous to the distinction which had emerged between presbyters and bishops.[129] In his exposé of papal office he stressed its pastoral role as one of guiding in love rather than teaching from on high. He deprecated the juridical function while seeing its necessity.[130] He also recognised the teaching office of the pope though looking with a questioning eye on those who advocated papal infallibility.[131] Erasmus confided his views on the papacy to More as we know from a letter he wrote in September 1529, 'Federibus principum admisceri Pon-

[126] See Thomas Starkey to Thomas Cromwell, c. June 1536, *LP* XI, 73, and the discussion of this letter together with the events which surrounded it in Breifne Walker, *Cardinal Reginald Pole, Papal Primacy and Church Unity 1529-1536*, M.A. thesis presented to University College, Dublin, 1972, 70-85. According to this view it was the deaths of More and Fisher which caused Pole to shift his ground. Interestingly enough the shift took the form of a shift of interpretation of ecclesial consensus, from looking on it in a juridical light as Henry tended to do in the *Assertio* to seeing it in theological and pneumatic terms as More did in the *Responsio* and later works; see Walker, *Cardinal Pole*, 18 ff. and 241-245.

[127] Erasmus, *Enchiridion*, ed. Holborn, 107/14-16; Kohls, *Die Theologie des Erasmus*, 164-165, 175.

[128] See Gebhardt, *Die Stellung des Erasmus zur römischen Kirche*, 263-277; Hentze, *Kirche*, 118-127. In particular see the notes to the 1516 edition of the new testament in Erasmus, *Novum instrumentum*, (1516), *LB* VI, 88F: 'Petrus saxeus solidam Ecclesiae fidem repraesentat.' See also *Ratio verae theologiae*, ed. Holborn, 198/4-8; idem, *Paraphrases in Mt*, (1522), *LB* VII, 92F.

[129] See Erasmus to Artlebus Boskowitz, 28 January 1521, Allen, *Erasmi epistolae*, IV, 440/72-78; *Ad monachos quosdam hispanos*, (1528), *LB* IX, 1067B. On this see in particular Harry J. McSorley, *Erasmus and the Primacy of the Roman Pontiff: Between Conciliarism and Papalism*, *ARG* 65 (1974) 37-54. For McSorley, Erasmus had come to accept primacy as a matter of faith rather than law by 1526. What he had regarded earlier as an evolution within a human community, he now looked on as a legitimate doctrinal development.

[130] See Erasmus, *Ad monachos quosdam hispanos*, (1528), *LB* IX, 1067A.

[131] Erasmus to Cardinal Lorenzo Campeggio, 19 January 1524, Allen, *Erasmi epistolae*, V, 384/19-27: '...Et tot aliis locis voco Petrum principem Apostolici ordinis, Pontificem Romanum, vicarium Christi et Ecclesiae principem, tribuens illi potestatem secundum Christum maximam.'; idem, *Apologia ad Stunicam*, (1521), *LB* IX, 365C; idem, *Responsio ad annotationes Ed. Lei*, (1520?), *LB* IX, 256D.

tificem, mihi nec Pontifici videtur expedire nec reipublicae Christianae. Ille maior est quam ut ullo federe sit astringendus, mea quidem sententia,' while the earlier *Enchiridion* (1504) was written at a period when he was spending a good deal of his time in England, 1499-1514.[132] Hence More could well have been informed of Erasmus's sentiments regarding the papacy. It was not all one way traffic. A recent study (see note 129 above) argues that by 1526 Erasmus had come to accept divine institution of the petrine primacy. What persuaded him was his growing awareness of the decrees of the council of Ferrara-Florence. It may well be that he learned of these from More's *Responsio* as well as Fisher's *Confutatio*.

Erasmus's restrained attitude towards Rome contrasted rather sharply with that of Fisher. The latter took a strong stand in his first sermon against Luther (1521) where he sought to establish that the pope *iure divino* is 'the heed of vnyersall chyrche of christ,' though the arguments offered were somewhat jejune.[133] His treatment in the *Assertionis Lutheranae confutatio* (1523) was a good deal more thoroughgoing. There he gave three major sets of arguments from scripture, the tradition including fathers and councils, concluding with a detailed analysis of Mt 16, 18 and Jn 21, 15-17, interpreted in a strongly petrine sense.[134] The pope like Christ, Fisher held, possesses the plenitude of power though he chooses not to exercise it. His main functions in the church are to settle controversies, to convene general councils and suppress the contumacious when bishops disagree.[135] At the same time, Fisher acknowledged without reserve the pope's primacy of jurisdiction if in somewhat metaphorical terms. The pope is the parent stem from which comes the common life of the body.[136] Or as he put it in another metaphor: 'Have we not observed that Christians are born of priests, priests of bishops and that bishops are generated by the sovereign pontiff.'[137]

While not going the whole way on papal infallibility,[138] Fisher exalted the role of the papacy in the church, even speaking of the pope as head of

---

[132] See Erasmus to Thomas More, 5 September 1529, Allen, *Erasmi epistolae*, VIII, 273/53-55.

[133] See Fisher, *Sermon, English Works*, 315 and *passim*.

[134] See Fisher, *Confutatio, Opera Omnia*, 530-580.

[135] See Fisher, *Confutatio, Opera Omnia*, 550-551.

[136] See Fisher, *Confutatio, Opera Omnia*, 565-566.

[137] See Fisher, *Confutatio, Opera Omnia*, 569.

[138] See Fisher, *Euersio munitionis quam Iodocus Clichtoueus erigere moliebatur*, Louvain, (Martens), 1519, sigs. Y4-A6: '...the authority of the sovereign pontiff is great, but it is still greater if the custom of the Roman see is added to it, and it is greatest if the consent of the whole church accrues to it.'

the mystical body of Christ in language reminiscent of Boniface VIII.[139] Fisher undoubtedly influenced More's thought on the primacy, as More acknowledged in the *Responsio*, where the shift in More's interpretation from *Baravellus* to *Rosseus* might well be seen as a shift from an Erasmian to a Fisherian view of primacy.[140] However, those influences notwithstanding, More remained a papal moderate even to his proud claim: '... I neuer entend....to pynne my soule at a nother mans backe, not euen the best man that I know this day liuing...' This was perhaps even truer with respect to papal primacy than to any other issue.

VII. COUNCIL

One of the major contributions to theology by the later middle ages was a theology of the general council. A general theory of council was not worked out in the church till the period of the western schism, though of course councils had been convened at irregular intervals in different areas in the church following the first council of Jerusalem. The first seven so-called 'ecumenical councils' were convened by the emperors though the bishops of Rome exercised as a rule a good deal of influence within them.[141] In the course of the middle ages, as the suzerainty of Rome grew, local synods of the Roman church grew into fully fledged councils of the western church.[142] Theorists, however, who ascribed the plenitude of jurisdiction to the pope failed to produce a satisfactory theory of council except in a purely advisory capacity. On the other hand, general corporation theory held within it the seeds of a later representative and pluralist conciliar theology.[143]

The greatest impetus to conciliar thinking before the schism was to be found in the works of two 'nonconformist' thinkers, Marsiglio of Padua and William of Ockham. As Marsiglio's ideas received currency once more among Henrician publicists, it may be worthwhile describing them

---

[139] 'Se here be thre heedes vnto a woman—god, chryst, & her husbande. & yet besyde all these she hath an heed of hyr owne...How moche rather our mother holy churche which is the spouse of christ. hath an heed of her owne. that is to saye the pope...' See Fisher, *Sermon, English Works*, 321.

[140] See *Responsio*, 138/29-140/3.

[141] See Odilio Engels, *Council*, in *Encyclopedia of Theology*, ed. K. Rahner, London, 1975, 298-302; H. Jedin, *Ecumenical Councils in the Catholic Church*, 14; H. Oberman, '*Et tibi dabo claves regni caelorum*'. *Kirche und Konzil von Augustin bis Luther. Tendenzen und Ergebnisse*, *Nederlands Theol. Tijdschrift* 25 (1971) 261-282; 29 (1975) 97-118.

[142] See Engels, *Council*, 302-304; Jedin, *Ecumenical Councils*, 60-104; G. Fransen, *L'Ecclésiologie des conciles médiévaux*, in *Le Concile et les conciles*, Paris, 1960, 139-141.

[143] See Tierney, *Foundations of the Conciliar Theory*, 23-95, 132-149.

in some detail. Marsiglio applied to society, conceived in a unitary way, principles drawn mainly from Aristotle's *Politics*. Sovereignty resides in the people but they delegate this to their representatives and ultimately the supreme legislator, the emperor. Supreme authority over all aspects of life including the spiritual resides in him. Hence the subordination of church to state. Analogously, within a church lacking jurisdiction, supreme authority resides in the council representing the *universitas fidelium*. The papacy is a purely human creation, subordinate to the council which itself is convened, not by the pope but by the supreme legislator.[144] Marsiglio's ideas did not greatly influence the evolution of conciliar theory in the fifteenth century but they were involved in the Henrician assumption of jurisdiction over the church. They probably received indirect acknowledgement in More's *Confutation* and may have been on his mind when discussing the council in his letters of the trial period. William of Ockham had a greater following among conciliarists. As his thought has been already discussed, we shall refer to it here only in a general way.[145]

Essentially conciliar theories grew out of different conceptions of the church which have been summarised above. While recognising a fundamental difference between those who emphasised the charismatic aspects of the church on the one hand and socio-institutional elements on the other, one can enumerate five main schools of thought regarding the primary trusteeship of sovereignty (i.e., grace or socio-juridical power depending on one's perspective) in the ecclesiastical community. This division of 'opinion grew out of an unresolved disagreement as to who succeeded to the twelve apostles.[146] The schools of thought enumerated below represent currents of ideas rather than clearly delineated positions. Hence in reality the lines of demarcation were not so evident as this schema might suggest.

1. The papal-monarchist view upheld in the medieval era by Thomists such as Turrecremata and Cajetan looked on the council as subordinate to the pope, deriving its authority from him and in Cajetan's view having no direct power over the papacy itself.[147]

---

[144] See Harry S. Stout, *Marsilius of Padua and the Henrician Reformation*, *CH* 43 (1974) 308-318.

[145] See Victor Martin, *Les Origines du Gallicanisme*, II, 32-41; G. de Lagarde, *La Naissance de l'esprit laïque*, II, 202-243; J. Quillet, *La Philosophie Politique de Marsile de Padoue*, 161-274.

[146] See K. A. Fink, *Die konziliare Idee im späten Mittelalter*, *Vorträge und Forschungen*, ed. T. Mayer, No. 9 (1965) 119-134. See Hans Küng, *The Church*, London, 1968, 354-359, though he omits an historical analysis of the various positions adopted in the course of church history.

[147] For a general survey of these ideological currents see P. de Vooght, *Le Conciliarisme aux Conciles de Constance et de Bâle*, 143-181; Jedin, *Bischöfliches Konzil oder Kirchenparlament*, 5-35;

2. The curialist, 'oligarchical' or 'aristocratic' view identified the *ecclesia romana* with the pope together with his college of cardinals. This corporation is the seat and source of all ecclesiastical authority to which the council is essentially subordinate. In the late medieval period this view was expounded by Peter Flandrin and St Vincent Ferrer.[148]

3. The 'episcopalist' view as expounded by Gerson, while recognising the divine right of both pope and bishops saw the papal office as exercised within the episcopal body. The council is essentially a meeting of the world episcopate including the pope. Both organs are necessary for its proper functioning though in certain situations the council is superior to the pope. This position was upheld within More's life span by Gabriel Biel the Tübingen theologian and Dionysius Carthusianus of Roermond.[149]

4. The 'populist' or 'democratic' view of the church proposed with such vigour by William of Ockham, while recognising the divine institution of episcopate and papacy ascribed ecclesiastical sovereignty to the Christian people. The council then as representing the whole Christian people possesses when in session, in this view, supreme ecclesiastical authority. It is superior to the pope. In More's time this view found expression in modified form in the writings of the Sorbonne professor Jacques Almain. It had been developed in a different theological perspective by the great German scholar Nicholas of Cusa in his earlier phase.[150] (Cusa belonged

Congar, *Ecclésiologie*, 290-352. See in particular, Turrecremata, *Summa de ecclesia*, lib. III, cap. 5, pp. 278rv; lib. III, cap. 11-12, pp. 286v-288v; Binder, *Wesen und Eigenschaften der Kirche*, passim; Congar, *Ecclésiologie*, 340-344; Cajetan, *De comparatione auctoritatis papae et concilii*, cap. VII, I, II, IV, in *Opuscula omnia*, I, 10-11, 5-6, 7-8, in Rocaberti, XIX, 455-456, 446-448, 450-451; ibid, cap. XVI, *Opuscula omnia*, I, 18-19, in Rocaberti, XIX, 469-471; *Apologia de comparata auctoritate papae et concilii*, cap. I, XXII, XXI ad 7um. in *Opuscula omnia*, I 31-48, in Rocaberti, XIX, 493-494, 516-520. O. de la Brosse, *Le Pape et le Concile*, 317-330; Congar, *Ecclésiologie*, 349-352.

[148] On Flandrin (+1384) see Merzbacher, *Wandlungen*, 348-349; Flandrin, *In facto schismatis*, ed. Bliemetzreider, *Literarische Polemik*, Vienna, 1909, 3-71; On Ferrer (+1419) see Merzbacher, *Wandlungen*, 351; Ferrer, *De moderno ecclesie schismate*, ed. Fages, *Oeuvres*, I, 27-38.

[149] See Gerson, *De auctoritate concilii*, *RHE* 53 (1958) 787; idem, *De potestate ecclesiastica*, Du Pin II, 231D, 238D; idem, *Propositio facta coram anglicis*, Du Pin II, 128B, 129 A-D; idem, *De unitate ecclesiastica*, Du Pin II, 114C-114D. See also J. B. Morrall, *Gerson and the Great Schism*, 81-84, 107-108. On Biel, see Oberman, *Harvest of Medieval Theology*, 415-419. See also Dionysius Carthusianus (Denis Rickel), *De auctoritate summi pontificis et generalis concilii libri tres*, *Opera minora* IV, Tournai, 1908, lib. I, art. 18, 19, 26, 29, 32, 39; 554-557; 567-575, lib. III, art. 8, 624-627; see Remigius Bäumer, *Nachwirkungen des konziliaren Gedankens*, 193, 205, 212, 250-251.

[150] See Jacques Almain, *De auctoritate ecclesiae et conciliorum generalium*, in *Gersonii Opera Omnia*, ed. Du Pin, II, 1003B-1005A. On Almain see de la Brosse, *Le Pape et le Concile*, 200-202 and *passim;* Bäumer, *Nachwirkungen des konziliaren Gedankens*, 62-63, 68-71, 100-101. Nicholas of Cusa, *De concordantia catholica*, II, 18 in *Opera* (Basle, 1565), 738-742, ed. Kallen, XIV,

to a neo-platonic current of thought; Almain had an Aristotelian-nominalist lineage.)

5. The 'constitutionalist' or 'pluralist' school saw the episcopate and papacy as well as the church as a whole as of divine institution. Divine authority is given directly to each order in its own right. Hence full ecclesiastical sovereignty is diffused throughout the whole body. The council represented the amalgamation of these reservoirs of authority in one single body. Each of these constituent members is essential to the council if it is to represent the whole church. Hence the superiority of council to pope in a conflict situation. This view at the time of Constance had been expounded by Gelnhausen and Zabarella, and in More's day was upheld by the Scottish-Parisian theologian John Major.[151]

6. Finally one must note the limiting case that ultimately ecclesiastical sovereignty in terms of the fidelity of the church to its Lord may be guaranteed by only one individual. For Ockham the council was not infallible in faith, nor was the *universitas fidelium*. This view influenced several conciliarists and was carried on into the fifteenth century by the Sicilian canonist Panormitanus, cited by Luther. It played a key part in the latter's devaluation of the authority of both consensus and council. It even found an echo in the writings of More though the latter balanced it by a positive and, for some, reassuring theology of consensus.[152]

Where did Luther fit into this picture? Assuming an evangelical conception of the church, Luther's appeal to the council from the pope had

---

189-203. See also Congar, *Ecclésiologie*, 330-334. See also the important work of A. J. Black, *Monarchy and Community. Political Ideas in Later Conciliar Controversy 1430-1450*, Cambridge, 1970, 7-52. Black pays special attention to John of Segovia the Spanish theologian from the school of Salamanca who was one of the principal advocates of the more extreme conciliarist position at Basle, an ally of Zabarella and Panormitanus.

[151] See Conrad of Gelnhausen, *De congregando concilio*, cap. III, in Martène and Durand, *Thesaurus novus anecdotorum*, II, 1217F-1218A; on Conrad see Martin, *La supériorité du concile sur le pape*, III, *Rev. Sc. Rel.* XVII (1937) 409-417. On Zabarella see Tierney, *Foundations of the Conciliar Theory*, 220-237; see Major, *Disputatio de auctoritate concilii*, in *Gersonii Opera Omnia*, ed. Du Pin, II, 1132A-1145A. On Major see Bäumer, *Nachwirkungen des konziliaren Gedankens*, 62, 67-68, 100, 197.

[152] See Ockham, *Dialogus*, Pars I, lib. 5, cap. 32-35, in Goldast, *Monarchiae* III, 503-506. Panormitanus (Nicholas de Tudeschis), *Commentaria in libros decretalium*, Lyon, I, de electione, 122r; '...plus credendum uni privato fideli quam toti Concilio aut Papae, si meliorem habeat autoritatem vel rationem' in *WA* 2, 404/26-31. See also *WA* 42, 334/30; *WA* 1, 568/19-23; More, *Confutation*, 555/4-17 where More refers to '...the comen opynyon of good Chrysten people, that the fayth abode at...(one) tyme onely in our lady...' Note that a large section of Ockham's *Dialogus* is taken up with the question of the possibility of error in the church. Ockham's conclusion here was that the faith of the church might be preserved in infants lacking the use of reason! '...errante tota multitudine Christianorum usum rationis habentium, possunt saluari promissiones Christi per paruuolos baptizatos.' In *ibid.*, 506.

significance within that context. It was not a purely opportunistic, move, utilising principles to which Luther no longer gave assent. Rather was it a question of supplying a new meaning, which he would have regarded as authentic, to a traditional institution. Whenever the church of Christ is gathered in visible form, the true inner, spiritual church is also present.

In Luther's conception, a council as such can never adequately represent this true hidden church nor make its decisions binding *ipso jure*.[153] On the other hand he recognised the value of the council in deciding disputed interpretations of scripture. In these matters the authority of the council does not derive from any divine right, nor from a canonically exact set of procedures, nor even a majority vote. Rather does it come from the assent of the hidden spiritual church which must inevitably be present in a truly universal council.[154]

Conformity to scripture is the acid test of conciliar authority. Only the spiritual hidden church has the capacity to judge this. The approval of this hidden spiritual church is what counts in the clarification of disputed questions.[155] This gives conviction to Luther's continued acceptance of the first four ecumenical councils as well as his citation of Pisa. On the other hand it leaves unanswered the question as to how the assent of the hidden spiritual church can be distinguished from that of other conciliar participants?

Uncertainty on this matter is increased by Luther's repeated citation of Panormitanus, the fifteenth century Sicilian canonist. Panormitanus, (1386-1445) or Nicholas de Tudeschis as he was christened, repeated Ockham's assertion that in the last resort the true church might well survive in one faithful follower of Christ.[156] Though the rest of the church might err, Christ's promise that his church would ever remain would be vindicated in one loyal believer.

---

[153] See *WA* 1, 568/19-32.

[154] See *WA* 8, 149/34-151/7. In practice this amounted to accepting only the first four councils as authentic. See also *WA* 50, 615, where he speaks rather contemptuously of conciliar authority as compared to that of one spiritual man.

[155] *WA* 6, 412/11-413/26; *WA* 9, 401-403.

[156] 'Si enim solus essem in toto orbe terrarum, qui retinerem verbum, solus essem ecclesia et recte iudicarem de reliquo toto mundo, quod non esset ecclesia.' See *WA* 42, 334/30. Cf. also *WA* 2, 404/26-31: '...plus credendum uni privato fideli quam toti Concilio aut Papae, si meliorem habeat autoritatem vel rationem.' Cf. also *WA* 1, 568/19-23; Panormitanus, *Commentaria in libros decretalium*, Lyon, 1524, I, de electione, 122r: 'vnde possibile est quod vera fides christi remaneret in vno solo: ita quod verum est dicere quod fides non deficit in ecclesia: sicut ius vniuersitatis potest residere in vno solo aliis peccantibus.' Panormitanus gives the archetypal example of the fidelity of the Virgin Mary following the death of Christ, subsequently used by More, *Confutation*, 555/4-17.

Luther made use of this authority to support his own stand against church authority. The implication was clear. He might well be that one true believer. In making use of this argument he was employing a relative commonplace of late medieval orthodox ecclesiology, one, as we have seen, which crops up even in More's writings. With hindsight one can say, however, that it completely undermines the authority of any council which fails to reach full, unanimous agreement from its participants. Moreover, even where such total agreement exists, it leaves open the possibility of the one true surviving believer not being present at the council.

Tyndale, who had adopted a far more fundamentalist interpretation of the *scriptura sola* axiom, had even less time for councils than Luther. The letter of scripture is always open and clear to the spiritual man. Scripture judges the church and its councils rather than the reverse: '...therefore were all things necessary to salvation comprehended in scripture ever to endure. By which scripture the councils general...have concluded such things as were in them determined...And by the same scripture we know which councils were true, and which false...'[157] Nor indeed did he view the councils as worthy of much trust or confidence any more than parliament. Here, curiously, his stance was the reverse of More the parliamentarian whose experience of constitutional assembly seems to have left him favourably disposed to conciliar thought. Thus Tyndale: 'Moreover, the general councils of the spiritualty are of no other manner, since the pope was a god, than the general parliaments of the temporalty; where no man dare say his mind freely and liberally, for fear of some one and of his flatterers. And look in what captivity the parliament be under the private councils of kings, so are the general councils under the pope and his cardinals.'[158]

In the course of the fifteenth century English theology had been markedly reticent on the subject of conciliarism. English ecclesiastics on the whole had supported the papal line in the conciliar controversy. Hence it is a little surprising to see a conciliar note re-emerging in the 1530's. It came not surprisingly in connection with 'the King's Great Matter'. Cromwell's campaign to win support for the king included a clever publicity campaign to build up support for his authority in church as well as state and to undermine that of the pope. Symptomatic of this trend was

---

[157] See Tyndale, *Answer*, 99-100; 135-137; 139.

[158] See Tyndale, *Answer*, 158-159; 99: 'Now, sir, if you gather a general council for the matter, the churches of France and Italy will not believe the churches of Spain and Dutchland, because they so say; but will ask how they prove it? Neither will Lovain believe Paris, because they say they cannot err; but will hear first their probation.'

a booklet, *Articles devised by the holle consent of the kynges most honourable counsaylles* published in 1533.[159]

This latter work contained two important series of arguments, one in favour of the king's divorce; the other claiming that the final court of appeal lay not with the pope but with the general council. Conciliarism had come to England and received an official welcome. Thomas Cromwell himself was personally responsible for the publication of Marsiglio of Padua's *Defensor Pacis* in English translation two years later. This work was of a far more profound and radical nature than the conciliar dabblings of Cromwell's pamphleteers. Nonetheless it was these developments rather than the views of Luther or Tyndale which appear to have stimulated More to systematic reflection on the council and its function in the church.[160]

More was first drawn to discuss the council ·in any detail by a scathing attack from Luther against false councils. These, he claimed, had ascribed powers to Roman pontiffs far in excess of any warrant from scripture.[161] More replied by pointing out that councils were in essence assemblies of the whole church, guaranteed the same divine assistance promised to the church in general. When problems arise, 'To whom should the people rather wish that business delegated than to the bishops?..'[162] It was only in the years leading up to the final 'show-down' with Henry that he dealt at any length with the conciliar issue, in the *Confutation* and in some of the correspondence leading to his trial.

More tended to speak of the council in language drawn from legal theories of representation, as well as drawing very definite analogies between the working of council and of parliament.[163] Representation for medieval thinkers was not the equivalent of democratic election, 'Symbolic' representation was a commonplace of ecclesiastical thought. The Lords in England's upper house as well as the Commons were thought to

---

[159] See *Articles devised by the holle consent of the kynges most honourable counsaylles*, pr. Berthelet, London, 1533, repr. Pocock, *Records of the Reformation, The Divorce 1527-1533*, Oxford, II, 1870, 521-531. For an account of this literature see P. Janelle, *L'Angleterre à la veille du schisme*, Paris, 1935, 232-319; F. Le Van Baumer, *The Early Tudor Theory of Kingship*, 49-56; W. G. Zeeveld, *Foundations of Tudor Policy*, 87-89; 130-131; 135-137; P. Hughes, *The Reformation in England*, I, 248-269; Elton, *Policy and Police*, 171-216.

[160] See Elton, *Policy and Police*, 186 and 186, n. 2.

[161] See *WA* 10/2, 218/13-21.

[162] See *Responsio*, 626/21-628/5, tr. 627/24-629/6.

[163] See *Confutation*, 146/15-20; ibid. II, 714/34-715/4; ibid. II, 872/23-29; ibid. I, 344/21-345/7; ibid. I, 345/29-346/5, and passim. More to Cromwell, *Correspondence*, 499/238-247; Roper to Alington, *Correspondence*, 524/393-525/418; More to Wilson, *Correspondence*, 537/136-140.

represent their localities in parliament.[164] Hence, though not necessarily democratic, More's conciliar theory was definitely representational in tone.

This implied that sovereignty, if the term may be applied to the church, lay ultimately with the people as a whole. The language and concepts he used in relation to the council derived in all likelihood from the juristic tradition best represented in an intellectual ancestry descending from Bracton and Sir John Fortescue.[165] In practice, however, perhaps without his being aware of it, this placed him in the school of thought numbered five above, which included among its exponents scholars such as Gelnhausen, Zabarella and, in More's day, the Parisian Scot, John Major.[166]

There is no suggestion that the council be placed above the pope. But equally the contrary was consciously excluded, that the pope is above the council.[167] Consequently More evidently looked on pope and council as correlative and co-responsible organs of authority. He insisted on 'lawful' assembly,[168] presumably implying convocation by the pope as well as papal approval for its acts on the parliamentary analogy. Conversely he recognised the possibility of the deposition of a pope for grave personal

---

[164] See for example, Tierney, *Foundations of the Conciliar Theory*, 108-116; 121-124; 186-188 and passim; Chrimes, *English Constitutional Ideas*, 81-126; Elton, "*The Body of the Whole Realm*", (Charlottesville, Va), 19-20, and *Studies in Tudor Politics* II, 32-33 and passim.

[165] See Margaret Hastings: *Thomas More and John Fortescue*, Moreana 36 (1972) 61-63; Schoeck, *Common Law and Canon Law*.

[166] Note the similarity between More's description of the origin of conciliar authority and those of some university delegates in Basle cited in Black, *Monarchy and Community*, 17-18 from H. Weigel and others, *Deutsche Reichstagsakten*, Hist. Komm.d. Bayer. Akad. d. Wiss., Stuttgart-Göttingen, 1935-63, xvii, 367, xvi, 499. '...the whole church, dispersed as it is over the world, cannot have the exercise of its power, which it holds immediately from Christ, for that activity which properly belongs to the whole church; for the whole church is assembled out of different members and hierarchical ranks, which cannot come together for the exercise of any one activity, unless they are joined together; and this cannot happen except by means of the assembly of a general council. Thus the power of the universal church is brought into activity through the existence of the general council. Such power exists in the dispersed church in the same way that the seed exists in the grass, or wine in the grape; but, in the general council, it exists in its formal and complete essence. Nor can it be said that such power can only be exercised through the pope; for then the universal church could not exercise its power through itself and in the first instance but only through a part and in a limited way... The whole church itself exercises its own jurisdiction through the council representing it.'

[167] '...yit neuer thowght I the Pope above the generall counsaile...' in More to Cromwell, Rogers, *Correspondence*, 499/252-264.

[168] See More to Cromwell, Rogers, *Correspondence*, 499/238-247; Roper to Alington, Rogers, *Correspondence*, 526/448-455; ibid., 524/399-525/404.

fault.[169] These views are consistent with a moderate 'constitutionalist' approach to the relation between pope and council and indeed to the structure of the church itself.

The council did not figure greatly in Henry VIII's *Assertio Septem Sacramentorum*. One reference, however, bears a certain affinity to More's thinking on council. Henry wrote: '...how ridiculous is that exclamation of his (Luther's) against the see of Rome!...as if many of the laws...were not ordained in former times by the holy fathers, and public consent of Christians in synods and general councils.'[170] Here Henry speaks of the institution of public law in the church through the presumably implicit consent of 'the holy fathers' as well as the formal public consent of Christian people through synods and general councils. This suggests a representative theory of church assembly, as if those who meet to discuss and draw up ordinances do so on behalf of the people they represent.

As in More's case this does not necessarily presuppose an elective system for the choice of delegates. It does however presume a view of sovereignty within the church which does not see it as the exclusive prerogative of the 'spiritualty' but diffused through the whole body of believing Christians. In consenting to laws in synods and councils their representatives do so on their behalf. Henry's treatment of the council was a mere aside. Yet in some respects this makes it all the more interesting as a reflection of implicit assumptions regarding the nature of the church which were apparently, like More's, constitutional in tendency.

While More's mentor, John Colet, said little on the subject of councils, his fellow disciple John Fisher dealt quite fully, if not exhaustively, with conciliar theory on a number of occasions. Showing himself more familiar with both the history and theological underpinning of general councils than More, Fisher adopted a more reserved attitude in regard to their authority, closer to that of papal monarchists like Torquemada and Cajetan than constitutionalists such as Gelnhausen or Zabarella. This derived in large measure from his 'high' view of papal power as the source and origin of other degrees in Christian hierarchy: 'Have we not observed that Christians are born of priests, priests of bishops, and that bishops are generated by the sovereign pontiff,'[171] a view which, if taken without qualification, could lead one back almost to Giles of Rome and Augustinus

---

[169] See *Confutation*, 590/13-15: 'There are orders in Christes churche, by which a pope may be bothe admonisshed and amended/and hathe be for incorrigible mynde and lacke of amendement, finally deposed and chaunged.'

[170] See Henry VIII, *Assertio*, sig. Mvl.

[171] See Fisher, *Confutatio, Opera Omnia*, 569; see also ibid., 565-566.

Triumphus. With characteristic English common-sense Fisher evaded the full rigour of his own logic, recognising real limits in practice to papal authority.

Fisher did not give blanket approval to conciliar decisions. He recognised that some may have erred, '...especially recent ones which were summoned in time of schism, where perhaps there 'had not been the greatest harmony of souls...'[172] Presumably he had in mind such assemblies as the later council of Basle (1437-1449) and the *conciliabulum* of Pisa (1511-1512). On the other hand he saw in this no reason to 'damne all the resydue'.

Fisher, too, applied the language of representation to councils: '...For these (beyond all controversy) represent the Catholic Church.'[173] This only in passing, however, and his usage might not stand up to rigorous analysis. At the same time he recognised both the value and authority of councils. The council has authority to legislate for the whole church. Similarly it can define doctrinal issues in such a way, however, as not to produce a new truth but to make an already revealed truth stand out more clearly.[174] This is merely another way of expressing the ministerial role of the church in relation to revelation. Church teaching does not make new truth. It simply points to what is the truth contained in divine revelation.

Fisher did not go at length into the composition of an ecumenical assembly but his reservations forced him to define clearly those councils he was prepared to accept. Referring to Mt 18, 17 he said: 'If he refuse to hear even the church let him be to thee as the heathen and the publican...But when are we to hear the church more than when the council agrees with the pope and the pope with the council?..'[175] Or as he put it elsewhere: '...I always view as suspect those where the pope differs from the council or where the council differs from the pope, unless the latter has happened through the very palpable fault of the pope.'[176]

---

[172] See Fisher, *Confutatio, Opera Omnia*, 292. Fisher also notes examples from the past of councils of dubious authenticity, those of the Donatists, the council of Rimini with its murdered bishops, that of Constantinople against the venerations of images, councils assembled by the papal authority without the Holy Spirit, such as that of Stephen VI against his predecessor Formosus. See *Confutatio, Opera Omnia*, 595-598.

[173] See Fisher, *Confutatio, Opera Omnia*, 583-584.

[174] loc. cit.

[175] See Fisher, *Confutatio, Opera Omnia*, 583-584.

[176] Ibid., 595-598. 'Even if the Sovereign Pontiff together with the council, that is the church catholic, cannot making anything either true or false, and hence establish new articles of faith, nevertheless whatever these propose for our obligatory belief as an article of faith, all persons truly Christian ought to believe not otherwise than as an article of faith.' See Fisher, *Confutatio, Opera Omnia*, 583. Fisher based himself on Scotus (Sent. IV, dist. 2, q. 3).

In this latter passage, without realising it, perhaps, Fisher drifted away from a papal monarchist ecclesiology, admitting the need for agreement of council with the pope before the full weight of church authority could be focused on any issue. He also made allowance, as did the papal monarchists, for conciliar action independent of the papacy in the event of grave personal error on the part of the papal incumbent. On the other hand, Fisher clearly provided for papal agreement with the council. In the historical context this implies the papal right of convocation and approval of the conciliar acts.

Hence in all of this Fisher was not entirely consistent with his own position on papal authority as being the source of that of other ranks in the church. He had allowed himself to slide into a constitutionalist view of the council, recognising at least two distinct organs of authority within the church, council and pope. In all of this More, even though he did not treat in depth of either papacy or council, seems to have been the more logical of the two, combining a moderate papalism with a constitutionalist view of council.

It is more difficult to come to grips with Erasmus's view of the council. Those who have written most recently on his ecclesiology have not devoted a great deal of attention to the topic.[177] In general Erasmus was more prone to cite scripture, patristic tradition or church consensus in support of his opinions. At the same time he was not averse to citing even medieval councils in support of his views. As early as 1495 in the *Antibarbari* he cited the decisions of medieval councils to back up his own recommendations regarding the use of literary arts such as grammar, rhetoric and dialectics.[178] On the other hand in the *Julius Exclusus*, (c. 1513), a work not certainly Erasmus's but probably his, at least in part, the author made fun of the Fifth Lateran Council as being little more than an instrument of papal diplomacy and consequently of little value as a guide in the interpretation of the divine word.[179] In his later works, nonetheless, Erasmus

---

[177] See Kohls, *Die Theologie des Erasmus*, 125 ff; 146ff; 148ff; 159ff; 168ff; 176ff; Gebhardt, *Die Stellung des Erasmus von Rotterdam zur römischen Kirche*, 52-58; see studies by McConica, Augustijn, De Vogel, Hyma and Pollet in Coppens, *Scrinium Erasmianum*, II, 77-195; Hentze, *Kirche und kirchliche Einheit bei Desiderius Erasmus von Rotterdam* is curiously reticent on this question.

[178] Kohls dates the composition of the *Antibarbari*'s essential content to 1495, even though, of course, part I was not printed till 1520 by Froben of Basle; see idem, *Theologie des Erasmus*, 37-38. There is some debate on this point. Conciliar references occur in Erasmus, *Antibarbari*, ed. Holborn, 107/4.

[179] See for example R. H. Bainton, *Erasmus and Luther and the Dialogue 'Julius Exclusus'* in *Festschrift für Franz Lau*, Göttingen, 1967, 17-26; James D. Tracy, *Erasmus, The Growth of a Mind*, Geneva, 1972, 137-138; C. Reedijk, *Érasme, Thierry Martens et le 'Iulius Exclusus'* in *Scrinium Erasmianum*, II, ed. J. Coppens, 1969, 351-378.

expressed firmer adherence to church authority in matters of doctrine including that of the general council. This attitude was already in evidence
in 1522 but was given firmer expression at least from 1527 onwards.[180]

Erasmus recognised the divine institution of ecclesiastical office in a
general way, while seeing the diversification of offices as an evolution
within Christian tradition.[181] He also ascribed to office holders, bishops in
particular, the task of teaching the gospel in Christ's name.[182] When,
however, he thought of church authority in relation to specific matters of
doctrine he turned to scripture, tradition and the consensus of the church
as his principal guidelines. It is in this context that his later statements on
the significance of conciliar teaching must be viewed. Conciliar teaching is
one way church consensus has of expressing itself. His tendency was to
refer to both in the same breath, as for example in *Lingua* when speaking of
his assent to revealed truth: 'Idem arbitror de Conciliorum decretis,
praesertim si consensus populi Christum profitentis accesserit.'[183] He
never allowed fathers, doctors or councils to be placed on a par with scripture.[184] At the same time he accepted conciliar decisions though with blind
rather than informed faith: '...in quibus si nihil definisset Ecclesia,
rogatus quid sentirem, responderem mihi non liquere, sed Deo cognitum
esse.'[185]

---

[180] See C. Augustijn, *The Ecclesiology of Erasmus*, in *Scrinium Erasmianum*, II, 153-155 and
passim. Augustijn cites the well known statement by Erasmus: 'How much the authority of
the Church means to others I do not know: to me it means so much that I could have the
same opinions as the Arians and Pelagians if the Church had accepted what they taught.
The words of Christ are enough for me, but people should not be surprised if I follow the
Church as their interpreter; convinced of its authority, I believe the canonical Scriptures.
Perhaps others are wiser or stronger; I for one find tranquillity in nothing safer than settled
decisions of the Church' in Allen, *Erasmi epistolae* VII, 216/62-70. See also C. J. De Vogel,
Erasmus and Church Dogma, Scrinium Erasmianum, II, 109-117; Gebhardt, *Die Stellung des
Erasmus*, 52-58; 359-376; Hentze, *Kirchliche Einheit*, 127-132; 150-159.

[181] 'Qui vero deliguntur ad mysticas functiones, iis per sacramentum Ordinis augetur
donum Spiritus ad digne administrandum munus delegatum' in *Explanatio symboli*, (1533),
LB V, 1176E; see also idem, *Christiani hominis institutum*, (1514), *LB* V, 1358D; idem, *Christiani matrimonii institutio*, (1526), *LB* V, 634D. 'Apostoli Episcoporum ac Sacerdotum per-
sonam gerunt, ipse Dominus Dei at hominis gerit', in idem, *Ecclesiastes*, (1535), *LB* V,
1056E.

[182] 'Non semper tingit, non semper ungit aut absolvit Sacerdos, sed docendi munus
perpetuum est, sine quo caetera (munia) sunt inutilia.', Erasmus, *Ecclesiastes*, (1535), *LB* V,
831D; see also ibid., 801C; 777E; 826D; 830E; 791E.

[183] 'Mihi gregario homunculo satis est Ecclesiae ductum sequi, praesertim cum Scripturarum auctoritas stet a nobis' in Erasmus, *Detectio prestigiarum*, (1526), *LB* X, 1563A-F.

[184] Erasmus, *Lingua*, (1525), *LB* IV, 703D.

[185] Erasmus, *Hyperaspistes*, (1526-27), *LB* X, 1258E. Erasmus was referring here to matters such as purgatory, baptism of infants, the immaculate conception of the Virgin Mary.

Though the myth of Erasmus's *adogmatismus* has been safely put to rest, it is still possible to see a real dogmatic minimalism at work. Thus while he looked to a council to promote and possibly bring about the reunion of Christianity, he did not offer any welcome to a further multiplication of dogmatic definitions.[186] Erasmus had unconsciously absorbed a historical dimension to all his thinking, a dimension which tends to relativise the dogmatic statements of any age in terms of its cultural forms, philosophy, language and profound concerns. Thus, what he might have been calling for, had he lived a few centuries later, was a hermeneutic of conciliar statements.

In any event J. Coppens, the Louvain Erasmian scholar, suggests that Erasmus might well have made his own the views of a present-day theologian: 'Every interpretation of God's word which does not regulate itself in accordance with the teaching of the magisterium, a magisterium itself conditioned by its past, empties historic Christianity of its substance.'[187] Erasmus accepted the teaching authority of the church unambiguously, at least in his later years. But he tended to refer its affirmations back to the twin springs from which it drew its inspiration, the sources of revelation and the consensus of the believing community. With these there must always be a strong and vital connection.[188]

More's attitude to the council till 'The Trial Proceedings' was not unlike that of Erasmus. The councils were there in consciousness but rather in the background. Faith was learned from the church especially where consensus existed. At the same time when the challenge was put, whether by Luther or Henrician apologists, he was prepared to debate even in a rudimentary way the nature and origin of conciliar authority, something Erasmus did not feel impelled to do at any length. In regard to the actual weight of conciliar authority, More's position was more simplistic than that of Erasmus. He had a clear-eyed vision of the development of doctrine within the church, but he welcomed the final stamp of approval by conciliar authority to any given proposition and readily attributed to this a degree of finality his humanist colleague would have been reluctant to afford.

---

[186] See Erasmus to the Town Council at Basle, Allen, *Erasmi epistolae* VI, no. 1539/105-114; Erasmus to Paul III, 23 Jan. 1535 in Allen, *Erasmi epistolae* XI, pp. 62-63, esp. 62/70-63/77.

[187] See J. Coppens, *Où en est le portrait d'Érasme théologien?* in *Scrinium Erasmianum*, II, 592, citing R. Draguet, *Arnold van Lantschoot (1889-1969)*, *Le Muséon* 82 (1969) 252.

[188] ibid., 593.

[189] See Klaus Oehler, *Der consensus omnium als Kriterium der Wahrheit in der antiken Philosophie und der Patristik. Eine Studie zur Geschichte des Begriffs der Allgemeinen Meinung*, in *Antike und Abendland* 10 (1961) 103-129.

VIII. CONSENSUS

Although More had conciliar leanings, they grew out of a deeper sense both of church and society as a common body made up of individuals each of whom is a person of significance in his own right. In day-to-day life this was evidenced in the courtesy and consideration More showed those who crossed his path. More profoundly, however, Sir Thomas More, social reformer, parliamentarian and incipient democrat had a deep sense of the value of the individual and the worth of his opinion. This was confirmed from a theological standpoint by his repeated refrain concerning the presence of the Spirit of God to each baptised Christian, and the new law inscribed in the heart of each individual by the abiding Spirit. These elemental landmarks within his vision of the world form part of a perspective which extended from the wisdom of Greece and Rome to the heritage of patristic lore, as well as the constitutional, legal and theological theories of the later middle ages. More's doctrine on consensus had its roots both in centuries-old tradition of consent as a basis for political sovereignty and in ecclesial consensus as a guide to Christian truth.

Klaus Oehler has traced the transition from the philosophical and juridical concept of consent in the Graeco-Roman world to its incorporation in Christian theology in patristic times.[189] Although the concept had its antecedents in Greek literature and early philosophy, Aristotle was the first to use the concept systematically as a principle of verification.[190] His axioms concerning the consent of all as a principle of truth were elaborated in his logic, and applied in his ethics and politics. These principles were taken over by Sophists, Epicurean, and Stoic philosophers. The latter gave the principle a psychological dimension in terms of certain inborn ideas native to man and therefore common to all, prior to all experience.[191] Stoic ideas greatly influenced Cicero's speculations in ethics and politics, providing him with a dialectical tool with which to carve out with Roman precision the foundations of his moral and legal system. Cicero's maxim: *omni autem in re consensio omnium gentium lex naturae putanda est* found its complement in his political ideal of *consensus omnium bonorum.*[192]

This doctrine on consent was taken over into the *Realpolitik* of Imperial Rome and proclaimed as the foundation of the Roman state, as, for example, when the Emperor Augustus had inscribed in the thirty fourth chapter of the *Monumentum Ancyranum: per consensum universorum potitus rerum om-*

---

[190] Oehler, *Der consensus omnium,* 103-108.
[191] Oehler, *Der consensus omnium,* 108-109.
[192] ibid., 109-111.

nium.[193] The doctrine of consent became a commonplace of Roman law in its varied ramifications. Through Justinian it was to arouse manifold echoes in medieval times in canonist thought. Medieval canonists had another source for consensus-theory in Germanic law. The customary law of the Franco-Germanic tribes required in many instances unanimous consent by an assembly for the ratification of decisions. Only slowly did the principle of majority rule emerge.

Even earlier, however, the Ciceronian doctrine of consent had passed into theology. This appeared already in Clement of Rome (c. 96 A D) who saw in the *consensus ecclesiae* or the *consensus presbyterorum* evidence of the unifying activity of the Holy Spirit and in consequence a firm indication of where truth lay.[194] Doctrinal unity as norm of authentic church life was stressed by Irenaeus, Tertullian and Hippolytus. The latter also used the language of consent concerning the election of bishops. Both of these themes recur in the writings of Cyprian, but it was not till the fifth century and the work of St Vincent of Lerins that a satisfactory formulation was found for the doctrinal aspect: '...quod ubique, quod semper, quod ab omnibus creditum est, hoc est etenim vere proprieque catholicum.'[195] Vincent like Augustine did not believe that all questions could be resolved by recourse to tradition. In some instances where division is to be found in tradition itself, a council may be called to determine where truth is to be found, 'quorum est in ecclesia saluberrima auctoritas' as Augustine put it.[196]

This tradition concerning the role of consensus in preserving unity of faith in the Christian community was maintained in the early middle ages by such luminaries as Hincmar of Rheims, archbishop of that diocese from 845-882.[197] Throughout the middle ages the concept of the inerrance of the church based on the agreement in faith of the *congregatio fidelium* was generally accepted. As this agreement was normally in evidence at least in public profession, its theological justification did not arouse the keenest interest. Attention was focused rather on issues concerning orders,

---

[193] ibid., 111-116.

[194] Oehler, *Der consensus omnium,* 117.

[195] Oehler, ibid., 118-123.

[196] Oehler, ibid., 123; Congar, *Ecclésiologie,* 22. See also F. Hofmann, *La signification des conciles pour le développement de la doctrine ecclésiale d'après saint Augustin,* in *Église et Tradition,* Le Puy et Lyon, 1963, 65-73; Heiko Oberman, *"Et tibi dabo",* Ned. Theol. Tijdschrift 25 (1971) 265-277.

[197] 'Nam si non est unius consensionis signum una communio, quid erit quod ad confitendam omnis Ecclesiae consonantiam mystice celebratur...?' Hincmar, *De praedestinatione,* c. 381, 1, cited Y. Congar, *L'Ecclésiologie du haut-moyen-âge,* Paris, 1968, 169.

episcopate and papacy. Hence it is in the practical sphere of the ordering
of church life that one must look for more significant influence of the
theory of consensus in medieval thought.[198]

The course of this development has been traced in a number of
remarkable studies of its effect both on canonical thought and civil theories
of representation and consent.[199] The Roman maxim 'quod omnes tangit
ab omnibus approbari debet' became a key principle governing the corporate life of Christian communities in the thirteenth century. The strong
sense of community inherent in Franco-Germanic society as well as in
other parts of Europe, nourished by Christian fraternal influence, found a
constitutional formulation in this axiom. Initially applied to the requirement of prior consent before taxes were levied, it gradually passed to matters of larger import affecting the corporate life of collegiate bodies, local
churches, and eventually the church in general. The cultivation of
Aristotelian philosophy especially the *Politics,* favoured this evolution.
Parallel developments took place in the civil sphere with the convocation of
councils and assemblies and the growth eventually of parliaments not
merely in Britain but throughout Christendom.[200]

---

[198] See in particular Yves Congar, *Quod omnes tangit, ab omnibus tractari et approbari debet,* in
Revue historique de droit français et étranger 104 (1958) 210-259. In this article Congar traces the
influence of Roman theories of consent on medieval legal, political and theological thought.
See in particular his citation of the second edition of the Code of Justinian: 'quod omnes
similiter tangit, ab omnibus comprobetur', C. 5, LIX, 5, cited by Congar, op. cit., 210, n.
2. He sees this axiom and others of its kind as playing a key role in the development of
medieval theories of consent and representation. See also Gaines Post, *Studies in Medieval
Legal Thought,* Princeton, N.J., 1964, 163-238 for a detailed analysis of the influence of the
same principle on English medieval constitutional thought, notably in Bracton and early
parliaments. In general see the classic study, P. Vinogradoff, *Roman Law in Medieval Europe,*
2nd ed., by F. de Zulueta, Oxford, 1929, passim; Gierke, *Political Theories of the Middle Ages,*
166-167; Tierney, *Foundations of Conciliar Theory,* 108-116; 121-124; 186-188 and passim.

[199] The remarks which follow are based mainly on the classic work of Gierke, *Political
Theories of the Middle Ages,* as well as more recent studies such as those of Tierney, *Foundations
of the Conciliar Theory;* Congar, *Quod omnes tangit;* idem, *Ecclésiologie,* 90-122; 176-352; for the
civil side see Post, *Medieval Legal Thought,* 61-238; Chrimes, *Constitutional Ideas,* 66-141; J. E.
A. Jolliffe, *The Constitutional History of Medieval England,* London, 4th ed. 1967, 304-495;
Elton, '*The body of the whole realm*', in *Studies in Tudor Government* II, 19-59. These writers provide ample directions to the wider literature.

[200] See Post, *Medieval Legal Thought,* 91-238; Elton, '*The body of the whole realm*', in *Studies in
Tudor Government,* II, 19-59; H. Cam, *Recent Work and Present Views on the Origins and Develop-
ment of Representative Assemblies,* in *Relazioni del X Congresso Internaz. di Scienze Storiche,* I,
Florence, 1955, 3-101; A. Marongiu, *Medieval Parliaments: A Comparative Study,* tr. S. J.
Woolf, London, 1968; D. Hanson, *From Kingdom to Commonwealth,* Boston, Mass., 1970,
217-252 and passim; B. Wilkinson, *The Creation of Medieval Parliaments,* New York, 1972; G.
O. Sayles, *The King's Parliament of England,* London, 1975, 88-93 who disagrees radically
with Post and Cam on the nature of representation in early English parliaments.

Subsequently criticism of papal absolutism, the controversy between Boniface VIII and Philip the Fair as well as that between John XXII and Louis of Bavaria, and most acutely of all, the great western schism led to the application on the broadest possible scale of this principle to the structure of the church. While Vincent of Lerins' maxim, *quod semper, quod ubique, quod ab omnibus* was generally accepted as a norm of faith, a general council representing the entire church was looked on as its supreme instance. A variety of conciliar theories has been described above. What is worth noting here is the fundamental assumption concerning the authority of popular consensus underlying some of these.

Gerson and the early Cusa made a direct application of the legal principle *quod omnes tangit...* to the life and action of the universal church.[201] At the same time they maintained full respect for its hierarchical order. Dietrich of Niem and later Zabarella went a stage further, arguing that the power of the church resides primarily in the full community, rather than in its organs. Hence with the consent of the community it may be withdrawn from any of these.[202] More extreme views were put forward by Marsiglio of Padua and William of Ockham. Marsiglio drew his inspiration mainly from Aristotle. For him the supreme authority in the church is the body of the faithful represented by the general council.[203] Ockham on the other hand moved into a rigorous individualism. While recognising that the supreme authority in the church lay with the entire body of the faithful, and that therefore in principle each believer could attend the general council, he nullified these assumptions by predicating the possibility of the church of Christ surviving in only one true believer. In the limiting case of total schism final authority would rest with him.[204]

Theories of consensus and consent were very much in the air in the late medieval era at the level of procedure, constitutional theory and

---

[201] See Fink, *Die konziliare Idee im späten Mittelalter, Vorträge und Forschungen,* ed. T. C. Mayer, No. 9 (1965) 119-134. For Gerson see *De considerationibus,* in Du Pin *Opera Omnia,* II, 232: 'Quid enim minus tolerabile quam si universam rempublicam una unius sententia presumeret pro libito versare reversareque; cum verissime dicit canon, "Quod omnes tangit ab omnibus debet approbari". Ab omnibus intellige, vel a major omnium saniorque consilio;' for Cusa see *De concordantia catholica,* III, pref., ed. Schardius, (1618), p. 354, cited Congar, *Quod omnes tangit,* p. 242, n. 123.

[202] See Dietrich of Niem, *De modo uniendi ac reformandi ecclesiam* in Du Pin II, 161-201; Francesco Zabarella, *Tractatus de schismate,* in S. Schardius, *De jurisdictione, auctoritate et praeeminentia imperiali ac potestate ecclesiastica,* Basle, 1566, 686-711.

[203] See Marsiglio, *Defensor pacis,* ed. Scholz, *Fontes juris German. in usum scholarum,* Hanover, 1932, 385 ff.; 393 ff.; 400; 603-604.

[204] See Ockham, *Dialogus,* p. 1, lib. 2, cap. 25 in Goldast, III, 429; lib. 4, cap. 9, in Goldast, III, 450-451.

theological principle. In civil life the growth of parliaments had brought
the doctrine of consent into the foreground in many European countries
including England. The classical nostalgia of the Renaissance was to
renew awareness in the minds of many of the Greco-Roman heritage.
Such was the cultural ambience in which Sir Thomas More and his adver-
saries took up their pens to turn them into spears.

Martin Luther's respect for the word of God did not begin in 1517,
though of course his attitude developed as time went on. For him the
gospel was the church's greatest possession, its proclamation her greatest
function. Christ founded the church through this word, and through it he
continues to nourish and support it.[205] God's word is in the church *passive
et ministerialiter,* passively in so far as the church receives the word on God's
authority, ministerially in so far as the church is used as an instrument for
the transmission of the word.[206] The gospel of course is not identical with
the scriptures, but in practice Luther tended to make the same claims for
the literal sense of scripture that he did for the transcendental word of
God. It is the gospel, then, whose principal expression is the written word
of God in the canonical writings that is in the church, and which is
transmitted by the church.

There is no question of the church possessing authority over the word of
God. The word possesses authority because it is God's word. Its authority
in no way depends on the church. The believer submits to the word
because it comes from God, not because it is transmitted by the church.

Scriptural truth therefore is the criterion for assessing the validity of
preaching and of doctrinal statements emanating from the church. All
didactic statements, oral as well as written, must derive their content from
scripture and submit to being assessed against the measuring-rod of holy
writ.[207] On the other hand this provides for a certain inerrancy in the faith
of the church. Her teaching is inerrant in so far as it is in conformity with
God's word found in scripture. Otherwise it is fallible. Certainty of faith
therefore is grounded in God's word, and the clear sense of scripture is the

---

[205] See *WA* 3, 32/2 ff; *WA* 4, 189/34 ff.

[206] '...verbum est verbum Dei originaliter et autoritative, non ecclesiae nisi passive et
ministerialiter. Ergo ecclesia est sub verbo et mandato Dei et non supra.' *WA* 30-II, 682/1-3;
ibid., 681-690 passim. On this see Karl Gerhard Steck, *Lehre und Kirche bei Luther,* Munich,
1963, 44-122; cp. Jaroslav Pelikan, *Luther the Expositor, Luther's Works, Companion Volume,*
Saint Louis, Mo., 1959, 48-88 and passim.

[207] 'Nolo omnium doctor iactari, sed solam Scripturam regnare, nec eam meo spiritu aut
ullorum hominum interpretari, sed per se ipsam et suo spiritu intelligi volo.' See *WA* 7, 98ff;
WA 7, 721; *WA* 39-I, 184-197.

surest pointer to this.[208] Otherwise the element of human corruption and inadequacy holds sway.

Does this mean that synthetic credal statements such as creeds, confessions, and catechisms are of no value? Such definitions of the content of belief are in no way excluded but their authority comes not from the church which draws them up but from the divine word they express; they possess authority only in so far as they express it.[209] The role of the church in regard to such statements is merely that of an editor or interpreter of biblical truth.

To a certain extent the consent of the believing church to any given set of propositions is a guarantee of their conformity to God's word. This testimony is never unquestionable as the existence of such a general assent is always difficult to establish. Even if established it does not constitute irrefragable testimony to the truth of the statements in question as Luther, like Ockham, Biel, and Panormitanus, admitted the limiting case where divine truth might be preserved alive by only one believer.[210] Consequently one dissenting voice from any given consensus might be conceivably the voice of the one authentic Christian witness. The authority of any didactic statement therefore derives not from the church as such but from the word of God which it transmits. But the church at any point of time might be reduced to one true believer.

Allowing for the limiting case where one Christian alone remains true, Luther did see some real utility in the consent of the church to doctrinal statements. Only the assent of the true believing church could guarantee their correspondence with scripture. Seen in this light creeds, catechisms, doctrinal statements have a value in the interpretation of obscure passages in the written word of God, and in placing its hidden depths at the disposal of the *rudes*, of whom not a few exist. Curiously enough, in his work against Henry, Luther used one of the texts of scripture More was fondest of quoting in favour of the value of consensus, Ps. 67, 7: '...ille, inquam, internus spiritus unanimes habitare facit in domo hic docet idem sapere, idem iudicare, idem cognoscere, idem probare, idem docere, idem confiteri, idem sequi. Ubi ille non fuerit, impossibile est, ut unitas sit.'[211] As

---

[208] *WA* 30-III, 342/1-343/1.

[209] *WA* 2, 427/8-11.

[210] 'Si enim solus essem in toto orbe terrarum, qui retinerem verbum, solus essem ecclesia et recte iudicarem de reliquo toto mundo, quod non esset ecclesia.', *WA* 42, 334/30. '...plus credendum uni privato fideli quam toti Concilio aut Papae, si meliorem habeat autoritatem vel rationem...' *WA* 2, 404/26-31; see also Panormitanus, *Commentaria in libros decretalium*, Lyon, 1524, 122r.

[211] See Luther, *Contra Henricum*, *WA* 10-II, 219/32-220/4.

More indicated in his comments on this passage, all of this made complete sense to him. On the other hand he pointed out that Luther had earlier already set the limits to the value of consensus even within this same work, having appealed from pope, to council, to people, and ultimately the judgment of one individual.[212] For Luther the acid test of any theological proposition remained its conformity to the word of God. In the final analysis judgment on this might rest with one. Hence though he valued consensus and in the later stages of his reforming campaign came to value once more the interpretations of the fathers, Luther retained an essential scepticism in the face of common opinion.

Tyndale took up an even more radical stance than his master. Taking the written word of scripture in its literal sense as an absolute norm of faith, and assuming its transparency to the mind of the true believer, he rejected any mediation of divine truth by the Christian community. '...the pith and substance in general of every thing necessary unto our souls' health, both of what we ought to believe, and what we ought to do, was written...' Anyone who feels injured by traditional belief should abandon it immediately.[213] Nor is the common consent of the body of believers a guide to the correct understanding of the gospel. Many of those who support the papists come '...with a story faith, a popish faith, a faithless faith, and a feigned faith of their own making...' No strength lies in numbers. If it did, the doctrine of Mahomet would be true, as it has the backing of even greater numbers of believers than More's faith.[214]

Faced with these objections, More, as I have indicated above, pointed out the inherent tensions in Luther's position. He himself opted for a firm doctrine of consensus. This consensus of the whole church may exist at any given moment of time.[215] It is even more convincing if spread throughout the ages, so that a constant tradition of consent extending to apostolic times confirms any particular assertion.[216] In this More stood within the broad lines of Augustine's argument from continuity in faith

---

[212] See *Responsio*, 620/33-624/26, tr. 621/38-625/31. See *Responsio*, 610-639, where More comments on some of the more relevant passages from *Contra Henricum*, notably *WA* 10-II, 218/6-36; 219/21-32.

[213] Tyndale, *Answer*, 26-28; 55.

[214] Tyndale, *Answer*, 70; 116: 'It is enough to prove their part, that it is a common custom, and that such a multitude do it. And so, by his doctrine, the Turks are in the right way.'

[215] *Responsio*, 96/12-16, tr. 97/11-16. More did not insist on total unanimity for consensus but implicitly accepted the medieval principle of the *maior et sanior pars* prevailing; see *Responsio*, 202/26-28, tr. 203/31-33 'almost all..'

[216] See *Responsio*, 128/3-12, tr. 129/3-14; ibid., 250/13-27, tr. 251/17-31.

and Vincent of Lerins' teaching on the universality of belief: *quod semper, quod ubique, quod ab omnibus.*

There is an interesting reflection of Roman juridical thought in the *Responsio* as well. It occurs in a legal discussion concerning the rights of property, though it has applications in theology as well as law, '...nisi rationi consensus accedat...qui consensus aut coalescens usu, aut expressus litteris, publica lex est.'[217] Consensus can grow out of custom and be expressed as eloquently in its tacit traditions as in its literary masterpieces. This principle explains More's defence of what would now be regarded as secondary elements of orthodox practice such as pilgrimages, devotion to saints and so on.

Beyond the definition of consensus, however, More had to determine more clearly for himself the subject of this consensus. Is it the elect, the just, the faithful or the clergy? In short, one of the factors which spurred him on to work out a definition of the church, and to go beyond that into a rudimentary apologetic, was his discovery that Luther too held a theory of consensus. On Luther's part this was the consensus of the hidden, spiritual church of true believers. Sir Thomas More's was the common known Catholic Church made up of saints and sinners, lay and cleric alike.[218] Guided by the Spirit and living in the security of Christ's promise to be with his church, it is the consensus of this broad community that More accepts as normative of faith. The consensus does not 'make law', to use a legal analogy, but interprets authoritatively a divine revelation to which it is subordinate. This conception is not too far removed from the medieval idea of the role of parliament and courts in relation to the fundamental natural and customary law of society.[219]

In his replies to Tyndale, More leaned as heavily as ever on the doctrine of consensus. He treated explicitly of the relation of church to revelation, making it abundantly clear that for him the church is subordinate to revelation. On the other hand as he did not identify revelation exclusively with scripture, he saw the church in its consensus 'canonising' scripture as well as acting as its interpreter.[220] In the *Confutation* he dealt more formally

---

[217] *Responsio*, 276/20-25, tr. 277/23-30. See also Headley's lucid discussion of these issues, *Responsio*, 752-760 and passim. On More's role as parliamentarian, an experience which undoubtedly influenced his thought, see J. S. Roskell, *The Commons and their Speakers in English Parliaments 1376-1523*, Manchester, 1965, 324-332.

[218] See *Responsio*, 624/5-12, tr. 625/6-14; ibid., 172/1-10, tr, 173/1-11.

[219] See C. H. McIlwain, *The Growth of Political Thought in the West from the Greeks to the End of the Middle Ages*, New York, 1932 (repr. 1968), 183-200.

[220] See for example *Confutation*, 133/31-35: '...though the chyrch be not aboue the scripture and holy wryt: yet yt is so taught by the spyryte of god and his holy secrete inwarde

with the problem raised by the development of doctrine, recognising that consensus might not always have existed in the church on any particular issue. Here he referred to both the role of the Spirit in continuing revelation and in guiding the church towards consensus. Furthermore, he adverted to the function of rational discourse in teasing out disputed questions. Hence although the Lerinian formula might not always apply, the consensus ultimately arrived at was equally binding.[221] This brought More to a more Augustinian position on this issue, a factor which may also have had some bearing on his more noticeable interest in the councils of the church both in the *Confutation* and the trial proceedings.

While More may have been influenced in his regard for scripture and living tradition by his spiritual father, John Colet, he can have learned little directly from him of a theology of consensus. For Colet, the rule of faith was scripture and tradition.[222] He did not deal extensively with the teaching office of the church, though in his Cabalist period bishops had a key role in transmitting this secret, oral tradition. Nor did Colet dwell at any length on the role of the general council nor even of the faith of the church as guide to truth. In keeping with the spirit of Renaissance humanism, the primary rule of faith is the written word of scripture. Beside this, however, unlike Luther and Tyndale, he set the living tradition of the church whose antecedents he vindicated in terms of a quasi-Cabalistic oral tradition. At the same time the doctrine of consensus which emerges in More's writing is fully consonant with the vision of the church held up by Colet as a spiritual communion of the redeemed with Christ, bound together by love: '...In this mutual love consists all order, duty and office in the Church; and the whole Ecclesiastical Hierarchy in it rests on the love of God and of our neighbour.'[223] Although the doctrine of consensus did not figure greatly in Colet's writings, it may well be that his spiritual conception of the church provided Thomas More with a basic perspective in which Spirit-signed Christians bound together in the corporate unity of Catholic fellowship form the primary model of the Chris-

worde vnwrytten, that yt can not be dampnably deceyued in the vnderstandynge of his holy scrypture wryten.' On all this see Flesseman-Van Leer, *The Controversy about Ecclesiology*, 69-79; 84-86; Prévost, *Thomas More*, 259-264; Marius, *Confutation*, 1292-1294.

[221]See *Confutation*, 337/27-33; ibid., 996/20-23; *Confutation*, 248/11-24; ibid., 249/9-16.

[222] See Hunt, *Dean Colet and his Theology*, 62-63; 88-102. Hunt underestimates Colet's appreciation of tradition. See Robert Peters, *John Colet's Knowledge and Use of Patristics, Moreana* no. 22 (1969) 45-59. See also Colet, *Enarratio I Cor,* 239, tr. 110; idem, *In ecclesiasticam hierarchiam,* 87; ibid., 105-107. On Colet's Cabalist tendencies see ibid., 56; 110-112; 135.

[223] Colet, *In ecclesiasticam hierarchiam,* 50-51; *Enarratio I Cor,* 87; *De corpore Christi mystico,* 44-45.

tian church. It is not a long step from there to see the consensus in faith of this body as the principal criterion of the content of faith.

On the other hand, Henry VIII in his *Assertio* had a relatively firm theory of consensus. Henry held for a two-fold transmission of revelation through scripture and unwritten traditions preserved in the faith of the church.[224] Like More he attributed this consistency of faith in the church to the action of the Holy Spirit.[225] When there was question of deciding obscure or disputed questions concerning the significance of divine revelation, Henry turned to scripture and tradition for support. The ultimate arbiter, however, is the common faith of the Christian community. Thus, for example, when discussing the sacrament of confirmation, Henry quotes scripture, some of the fathers, and concludes his argument pointing out the support he has from 'the faith of the whole church which is nowhere stronger than in the sacraments.'[226] This 'consensus' of the whole church, though Henry does not use the word, is unfailing. For '...Christ's care is not that his church may not err after this or that manner; but that it may not err in any manner whatsoever.'[227]

Henry's brief reference to councils brings out an explicit use of the terminology of consent. Referring to Luther's condemnation of restrictive legal practice in the established church, he rejected the criticism on dual grounds of tradition and public consent: '...as if many of the laws, which he (Luther) calls murdering laws were not ordained in former times by the holy fathers and public consent of the Christians in synods and general councils.'[228] Without any real analysis of the nature and structure of conciliar assembly, Henry assumed it to possess a certain representative character and its decisions to represent the 'public consent' of the whole Christian people. Is this not an unconsidered application to ecclesiastical matters of a doctrine of consent which had governed the convocation of parliament at least since the time of Edward III?[229] Even if it came from

---

[224] See Henry VIII, *Assertio,* sig. Mv3: 'Many other things done by Jesus have been omitted by all (the new testament writers), which...are not written in this book (John's gospel), and which the whole world could not contain; some of which have been delivered to the faithful by the mouth of the apostles, and have been ever after conserved by the perpetual faith of the holy Catholic Church...'

[225] Henry VIII, *Assertio,* sig. Mrv4: The church is guided and directed by the Holy Spirit so that '...what was to be done might be taught by the Holy Spirit of whom Christ said: "But when the Paraclete comes, whom I will send you from the Father, the Spirit of truth, he shall give testimony of me."'

[226] Henry VIII, *Assertio,* sig. Mr4.

[227] Henry VIII, *Assertio,* sig. Qr1.

[228] Henry VIII, *Assertio,* sig. Mv1.

[229] See Post, *Medieval Legal Thought,* 230-238.

the prompting of one or other of his mentors, one can see a certain likeness between this mode of expression and that of Thomas More in relation to the general council as a means of crystallising the consent of the whole Christian people both in matters of church order and of belief.[230]

John Fisher did not stress the role of consensus in the determination of faith and praxis in the Christian community. For him the mainsprings of the church's activity in relation to revelation and the regulation of Catholic life were the episcopate, the papacy and the general council. This is not to say he ignored the role of consensus but rather that he confined it to a minor key.[231] Fisher used the argument from consensus quite early in his theological career, in *The Destruction of Clichtove's Bulwark* (1519), part of his trilogy of works arguing in favour of the identity of 'the three Marys', spoken of in the gospels, with the traditional figure of Mary Magdalen.[232] Its use here is symptomatic of Fisher's method. His case for their identity with Mary Magdalen rests first on the authority of the supreme pontiff; second on Roman usage (the liturgical office in honour of Mary Magdalen, and the washing of feet on the eve of Palm Sunday); thirdly the consensus of the church. The general consent of the church may be explicit or tacit. One instance of the latter is the general agreement on the blessed Virgin's assumption. A formal consensus appears to exist for the unicity of Mary Magdalen of a similar kind.[233]

John Headley discussed Fisher's theory of consensus in the *Assertionis Lutheranae confutatio* and made some interesting points. He noted: '...Fisher gives *consensus* a significant role, but the overtones of the term are human and legal. *Consensus* is that human agreement, sometimes episcopal, sometimes unanimous, which gives approval and support to the received practices of the church.'[234] Fisher understands consensus as a term which pertains to human things that are made by the light of reason.

---

[230] See for example: '...counsayles do represent the whole chyrch...lyke wise as a parliament representeth ye hole reame...', in *Confutation*, 146/15-20; and speaking of the binding power of conciliar decisions: '...But when the counsayle and the congregacion agreeth and consenteth vppon a poynt/...it must stand tyll yt be by a nother lyke authoryte chaunged' in *Confutation*, 923/5-11 and passim.

[231] See in particular, Surtz, *John Fisher*, 52-81; Duggan, *The Church in the Writings of St. John Fisher*, 84-148; 157-272.

[232] The controversy arose because the French humanist Lefèvre d'Étaples questioned the identity of the woman who anointed Jesus' feet in the pharisee's house (Lk 7, 36-50) with Mary Magdalen from whom seven devils were cast out (Lk 8, 2) and with Mary, the sister of Martha and Lazarus, who also anointed Jesus' feet (Jn 12, 1-9). Fisher wrote two works against Lefèvre d'Étaples and one against the latter's associate, Josse Clichtove. It is this last work which is under discussion here: *Euersio munitionis quam Iodocus Clichtoueus erigere moliebatur aduersus unicam Magdalenam*, Louvain, Martens, 1519.

[233] See Fisher, *Euersio munitionis Clichtoueus*, sigs. G 3v-4v.

[234] See Headley, *Responsio*, 744, citing *Confutatio*, Antwerp, 1523, 6, 7, 11, 221.

To describe the unifying effect of the Spirit's action he introduces a concept which goes back to Stoicism but which had been given recent currency by Erasmus under a different name: *concordia*. According to Headley
this term is reserved by Fisher for agreement reached in the Spirit concerning truths of faith. Thus it is by the term *concordia* rather than *consensus*
that Fisher understands the action and impact of the Holy Spirit in the
church.[235]

While Dr Headley's exegesis of Fisher might be questioned, it is
perhaps more appropriate here to note that in his English writings More
used *concord* and *consensus,* indifferently, as synonyms one for another.[236]
Hence there is no direct dependence in evidence on this point, assuming
Headley's interpretation of Fisher to be correct. However, it was not only
in terminology that a discrepancy existed between the two authors. There
is a marked contrast in emphasis in their respective approaches to the
authority of the church in matters of belief. Putting it briefly, Fisher's
priorities were: pope, council and concord, in that order. More accepted
the papacy, and in his latter years especially spoke highly of councils, but
throughout his theological career underlined unambiguously the authority
of church consensus as the key criterion for assessing the church's presentation and interpretation of revelation. One might say he remained an
unrepentant 'populist' to the end for it was this very doctrine which
obliged him in conscience to face the scaffold. In short his priorities were
the reverse of Fisher's: consensus/concord, council, pope.

Although information is scarce concerning Erasmus's views on consensus in his early period, it is clear that from the time of Luther's breach with
Rome this doctrine surfaced in his mind in various forms and with increasing vigour.[237] Initially sympathetic to Luther's desire for church reform,

---

[235] See Headley, *Responsio,* 744-745, citing *Confutatio,* Antwerp, 1523, 15, 17, 20.

[236] More for example, speaking of God's action in the minds and hearts of believers, said:
'...tyll that he rewarde theyr vertuouse dylygence wyth ledyng them secretely in to the consent and concorde and bylyef of the trouth by his holy spirite *qui facit unanimes in domo...*' in
Confutation, 248/20-24; speaking of the gradual development of consensus he said: '...it is
trew and taught vnto the chyrche by the spyryte of god,...and the chyrche growen *into the consent and agrement therof by the same spiryte of concorde and agrement,* whych maketh all the house of
one mynde...' in *Confutation,* 285/10-16.

[237] On this as on most matters concerning Erasmus the literature is immense. I refer the
reader to more recent studies where references will be found to a wider bibliography. See in
particular G. Gebhardt, *Die Stellung des Erasmus,* 52-72; 234-301; 359-376; J. Coppens,
Scrinium Erasmianum, II contains the following relevant studies: C. J. de Vogel, *Erasmus and
His Attitude towards Church Dogma,* ibid., 101-132; C. Augustijn, *The Ecclesiology of Erasmus,*
ibid., 135-155; A. Hyma, *The Contributions by Erasmus to Dynamic Christianity,* ibid., 157-182;
J. V. Pollet, *Origine et Structure du 'De Sarcienda Ecclesiae Concordia' (1533) d'Érasme',* ibid.,
183-195; J. Coppens, *Où en est le portrait d'Érasme théologien,* ibid., 569-593. In preparing the

he also warned him against provoking dissension. In explaining his own attitude to Luther to Archbishop Albert of Brandenburg he affirmed unequivocally that he himself would never deliberately teach error or cause confusion and would do anything to avoid dissension.[238] This is a recurrent theme in subsequent writings; every effort must be exerted to preserve *pax* and *concordia*.

Concordia is obviously a broader concept than *consensus*, embracing as it does the whole of human life. *Consensus* is *concordia* as it applies to matters of thought and principles of human behaviour. Erasmus used the concept before Luther's emergence, e.g., in his gloss on Mt 11, 28-30 he declared that Christendom would return to its true course when teachers and preachers concentrated on those matters on which there exists a broad consensus (*magno consensu*) rather than losing time in irrelevant debate.[239] Nonetheless it was his conflict with Luther which crystallised his ideas on this issue. His open confrontation with the latter began with his *De libero arbitrio* published in Basle, 1524. A year later he wrote to the town council of Basle concerning Oecolompadius's work on the eucharist: '...*Concerning the words of the Supper of the Lord,* which in my opinion is learned, eloquent and diligent; and I would also add, devout, if that could be devout which conflicts with the opinion and consensus of the church, to depart from which I judge to be most perilous.'[240] Surely a characteristically oblique Erasmian bow in the direction of consensus! Subsequently Erasmus was accused of embracing Oecolompadian eucharistic theology, denying any real presence of Christ in the sacrament. Once more he reiterated his position that he could not see his way to depart from the harmonious agreement of the Christian people. Erasmus associated the authority of the general council with the 'consensus omnium ecclesiarum ac gentium' in this protestation. He made the same point to Willibald Pirckheimer in a letter of 30 July 1526: 'Ecclesia autem voco consensum populi Christiani per universum orbem.'[241]

---

subsequent account of Erasmus's views on consensus J. K. McConica, *Erasmus and the Grammar of Consent,* ibid., 77-99 was of special value. A more recent study also proved useful: Willi Hentze, *Kirche und kirchliche Einheit bei Desiderius Erasmus von Rotterdam,* Paderborn, 1974, 127-132; 203-207; 217-221 and passim.

[238] Erasmus to Luther, (30 May 1519), Allen, *Erasmi epistolae III,* 606/47-49; Erasmus to Albert of Brandenburg, (19 October 1519), ibid., IV 100/27-28; 48; ibid., IV, 107/256-260.

[239] Erasmus, *Novum instrumentum,* (1516), *LB* 6, 64F-65D.

[240] Erasmus to the Town Council of Basle, (c. October 1525), Allen, *Erasmi epistolae VI,* 206/2-5: '...cum sententia consensuque Ecclesiae: a qua dissentire periculosum esse iudico.'

[241] Erasmus to Conrad Pellican, (c. 15 October 1525), *Erasmi epistolae VI,* 210/66-67; ibid., 209/28-32; Erasmus to Willibald Pirckheimer, (30 July 1526), Allen, *Erasmi epistolae VI,* 372/25-29.

This doctrine of consensus had its origins in a definitively pneumatic and communitarian view of the church. The former had been already sketched out in the earlier writings, notably the *Enchiridion militis christiani* (1503).[242] An outline of a strictly personalised view of the latter is found in his *Ratio verae theologiae* in 1518 where the Christian community is presented as three concentric circles. The inner circle consists of priests, bishops, cardinals, the pope etc. The second circle consists of secular princes whose administration must be devoted to Christ's service. The outer circle consists of the *crassissimam huius orbis partem,* baptised but semi-committed Christians.[243] Unanimity is a characteristic of this community which is bound together by the Spirit of God, the Word of God, and the sacraments of divine grace.[244] What is in question, therefore, is not a consensus of a purely human or political order but a unanimity of mind and heart brought about by the inner action of the Spirit of God.

In adopting this position Erasmus was not basing himself exclusively on scripture. His theological outlook was greatly influenced both by Stoic and Platonic ideas derived from the early fathers.[245] His fundamental assumption was that behind the world lies the order of the divine Logos. The world has been created according to a rational plan. A rational though obscure order underlies the confused experience of daily living. One is in contact with this unchanging order when one is at peace with God, one's neighbour and oneself.[246] Harmony therefore is a sure sign of the achievement of real identity with the perennial and the divine. Harmony expresses itself in the Christian community in relation to doctrine in terms of an ongoing consensus concerning the content of revelation. The world of Vincent of Lerins, *quod semper, quod ubique, quod ab omnibus* was much more that of Erasmus than Luther's personalised interpretation of Paul's phrase *spiritualis autem iudicat omnia* (1 Cor 2, 15). Hence although like Luther, Erasmus called for a return to the sources especially scripture, and like the Wittenberger called for a radical reform of the church, when it came to determining disputed doctrinal questions there was a radical divergence of view between the two. For Luther truth might well be found in the words

---

[242] See Kohls, *Die Theologie des Erasmus,* 161-165 and passim.

[243] Erasmus, *Ratio verae theologiae,* (1518), *LB* 5, 88C ff.

[244] See Erasmus, *Querela pacis,* (1517), *LB* 4, 632 B: 'Nam quod populum Christianum Ecclesiam vocari placuit, quid aliud quam unanimitatis admonet?'; idem, *Ecclesiastes,* (1535), *LB* 5, 772C; idem, *Julius exclusus,* ed. W. K. Ferguson, *Erasmi opuscula,* 115/977-980: 'Ecclesia est populus Christianus, Christi spiritu conglutinatus...' (Authorship of the last work is disputed).

[245] See McConica, *Consent,* in Coppens, *Scrinium Erasmianum* II, 86-94; 96-99.

[246] See Erasmus, *Ecclesiastes,* (1535), *LB* 5, 1099B.

of one prophetic individual. For Erasmus it was found ultimately in the general belief of the Christian community as a concrete expression of the ultimate harmony underlying the universe. Harmony of thought points to a real contact with the order underlying the shifting appearances of the world.

Erasmus acknowledged the difficulty of determining the existence of consensus on any particular issue. He also recognised different forms of consensus—one given over a period of time and whose origins are at least remote, the other given more proximately at a general council.[247] This led him to distinguish three modes of expressing consensus: the consent of the fathers, consent of general councils, and the consent of the faithful.[248] The consent of the Christian people as 'consensus populi Christiani per universum orbem' was used more frequently as an authority in Erasmus's latter years after his breach with Luther.[249] However, for Erasmus the consent of Christians was not merely that of the mass of believers but also that of the enlightened and cultivated among them. Indeed at one stage he 'floated' the idea of a senate of one hundred or at least fifty to represent the body of what one must term learned opinion.[250] This idea, implicitly at least, harks back to the *magisterium doctorum*, a concept which surfaced in the middle ages and reached perhaps its highest point in the influence of theologians on the deliberations of Constance.[251] Such was Erasmus's respect for learning that he admitted that the number of cultivated people who followed Luther nearly won him over.[252] In the last resort, however, he held on to his basic principle of consent, not of the learned few, but also of the body of believers as well as the fathers of tradition and the general councils themselves.

In his attitude to the standard of ultimate Christian truth Erasmus found himself in close sympathy with Thomas More. Neither proposed an

---

[247] See Gebhardt, *Die Stellung des Erasmus*, 55.

[248] Erasmus, *Preface to Hyperaspistes*, Vol. II (1527), in Allen, *Erasmi epistolae* VII, 116/6-9.

[249] See Gebhardt, *Die Stellung des Erasmus*, 56.

[250] Erasmus to Julius Pflug, (20 August 1531), Allen, *Erasmi epistolae* IX, 319/31 ff.

[251] See Congar, *Ecclésiologie*, 241-244. Congar notes that this tradition stretches at least from the 12th century through the Döllinger school at Vatican I to the present day. He cites Peter d'Ailly at Constance: 'Non sunt excludendi a voce diffinitiva sacrae Theologiae doctores ac iuris canonici et civilis: quibus, et maxime theologicis, datur auctoritas praedicandi et docendi ubique terrarum, quae non est parva auctoritas in populo christiano, sed multo maior quam unius episcopi vel abbatis ignorantis, et solum titulati' in I. D. Mansi, *Sacrorum conciliorum collectio*, XXVII, 561, cited Congar, *Ecclésiologie*, p. 243, n. 14.

[252] See Erasmus to George of Saxony, (12 December 1524), Allen, *Erasmi epistolae* V, 604/110-114: '...quoties meo cum animo reputabam tot hominum milia in Luteri fauorem consentientia...'

infallible papal authority. Both accepted conciliar decisions but it was only in his last, '*Confutation* phase', and probably in reaction to the contrived conciliarism of Henry's propagandists that More went significantly beyond Erasmus in his emphasis on council. Hence the large measure of agreement between them in recognising the significance of universal consensus as a pointer to divine truth. Both recognised the value of a consensus stretching in time to the early, preferably apostolic church, as well as a consensus in the present time throughout the known Christian world. Both thinkers recognised the possibility of doctrinal development from diversity of thought to final consensus.

Here however one must note a difference in stress. More was ready to recognise consensus rather promptly and to attach its authority to matters of little as well as of great moment, to use it to defend devotional customs such as pilgrimages and honouring images as well as the central doctrines of the creed. On the other hand the sceptical Roterodamus was loath to see certainty where any doubt existed. Hence in his scheme of things the areas where such a consensus could be established were not great in number. His list of truths attested by universal consensus was not great in length.

One reason for this divergence lay, perhaps, in divergent concepts as to who the subject of consensus was. For More unmistakably it was the common corps of Christendom, the great mass of baptised believers marked by the Holy Spirit. Erasmus on the other hand, though stressing the role of the Spirit in each man's heart, influenced perhaps by a neo-platonic ecclesiology fathered on him possibly by Dean Colet, tended to restrict the bearers of consensus to the enlightened and intelligent few. Hence, possibly unconsciously, he fell into an intellectually aristocratic approach to the church as well as to his theory of consensus. More on the other hand remained firmly populist, pledging his faith in the great mass of mankind not merely because of respect for the common man but also from a profound belief in the power and influence of the Spirit of God in the simplest and least cultivated of Christians.

If one were to look at the question of mutual influence, it would be difficult to evolve any clear line of direct priority of one over the other. More's theology of consensus had its roots in a democratic predilection already in evidence in the *Epigrams* and which was given philosophical expression in the political forms of the *Utopia*. Erasmus's theology of *concordia* and *consensus* is in evidence in his early commentaries on scripture. It has its roots in a philosophical and theological persuasion which goes back to his earliest works in theology, such as the *Epistola de contemptu mundi* (c. 1487), the *Antibarbari* composed about 1495, and the *Enchiridion militis christiani* (1503).

Nonetheless it is unlikely that the firm stand More took against Luther in his *Responsio* and his rebuttal of the Reformer's assertions largely on the basis of a theory of consensus failed to reinforce Erasmus's conviction concerning the essential nature of truth and the value of consensus as a test of its valid appropriation by the Christian community. This ultimately was the basis of his radical separation from the Lutheran schism and the ground of a polarisation which became evident in the late fifteen twenties. On the other hand the freedom with which More interchanged the terms *concorde* and *consent*, notably in the *Confutation*, suggests a real and active awareness of his friend's writings on the subject. Hence, as anyone familiar with both figures might well have suspected, although one cannot ascribe a paternal role to either, there is evidence of a lasting fraternal enrichment extending to the very criterion on which each one based his radical separation from the path the Reformation was taking both in continental Europe and in Britain.

IX. Subsequent influence

It is impossible to describe adequately the subsequent influence of the writings of Sir Thomas More. The simple fact is that the basic research has not been done. Only two things can be remarked at this stage. The first is to say a few words about his impact on English recusants in the sixteenth century; the second, to show his place in the broad stream of Roman Catholic ecclesiologies of the same period.

In outlining More's subsequent reputation among English Catholic scholars one must depend heavily on the work of J. K. McConica.[253] In a highly literate article he has studied More's impact on his immediate circle of friends and their later successors in the English recusant circle which established itself mainly in the Low Countries in the latter years of Henry VIII's reign. Dr McConica notes that even More's family circle failed to follow him initially in his blank refusal to take the oath of succession. It is a commonplace of *Moreana* that his wife Alice looked on his refusal as bordering on the vagary of an over-scrupulous child.[254] What receives

---

[253] See James K. McConica, *The Recusant Reputation of Thomas More*, in R. S. Sylvester and G. P. Marc'Hadour, *Essential Articles for the Study of Thomas More*, Hamden (Conn.), 1977, 136-149. See also Marie Delcourt, *L'amitié d'Érasme et de More entre 1520 et 1535*, Bulletin de *l'Association Guillaume Budé* no. 50 (1936) 7-29; *Recherches sur Thomas More: la tradition continentale et la tradition anglaise*, Humanisme et Renaissance 3 (1936) 22-42; W. Egan, *Rule of Faith*, 69-78.

[254] 'What the good yere, master Moore,' quoth she, 'I mervaile that you, that have bine alwaies hitherto taken for so wise a man, will nowe so play the foole to lye heare in this close, filthy prison, and be content thus to be shut vpp amongst mise and rattes...'—a dialogue between Mistress Alice and More reported in Roper, 82/3-21.

somewhat less attention is his favourite daughter Margaret's inability to grasp the reasoning behind his refusal.

Margaret Roper's questions were spelled out in her letter to Alice Alington, More's step-daughter and married to Sir Giles Alington, a friend of Sir Thomas Audley, More's successor as Lord Chancellor. Margaret could not see how it was contrary to Christian faith to accept the oath of succession.[255] Eventually she did take the oath with the saving clause 'as far as the law of Christ allows.' At a later date she tried to hire a distinguished Protestant humanist, Roger Ascham, as tutor to her children.

Her attitude, however, involved no personal disloyalty to her father. Indeed the family took every care to preserve his memory by collecting all known records and keeping them in safety. It is largely due to their efforts that we have the large collection of his letters as well as the early collected editions of his printed works. Moreover, within ten years of More's death not only his family circle but a number of other scholars openly rejected royal supremacy or simply took flight to the continent. Among the latter were Richard Smith D. D., first regius professor of divinity at Oxford; John Harpsfield, brother of More's biographer Nicholas and classics lecturer at Oxford, and his fellow don George Etherige.

Members of More's own family circle took their stand in the 'Plot of the Prebendaries' (1538-1544) against Thomas Cranmer, Archbishop of Canterbury.[256] Cranmer's evident leaning towards continental Protestantism threatened traditional Catholic doctrines on justification, grace, and the sacraments. Cranmer's enemies, among them traditionalists inside the Canterbury chapter, a number of Kentish gentry, as well as opponents of the archbishop within the King's council itself collected evidence against him and presented it to the council. Henry VIII treated the matter with a certain degree of ironic humour in handing over the task of investigating the charges against him to Cranmer himself.

The outcome of the investigation was less than humorous. Sir Thomas

---

[255] The whole touching relationship and correspondence between More and his daughter Margaret brings out these points. Note in particular the lengthy, elegant letter from Margaret Roper to Alice Alington, (August 1534), Rogers, *Correspondence,* 514-532; see also Reynolds, *Margaret Roper,* 44-111.

[256] McConica, *Recusant Reputation,* 137; A. F. Pollard, *Thomas Cranmer and the English Reformation 1489-1556,* London, 1904, repr. 1965, 124-160; Hughes, *Reformation,* II, 22-62; Jasper Ridley, *Thomas Cranmer,* Oxford, 1962, 229-257; M. L. Zell, *The Prebendaries' Plot of 1543; A Reconsideration, JEH* 27 (1976) 241-253; E. E. Reynolds, *Margaret Roper,* London, 1960, 112-140.

More's son John, his surviving sons-in-law William Daunce and William Roper together with other associates such as John Heywood—married to a niece of More's,—John Larke, parish priest of Chelsea, and John Ireland, a chaplain to the Roper family, were indicted with a number of others on charges of having denied royal supremacy. Larke, Ireland, and Bishop Stephen Gardiner's nephew Germayn Gardiner were executed on 15 February 1544. Another son-in-law of More's, Giles Heron, had already perished on 4 August 1540 on a separate charge of treason at Thomas Cromwell's behest. The loyalty of the family group to the main stream of Catholic orthodoxy could hardly be called in question whatever nuances of attitude might be found within the consciences of individual members.

The most concrete evidence of the indebtedness of this group to More was the publication of two editions of his work, the fine black letter 1557 *English Works*, one of the more impressive typographical achievements of the sixteenth century, brought out by his nephew William Rastell in the safety of Mary's reign, and the *Latin Works* published by Elizabethan Catholic refugees in Louvain in 1565. The principal editor of the *Latin Works* seems once more to have been William Rastell then in exile under Elizabeth, though the work was published after his death.[257]

The controversy over the contrast between these collections and the Basle edition of More's *Latin Works* printed at the press of Episcopius in 1563 need not delay us here. Dr McConica points out that the bias in so far as it existed in the work of More's English disciples points to their retrospective wish to create the impression of sustained and unswerving opposition to royal supremacy among all its eventual opponents.[258] Of more significance were the biographies of More written during this period which signalled the continuing iconic impact of More's personality on these generations, notably William Roper's about 1552, Nicholas Harpsfield's somewhat later, and the second generation of exiles' contributions: Thomas Stapleton's in Douai, 1588, and the anonymous Ro. Ba. about 1600. Their interest was more than biographical. As McConica puts it, 'What interested them was More the martyr statesman, the great humanist who became the most widely-respected Englishman of his day and died for the tie with Rome, as proto-martyr of the English laity.' Who could better bolster up the courage of a small group of exiles living on the margin of a powerful establishment?

---

[257] McConica, *Recusant Reputation*, 143-147. See A. W. Reed, *William Rastell and More's English Works*, in Sylvester and Marc'Hadour, *Essential Articles*, 446.
[258] McConica, *Recusant Reputation, 143-149.*

More's reputation as theologian

This leaves unanswered the immediate question concerning More's theological influence, more precisely in matters concerning the church. This is largely unexplored territory since the ecclesiology of the English recusants has been as little studied as that of the opponents of Wyclif and Lollardy in the previous century. This does not prevent our recognising three theologians of note in the English recusant tradition, Cardinal Reginald Pole (1500-58), Nicholas Sanders (1527-81), and Thomas Stapleton (1535-98). Of these Pole is the key link.

Of royal blood by his mother Margaret, niece of Edward IV, Reginald Pole was born in 1500.[259] A correspondent of More's and Erasmus's, in 1521 he went to Padua soon coming under the influence of the humanist reformers of Gasparo Contarini's (1483-1542) Venetian circle. Pole opposed Henry both over the divorce and royal supremacy. In his *Pro ecclesiasticae unitatis defensione* composed in 1534-36, Pole made a strong plea for the traditional unity of the church around the bishop of Rome.[260]

The *De unitate*, as Pole's tract is more frequently named, was written in particular to counteract Richard Sampson's *Oratio*,[261] one of the early apologies for the Henrician regime, and in general as a counter-weight to Henry's assumption of supreme ecclesiastical authority. Its theological background was the Christian biblical humanism shared by Erasmus and More. Pole was influenced particularly by the neo-platonic philosophy of the Contarini circle, espoused later by the group he gathered around himself at Viterbo. This perspective bore some resemblance to Luther's in that it too started with justification of the individual, the centrality of faith in determining the Christian's approach to life, and the guidance of the Holy Spirit in determining the content of belief. However, when he came

---

[259] For Pole's career see: F. A. Gasquet, *Cardinal Pole and His Early Friends*, London, 1927; W. Schenk, *Reginald Pole*, London, 1950; for Pole's theological and humanist background see in particular the monograph by Dermot Fenlon, *Heresy and Obedience in Tridentine Italy. Cardinal Pole and the Counter Reformation*, Cambridge, 1972, 1-68 and passim.

[260] He remained a layman till 1556 when he was ordained priest at Greenwich and consecrated Archbishop of Canterbury. Three years previously, on Mary's accession to the English throne, he had been appointed legate to England by Julius III and negotiated England's return to communion with Rome. He died in 1558, only twelve hours after the queen.

[261] Richard Sampson (+ 1554) was a doctor of law who had studied for six years in Paris. Belonging to Wolsey's household, he acted as a *peritus* to Henry VIII both in the divorce case and the supremacy controversy. In June 1536 he was made Bishop of Chichester. The *Oratio*, a controversial work defending Henry's position, was printed by Berthelet in 1535. It is available in a later edition in J. Strype, *Ecclesiastical Memorials*, I, 2, 162-175.

to the core issue for Englishmen, the primacy of the pope, Pole's argumentation bore a marked similarity to that of both More and Fisher.[262]

Pole's case for papal primacy was based mainly on scriptural arguments, in particular a straightforward interpretation of Mt 16, 18 in terms of the direct establishment of the church on Peter as its foundation stone. In this Pole could well have been influenced by Fisher. The other two arguments put forward relate rather to More's positions on consensus and continuity in papal office.

Pole locates the discussion within a general view of the church.[263] In this one can see the neo-platonic influence at work. The organisation of the church reflects the underlying order of the universe. 'Who could possibly have conceived a constitution better than that of nature itself (for the church)? With the greatest admiration, we behold its most beautiful order: from the lowest to the intermediate to the highest, as if by a certain step, all things are led to the government and control of one man. Is not this constitution, this order, most beautiful?'[264] This image of the church expressed itself in Pole's thought in the biblical symbol of the temple, God's house. Peter is the foundation stone.[265] Remove the stone and the building collapses.

In the hands of medieval theologians, such as Giles of Rome and Augustinus Triumphus, this type of imagery had led to an extreme exaltation of the papal office. In the gentler neo-platonism of Northern Italy the emphasis is on the spiritual. The centre of the church is Christ. It is his Spirit who guides the church. The Spirit of God pervades the activities of all orders of the church, inspiring the scriptures, guiding its rulers, enlivening its worship.

The focal point of Pole's argument concerned precisely the papal primacy. The arguments he marshalled were in no way novel. '...for proof of this there are the authority of the church, the authority of the scriptures, the authority of all the holy and learned men who have ever written or spoken about these matters. In addition the course of events for many centuries from Peter's time down to our own age, fully conforms with this testimony.'[266]

---

[262] For Pole's ecclesiology see Breifne V. Walker, *Cardinal Reginald Pole, Papal Primacy and Church Unity 1529-1536,* unpublished MA thesis, University College, Dublin (NUI), 1972, 54-262.

[263] Walker, *Cardinal Pole,* 196-240.

[264] Pole, *De unitate,* ff. xxxvii v and passim.

[265] Pole, *De unitate,* xl v passim.

[266] Pole, *De unitate,* ff. xl v-xli r.

In scripture Pole singled out the Matthean pericope Mt 16, 13-20. An equally clinching argument for him was, however, the consensus of the church. 'Should not that multitude in the church be brought to mind who with such great and constant determination obeyed that person who holds the place of Christ...not only ordinary folk, but princes of state, kings and emperors...'[267] or again 'What if I leave the opinions of men and consider only the tradition of the universal church? This tradition has for many centuries confirmed the authority of the Roman pontiff. Will the name of Sampson and his doctrinal opinion be of such value that it will be given greater credence than that of the whole church?'[268] In this emphasis on consensus brought about by the Holy Spirit Pole is in tune with the line set by More in the *Responsio* and his subsequent writings, as well as Fisher. It must be added, however, that Pole did not make More's subtle distinctions between law and doctrine. For him there was no doubt whatever about the divine institution of the Roman primacy as such. It is indisputable. In this he was closer to Fisher than More as well as to the subsequent course of Counter Reformation apologetic.

Running through the *De unitate* is a sustained lament for the deaths of Fisher and More. While there is no explicit citation from their works, it is not unreasonable to assume familiarity on Pole's part with their writings. Towards the end of the first book he describes them both as his dearest friends. Without the slightest hesitation he acknowledges his indebtedness to the two martyrs: '...ego vero agnosco, et praedico libenter, eos mihi amicos omnium charissimos fuisse... Ego vero cum ex illorum vita magnum capiebam fructum, tum ex morte multo cepi maiorem.'[269]

Nicholas Sanders (1527-1581) belongs to the next generation of English recusants, those who went into exile after the Elizabethan settlement of 1559.[270] Together with a large number of refugees he took up residence in Louvain where he eventually became regius professor of theology in 1565. Subsequently, in 1572, he moved to Rome to represent English Catholics at the Vatican. Among Sanders's fellow exiles were friends and acquaintances of Sir Thomas More, including his nephew and publisher, William Rastell.

---

[267] Pole, *De unitate,* ff. xxxviii r and passim; ff. xliii v.

[268] ibid. ff. xxxvi v.

[269] Pole, *De unitate*, ff. xxx r.

[270] See Thomas Veech, *Dr. Nicholas Sanders and the English Reformation (1530-1581)*, Louvain, 1935; see also John Pollen, *The English-Catholics in the Reign of Queen Elizabeth*, London, 1920; A. C. Southern, *Elizabethan Recusant Prose*, London, 1950. For general background see Patrick McGrath, *Papists and Puritans under Elizabeth I*, London, 1967, 57-72; 100-124; John Bossy, *The English Catholic Community 1570-1850*, London, 1975, 11-76 and passim.

Mary's reign had seen the publication of the black letter edition of More's English works in 1557. As we have noted, the Latin works appeared first at Basle in 1563 while a somewhat different selection was published at Louvain two years later, in 1565. This last project was most probably directed by More's nephew William Rastell. The different flavour of the Basle collection came from someone with Erasmian sympathies whose identity remains unknown.[271] All this took place during a period when the memory of the executed chancellor was very much alive. What of the influence of his ideas?

Sanders was author of a large collection of treatises. His main work of controversy, *De visibili monarchia ecclesiae* ran to eight books.[272] The title itself indicates how the centre of debate had shifted from More's *Confutation of Tyndale*, through Pole's *De unitate ecclesiae* to a direct confrontation on the issue of church government and specifically its supreme ruler. This was due partly to a shift in Catholic controversial theology in the period following the Council of Trent's first session to a clearcut emphasis on the external institution of the church and the papacy in particular. The lines of battle had been clarified and their contours more sharply defined. In Sanders's case a further reason can be found in the line taken by Anglican apologetic in defence of the Elizabethan settlement. 'The upholders of the Established Church's conception of the royal supremacy in matters spiritual, devoted more attention to repelling the papal claims than in attempting to define their own positions...'[273]

Sanders's extensive treatment of the papacy covers the entire ground of church disciplines, scripture, patristics, history of theology and church history. He quotes from More, along with other controversial writers such as Fisher, Pole, Eck, Hosius, Driedo, Contarini and Sadoletus. These were quotations *in extenso* of corroborative testimony. When Sanders came, however, to compare his work with other controversialists of note, More did not even figure in the list.[274] Hence the immediate result of this brief enquiry is rather negative. More's figure certainly stood before the eyes of the Elizabethan recusant exiles. His theological position was also

---

[271] On the comparison of these various editions, see McConica, *Recusant Reputation*, 143-149; see also the earlier works of Marie Delcourt, *Recherches sur Thomas More*; idem, *L'Amitié d'Érasme et de More entre 1520 et 1535*.

[272] Nicholas Sanders, *De visibili monarchia ecclesiae libri VIII*, Louvain, 1571, a folio volume of 844 pages. This work of Sanders was but one contribution to a longstanding controversy surrounding the Elizabethan settlement. See P. Hughes, *Rome and the Counter-Reformation in England*, London, 1942, 144-159; Southern, *Recusant Prose*, 60-180.

[273] Veech, *Nicholas Sanders*, 113.

[274] Veech, *Nicholas Sanders*, 96.

acknowledged, but as little more than a link in a chain rather than the raw material from which the bonds of loyalty to Rome and its tradition were fashioned. His was one voice among many, a prophetic voice indeed, but not that of the founder of a school of thought.

That More retained his place in recusant iconography is evident in the writings of another theologian whose career overlapped with Sanders, namely Thomas Stapleton (1535-1598).[275] Stapleton left England in 1559 and became professor of catechetics at Douai University in 1571 and later of scripture in Louvain, in 1590. His theological writings, mainly controversial, were voluminous, though he is best remembered for his biography of Thomas More in his work *Tres Thomae* published at Douai in 1588.[276] This full scale biography, though it lacks the simplicity and fresh, witness quality of Roper's, is indicative of the esteem in which More was still held over fifty years after his death.

Most of Stapleton's time was given to theological controversy. Among his writings two works stand out for their treatment of the church.[277] More does not figure greatly as a mentor in these. The approach adopted by Stapleton is, indeed, the reverse of More's who passed from concrete issues to the nature of the church. Stapleton's starting point is the church, its definition, power and authority. In other words he begins where More left off. His method and sources though broadly traditional and historical belong to a new phase of apologetic. The broad context within which More viewed the church, its spiritual and popular nature, mission and authority have gone back stage. The ecclesiastical institution, its validity, power and authority dominate the scene to such an extent that other, more spiritual aspects of the church can be easily overlooked. As a fevered patient's focus of consciousness centres on an inflamed or threatened limb, so Roman Catholic theology allowed itself to be mesmerised by the sallies of the opposition rather than concentrate on its own proper sources and deeper concerns.

---

[275] See Marvin R. O'Connell, *Thomas Stapleton and the Counter Reformation*, New Haven and London, 1964; Southern, *Recusant Prose*, 126-135; 526-532; H. Schützeichel, *Wesen und Gegenstand der kirchlichen Lehrautorität nach Thomas Stapleton, Ein Beitrag z. Geschichte der Kontroverstheologie im 16. Jahrhundert*, Trier, 1966.

[276] Thomas Stapleton, *Tres Thomae, Seu de S. Thomae Apostoli...De S. Thoma Archiepiscopo Cantuariensi... D. Thomae Mori...vita*, Douai, 1588, tr. P. E. Hallett, *The Life and Illustrious Martyrdom of Sir Thomas More*, London, 1928.

[277] Thomas Stapleton, *Principiorum fidei doctrinalium demonstratio methodica*, Paris, 1578 filled 452 pages in the *Opera Omnia*, Paris, 1620. Most of this work was given over to questions of ecclesiology: *Principiorum fidei doctrinalium relectio scholastica et compendiaria*, Antwerp, 1596, was his major contribution to a debate with an Anglican divine, William Whitaker, regius professor of divinity at Cambridge.

European developments

English recusant theology remained in step with the broad trend of European writing on the church in the sixteenth century.[278] Pretridentine controversialists had initially centred their defence on the Roman primacy but quickly came to see that more general questions of ecclesiology lay in the background. Handbooks of controversial theology followed Johann Eck's *Enchiridion locorum communium* in providing a chapter on the church whose role as validating scripture is stressed.[279] 1529 saw Nicholas Herborn launch the first monograph on the marks of the church. Nine years later in 1538 the Louvain theologian Albertus Pighius published a strictly curialist ecclesiology, *Hierarchiae ecclesiasticae assertio*. Apostolic succession guarantees the authenticity of tradition, while the pope rather than the council is indefectible is their message. The institutional church has become the focus of both apologetic and systematic theology. In this connection it is interesting to note the reference to More's position on the papacy in Pedro de Soto's *Defensio catholicae confessionis* published in Antwerp in 1557.[280]

Although ecclesiology lay close to the core of Luther's innovations, the Council of Trent abstained from an explicit treatment of the church or even of the much-assaulted papal primacy.[281] This omission came about partly on pragmatic grounds. The council decided to limit itself as far as possible to strictly practical issues of reform. Underlying the decision, however, was a deep-seated ideological tension coming from late medieval thought between episcopalist and curialist conceptions of the church. (It was left mainly to the reformers to carry forward the populist and spiritual currents of thought.) In the circumstances it was deemed more opportune by Trent to get on with the business of institutional and moral reform and to leave more theoretical issues for some later date. The practical compromise worked out was to reinforce episcopal authority in pastoral mat-

---

[278] See Hubert Jedin, *Zur Entwicklung des Kirchenbegriffs im 16. Jahrhundert, Relazioni del X Congresso Internazionale di Scienze Storiche,* Vol. 4, Rome, 1955, 59-73; repr. idem, *Kirche des Glaubens, Kirche der Geschichte,* Vol. 2, Freiburg, 1966, 7-14; Congar, *Ecclésiologie,* 349-389.

[279] Johann Eck, *Enchiridion locorum communium adversus lutteranos,* Landshuti, 1525. See Pierre Fraenkel, *Johann Eck und Sir Thomas More 1525-1526. Zugleich ein Beitrag zur Geschichte des 'Enchiridion locorum communium' und der vortridentinischen Kontroverstheologie,* in *Von Konstanz nach Trient, Festschrift August Franzen,* ed. R. Bäumer, Munich, Paderborn, Vienna, 1972, 481-494.

[280] Nicholas Herborn, *Tractatus de notis verae ecclesiae,* Cologne, 1529; Albertus Pighius, *Hierarchiae ecclesiasticae assertio,* Cologne, 1538; Pedro de Soto, *Defensio catholicae confessionis,* Antwerp, 1557, 79-80, repr. More, *Treatise On The Passion,* 1069-1073.

[281] Jedin, *Zur Entwicklung des Kirchenbegriffs,* 68-70; Congar, *Ecclésiologie,* 364-368.

ters, not by reason of its own divine right but rather as delegated by the apostolic see of Rome.

Bellarmine's *Disputationes de controversiis christianae fidei,* published in Ingolstadt, 1586-93 mark the end of a cycle in the development of Roman Catholic ecclesiology reaching as far back as Augustine. The church for Bellarmine is '...the congregation of believers, who are bound together by sharing the same sacraments under the guidance of lawful pastors and especially that of Christ's vicar on earth the Roman pontiff.'[282] The bond with the spiritual is maintained by the mention of faith and sacrament in this definition but the stress is laid on the external elements of outward profession of faith, visible participation in the sacraments and the rule of lawful pastors especially 'Christ's vicar the Roman pontiff.' The test of orthodoxy for Bellarmine is communion with Rome. The Roman church is the true church because it is ruled by the pope. The view of the church bequeathed by Bellarmine to his heirs emphasised its nature as a perfect society, organised like the state, having at its summit the pope assisted by Roman congregations made up of cardinals and officials. Royal absolutism which triumphed in the nation states of sixteenth century Europe was reflected in this image of the church. In a movement which reached its peak in the nineteenth and early twentieth centuries, papal Rome became the norm of Christian life. The trend later caricatured by J. A. Möhler was in full flight: 'God created the hierarchy and so provided more than adequately for the needs of the church till the end of the world.'

This latter view can justly be described as 'papist' as distinct from the 'papalism' of More's carefully measured loyalty to papal 'prefecture' (his own term), which he saw as essentially subordinate to Christ's in service to a large popular assembly striving to live according to the Spirit. This Spirit, given to each one individually as well as exercising a creative influence within the whole body of believers, lies at the core of More's view of the church and his understanding of Christian experience. It is true that the logic of debate brought Sir Thomas More to see the importance of the church and within the church the threatened aspects of visible form and pastoral office. Similarly, argument brought him to the point of clearly affirming the identity of the church of Christ with the common corps of Christendom in all its triumphs and all its failures. But for him this was the

---

[282] Robert Bellarmine, *Disputationes de controversiis christianae fidei,* 3 Vols, Ingolstadt 1586-93, repr. 12 Vols., Paris, 1870-1874. Citation from idem, *De controversiis,* II, 100 in Jedin, *Zur Entwicklung des Kirchenbegriffs,* 70-73; Congar, *Ecclésiologie,* 370-375; J. B. Biciunas, *Doctrina ecclesiologica S. Roberti Card. Bellarmini cum illa Joannis Card. de Turrecremata comparata,* Rome, 1963.

end of the argument not the beginning. Balance was lost only when a later generation turned the conclusion into the premise, the shell into the core and so made of servant-office a baroque, absolutist principality.

As yet there is no evidence to show that Sir Thomas More's theology of the church exercised great influence on subsequent developments within Roman Catholic circles. It remains perhaps for students of the present day to draw the full benefit of his balanced, humane and fundamentally spiritual conception of the Christian commonwealth. At the time of his canonisation in 1935, Luther's not too warmly remembered biographer, Hartmann Grisar, said of More's theological writings 'vera scientifica investigatio operum nondum facta est.' In view of the flowering of More studies over the past thirty years, this is no longer true. Yet perhaps we are only at the beginning of a new cycle of reflection as students on all sides of the confessional divide weigh the implications of Sir Thomas More's keenest perceptions.

To apologists of royal supremacy in the Church of England Sir Thomas More posed the question of doctrinal development and authentic teaching authority within the church, as well as the specific issue of papal primacy. Against the Evangelical's emphasis on the Spirit-guided prophetic individual he placed the countervailing value of the Spirit-guided community finding its voice in the common consensus of belief. In contrast with the reformers' concept of a fleetingly visible church of the elect was More's conviction concerning the character of the Christian community, not as a hidden body of the just but as a mixed, sprawling mass of sinners and saints in 'the common knowen church'. For theologians of all schools More raised the issue of divine revelation, its nature and its relation to scripture, tradition, the individual believer and the believing community. Pehaps indeed in recognising '...that all the varyaunce between theym and vs, ryseth vpon the suretye of suche thinges as are to be belieued vppon the losse of saluacion' he had come to the central question, the answer to which largely determines subordinate issues regarding faith, justification, scripture, tradition, and church.

BIBLIOGRAPHY

A glasse of the truthe, pr. Berthelet, London, 1531.

Ames, Russell, *Citizen Thomas More and his Utopia*, Princeton, 1949.

Bainton, Roland H., *Erasmus of Christendom*, New York, 1969.

Barnes, Robert, *The Reformation Essays of Dr. Robert Barnes*, ed. by Neelak S. Tjernagel, London, 1963.

Bäumer, Remigius, *Nachwirkungen des konziliaren Gedankens in der Theologie und Kanonistik des frühen 16. Jahrhunderts*, Münster Westf., 1971.

Bietenholz, Peter G., *Erasmus' View of More*, in *Moreana* no. 5 (1965) 5-16.

Birchenough, E. and J., and Marc'Hadour, G., *More's Appointment as Chancellor and his Resignation*, in *Moreana* no. 12 (1966) 71-80.

Black, A. J., *Monarchy and Community. Political Ideas in the Later Conciliar Controversy 1430-1450*, Cambridge, 1970.

Botte, B. et al., *Le Concile et les Conciles, contribution à l'histoire de la vie conciliaire de l'église*, Chevetogne, Cerf, Paris, 1960.

Bridgett, Thomas E., *The Life and Writings of Sir Thomas More*, London, 1891.

Brosse, Olivier de la, *Le Pape et le concile. La comparaison de leurs pouvoirs à la veille de la réforme*, Paris, 1965.

Byron, Brian, *The Fourth Count of More's Indictment*, in *Moreana* no. 10 (1966) 33-46.

——, *Loyalty in the Spirituality of St. Thomas More*, *Bibliotheca Humanistica et Reformatorica*, Vol. IV, Nieuwkoop, 1972.

Chambers, Raymond W., *Thomas More*, London, 1935, repr. 1963.

Chrimes, S. B., *English Constitutional Ideas in the Fifteenth Century*, Cambridge, 1936.

Clebsch, William Anthony, *England's Earliest Protestants, 1520-1535*, New Haven and London, 1964.

Congar, Yves M.-J., *La Tradition et les traditions*, Paris, 2 Vols, 1960, tr. M. Naseby and T. Rainborough, *Tradition and Traditions. An historical and a theological essay*, London, 1966.

——, *L'Église de saint Augustin à l'époque moderne*, Paris, 1970.

Coppens, Joseph, *Scrinium Erasmianum. Mélanges historiques publiés sous le patronage de l'université de Louvain à l'occasion du cinquième centenaire de la naissance d'Érasme*, 2 Vols, Leyden, 1969.

Delcourt, Marie, *L'Amitié d'Érasme et de More entre 1520 et 1535*, in *Bulletin de l'Association Guillaume Budé* no. 50 (1936) 7-29.

——, *Recherches sur Thomas More, la tradition continentale et la tradition anglaise*, in *Humanisme et Renaissance* 3 (1936) 22-42.

Derrett, J. Duncan M., *Neglected Versions of the Contemporary Account of the Trial of Sir Thomas More*, BIHR 33 (1960) 202-223.

——, *The Trial of Sir Thomas More*, EHR 79 (1964) 449-477.

——, *The 'New' Document on Thomas More's Trial*, in *Moreana* no. 3 (1964) 5-19.

Dickens, Arthur Geoffrey, *The English Reformation*, London, 1967.

Donnelly, Gertrude J., *A Translation of St. Thomas More's 'Responsio ad Lutherum'*, Washington, 1962.

Egan S.J., Willis J., *The Rule of Faith in St. Thomas More's Controversy with William Tyndale, 1528-1533*, Los Angeles, 1960.

Elton, G. R., *England under the Tudors*, London, 1962.

——, *Policy and Police. The Enforcement of the Reformation in the Age of Thomas Cromwell*, Cambridge, 1972.

——, *Reform and Renewal. Thomas Cromwell and the Commonweal*, Cambridge, 1973.

——, *Studies in Tudor and Stuart Politics and Government. Papers and Reviews 1946-1972*, 2 Vols, Cambridge, 1974.

——, *Reform and Reformation, England 1509-1558*, London, 1977.

England/King's Council, *Articles deuisid by the holle consent of the kynges counsayle*, pr. Berthelet, London, 1533.

Erasmus, Desiderius, *Desiderii Erasmi Roterodami opera omnia emendatiora et auctiora, ad optimas editiones praecipue quas ipse Erasmus postremo curauit summa fide exacta, doctorumque virorum notis illustrata. Quorum primo, in hac editione, praefixa sunt elogia et epitaphia Erasmi, à viris doctis conscripta, nec conjunctim unquam antea sic edita. Cum indicibus totius operis copiosissimis*, ed. E. du Pin, 10 Vols, Leyden, 1703-1706.

——, *Opus Epistolarum Des. Erasmi Roterodami*, edited by P. S. and H. M. Allen and H. M. Garrod, 12 Vols, Oxford, 1906-1958.

Expositio fidelis de morte D. Thomae Mori & *quorundam aliorum insignium uirorum in Anglia*, Froben, Basle, 1535.

Fenlon, Dermot, *Heresy and Obedience in Tridentine Italy. Cardinal Pole and the Counter Reformation*, Cambridge, 1972.

Fischer, John, *Opera, quae hactenus inueniri potuerunt omnia*, VVirceburgi, apud Georgium Fleischmannum, Anno MDXCVII; repr. 1967.

——, *The English Works of John Fisher*, Part I, ed. J. E. B. Mayor, London, Early English Text Society, 1876; repr. 1935.

Flesseman-Van Leer, E., *The Controversy about Scripture and Tradition between Thomas More and William Tyndale*, in *Nederlands Archief voor Kerkgeschiedenis* Nieuwe Serie 43 (1959) 143-165 .

——, *The Controversy about Ecclesiology between Thomas More and William Tyndale* in *Nederlands Archief voor Kerkgeschiedenis* Nieuwe Serie 44 (1960) 65-86.

Gebhardt, Georg, *Die Stellung des Erasmus von Rotterdam zur römischen Kirche*, Marburg, 1966.

Geiselmann, Josef Rupert, *The Meaning of Tradition*, tr. W. J. O'Hara, London, 1966.

Gerlo, Alois et al., *Thomas More 1477-1977. Colloque de novembre 1977*, Brussels, 1980.

Gibson, Reginald Walter, *St. Thomas More: A preliminary bibliography of his works and of Moreana to the year 1750. With a bibliography of Utopiana* compiled by R. W. Gibson and J. Max Patrick, New Haven and London, 1961.

Grimm, Harold John, *The Reformation Era, 1500-1650*, 2nd edn, New York, 1973.

Guy, John, *The Public Career of Sir Thomas More*, Harvester Press, Brighton, Sussex, 1980.

Harpsfield, Nicholas, *The life and death of Sir Thomas Moore, knight, sometymes Lord high Chancellor of England, written in the tyme of Queene Marie*, edited by Elsie Vaughan Hitchcock, E.E.T.S., London, 1932.

Hay, Denys, *A Note on More and the General Council*, in *Moreana* no. 15 (1967) 249-251.

Headley, John M., *Thomas Murner, Thomas More, and the First Expression of More's Ecclesiology*, *Studies in the Renaissance* 14 (1967) 73-92.

——, *More Against Luther: On Laws And the Magistrate*, in *Moreana* no. 15 (1967) 211-223.

——, *Thomas More and the Papacy*, in *Moreana* no. 41 (1974) 5-10.

——, *The 'Nos Papistae' of Thomas More*, *Moreana* no. 64 (1980) 89-90.

Hendrix, Scott H., *Ecclesia in Via. Ecclesiological developments in the medieval psalms exegesis and the 'Dictata super psalterium' (1513-1515) of Martin Luther*, Leyden, 1974.

Hentze, Willi, *Kirche und Kirchliche Einheit bei Desiderius Erasmus von Rotterdam*, Paderborn, 1974.

Henry VIII, *Assertio septem sacramentorum*. See *Libello huic regio haec insunt*.

——, *Libello huic regio haec insunt. Oratio J. Clerk apud Ro. pon. in exhibitione operis regii. Responsio roman. pont. ad eandem ex tempore facta. Bulla ro. pon. ad regiam maiestatem pro eius operis confirmatione. Summa indulgentiarum, libellum ipsum regium legentibus concessarum. Libellus regius (Assertio septem Sacramentorum) aduersus Martinum Lutherum haeresiarchon. Epistola regia ad illustrissimos Saxoniae duces pia admonitoria*, In aedibus Pynsonianis, apud Londinum, 1521.

——, *Serenissimi ... regis Angliae ad Saxoniae principes ... epistola*, Cologne, 1523.

——, *Literarum ... quibus ... Henricus octavus ... respondit ad quandam epistolam Martini Lutheri*, pr. Pynson, London, 1526.

Hitchcock, James, *Thomas More and the Sensus Fidelium*, in *Theological Studies* 36 (1975) 145-154.

Holeczek, Heinz, *Die humanistische Bildung des Thomas More und ihre Beurteilung durch Erasmus von Rotterdam*, in *Zeitschrift der historischen Forschung* 3 (1976) 165-204.

Huber, Paul, *Traditionsfestigkeit und Traditionskritik bei Thomas Morus. Inaugural-Dissertation zur Erlangung der Doktorwürde der Philosophisch-Historischen Fakultät der Universität Basel*, Basle, 1953.

Hughes, Philip, *The Reformation in England*, rev. edn, 3 Vols in one, London, 1963.

Hume, Anthea, *A Study of the English Protestant Exiles 1525-35*, (Ph. D. thesis), University of London, 1961.

Hunt, Ernest William, *Dean Colet and his Theology*, London, 1956.

Hyma, Albert, *Erasmus and the Oxford Reformers, (1493-1503)*, in *NAKG* n.s. 25 (1932) 69-92; 97-134; *Erasmus and the Oxford Reformers (1503-1519)*, *NAKG* n.s. 38 (1951) 65-85.

Jedin, Hubert, *Geschichte des Konzils von Trient*, 4 Vols, Freiburg, 1949-75, translated E. Graf, *A History of the Council of Trent*, 3 Vols, London, 1957-.

——, *Zur Entwicklung des Kirchenbegriffs im 16. Jahrhundert*, *Relazioni del X Congresso Internazionale di Scienze Storiche (Roma 4-11 Sett. 1955)*, Vol. IV, Rome, 1955, 59-73; in idem, *Kirche des Glaubens, Kirche der Geschichte*, Vol. II, *Konzil und Kirchenreform*, Freiburg, 1966, 7-14.

——, *Bischöfliches Konzil oder Kirchenparlament? Ein Beitrag zur Ekklesiologie der Konzilien von Konstanz und Basel*, Basle, 1963.

——, *Reformation und Kirchenverständnis*, in *Probleme der Kirchenspaltung im 16. Jahrhundert*, edited by Raymund Kottje & Joseph Staber, Regensburg, 1970, 59-84.

Knappen, Marshall Mason, *William Tindale, First English Puritan*, in *Church History* 5 (1936) 201-215.

——, *Tudor Puritanism. A Chapter in the History of Idealism*, Chicago, 1939.

Koebner, Richard, *'The Imperial Crown of the Realm'. Henry VIII, Constantine the Great, and Polydore Vergil*, in *Bulletin of the Institute of Historical Research* 26 (1953) 29-52.

Lehmberg, Stanford E., *The Reformation Parliament, 1529-1536*, London, 1970.

Lortz, Joseph, *Die Reformation in Deutschland*, 2 Vols, Freiburg, Basel, Wien, 4th edn, 1962; translated by R. Walls, 2 Vols, London, 1968.

Luther, Martin, *Resolutio Lutheriana super propositione sua decima tertia de potestate papae*, (1519), *WA* 2, 183-240.

——, *Assertio omnium articulorum M. Lutheri per bullam Leonis X damnatorum*, (1520), *WA* 7, 94-151.

——, *De captivitate babylonica ecclesiae praeludium*, (1520), *WA* 6, 497-573.

——, *Acta et res gestae D. Martini in comitiis principum Wormatiae*, (1521), *WA* 7, 825-857.

——, *Ad librum eximii magistri nostri Mag. Ambrosii Catharini ... responsio*, (1521), *WA* 7, 705-778.

——, *Contra Henricum regem angliae*, (1522), *WA* 10/2, 180-222.

McConica, J. K., *English Humanists and Reformation Politics under Henry VIII and Edward VI*, Oxford, 1965.

——, *The Recusant Reputation of Thomas More* in *Essential Articles for the Study of Thomas More*, edited by R. S. Sylvester and G. P. Marc'Hadour, Hamden, Conn., 1977, 136-149.

Marc'Hadour, Germain, *L'Univers de Thomas More. Chronologie critique de More, Érasme et leur époque (1477-1536)*, Paris, 1963.

——, *Thomas More et la Bible. La place des livres saints dans son apologétique et sa spiritualité*, Paris, 1969.

——, *The Bible in the Works of St. Thomas More*, 5 Vols, Nieuwkoop, 1969-1971.

Marius, Richard C., *The Pseudonymous Patristic Text in Thomas More's Confutation*, in *Moreana* no. 15 (1967) 253-266.
——, *Thomas More and the Early Church Fathers, Traditio* 24 (1968) 379-407.
——, *More the Conciliarist, Moreana,* no. 64 (1980) 91-99.
Martz, Louis L., *Thomas More: The Tower Works,* in *St. Thomas More: Action and Contemplation,* edited by R. S. Sylvester, New Haven and London, 1972, 57-83.
Meinhold, Peter, *Das Konzil im Jahrhundert der Reformation,* in *Die ökumenischen Konzile der Christenheit,* ed. H. J. Margull, Stuttgart, 1961, 201-236.
Merzbacher, Friedrich, *Wandlungen des Kirchenbegriffs im Spätmittelalter, Grundzüge des ausgehenden 13. des 14. und 15. Jahrhunderts* in *Zeitschrift der Savigny-Stiftung für Rechtsgeschichte,* Vol. 70, *kanonistische Abteilung* 39 (1953) 274-361.
Meyer, Carl S., *Henry VIII Burns Luther's Books, 12 May 1521,* in *The Journal of Ecclesiastical History* 9 (1958) 173-187.
More, Cresacre, *The Life of Sir Thomas More.* With a biographical preface, notes and other illustrations by the Rev. J. Hunter, London, 1828.
More, Thomas, *Here is conteyned the lyfe of Johan Picus Erle of Myrandula a grete lord of Italy an excellent conning man in all sciences.* & *verteous of lyuing. with dyuers epistles* & *other warkis of the seyd Johan Picus full of grete science vertew and wysedome. whos lyfe* & *warkys bene worthy* & *digne to be redd* & *oftyn to be had in memorye.* London, (undated, c. 1510); *EW,* 1-34.
——, *The history of king Richard the thirde, EW,* 35-71; *The History of King Richard III,* edited by Richard S. Sylvester, New Haven and London, 1963, *CW* 2.
——, *Opuscula,* Paris, 1506; *Dialogi et alia emuncta,* Paris, 1514; *Opuscula,* Venice, 1516; *Translations of Lucian,* edited by Craig R. Thompson, New Haven and London, 1974, *CW,* Vol. 3, Part I.
——, *Libellus vere aureus nec minvs salvtaris qvam festiuus de optimo reip. statu, deque noua Insula Vtopia authore clarissimo viro Thoma Moro inclytae ciuitatis Londinensis ciue* & *vicecomite cura M. Petri Aegidii Antuerpiensis,* & *arte Theodorici Martini Alustensis, Typographi almae Louaniensium Academiae nunc primum accuratissime editus,* Louvain, 1516; *Utopia,* edited with an introduction and notes by Edward Surtz, S. J., and J. H. Hexter, New Haven and London, 1964, *CW* 4.
——, *De optimo reip. statv deqve noua insula Vtopia libellus uere aureus, nec minus salutaris quam festiuus, clarissimi disertissimique uiri Thomae Mori inclytae ciuitatis Londinensis ciuis* & *Vicecomitis. Epigrammata clarissimi difertissimique uiri Thomae Mori, pleraque e Graecis uersa. Epigrammata. Des. Erasmi Roterodami,* Basle, 1518; *The Latin Epigrams of Thomas More,* edited with translations and notes by Leicester Bradner and Charles Arthur Lynch, Chicago, 1953.
——, *Ervditissimi viri Guilielmi Rossei opus elegans, doctum, festiuum, pium, quo pulcherrime retegit, ac refellit insanas Lutheri calumnias: quibus inuictissimum Angliae Galliaeque regem Henricvm eius nominis octauum, Fidei defensorem, haud literis minus quam regno clarum, scurra turpissimus insectatur: excusum denuo diligentisisime, digestumque in capita, adiunctis indicibus opera uiri doctissimi Ioannis Carcellij,* London, 1523; *Responsio ad Lutherum,* edited by John M. Headley, translated by Sister Scholastica Mandeville, New Haven and London, 1969, *CW* 5.
——, *A dyaloge of syr Thomas More knyghte: one of the counsayll of our souerayne lorde the kyng and chauncelloure of hys duchy of Lancaster. Wheryn he treatyd dyuers maters/as of the veneracyon* & *worshyp of ymagys* & *relyques/prayng to sayntis/* & *goynge on pylgrymage. Wyth many other thyngys touchyng the pestylent secte of Luther* & *Tyndale/by the tone bygone in Saxony/* & *by the tother laboryd to be brought in to England. Newly ouersene by the sayd syr Thomas More chauncellour of England,* London, 1531; reprinted from *EW* in facsimile and in modern spelling, *A Dialogue Concerning Heresies,* edited by W. E. Campbell with introduction and notes by A. W. Reed, London, 1927, repr. 1931; *A Dialogue Concerning Heresies,* edited by Thomas Lawler, Germain Marc'Hadour and Richard Marius, 2 Vols, New Haven and London, 1981, *CW* 6.

——, *A dialoge of comfort against tribulacion, made by Syr Thomas More knyght, and set foorth by the name of an Hungarien, not before this time imprinted*, London, 1531; *A Dialogue of Comfort against Tribulation*, edited by Louis L. Martz and Frank Manley, New Haven and London, 1977, *CW* 12.

——, *The confutacyon of Tyndales answere made by syr Thomas More knyght lorde chauncellour of Englonde*, 2 Vols, London, 1532-33; *The Confutation of Tyndale's Answer*, edited by Louis A. Schuster, Richard C. Marius, James P. Lusardi, and Richard J. Schoeck, New Haven and London, 1973, *CW* 8.

——, *The debellacyon of Salem and Bizance*, London, 1533.

——, *The apologye of syr Thomas More knyght*, London, 1533, edited with introduction and notes, by Arthur Irving Taft, Ph. D., London, 1930; *The Apology*, edited by J. B. Trapp, New Haven and London, 1979, *CW* 9.

——, *Treatise On The Passion, Treatise On The Blessed Body, Instructions And Prayers*, edited by Garry E. Haupt, New Haven and London, 1976, *CW* 13.

——, *The workes of Sir Thomas More Knyght, sometyme Lorde Chauncellour of England, wrytten by him in the Englysh tonge*, London, 1557.

——, *Thomae Mori, Angliae ornamenti eximii, lucubrationes, ab innumeris mendis repurgatae*, Basle, 1563.

——, *The Correspondence of Sir Thomas More*, edited by Elizabeth Frances Rogers, Princeton, 1947.

——, *St. Thomas More: Selected Letters*, edited by Elizabeth Frances Rogers, Selected Works of St. Thomas More, Vol. 1, New Haven and London, 1967.

——, *Neue Briefe. Mit einer Einführung in die epistolographische Tradition*, edited by Hubertus Schulte Herbrüggen, Münster, 1966.

Moreau, E. de, Jourda, P., Janelle, P., *La Crise Religieuse du XVIe siècle*, (*Histoire de l'Église*, edited by A. Fliche et V. Martin, Vol. XVI), Paris, 1950.

Mozley, J. F., *William Tyndale*, London, 1937.

Oakley, Francis, *Headley, Marius and Conciliarism*, Moreana, no. 64 (1980) 82-88.

Oberman, Heiko Augustinus, *The Harvest of Medieval Theology. Gabriel Biel and Late Medieval Nominalism*, Cambridge, Massachusetts, 1963.

——, *Forerunners of the Reformation. The Shape of Late Medieval Thought, Illustrated by Key Documents*, London, 1967.

——, *The Shape of Late Medieval Thought: the Birthpangs of the Modern Era*, in *The Pursuit of Holiness in Late Medieval and Renaissance Religion*, edited by Charles Trinkhaus with Heiko Oberman, Leyden, 1974, 3-25.

——, *Werden und Wertung der Reformation, Vom Wegestreit zum Glaubenskampf*, Tübingen, 1977.

Paris Newsletter, Discours sur le procez et execution de Thomas Morus, chancellier d'Angleterre, in Nicholas Harpsfield, *The life and death of Sr Thomas Moore*, E.E.T.S., London, 1932, 253-266.

Parmiter, G. de C., *The Indictment of St. Thomas More*, in *The Downside Review* 75 (1957) 149-166.

——, *Saint Thomas More and the Oath*, *The Downside Review* 78 (1960) 1-13.

——, *Tudor Indictments, Illustrated by the Indictment of St. Thomas More*, Recusant History 6 (1961-62) 141-156.

——, *The King's Great Matter. A Study of Anglo-Papal Relations 1527-1534*, London, 1967.

Peters, Robert, *Utopia and More's Orthodoxy*, in Moreana nos 31-32 (1971) 147-155.

Pineas, Rainer, *Thomas More and Tudor Polemics*, Bloomington, Indiana, 1968.

Porter, Harry Culverwell, *Puritanism in Tudor England*, London, 1970.

——, *Reformation and Reaction in Tudor England*, Cambridge, 1958.

Prévost, André, *Thomas More, 1477-1535, et la crise de la pensée européene*, Tours, 1969.

Reed, A. W., *William Rastell and More's English Works*, in R. W. Sylvester and G. P. Marc' Hadour, *Essential Articles for the Study of Thomas More*, Hamden (Conn.), 1977, 436-446, repr. from *The English Works of Sir Thomas More*, Vol. 1, London, 1931, 1-12.

Reynolds, E. E., *The Trial of St. Thomas More*, London, 1964.
——, *The Field is Won. The Life and Death of Saint Thomas More*, London, 1968.
RO: BA:, *The Lyfe of Syr Thomas More Sometymes Lord Chancellor of England*, edited by Elsie Vaughan Hitchcock and P. E. Hallett, London, 1950.
Roper, William, *The Lyfe of Sir Thomas Moore, knighte*, edited by Elsie Vaughan Hitchcock, E.E.T.S. (Original Series no. 197), London, 1935.
Rouchausse, Jean, *La Vie et l'œuvre de John Fisher evêque de Rochester, 1469-1535*, Nieuwkoop, 1972.
Rupp, E. Gordon, *Studies in the Making of the English Protestant Tradition*, Cambridge, 1949.
——, *The Righteousness of God, Luther Studies*, London, 1953.
Sawada, Paul Akio, *Two Anonymous Tudor Treatises on the General Council*, in *The Journal of Ecclesiastical History* 12 (1961) 197-214.
——, *Das Imperium Heinrichs VIII. und die erste Phase seiner Konzilspolitik*, in *Reformata Reformanda. Festgabe für Hubert Jedin*, edited by E. Iserloh and K. Repgen, Münster Westf., Vol. 1, 1965, 476-507.
Scarisbrick, John Joseph, *Henry VIII*, London, 1968.
Schenk, William, *Reginald Pole, Cardinal of England*, London, 1950.
Schoeck, Richard J., *Canon Law in England on the Eve of the Reformation*, in *Mediaeval Studies* (Toronto) 25 (1963) 125-147.
——, *Common Law and Canon Law in Their Relation to Thomas More*, in *St. Thomas More: Action and Contemplation. Proceedings of the Symposium Held at St. John's University October 9-10, 1970*, 15-56, edited by Richard S. Sylvester, New Haven and London, 1972.
Sheldrake, Philip, *Authority and Consensus in Thomas More's Doctrine of the Church*, *The Heythrop Journal* XX (1979) 146-172.
Smith, H. Maynard, *Henry VIII and the Reformation*, London, 1962.
——, *Pre-Reformation England*, London, 1963.
Smith, Preserved, *Englishmen at Wittenberg in the Sixteenth Century*, *The English Historical Review* 36 (1921) 422-433.
Stapleton, Thomas, *Tres Thomae. Seu de S. Thomae Apostoli rebus gestis. De S. Thoma Archiepiscopo Cantuarensi... D. Thomae Mori ... vita*, Douai, 1588, translated by P. E. Hallett, *The Life and Illustrious Martyrdom of Sir Thomas More*, London, 1928.
Stout, H. S., *Marsilius of Padua and the Henrician Reformation*, in *Church History* 43 (1974) 308-318.
Sullivan, Frank and Majie Padberg, *Moreana — Materials for the Study of Saint Thomas More*, Loyola University of Los Angeles, Los Angeles, California, (separate fascicules) 1964-1971.
Surtz, S. J., Edward Louis, *The Works and Days of John Fisher. An Introduction to the Position of St. John Fisher (1469-1535), Bishop of Rochester, in the English Renaissance and Reformation*, Cambridge, Mass., 1967.
Sylvester, R. S. and Marc'Hadour, G. P., *Essential Articles for the Study of Thomas More*, Hamden, Connecticut, 1977.
Sylvester, Richard, *Thomas More: Humanist in Action*, in *Medieval and Renaissance Studies*, edited by O. B. Hardison Jnr, Chapel Hill, 1966, 125-137.
——, *St. Thomas More: Action and Contemplation. Proceedings of the symposium held at St. John's University, October 9-10, 1970*, New Haven and London, 1972.
Thomson, John A. F., *The Later Lollards 1414-1520*, Oxford, 1965.
Tierney, Brian, *Foundations of the Conciliar Theory, The Contribution of the Medieval Canonists from Gratian to the Great Schism*, Cambridge, 1953.
——, *Origins of Papal Infallibility 1150-1350, A Study on the concepts of infallibility, sovereignty and tradition in the middle ages*, Leyden, 1972.
Tjernagel, Neelak Serawlook, *Henry VIII and the Lutherans, A Study in Anglo-Lutheran relations from 1521-1547*, Saint Louis, Mo., 1965.
Trinterud, L. J., *A Reappraisal of William Tyndale's Debt to Martin Luther*, in *Church History* 31 (1962) 24-45.

Tyndale, William, *The parable of the wicked mammon*, Marburg, 1528.

——, *An answere vnto Sir Thomas Mores dialoge made by Vvillyam Tindale*, n.p., 1531.

——, *The Obedience of a Christen man and how Christen rulers ought to gouerne where in also (yf thow marke diligently) thou shalt fynde eyes to perceaue the crafty conueyaunce of all iugglers*, (1st edn, Marburg, 1528), 2nd edn, Marburg, 1535.

——, *A Pathway into the Scripture*, (probably Antwerp, c. 1530-31).

——, *Doctrinal treatises and introductions to different portions of the holy scriptures*, edited for The Parker Society by the Rev. Henry Walter, B.D., F.R.S., Cambridge, 1848.

——, *Expositions and notes on sundry portions of the holy scriptures, together with the practice of prelates*, edited for The Parker Society, by the Rev. Henry Walter, B.D. F.R.S., Cambridge, 1849.

Ullmann, Walter, *The Growth of Papal Government in the Middle Ages. A study in the ideological relationship of clerical to lay power*, 3rd edn, London, 1970.

Vocht, Henry de, *Acta Thomae Mori; History of the Reports of his Trial and Death with an Unedited Contemporary Narrative*, Louvain, 1947.

Vooght, Paul de, *Les Sources de la doctrine chrétienne, d'après les théologiens du xive siècle et du début du xve avec le texte intégral des xii premières questions de la summa inédite de Gérard de Bologne (+ 1317)*, Desclée de Brouwer, 1954.

Watt, John, *The Theory of Papal Monarchy in the Thirteenth Century*, London, 1965.

Wilkinson, Bertie, *Constitutional History of England in the Fifteenth Century (1399-1485) with illustrative documents*, London, 1964.

INDEX OF SUBJECTS

INDEX OF NAMES

x, 1, 2, 4, 87, 171, 236, 251, 252, 253, 254, 264, 288, 290; *Assertio Septem Sacramentorum*, 2, 81-2, 86-7, 91, 92n, 95n, 97n, 106, 107, 108, 110, 125, 126, 146, 202, 203, 244n, 251-2, 253, 261, 267, 272, 287, 292, 313-14, 326n, 330, 338, 339n, 349, 363

Henry of Langenstein, 38n, 335n

Hentze, W., 321n, 327n, 328n, 332n, 351n, 352n, 366n

Herborn, Nicholas, 378

Herbruggen, H. S., 129n

Heron, Giles, 372

Hexter, J., 80

Heywood, John, 372

Hierom, *St, see St* Jerome

Hilary of Poitiers, 71, 72n, 75n

Hilton, Walter, 78

Hincmar of Rheims, 355

Hippolytus, 355

Hitchcock, E. V., 7n, 73n

Hitchcock, James, 16n

Hödl, L., 24n

Hofmann, Fritz, 20n, 21n, 355n

Hofmann, L., 46n

Holeczek, Heinz, 80n

Holl, Karl, 319n

Holt, John, 73, 325n

Hosius, 376

Huber, Paul, 10, 14, 252-3, 264n, 303n

Hugh of St Cher, 77

Hugh of St Victor, 26, 318, 323

Hughes, Philip, 129n, 172n, 237n, 239n, 240, 250n, 251n, 257n, 258, 347n, 371n, 376n

Huguccio, 29

Hume, Anthea, 3n, 131n, 134n, 172n

Hunne, Richard, 133

Hunt, Ernest W., 362n

Hurley, M., 55n

Hus, John, 49, 51, 53-4, 56, 60, 63, 336

Hyma, Albert, 80n, 351n, 365n

Ignatius, *St*, 75n, 224, 259-60, 305

Innocent III, *Pope*, 29, 334n

Innocent IV, *Pope*, 29, 334

Ireland, John, 372

Irenaeus, 75n, 355

Isidorus Mercator, 24n

Iwand, H. J., 319n

Jacob, E. F., 38n, 117n, 239n

James of Viterbo, 30n

Janelle, P., 172n, 240n, 347n

Jedin, Hubert, 8, 37n, 41-5 (notes), 105n, 190, 250n, 336n, 341n, 342n, 378n

Jerome, St, 55, 58, 65, 75n, 143, 205

Jesus Christ, 14, 31, 67, 85, 130, 241-2, 271-2; and his church, 21, 27, 39, 40, 41, 42, 43, 51-2, 54, 56, 91n, 95, 97, 105, 115, 125, 136-8, 148-54, 157-8, 165-8, 170, 173, 177-9, 181, 187, 206, 222-3, 224-6, 233, 266, 277, 279-81, 284-6, 287, 305, 321, 323, 324, 330, 331, 345, 374; message of, 50, 92, 93, 94, 98, 101, 117, 118-19, 124, 126, 141-2, 144, 162-3, 193, 198, 200, 202, 208, 213-14, 219-20, 228, 232, 269, 274, 284,